D1219028

ECONOMIC EFFECTS OF FUNDAMENTAL TAX REFORM

ECONOMIC EFFECTS OF FUNDAMENTAL TAX REFORM

Henry J. Aaron
William G. Gale
Editors

BROOKINGS INSTITUTION PRESS
Washington, D.C.

Copyright © 1996
THE BROOKINGS INSTITUTION
1775 Massachusetts Avenue, N.W., Washington, D.C. 20036

Library of Congress Cataloging-in-Publication data

Economic effects of fundamental tax reform / Henry Aaron, William Gale, eds.
   p. cm.
   Papers presented at a conference sponsored by the Brookings Institution.
   Includes bibliographical references and index.
   ISBN 0-8157-0058-X (cloth : alk. paper). — ISBN 0-8157-0057-1
(pbk. : alk. paper)
   1. Taxation—Economic aspects—United States—Congresses.
2. Income tax—United States—Congresses. 3. Tax incidence—United
States—Congresses. I. Aaron, Henry J. II. Gale, William G.
III. Brookings Institution.
HJ2381.E226 1996
336.2'05'0973—dc20   96-27074
                                                           CIP

9 8 7 6 5 4 3 2 1

The paper used in this publication meets the minimum requirements of the
American National Standard for Information Sciences—Permanence of Paper
for Printed Library Materials, ANSI Z39.48-1984

Typeset in Sabon

Composition by Harlowe Typography, Inc.
Cottage City, Maryland

Printed by R. R. Donnelley and Sons, Co.
Harrisonburg, Virginia

THE BROOKINGS INSTITUTION

Dedicated to
Joseph A. Pechman
1918–1989

Foreword

T AX REFORM has returned to the national political agenda. Ten years ago the issue was how to reform the personal and corporation income taxes. Today the question is whether to replace the income tax with one form or another of consumption taxation. Putting the issue this way is a bit misleading, because the current tax system is a complex hybrid between an income and consumption tax, with some features that violate the principles of either system.

Much public debate on tax reform focuses on broad principles and takes place at a high level of generality. The tax system, however, comprises the most specific of laws with special provisions formulated to achieve a host of narrowly defined objectives. Reform of the current system will therefore have myriad effects. To judge the desirability of reform proposals, one must evaluate the consequences of change not only for the economy as a whole but for the individuals and businesses on whom current tax law has such an important bearing.

On February 15 and 16, 1996, the Brookings Institution convened a conference to examine in detail the effects of the major tax reform proposals currently under discussion. Conference participants listened to twelve papers and the responses of twelve discussants who addressed the probable effects of tax reform on economic growth, saving, labor supply, health insurance, housing, charitable giving, financial institutions, international trade, administrative costs, income distribution (instantaneous and long term), and the special problems of transition. This volume presents those papers and the discussants' comments, along with an introductory chapter by the editors, senior fellows Henry J. Aaron and William G. Gale.

These papers show that fundamental tax reform presents the American public with fundamental choices. The current system is extraordinarily complex. Its complexity is a consequence of a variety of provisions designed to encourage homeownership, charitable contributions, employer-financed health insurance, and many other activities. The personal income tax system is also progressive. Replacing the current tax system could bring the virtues of simplicity yet eliminate incentives for many socially beneficial activities that current provisions of the tax code promote. The flat tax would promise some increase in output, labor supply, and savings, but at the cost of diminished productivity. Readers of this volume can find the most up-to-date estimates of all of those effects. With this information, they can judge whether the trade-offs that fundamental tax reform would bring are worth making.

Theresa Walker, Nancy Davidson, Caroline Lalire, James Schneider, and Deborah Styles edited the volume. Joseph Milano and Jasper Hoek provided research assistance, Cynthia Iglesias and Gerard Trimarco verified the manuscript, and Kathleen Elliott Yinug handled conference arrangements and prepared the manuscript for editing. Mary Mortensen constructed the index.

This project was supported by the Aspen Institute, the Carnegie Corporation of New York, and the Joseph A. Pechman Fund. Brookings gratefully acknowledges that support.

The views expressed in this volume are those of the authors and should not be ascribed to the organizations whose assistance is acknowledged above or to the trustees, officers, or other staff members of the Brookings Institution.

Michael H. Armacost
President

September 1996
Washington, D.C.

Contents

Tables

Figures

CHAPTER 1

Introduction

Henry J. Aaron and William G. Gale

T AX REFORM has returned to the national political agenda. Leading members of both parties have proposed to alter or replace the current personal and corporation income taxes. These proposals come barely a decade after President Reagan signed the Tax Reform Act of 1986. The 1986 tax act was the culmination of a decades-long effort to broaden the bases and cut rates of the personal and corporation income taxes. Tax reform, many observers thought, had been achieved, and the nation could move on to other issues. It hasn't turned out that way.

The forces leading to the 1986 tax act and the reasons why tax reform has reentered the political debate are instructive. In the decades before 1986, Congress enacted a succession of deductions, credits, allowances, and exclusions, each intended to advance particular economic or social objectives. Whether the provisions were effective was unclear, but two effects were beyond dispute. The provisions made the tax system more complicated; and they narrowed the tax base, thus requiring higher tax rates. As a result, efforts to shelter income also increased. To compound the problem, the proliferation of special tax provisions undermined the efficacy of each—to encourage every sort of behavior is to encourage none.

A small cadre of economists and lawyers, including Joseph A. Pechman, former director of the Brookings Economic Studies program, to whom this book is dedicated, urged sharp cuts in marginal tax rates financed by repeal of most of the base-narrowing tax provisions. Until the mid-1980s their views had been treated as ivory tower speculations, since efforts to curtail deductions and shelters often failed in the face of impassioned opposition from powerful tax lobbies.

Against this backdrop, the enactment of the Tax Reform Act of 1986 became possible because of widening recognition of the general benefits of lower rates and base broadening. The act was the culmination of bills submitted by both Democrats and Republicans and achieved some but not all of the objectives sought by advocates of base broadening and rate reduction. It simplified tax filing for millions of filers by raising personal exemptions and the standard deduction. It lowered the maximum statutory individual rate from 50 percent to 28 percent and the maximum corporate rate from 46 percent to 34 percent.[1] It reduced tax avoidance by eliminating shelters, ending the exclusion of half of long-term capital gains, and restricting IRA deductions for individual retirement accounts (IRAs). And it raised "minimum taxes" on individuals and corporations who made what the law defined as excessive use of tax avoidance provisions. Liberals applauded the more generous treatment of the poor and the closing of tax shelters; conservatives valued the reduction in marginal tax rates.

Since then, the fragile political compromise underlying the tax reform act has frayed. First, Congress raised statutory tax rates in 1990 and 1993. New rates of 31, 36, and 39.6 percent on high-income households moved the top marginal rate about halfway back to its 1986 level and indirectly recreated a tax advantage for capital gains, the maximum rate on which remained at 28 percent. Phaseouts of personal exemptions and deductions at high-income levels raised effective rates by about 2 percentage points more for some high-income taxpayers. Second, although taxes became simpler for individuals whose income came from earnings, the 1986 act probably increased complexity for individuals with significant capital income and for businesses. Third, the U.S. economy has not performed well since 1986. Poor economic performance has spawned numerous suggestions for increasing growth, with tax proposals in the vanguard.

Most of the new proposals, however, differ fundamentally from past efforts. Rather than tinker with the existing tax system, many of the new proposals would scrap the personal and corporation income taxes and start over with a whole new tax system, based on consumption rather than income. Advocates claim that fundamental tax reform would drastically simplify compliance and raise economic growth by boosting saving, investment, work, and entrepreneurship. If these claims are valid, the United States should identify the most promising proposal and move

---

1. The maximum *effective* rate in the personal income tax was 33 percent over a range in which personal exemptions were phased out.

ahead. If the claims are overstated or omit important considerations, these issues should be explained. In either case, examining fundamental tax reform can raise understanding of how the current system influences economic activity.

To address these issues, the Brookings Institution organized a conference attended by leading economists and lawyers, including authors and supporters of some of the reform plans. The conference revolved around twelve papers addressed to various specific effects of the major reform proposals. This volume brings together those papers and formal comments by discussants.

Elements of Tax Reform

Fundamental tax reform revolves around changes in three main features of the tax system: the tax base, allowable deductions from the base, and tax rates. Revenue needs constrain these choices; narrower bases and more generous deductions typically require higher tax rates to raise a given amount of revenue. Tax systems differ in other important ways— how visible the tax system is to the public; who sends the tax payments to the government (business or households, for example); and how easy the tax system is to comply with and enforce.

The Tax Base

The current federal "income" tax is a complex hybrid between an income and consumption tax, with some features that violate the principles of either system. A pure income tax would tax all labor earnings and capital income, whether obtained in cash or other forms. The current tax system, however, does not tax the imputed rental income on owner-occupied homes. Nor does it tax fringe benefits such as employer-financed health insurance. The appreciation of assets that are not sold represents income but is usually not taxed until the asset is sold.[2] If the asset is not sold during the owner's lifetime, appreciation will never be taxed under the income tax (but may be under the estate tax). Contributions to qualified pension plans are part of compensation but are not

2. There are some important exceptions. Accruing value on zero-coupon bonds is imputed and taxed annually. Futures contracts are "marked to market," and the change in value is subject to tax each year.

included in current taxable income; instead, individuals pay tax on pensions when received. In addition to not taxing many forms of income, the current income tax taxes some forms twice or more: corporate earnings are taxed at the corporate level and again at the individual level when they are remitted as dividends. The system also taxes some items that are not properly considered income: for example, the inflationary component of interest payments or of realized capital gains.

The various consumption tax proposals described below would essentially abandon the taxation of new saving—saving initiated after the taxes take effect.[3] Under the USA tax (unlimited savings allowance), new saving would be treated much like "sheltered" saving in pensions or 401(k)s is treated today: a deduction would be provided for net contributions and net withdrawals would be taxed. Under a retail sales tax or a value-added tax, a similar treatment is provided: no tax is due on saved income, but money that is withdrawn and spent on consumption goods would be taxed. These plans provide what is called "front-loaded" tax treatment of saving: a deduction is provided for the initial saving, and the withdrawal is taxed. The alternative, "back-loaded" treatment, would provide no initial deduction for saving, but then impose no tax on the withdrawal of funds. The flat tax applies this treatment to nonpension saving, while allowing front-loaded treatment of pension saving. If tax rates remain constant over time, these two methods of taxing saving result in equivalent after-tax amounts left in the hands of the saver.[4]

In contrast to the treatment of new saving, all of the plans except the USA tax would tax consumption financed out of the returns from previously existing wealth. The USA tax contains elaborate transition rules to eliminate taxes on up to $50,000 of consumption financed by drawing down old assets. To the extent that such assets were financed out of income previously taxed under the income tax, the logic is that such assets should be exempted from additional tax burdens upon being cashed in. The treatment of consumption financed by old saving is crucial to tax reform. Taxing consumption out of old saving will seem unfair to many participants. But exempting such consumption will require higher

---

3. There are some qualifications to these conclusions, however. See chapter 3 by Eric M. Engen and William G. Gale in this volume.

4. Under front-loaded treatment, $X of saving that earns returns of $100i$ percent for n years accumulates to $X(1+i)^n$. On withdrawal and taxation at the rate t, $X(1+i)^n(1-t)$ remains. Under back-loaded treatment, the taxpayer sets aside $X, but after tax at rate t has only $X(1-t)$ to save. After earning returns at rate i for n years, the taxpayer has $X(1+i)^n(1-t)$, the same as in the front-loaded case.

tax rates on all other consumption to reach a revenue target. These higher taxes would reduce the efficiency and growth effects of tax reform. Transitional relief for old capital fundamentally changes the nature of a consumption tax. Broadly speaking, future consumption can be financed from two sources: existing assets and future wage income. If consumption out of existing assets is exempted from the tax, then the "consumption" tax with transitional relief becomes essentially a wage tax.

Deductions, Credits, and Allowances

Current tax law permits dozens of allowances, credits, exemptions, and deductions. Each provides tax relief that supporters believe improves tax equity (such as the authorization to deduct medical expenses in excess of 7.5 percent of income) or encourages some meritorious activity (such as the charitable contributions deduction). Taken together they reduced the individual tax base by an estimated $1,270 billion in 1993 or about 50 percent of the actual base. If these provisions were all eliminated, tax rates could be reduced across the board by about one-third, from the current 15 to 39.6 percent to a range from 10 to 27 percent. The same amount of revenue could be raised from the personal income tax with a flat tax rate of 13.5 percent. Repealing some of these provisions would also simplify compliance and administration.

These provisions also impose costs. The higher tax rates required to collect a given amount of revenue raise the distortions imposed by any tax system. They complicate record-keeping and enforcement and add to complexity in a more subtle way since raising rates raises the return to tax avoidance.

Rates

Tax rates raise several important issues. The first concerns the effects of taxes on economic decisions. The higher the tax rate, the greater the distortion created by the tax system. A deduction that would matter little if the tax rate were 10 percent becomes powerful when the rate is 40 percent. The second issue concerns the effects of taxes on the distribution of tax burdens across the income distribution. The current personal income tax has six rates: 0, 15, 28, 31, 36, and 39.6 percent, at successively higher taxable income. Taxpayers with taxable incomes over stipulated thresholds lose portions of their personal exemptions and certain itemized deductions. Together, these two phaseouts can raise marginal tax rates by nearly 2 percentage points. Once the phaseout is complete, the top marginal rate returns to 39.6 percent.

Legislators use multiple positive rates in personal taxes to achieve a desired distribution of tax burdens among people or households. A zero rate under personal taxes for those with little income or consumption also simplifies administration and compliance by excusing households with few resources and little potential tax liability from the need to file returns or maintain records. Multiple positive rates increase progressivity but raise compliance and administrative costs. Contrary to popular lore, the computational burden posed by multiple rates is trivial. Most people look up their income tax liability from a tax table. But multiple rates greatly increase transactional complexity. The effect is most apparent with capital transactions, which typically consist of partially offsetting expenses and income flows that occur over time. Regardless of the rate, taxpayers have incentives to accelerate deductions and defer income. Multiple rates also make it profitable to split capital transactions into separate components. Allocating deductions to high-bracket taxpayers and income to low-bracket taxpayers can reduce or defer taxes, sometimes dramatically. Such splitting of transactions underlay many tax shelters before 1986 and sometimes turned the tax system into a subsidy system.

The Major Reform Plans

Most of the major reform plans would replace the existing system with taxes on consumption, wipe out deductions, and flatten rates. But the taxes also differ in many ways. Table 1-1 shows the broad features of each proposal.

National Retail Sales Tax

A retail sales tax (RST) is perhaps the clearest example of a consumption tax. In its purest form, a national RST would apply at a single rate to all business sales to households. Sales from one business to another would be exempt because these sales are purchases of inputs for business use, rather than personal consumption.

Retail sales taxes are imposed by forty-five states and the District of Columbia. They relieve everyone other than retailers of the burdens of tax compliance. However, they suffer from a number of practical shortcomings.

A high-rate, retail sales tax is subject to serious and possibly insuperable administrative problems. Many retail establishments sell to both households and businesses. It is easy to exempt business sales if one is indifferent to tax evasion by households using businesses as cover for their own purchases. Exempting business while preventing evasion by households is administratively difficult. Some activities are cumbersome to tax at any rate. Small retailers keep poor records and enforcement is costly. Some services are hard to tax—banking services, for example—and others are unpopular to tax—education and medical services, for example. At the relatively low rates in effect in the various states, these problems are manageable. At rates above 20 percent, which would be necessary to replace the personal and corporation income taxes along with state income taxes that would likely have to be converted to sales taxes, these problems become extremely difficult. Perhaps for these reasons, no country in the world now imposes a retail sales tax of more than 10 percent.

Retail sales taxes also claim a larger share of the incomes of low-income households than of high-income households. Various methods have been proposed to provide tax relief for low-income households. However, any method that required households to provide information on income would substantially complicate the tax. Some states exempt food and other necessities from tax, but this approach is inefficient, because most households consume a mix of goods, and each commodity exemption raises the tax rate necessary to reach a given revenue target.

The Value-Added Tax

The value-added tax (VAT) applies to the same tax base as the retail sales tax but is collected differently—the VAT would apply to all businesses. The base is gross receipts from sales, less purchases (including investments) from other businesses. Thus, the increment in value of a product at each stage of production is subject to tax. Since the increment in value, cumulated over all stages of production, just equals the value of final sales the VAT base is total sales to consumers—that is, consumption. Because the tax is collected at each stage of production, the revenue loss from exemptions or evasion by a given seller is smaller than it is under the retail sales tax. For example, exemption of hospital services to consumers would not remove tax collected from manufacturers of hospital supplies.

Table 1-1. *Comparing the Tax Plans*

Tax provision	Current law	Retail sales tax	Value-added tax	Armey-Shelby flat tax	USA tax	Gephardt
Change in system	None	Replaces individual and corporate income tax and estate tax	Replaces individual and corporate income tax	Replaces individual and corporate income tax and estate tax	Replaces individual and corporate income tax; offsets payroll taxes	Modifies current system
Individual-level tax						
Summary	Imposes graduated-rate tax on wage and capital income with exemptions and deductions	Eliminates individual-level income tax	Eliminates individual-level income tax	Imposes single-rate tax on wages and pension distributions with large exemptions and no deductions	Imposes graduated-rate tax on wage and capital income less saving and other deductions, with a credit for employee payroll taxes	Broadens base and reduces rates relative to current system
Tax base						
Wages and salaries	Yes	...	...	Yes	Yes	Yes
State and local bond interest	No	...	...	No	No	Yes
Other interest, dividends, rent, royalties	Yes	...	...	No	Yes	Yes
Realized capital gains	Yes (at preferred rates)	...	...	No	Yes	Yes
Health insurance	No	...	...	No	No	Yes

Employer pension contribution	No	No	No	Yes
Employee pension contribution	No	No[a]	No	Yes
Accumulation in pensions	No	No	No	No
Pension receipts	Yes	Yes	Yes	Yes
Social security	Yes	No	Yes	Yes
Deductions				
Nonpension saving	No	No	Yes	No
Mortgage interest	Yes	No[b]	Yes	Yes
Charitable contributions	Yes	No[b]	Yes	No
Property taxes	Yes	No	No	No
State and local taxes	Yes	No	No	No
Tax rates (percent)	15, 28, 31, 36, and 39.6[c]	20 in 1996–97, 17 thereafter	After 1999, rates are 8, 19, and 40[d]	10, 20, 26, 32, and 34[c]
Exempt range (dollars)[f]	...	...	...	...
Single person	6,400	10,700	6,950	7,750
Married couple	11,550	21,400	12,500	13,850
Family of four	16,550	31,400	17,600	19,350
EITC	Yes	No	Yes	Yes
Payroll tax credit	No	No	Yes	No
Child care credit	Yes	No	No	No

Table 1-1 (continued)

Tax provision	Current law	Retail sales tax	Value-added tax	Armey-Shelby flat tax	USA tax	Gephardt
Business-level tax						
Summary	Corporations pay essentially flat-rate tax on net income; other businesses pay taxes under individual income tax	Imposes flat-rate tax on sales to consumers by all businesses	Imposes flat-rate tax on all business sales to consumers and other businesses less costs of inputs and capital goods	Imposes flat-rate tax on value-added base less wages and employer pension contributions	Imposes flat-rate tax on value-added base with export exemptions plus refundable credit for payroll taxes paid by employer	Retains current tax and cuts "corporate welfare" by $50 billion (no details specified)
Tax base						
Sales of goods and services^g	Yes	Yes	Yes	Yes	Yes	Yes
Financial income	Yes	No	No	No	No	Yes
Foreign-source income	Yes	No	No	No	No	Yes

Deductions					
Wages and salaries	Yes	No	No	Yes	No	Yes
Employer pension contribution	Yes	No	No	Yes	No	Yes
Investment	Depreciated	No	Expensed	Expensed	Expensed	Depreciated
Payroll taxes	Yes	No	No	No	Credit	Yes
Other taxes	Yes	No	No	No	No	Yes
Interest paid	Yes	No	No	No	No	Yes
Health insurance	Yes	No	No	No	No	Yes
Tax rates (percent)	35[h]	17[i]	17[i]	20 in 1996–97, 17 thereafter[i]	11	Same as current law
Foreign trade	In general, taxes export sales	Taxes imports; exempts exports	Taxes imports; exempts exports	Taxes exports; exempts imports	Taxes imports; exempts exports	Same as current law

a. The legislation is unclear, but if all pension receipts are taxed, all pension contributions should be untaxed.

b. A flat-tax plan submitted by Senator Arlen Specter (Republican of Pennsylvania) would retain this deduction.

c. In 1995 taxable income brackets were $0–$23,350, $23,350–$56,550, $56,550–$117,950, $117,950–$256,500, and over $256,500 for single filers; $0–$39,000, $39,000–$94,250, $94,250–$143,60, $143,600–$256,500, and over $256,500 for married filers; and $0–$31,250, $31,250–$80,750, $80,750–$130,800, $130,800–$256,500, and over $256,500 for heads of household.

d. The rates would originally be set at 19, 27, and 40 percent but would fall over time. After 1999 rates would be set at 8, 19, and 40 percent. For years 2000 and beyond, taxable income brackets are $0–$3,200, $3,200–$14,400 for single filers; $0–$5,400, $5,400–$24,000, and over $24,000 for married filers; and $0–$4,750, $4,750–$21,110, and over $21,100 for heads of household.

e. Taxable income brackets are $0–$24,050, $24,050–$58,300, $58,300–$121,600, $121,600–$264,450, and over $264,450 for single filers; $0–$40,200, $40,200–$97,150, $97,150–$148,150, $148,150–$264,450, and over $264,450 for married filers; $0–$32,250, $32,250–$83,250, $83,250–$134,850, $134,850–$264,450, and over $264,450 for heads of household.

f. This range ignores the EITC and payroll tax credit and is the sum of personal and dependent exemptions and the standard deduction in the income tax; personal and dependent exemptions in the flat tax; personal and dependent exemptions plus a "family living allowance" in the USA tax; and personal and dependent exemptions in the Gephardt plan.

g. For the retail sales tax only goods and services sold to consumers would be taxed. For the other plans all sales are included in the tax base.

h. Taxable income brackets are $0–$50,000, $50,000–$75,000, $75,000–$100,000, $100,000–$335,000, $335,000–$10,000,000, $10,000,000–$15,000,000, $15,000,000–$18,333,333, and over $18,333,333. The respective tax rates are 15 percent, 25 percent, 34 percent, 39 percent, 34 percent, 35 percent, 38 percent, and 35 percent. Almost all corporate income is taxed at the 34 percent rate or higher.

i. At this rate, the new system would raise less revenue than the current system.

European nations have shown that value-added taxes can be enforced at rates sufficient to generate enough revenues to replace the personal and corporation income tax. But the value-added tax, like the retail sales tax, imposes disproportionate burdens on low-income households. European nations typically offset this effect with public services, family allowances, and other forms of assistance at levels well above those provided in the United States.

The Flat Tax

The flat tax is a two-part value-added tax. The tax base for businesses is identical to the VAT base, except that businesses also subtract wage payments and pension contributions to workers. Households pay tax on earnings and pension benefits at the same rate applied to businesses, but only above some threshold. Unlike the retail sales and value-added taxes, the earnings component of the flat tax is a personal tax. By splitting the value-added tax into two pieces and providing personal exemptions, the flat tax is able to eliminate direct tax on households with modest earnings. In its pure form, the flat tax would repeal all itemized deductions.

The USA Tax

Unlike the preceding plans, the USA tax combines two distinct and separate elements. Households would be subject to a personal consumption tax. Each household would pay tax on income less certain itemized deductions and exclusions and less an *unlimited savings allowance* (hence, the name). Households would calculate income much as they do now under the personal income tax. Net additions to savings would be deductible without limit and net depletion of savings would be taxable, except that households would be permitted to consume up to $50,000 of wealth in their possession at the time the new tax takes effect. Expenditures from assets above this level would be treated as negative saving and would add to the tax base. Deductions for mortgage interest, charitable contributions, alimony, and a limited amount of tuition would apply to all taxpayers, not just itemizers. Exemptions based on family size would be allowed. In the initial year, tax rates would be applied at graduated rates of 19 percent, 27 percent, and 40 percent. In later years the bottom two rates would be reduced to 8 and 19 percent. The USA tax would also give households a refundable credit for the worker's component of payroll taxes. A separate value-added tax would be collected from businesses at a rate of 11 percent on value added, less a credit for the employer portion of payroll taxes.

The USA tax raises administrative problems not present in the current system or other proposed reforms. Many of these problems revolve around the need to keep track of assets in existence at the time the new tax would take effect and to distinguish them from assets created later. For example, taxpayers would have powerful incentives to conceal old wealth, perhaps by moving it offshore, and to bring it back after the new tax comes into effect, thereby qualifying for the unlimited savings allowance.

Income Tax Reform

The principle underlying the Tax Reform Act of 1986 was to broaden the income tax base by terminating or limiting a wide variety of deductions, exclusions, allowances, and credits and use the additional revenue to cut rates. Representative Richard Gephardt (Democrat of Missouri) proposes a reprise of that approach to tax reform. His plan would eliminate deductions for state and local taxes and charitable contributions, various deductions for pension contributions, and the exemption of interest paid on municipal bonds, but would retain the earned income tax credit and the mortgage interest deduction. Employer-provided health insurance would be part of the employee's taxable income. Base broadening would permit a rate of 10 percent for income of most taxpayers above an exempt level, with rates rising to a maximum of 34 percent. The plan would make modest changes in the corporation income tax with an emphasis on cutting what is often called corporate welfare.

Comparing the Plans

The five plans represent prototypical approaches to tax reform. Some of the elements of each plan could be grafted onto others. The flat tax could be modified to accommodate payroll tax credits, deductions for charitable contributions or state and local taxes, or even graduated tax rates. The income tax could be modified to have flat rates and no deductions.

But some provisions are simply inconsistent with the basic principles of particular reforms. Plans, like the flat tax, that exclude asset income from personal tax, cannot allow a mortgage interest deduction without creating a tax loophole, since households could borrow against their house, deduct the interest payments, and use the proceeds to buy assets whose income would be exempt. This example illustrates a fundamental constraint on any tax reform plan: the tax system is a *system*, the pieces of which must be related to one another in a logically consistent fashion.

Chapter Summaries

Whether to adopt a particular tax reform should hinge on how it affects individuals and businesses, not just on broad philosophical principle. The broad principles are important guideposts for tax reform, but they frequently bend before the complexities of modern economies and the pressures of political compromise. Thus the studies in this book take up not only the long-run effects of relatively pure forms of the various reform proposals but also examine details that are often ignored.

Investment and Growth

Alan J. Auerbach calculates the overall effect of major tax reform plans on aggregate performance of the economy. He uses a general equilibrium model to calculate the many simultaneous and interacting responses to changes in tax policy to differentiate between short- and long-run effects of reform.

Auerbach explains that a difficult part of analyzing tax reform is characterizing the existing system. Taxes on capital income vary depending on the type of asset, the owner, how the asset is financed, and whether the alternative minimum tax applies. He finds that the current system distorts investment principally by penalizing future consumption and by favoring the two-fifths of the total capital stock devoted to housing over other investment. Thus, he cautions, comparing a pure consumption tax with a pure income tax misrepresents the actual policy choice.

Auerbach finds that each of the pure alternative systems—the retail sales tax, the VAT, the flat tax, and the USA tax—would eventually raise output, capital, wages, and economic welfare, and reduce interest rates. The results are sensitive to whether transitional relief for old capital is provided; how large the personal exemptions are; whether adjustment costs impede changes in investments; how linked the U.S. economy is to the rest of the world; whether tax rates are proportional or progressive; and the sensitivity of labor supply to reduced tax rates. In particular, plans that provide transition relief or retain personal exemptions and models that allow for adjustment costs in investment eliminate much of the long-run gain in growth and efficiency and almost all of the gain over the first ten years.

Saving

The primary way to raise economic growth is to boost national saving, and advocates have claimed that fundamental tax reform would dramatically boost saving by reducing the effective tax rate on capital income. Eric M. Engen and William G. Gale note several factors that suggest a small impact on saving. First, much U.S. saving occurs in tax-preferred forms such as pensions, 401(k)s, IRAs, and life insurance vehicles. This saving already receives the tax treatment it would face under a consumption tax. If tax reform caused interest rates to fall, the return on such investments would decline, which may reduce saving. Second, people save for a variety of reasons, including precautionary motives, which may be less sensitive than long-term saving to taxes and interest rates. Third, transition relief for old capital would require higher tax rates and reduce saving.

Engen and Gale, accounting for these factors in a general equilibrium framework, find that tax reform would raise saving but not by very much. If a flat consumption tax, providing transitional relief and personal exemptions, replaced a hybrid income-consumption tax, the saving rate would rise from 6.1 percent to 6.6 percent five years after the reform took effect and to 6.4 percent in the steady state. The steady-state ratio of capital to income would rise 4.7 percent and steady-state utility by 0.2 percent.

Engen and Gale caution that the results do not account for changes in pension coverage. Reform would remove most of the current tax preference for pensions relative to other saving. This would likely cause a decline in pension coverage that would reduce the impact on saving. In particular, how tax reform would treat nondiscrimination rules and withdrawal restrictions is a critical but uncertain element of the full impact on saving.

Health Insurance

Proposals for fundamental tax reform would slash current tax incentives for employers to buy health insurance for their employees. Jonathan Gruber and James Poterba estimate the effect of such changes on health insurance coverage and benefits. The current exclusion of employer-financed health insurance from both income and payroll taxes reduces the price of employer-purchased health insurance relative to self-insurance by one-fourth to one-third. The flat tax, the retail sales tax, and Representative Gephardt's income tax reform would all reduce this incentive by about half by ending the income tax exclusion. The USA tax eliminates the payroll tax advantage as well.

Gruber and Poterba model these tax changes as increases in the price of insurance and use estimates of the responsiveness of health insurance purchases to price to measure the effect of tax reform. Unfortunately, these estimates vary widely, and it is uncertain whether the response varies by income class and the extent to which changes in demand show up as changes in people insured or insurance per person. Estimates of the decline in demand for insurance range from 11 percent to 38 percent. The number of uninsured people would rise by 5.5 million to 24 million, an increase of 14 percent to 60 percent.

Gruber and Poterba review the effects on the demand for auxiliary coverage, increases in deductibles and cost sharing, and encouragement of managed care. The largest, and potentially most important, uncertainty concerns whether workplace pooling of health risks would remain common practice. Gruber and Poterba also examine whether the decline in employer-financed health insurance would raise medicaid spending, reduce growth of overall health care spending, and raise growth of cash wages. In each case, they conclude the effects would be small.

Land and Residential Housing Prices

The impact on housing prices is one of the most controversial aspects of tax reform. The current tax system favors investments in owner-occupied housing over other assets. The advantage, though, is not given by the very popular mortgage interest deduction—interest payments should be deductible in an income tax. Rather, the advantage is provided by generous capital gains rules and the exclusion of the imputed rents from taxable income. Though imputed, the income flow is real: owners who rent houses to other people pay taxes on the rent. If the owner and "renter" are the same person, the value of the rental payment is still income, but it is implicit and not taxed.

The flat tax would end both the mortgage interest and property tax deductions and put housing on equal terms with other assets. The USA tax would continue the mortgage interest deduction and retain the current tax preference for housing. Retail sales taxes and value-added taxes could apply to housing services but probably would not. Deductions for property taxes or mortgage interest could also be removed within the existing system.

Dennis R. Capozza, Richard K. Green, and Patric H. Hendershott examine the effects on land and housing prices and housing finance. They find that current incentives primarily act to raise the price of residential land. Because houses and land are linked, removing the incentives would reduce the price of the structure plus land. Prices would fall most in communities where income and tax rates are relatively high since the incentives matter most at the highest tax rates.

Using 1990 data, they estimate that repealing the property tax deduction would reduce housing prices nationwide by an average of 5 percent. Repealing the mortgage interest deduction as well would reduce housing prices by an additional 12 percent. The USA tax would reduce prices by 20 percent. The flat tax would reduce prices by 29 percent if interest rates held steady, by 20 percent if rates fell 1 percentage point, and by 9 percent if interest rates fell 2 percentage points. The results are sensitive, however, to initial conditions. In each case, there is a dramatic range across cities, reflecting differences in local property tax rates and tax brackets of homeowners. The authors note that price declines could have serious consequences for mortgage lenders, since many initial mortgages equal or exceed 80 percent of market value and housing prices have recently fallen in many housing markets.

Because the USA tax continues to treat mortgage borrowing more favorably than other borrowing, the authors estimate that homeowners would raise the average loan-to-value ratio to 0.8. This increase in borrowing, combined with continued deductibility of mortgage interest, would reduce revenues about $50 billion over the first three years after the new tax took effect and raise the rates necessary to maintain revenue. They also predict that the impact on homeownership rates would be small.

Charitable Contributions

Charles T. Clotfelter and Richard L. Schmalbeck note that nonprofit organizations may be like innocent bystanders at a gunfight, not intended targets, but in grave danger of being hit. The current tax system encourages charitable organizations in numerous ways. Fundamental reform proposals could remove the deduction for individual and corporate charitable contributions. Even if the deduction remained, however, tax reform would affect giving by changing marginal tax rates, which affect the price of giving.

Unfortunately, analysts disagree on how responsive charitable giving is to its price. Using two estimates of the responsiveness, Clotfelter and Schmalbeck calculate that the flat tax and the Gephardt proposal, both of which repeal the charitable contributions deduction, would reduce individual charitable giving by 10 percent to 22 percent. The USA tax, which raises marginal rates and retains a deduction for charitable contributions, would increase giving by 11 percent to more than 30 percent. The authors expect little impact on volunteering.

The Armey-Shelby flat tax would also repeal estate and gift taxes. The full effects are uncertain because repealing the estate tax would affect gifts by living persons as well as testamentary gifts. Clotfelter and Schmalbeck estimate that testamentary gifts would fall 24 percent to 45 percent. The impact on corporate contributions is even less certain. It is unclear how responsive corporations are to the price of giving and the extent to which corporations would recharacterize charitable contributions as advertising or other deductible expenses. The authors calculate that repeal of deductibility would reduce corporate donations by 15 percent to 45 percent.

Labor Supply

Most tax reform plans would reduce marginal tax rates on earnings and change the form of employee compensation by reducing incentives for employers to provide pensions or health insurance. These changes could affect decisions on when to enter the labor force and when to retire. Some advocates also claim that reform would encourage entrepreneurship by raising returns to risk taking and to investments in training and education. Unfortunately, little research is available to support estimates of the size of such effects. In contrast, a large body of research is available to estimate how tax reform would change hours worked by people in the labor force. Robert Triest uses this research to estimate the effect of tax reform on hours worked.

Triest shows that labor supply incentives are influenced by the income tax, the payroll tax, the earned income tax credit, tax avoidance behavior, and phaseouts of government means-tested spending programs. Disagreement remains on how taxes affect work effort of men and women. Triest uses three sets of behavioral responses. In the intermediate case, the flat tax would raise labor supply by 1.1 percent; the flat tax with an earned income tax credit by 0.9 percent; and the Gephardt modified income tax by 0.9 percent. With small behavioral responses, the flat tax raises hours worked by 0.4 percent; with high assumed responses, the increase is 6.5 percent. The reforms would generally raise labor supply most among households in the top income decile, who would receive the largest cut in marginal tax rates.

Distribution of Income

Who gains and who loses is at the forefront of every debate on tax reform. Congress and the public pay most attention to the distribution of burdens imposed in a given year. But economists point out that longer-term measures may be more revealing. Low-income households in any given year will include some who are temporarily poor—young taxpayers just starting out, retirees who once had higher incomes, households with short-term earnings drops or capital losses—as well as the permanently poor who never have earned much.

William G. Gale, Scott Houser, and John Karl Scholz examine the distributional effects of tax reform in a single year. Don Fullerton and Diane Lim Rogers focus on the effects over the full lifetimes of households with typical characteristics.

Gale, Houser, and Scholz find that the current tax system—including personal and corporate income taxes, the payroll tax, and state income taxes—is strongly progressive. Replacing the personal and corporate income taxes with a flat tax would generate modest effects except at the very top and the very bottom. Average tax rates would rise by 2–3 percentage points for households in the bottom 40 percent of the income distribution. For households in the top 1 percent, tax rates would fall by 7 percentage points, and tax payments would fall by more than $37,000 a year.

To eliminate some of the problems connected with looking at annual distributions of tax burdens, the authors also examine married couples in which the husband is between ages 40 and 50, who should thus be near the lifetime income peak. The effects of the flat tax for this group are even more pronounced at the bottom of the income distribution. Various modifications, such as retaining the earned income tax credit and some itemized deductions, or permitting a deduction for payroll taxes, ameliorate these effects. But under all variants, the flat tax does just what its name promises. It flattens current progressivity. If revenues are maintained, taxes rise for low-income families and fall for high-income families.

A value-added tax contains no personal exemptions for low earnings and flattens distribution even more than the flat tax. The USA tax keeps taxes relatively constant at the bottom of the distribution and slightly reduces them for households in the tenth to seventieth percentiles. Average tax rates increase by 3–7 percentage points for households in the top 5 percent. A base-broadening, rate-reducing income tax reform described by the authors would slightly reduce taxes for families in the lower 80 percent of the income distribution and raise taxes for families with higher incomes.

To complement these annual estimates, Fullerton and Rogers examine long-term distributional effects. They find that shifting to a proportional consumption, wage, or income tax would reduce welfare of the current elderly and improve welfare of the current young, with the largest effects under a proportional consumption tax. Allowing personal exemptions or commodity exemptions does not materially alter the result.

Fullerton and Rogers classify people based on the present value of lifetime income and find that replacing the current income tax with a single-rate tax with no exemptions reduces welfare of the poorest 2 percent of the population by 4 to 6 percent and increases welfare of the richest 2 percent by 9 percent to 10 percent. Adding an exemption changes the results dramatically—all income groups gain from replacement of the current tax system with a single-rate wage, consumption, or income tax above an exempt level.

Simplification

Joel Slemrod evaluates claims that tax reforms would simplify compliance and administration. He emphasizes that simplicity and compliance costs can not be evaluated independently of some standard of tax enforcement and intrusiveness. Moreover, complexity exists for very practical reasons. Many of the provisions that complicate the tax system arose because people thought that they added to fairness or promoted some socially or economically desirable objective. Thus, simplifying the tax system can create trade-offs with fairness, social goals, and tax enforcement.

The personal and corporation income taxes are extremely complex for some taxpayers. Slemrod estimates that total administrative and compliance costs are about $75 billion, or 10 percent of revenue collected. These estimates, though, are fraught with uncertainty. Estimates for systems that exist only on paper are even more hazardous.

The retail sales tax raises particular problems. Administrative and compliance costs of actual U.S. retail sales taxes range from 2 percent to 4 percent of revenue collected. None of these taxes has a rate above 7 percent. To replace the personal and corporation income taxes would require rates above 20 percent, given likely exemptions and the likely conversion of state income taxes to sales taxes. At these rates, Slemrod argues, the retail sales tax would not be administrable because incentives to evade the tax would all be focused on retailers and would not be containable. In contrast, experience in European countries shows that value-added taxes can be administered at the rates needed to replace the personal and corporation income taxes, even with some complications of multiple rates, exemptions, and so-called zero rating. Evasion varies in the European Community from an estimated 2.4 percent in the United Kingdom to 40 percent in Italy. Administrative and compliance costs of VATs range from 5 percent to 6 percent of revenue collected.

Because the flat tax combines a VAT with a personal tax on wages, collection costs would exceed those of a VAT. Slemrod estimates that after the expiration of any transition provisions, the flat tax would lower business compliance costs by 30 percent and personal compliance costs by 70 percent, relative to the corporate and personal income taxes respectively, cutting total collection costs approximately in half. Slemrod judges a personal consumption tax, such as the USA tax, to be unenforceable at acceptable standards of fairness and intrusiveness. The transition provisions would be particularly onerous because they require valuation and tracking of all assets, something no tax system has ever done.

Income tax reform holds out limited potential for simplification. He estimates that a variety of reforms could reduce personal compliance costs by 15 percent and business costs by 5 percent. In short, income tax reform could achieve sizable savings for people with simple returns, but little simplification for people with returns complicated by significant flows of business or other capital income.

Transition

Transitional issues are central to any tax reform effort. Tax legislation often contains provisions to compensate those who are penalized by the change in rules. These provisions may last many years, are often complicated, and can have significant adverse impacts on revenues and economic growth, but they seldom receive much advance consideration.

Ronald A. Pearlman argues that the principle of "reliance"—taxpayers making choices on the assumption that the tax laws would continue to apply—is necessary to justify transition relief. It is not sufficient, however, as other provisions of a new tax law may provide relief to the very taxpayers who suffer from the provision for which transition relief is claimed. Transition relief may grandfather affected taxpayers, delay or phase in new rules, or directly compensate affected taxpayers. The Armey-Shelby flat tax explicitly disavows transition relief, the USA tax contains elaborate transition relief, and the other plans have not addressed the issue. Pearlman argues that flat-tax advocates are wrong to dismiss transition relief and that the relief in the USA tax is poorly designed.

The most important transition issue is the so-called capital levy on consumption out of existing wealth. Taxing old wealth may not seem fair but is critically important to some of the goals of tax reform, because doing so raises considerable revenue and thus allows lower tax rates in the rest of the tax system. Another issue involves the treatment of contract interest. The income tax permits interest deductions and includes interest receipts in taxable income. The retail sales tax, value-added tax, and flat tax would end both provisions, so that interest payers would suffer windfall losses, while interest recipients would enjoy windfall gains. In addition, many businesses now have net operating losses that they can carry forward as offsets against any profits they may earn. Their status under a new tax system remains an open question.

Pearlman argues that transition relief of some form is almost inevitable and will prove complicated and that these concerns should not be used as an argument against fundamental tax reform but rather as a warning that transition issues deserve careful and early consideration.

Financial Institutions

Many people have suggested that taxing financial institutions raises particular problems for consumption taxes. But David F. Bradford points out that functionally identical problems exist under income taxes. Households accept lower cash returns on checking accounts than they could earn on other investments of equal risk because banks provide valuable services in kind along with whatever cash returns they offer. These services should be taxed as household income under an income tax or as consumption under a consumption tax, but the value of these services is difficult to measure. This is a problem only for financial services provided to households, however. For businesses, the failure to measure the value of financial services understates business income and expenses by the same amount, so business taxable income is unaffected as long as a single tax rate applies to all businesses.

In practice, U.S. retail sales taxes typically exempt financial services. Foreign countries with value-added taxes often exempt financial institutions. These institutions do not pay value-added tax directly, but pay some tax indirectly because they lose credits for taxes levied on their suppliers. In addition, value-added taxes create certain perverse incentives in nonfinancial businesses. VATs are intended to apply to real, not financial, transactions. This distinction creates an incentive for business to convert real transactions into financial ones, for example, by decreasing prices on goods sold and compensating for the loss by insisting on deferred payment at inflated interest rates. To solve this problem, Bradford suggests treating all receipts from installment sales on a cash-flow basis. Bradford concludes that cash-flow approaches can tax consumption of financial services at rates similar or identical to those applied to other consumer goods.

International Taxation

With the growth of international trade and capital movements, the international consequences of tax policy are of increasing importance. James R. Hines describes current tax rules and explains the ramifications of various tax reform proposals for international economic transactions. The United States currently taxes residents on their worldwide income. Foreign subsidiaries of U.S. corporations may defer U.S. tax on income earned abroad until it is repatriated if they satisfy certain conditions. U.S. businesses receive credits, subject to certain limits, for taxes paid abroad.

The plans differ from current law and one another in their treatment of imports and exports. The retail sales tax and USA tax would tax imports and exempt export sales of U.S. companies. The Armey-Shelby flat tax would tax exports and permit businesses to deduct the costs of imports. Hines reports the well-established theoretical conclusion that the effects of these two methods of border adjustment on trade should be the same, but notes that a new system might cause an extended adjustment period during which this theoretical outcome would not be fully realized. He also points out that tax reform plans that discourage investment in housing would encourage investment elsewhere, in the United States and abroad.

Hines highlights a range of questions that seldom arise in popular discussions of tax reform. One issue is "transfer prices," the internal prices used in transactions between the parent company and its subsidiaries or among subsidiaries. Transfer prices determine the international distribution of reported costs, revenues, and profits. The retail sales tax would give companies incentives to report profits in the United States, while the flat tax and USA tax would give incentives to report revenues and sales outside the United States. Another issue is that tax reform would also change incentives for individuals to live or work abroad. International considerations also create special transition issues. Foreign subsidiaries of U.S. companies have unrepatriated profits, the tax on which would be due when the profits were repatriated. Repealing the corporation income tax would eliminate these taxes.

Conclusion

The U.S. tax system imposes graduated tax rates on a base that is neither income nor consumption and allows numerous special deductions, allowances, and credits. Fundamental tax reform could alter the rates, the base, or the exemptions from the base, but the chapters in this volume suggest that a tax reform plan that could win congressional and presidential approval may not look exactly like any of the plans on the table. If Slemrod is correct, the retail sales tax and the USA tax will not survive close scrutiny in current form because of implementation issues. Pearlman's consideration of transition issues suggests that any approved plan will provide relief for people and businesses who stand to lose significantly. If so, the analysis of Capozza, Green, and Hendershott suggests homeowners will receive some sort of relief, the simplest of which is to retain current deductions for mortgage interest and property tax. If Clotfelter and Schmalbeck are right that eliminating the charitable deduction would seriously damage nonprofits, Congress may well retain the deduction. If taxing health insurance is seen as likely to curtail insurance as much as Gruber and Poterba estimate, pressure for continuing the exclusion will be strong. If these provisions are too strong to resist, other existing provisions—the earned income tax credit, the deduction for state and local income taxes, business deductions of payroll taxes—may also turn out to be indispensable.

Each of these changes would narrow the tax base and necessitate higher rates to sustain revenues. The revenue-neutral rate for the Armey-Shelby flat tax with no deductions or exclusions is about 21 percent. Allowing transition relief would raise the required rate to 23 percent. Adding deductions for mortgage interest, charity, and health insurance would raise the revenue-neutral rate to 27 percent. Adding in the EITC and deductions for state and local taxes and payroll taxes would raise the rate to about 32 percent.[5] Since most taxpayers now face a 15 percent rate and nearly all face a rate no higher than 28 percent, the flat tax may diminish considerably in appeal, or a system with multiple rates or smaller personal exemptions would attract consideration.

The studies in this volume of the effects of tax reform on output, labor supply, and saving all refer to relatively low-rate, "clean" reforms not cluttered by mortgage interest or charitable contributions deductions or by exclusion of employer-financed health insurance. Even if the reforms stay pure, Auerbach, Engen and Gale, and Triest estimate modest effects on output, saving, and labor supply, especially if transitional relief is provided. If the popular deductions were retained, tax rates would rise, and the predicted effects on saving, investment, and labor supply would shrink.

Thus, the studies in this volume, taken together, indicate why tax reform debates that proceed only in broad generalities are not as helpful or instructive as they could be. Tax laws balance a number of considerations: revenue, economic efficiency, fairness, social policy objectives, simplicity, and other goals. It would be surprising if the current system ideally balanced these criteria, but it should not be surprising that changing the system to emphasize one or more of these goals sacrifices others. None of this means that fundamental tax reform could not simplify the system and generate more economic growth. But the chapters show that the gains from realistic reforms may not be as large as advocates have hoped and that the process of adjustment to a new system will not be easy.

Reference

Aaron, Henry J., and William G. Gale. 1996. In *Setting National Priorities: Budget Choices for the Next Century*, edited by Robert D. Reischauer. Brookings.

5. These figures are based on calculations in Aaron and Gale (1996).

PART ONE

Saving, Investment, and Economic Growth

CHAPTER 2

Tax Reform, Capital Allocation, Efficiency, and Growth

Alan J. Auerbach

A CENTRAL focus of the current congressional debate about tax reform is the effect of taxes on U.S. national saving and investment. Most proposals aim to increase private saving by taxing consumption, rather than income, which would in turn boost national saving. These proposals also strive to generate more capital investment and to improve its allocation. The objective is to increase growth of the economy and the standard of living. Some people call these goals "increased competitiveness."

Tracing how additional capital formation (or other changes in economic behavior produced by a tax reform) affects growth and income is a task in itself, but a greater challenge lies in predicting how any particular tax reform will influence behavior.

One can break this puzzle into three parts. First, what incentives does the current tax system generate? Second, how would proposed reforms change these incentives? And, third, how will these changed incentives affect economic behavior? Economic debate too often proceeds as if the characteristics of both the current and proposed tax systems are simple, straightforward, and easily summarized. For example, some economists compare a proportional consumption tax with a proportional income tax. They further simplify the question by comparing the effect of the two tax regimes on the behavior of a representative individual. But these simplifications make such analysis almost useless. People and businesses are heterogeneous. Transition problems are important. Most significantly, neither the current tax system nor any realistic alternative resembles a simple, broad-based, proportional tax on income or consumption. Put simply, one needs to focus on far more than the changed incentives to consume now rather than later in determining whether a shift from today's income tax to a proposed consumption tax will increase national saving. A similar warning applies to inferences about improvements in the allocation of capital.

This chapter addresses the questions listed above in terms of the current tax reform debate. First, how much does the current U.S. tax system distort saving and investment and the allocation of capital? Who bears the burden of the current tax system and how does it affect asset prices? Second, how would different proposed reforms alter these distortions? How would such reforms affect incomes and wealth of different groups? Third, how would these changes be expected to alter economic behavior, in particular saving and its allocation among alternative investments?

A Framework for Analysis

Each household faces a budget constraint. In the absence of taxes, current consumption (C) equals wage income (W) plus current capital income (R) less saving (S), where both capital income and saving are defined net of depreciation: $C = W + R - S$. An income tax would be levied on $W + R$; a consumption tax on $W + R - S$; a wage tax on W.

New Saving and Old Capital

A wage tax and a consumption tax differ primarily in their treatment of existing assets. Both may be neutral with respect to the choice between current and future consumption; in other words, they do not distort the saving decision.[1] However, the consumption tax falls on asset income less saving (the $R - S$ term), thereby imposing what essentially is a capital levy on existing assets. The deduction for saving under a consumption tax (today's S) just offsets taxes on future cash flows from these assets (future R). Together these two provisions impose no net tax burden on *new* saving.[2] But no deduction for saving done in the past exists to offset taxes on current and future cash flows of existing assets. The taxpayer

---

1. A wage tax of, say, 10 percent reduces maximum possible current consumption by 10 percent if all earnings are consumed. It has the same proportionate effect on future consumption if all earnings are saved. Similar reasoning applies to a consumption tax.

2. This conclusion follows from the fact that the initial cost of an asset should, at the margin, equal the present value of that asset's future cash flows. Thus, by giving a deduction for an asset's cost and then taxing that asset's future cash flows at the same rate, the government is, essentially, simply making a loan to the taxpayer.

simply pays tax on the consumption-financed income and principal of existing assets. Because asset values equal the present value of expected future cash flows, this tax is equivalent to a one-time levy on the value of these assets.

Equivalent Taxes

As explained in the editors' introduction, many taxes that look different from one another are really equivalent. The government can tax consumption directly (as under a sales tax) or indirectly, either through separate taxes on wages (W) and cash flows ($R - S$), or through taxes on income ($W + R$) less saving (S). Likewise, whether a tax is imposed on businesses or individuals should not, in itself, influence the impact of the tax. The economic effects of an income tax, for example, should be the same whether employers withhold it or employees pay it directly.[3] For example, the capital levy imposed by the cash-flow component of the consumption tax would depress asset values if collected from businesses because it would reduce the net cash flow to individual owners of the businesses. Collecting the same tax at the individual level would leave asset values unchanged. But the incidence of the two taxes would be the same.[4]

Price-Level Effects

Although the initial equation makes no explicit mention of the price level, assets such as government bonds have fixed nominal values. Tax changes that alter the price level affect the real value of such assets. Assets not directly subject to cash-flow taxation still may bear the equivalent capital levy if a consumption tax translates into a price-level increase. The effect occurs because inflation erodes the real purchasing power of assets with fixed nominal returns.

Thus the initial equation should be expanded to include two assets and a term for the price level (p):

---

3. Of course, compliance and administrative costs may differ in important ways, depending on the point of collection.

4. As an analogy, imagine that the taxes one would owe on distributions from an individual retirement account were payable by the financial institution holding the account. Then the value of that account would be reduced by the amount of the anticipated tax liability.

(1) $$pC = pW + p(R_1 - S_1) + p(R_2 - S_2).$$

Now, suppose the government imposes a tax on wages and cash flows from only asset 1. Investors in asset 2 receive no deduction for purchases and pay no tax on income and sales proceeds. Taxing wages and the cash flows from asset 1 at rate τ has the effect of multiplying the first two terms on the right-hand side of equation 1 by the term $(1 - \tau)$. In addition, introducing the tax may cause the price level to rise from p to p'. Such a change will induce a proportional rise in the price of consumption goods, nominal wages, and, normally, the cash flows from assets. However, some assets, such as outstanding government bonds, may have fixed nominal cash flows. If so, the budget constraint becomes

(2) $$p'C = (1 - \tau)p'W + (1 - \tau)p'(R_1 - S_1) + p(R_2 - S_2).$$

It is sometimes assumed that the introduction of a consumption tax causes the general price level to rise enough to keep after-tax wages, $(1 - \tau)p'W$, constant, that is, by a factor $1/(1 - \tau)$. If this occurs, then expression 2 may be rewritten:

(3) $$p'C = (1 - \tau)p'W + (1 - \tau)p'(R_1 - S_1) \\ + p'(1 - \tau)(R_2 - S_2).$$

The price-level increase has the effect of spreading the cash-flow tax to this asset as well, by reducing the real after-tax values of its nominal cash flows through the price increase.[5]

Behavioral Effects

Behavioral changes resulting from tax changes will also alter wealth holdings. For example, increased saving under a consumption tax raises the demand for capital, which may boost asset prices. The size and duration of this effect will also depend crucially on the openness of capital markets and the treatment of international capital flows. Changes in incentives facing domestic residents need not translate into changes in the demand for only domestic assets.

5. For further discussion, see U.S. Congress (1993, pp. 53–54).

Timing

In addition, tax systems differ not only in their marginal (substitution) and inframarginal (income) effects, but also in their timing. For example, a consumption that exempts the cash flows from existing assets would be equivalent to a tax on wages alone, because it would collect no tax on existing assets and no *net* tax on new assets. But the timing of tax payments will differ from those of a wage tax. New saving will generate deductions and trigger future taxes of equal present value (discounted at the rate of return on the investment). Because the timing of tax payments under alternative tax systems differs, it is confusing to evaluate effects on saving by looking at annual private saving under the two tax regimes: when one compares the consumption with the wage tax, private saving would be higher but government revenues would be lower, with the government implicitly providing through tax deductions some of the funds being saved.[6]

As this example emphasizes, policymakers should be interested in *national* saving, not arbitrarily defined private saving. National saving equals net national product minus consumption by government and households. If government consumption is fixed, what matters for national saving is how tax policy affects output and personal consumption. Unless tax changes boost labor supply and output, an increase in national saving can come from only two sources: reduced consumption, which will directly increase current saving and raise future national saving by increasing output, or improved capital allocation, which can increase the productivity of a given stock of capital. Hence, if one is interested in national saving, relevant questions to ask for each tax change are whether it discourages consumption and whether it improves the allocation of capital.

The Current U.S. Federal Income Tax

The taxation of capital depends on at least four considerations. First, tax rules vary among assets. For example, depreciation deductions for tangible capital are spread over a period approximating the asset's economic lifetime. Research and development expenditures, which may provide

---

6. The present value of government revenue would be the same in the long run, discounted at the average return on private investment.

benefits for several years, may be deducted fully in the year the expenditures are made. Second, tax rules differ among classes of owners. The major distinction is between corporate and noncorporate businesses for business assets and between households and businesses for housing. Third, tax rules vary according to the nature of financial claims on assets. The most familiar is the distinction between rules applicable to corporate debt and those governing corporate equity. Fourth, any particular combination of owner, asset, and method of finance may be subject to more than one tax regime, as certain rules, such as minimum taxes, apply only under certain circumstances. I consider below the impact of taxation for each important combination of these different elements. Comparing the alternative treatments provides a sense of the distortions of asset choice, ownership patterns, and financial policy. Combining them provides a measure of the overall tax burden imposed on capital income.

Investment Incentives and Valuation under the Corporate Tax

Since 1993, the top corporation income tax has been 35 percent. That rate applies to virtually all corporate income not subject to the alternative minimum tax. Depreciation rules have evolved over the years. The most recent change, also in 1993, lengthened depreciable lives for nonresidential business structures to thirty-nine years.

Since economic income equals receipts less expenses, one of which is the loss of value of capital goods used in producing that income, depreciation allowances that match actual economic depreciation are necessary to reach a tax base equal to net income. In general, tax depreciation differs from true economic depreciation, leaving the investor with a lower or higher tax burden than would occur if "true" income were subject to tax. The size of the resulting distortion equals the difference between the statutory rate and an "effective tax rate," defined as the tax rate that, if combined with economic depreciation allowances, would generate the same marginal tax burden. If depreciation allowances are larger (smaller) in present value than economic depreciation, the effective tax rate will be lower (higher) than the actual tax rate.[7]

Under the tax law that prevailed before the Tax Reform Act of 1986, effective tax rates were generally much lower than the statutory tax rate of 46 percent then in effect. The differences between equipment and structures were quite large (because of the investment tax credit) and

---

7. This concept is discussed further in Auerbach (1983a).

quite dispersed. However, since 1986, effective tax rates have differed less and have been closer to the statutory tax rate. For example, Jane Gravelle finds that when the statutory corporate rate was 34 percent in early 1993, effective tax rates on different equipment classes ranged from 21 percent for railroad equipment to 39 percent for engines and turbines and autos. The effective tax rate for structures averaged 32 percent and ranged from 28 percent to 36 percent (except for mining and oil and gas structures, which faced an effective rate of just 11 percent as the result of special tax provisions not eliminated by the Tax Reform Act). She finds little variation in effective tax rates across industries after taking asset composition into account.[8]

Taken alone, this variation in effective tax rates imposes little inefficiency beyond that caused by uniform capital income taxation. I found that the lost productivity due to misallocation of corporate equipment and structures was equivalent to a loss of a fraction of 1 percent of the corporate capital stock every year from 1953 to 1962, a period during which the investment tax credit was not in effect and dispersion of effective tax rates was similar to what it is now.[9] Since the corporate capital stock accounts for only a fraction of corporate value added and corporate value added accounts for only a fraction of overall GDP, the distortion is therefore of a magnitude of 0.1 percent of GDP or less. Clearly, if the current tax system causes serious distortions, the problem must lie elsewhere.[10]

Even with complete uniformity of effective tax rates, though, the current treatment of corporate assets differs from that of a "pure" income tax. Tax burdens on older assets are higher than on comparable newer assets, mostly because depreciation allowances on older assets are worth less than depreciation on comparable newer assets. This difference in the value of depreciation deductions arises from two sources. First, depreciation allowances are "accelerated," in the sense that new assets receive deductions larger than economic depreciation and older assets receive smaller deductions. Second, depreciation deductions are based on the original purchase price of an asset. Inflation erodes the real value of fixed nominal depreciation deductions.

8. Gravelle (1994, pp. 54–55).
9. Auerbach (1983a).
10. These calculations focus on tangible, nonresidential corporate capital and exclude the intangible capital produced by research and development spending and the small amount of housing held in corporate form.

If, as suggested above, new capital faces an effective tax rate near the statutory rate, this outcome results from relatively low taxation of income early in asset lives followed by heavier taxation later on. Thus older assets face higher rates of taxation and should be valued at a discount precisely analogous to that imposed by the implicit capital levy under a consumption tax that provides no transition relief to protect owners of old assets. In each instance, existing assets face higher net taxes than new assets, and for essentially the same reason: new assets receive greater deductions than existing assets. Under the cash-flow tax, the difference is stark: new assets are immediately written off. Existing assets receive no deductions at all. The difference under the current tax system is smaller: new assets are not immediately written off, and existing assets receive some depreciation deductions. In effect, the current tax system imposes its burden in two stages: the first is an income tax at the effective rate on new investment; the second is a tax surcharge on the cash flows from existing assets that rises with the age of the asset. This second piece is like the cash-flow tax already analyzed, affecting asset values (and revenues), but not the incentive to invest.

My calculations indicate that equipment and structures currently face effective corporate tax rates of 28 percent and 33 percent, respectively (with an average of 31 percent)—near the statutory rate of 35 percent.[11] These calculations also suggest that the existing corporate fixed capital stock should carry a discount below market value averaging approximately 8 percent—smaller than before 1986, but still not negligible. In terms of the framework laid out in the previous section, one can think of the current corporate tax as imposing a nearly uniform tax on capital income (R) of 31 percent, plus a tax on cash flow $(R - S)$ of 8 percent. Eliminating the corporate tax would do away with both the marginal tax wedge and the cash-flow tax.

Financial Policy and Individual Taxes

The actual burdens imposed on corporate investment differ from those just presented. Individuals who own corporate equity pay not only the corporation income tax (an indirect burden) but also personal taxes on dividend income and capital gains from sale of shares. Individuals also

---

11. The methodology used is described in detail in Auerbach (1983a). The calculations here use updated capital stock weights from Auerbach and Hassett (1991), and include only federal income taxes. The results are in line with Gravelle's.

pay taxes on interest from corporate debt, but corporations pay no tax on returns to capital paid out as interest. To calculate the effects of these additional elements of taxation requires not only data on tax rates and asset ownership, but also assumptions about the determinants of financial policy.

First, although the tax treatment of debt and equity differs, companies use both methods of finance. Under current tax rules, with the corporate tax rate nearly as high (at 35 percent) as the highest individual rate (at 39.6 percent), nearly all individual investors would face lower overall tax rates if they received their corporate source income as interest payments rather than as dividends and capital gains. Many considerations explain the coexistence of debt and equity.[12] Analysts customarily assume that companies finance investment with fixed ratios of debt and equity, based on observed debt-equity ratios and the ownership of these securities. Taking this approach, I calculate the net additional tax on corporate source income arising from interest deductibility at the corporate level and personal taxes (see appendix A).

Even with the assumption of fixed financial policy and asset ownership patterns, a problem remains in the interpretation of the tax treatment of dividend income. Under the "traditional" view of equity-income taxation, the shareholder tax rate on equity-source income is a weighted average of the tax rate on dividends and the effective rate on capital gains (taking the advantage of deferral into account). However, an alternative or "new view" argues that, because taxes on dividends are essentially unavoidable, they should be capitalized into the value of shares (to the extent that they exceed the effective rate of tax on capital gains that would result were dividends not paid). On this view, dividend taxation imposes no burden on marginal investment decisions, because the presence of dividend taxation causes asset prices to be reduced by an amount equal to the future taxes on the dividends that this investment produces. This argument suggests another component of the current tax system that should be capitalized into the value of existing assets.[13] Because analysts remain divided on whether the traditional view or the new view is correct, I provide calculations corresponding to both.

Roughly a third of debt and equity is held not by individuals but by financial intermediaries and other entities, most notably insurance companies, pension funds, and nonprofit institutions. I follow the customary

12. Auerbach (1983b).
13. For further discussion, see Auerbach (1983b).

procedure of netting out the banking sector and treating the income from nonfinancial corporations as flowing directly to the ultimate individual asset holders, each with its own tax treatment.[14]

Under these assumptions, I conclude that these additional factors contribute essentially no added burden under the traditional view of dividend taxation and actually reduce the net burden under the new view, yielding overall tax rates on corporate source income of 31 percent and 26 percent, respectively.[15] To the extent that the "new" view of dividends holds, the market value of corporate assets should reflect the capitalization of the relatively unfavorable treatment of dividends, or roughly an additional 10 percent of the value of corporate assets (for a total of 18 percent, including the previously discussed amount attributable to accelerated depreciation).

One further element of "cash-flow" taxation under the current tax system is of some importance, in addition to accelerated nominal depreciation allowances and the tax treatment of dividends. Pension fund assets already face cash-flow tax treatment, as contributions to pension funds and their asset income are excluded from individual taxation, while benefit payments are taxed to individuals. Although new pension fund accumulations face no net tax, existing pension fund assets should (from the point of view of their ultimate beneficiaries) incorporate the capitalized value of future tax payments on withdrawals.

The Corporate–Noncorporate Distinction

I have suggested that distortions *within* the corporate sector are now rather insignificant. A second distinction is the allocation of capital *between* the corporate and noncorporate sectors. My calculations, paralleling those reported above for the corporate sector, yield an overall tax rate of 18 percent for new noncorporate investment under current tax rules. The corresponding cash-flow tax on old investments is 6 percent.

Thus new noncorporate investment faces an average marginal tax rate of approximately 18 percent, compared with a range of 26 percent to 31 percent on corporate investment. The gap is somewhat larger than that among different corporate-owned assets. The size of the inefficiency

---

14. King and Fullerton (1984).

15. This result derives from the considerable gap between the tax rate at which interest is deducted and the rate at which it is taxed. See Gordon and Slemrod (1988) for further discussion.

or "deadweight loss" associated with this gap depends crucially on the "elasticity of substitution," the degree to which capital moves between corporate and noncorporate production when the return differs. Traditional calculations found little loss—about 0.5 percent of GDP, according to Arnold Harberger and John Shoven.[16] These estimates were based on much larger gaps between the corporate and noncorporate tax burdens than currently exist. They did not take into account interest deductibility and the favorable treatment of capital gains. Using current tax rates would generate still smaller estimates of efficiency losses. On the other hand, Gravelle and Laurence Kotlikoff have argued that the elasticity of substitution between corporate and noncorporate production is effectively much larger than Harberger and Shoven supposed and have found much larger estimates of the deadweight loss of differential taxation between corporate and noncorporate sectors.[17]

Further Complications: Tax Losses, Passive Losses, and Minimum Taxes

The effective tax rate calculations presented thus far exclude such complications as the corporate and individual alternative minimum taxes (AMT), the restriction on individual deductions for passive losses, and the limitation on claims of refunds on credits due for active losses. Particularly during recessions, many companies have found themselves subject to limits on tax refunds for losses.[18] In 1991, 24.2 percent of the assets of active corporations were held by firms subject to the corporate AMT.[19]

A naive calculation might fix the effective tax rates of firms under these restrictions as if the restrictions applied permanently, meaning a tax rate of 0 for firms with losses and 21 percent for firms subject to the AMT. However, these restrictions are usually temporary, and companies can carry losses and excess AMT payments forward. The incentives to invest in the presence of tax losses or under a minimum tax depend on the pattern of statutory tax liabilities, as well as the transition probabilities between constrained (facing the minimum tax, having tax losses) and unconstrained states.[20] These provisions may either raise or lower

16. Harberger (1966); Shoven (1976).
17. Gravelle and Kotlikoff (1989).
18. Altshuler and Auerbach (1990).
19. U.S. Internal Revenue Service (1994a).
20. Auerbach (1983a); Lyon (1992).

Table 2-1. *Current Effective Tax Rates, by Industry*
Percent

Industry[a]	Corporate		Noncorporate	Overall		Corporate share[b]	Debt-assets ratio[c]
	Traditional	New		Traditional	New		
Agriculture	28	24	17	19	18	23	36
Mining	21	16	9	19	14	83	27
Construction	32	27	18	28	24	70	27
Manufacturing	31	27	18	31	27	100	34
Transportation, communication, and utilities	27	22	15	26	22	98	35
Trade	33	29	21	30	27	79	38
Services	32	28	21	28	25	64	39
Total	31	26	18	28	24	79	35

a. Computed by Auerbach and Hassett (1991), based on 1985 capital stock data.
b. Gravelle (1994, table B.6).
c. Ratio of interest deductions to assets from U.S. Internal Revenue Service (1994a), scaled by aggregate debt-assets ratio from Federal Reserve System (1995).

the effective tax rate an asset faces, depending on the extent to which that asset has deductions in the short run that must be deferred by constrained firms. Generally, these rules affect equipment investment more than structures, narrowing even further the difference in effective tax rates between equipment and structures. However, no serious calculations have been done on a disaggregate basis to indicate the relative importance of these restrictions on effective tax rates.

Restrictions on individual deductions for passive losses apply primarily to investment in residential construction. More generally, as noncorporate investment still is currently tax-favored, these restrictions probably narrow the gap between corporate and noncorporate investment.

Summary: Nonresidential Business Investment

The results thus far suggest little variation in effective tax rates among different assets and only a moderate gap between corporate and noncorporate sectors. However, industries vary in a number of respects simultaneously, including asset mix, share of assets in corporate form, and the share of capital raised by borrowing, sale of shares, or retention of earnings.[21] Therefore it is useful to take all of these factors into account in comparing the impact of the current tax system across industries. Table 2-1 provides such a comparison, in addition to a summary of the results given above. The table indicates that the overall variation in effective tax rates across industries is small. Except for agriculture and mining, which account for less than 15 percent of the nonresidential fixed capital stock, effective tax rates fall within a range of 5 percentage points.

One can conclude that, on balance, the distortion between assets (equipment and structures), sectors (corporate and noncorporate), and industries is lower than it was before the Tax Reform Act of 1986 and is not a major source of economic distortion—perhaps a fraction of 1 percent of GDP, given the order of magnitude for distortions within the corporate sector discussed above. Of course, assumptions are important, and uncertainties about behavior remain.

I have not discussed other distortions, including those revolving around the choice between debt and equity finance and when to realize capital gains and rebalance portfolios. It is difficult to know how large such distortions are. Some might argue that the tax incentive to borrow is desirable because increased leverage and its required interest payments

21. The ratio of debt to total capital measures the degree of "leverage."

force corporate executives to commit themselves to more efficient management. The lock-in effect of the capital gains tax discourages portfolio rebalancing but does not alter the underlying allocation of capital among companies. Further, alleviating the lock-in effect may actually reduce saving: individuals who acquire just the right mix of investments may find themselves meeting their goals with a smaller portfolio.[22]

The main distortion of the taxation of nonresidential fixed investment under the present tax system lies in the overall taxation of capital income. The calculation in table 2-1 puts this tax rate at between 24 and 28 percent. The additional implicit cash-flow tax on existing assets in excess of that faced by new investment of between 8 and 16 percent (depending on the appropriate view of the capitalization of dividend taxes) applies only to existing capital and therefore causes no inefficiency.

Other Investment Decisions

Aside from corporate and noncorporate fixed investment, the other major investment in the United States is housing. Most housing— 76 percent—is owner-occupied.[23] Given that the imputed rent on housing is not taxed, one can conclude that the effective tax rate on housing investment is very low—perhaps 5 percent.[24]

Finally, I have yet to touch on the complicated rules governing foreign investment, including the foreign tax credit, the different classes of income, and the rules for allocating interest and research and development expenses. I will return to these issues below when considering the impact of tax reform on interest rates.[25]

22. Auerbach (1992).

23. At the end of 1994, according to the Federal Reserve's Board of Governors (1995a), residential structures were valued at $5.856 trillion, owner-occupied housing at $4.448 trillion.

24. This number equals the ratio of housing that is not owner-occupied, 0.24, times an effective tax rate on rental housing of about 20 percent, according to Gravelle (1994). Two other factors not incorporated in the simulations below might reduce further the effective tax rate on housing. The first is the deductibility of state and local property taxes. If property taxes at least in part are a cost of providing housing (as opposed to purchasing local public services), then their deductibility makes the effective tax rate on housing negative: the gross returns are tax-exempt and some of the expenses are deductible. The second is the possibility that the ability to leverage housing investments significantly may convey an extra benefit to the extent that, as appears to be the case, borrowers are in a higher tax bracket than lenders.

25. See chapter 13 by James Hines in this volume.

Tax Reform: The New Proposals

Tax reform proposals currently being discussed differ in progressivity, treatment of existing assets, treatment of financial flows and foreign investment, and method of collection. Some of these differences are cosmetic, while others are of greater substance. Because many details must be resolved before most proposals can be put into legislative language, some of the analysis that follows is based on my own interpretation of the proposals.

National Sales Tax

A national sales tax (NST) would replace the current individual and corporation income taxes with a national tax on retail sales. Unlike most current state retail sales taxes, the NST would also cover services but exclude investment goods. It would approximate a consumption tax—a tax on labor income plus the cash flows from different assets.[26]

However, the cash-flow component associated with existing residential real estate would be left out of the tax base unless the tax applied to the sales of existing homes. The treatment of government bonds would depend on how prices responded to the tax shift. If prices rose, then all existing nominal assets would decline in value. The result would be equivalent to a cash-flow tax on existing federal debt. On the other hand, if the tax were absorbed through a decline in nominal wages, consumption out of existing federal debt would not be taxed.

In the case of tax-exempt debt, a decline in its value would have little if any impact on the value of existing household assets, to the extent that the liabilities of state and local governments were capitalized into property values. While there would still be redistributions among asset holders, the overall effects on wealth would be small, as in the case of corporate debt and other debt issued by intermediaries.

Value-Added Tax

Many variants of the value-added tax (VAT) differ in their administration. However, for the purposes of this discussion, one can lump together all destination-based value-added taxes on consumption

---

26. Joel Slemrod (in chapter 10 in this volume) questions the administrative feasibility of imposing a national retail sales tax at the rate that would be required.

goods.[27] As proposed by many in Congress, including Representative Sam Gibbons, the senior Democrat on the House Ways and Means Committee, a VAT would be essentially equivalent to the NST. It would tax the cash flows from existing assets except housing and, depending on what happened to prices, government debt.

Flat Tax

As originally designed by Robert Hall and Alvin Rabushka and proposed by Representative Dick Armey and Senator Richard Shelby and former presidential candidate Steve Forbes, the flat tax resembles the VAT in most respects.[28] In contrast to the VAT, it taxes wages at the individual level, thereby permitting retention of personal exemptions and a standard deduction.[29]

The Hall-Rabushka tax treats pensions differently from the way they are handled under a value-added tax. Under the VAT, pension contributions are part of labor compensation and are taxed at the business level. Pension payments to households are subject to no further direct tax. Under the flat tax, businesses may take a deduction for payments to pension plans, but households do not have to pay tax on the contribution when it is made. When pension benefits are paid, however, households must pay tax on the benefits to the extent that the sum of earnings and pensions exceeds the exemption level. This difference does not affect the incentive to save and invest because the after-tax return to the pensioner for each dollar of pension contribution is the same in either case. But the rules have different effects on existing pension fund assets. The burden under the flat tax is higher than it would be if pension benefits and

27. A destination-based tax is imposed on all items *purchased* in the taxing jurisdiction. By contrast, an origin-based tax is imposed on all such items that are *produced* in the taxing jurisdiction. A destination-based VAT is implemented through "border adjustments" that impose the tax on imports and relieve the tax on exports. An origin-based VAT requires no adjustments.

28. See Hall and Rabushka (1995).

29. Some, for example, Hall (1996), have argued that the flat tax also would affect prices differently from either the NST or the VAT—that while each of those taxes would translate into a higher price level, the flat tax would not. This argument hinges on a difference in national income accounting convention having real effects. Indirect business taxes, which would include a standard sales or value-added tax, are subtracted from output before factor incomes are calculated; direct taxes, including the current income tax and, arguably, both the business and individual components of the flat tax, are not. Thus, a Federal Reserve monetary policy based on maintaining nominal wage levels (gross of direct taxes but net of indirect taxes) would lead to an increase in nominal output—a price-level increase—under the introduction of an indirect tax but not under a direct tax.

contributions were simply left out of the individual tax base. Thus the personal tax under the Hall-Rabushka plan is a hybrid of a wage tax (on earnings) and a consumption tax (on pensions), both at the flat tax rate.

A third way that the Hall-Rabushka flat tax differs from the NST and VAT is that it is an origin-based tax, not exempting export sales or taxing import sales, while the NST and VAT are destination-based taxes. Taxing imports and giving a deduction for exports, as is done under the VAT, is equivalent to cash-flow treatment of net foreign investment. Thus the difference between this approach and the origin-based approach is one not of incentives, but of wealth effects, equal to the capitalized value of cash-flow taxes on net foreign assets. Given that the United States is now a net debtor nation, its net foreign asset holdings are negative. Thus the present value of associated cash flows is also negative, and excluding them from the tax base—as under the origin-based approach—provides a *broader* tax base.[30] This distinction has nothing to do with "competitiveness" as it is usually understood in the debate about value-added taxes, which appears to derive from an assumption that real exchange rates would be different under otherwise equivalent tax systems.

USA Tax System

The Nunn-Domenici USA (unlimited savings allowance) tax combines what appears to be, respectively, a subtraction method value-added tax on business and a progressive consumption tax on individuals. However, both taxes deviate from their prototypes.

The business-level value-added tax provides a credit for employer social security taxes. The individual tax allows a credit for individual social security taxes. In addition, the treatment of existing assets under both levels of tax and the treatment of borrowing under the individual tax deviate from a pure consumption tax approach.[31] Under the business tax, companies may amortize the basis of existing depreciable assets. The individual tax also preserves the basis of existing assets, meaning that taxable proceeds from sales of these assets are reduced by the tax basis. However, individuals with more than $50,000 in assets must defer use of this deduction until they are net dissavers. This combination not only shields some existing wealth from cash-flow taxation but also encourages

30. Auerbach (1995).
31. See Ernest S. Christian and George J. Schutzer, "USA Tax System," vol. 66, *Tax Notes*, March 10, 1995, special supplement.

households to dissave by imposing what amounts to a positive tax on saving. Borrowing is also treated in an anomalous manner. Borrowing is included in the tax base when households are net savers but not when they are net dissavers.[32]

Because the USA tax allows recovery of basis and provides credits for payroll taxes, its marginal rates are considerably higher than those of the flat tax, which also provides some relief for low-income citizens. Hall and Rabushka estimate that their system would require a 19 percent tax rate to match current revenues.[33] Initial Treasury estimates indicate that the Armey-Shelby flat tax, which has higher exemption levels than Hall and Rabushka proposed, would require a marginal rate of 25 percent.[34] By contrast, the marginal rates under the USA tax system are 11 percent at the business level plus up to 40 percent at the individual level. Unlike the flat tax, the USA tax would subject government debt to individual taxation. The business-level component of the USA system would treat foreign assets under the destination principle.

The 10 Percent Tax

Representative Richard Gephardt's "10 percent tax" is not based on the principle of taxing consumption. It would conform to the existing tax system much more closely than would the other plans. Contrary to its name, the 10 percent tax would have five graduated individual tax rates (10, 20, 28, 32, and 34) and would preserve the corporate tax. It would reduce marginal rates for most taxpayers by broadening the base to include more fringe benefits (mainly health insurance) and capital income than the current system does. Taxable capital income would include all realized capital gains and interest on state and local government obligations. In addition, it would end the exclusion from personal tax of pension contributions but retain deferral of tax on the income accruing to pension fund assets (comparable to that of today's nonde-

32. For further discussion, see Alvin C. Warren Jr., "The Proposal for an Unlimited Savings Allowance," *Tax Notes*, vol. 68, August 28, 1995, pp. 1103–08; and Louis Kaplow, "Recovery of Pre-Enactment Basis under a Consumption Tax: The USA Tax System," *Tax Notes*, vol. 68, August 28, 1995, pp. 1109–18.

33. Hall and Rabushka (1995).

34. Barbara Kirchheimer, "Armey Flat Tax Plan Panned by Treasury," *Tax Notes*, vol. 65, November 7, 1994, pp. 655–56. A more recent Treasury estimate of a modified version of the Armey proposal with generous low-income relief puts the break-even tax rate at 21 percent. See "'New' Armey-Shelby Flat Tax Would Still Lose Money, Treasury Finds," *Tax Notes*, vol. 70, January 22, 1996, pp. 451–61.

ductible IRAs). Thus the Gephardt plan is comparable to today's tax system, with somewhat higher effective tax rates on capital income.

The Impact of Tax Reform on Asset Values and Interest Rates

Taxes influence both the value of newly acquired assets and the relative values of new and existing assets. I explained above how the imposition of a cash-flow tax on existing assets (either directly or through a price-level increase applied to assets fixed in nominal terms) lowers the value of existing assets *relative* to the value of new assets. New assets receive larger tax deductions than old assets do.[35]

The effect on market value of a cash-flow tax depends on whether the tax is assessed at the firm level or at the household level (see note 4 above). Company-level taxes affect market values as just described, but individual-level taxes do not, even though both identically affect the after-tax value of the asset *to the investor*. For example, a cash-flow tax at the rate τ on individuals who owned an asset worth q would lower the value of that asset to the investor to $q(1 - \tau)$ since selling the asset at its market value of q would occasion a tax payment of $q\tau$. Because of this difference, I take care, when simulating the effects of the different tax systems, to distinguish the level (company or household) at which taxes are imposed.

Taxes also affect the values of existing assets by changing the cost and valuation of new assets. If new assets become more expensive, the price of comparable existing assets also rises. These changes in the value of new assets come through changes in the incentive to save and invest. Apart from the effects of tax reform on international capital movements, most of the proposals discussed above would lower the income tax on new investment. Such changes should reduce consumption and increase saving and investment. They should also shift investment to business plant and equipment from housing, which would receive no added benefits relative to the current tax system. In a world of homogeneous output and instantaneous adjustment of the capital stock, no changes in the

---

35. For example, if a new piece of equipment costs q, and a cash-flow tax at rate τ is in force, then an otherwise identical piece of existing capital will be worth $q(1 - \tau)$, the value of the new asset less the value of the immediate deduction on the new asset. Note that this differential will continue to apply, even in the future, because existing assets, even if acquired after the imposition of a cash-flow tax, will already have received a tax deduction and will not offer owners any additional one.

value of new capital goods would result, as quantity changes would erode any incipient changes in asset values by driving down before-tax returns on newly favored assets and pushing up the before-tax returns on assets whose purchases had been discouraged.

Since adjustments take time, changes in relative asset values might persist until the economy adjusted fully to the new tax system. With lags in adjustment, changes in an asset's quantity would only gradually erode the effects of tax changes on asset prices. In the aggregate, demand for capital would increase, causing a temporary increase in the value of new assets. The values of assets that become relatively less tax-favored, such as housing, would face reduced demand and lower prices.[36] The after-tax rate of return on investment would rise because of the lowered taxes on new investment in general. The before-tax return on business assets would fall as the stock of these assets increased, and both the before-tax and after-tax return on housing would rise.

The speed of adjustment would depend on both technology and individual responsiveness to the altered incentives. For example, if the demand for housing services is not very sensitive to price, then a small adjustment in the housing stock might allow before-tax returns to housing investment to rise enough to offset the decline in the relative tax advantage of housing.

Interest Rates in a Closed Economy

The interest rate would equal the before-tax return to capital only under very restrictive and inappropriate conditions: if all investment were financed by debt, if prices were completely stable, and if all assets faced an effective tax rate on investment income equal to the statutory rate at which interest payments were deducted. In this rather extraordinary case, the interest rate would equal the before-tax return to capital under the present tax system, and it would continue to do so after tax reform, when effective tax rates on all capital income were zero. In this case, the interest rate would track movements in the before-tax rate. The before-tax rate of return to capital would fall with a tax reform that raises investment, and the interest rate would fall to the same extent.

However, the current tax system does not satisfy these restrictive conditions, because it applies different rules to different investors, assets,

---

36. See chapter 5 by Dennis Capozza, Richard Green, and Patric Hendershott in this volume.

forms of financial claims, and types of business organizations. Without going into a very general analysis of the portfolio decisions of households and the financial decisions of companies, one can still get a sense of how the interest rate will move by aggregating capital into a single, representative asset and considering its overall tax treatment and how this compares with that of interest. I follow this procedure in the simulations reported below. Because the overall effective tax rate on capital may be higher (or lower) than the effective tax rate on interest income, the real interest rate can be below (or above) the overall before-tax rate of return to capital. Thus the interest rate may fall by less (more) than the before-tax return to capital as taxes on capital income are eliminated and the before-tax returns on capital and interest converge because their tax treatment is equalized.

Indeed, tax reform may cause interest rates to rise if the before-tax return to capital falls relatively little and the initial tax rate on interest income is much lighter than that on capital. Martin Feldstein argues that this outcome is likely.[37] I present calculations in appendix B suggesting that the interest rate may fall more than the rate of return to capital, as estimates suggest that the effective tax rate on interest income is higher than that on capital as a whole (including housing). In any event, the simulations presented below, which do not distinguish among types of finance or types of asset, equate the projected declines in before-tax returns and in interest rates.

Interest Rates in an Open Economy

Relaxing the closed-economy assumption could also temper the estimated drop in interest rates. The key issue is the extent to which foreign investors in the United States are faced with the same change in incentives as U.S. investors. If they lend to U.S. businesses and face only home country taxation, they would not be directly affected by U.S. tax changes. To the extent that before-tax interest rates fall, foreigners will tend to reduce lending to U.S. borrowers, thereby offsetting any increase in U.S. investment demand. The curtailment of foreign lending to U.S. borrowers would also reduce asset values relative to the predictions given above for the closed-economy case. This intuition underlies the "open-economy" simulations presented below, which assume a fixed U.S. interest rate.

37. Feldstein (1995).

Tax reform might encourage other investment in the United States by foreigners. Foreign owners of U.S. subsidiaries would have their U.S. taxes reduced. If foreign tax authorities do not impose offsetting tax increases in their home countries (as they would under a tightly applied "worldwide" or residence-based tax system), these foreign investors would wish to invest more in the United States at the pre-reform, before-tax rate of return. Whether they would invest more even at the lower rate of return induced by added U.S. household saving is less clear. If U.S. household saving were relatively unresponsive, capital inflows could result, financing any rise in U.S. investment demand that might occur and contributing to higher asset values. Again, a more complicated model than is used here would be necessary to trace out the changes in relative asset prices and investment.[38]

Simulating the Effects of Tax Reform

To simulate the effects of tax reform proposals on saving, investment, and growth, I use the Auerbach-Kotlikoff dynamic simulation model, described in more detail in appendix C. The model is a general equilibrium growth model with one production sector; a government that raises revenue, runs deficits, and provides goods and services and social security benefits; and fifty-five overlapping generations of households, with an exogenous rate of population growth. Households supply labor and consume in each year according to an optimal lifetime profile for each activity based on specified preference parameters that help determine the sensitivity of saving and labor supply with respect to the after-tax rate of return and the after-tax wage rate.

The model permits a fairly general specification of the tax system, with a payroll tax-based social security system and separate taxes of variable progressivity on total income, labor income, capital income, and consumption and, under the income and capital income tax bases, fractional expensing of new investment that can represent a range of investment incentives that apply only to new capital. It also permits one to set the level of adjustment costs facing new investment and has an open-economy option that keeps the interest rate fixed via international capital flows.

---

38. For further discussion of this issue, see Grubert and Newlon (1995).

Because the model has one production sector and homogeneous capital, it is impossible to consider two important aspects of tax reform: the impact of the shift away from housing investment that most of the proposals would encourage, and the reduced tax differential between corporate and noncorporate activities. The omission of these two factors may understate the efficiency gains from the reforms.[39] On the other hand, political pressures may cause supporters of all of the plans to follow the lead of the USA tax in supporting continuation of the mortgage interest deduction, which would reduce this downward bias.

The simulations describe the transition path from one steady state to another, as the economy responds under a variety of behavioral assumptions to each tax reform. The first step in performing these simulations is to specify the tax parameters associated with the current tax system and each reform (table 2-2). I omit the "10 percent tax" from this simulation exercise because it closely resembles the current system at the simulation model's level of abstraction and because little information is available about it

The Current System

Based on the calculations presented in table 2-1 and the associated text, I combine a midrange estimate of 26 percent for the marginal effective tax rate on nonresidential capital with an assumed low effective rate of 6 percent on residential capital and assume capital is half residential and half nonresidential to arrive at an effective marginal rate of 16 percent. Existing depreciation provisions should cause a discount of about 8 percent on nonresidential capital relative to new investment. Taking account of housing, the discount for the total existing stock of fixed capital relative to new investment in nonresidential capital is 4 percent.[40] To simulate this differential in the model, I assume that new investment receives an investment incentive, in the form of partial immediate deductibility above true economic depreciation that causes ex-

39. The model also does not incorporate any additional efficiency gains that might result from induced growth in technology spurred by capital deepening. See, for example, Stokey and Rebelo (1995).

40. I ignore the possibility that the taxation of dividends leads to additional capitalization, as would be true under the "new" view of dividend taxation. Under this alternative, the efficiency gains from moving to a new tax system would be smaller than those presented below, because the elimination of taxes on dividends would bestow larger windfalls on shareholders and smaller reductions in marginal tax rates..

Table 2-2. *Simulation Parameters of Current Tax System and Proposed Reforms*[a]

Percent

Parameter	Current system (1)	NST/VAT (2)	Hall-Rabushka		Armey-Shelby		USA system (7)
			No transition[b] (3)	Transition[b] (4)	No transition[b] (5)	Transition[b] (6)	
Wage tax							
a. Marginal rate	21.7	12.0	15.8	18.1	20.5	23.5	16.7
b. Average rate	7.5	12.0	10.2	11.7	9.8	11.7	6.2
Capital income tax							
c. Rate	20.0	6.0	9.5	5.6	12.5	7.4	2.8
d. Fraction expensed	20.0	100.0	100.0	100.0	100.0	100.0	100.0
Consumption tax							
e. Marginal rate	2.5	0	2.5	2.5	2.5	2.5	16.3
f. Average rate	2.5	0	2.5	2.5	2.5	2.5	8.2

a. Parameters for current system are for initial steady state. Those for alternative systems are for final steady state, and so are based on different aggregates.
b. With or without transition relief for existing capital.

isting capital to bear a discount of 4 percent relative to new capital. Specifically, I assume that the statutory capital income tax rate is 20 percent and that 20 percent of investment is expensed at the instant the investment is made. The result is an effective tax rate of 16 percent for new capital and 20 percent on existing capital.

The labor income tax in the model applies to all compensation. However, income taxes do not, in fact, apply to pension contributions, which are taxed only upon the receipt of benefits. I represent this practice by treating the existing tax, excluding the taxes on capital income already considered, as a hybrid of a wage tax on direct compensation and a consumption tax on pension contributions and benefits. Because household pension reserves equal about one-fourth of household wealth, I set the average consumption tax rate at one-third the average wage tax rate, calibrated so that the total tax on compensation equals that of the actual tax system.

To account for the progressivity of the income tax, I set the average marginal wage tax rate above the average wage tax rate. I set the average wage tax based on the overall revenue target and the average marginal rate so that, in combination with the consumption tax rate, it yields a total effective marginal tax rate on labor income equal to 23.6 percent, the current value for the United States based on estimates from the TAXSIM model of the National Bureau of Economic Research.[41] This procedure yields an average wage tax of 7.5 percent, an average consumption tax rate of 2.5 percent, and an average marginal wage tax rate of 21.7 percent.

These assumptions (and others discussed in appendix C) yield a before-tax rate of return to capital of 9.5 percent and a national saving rate of 4.1 percent. Both are realistic, a striking finding given the many simplifications of the model.[42]

National Sales Tax and Value-Added Tax

In terms of the simulation model, the national sales tax and the value-added tax are identical: a business-level, proportional tax on wages and returns to capital, with investments fully expensed. Since the resulting

---

41. The effective marginal wage tax, t, taking account of both wage and consumption tax effects, is defined by the expression $(1 - t) = (1 - t_w)/(1 + t_c)$, where t_w is the average marginal wage tax rate and t_c is the consumption tax rate.

42. Because the model ignores risk, there is only one rate of return, typically calibrated to correspond to the observed return to capital, rather than to a "safe" rate of interest.

tax base is consumption, these taxes could also be represented in the model simply as taxes on consumption with an equivalent revenue yield. However, while the NST and VAT have the same effects on real disposable incomes, they would affect asset values differently. The NST and VAT make existing capital less valuable to households than new capital. But this difference is capitalized into the market value of existing assets only when the tax on cash flow is collected at the company level. Because the model treats consumption taxes as being imposed at the household level and capital income taxes as being imposed at the business level, it is more accurate to represent the NST or the VAT in the wage tax-capital income tax-expensing form, with the consumption tax rate set to zero.

Two additional complications must be faced. First, because investments in housing are untaxed, the effective cash-flow tax rate on assets as a whole is lower than the rate on wages. Second, government debt faces an implicit capital levy only if prices increase. Since housing represents roughly half of all capital, I assume that half of assets, including government debt, face the cash-flow tax. With a wage tax rate of 12 percent, capital bears a tax rate of 6 percent (see table 2-2).[43]

The Flat Tax

I consider four versions of the flat tax: the basic Hall and Rabushka plan; the same plan modified to provide transition relief for existing assets; and two versions (with and without transition relief) of the Armey-Shelby flat tax that provide higher personal exemptions and standard deductions.

Hall and Rabushka propose a 19 percent statutory marginal tax rate. As under the NST/VAT, I assume half of existing capital is housing, which will not be taxed, and half is other capital, for which cash flow will be taxed. As a result, the average tax rate on capital is 9.5 percent. Since not every taxpayer will face the positive marginal tax rate on labor supply, I translate the 19 percent statutory rate into an average marginal tax rate, as described in appendix D, and estimate the average marginal tax rate on wages at 17.9 percent.

The exclusion of pension contributions from current tax (benefits are taxable when received) reduces the effective wage tax on compen-

---

43. I make the same assumptions for the remaining tax systems, because it seems inappropriate to impose differences among tax regimes by assuming differences in monetary accommodation.

sation to 15.8 percent. I set the consumption tax rate on pensions at 2.5 percent, which restores the marginal tax rate on all compensation to 17.9 percent.[44] Finally, the average tax rate is set to hold revenue unchanged.

The original Hall-Rabushka plan offers no transition relief for existing assets. In particular, assets acquired before the tax change receive no depreciation deductions. Hall and Rabushka have come to recognize that such relief may be politically necessary.[45] As an alternative to the basic Hall-Rabushka simulation just described, I assume that all assets are allowed to continue receiving depreciation allowances, a procedure roughly equivalent to allowing half of the value of such assets to be expensed: accordingly, I halve the effective cash-flow tax rate, to 4.8 percent.[46] I raise the cash-flow tax rate and the average and marginal tax rates on labor income proportionately to make up the lost revenue (see table 2-2, column 4).

The third and fourth flat-tax simulations are for the Armey-Shelby proposal, with and without transition relief, respectively. The Treasury estimates that a 25 percent tax rate would be necessary to match revenues under current law, given the Armey-Shelby tax base.[47] The average marginal tax rate on labor income is 22.4 percent, which, allowing for the assumed consumption-tax component (due to the taxation of pension benefits), yields a direct marginal tax rate on wages of 20.5 percent. In preparing this estimate I use the same methodology as for the Hall-Rabushka plan (see appendix D). However, the *average* labor income tax rate would be lower under the Armey-Shelby plan than it would be under the basic Hall-Rabushka plan, because the Armey-Shelby plan has a higher tax rate on business cash flows.

Providing transition relief under the Armey-Shelby plan lowers the effective cash-flow tax and raises the average and marginal tax rates on labor income to compensate for the revenue loss, just as it did under the Hall-Rabushka plan (see table 2-2, column 6).

44. The calculation is based on the expression given in note 41 above.
45. Hall and Rabushka (1995, pp. 78–79).
46. Under current law with current inflation, the present value of remaining depreciation allowances per dollar of net nonresidential capital is approximately half the value of the assets. Permitting these depreciation allowances to be taken has the same impact as forgiving half of the cash-flow tax on existing assets.
47. While I have no way of determining the accuracy of this estimate of the original Armey plan's revenue-neutral rate, this simulation, combined with the earlier one based on a 19 percent marginal tax rate, provides a sense of the plausible range of flat-tax outcomes.

The USA Tax

The USA tax system contains several important provisions that other proposals do not have. The 11 percent business tax is essentially a VAT. Accordingly, I treat this component of the plan as I did the NST/VAT, assuming a labor income tax of 11 percent and a cash-flow tax of 5.5 percent to account for housing. I estimate that basis recovery of depreciable assets is half as valuable as expensing, halving the remaining cash-flow tax to 2.8 percent. Then, to take account of the payroll tax credits, I subtract the full payroll tax from the 11 percent labor income tax, leaving a rate of −4.3 percent.

The individual tax has progressive rates, with a top marginal rate of 40 percent. This rate would apply to a large share of the population and leads to an average marginal rate of 35 percent (see appendix D). To deal with the exemption of existing housing and the partial basis exclusion for other assets, I treat this personal tax as 60 percent wage tax and 40 percent consumption tax. That is, I assume the individual tax imposes an average marginal wage tax rate of 21.0 percent (for a total marginal wage tax rate of 16.7 percent) and an average marginal consumption tax rate of 14.0 percent, which equals 16.3 percent on a tax-exclusive basis. I assume that the wage and consumption taxes are equally progressive, in terms of the relationship between the average and average marginal tax rates, after adding in the proportional 4.3 percent wage subsidy from the payroll-tax offset (see table 2-2, column 7).

A Comparison

All the reforms encourage saving by lowering the effective capital income tax rate to zero. However, the actual effects on saving would probably differ because the plans place different fiscal burdens on young and old generations. Relief for existing assets under the flat tax plans and the USA plan shifts resources from the young to the old. Under the model's life-cycle assumptions, this shift reduces aggregate saving because the old have a higher propensity to consume available resources than the young do. On the other hand, the credit for payroll taxes under the USA tax and its much greater reliance on consumption taxes shift the tax burden back toward the old, contributing to increased aggregate saving.

The combined taxes on labor income and on consumption (approximately the sum of rows a and e in table 2-2) govern labor supply under any of the proposals. The lack of progressivity under the NST/VAT keeps this marginal burden much smaller than under the current system. The burden rises a bit under the Hall-Rabushka plan without transition relief and still more with transition relief, but remains well below that under current law. The burden under the Armey-Shelby plan without transition relief is close to that under current law, while the Armey-Shelby plan with transition relief and the USA plan, with its progressive rates, actually increase this distortion.

Initial Results

Table 2-3 shows the macroeconomic and welfare effects of switching immediately to each of the six alternative tax reform proposals with rates on the primary tax bases of the respective systems adjusted in the short run to maintain budget balance. The table presents the percentage change in wages, the interest rate, the national saving rate, output per capita, and asset values at three points during the transition: in year 2 (that is, immediately after the change), in year 10, and in the long run ("year infinity"). (The changes in the saving and interest rates are in percentage points, not percentage of initial values.) It also reports changes in welfare of members of representative generations.[48] Welfare is measured as a percentage of the present value of that generation's lifetime consumption and leisure. The last line of the table presents a measure of the gain in economic efficiency associated with adoption of each proposal. The gain is the sustainable percentage increase in welfare for all future generations that would be possible if lump-sum transfers and taxes kept welfare constant for everyone alive at enactment. The measures of welfare and efficiency are expressed as a percentage of consumption plus leisure (which in the model, accounts for about 60 percent of the household's time); thus they translate into percentages of consumption alone that are about 2½ times greater, or of gross output about 1⅔ greater, than those in the table.

Wages

Under all plans wages eventually rise because added saving increases the economy's capital-labor ratio. However, capital accumulation takes

48. I assume here that individuals enter the model at age 20, so that a person entering the model in year 0 is born in year -20.

Table 2-3. *Macroeconomic and Welfare Effects of Tax Reforms,
with No Adjustment Costs*[a]

Percent

		Hall-Rabushka		Armey-Shelby		
Parameter	NST/VAT (1)	No transition[b] (2)	Transition[b] (3)	No transition[b] (4)	Transition[b] (5)	USA system (6)
Wage						
Year 2	-1.3	-0.6	-0.4	0.2	0.4	0.5
Year 10	2.2	2.2	2.0	2.5	2.2	3.4
Year infinity	4.8	5.3	4.5	5.4	4.3	6.0
Interest rate						
Year 2	0.3	0.1	0.1	-0.1	-0.2	-0.2
Year 10	-0.6	-0.7	-0.6	-0.7	-0.7	-1.0
Year infinity	-1.3	-1.4	-1.2	-1.4	-1.2	-1.6
Saving rate						
Year 2	3.8	4.8	4.1	4.4	3.4	4.7
Year 10	1.9	3.2	2.6	2.9	2.0	2.7
Year infinity	-0.8	0.8	0.6	1.0	0.6	0.7
Output per capita						
Year 2	6.8	4.7	3.3	2.7	0.6	0.3
Year 10	9.0	6.8	5.0	4.3	1.8	1.6
Year infinity	9.7	8.4	6.3	6.1	3.2	2.7
Asset values						
Year 2	-3.6	-5.7	-1.7	-8.9	-3.5	1.3
Year 10	-3.4	-5.7	-1.7	-8.9	-3.5	1.3
Year infinity	-3.2	-5.7	-1.7	-8.9	-3.5	1.3
Welfare (by year of birth)[c]						
-60	0.1	-0.01	0.03	-0.04	0.02	-0.1
-40	0.6	0.3	0.3	0.1	0.2	0.02
-20	1.2	0.5	-0.3	0.4	-0.8	0.6
0	2.2	1.6	0.7	1.3	0.02	1.6
Infinity	1.9	1.6	0.6	1.5	0.2	1.8
Efficiency gain	6.4	2.8	2.2	1.4	0.4	0.1

a. All changes reported are percentage increases over baseline steady state, except for changes in the saving and interest rates, which are already expressed as percentages.
b. With or without transition relief for existing capital.
c. Change as a percentage of the present value of lifetime consumption and leisure.

time even with an immediate rise in saving. In the short run, effects on labor supply govern changes in wages. Because the incentive to work rises, the real wage falls under the NST/VAT and the two Hall-Rabushka plans, as increased labor supply temporarily swamps saving-induced increases in capital. The largest long-run increase, under the USA plan, reflects both labor supply disincentives and increased saving and capital accumulation.

Interest Rates

In these initial simulations without costs of adjustment, the interest rate equals the before-tax return to capital. Thus, as determined by the aggregate production function and competitive factor pricing, the interest rate and the wage rate move in opposite directions. For that reason, the rise in labor supply initially reduces the size of increases in the interest rate under the NST/VAT and Hall-Rabushka plans. Eventually, increased saving pushes up capital-labor ratios under all plans, forcing down the return to capital and the interest rate.The biggest fall occurs under the USA plan—a long-run drop of 1.6 percentage points. About half the decline occurs within ten years.

Saving Rates

The saving rate jumps under each plan, in accord with the increased incentives to save. The increase is smaller under the Hall-Rabushka and Armey-Shelby plans with transition relief than without it because transition shifts resources from the relatively high-saving young to the relatively low-saving old. Saving rises more under the USA plan than under other plans with transition relief as the depressing impact of transition relief is offset by that of payroll tax credits financed by the consumption tax. Under all plans the saving rate trends down over time but remains above initial levels, except under the NST/VAT plan.

Output

Most of the long-run gain occurs within ten years. Output increases quite strongly—by 5.0 to 9.0 percent—under the NST/VAT and Hall-Rabushka plans, because both labor supply and saving increase. The two Armey-Shelby plans and the USA plans produce smaller output gains because labor supply rises little or falls and because capital accumulation occurs only gradually.

Asset Values

The price of the existing capital stock falls immediately because of changes in the relative treatment of new and existing capital. The cash-flow tax imposes more of a burden on existing capital than on new capital. Because the NST/VAT, Hall-Rabushka, and Armey-Shelby plans all include a larger cash-flow tax than that implicit in the current tax system, these plans all reduce the value of existing assets.[49] However, transition relief substantially mitigates the decline. The USA system boosts asset values slightly, but this result is misleading becasue this system imposes an additional tax burden at the individual level that is not incorporated in market values. The welfare effects on older genera-tions provide a clearer picture of this additional burden.

Welfare and Efficiency

The NST/VAT raises welfare for all generations. Wage taxation helps older generations at the expense of younger generations, while a shift to consumption taxation does the opposite. The combination of these two taxes balances the effects and, with some efficiency gains also present, permits both young and old to gain. In particular, the temporary increase in interest rates resulting from additional labor supply more than offsets the capital levy the old face, leaving them slightly better off. This 6.4 percent efficiency gain exceeds the gain of any generation because the efficiency calculation shifts all the gains from current generations to the future.

This reform seems to confirm that a tax reform can make everyone better off if it improves economic efficiency. However, the breakdown of the population in the model by age cohort ignores differences by income class.[50] A major reason for the formulation of the other alternatives is precisely to preserve some tax progressivity.

The Hall-Rabushka plan without transition relief produces a genera-tional pattern of welfare effects similar to that of the NST/VAT plan.

---

49. With one exception, these changes are constant over time because, for technical reasons, the simulations fix the cash-flow tax rate at its long-run value (given in table 2-2) and allow only the tax on wage income to vary over time in order to satisfy changes in annual revenue requirements during the transition. This minor simplification is not neces-sary under the NST/VAT, because of its simpler structure.

50. These effects are considered in detail in chapter 8 by William Gale, Scott Houser, and John Karl Scholz in this volume.

The gains are smaller, however, and only those born after the reform is instituted experience any noticeable improvement, as the introduction of progressivity reduces efficiency gain by more than half. Still, this gain is nearly 3 percent of lifetime resources for each future generation. Adding transition relief helps older generations at the expense of younger ones. The higher long-run tax rate on labor income required to make up the cost of transition relief also reduces the efficiency gain, to just over 2 percent of lifetime resources—still a significant gain.

The Armey-Shelby plan has more progressivity than the Hall-Rabushka plan and reduces efficiency gains still further. Combining greater progressivity and transition relief under the Armey-Shelby plan and the USA tax very nearly eliminates the efficiency gains from tax reform. These plans have similar effects on overall efficiency but different generational patterns. The USA system involves a greater shift in the tax burden from the young to the old, resulting in a sizable increase in welfare for the young, financed mostly by transfers from older generations rather than by efficiency gains. The modified Armey plan places a lower burden on the old than the USA tax does. Instead, its losers are those born just before the reform, who are too young to have substantial assets to benefit from transition relief and increased short-run interest rates and too old to be around when real wages rise enough to offset the increased taxes on labor.

Sensitivity Analysis

The magnitude of estimated effects clearly depends on the assumed behaviors expressed in the model parameters. It is important to get some idea of the sensitivity of results to these assumptions.

Adjustment Costs

The actual effects of any of these tax changes on the economy would depend on the speed of adjustment and the openness of the economy. Table 2-4 presents alternative simulations to those in table 2-3 for the case in which adjustment costs are moderate: an increase of 1 percentage point in the investment-capital ratio increases the cost of investment

Table 2-4. *Macroeconomic and Welfare Effects of Tax Reforms, with Adjustment Costs*[a]

Percent

Parameter	NST/VAT (1)	Hall-Rabushka		Armey-Shelby		USA system (6)
		No transition[b] (2)	Transition[b] (3)	No transition[b] (4)	Transition[b] (5)	
Wage						
Year 2	−1.2	−0.7	−0.3	−0.2	0.3	0.5
Year 10	0.4	0.7	0.7	1.1	1.1	2.0
Year infinity	4.1	4.5	3.7	4.6	3.5	5.2
Interest rate						
Year 2	0.2	0.3	1.1	−0.8	0.2	−0.7
Year 10	−0.7	−0.7	−0.6	−0.7	0.1	−1.0
Year infinity	−1.4	−2.0	−1.5	−2.1	−1.5	−1.8
Saving rate						
Year 2	0.9	2.3	2.1	1.9	1.7	1.0
Year 10	0.1	1.6	1.2	1.5	1.0	1.3
Year infinity	−1.0	0.7	0.5	0.8	0.5	0.5
Output per capita						
Year 2	4.5	2.9	1.7	1.0	−0.6	−2.0
Year 10	6.0	4.4	3.0	2.3	0.3	−0.5
Year infinity	8.9	7.6	5.6	5.3	2.5	2.0
Asset values						
Year 2	6.1	3.0	4.9	−0.3	2.3	12.5
Year 10	5.7	1.9	5.2	−2.4	1.9	8.3
Year infinity	0.1	−3.6	0.6	−6.9	−1.4	3.5
Welfare (by year of birth)[c]						
−60	0.1	0.1	0.1	−0.01	0.1	−0.1
−40	0.6	0.3	0.3	0.1	0.2	0.02
−20	0.3	−0.3	−1.0	0.3	−0.6	−0.02
0	1.4	0.9	0.1	0.6	−0.6	1.0
Infinity	1.5	1.3	0.3	1.2	−0.1	1.5
Efficiency gain	5.7	2.2	1.6	1.0	−0.00	−0.3

a. With adjustment costs, the total price to the firm of one dollar of new capital goods is $1 + \Phi \ (I/K)$, where I/K is the investment-capital ratio and Φ is an adjustment cost. Parameters set equal to ten in these simulations. All changes reported are percentage increases over baseline steady state, except for changes in the saving and interest rates, which are already expressed as percentages.

b. With or without transition relief for existing capital.

c. Change as a percentage of the present value of lifetime consumption and leisure.

goods to the firm by 10 percent. This cost is below some estimates and higher than others.[51]

51. For example, it is lower than Summers (1981) and higher than Cummins, Hassett, and Hubbard (1994). Because I have not altered any other parameters, some of the other characteristics of the initial steady state are slightly different. Most notable is that the national saving rate is initially 3.3 percent rather than 4.1 percent.

Adjustment costs slow capital accumulation and temporarily increase the value of existing assets because quantity adjustments only partially satisfy the increased demand for investment goods. The national savings rate in year 2 rises by less in each simulation than under the corresponding simulation without adjustment costs—by a range of 0.9 to 2.3 percentage points, rather than 3.4 to 4.8 percentage points. Adjustment costs explain the large jumps in asset values under most of the plans, most notably the USA tax system. Only under the basic Armey-Shelby plan do asset values still fall initially. Under the other plans, the increased demand for assets that pushes values up more than offsets the depressing effect of the business cash-flow tax.

This impact on asset values changes the pattern of welfare gains, raising the welfare of older generations of asset holders. Under even the Hall-Rabushka plan without transition relief, the old now gain, suggesting that transition relief may not be necessary to spare these generations harm from tax reform. However, with slower capital accumulation, the slower growth of real wages and output reduces the welfare gains of younger generations. Indeed, under the Armey-Shelby plan with transition relief and the USA plans, output actually falls initially. The delay in adjustment not only reduces the welfare gains of younger generations, but results in overall efficiency losses.

These results underscore the uncertainties associated with fundamental tax reform. They indicate that a change in even one parameter can cause sharp changes in estimated effects or even reverse the sign. In fact, substantial uncertainty surrounds most of the parameters. Whether the resulting uncertainties cancel one another or cumulate into even greater total uncertainty is unclear.

International Capital Flows

The estimates presented so far assume that tax reform has no effect on international capital movements or that such induced capital movements modify the domestic effects of tax reform. This assumption is clearly false, but modeling of international capital flows is complicated because reforms may encourage investment by some investors and discourage it by others. For purposes of illustration, I assume that before-tax returns are determined in international capital markets and remain unchanged despite U.S. tax reform and its effects on behavior of U.S. savers and investors. This situation could occur if foreign investors' tax liabilities were unaffected by U.S. tax reform, if all assets were perfect

Table 2-5. *Effects of Two Tax Reforms on an Open Economy*[a]

Parameter	Hall-Rabushka (transition)[b]	USA system
Saving rate		
Year 2	6.3	7.6
Year 10	5.1	6.3
Year infinity	1.5	2.1
Output per capita		
Year 2	5.5	2.3
Year 10	5.9	2.9
Year infinity	9.3	8.8
Welfare (by year of birth)[c]		
−60	0.03	−0.1
−40	0.5	0.2
−20	−0.3	0.6
0	−0.6	0.9
Infinity	−0.4	1.7
Efficiency gain	2.7	0.4

a. Simulations based on the assumption of constant interest and wage rates. All changes reported are percentage increases over baseline steady state, except for changes in the saving rate, which is already expressed as a percentage.
b. With transition relief for existing capital.
c. Change as a percentage of the present value of lifetime consumption and leisure.

substitutes, and if international capital flows instantaneously eliminated all differences in after-tax returns.

Table 2-5 provides simulations under this assumption for the Hall-Rabushka plan with transition relief and for the USA plan.[52] The results reflect the assumption of frictionless capital mobility. With the before-tax rate of return fixed, the national savings rate nearly triples by year 2, and stays very high, as most of the capital created by this saving flows out of the country. The current account, initially assumed to be unaffected by reform, develops a large surplus. These surpluses are very high—8 percent of national income under the Hall-Rabushka plan and 9 percent under the USA tax. Per capita *national* product rises much more than in the base case. Per capita *domestic* product, in contrast, actually *falls* in the long run by 4.0 percent and 10.4 percent, respectively. Without domestic capital deepening, domestic product changes in proportion to labor supply; this is reduced in the long run by higher levels of income and, under the USA plan, a higher marginal tax rate as well. Older generations gain as their capital earns the higher, worldwide return to capital. Younger and future generations lose because the export of capital

52. I had difficulty getting the simulation model to converge for some of the other reforms.

Table 2-6. *Effects of Tax Reforms, Assuming Alternative Labor Supply Responsiveness*[a]

Parameter	NST/ VAT (1)	Hall-Rabushka		Armey-Shelby		USA system (6)
		No transition[b] (2)	Transition[b] (3)	No transition[b] (4)	Transition[b] (5)	
Output per capita						
Base case[c]						
Year 10	9.0	6.8	5.0	4.3	1.8	1.6
Year infinity	9.7	8.4	6.3	6.1	3.2	2.7
Lower elasticity[d]						
Year 10	4.0	4.1	3.2	3.3	2.1	2.1
Year infinity	4.3	4.8	3.7	4.0	2.6	2.5
Difference						
Year 10	−5.0	−2.7	−1.8	−1.0	0.3	0.5
Year infinity	−5.4	−3.6	−2.6	−2.1	−0.6	−0.2
Efficiency gain						
Base case[c]	6.4	2.8	2.2	1.4	0.4	0.1
Lower elasticity[d]	4.8	1.4	1.2	0.7	0.5	0.1
Difference	−1.6	−1.4	−1.0	−0.7	0.1	0.04

a. Changes reported are percentage increases over baseline steady state.
b. With or without transition relief for existing capital.
c. Simulations incorporating an elasticity of substitution between consumption and leisure of 0.8.
d. Simulations based on an elasticity of 0.3.

denies them the benefit of real-wage growth. The opportunity to benefit from improved worldwide capital allocation increases overall efficiency.

While the simple open-economy assumption leads to implausible results, it is clearly wrong to ignore the effects of tax reform on international capital flows and their consequences for the domestic economy. The large differences indicate yet another area of uncertainty about the consequences of fundamental tax reform.

Labor Supply

The parameter that determines the labor supply response to changes in the after-tax wage is the elasticity of substitution between labor and leisure. In all preceding simulations, this key parameter equals 0.8, a reasonable value that generates plausible aggregate labor supply. Table 2-6 presents the growth and efficiency effects if this key parameter is reduced to 0.3, indicating that labor supply is far less sensitive to variations in wages than in the base case. These simulations do not allow for adjustment costs or for tax-induced international capital movements.

In evaluating these results, it is useful to keep in mind that some of the plans (notably the NST/VAT) increase output both through increased capital formation and increased labor supply, while others (notably the modified Armey and USA plans) increase output primarily through increased capital formation. A reduction in labor supply responsiveness should matter more for output growth in the first group of plans than in the others. Table 2-6 confirms this intuition. The change in assumption reduces estimated output growth by more than half under the NST/VAT plan, with progressively smaller effects in plans with higher marginal tax rates on labor supply and, hence, less improved incentive for labor supply. In fact, the reduced reponsiveness of labor supply actually raises output growth after ten years under the modified Armey and USA plans. Because these plans discourage labor supply relative to the current system, the lower labor supply response works in their favor. The same general picture holds for changes in economic efficiency: the reduction in efficiency growth declines as one moves to the right in the table, and efficiency is actually improved under the modified Armey and USA systems.

In summary, a much smaller labor supply responsiveness reduces output growth and efficiency gains considerably under the plans that produce the largest gains, but it leaves gains in output and efficiency under all plans.

Conclusion

The intricacy of proposed reforms and the current tax system complicates analysis of their effects. I reach four major conclusions.

First, the current tax system distorts investment, principally by confronting would-be savers with a tax that distorts their choice between current and future consumption and by imposing very different rates on residential and nonresidential investment.

Second, the current debate is not about a switch from a pure income tax to a pure consumption tax. The U.S. tax system already has certain elements of consumption tax treatment. No proposal under review would tax all consumption financed by existing assets. Third, the welfare, saving, and output gains from a switch to a VAT, NST, the many variants of the flat tax, or the USA tax depend sensitively on how they are drafted and on such poorly understood factors as the ease with which capital adjusts, the openness of the economy, and the responsiveness of household behavior. All simulations point to a short-run increase in national saving, but not necessarily to a sizable increase in output or welfare.

Fourth, transition relief and progressivity—two realistic components of a prospective tax reform—each reduce output growth and efficiency gains. Combining these two features, as under the Armey-Shelby system with transition relief and the USA tax system, reduces output growth substantially and eliminates much or all of the gain in economic efficiency.

Any of these proposals to shift toward consumption taxation would increase national saving, at least in the short run. But the gains in economic efficiency may be small or nonexistent, and the long-run increase in output may be modest if the plans preserve progressivity and provide transition relief. Although my analysis has not considered the additional efficiency gains from an improved allocation of the capital stock, primarily through a reduction in the relative tax preference for owner-occupied housing, these gains are available through much simpler measures without a major change in the tax system.

Appendix A: The Derivation of Effective Tax Rates

I derive corporate effective tax rates in two stages. First, I compute the tax burden at the corporate level and then the additional burden from interest deductibility and personal taxes.

The calculation starts with an expression for the user cost of capital, relating the before-tax, before-depreciation rate of return, c, to the required real rate of return, r; the rate of economic depreciation, δ; the corporate tax rate, τ; and the present value of depreciation allowances, z:

$$(A1) \qquad c = \frac{(r + \delta)(1 - \tau z)}{(1 - \tau)}.$$

The effective corporate tax rate is then $[(c - \delta) - r]/(c - \delta)$.

The next step relates the firm's real cost of funds (r) to the net real return received by holders of debt and equity (n) by the expression

$$(A2) \quad r = n\left[b\frac{1 - \tau}{1 - \Theta} + (1 - b)\frac{1}{1 - \Phi}\right]$$
$$+ \pi\left[b\frac{\Theta - \tau}{1 - \Theta} + (1 - b)\frac{\Phi}{1 - \Phi}\right],$$

where b is the share of debt finance and π is the inflation rate.[53] This expression recognizes that corporations deduct interest payments at the corporate tax rate, τ; that individuals pay tax on interest at the rate, Θ, and that equity income is taxed at a rate, Φ, that depends on the tax rates on dividends and capital gains (only the latter under the assumption of the "new view"). The inflation rate affects the tax burden because the tax system is not indexed. The tax rate at this level is measured by comparing r and n; the total tax rate on corporate source income equals $[(c - \delta) - n]/(c - \delta)$. For noncorporate investment, I follow the approach just given, but replace the corporate tax rate, τ, with the individual tax rate on dividends and set the tax rate on equity income, Φ, to zero, because there is no second level of tax on noncorporate equity income.

Following King and Fullerton and Fullerton and Karayannis, I assume that asset holders comprise three groups: households, tax-exempt institutions, and insurance companies.[54] I use the ownership weights for debt and equity given in table 10-3 of Fullerton and Karayannis, the tax rates for insurance companies they provide in table 10-4 (updated for the 1993 increase in the corporate tax rate), and tax rates on individuals for 1993 derived from the NBER's TAXSIM program and kindly provided by Daniel Feenberg and Andrew Mitrusi. These data are summarized as follows:

Asset holder	Debt share	Equity share	Tax rate on interest	Tax rate on dividends	Tax rate on capital gains
Households	0.61	0.74	0.218	0.270	0.245
Tax-exempt institutions	0.24	0.22	0	0	0
Insurance companies	0.15	0.04	0.35	0.07	0.35
Total	1.00	1.00	. . .	. . .	. . .

For the aggregate corporate sector, I assume a debt-value ratio of 0.35 (the value for the nonfinancial corporate sector at the end of 1994,

53. See Auerbach (1983a).
54. King and Fullerton (1984); Fullerton and Karayannis (1993).

according to the Board of Governors of the Federal Reserve), an inflation rate of 3 percent, and a cost of funds to the corporation of $r = 0.04$.[55] I further assume that the effective capital gains rate is one-fourth the statutory rate and that the share of nominal equity income distributed as dividends is 0.3.[56] These assumptions yield the values of $(r - n)/n$, the additional tax wedge defined in equation A2. Under either the "traditional" view or the "new" view of dividend taxation, individual taxes impose little additional burden on corporate source income, as the gap between corporate and individual tax rates on interest income roughly offsets the positive tax burden on equity income. Even though these additional tax provisions add little to the overall tax wedge on corporate source income, they do affect the value of corporate assets to individuals. At the margin, pension fund earnings are effectively untaxed, not simply through exemption, but also through cash-flow rules. Thus withdrawals from pension funds will be taxed, and this future burden should be capitalized—not in share values themselves (because the taxes will not be paid by firms), but in the values individuals place on assets held in pension funds. In addition, to the extent that the "new" view of dividends holds, corporate equity should be discounted by the ratio $(1 - \Theta_D)/(1 - c)$, where Θ_D is the tax rate on dividends and c the accrual-equivalent capital gains tax rate. Based on the tax rates and corporate debt-equity ratio given above, this discount would amount to just over 10 percent of the value of corporate assets, for a total undervaluation (taking account of the 8 percent due to accelerated depreciation) of about 18 percent.

Appendix B: Tax Reform and Interest Rates

One can get a sense of the relationship between the real return to capital and the real interest rate by considering the overall tax wedges facing capital and interest. If R equals the aggregate real return to capital (net of depreciation) and n represents the net return, then $R(1 - \mu) = n$, where μ is the total tax wedge facing investment. For debt to deliver the after-tax return, n, the nominal interest rate, i, must satisfy the expression $n = i(1 - \Theta) - \pi$, where π is the inflation rate and Θ is the tax rate on

55. Federal Reserve System, Board of Governors (1995a).
56. See Auerbach (1989).

nominal interest payments. Thus the interest rate and the return to capital are related by the expression

(B1) $$i = \frac{R(1 - \mu) + \Theta\pi}{1 - \Theta} + \pi.$$

As noted in the text, if $\Theta = \mu$ and $\pi = 0$, then the real interest rate, $1 - \pi$, equals the before-tax return, R. With $\pi > 0$, the effective tax rate on real interest rises above Θ because nominal interest is taxed, and this raises $1 - \pi$ relative to R. Of course, inflation affects μ as well.

After the tax reform, the tax rates Θ and μ are set to zero and the new interest rate, i', equals $R' + \pi$, where R' is the new return to capital. Thus the changes in i and R are related by

(B2) $$\Delta i = \Delta R + \frac{R(\mu - \Theta) - \Theta\pi}{1 - \Theta}.$$

In the text, I use a value of $\mu = 0.16$ for investment overall, including residential investment (based on a value of 0.26 for nonresidential investment), and assume a value of $\pi = 0.03$. The average value of Θ, based on data in appendix A, is 0.185. For $R = 0.06$ (roughly consistent with the assumed real cost of funds to the firm of 0.04 on which the calculation of μ is based), this yields the numerical solution to equation B2 of $\Delta i = \Delta R - 0.009$. That is, the interest rate falls by 0.9 percentage points *more* than the before-tax return to capital. Even with housing omitted, that is, using a value of $\mu = 0.26$, the interest rate drops by slightly more than the before-tax return to capital.

Appendix C: The Auerbach-Kotlikoff Simulation Model

I use the Auerbach-Kotlikoff simulation model to simulate the macroeconomic effects of tax changes.[57] This is a dynamic model that, at each date, has fifty-five overlapping generations of individuals who save and supply labor to maximize lifetime utility, with no bequest motive. Unless otherwise reported, all simulations reported in the chapter use the base-case parameter assumptions of Auerbach-Kotlikoff, including a pure rate of time preference of 0.015, a population growth rate of 0.015, an inter-

---

57. See Auerbach and Kotlikoff (1987). For additional simulations of the impact of tax reform using this model, see Kotlikoff (1995).

temporal elasticity of substitution of 0.25, an intratemporal elasticity of substitution (between leisure and goods) of 0.8, a relative weight of 1.5 for leisure in each period's utility subfunction, and a Cobb-Douglas production function.

The intertemporal elasticity of substitution of 0.25 is relatively low among empirical estimates, suggesting a small savings response. However, as Eric Engen and William Gale discuss in their chapter, there are other features of this model, including the absence of uncertainty and a bequest motive, that make the savings response larger than in their analysis, despite their use of a somewhat larger intertemporal elasticity (0.33). A precise comparison of the responsiveness of saving in the two models is made difficult because of the many other differences in preferences, including differences in the rate of time preference, and their assumption of exogenous labor supply. Similarly, it is difficult to translate the behavior implied by this model's intratemporal elasticity of substitution (between consumption and leisure) into standard labor supply elasticities (such as those used by Robert Triest in his chapter) that are not based on life-cycle behavior.

The initial steady state is calibrated so that the payroll tax rate is 0.153, the sum at present of employer and employee contribution rates. I assume that one-quarter of this tax rate is viewed by households as being offset by associated marginal social security benefits. The initial level of the national debt equals 55 percent of one year's net output (roughly its current level), and federal revenue (excluding social insurance contributions) equals 13.5 percent of net output, also roughly in line with its current level.

The model incorporates tax progressivity by allowing the marginal rate structure for each type of tax to be quadratic. While this does not precisely replicate the type of progressivity under a flat tax, it does allow a reasonable approximation, in that one can determine separately the average tax rate and the average marginal tax rate.

Appendix D: Estimating Average Marginal Tax Rates under Proposed Reforms

Under each of the tax reforms considered above (except the NST/VAT), the marginal tax schedule facing labor income is progressive. Even under a flat tax, labor income may face one of two marginal tax rates, including zero. To compute the average marginal tax rate, defined as how much taxes would rise if labor income rose proportionally, one must calculate the share of labor income subject to each marginal tax rate. For each proposal, I form estimates of these shares, starting with data from the Statistics of Income on the shares of adjusted gross income by income bracket for 1991 and inflating these brackets by the degree of income growth between 1991 and 1995.[58] Then, for each tax system, I use the following algorithm:

1. Calculate the rate schedule for two classes of taxpayers: single and married filing jointly with two minor dependents, including the amount in the zero bracket.

For Hall-Rabushka, this yields zero-bracket amounts of $9,500 for single filers and $25,500 for joint filers (a $16,500 standard deduction plus $9,000 for two dependents). For the Armey plan, as analyzed by the Treasury, the corresponding levels are $12,350 (singles) and $34,700 (joint filers—a $24,700 standard deduction plus $10,000 for two dependents). For the USA system, as introduced into legislation in 1994 (S. 722), the zero-bracket amounts are $6,950 for singles (a $4,400 family allowance plus one $2,550 personal exemption) and $17,600 for joint filers (a $7,400 family allowance plus four $2,550 personal exemptions). Above these levels, rates of 8 percent and 19 percent, respectively, apply to the next $3,200 and $11,200 (singles) and $5,400 and $18,600 (married, filing jointly), with a 40 percent rate applicable to all higher amounts.

2. Ignoring other differences between AGI and the tax base, estimate the share of AGI in each tax bracket, starting from zero (using table 1.2 from the Statistics of Income and interpolating to align SOI income categories and bracket break-points). Use these shares as weights to calculate an average marginal tax rate for each group; then weight by the relative share of AGI accounted for by each type of return. This procedure essentially assumes that the differences between AGI and the new tax bases are distributed proportionately to AGI, which probably assigns too much weight to higher-AGI individuals (who have disproportionately more capital income).

3. Redo the calculation in step 2, with different weights, by subtracting the total amount of AGI for each filing status that is not attributable to wages, salaries, or pension income (derived from table 1.3 of the Statistics of Income) from the AGI of the highest income class. This procedure essentially assigns the elements of AGI that would not be taxed under

58. U.S. Internal Revenue Service (1994b).

the flat tax proposals to the highest income class, which assigns too little weight to this class.

4. Use a simple average of the values calculated in steps 2 and 3, which vary by between 1 and 2 percentage points.

Comment by R. Glenn Hubbard

Much of the current debate over tax reform in the United States centers on "consumption taxes." Many economists argue that a shift from the current tax system to a broad-based proportional consumption tax would increase saving and investment and economic well-being. A critical element of such an argument is that changes in tax incentives have significant and predictable behavioral effects.

Alan Auerbach's chapter focuses on how researchers and policymakers might predict the effects of particular tax reforms on behavior. I would characterize the design of his paper as follows. One can, in principle, decompose "tax reform"—the shift from the current tax system to a broad-based consumption tax—into two parts. The first part eliminates differential capital taxation, moving the current tax system toward a uniform broad-based income tax. The second part permits expensing of capital goods rather than depreciation, shifting a uniform broad-based income tax to a uniform broad-based consumption tax. Having made this decomposition for analytical purposes, one can attribute efficiency gains (and, for that matter, changes in fairness or tax simplicity) and transition gains or losses to the two parts of fundamental tax reform.

The two-part approach suggests strongly that one cannot speak of fundamental tax reform as simply a contest between "income taxes" and "consumption taxes." An important set of efficiency issues surrounds the first part—distortions in the allocation of capital and financial distortions, for example; these issues are part of a debate regarding income tax reform. Economic analysis of the second part of tax reform focuses on the magnitude of saving and investment responses to the shift toward consumption taxation.

Auerbach organizes his chapter nicely to fit this logical framework. He begins by posing a simple accounting framework to highlight key marginal (substitution) and inframarginal (income) effects of tax reform. He then describes incentives for economic and financial decisions under the current U.S. federal income tax. Auerbach also offers a clear discussion of leading tax proposals, including a national sales tax, a value-added tax, a flat tax,[59] and the "10 percent tax" of Representative Richard Gephardt.[60] The two principal analytical sections of the chapter—on which I focus my remarks—discuss the impact of tax reform on asset values and interest rates and present simulations of the effects of tax reform on saving and economic well-being.[61]

Before I comment on these analytical sections, let me make two observations about Auerbach's descriptions of distortions under the current federal tax. The theme of his discussion is that *allocation* distortions are relatively minor in the post-1986 period, so that analysis of fundamental tax reform should emphasize distortions of the *level* of capital. Although effective tax rates do not vary substantially across types of business capital, there is still an important variation between the tax treatment of business capital and owner-occupied housing, suggesting the possibility of efficiency gains from improved allocation of capital.[62] Second, some models of corporate leverage and corporate payout policy suggest efficiency gains from removing the financial distortions in the current tax system.[63]

Tax Reform, Asset Valuation, and Rates of Return

Auerbach's description of likely valuation consequences of tax reform can be described as follows. First, in a closed economy, stock market valuation of business assets falls in response to the introduction of expensing (though tempered in the short run owing to costs of adjusting the capital stock). Second, interest rates will likely fall by (at least) the amount of the tax wedge because interest income currently faces a higher effective tax rate than capital as a whole. Third, if the United States could

59. The "national sales tax" is a uniform retail sales tax on goods and services. The "value-added tax" studied is a uniform destination-based value-added tax on consumption goods. The "flat tax" is a hybrid of a wage tax and a subtraction-method value-added tax. The "USA tax" combines variants of a subtraction-method value-added tax and a progressive individual consumption tax.

60. With the exception of the Gephardt plan, these proposals represent variants of a broad-based consumption tax. The 10 percent tax—which is, in fact, a five-bracket graduated tax system—resembles more closely the current tax system, though with higher effective tax rates on capital income.

61. The familiar model of Auerbach and Kotlikoff (1987) is used.

62. See, for example, Jorgenson (1996).

63. See, for example, Gertler and Hubbard (1993), the "traditional view" of dividend policy summarized in Poterba and Summers (1995), and the calculations in U.S. Department of Treasury (1992).

be considered a price taker in the international capital market, U.S. interest rates would not change.

I suspect that assessing the effects of tax reform on rates of return and asset prices is more complicated than Auerbach suggests. Because investment incentives accompany the switch from an income to a consumption tax, the level of business fixed investment in the United States will likely increase. Effects on the capital stock and net capital flows—and ultimately on rates of return and asset prices—are more difficult to gauge, however, on account of differences in consequences for debt- and equity-financed investment returns and the importance of sectors and entities already receiving favorable tax treatment, for example, noncorporate business, owner-occupied housing, pension funds, and many foreign investors.

Predicting the Change in Future Returns in a Closed Economy

For the corporate sector by itself, a shift to a consumption tax increases the after-tax return on equity-financed investment. Investors no longer face the double tax on corporate income from the corporate income tax and the tax on dividends and capital gains; at the margin, the pre-tax return to capital is paid to investors.

What about debt-financed investments and interest rates? Like equity investors, debt investors benefit from the removal of the personal tax on capital income; the after-tax return on debt rises. The equilibrium change in market interest rates depends, however, both on investors' portfolio decisions and the interest rates firms are willing to offer to raise funds for investment.

To see this tension, start with the case of a marginal investment financed with debt. (For simplicity, abstract from inflation.) Under the income tax, debt holders receive the pre-tax return to capital upon which they pay personal taxes, because interest is deductible by corporate borrowers. Under the consumption tax, the value of immediate expensing just offsets the present value of now forgone interest deductions. From the perspective of the firm, there is no change in the interest rate that is offered to debt holders. Hence the prima facie case for a fall in interest rates because taxes levied on corporate-generated capital income are eliminated is not necessarily compelling. Indeed, considering only the corporate sector and debt-financed investments, interest rates decline only to the extent that an increase in household saving reduces the pre-tax return to capital in the economy.

Once equity finance is back in the picture to finance marginal investments, interest rates may rise or fall depending on portfolio adjustments by suppliers of capital and financing choices of demanders of capital. On the one hand, the corporate-level tax treatment of dividends is not changed by the consumption tax, while interest payments are no longer deductible; firms will issue more equity and less debt, lowering interest rates, all else equal. On the other hand, suppliers of capital now receiving higher after-tax returns on equity require higher returns—a higher interest rate—on debt. The net effect of these two portfolio decisions on interest rates is ambiguous. As is often noted, the nondeductibility of corporate interest payments under a consumption tax should lower interest rates relative to expected returns on equity.[64] However, the positive effect of expensing on the overall return to capital may still lead to an absolute increase in interest rates.[65]

Now let's add tax-favored sectors and entities to the analysis. As of 1995, approximately 9.3 percent of outstanding debt in credit-market instruments is in the form of tax-exempt bonds.[66] Moreover, the elimination of mortgage interest deductibility reduces the tax-favored status of owner-occupied housing. This change in tax treatment in the switch from an income tax to a consumption tax causes households to shift capital to the business sector from the state and local government and housing sectors. As a result, the rise in equity returns brought about by the elimination of capital income taxes would be mitigated, reducing interest rates for business investment. Because the elimination of the corporation income tax eliminates the relative tax advantage of the noncorporate business sector, capital would also flow from the noncorporate to the corporate sector, also mitigating the increase in after-tax corporate equity returns and reducing interest rates, all else equal.

As of 1995, 32.9 percent of corporate equity and 72.4 percent of corporate debt is held by tax-exempt institutions and foreign investors.[67] Hence, because a significant fraction of corporate investment income already effectively receives "consumption tax" treatment at the investor level, the increase in saving brought about by the consumption tax may be less than a first-pass guess might suggest. All else equal, this effect would augment the increase in equity returns and weaken pressure to reduce interest rates.

64. See, for example, Hall and Rabushka (1995).
65. See, for example, Feldstein (1995).
66. This calculation is based on data from Federal Reserve System (1995b).
67. This calculation is based on data from Federal Reserve System (1995b).

To the extent that the offset to the saving effect is smaller than the capital movement from previously tax-favored sectors to the corporate sector, gross interest rates will probably rise but by less than the analysis of the corporate sector alone would suggest.

Predicting the Change in Future Returns in an Open Economy

Although the polar closed-economy case presented above does not accurately describe capital markets, the extent to which capital is internationally mobile is the subject of vigorous debate.[68] Available data suggest that the volume of cross-border lending in U.S. dollars is similar to borrowing by U.S. businesses.[69] Hence, the worldwide supply of debt to U.S. businesses may be quite elastic.

One must also estimate the extent to which portfolio debt capital is internationally mobile to assess the response of U.S. interest rates to a switch from an income tax to a consumption tax. Suppose, for example, that the reduction in demand for debt capital by the U.S. state and local government and housing sectors puts downward pressure on domestic interest rates. All else equal, there would be an outflow of debt capital from the United States to the international capital market. Foreign debt investors are not made better off under the consumption tax: no withholding tax is currently paid on portfolio interest and, because of interest deductibility, returns on debt escape tax at the corporate level. These considerations suggest that foreign-currency debt may become more attractive to international investors.

If portfolio debt capital were perfectly internationally mobile, U.S. interest rates would not decline in response to the shift of capital out of the state and local government and housing sectors. Alternatively, as already discussed, in the absence of capital mobility, U.S. interest rates would likely fall.

To predict the net response of U.S. interest rates to the change in tax regime, one would need to compare the interest elasticity of demand for capital in the business sector in the United States. On the equity side, the rise in after-tax equity returns in the United States under the consumption tax regime would induce an inflow of equity capital from abroad.

---

68. See, for example, the review in U.S. Department of the Treasury (1992).

69. For the end of 1994, the Bank for International Settlements estimates that cross-border claims in dollars were $2,345 billion, and Eurobonds and notes in dollars totaled $915 billion. For U.S. nonfinancial businesses at the same time, the Federal Reserve estimates credit-market borrowing to be $3,885 billion.

Transition Tax and Asset Prices

Wealth holders bear the short-run burden of the transition to a consumption tax.[70] The transition effect on stock prices depends on the relative importance of: the "tax on old basis" effect of expensing ($-$), the possibility that the dividend tax was capitalized in share prices ($+$), and the presence of adjustment costs ($+$). Another consideration—which has received little attention by economists—is that life insurance companies and pension funds will likely see their assets shrink after tax reform. Whether this shrinkage affects stock prices depends on whether households offset any decline in contractual saving with saving in other forms and whether households allocate their portfolio in a manner roughly similar to that of institutional asset managers. Finally, a consumption tax is accompanied by a one-time increase in the price level, and nominal debt holders share in any transition loss in asset values.

Simulating the Effects of Tax Reform

Auerbach uses a representative-agent, one-capital-good, dynamic life-cycle simulation model to estimate effects of tax reform proposals on saving, investment, and growth. All of the consumption tax proposals Auerbach considers reduce the effective tax rate on capital income to zero,[71] thereby encouraging saving. The flatter rates under most of the plan also increase household labor supply.

Four basic points summarize the simulation exercises. First, the current tax system embodies features of both income and consumption taxation; hence gains from consumption tax elements of tax reform are likely to be smaller than one might guess. Second, reforms generate real effects via lower marginal tax rates—in general and on capital income in particular—financed in part by a transition tax. Third, efficiency gains are significant in many cases. Fourth, the magnitude of efficiency gains from tax reform depends in part on the extent of transition relief.

More specifically, the simulations indicate that household saving rates rise under each plan, though the amount of the increase depends on

70. Offsetting this, to the extent that wealth holders have long horizons for future consumption, an improvement in rates of return may still leave them better off over their lifetimes.

71. The consumption tax exempts only the opportunity cost of capital from taxation. See Gentry and Hubbard (1995). Inframarginal returns are treated similarly under a broad-based income tax and a broad-based consumption tax. This is consistent with Auerbach's treatment, because there are no inframarginal returns in the Auerbach-Kotlikoff model.

whether transition relief is offered, thereby requiring higher tax rates. Because the additional saving in response to tax reform increases the capital-labor ratio, wages rise in the long run. Interest rates decline in the long run (though in plans with low marginal tax rates such as the flat tax, the short-run increase in labor supply puts upward pressure on the interest rate immediately following tax reform). Output gains are significant and relatively soon in coming—particularly under the flat tax (Hall-Rabushka version) and value-added tax plans. Asset prices fall because most of the consumption tax proposals include a cash-flow tax of greater magnitude than that in the current system. Again, efficiency gains are significant for the value-added tax and flat-tax reforms though these gains are reduced when transition relief is provided.

Auerbach also presents a description of the sensitivity of his simulation results to key parameters in the model. In particular, he shows that lower costs of adjusting the capital stock make possible greater gains in saving and efficiency from tax reform. Higher adjustment costs temporarily increase the value of existing assets and slow the rate of saving and capital accumulation. Variations in the "openness" of the capital market (an open capital market is modeled by fixing the real interest rate) affect the results. The unchanged interest rate in the (small) open economy simulation implies a higher interest rate and lower steady-state capital stock than in the base case. Alternative values of the elasticity of substitution between goods and leisure lead to different results. A lower value of the goods-leisure elasticity dampens the responsiveness of labor supply to tax reform, generally reducing the efficiency gains from tax reform.

The simulation exercises and sensitivity analysis yield no surprises. They follow from the basic intuition of the life-cycle framework from which Auerbach has taught us much over the years. Rather than suggest additional exercises, let me ask whether this model—with its assumptions of representative agents within cohorts, perfect lending and insurance markets, no financial structure distortions, and no heterogeneity in capital markets—is the "right model" for this sort of analysis.

The obvious and cheap answer is "probably not." To be fairer, are these missing features subtleties or important qualifications? I suspect that the latter is true. At least four limitations come to mind. First, the model abstracts from intragenerational variation (for example, differences in lifetime income and savings propensities), a topic central to the actual policy debate over tax reform. Second (and a related point), distributional implications of the transition between tax regimes depend only on household age. Third, increases in productive capital investment are financed only by new saving; "capital flows" from currently tax-favored sectors (in particular, housing) are not modeled. Finally (and more technically), the model abstracts from any link between capital deepening and technological advance that is emphasized in much of the new growth economics analysis. Having said this, I believe that the simulations still provide a useful basis for starting to analyze the economic consequences of tax reform.

Conclusion

Auerbach's chapter frames well the key issues in analyzing fundamental tax reform. Indeed, apart from the chapter's modeling exercises, three warnings to tax reform analysts bear attention. Understand the sources of tax-related distortions of economic decisions and their relative importance. Examine gains and losses between realistic tax systems. Finally, do not forget the political economy—as well as the economics—of tax reform, particularly in studying the transition between tax regimes.

More thorough analysis of efficiency and distributional analysis of tax reform is still needed to guide the policy debate. Research on broader life-cycle models and on empirical studies of household saving, household portfolio allocation, and business investment should complement Auerbach's analysis in formulating policy evaluation.

References

Altshuler, Rosanne, and Alan J. Auerbach. 1990. "The Significance of Tax Law Asymmetries: An Empirical Investigation." *Quarterly Journal of Economics* 105 (February): 61–86.

Auerbach, Alan J. 1983a. "Corporate Taxation in the United States." *Brookings Papers on Economic Activity* 2: 451–513.

———. 1983b. "Taxation, Corporate Financial Policy, and the Cost of Capital." *Journal of Economic Literature* 21 (September): 905–40.

———. 1989. "Capital Gains Taxation and Tax Reform." *National Tax Journal* 42 (September): 391–401.

———. 1992. "On the Design and Reform of Capital-Gains Taxation." *American Economic Review* 82 (May): 263–69.

———. 1995. "Flat Taxes: Some Economic Considerations." Testimony before the Committee on Finance, U.S. Senate (April).

Auerbach, Alan J., and Kevin Hassett. 1991. "Recent U.S. Investment Behavior and the Tax Reform Act of 1986: A Disaggregate View." *Carnegie–Rochester Conference Series on Public Policy* 35 (Fall): 185–216.

Auerbach, Alan J., and Laurence J. Kotlikoff. 1987. *Dynamic Fiscal Policy.* Cambridge University Press.

Cummins, Jason G., Kevin A. Hassett, and R. Glenn Hubbard. 1994. "A Reconsideration of Investment Behavior Using Tax Reforms as Natural Experiments." *Brookings Papers on Economic Activity* 2: 1–74.

Federal Reserve System, Board of Governors. 1995a. *Balance Sheets for the U.S. Economy.* Washington.

———. 1995b. *Flow of Funds Accounts, Flows and Outstandings: Second Quarter 1995.* Washington.

Feldstein, Martin. 1995. "The Effect of a Consumption Tax on the Rate of Interest." Working Paper 5397. Cambridge, Mass.: National Bureau of Economic Research (December).

Fullerton, Don, and Marios Karayannis. 1993. "United States." In *Tax Reform and the Cost of Capital: An International Comparison*, edited by Dale W. Jorgenson and Ralph Landau, 333–67. Brookings.

Gentry, William M., and R. Glenn Hubbard. 1995. "Distributional Implications of Introducing a Broad-Based Consumption Tax." Mimeograph. Columbia University.

Gertler, Mark, and R. Glenn Hubbard. 1993. "Corporate Financial Policy, Taxation, and Macroeconomic Risk." *RAND Journal of Economics* 24 (Summer): 286–303.

Gordon, Roger, and Joel Slemrod. 1988. "Do We Collect Any Revenue from Taxing Capital Income?" In *Tax Policy and the Economy*, vol. 2, edited by Lawrence H. Summers, 89–130. MIT Press.

Gravelle, Jane. 1994. *The Economic Effects of Taxing Capital Income.* MIT Press.

Gravelle, Jane, and Laurence J. Kotlikoff. 1989. "The Incidence and Efficiency Costs of Corporate Taxation When Corporate and Noncorporate Firms Produce the Same Goods." *Journal of Political Economy* 97 (August): 749–80.

Grubert, Harry, and T. Scott Newlon. 1995. "The International Implications of Consumption Tax Proposals." *National Tax Journal* 48 (December): 619–47.

Jorgenson, Dale W. 1996. "The Economic Impact of Fundamental Tax Reform." In *Frontiers of Tax Reform*, edited by M. J. Boskin, 181–95. Stanford, Calif.: Hoover Institution Press.

Hall, Robert. 1996. "The Effects of Tax Reform on Prices and Asset Values." In *Tax Policy and the Economy*, vol. 10, edited by James Poterba, 71–88. MIT Press.

Hall, Robert, and Alvin Rabushka. 1995. *The Flat Tax*, 2d ed. Stanford, Calif.: Hoover Institution Press.

Harberger, Arnold C. 1966. "Efficiency Effects of Taxes on Income from Capital." In *Effects of Corporation Income Tax*, edited by Marian Krzyzaniak, 107–17. Wayne State University Press.

CHAPTER 3

The Effects of Fundamental Tax Reform on Saving

Eric M. Engen and William G. Gale

A PRIMARY GOAL of fundamental tax reform is to increase saving. Higher saving would increase economic growth, improve future living standards, and help ensure that households are adequately prepared for retirement. Concerns about U.S. saving have become more intense as net national saving has fallen from an average of almost 11 percent of net national product in the 1950s through the 1970s to about 4 percent since 1990. Personal saving also has declined from an average of more than 7 percent of disposable income in the 1950s through the 1970s to 5 percent since 1990.

The effects on saving of switching to a consumption tax depend on several issues. First, the magnitude of the tax burden placed on saving in the current system is crucial for determining the degree to which the tax distortion on saving would be reduced under a consumption tax. Second, the effect depends on how rates of return to capital would respond to tax reform and the sensitivity of saving to changes in after-tax returns. Third, the effect would be influenced by the redistribution of tax burdens across groups with different propensities to save, including any windfall gains and losses created in the transition to the new system.

These issues are examined with a simulation model of households' saving behavior. The simulation model uses estimates of behavioral parameters and economic characteristics of households and the economy to develop quantitative predictions of saving behavior and its response

We thank David Bradford, Jon Skinner, and conference participants at Brookings and Dartmouth for helpful comments, and the National Institute on Aging for financial support. The views expressed here are ours and do not necessarily reflect the views of the Federal Reserve, the Brookings Institution, or their staffs.

to various types of tax reforms. The existing U.S. tax system is modeled as a progressive tax with a base that is a hybrid between a consumption tax and an income tax. Our simulation results indicate that moving from the existing system to a flat-rate consumption tax would raise the long-term saving rate by 0.3 to 0.8 percent of GDP. This result reflects the interaction of several effects. Moving to a consumption tax would reduce tax rates on new saving, raising the after-tax return to saving, and would lighten tax burdens on households that save more. These effects would increase saving. But these positive effects would be moderated by several factors. First, the current tax system already taxes a substantial portion of household saving as it would be taxed under a consumption tax. Funds placed in 401(k)s and other pension plans, Keoghs, and most individual retirement accounts (IRAs) are tax deductible at the time of the contribution, and the earnings on these funds accrue tax free. Contributions and investment earnings are taxed only when they are withdrawn. For saving that is tax-preferred in the current system, there is no first-order effect of tax reform, as it already receives consumption-tax treatment. Moreover, if tax reform causes a drop in before-tax rates of return, as many forecast, returns to this category of saving would fall. Second, saving that is done for precautionary reasons is relatively insensitive to the rate of return, so a portion of household saving would be unresponsive to an increase in the after-tax return induced by tax reform. Third, transition rules may eliminate taxes on consumption financed with assets accumulated before tax reform. These transition rules would shift some of the tax burden from older cohorts with lower saving propensities to younger cohorts with higher saving propensities, which would further reduce the positive saving effects of switching to a consumption tax.

The actual effects of tax reform may be somewhat smaller than those indicated by the model because of several factors that are outside the scope of the simulation. For example, pensions would lose their current tax-advantaged status under a consumption tax, and pension coverage and benefits would probably shrink, which could decrease saving. Moreover, assets currently in pensions and other tax-sheltered saving face restrictions on withdrawals. It is unlikely that these restrictions would survive under a consumption tax, and their removal could cause a spurt in consumption as households gained access to some of these funds. Thus our main conclusion is that replacing the current tax system with a consumption tax is not likely to raise the saving rate by very much, and under plausible circumstances, the change in saving could be negligible.

Taxes and Saving: Current Law

In principle, the current U.S. tax system taxes household income at progressive rates. Labor income includes wages, salaries, and bonuses. Capital income includes interest, dividends, rent, and capital gains, minus depreciation. The corporation income tax also taxes corporate profits, resulting in the double taxation of corporate income.[1] In practice, the U.S. income tax contains numerous provisions that are consistent with a consumption-based tax, thus making the current system a hybrid rather than a pure income tax.[2]

Tax-Preferred Saving Accounts

The U.S. tax code currently provides a variety of tax-preferred retirement saving accounts.[3] The important features common to these saving accounts are that contributions are usually tax deductible and, in all cases, investment income on the account balances accrues tax free. Tax-deductible contributions and earnings are taxed at ordinary income tax rates only upon withdrawal. Withdrawals for unapproved purposes before the account holder reaches age 59½ can trigger an added penalty. An individual can set up an IRA or a Keogh plan (if self-employed). In addition, the cash value of whole life insurance—the so-called inside buildup—enjoys significant tax advantages; the premiums paid by individuals are not tax deductible, but the earnings on reserves are tax exempt. Employers provide tax-sheltered saving to employees through qualified defined-benefit (DB) and defined-contribution (DC) pension plans, which include 401(k) plans. Tax-preferred savings accounts now constitute more than one-third of aggregate household financial assets (table 3-1). In 1994 the asset balances of IRAs and Keoghs are estimated to have been about $1 trillion, and the value of life insurance reserves were almost $500 billion. The value of qualified pension fund assets—including 401(k) plans—totaled approximately $5 trillion in 1994.[4]

---

1. The nature of the burden of the corporate income tax is affected by one's interpretation of the tax treatment of corporate dividend income. See chapter 2 by Alan Auerbach in this volume for more discussion of this issue.

2. Aaron, Galper and Pechman (1988) discuss other issues involving hybrid income-consumption taxes.

3. See Engen, Gale, and Scholz (1994) for more details on the structure of saving incentives.

4. Estimates of the asset values for IRAs and Keoghs in 1994 are based on data from

Table 3-1. Tax-Preferred Saving Incentive Accounts and Household
Financial Assets, 1976–94

	Percent of household financial assets			
Type of asset	1976–80	1981–85	1986–90	1991–94
IRA and Keogh assets	n.a.	1.4	3.4	4.8
Life insurance reserves	4.0	3.0	2.6	2.7
Pension reserves	14.1	18.3	23.6	27.6
Total saving incentive assets	18.1	22.8	29.7	35.1
Total financial assets (percent of net worth)	66.8	67.3	71.7	75.4

Sources: Federal Reserve Board, *Balance Sheets for the U.S. Economy 1945–94*, 1995. Employee Benefit Research Institute, *EBRI Databook on Employee Benefits*, 1995.

Table 3-2. Decomposition of U.S. Personal Saving, 1971–93
Percent of net national product

Type of saving	1971–80	1981–85	1986–90	1991–93
Net personal saving	7.2	8.1	5.8	5.9
Retirement	3.7	6.7	5.7	5.6
Pensions	3.7	5.4	4.4	4.2
Individual	n.a.	1.3	1.3	1.4
Life insurance	0.5	0.3	0.6	0.5
Other	3.0	1.1	−0.5	−0.2

Source: Sabelhaus (1996).

Aside from saving in tax-sheltered accounts, U.S. net personal saving is negligible (table 3-2).[5] Over the last twenty years, while the personal saving rate has declined, the rate of tax-preferred retirement saving has risen, but other net personal saving has vanished.[6] In the 1970s, tax-preferred retirement and life-insurance saving constituted less than 60 percent of total personal saving. Since the mid-1980s, they have made up more than 100 percent of personal saving.

Tax-Preferred Assets

The current tax system does not fully tax income from whole classes of assets. For example, the interest paid on municipal bonds is untaxed

1980 to 1992 provided by Employee Benefit Research Institute (1995). Data on life insurance reserves and pension assets are compiled by the Federal Reserve Board (1995).

5. These calculations are reported in Sabelhaus (1996). Retirement and life-insurance saving includes contributions plus reinvested earnings less withdrawals. Capital gains are excluded from this measure because they are also excluded from measures of personal saving and from national income.

6. For example, see Congressional Budget Office (1993) for an examination of studies and evidence on the decline in U.S. saving rates.

by the federal income tax. More important, the imputed rent on owner-occupied housing is not subject to tax, the taxation of capital gains on home sales can be deferred, and up to $125,000 in capital gains on home sales is tax exempt for taxpayers age 55 and older.[7] In fact, all assets that generate returns as capital gains are tax favored in the individual income tax because the tax on capital gains is deferred until gains are realized, reducing the present value of taxes owed.[8] Moreover, the maximum rate on capital gains—28 percent—is below the ordinary marginal tax rate faced by the recipients of a substantial portion of capital gains, and capital gains assets enjoy a step-up in basis at death that bequeathed funds in saving incentive accounts do not receive. Thus assets that generate returns in the form of capital gains can sometimes provide more favorable tax advantages than assets kept in tax-preferred savings accounts.

Unrealized capital gains on residential and investment real estate, noncorporate business equity, and stocks and mutual funds held outside retirement accounts constituted about 40 percent of household net worth in 1989 and 37 percent in 1992.[9] In 1989 about one-third of the gross asset value of households' mutual fund holdings and directly held corporate equities (outside of retirement accounts) were unrealized capital gains.[10] Directly held corporate equities and mutual funds constituted a growing proportion of household net worth over the past twenty years (table 3-3).[11] In 1989 almost 70 percent of the gross asset value of households' direct holdings of noncorporate businesses were unrealized capital gains.[12] Unrealized capital gains represented an estimated 46 percent of

7. For a fuller explanation of the tax advantages of housing, see chapter 5 by Capozza, Green, and Hendershott in this volume and Rosen (1985).

8. The value of deferral of capital gains taxes in the individual income tax is considerable. At a discount rate of 6 percent, deferring tax five, ten, or twenty years reduces the present value of the ultimate tax payments by 25 percent, 44 percent, and 69 percent, respectively. However, the value of corporate equities is reduced by the corporate income tax.

9. Kennickell and Starr-McCluer (1994).

10. Kennickell and Wilcox (1992).

11. Although some of these stock and mutual fund holdings are in tax-preferred saving accounts, a significant portion are not. Mack (1993) shows that about 15 percent of mutual fund assets were held in household-directed retirement accounts (IRAs and Keoghs) in 1992. Moreover, the Employee Benefit Research Institute (1995) reports that $202 billion of IRA and Keogh assets in 1992 were held in self-directed stock brokerage accounts, which accounts for only 7 percent of the direct holdings of corporate equities recorded in households' balance sheets by the Federal Reserve Board (1995).

12. Kennickell and Wilcox (1992).

Table 3-3. *Tax-Preferred Assets, Debt, and Household Net Worth, 1976–94*

	Percent of net worth				Percent of asset value attributable to unrealized capital gains[a]
Type of asset or debt	1976–80	1981–85	1986–90	1991–94	1989
Stocks + mutual funds	9.6	9.0	11.2	16.3	32.8
Noncorp. business equity	19.2	17.6	13.9	11.0	68.8
Residential housing	33.3	33.9	32.4	30.8	46.1
Tax-exempt bonds	0.9	1.3	2.1	2.0	...
Mortgage debt	9.3	9.4	11.6	12.9	...
Consumer debt	4.1	3.8	4.3	3.8	...

Source: Federal Reserve Board, *Balance Sheets for the U.S. Economy 1945–94*, 1995.
a. Kennickell and Wilcox (1992).

the value of primary residences in 1989.[13] Households held over $7 trillion in residential housing in 1994. In 1994 interest on $388 billion in tax-exempt municipal bonds, about 2 percent of households' financial assets, was exempt from federal income tax.

These statistics indicate that the current tax system is not a pure income tax in its treatment of capital income. Instead, it is a complex hybrid income-consumption tax, as a substantial proportion of households' assets and saving currently receives tax-preferred treatment similar to the tax treatment of saving under a consumption tax.

Taxes and Debt

In a comprehensive income tax, all capital income should be taxed and all interest expense should be deductible. Variants of a consumption tax that exempt interest income should also deny deductions for interest expense. The appropriate treatment of interest expenses in a hybrid income-consumption tax is unclear. The central problem is that allowing the deductibility of some, or all, of interest paid when not all capital income is taxed creates opportunities for tax arbitrage.[14]

13. Kennickell and Wilcox (1992).
14. Tax arbitrage can arise if the after-tax interest rate on debt is less than the after-tax rate of return on saving even if the before-tax interest rate on debt is greater than the before-tax rate of return on saving. For example, borrowing funds that are allowed an immediate tax deduction for interest paid and investing the funds in an asset with income that is tax deferred can potentially generate an after-tax profit. Engen and Gale (1995)

The hybrid character of the current tax system is evident in its treatment of debt payments as in the taxation of income. The Tax Reform Act of 1986 phased out the deductibility of interest paid on consumer debt but retained almost complete deductibility of interest paid on mortgage debt and investment loans. In 1994 home mortgages composed about 76 percent of the $4.6 trillion in total household debt, or 13 percent of household net worth (table 3-3). Consumer credit, interest on which is not tax deductible, accounted for about 20 percent of household debt.[15] Although the majority of household debt currently receives income-tax treatment, a substantial portion encounters consumption-tax treatment.

Household Saving under Tax Reform

A consumption tax either taxes consumption directly (a retail sales tax, for example) or allows a deduction from income for net saving. The deduction can be introduced in either of two ways. In the first approach, net contributions to saving accounts and reinvested asset income are excluded from taxes, but net withdrawals are taxed.[16] Under the second approach, the net contribution is not tax deductible, but investment earnings and withdrawals are tax exempt. If the tax rate is held constant, the two approaches reduce the present value of consumption possibilities by the same percentage.[17] This equivalence is often used to suggest that wage taxes—which essentially tax saving according to the second approach—are equivalent to consumption taxes, which essentially use the

---

present recent evidence on the interaction between tax-preferred mortgage debt and tax-preferred 401(k) plans. Steuerle (1985) provides a general explanation of tax arbitrage.

15. Evidence suggests that the shift in tax treatment of debt enacted as part of the Tax Reform Act of 1986 led households to rely increasingly on mortgage debt, but appears to have done little in restraining total household debt. Engen and Gale (1995) and Maki (1995) describe these trends in household debt more fully.

16. These rules are similar but by no means identical to those governing current tax-preferred saving accounts such as IRAs or 401(k)s. For saving incentives, the contribution is deductible regardless of whether it represents a net increase in saving, and the withdrawal is subject to tax, regardless of whether it is used for consumption. Withdrawals from these accounts must be made after age 70½ according to a formula set forth in regulations.

17. A tax rate of t percent on withdrawals reduces consumption possibilities t percent. A tax on deposits at the rate of t percent reduces deposits, subsequent interest earnings, and amounts available for withdrawal also by t percent.

first approach. However, there are at least two important differences between consumption taxes and wage taxes.[18]

Future consumption can be financed from two sources: existing assets or future wages. Thus the first difference is that the base of a consumption tax includes consumption financed from capital existing at the time of the tax reform, whereas the base of a wage tax would not. Consumption from existing capital includes not only consumption out of the return to previously existing capital (which would also be taxed under an income tax), but also consumption financed by cashing in the *principal* of previously existing assets. To the extent that the principal of previously existing capital did not receive a tax deduction when it was initially saved, it would not be taxed again when consumed under an income tax, but would be taxed a second time when consumed under a consumption tax. The tax levy on the principal of existing capital is economically important because it raises the consumption tax base and hence lowers the rate that has to be applied to other consumption. Moreover, this tax levy imposes more of the total tax burden on older cohorts with relatively low saving propensities while reducing the necessary tax burden on younger cohorts with relatively higher saving propensities.[19] Furthermore, if the levy is unanticipated, and if it is also believed that the imposition of a capital levy does not change the probability that a levy will be enacted in the future, then the levy raises substantial revenue in a distortion-free manner and so improves the efficiency of the consumption tax. Nonetheless, it may be considered unfair. Allowing deductions for consumption financed by the principal of old capital would remove the levy. Switching to a wage tax would remove the levy as well as the tax on consumption financed from the return of existing capital.

A second difference between a wage tax and a consumption tax concerns the treatment of capital income from new saving. It is simplest here to assume there is no pre-existing capital. If everyone earns the same return—for concreteness, assume it is the risk-free rate of return—on his or her saving, there is no difference here between the wage tax and the

18. The present value of taxes paid under a consumption tax and those paid under a wage tax would be equivalent if there were no existing assets at the time either tax was imposed, the interest rate was the same in both regimes, and the tax rates were set appropriately. However, the timing of tax payments would be different. See Bradford (1984, 1986, 1996) for more discussion of the general principles of consumption taxes.

19. Older cohorts generally have accumulated substantial life-cycle and precautionary saving, and thus are either accumulating little in additional saving or are dissaving. Younger cohorts are generally adding to their stocks of retirement and precautionary assets and have a higher propensity to save.

consumption tax. Two people with equal wages would pay equal present discounted value of taxes under a wage tax or consumption tax, regardless of how much they saved. If everyone earns the same rate of return, saving more does not change the present value of consumption because the rate of return earned is exactly equal to the discount rate. The tax deduction for *new* saving under a consumption tax just offsets the present discounted value of the future tax liability when this saving, plus a risk-free rate of return, is consumed.[20] Thus the opportunity cost component of the return on saving (or the risk-free return to compensate for deferring consumption) is untaxed under a consumption tax or a wage tax.[21]

Now let rates of return vary across investments. To be specific, assume that risk is held constant, so returns vary only because one investor is more astute or productive in investing than another. In economists' parlance, one of the investors earns "rents" or excess returns. The key difference is that under a wage tax, these extra returns are not taxed, while under a consumption tax they are. To see this, note that, assuming that each investor saves the same amount, the investor who receives excess returns has a higher present value of consumption than the other. Under a wage tax, this difference does not matter; if investors earn the same wage, they pay the same taxes. In contrast, under a consumption tax, the investor with excess returns raises the present value of his or her consumption and so raises the present value of consumption taxes paid. The portion of the overall return to capital over and above the risk-free return, controlling for risk, generates a positive present value of tax revenues.[22] Thus both consumption taxes and wage taxes remove the tax distortion imposed by an income tax on the opportunity cost of saving,

20. The tax deduction for saving (S) reduces an individual's tax liability by tS, where t denotes the effective tax rate. If this saving earns a risk-free return equal to r_f, and the individual consumes the principal plus earnings after n years ($S(1+r_f)^n$), then the present value of the future consumption tax liability is equal to $t\{S(1+r_f)^n]/(1+r_f)^n\}$, which equals tS. Thus the capital income reflecting the risk-free return on this saving is untaxed under a consumption tax.

21. Under a consumption tax, the return to saving that compensates for risk is untaxed also. However, the analysis of this point is more complicated. See Bradford (1996) for a discussion.

22. As before, the deduction for saving (S) reduces an individual's tax liability by tS, where t denotes the effective tax rate. If this saving earns a return of r^*, greater than the risk-free return of r_f, and the individual consumes the principal plus earnings after n years ($S(1+r^*)^n$), then the present value of the future consumption tax liability is equal to $t\{S(1+r^*)^n]/(1+r_f)^n\}$, which exceeds tS. Thus capital income above the risk-free return on this saving is taxed at rate t under a consumption tax, while capital income up to the opportunity cost is untaxed.

but the consumption tax captures taxes on excess returns to new capital investment, while a wage tax does not.[23]

The Effects of Tax Reform on Saving in a Simulation Model

In this section, we report the results of using a simulation model to examine the effects of switching from a progressive hybrid income-consumption tax to a flat-rate consumption tax. Simulation analyses are particularly helpful for analyzing policies where data are limited or unavailable and where the distinction between short- and long-term effects matters. Fundamental tax reform is such a policy because it involves changes outside the range of historical experience and economic behavior, and the short-term effects of a new tax system may be quite different from the ultimate impact.

The manner in which taxes affect saving in a simulation depends crucially on the model's assumptions concerning a household's motives for saving and the time horizon over which it plans. In the simplest life-cycle models, consumers are posited to save only for retirement.[24] Since the interest rate determines the price of future consumption relative to current consumption, changes in the interest rate alter life-cycle retirement saving. However, the theoretical effect of a change in the after-tax rate of return on saving is ambiguous. An increase in the after-tax return reduces the price of future consumption and leads to increased future consumption. But the increased return also reduces the amount of current saving necessary to support any given level of future consumption. The saving elasticity depends on the relative magnitudes of each effect.

Simulation studies that rely on a life-cycle framework and assume certainty in the economic environment usually imply a large, positive saving elasticity that is substantially greater than that suggested by em-

23. See Bradford (1996) and Hubbard and Gentry (1996) for more discussion of this point.
24. A motive to save for bequests can arise if it is assumed that households care about their heirs as well as themselves. If this concern about their heirs is purely altruistic—that is, parents do not demand anything in return for their bequests—then the planning horizon for a saver can become infinite. See Barro (1974). However, the assumed intergenerational altruism underlying this bequest model is strongly rejected by the evidence. See Bernheim (1987), Altonji, Hayashi, and Kotlikoff (1992, 1995), and Hayashi, Altonji, and Kotlikoff (1996).

pirical evidence.[25] It is neither surprising nor convincing that such models predict large increases in aggregate saving from replacing a comprehensive income tax with a comprehensive consumption tax.[26]

The precautionary saving model adds to the life-cycle framework the realistic considerations that people may save not only for retirement, but also to protect themselves against such unforeseen future circumstances as a cut in wages, unemployment, disability, or illness, and that people may hold onto some wealth during retirement as a precaution against the possibility of outliving their financial assets. Recent theoretical developments suggest that precautionary saving can be a powerful influence on household saving behavior.[27] Empirical research confirms this intuition.[28] The presence of precautionary saving has also been shown to provide at least partial resolutions to several features of actual consumption and saving behavior that are puzzles when viewed from the perspective of a certainty model.[29]

Because precautionary saving usually provides for short-term contingencies, it is less sensitive to changes in the rate of return than pure life-cycle saving. A model that incorporates precautionary motives for saving

25. Empirical estimates of the saving elasticity and simulated saving elasticities are discussed in more detail below.

26. Feldstein (1978), Summers (1981), Evans (1983), Auerbach and Kotlikoff (1983, 1987), Auerbach, Kotlikoff, and Skinner (1983), Seidman (1983, 1984), Hubbard and Judd (1986), Starrett (1988), McGee (1989), Gravelle (1991), chapter 2 in this volume by Alan Auerbach, and chapter 9 in this volume by Fullerton and Rogers and (1993) are examples of studies that use a certainty version of the life-cycle model for analysis of capital income taxation. Most of these studies report large increases in saving by switching to a consumption tax. For example, Summers (1981) reports that switching from an income tax to a consumption tax would raise consumer well-being by 6 to 16 percent of lifetime income, and boost the capital-income ratio 40 to 60 percent. Auerbach and Kotlikoff (1987) report smaller, but still substantial, gains to saving.

27. Skinner (1988), Zeldes (1989), Caballero (1991), Deaton (1991), Carroll (1992), Hubbard, Skinner, and Zeldes (1994, 1995), and Engen (1994).

28. The 1992 Survey of Consumer Finances (SCF) reported that the most frequently cited reason for saving by households in the survey was precautionary saving, which included affirmative responses to "saving for reserves against unemployment" and "saving in case of illness." Forty-two percent of households cited precautionary reasons as an important reason for saving, while about 27 percent cited retirement as an important reason for saving. See Kennickell and Starr-McCluer (1994). Similar frequency of responses to these saving questions was also reported in the 1986 SCF, Engen and Gale (1993) and the 1989 SCF, Kennickell and McCluer (1994). Other empirical research includes Carroll and Samwick (1995) and Engen and Gruber (1996).

29. For example, precautionary saving can help explain the sensitivity of consumption to changes in current income and the relationship between consumption and income over the life-cycle. See Deaton (1992) and Browning and Lusardi (1995) for surveys of these issues.

can imply a substantially smaller and more plausible saving elasticity.[30] Previous analysis of the effects of consumption taxes within a stochastic life-cycle model yields increases in saving that are as much as 80 percent smaller than those produced by a certainty life-cycle model.[31]

The Model

The simulation model used here modifies the standard life-cycle framework by having consumers face uncertain labor earnings and an uncertain life span. Individuals save for retirement and as a precaution against downturns in future earnings and outliving their assets. The model consists of five parts: a framework for describing consumers' preferences for consumption and saving; the budget constraints faced by consumers; a formalization of the uncertainties facing consumers; government taxes and spending structures; and an overlapping generations framework, which recognizes that the population consists of people of different ages.[32]

People enter the model at age 21. The probability of dying increases with age, and the maximum life span is 90. Each year people maximize their expected well-being over the rest of their lifetime by choosing how much to consume and save; how to allocate their assets between a tax-preferred saving incentive asset or a conventional, fully-taxed asset; and deciding whether to work full time or not at all.[33] No one intentionally leaves bequests, but accidental bequests occur because people cannot predict exactly when they will die.[34] Consumers are assumed to be risk averse and "prudent," which means in the model that uncertainty about future earnings leads to precautionary saving.[35]

---

30. Engen (1994).

31. Engen (1994).

32. Descriptions of most elements of this simulation model appear in Engen (1994), Engen and Gale (1993), and Engen, Gale, and Scholz (1994).

33. To simplify the computation of the model, individuals are not given a choice of part-time work or a range of hours to work.

34. To simplify the solution of the model, all accidental bequests are effectively confiscated, that is, no other generation receives them. This simplifying assumption was also made in Hubbard, Skinner, and Zeldes (1994, 1995).

35. Uncertainty in the rate of return from saving would generate an additional precautionary saving motive. However, for most households, human wealth is substantially greater than financial wealth, and thus uncertainty about expected wages is quantitatively more important than uncertainty about rates of return on assets. Skinner (1988) showed that empirically plausible interest rate uncertainty generates only a small amount of precautionary saving relative to labor earnings uncertainty.

Consumption can be financed in three ways: by after-tax labor earnings; by annuity income from social security, which people cannot collect until they are at least age 65 and have retired; and by balances in the two assets. Both assets earn the same certain pre-tax rate of return.[36] The return on conventional assets is fully taxed. For the saving incentive account, contributions are deductible and constrained by an annual limit, and contributions and investment earnings are not taxed until withdrawn. Funds withdrawn before the account holder reaches age 60 are subject to a 10 percent penalty.[37]

In the model, government revenues equal expenditures, which include social security benefits and a government-provided good that is allocated equally to all individuals. The baseline tax system is a progressive hybrid income tax, similar to the U.S. system, with tax brackets of 15, 30, and 40 percent.[38] Individuals are allowed a personal exemption ($2,500) and a standard deduction ($3,500). Deductions for tax-sheltered saving are subject to an annual limit of $7,500. When the tax structure changes, new tax rates are determined in order to raise the same aggregate revenue in each year.

Cohorts of different ages are incorporated in an overlapping generations framework that accounts for mortality and for population growth of 1 percent a year. The model contains a simple production sector that demands labor and capital from the household sector and helps determine the pre-tax rate of return to capital and expected wages in the model. Labor productivity rises by an average of 0.5 percent a year. Workers are uncertain about their individual wages, but there are no business cycles in the model. This simple general equilibrium framework allows for feedback effects of broad tax policy changes in the return to capital and wages owing to changes in the capital stock and labor supply while maintaining the focus of the analysis on individual saving behavior.

36. Because there are no excess returns to capital in this model, the issues concerning the treatment of capital "rents" under a consumption tax—discussed above—do not arise here.

37. We ignore mandatory withdrawals required starting at age 70½ and the loan provisions of some 401(k) plans.

38. These tax rates correspond to the following tax brackets: $20,000–$55,000, $55,000–$120,000, and above $120,000 (1995 dollars). The five tax brackets in the current tax system are approximated by these three tax rates in order to ease the computational burden.

The Interest Elasticity of Saving

Simulated effects of taxes on saving depend crucially upon the implied saving elasticity in the simulation model. However, a standard empirical benchmark for the saving elasticity is difficult to determine. Results from empirical studies using aggregate time-series data have been inconclusive, although many estimates fall in a range from 0 to 0.4.[39] Virtually no empirical study suggests a large saving response by households to changes in the after-tax return. But any study based on aggregate data faces formidable econometric problems. Some studies have used nominal rates of return rather than inflation-adjusted interest rates, and most studies have not used an after-tax rate of return. Moreover, estimating the saving elasticity is difficult with aggregate time-series data because of the problems involved in measuring changes in expected real after-tax returns and in holding constant the other factors that affect saving. In fact, the Lucas critique implies that a stable aggregate saving function may not even exist.[40] The problems with studies based on time-series evidence introduce substantial uncertainty into determining the empirical responsiveness of household saving to changes in the after-tax return.[41]

Many scholars have studied the effects of tax-preferred saving incentives using household-level data.[42] No consensus has emerged. It is not clear, in any event, what lessons could be drawn from the saving effects

39. The estimated elasticity of 0.4, based on research by Boskin (1978) and Boskin and Lau (1978), is usually considered an upper bound. Blinder (1975), Howrey and Hymans (1980), Carlino (1982), and Friend and Hasbrouck (1983) reported estimates close to zero. Wright (1967, 1969), Juster and Wachtel (1972), and Gylfason (1981) reached intermediate values. Bosworth (1984), demonstrating the fragility of these results, found a range of estimates from zero to small positive elasticities. Gylfason (1981), Bosworth (1984), Ballard (1990), and Gravelle (1994) provide surveys of this literature, and Bernheim (forthcoming) discusses some of the econometric problems.

40. Lucas (1976).

41. Another empirical approach to estimating the sensitivity of saving to changes in the after-tax return has focused upon analyzing the relationship between the growth rate of consumption—rather than the level of consumption—and changes in the after-tax rate of return. Unfortunately, empirical analysis of this intertemporal elasticity of substitution for consumption does not yield any clear consensus on the responsiveness of saving to changes in its after-tax return. Bernheim (forthcoming) provides a discussion of the econometric problems in estimating the intertemporal elasticity of substitution. Engen (1994) shows that the saving elasticity can vary substantially even while holding constant the intertemporal elasticity of substitution depending on the importance of precautionary saving.

42. Hubbard and Skinner (1995), Bernheim (forthcoming), Engen, Gale, and Scholz (1996), and Poterba, Venti, and Wise (1996) provide surveys of the literature on saving incentives.

of IRAs and 401(k)s for fundamental tax reform. Shifting of existing assets and intended saving from taxable to sheltered accounts, so important in the analysis of saving incentives, is not a major issue in evaluating the effects of switching from the current tax system to a pure consumption tax. Furthermore, saving incentives have contribution limits; a consumption tax does not. Savers at the contribution limit for sheltered accounts face no marginal tax incentive to increase saving.[43] Contributors who are not at contribution limits face a marginal incentive to increase saving similar to that provided under a consumption tax, but no study of saving incentives has focused solely upon the marginal saving of non-limit contributors, controlling for any asset shifting, before and after the introduction of saving incentives.

An alternative to empirical estimates of the saving elasticity has been to simulate the saving elasticity in a stylized economic model.[44] For example, Lawrence H. Summers found that within a multiperiod certainty life-cycle model the interest elasticity of saving is usually large and positive—generally greater than 1 and often above 2.[45] Don Fullerton and Diane Lim Rogers calculate a saving elasticity of 1.3 in their baseline model which includes bequests, and the elasticity increases to above 2

43. See Gale and Scholz (1994) for further discussion of this issue regarding IRAs. Evidence on the proportion of 401(k) contributions that are constrained by a contribution limit is generally unavailable. This issue is complicated by the fact that although the IRS imposes an annual dollar limit on 401(k) contributions, many workers face different lower limits because of nondiscrimination rules or rules set by their employer. However, given their higher contribution limits, it is likely that fewer 401(k) contributors than IRA contributors are constrained by a contribution limit.

44. See Gravelle (1994) and Elmendorf (1996) for surveys of this literature.

45. Summers (1981). Evans (1983) showed that if individuals are assumed to have a negative rate of time preference—that is, they value future consumption above current consumption—then the interest elasticity of saving can be smaller than in Summers' model. However, economists generally accept the premise of a positive time preference rate on the basis of observing positive interest rates. Both Evans (1983) and Starrett (1988) have suggested that a specific type of bequest motive can reduce the implied saving elasticity. Evans (1983) demonstrated that this result depends crucially on the assumption that bequests are made without taking account of the well-being of the recipient. An alternative approach is based on the assumption that households care about their heirs in a purely altruistic manner and the savers' planning horizon becomes infinite. In this case, the predicted saving elasticity usually goes to infinity—small changes in the after-tax rate of return yield huge increases in saving. Without any guideline for determining the appropriate bequest motive, the effect of bequests on the saving elasticity is unclear. Starrett (1988) also showed that an economic model that introduces a subsistence level of consumption for individuals can decrease the saving elasticity. However, the amount of consumption necessities must rise proportionally with income, and a high level of necessities—approximately 50 percent of average consumption—is required in order to generate a substantial decrease in the saving elasticity.

Table 3-4. *Interest Elasticity of Saving and Saving Rates in the Precautionary Saving Model*

| | Household preferences for saving | | | | | |
| | Baseline parameter specification[a] | | Less prudent households[b] | | More prudent households[c] | |
Item	(1)	(2)	(3)	(4)	(5)	(6)
Real after-tax rate of return to capital	0.03	0.05	0.03	0.05	0.03	0.05
Aggregate saving elasticity	0.26	0.39	0.40	0.64	0.15	0.22
Aggregate saving rate (percent)	5.7	6.0	4.9	5.8	6.7	6.8
Aggregate asset-income ratio	3.94	4.25	3.44	4.08	4.68	4.71

Source: Authors' calculations.
a. Intertemporal elasticity of substitution = 0.33; relative risk aversion coefficient = 3; and time-preference rate = 0.04.
b. Less prudent: intertemporal elasticity of substitution = 0.5; relative risk aversion coefficient = 2; and time-preference rate = 0.04.
c. More prudent: intertemporal elasticity of substitution = 0.2; relative risk aversion coefficient = 5; and time-preference rate = 0.04.

when bequests are omitted.[46] These studies illustrate the point that certainty life-cycle models usually generate implausibly large saving elasticities and therefore will overstate the increase in saving from switching to a consumption tax.[47]

In the baseline specification of our precautionary saving model, where households are characterized as having an "average" amount of prudence, the aggregate interest elasticity of saving is 0.26 if the real after-tax interest rate is 3 percent and 0.39 if the real after-tax interest rate is 5 percent (table 3-4). Associated with these saving elasticities are aggregate household saving rates of 5.7 to 6.0 percent and aggregate asset-income ratios of 3.94 to 4.25 that are close to values actually observed.[48] Households that are less risk averse than assumed in our baseline simulations save relatively less for precautionary reasons and relatively more for retirement. As a result, saving falls, but its sensitivity to the rate of return rises (table 3-4, columns 3 and 4). Households that are more risk

46. Fullerton and Rogers (1993).
47. Moreover, none of the previous studies of consumption taxes (see footnote 26) explicitly accounted for the fact that the current tax structure is a hybrid income-consumption tax where some saving already escapes taxation. The assumption of switching from a pure income tax tends to overstate the reduction in the tax distortion on saving from the current system.
48. We also ran the model without precautionary savings, with the baseline parameter specifications in table 3-4, and both a 3 percent and 5 percent real rate of return. The resulting saving elasticities are high (1.94 and 1.47), and the saving rates (1.3 percent and 2.9 percent) and the asset-income ratios (0.87 and 1.96) are low relative to observed ratios.

averse save more for precautionary reasons, raising the aggregate saving rate and reducing the saving elasticity (table 3-4, columns 5 and 6).

Effects of Tax Reform on Saving

The simulations indicate that replacing the current hybrid tax with an immediate, permanent, and unanticipated consumption tax would boost saving and economic welfare (table 3-5). Our initial simulations examine the effects of replacing the current tax with a proportional consumption tax with neither transition relief for existing capital nor an exemption for a consumption allowance. This simulation also assumes that all changes in saving show up as changes in U.S. domestic investment.

Based on these assumptions, the required consumption tax rate would be about 21 percent. Our model indicates that saving would rise immediately by more than 1 percent of GDP, but the surge would subside and settle down to an increase of 0.8 percent of GDP (table 3-5, column 1). The ratio of assets to income would grow steadily and level out 13 percent larger than in the baseline case. Pre-tax interest rates would fall steadily and end 0.7 percentage point below the baseline case. Lifetime utility rises because added capital boosts wage rates and because adopting the consumption tax removes a tax wedge between current and future consumption.[49]

The presence of tax-preferred saving in the baseline hybrid tax system tempers the gains in saving from switching to a consumption tax. Prior to tax reform, approximately half of the saving in the model is in the tax-preferred asset. These accounts provide tax treatment for saving similar to a consumption tax. In addition, these accounts restrict access to funds placed in these investment vehicles and, therefore, are more likely to attract long-term retirement saving, which tends to be more interest sensitive. In contrast, short-term precautionary saving, which is less sensitive to the interest rate, tends to accumulate in taxed, but liquid, saving instruments. Removing the tax on assets held for precautionary reasons has a relatively small effect on saving.

Because saving incentives are available under current law, people would respond in different ways to a consumption tax. Some savers currently have exhausted opportunities to save in tax-sheltered accounts. If their additional (or "marginal") saving bears the full brunt of the

---

49. Another reason is that the discrete labor supply choice in the model implies a relatively small labor elasticity of less than 0.1.

Table 3-5. *Interest Rate, Saving, and Household Welfare Effects in a Switch from Hybrid Income-Consumption Tax to Consumption Tax*

Item	(1)	(2)	(3)	(4)
	Features of the tax structure and the economy			
Transition relief	no	yes	yes	yes
Personal allowance	no	no	yes	no
Economy	closed	closed	closed	open
	Results			
Pre-tax interest rate (percent)				
Initial	6.3	6.3	6.3	6.3
Year 2	6.2	6.2	6.2	6.3
Year 5	5.9	6.1	6.1	6.3
New steady state	5.6	5.9	6.0	6.3
Saving rate (percent)				
Initial	6.1	6.1	6.1	6.1
Year 2	7.5	6.9	6.8	7.6
Year 5	7.2	6.7	6.6	7.3
New steady state	6.9	6.5	6.4	6.9
Asset-income ratio				
Initial	4.27	4.27	4.27	4.27
Year 2	4.33	4.30	4.29	4.35
Year 5	4.48	4.38	4.35	4.52
New steady state	4.83	4.54	4.47	4.89
Change in utility[a]				
80[b]	−0.2	0.1	0.2	0.2
60[b]	0.2	0.2	0.1	0.3
40[b]	0.8	0.3	0.2	0.3
20[b]	1.2	0.6	0.5	0.2
New steady state	1.0	0.5	0.4	0.3

Source: Authors' calculations.
a. Percent of lifetime income.
b. Age at transition.

current capital income tax, conversion to a consumption tax would increase their net yield from the current after-tax rate of return to the pre-tax rate of return under the new system. If the saver has not exhausted opportunities to save in sheltered accounts, the saver would earn the pre-tax rate of return on the margin before tax reform. Eliminating the capital income tax has no first-order effect for such "inframarginal" savers. However, if, as our simulations suggest, the pre-tax rate of return falls as other people increase saving, then the second-order (general equilibrium) effect for inframarginal savers is likely to *reduce* saving. The positive effect we find on overall saving is the difference between the increase in saving by the "marginal" group of savers and reductions in saving by the "inframarginal" group.

The effects on welfare are unevenly distributed across age groups at the time of the reform. The very oldest age cohort suffers a welfare loss as their tax burden rises because consumption under current law is untaxed to the extent that it is financed by assets accumulated from already taxed income. Under the new law, all of their consumption would be taxed. The welfare gains rise inversely with age. Compared with older workers, younger workers benefit from longer periods of accumulation under the new system and have less accumulated capital that is subject to full taxation under the new system.

Allowing transition relief for existing capital would require a higher tax rate of almost 24 percent to preserve revenue neutrality. This higher rate reduces all behavioral effects of tax change (table 3-5, column 2). Saving increases about half as much as it does without transition relief. The eventual increase in the capital stock is about half as large. Interest rates fall about half as much, and welfare gains are reduced by half. The only significant difference is that even the very elderly enjoy lifetime welfare gains if transition relief is included.[50]

Unlike the current tax system, the consumption tax simulated in columns 1 and 2 provides no personal or dependent exemptions or standard deduction. The first dollar of consumption is subject to tax. To test the consequences of allowing a base level of consumption to be untaxed, we introduced a $15,000 personal allowance to the consumption tax while maintaining the transition relief for existing capital. This personal allowance means that the consumption tax has two brackets: zero on consumption up to $15,000 and a positive rate of 27 percent on consumption above $15,000. To sustain revenue, the marginal tax rate must increase. These changes convert a proportional consumption tax into a progressive one, based on average tax rates. These changes slightly reduce the increases in welfare and saving (table 3-5, column 3). The differences between the effects shown in columns 2 and 3 are small because labor is supplied very inelastically in the model.[51]

The three simulations shown so far impose an unrealistic assumption on economic behavior; all of the additional saving in these simulations would be invested in the United States. Although domestic rates of return fall, these simulations do not allow investors to seek higher returns

---

50. Appendix table 3A-1 shows results corresponding to those in table 3-5, column 2, for households that are more prudent and less prudent than we posit for our main simulations.

51. See chapter 7 in this volume by Robert K. Triest for an analysis of the effect of tax reform on labor supply.

abroad. In fact, U.S. investors have been earning returns abroad similar to those they earn at home. They might well invest much of any increase in saving in foreign assets. To illustrate the range of possible effects, we restricted our model to fix the pre-tax interest rate at its baseline value, a result that can occur in our model only if all increased saving flows abroad. Thus we would expect that the "real-world" results should be somewhere between the open and closed economy cases.[52] In this simulation we maintain transition relief but eliminate the personal allowance. The results of this simulation (table 3-5, column 4) show that saving and the capital stock increase about as much as in column 1, but the change in utility is reduced about two-thirds. The reason for this pattern is that the increased capital stock is held abroad and cannot increase productivity of U.S. workers. Recipients of capital income do better than if the rate of return fell, but wage earners enjoy no welfare gains.

In general, these simulations suggest that tax reform would increase household saving and welfare. Our results are not as large as those produced by some other models principally for two reasons. We take explicit account of the hybrid character of the current tax system—the presence of consumption tax elements in what is called an income tax. We also incorporate precautionary saving, which reduces the implied saving elasticity. Both considerations should be integral to the analysis of tax reform and both reduce the saving response to tax reform.

Simulation models have advantages in studying saving behavior because they formalize complex and interactive responses, but they suffer from at least two important shortcomings. First, not all economic agents behave as in formal economic models. Second, the results exclude consideration of a variety of issues that would make the model excessively complicated or unwieldy or that cannot readily be modeled. These problems should come as no surprise, as the purpose of an economic model is to extract the most important elements of a situation and omit others. We turn now to a variety of issues not included in our model that we think would be important in appraising the effects of tax reform on saving and economic welfare.

---

52. The before-tax interest rate could remain constant with increased domestic investment if tax reform, technological change, or some other effect increased domestic demand for capital. We have not included these effects in our model. In addition, a large increase in capital exports would necessitate a shift in the U.S. current account balance that could occur only if U.S. terms of trade deteriorated. Our model does not include these effects either, an omission that has some bearing on our welfare calculations.

Employer-Provided Pensions

The simulations can be thought of as including voluntary defined contribution (DC) plans, such as 401(k)s,[53] but not more traditional DC plans or any defined benefit plans. Contributions and earnings in the omitted plans accounted for a significant share of personal saving over the last decade. These plans would be adversely affected by tax reform. This section explores the impact of tax reform on non-401(k) pensions and how the effect on pensions might influence the ultimate effect on saving.

Pensions are treated favorably relative to other forms of saving under the tax system. Pension contributions are generally tax deductible and the earnings accrue tax free. Withdrawals are taxed as ordinary income. Under a consumption tax, all saving would receive equivalent treatment, except that other saving would likely not be exempt from payroll taxes, while pension contributions would likely remain exempt from payroll taxes.

While the decline in tax-favored status would reduce interest in pensions, there may be other reasons why employees or employers might wish to retain pensions. Per person administrative costs are smaller for pension plans that apply to large groups than for individuals who make their own arrangements. Defined benefit plans encourage long-term attachment to a given job. Pensions offer deferred benefits and so may be relatively more attractive to employees who have long-term planning horizons, a characteristic many employers find attractive in workers. Pensions can also be used to encourage workers to retire at times management thinks appropriate. Some managers feel an obligation to make sure that employees accumulate sufficient income for a decent retirement, even if employees do not wish to save. However, it is uncertain how compensation arrangements would adjust if employers wanted to continue to offer pensions, but employees preferred to control their own retirement saving.

Pensions currently are subject to extensive regulation concerning coverage, asset management, minimum and maximum funding rules, pension insurance, vesting rules, limits on the size of benefits, and equitable dis-

---

53. Strictly speaking, 401(k) plans are only available at private firms, but 403(b) plans, 457 plans, and other deferred compensation arrangements are available for employees of nonprofits, state and local governments, and other types of employers, respectively. We view the simulation model as implicitly including all of these plans.

tribution of benefits among employees. Frequent rule changes in recent years have further raised the cost of compliance.[54] Currently, pension regulations not only impose costs on employers but also deny workers free access to funds accumulated in their names. For these reasons, it is unclear, first, how the removal or reduction of the tax preference will influence firm decisions to maintain pensions and employee decisions to accept pensions, and second, how a change in pensions will affect overall saving. We address each issue in turn.

Pension Coverage and Tax Reform

A pure consumption tax would accord certain advantages to ordinary saving over pensions. The most obvious advantage is the absence of complex and costly regulation. A second is liquidity. Under a consumption tax, all saving would enjoy tax treatment as favorable as pensions now receive (other than the treatment of payroll taxes), and nonpension saving would be accessible at any time.

In prior research, Patricia B. Reagan and John A. Turner estimate that reducing the taxation of nonpension saving by 1 percentage point would reduce pension coverage rates by 0.4 percentage points for men and by smaller and more uncertain amounts for women.[55] William M. Gentry and Eric Peress estimate that a 1 percentage point fall in the tax on nonpension saving would reduce pension coverage rates by 0.89 percentage point.[56]

Effects of Pensions on Saving

The theoretical analysis of how pensions might affect saving is extremely complex, and various analysts have shown that pensions can have any effect from reducing nonpension wealth by more than pension wealth (an offset of more than 100 percent) to raising nonpension wealth (an offset of less than zero). Most empirical studies find offsets of 20 percent or less. Almost half find no offset at all or a positive effect of pensions on other wealth. On balance, past research shows little offset between pensions and other wealth. However, Gale has shown that econometric biases have caused past empirical work to understate offsets.[57]

54. See Shoven (1991), Hay-Huggins (1990), or Gale (1994).
55. Reagan and Turner (1995).
56. Gentry and Peress (1994).
57. Gale (1995).

Some of the biases are so serious that empirical research can find that pensions increase nonpension wealth even if pensions in fact cause nonpension wealth to fall by the full amount of pension saving. After correcting for most of the biases, Gale estimates that between 20 percent and 60 percent of pension contributions are net additions to saving.[58]

Illustrative Calculations

Given the heterogeneity of empirical research and the still-unresolved econometric problems, any estimate of how much pensions reduce nonpension saving is uncertain. Even more uncertain are estimates of the extent to which adoption of a consumption tax would discourage the continuation of old pension plans or the adoption of new ones. In this light, we present some illustrative calculations of the effects of adopting a consumption tax on pensions and pension-induced net saving.

The following calculation is shown in table 3-6, column 7. Suppose that non-401(k) pensions account for half of saving; 50 percent of pension contributions and earnings are new saving; moving to a consumption tax reduces the tax on nonpension saving by 20 percentage points; a 1 percentage point rise in tax on nonpension saving raises pension coverage by 0.25 percentage point; the initial pension coverage rate is 50 percent; and the initial saving level is 100 units, 50 in pensions and 50 in nonpensions. Then switching to a consumption tax would reduce pension coverage by 5 percentage points (20 × 0.25). This would be a 10 percent decline in pension coverage from the initial level of 50 percent, and assuming all pensions are the same size, would reduce pension saving by 10 percent or 5 units. Since 50 percent of the decline is saving that would have occurred anyway (that is, the other 50 percent is new saving), other saving rises by 50 percent of the 5 units, or by 2.5 units. Hence, the net effect of tax reform on pension saving and via pensions on other saving is −2.5 units (−5 + 2.5), or 2.5 percent of the original level of personal saving. Using a baseline personal saving rate of 6.1 percent of GDP, as shown in the simulations in table 3-5, this suggests that the personal saving rate would decline by about 0.15 percentage point of GDP (6.1 percent × 2.5 percent) owing to consideration of the direct effect on non-401(k) pensions and the induced effect on nonpension saving. This should be compared

58. The results vary across estimation techniques. The estimates reported above may still overstate the impact of pensions on saving because Gale (1995) does not correct for all biases.

Table 3-6. *Effects of Tax Reform on Pension Coverage and Pension-Induced Changes in Total Saving, Exploratory Calculations*[a]

Item	(1)	(2)	(3)	(4)	(5)	(6)	(7)	(8)	(9)	(10)	(11)	(12)
Condition												
Percent of pension saving that is a net addition to saving	20	20	20	20	50	50	50	50	80	80	80	80
Percentage point change in tax on nonpension saving	20	10	20	10	20	10	20	10	20	10	20	10
Percentage point change in coverage rate due to 0.01 change in taxes	0.5	0.5	0.25	0.25	0.5	0.5	0.25	0.25	0.5	0.5	0.25	0.25
Result												
Percentage point change in pension coverage rate	−10	−5	−5	−2.5	−10	−5	−5	−2.5	−10	−5	−5	−2.5
Percent change in total saving due to change in pension	−2	−1	−1	−0.5	−5	−2.5	−2.5	−1.25	−8	−4	−4	−2
Pecentage point change in personal saving rate	−0.12	−0.06	−0.06	−0.03	−0.30	−0.15	−0.15	−0.08	−0.49	−0.24	−0.24	−0.12

Source: Authors' calculations.
a. It is assumed that the initial pension coverage rate is 50 percent and that 50 percent of all saving pre-tax reform occurs through pensions.

with the long-term estimated increases of 0.3 to 0.8 percent of GDP in table 3-5 that ignored pension considerations.

Given the uncertainty about underlying parameter estimates, the range of variation in plausible results is large. For example, table 3-6, column 9, shows that if 80 percent of pension saving is a net addition to saving, if taxes on nonpension saving fall by 20 percentage points, and if pension coverage falls by 1 percent for each 2 percentage point decrease in the tax rate on nonpension saving, the net reduction in pension saving and in pension-induced other saving would be 0.5 percentage point of GDP: that is, of roughly the same magnitude as the estimated increase in saving in the simulation models.

Three conclusions emerge from these calculations. First, the effect on pensions, even adjusting for the induced increase in nonpension saving, could offset much or all of the increase in saving projected by our simulation model. Second, the pension system could shrink significantly under plausible assumptions. Third, fears that tax reform will largely eliminate the pension system cannot be supported using the parameter estimates in the literature.

Removing Withdrawal Restrictions

Current regulations generally prohibit pension beneficiaries from gaining access to funds before particular ages or unless they change jobs. Employees normally may not withdraw funds from defined contribution pension plans unless they change jobs, and sometimes not even then. Rules limiting access to defined benefit assets are even more restrictive. The rationale for all of these restrictions would come into question under a consumption tax, because all of the tax advantages enjoyed by current pensions would be generally available. Though it is possible that regulations limiting access to funds accumulated before the new tax took effect would remain in force, they might well be relaxed or suspended. If so, households may have access to some retirement funds previously closed to them. While most households might leave such funds alone, some might use them to finance current consumption. It is hard to know exactly how much consumption would result, but the increase could be considerable. In 1992 pension reserves totaled $4.5 trillion. Most of these assets were either in DB plans or in group insurance contracts within DC plans, funds that may not be readily available to pension holders even in the absence of withdrawal restrictions. But about $500 billion were in private non-401(k) DC pension funds (excluding funds allocated to group insurance contracts). If these non-401(k) DC assets became accessible without any penalty, and households consumed as little as 4 percent of these assets in the first year after adoption of a consumption tax, the increase in consumption, $20 billion, would be equal to about one-quarter of a percent of GDP, which would cut into any increase in saving created by a consumption tax.

Other Pension Issues

If tax reform reduces pre-tax interest rates, then at the same time that they would lose their tax-preferred status, defined benefit plans would also face a deterioration in their funding status, as liabilities would rise owing to the simple mechanics of discounting. A second issue is the status of nondiscrimination rules under tax reform. Under an income tax, non-discrimination rules attempt in principle to ensure that the benefits of the tax preference for pensions are equitably distributed across workers. Many analysts believe that the rules have the effect of raising saving by encouraging pension contributions among those who would otherwise be least likely to contribute to pensions or any other saving. Under a consumption tax, however, there is no longer any tax preference for pensions, so at least the tax rationale for having nondiscrimination rules would disappear. If the rules were eliminated, this would reduce pension regulation tremendously but also might cause employers to drop pension coverage or reduce pension incentives—such as matching contribu-tions—for certain groups of workers.[59]

Other Issues outside the Model

The impact of tax reform on saving will be influenced by several other factors not discussed above. Some of these factors may boost the positive saving effects of tax reform while others may tend to dampen any increase in saving.

First, because saving is a net concept encompassing the accumulation of both assets and debt, a properly designed consumption tax could encourage saving not only because it reduces the tax on the return to saving but also by not allowing interest on borrowing to be tax deduct-ible. However, if political realities require that the mortgage interest

---

59. See Engen and Gale (1996) for more discussion of pensions and tax reform.

deduction be maintained under a new consumption-type tax, then not only would tax reform not discourage household borrowing, but it also increases the possibilities of tax arbitrage (see note 15).

Second, an important feature of recent tax reform proposals is that they usually involve removing the double taxation imposed by the current corporate income tax. Integration of the individual and corporate tax systems could be achieved under either an income tax or a consumption tax.[60] However, the positive benefits of corporate tax integration under either tax system include removing the double taxation on capital income from the corporate sector and eliminating this tax distortion on the allocation of capital and corporate financing decisions.[61]

Third, tax reform could end the relatively generous tax treatment now accorded to owner-occupied housing relative to other assets. The elimination of this tax distortion could lead to a more efficient allocation of capital yielding positive economic benefits in the long run.[62] However, the relationship between housing values and other financial assets held by households is uncertain. For example, Jonathan Skinner and Hilary Hoynes and Daniel McFadden find little relationship between house values and other financial assets.[63] Eric Engen and William Gale find no offset between house values and 401(k) balances, although they find a significant offset between mortgage debt and 401(k)s.[64]

Fourth, we have not modeled the interaction between inflation and the tax code. Accounting for this would raise effective tax rates in the current system. Moving to a consumption tax resolves issues concerning the tax treatment of the inflationary component of capital income so that the fall in the effective tax rate on capital income would be larger if inflation were accounted for, and the impact on saving may be larger as well.[65]

Fifth, moving to a consumption tax would remove the "lock-in"effect on assets that generate capital gains. This could create a short-term binge of consumption, similar in nature to the impact of removing the early withdrawal restrictions on pensions discussed above. It is estimated that in 1994 households held about $1 trillion in unrealized capital gains in

60. See U.S. Department of the Treasury (1992) for discussion and proposals to integrate the corporate income tax.

61. See chapter 2 by Alan Auerbach in this volume for more discussion of these issues.

62. See chapter 5 by Capozza, Green, and Hendershott in this volume.

63. Skinner (1988); Hoynes and McFadden (1994).

64. Engen and Gale (1995).

65. See Feldstein (1996) for more discussion of this issue.

stocks and mutual funds (outside of retirement accounts).[66] If households consumed as little as 4 percent of these unrealized capital gains in the first year after adoption of a consumption tax, the increase in consumption, $40 billion, would be equal to about one-half of a percent of GDP, which would cut substantially into any increase in saving created by a consumption tax.

Sixth, we have modeled the effects of a consumption tax that is immediate and completely unanticipated. These features influence the magnitude of the "lump-sum" tax levy on existing capital that is an important component of the saving and efficiency effects of tax reform. Allowing for a phased-in or anticipated move to a consumption tax would tend to reduce the impacts on saving. For example, households would have the incentive to spend down a portion of their existing assets in anticipation of moving to a consumption tax, reducing saving and diminishing the efficiency gains from the tax levy on existing capital following tax reform.[67]

Seventh, some economists have suggested that saving decisions are strongly influenced by psychological or behavioral factors not normally included in economic analyses, and doubt that at least some people have the time-consistent preferences assumed in life-cycle models. Recent "behavioral" models of saving have assumed that people have conflicting preferences.[68] One set of preferences is that of a farsighted, patient planner, while the other set of preferences characterizes a myopic, impatient spender. Tax policy that supports one set of preferences over the other can have a large effect on saving. B. Douglas Bernheim explains how public policy could encourage saving by changing the way saving decisions are framed, facilitating simple mental calculations, providing education, and encouraging agents that have a selfish interest in promoting saving by others. He notes, for example, that to the extent that the tax

---

66. In 1994 the household sector held $1.1 trillion in mutual funds and $2.9 trillion in corporate equities. Federal Reserve Board (1995). It is estimated that about 15 percent of mutual fund assets and approximately 7 percent of corporate equities were in self-directed retirement saving accounts—IRAs and Keoghs (see footnote 11). Thus households held about $3.6 trillion in stocks and mutual funds (outside of retirement accounts), of which about one-third, or $1.2 trillion, is estimated to be unrealized capital gains. Kennickell and Wilcox (1992).

67. The possibility that a lump-sum tax levy on existing capital would raise savers' subjective assessment of the probability of another tax levy in the future could reduce the positive impact of tax reform on saving. (See the comment by Robert Hall in chapter 11 in this volume.)

68. See Thaler and Shefrin (1981), Shefrin and Thaler (1988), and Laibson (1995).

system favors the development of institutions to encourage saving (for example, pensions) and to the extent that these institutions affect saving in a positive manner, moving to a consumption tax might have only a small positive impact and possibly a negative impact on saving.[69]

Conclusion

Our formal analysis indicates that, in a closed economy, tax reform could increase household saving by up to 0.8 percent of GDP. If one includes transition relief and an exempt consumption amount, the marginal tax rates necessary to sustain revenues increase and the effects of tax reform on saving fall to 0.3 percent of GDP. Modeling the United States as a small, completely open economy raises the estimated impact to 0.8 percent. Because the United States is neither a closed economy nor a small, completely open economy, the simulations suggest an impact on the saving rate of about 0.5 percentage point of GDP.

Our analysis does not capture all the potential effects of tax reform. In particular, curtailments in the private pension system could offset much of whatever increase in saving occurs generally. A spurt in consumer spending caused by both releasing the withdrawal restrictions on pension accumulations and removing the tax-induced lock-in effect on unrealized capital gains could also reduce the saving impact, at least for a period. Finally, if one considers the possibility that groups will lobby for, and win the continuation of, particular tax advantages, the marginal tax rates necessary to sustain revenue would rise, tax-arbitrage opportunities may open up, and the potential increase in saving could be smaller. Thus, while a carefully designed tax reform may be able to boost the saving rate modestly relative to the decline in recent decades, a poorly designed reform could have a negligible effect on saving.

69. Bernheim (forthcoming).

Table 3A-1. *Interest Rate, Saving, and Household Welfare Effects in Switch from Hybrid Income-Consumption Tax to Consumption Tax, Accounting for Sensitivity to Households' Saving Preferences*[a]

Effects of change in tax	Less prudent households[b]	More prudent households[c]
Pre-tax interest rate (percent)		
Initial	6.6	6.0
Year 2	6.4	5.9
Year 5	6.3	5.8
New steady state	6.0	5.7
Saving rate (percent)		
Initial	5.9	6.8
Year 2	6.9	7.3
Year 5	6.7	7.2
New steady state	6.6	7.1
Asset-income ratio		
Initial	4.12	4.72
Year 2	4.31	4.33
Year 5	4.42	4.49
New steady state	4.60	4.93
Change in utility[d]		
80[e]	0.2	0.1
60[e]	0.3	0.1
40[e]	0.4	0.2
20[e]	0.7	0.4
New steady state	0.6	0.3

Source: Authors' calculations.
a. The simulations assume transition relief, no personal allowances, and a closed economy.
b. Intertemporal elasticity of substitution = 0.5; relative risk aversion coefficient = 2.
c. Intertemporal elasticity of substitution = 0.2; relative risk aversion coefficient = 5.
d. Percent of lifetime income.
e. Age at transition.

Comment by B. Douglas Bernheim

This chapter is concerned with the positive and normative effects of replacing the current hybrid income tax system with a flat consumption tax. The authors reach two central conclusions: first, that this reform would stimulate relatively little new saving, and second, that the resulting impact on welfare, though positive, would be minor. I am sympathetic with the first conclusion (though for somewhat different reasons) but skeptical of the second. Ultimately, I draw rather different lessons for public policy.

Effects of Consumption Taxation on Household Saving

In a recent survey paper, I have provided a detailed review of the existing literature on the *generic* interest elasticity of saving (that is, the responsiveness of saving to changes in the after-tax, risk-compensated rate of return available on all investments).[70] I agree with Engen and Gale that there is no theoretical reason to presuppose that this generic elasticity is substantial, though (unlike the authors) I would not be inclined to single out precautionary saving as the chief candidate for explaining a low elasticity. I also agree that it is difficult to find any reliable evidence that points to a substantial elasticity. However, my interpretation of the literature differs slightly from Eric Engen and William Gale's, in that I am less willing to embrace a simulation model in which the elasticity of saving is small. Owing to the inherent and severe flaws in the empirical methodologies that have been used to measure the interest elasticity of saving (that is, correlations between the after-tax rate of return and either saving or consumption, or estimation of Euler equations), I am inclined to conclude that enormous uncertainty is associated with the best estimate of this parameter.

Even if the generic interest elasticity of saving is small, saving may nevertheless respond strongly to narrowly focused tax incentives, such as those embodied in IRAs and 401(k)s. There are a variety of reasons for this response.[71] Engen and Gale's analysis suggests one reason: that tax-favored retirement accounts segregate interest-sensitive saving (retirement saving) from interest-insensitive saving (precautionary saving). Narrow tax incentives may also influence behavior through more subtle psychological channels. And perhaps most important, narrow tax incentives may shape saving indirectly by fostering the growth and development of pro-saving institutions and activities (for example, the pension system, promotion of long-term investment vehicles, and so on). It is therefore possible that the adoption of a consumption tax could undermine conditions and institutions that promote saving. One of the most thought-provoking sections of this chapter contains a back-of-the-envelope calculation, indicating that the removal of special tax advantages for pensions could have an adverse impact on total saving. If anything, I think that the calculation is conservative and understates the

70. Bernheim (forthcoming).
71. See Bernheim (forthcoming) for an elaboration.

potential adverse impact. According to Engen and Gale, "fears that tax reform will largely eliminate the pension system can not be supported using the parameter estimates in the literature." But these parameter estimates are based on relatively limited historical and cross-state variation in the tax treatment of pensions. There is no precedent in the pertinent data for the complete *elimination* of tax-favored status—to extrapolate consequences based on available estimates therefore requires an enormous leap of faith.

The central lesson that I draw from this discussion is that any estimates of the effect of consumption taxation on saving are subject to enormous uncertainty. There is very little reliable evidence on the generic interest elasticity of saving, and practically nothing is known about the psychological effects of taxation on saving or about the indirect effects of taxation on saving through the evolution of institutions. By focusing on point estimates, Engen and Gale fail to emphasize the substantial risks and unknowns associated with large-scale, fundamental tax reform.

Flat tax consumption proposals might also be expected to alter the rate of national saving because, aside from changing tax bases, they would reduce the progressivity of the tax system. Yet Engen and Gale's simulations indicate that a change in progressivity (accomplished through the introduction of a personal allowance) would have little effect on household saving. I am skeptical of this conclusion, primarily because Engen and Gale's model omits many features that strike me as central to a proper evaluation of progressivity. First, they assume that labor supply is very inelastic. Labor supply elasticities feature prominently in other simulation studies of fundamental tax reform, such as the work of Alan Auerbach and Larry Kotlikoff. One might imagine that an increase in progressivity might flatten the age-earnings profile, thereby increasing saving early in the life-cycle and reducing saving later in the life cycle. Second, Engen and Gale abstract from heterogeneity of saving behavior within generations.

High-income individuals may well have higher interest elasticities of saving because they are less vulnerable to income fluctuations and therefore less motivated by precaution, they spend smaller fractions of their resources on necessities and therefore undertake less "target saving," or they have greater education and financial sophistication and are therefore more inclined to understand and respond to the greater economic rewards associated with compounding at higher after-tax rates of return.

The Effects of Consumption Taxation on Welfare

Engen and Gale's welfare analysis is predicated on simulations of rational, farsighted decisionmakers who form complex, long-term financial plans in an uncertain environment. Since I have criticized the realism of this kind of simulation elsewhere, I will not repeat my concerns here.[72] Even those who are sympathetic to this kind of simulation exercise must recognize that the usefulness of any particular model depends on the nature of the question that one is trying to answer. Models aren't just good or bad. A model may, for example, be reasonably good in reproducing actual levels of consumption, spending, and so on but rather poor at predicting the manner in which these levels would respond to changes in the tax code. More important (in the current context), even if a model accurately predicts levels and derivatives, there is no reason to believe that it provides accurate measures of consumer welfare.

This point requires further clarification. The authors' model reproduces several salient features of the economy (for example, rates of saving and, to the extent one believes any of the estimates, interest elasticities of saving) rather well. It does this by invoking precautionary saving motives for rational, farsighted planners. The authors' simulations imply that, if one accepts this interpretation of the data, then the welfare effects of fundamental tax reform are small. Yet Engen and Gale have provided us with very little reason to believe that this is the correct interpretation of the data for the purposes of making welfare evaluations. If one adopts what is, in my view, more plausible "behavioral" hypotheses about saving behavior, it may still be possible to replicate the same salient features of the economy, but the welfare implications of tax reform may be very different.

To illustrate, imagine that saving is primarily determined by an internal struggle to impose self-control. Considerable evidence exists that individuals discipline their own behavior by imposing simple private rules.[73] A rule might, for example, specify that the individual must save 5 percent of income, regardless of circumstances. Such a rule could obviously explain both the level of saving and the insensitivity of saving to the rate of return. However, it is also consistent with the view that consumption taxation could greatly enhance consumer welfare. This is

72. Bernheim (1994).
73. See Bernheim (forthcoming).

because an increase in the after-tax rate of return leads to greater retirement consumption, even with fixed saving. If retirement consumption is significantly below the optimum to begin with (as one might well expect in a model of self-control), then any increase in this consumption could have a much larger first-order effect than in the Engen-Gale simulations.

Discussion

Ultimately, the authors and I draw different lessons for public policy. My central concern about current consumption tax proposals is that they could undermine institutions (such as the pension system) and activities (such as promotion of long-term saving vehicles) that encourage personal saving. This is not, however, an *inherent* problem with consumption tax proposals. It is certainly possible to retain special provisions that would favor contributions to pension funds or other kinds of savings accounts. For example, if one implemented a consumption tax as a wage tax, one could simply make these contributions deductible while continuing to impose no tax on withdrawals. This would amount to subsidizing certain forms of saving.

Thus the choice between income taxation and consumption taxation is not a choice between a system that permits special saving incentives and one that does not. Rather, it is a choice between a system in which special incentives reflect a departure from a baseline that penalizes saving and a system in which special incentives would reflect a departure from a baseline that is neutral toward saving.

Whenever I think about this choice, I am struck by the arbitrariness of income taxation. Income taxes are, after all, simply indirect taxes on consumption. Given an income tax, it is possible to construct a consumption tax that has the same effect on a household's lifetime budget constraint. Generally, this requires the use of age-specific tax rates (as well as appropriate transfer taxes). To appreciate the peculiarity of income taxation, suppose hypothetically that the United States adopted a broad-base consumption tax, as well as a constitutional amendment banning income taxation. Would current proponents of income taxation advocate the introduction of age-specific tax that imposed the greatest penalties on the consumption of the aged, while heavily favoring consumption among young taxpayers? I suspect that this proposal would be highly unpopular, even among those who currently favor income taxation. Stated in this way, the justification for income taxation is difficult to discern. One might defend consumption tax rates that rise with age on the grounds that those with greater ability to pay tend, on average, to defer consumption to a greater extent than those with less ability to pay. But the extent to which a household defers consumption strikes me as an extraordinarily poor proxy for ability to pay—why not simply apply a progressive tax schedule?

While I therefore tend to favor a properly designed consumption tax over an income tax, this endorsement is heavily qualified. Perhaps most important, I think that economists—including Engen and Gale—have understated the risks and unknowns associated with fundamental tax reform.

References

Aaron, Henry J., Harvey Galper, and Joseph A. Pechman, eds. 1988. *Uneasy Compromise: Problems of a Hybrid Income-Consumption Tax.* Brookings.

Altonji, Joseph G., Fumio Hayashi, and Laurence J. Kotlikoff. 1992. "Is the Extended Family Altruistically Linked? Direct Tests Using Micro Data." *American Economic Review* 82 (December): 1177–98.

Altonji, Joseph, Fumio Hayashi, and Laurence Kotlikoff. 1995. "Parental Altruism and Inter Vivos Transfers: Theory and Evidence." NBER Working Paper 5378 (December).

Auerbach, Alan J., and Laurence J. Kotlikoff. 1983. "National Savings, Economic Welfare, and the Structure of Taxation." In Martin Feldstein, ed., *Behavioral Simulation Methods in Tax Policy Analysis*, 459–98. University of Chicago Press.

———. 1987. *Dynamic Fiscal Policy.* Cambridge University Press.

Auerbach, Alan J., Laurence J. Kotlikoff, and Jonathan Skinner. 1983. "The Efficiency Gains from Dynamic Tax Reform." *International Economic Review* 24 (February): 81–100.

Ballard, Charles L. 1993. "Taxation and Saving." In *Taxation Issues in the 1990s*, edited by John Head. Sydney, Australia: Australian Tax Research Foundation.

Barro, Robert J. 1974. "Are Government Bonds Net Wealth?" *Journal of Political Economy* 82 (November–December): 1095–1117.

Bernheim, B. Douglas. 1987. "Ricardian Equivalence: An Evaluation of Theory and Evidence." *NBER Macro Annual* 2: 263–304

———. 1994. "Comment." *Brookings Papers on Economic Activity* 1: 152–66.

———. Forthcoming. "Rethinking Saving Incentives." In *Fiscal Policy: Lessons from Economic Research,* edited by Alan Auerbach. MIT Press.

Board of Governors of the Federal Reserve System. 1995. *Balance Sheets for the U.S. Economy 1945–1994.* Table B.100: 22–25 (June).

Boskin, Michael J. 1978. "Taxation, Saving, and the Rate of Interest." *Journal of Political Economy* 86 (April): S3–S27.

Boskin, Michael J., and Lawrence J. Lau. 1978. "Taxation and Aggregate Factor Supply: Preliminary Estimates." In *1978 Compendium of Tax Research*, U. S. Department of the Treasury, 3–15. Washington.

Blinder, Alan S. 1975. "Distribution Effects and the Aggregate Consumption Function." *Journal of Political Economy* 83 (June): 447–75.

Bosworth, Barry P. 1984. *Tax Incentives and Economic Growth*. Brookings.

Bradford, David F. 1986. *Untangling the Income Tax*. Harvard University Press.

———. 1996. "Consumption Taxes: Some Fundamental Transition Issues." In *Frontiers of Tax Reform*, edited by Michael Boskin, 123–50. Hoover Institution Press.

Bradford, David F., and the U.S. Treasury Tax Policy Staff. 1984. *Blueprints for Basic Tax Reform*. Arlington, Va.: Tax Analysts.

Browning, Martin, and Annamaria Lusardi. 1995. "Household Saving: Micro Theories and Micro Facts." Mimeo. Dartmouth College (April).

Caballero, Ricardo J. 1991. "Earnings Uncertainty and Aggregate Wealth Accumulation." *American Economic Review* 81 (September): 859–71.

Carlino, Gerald A. 1982 "Interest Rate Effects and Temporary Consumption." *Journal of Monetary Economics* 9 (March): 223–34.

Carroll, Christopher D. 1992. "Buffer Stock Saving and the Permanent Income Hypothesis." Mimeo. Federal Reserve Board.

Carroll, Christopher D., and Andrew A. Samwick. 1995. "The Nature and Magnitude of Precautionary Wealth." Mimeo. Federal Reserve Board.

Congressional Budget Office. 1993. "Assessing the Decline in the National Saving Rate." Washington (April).

Deaton, Angus. 1991. "Saving and Liquidity Constraints." *Econometrica* 59 (September): 1221–48.

Deaton, Angus. 1992. *Understanding Consumption*. Oxford: Oxford University Press.

Elmendorf, Douglas W. 1996. "The Effect of Interest-Rate Changes on Household Saving and Consumption: A Survey." Mimeo. Federal Reserve Board.

Employee Benefits Research Institute. 1995. *EBRI Databook on Employee Benefits*, 3d ed. Washington: EBRI-ERF.

Engen, Eric M. 1994. "Precautionary Saving and the Structure of Taxation." Mimeo. Federal Reserve Board.

Engen, Eric M., and William G. Gale. 1993. "IRAs and Saving in a Stochastic Life-Cycle Model." Mimeo. UCLA.

———. 1995. "Debt, Taxes, and the Effects of 401(k) Plans on Household Wealth Accumulation." Mimeo. Federal Reserve Board and Brookings.

Engen, Eric M., and William G. Gale. 1996. "Comprehensive Tax Reform and the Private Pension System." In Employee Benefits Research Institute, *Com-*

prehensive Tax Reform: Implications for Economic Security and Employee Benefits. Washington (forthcoming).

Engen, Eric M., and Jonathan Gruber. 1996. "Unemployment Insurance and Precautionary Saving," Mimeo. Federal Reserve Board and MIT.

Engen, Eric M., William G. Gale, and John Karl Scholz. 1994. "Do Saving Incentives Work?" *Brookings Papers on Economic Activity* 1: 85–151.

———. 1996. "Effects of Tax-Based Saving Incentives on Saving and Wealth: A Critical Review of the Literature." Mimeo. Federal Reserve Board, Brookings, and University of Wisconsin (May).

Evans, Owen J. 1983. "Tax Policy, the Interest Elasticity of Saving, and Capital Accumulation: Numerical Analysis of Theoretical Models." *American Economic Review* 73 (June): 398–410.

Feldstein, Martin. 1978. "The Welfare Cost of Capital Income Taxation," *Journal of Political Economy* 86 (April): S29–S51.

———. 1996. "The Costs and Benefits of Going from Low Inflation to Price Stability." Working Paper 5469. Cambridge, Mass.: National Bureau of Economic Research (February).

Friend, Irwin, and Joel Hasbrouck. 1983. "Saving and After-Tax Rates of Return." *Review of Economics and Statistics* 65 (November): 537–43.

Fullerton, Don, and Diane Lim Rogers. 1993. *Who Bears the Lifetime Tax Burden?* Brookings.

Juster, F. Thomas, and Paul Wachtel. 1972. "Inflation and the Consumer." *Brookings Papers on Economic Activity* 1: 71–114.

Gale, William G. 1994. "Public Policies and Private Pension Contributions." *Journal of Money, Credit, and Banking* 26 (August, part 2): 710–32.

———. 1995. "The Effects of Pensions on Wealth: A Re-Evaluation of Theory and Evidence." Mimeo (June).

Gale, William G., and John Karl Scholz. 1994. "IRAs and Household Saving." *American Economic Review* 84 (December): 1233–60.

Gentry, William M., and Eric Peress. 1994. "Taxes and Fringe Benefits Offered by Employers." Working Paper 4764. Cambridge, Mass.: National Bureau of Economic Research (June).

Gravelle, Jane G. 1991. "Income, Consumption, and Wage Taxation in a Life-Cycle Model: Separating Efficiency from Redistribution." *American Economic Review* 81 (September): 985–95.

———. 1994. *The Economic Effects of Taxing Capital Income.* MIT Press.

Gylfason, Thorvaldur. 1981. "Interest Rates, Inflation, and the Aggregate Consumption Function." *Review of Economics and Statistics* 63 (May): 233–45.

Hall, Robert E., and Alvin Rabushka. 1995. *The Flat Tax*, 2d ed. Stanford, Calif.: Hoover Institution Press.

Hayashi, Fumio, Joseph Altonji, and Laurence Kotlikoff. 1996. "Risk Sharing between and within Families." *Econometrica* 64 (March): 261–94.

Hay-Huggins Company, Inc. 1990. "Pension Plan Expense Study for the Pension Benefit Guaranty Corporation" (September).

Howrey, E. Philip, and Saul H. Hymans. 1980. "The Measurement and Determination of Loanable-Funds Saving." In *What Should Be Taxed: Income or Expenditure?*, edited by Joseph A. Pechman, 1–48. Brookings.

Hoynes, Hillary Williamson, and Daniel McFadden. 1994. "The Impact of Demographics on Housing and Non-Housing Wealth in the United States." Working Paper 4666. Cambridge, Mass.: National Bureau of Economic Research (March).

Hubbard, R. Glenn, and William M. Gentry. 1996. "Distributional Implications of Introducing a Broad-Based Consumption Tax." Mimeo. Columbia University.

Hubbard, R. Glenn, and Kenneth L. Judd. 1986. "Liquidity Constraints, Fiscal Policy, and Consumption." *Brookings Papers on Economic Activity* 1: 1–50.

Hubbard, R. Glenn, and Jonathan Skinner. 1995. "The Effectiveness of Saving Incentives: A Review of the Evidence." Mimeo. Columbia University and Dartmouth College (June).

Hubbard, R. Glenn, Jonathan Skinner, and Stephen P. Zeldes. 1994. "The Importance of Precautionary Motives in Explaining Individual and Aggregate Saving." *Carnegie-Rochester Conference Series on Public Policy* 40 (June): 59–126.

Hubbard, R. Glenn, Jonathan Skinner, and Stephen P. Zeldes. 1995. "Precautionary Saving and Social Insurance." *Journal of Political Economy* 103 (April): 360–99.

Kennickell, Arthur, and Martha Starr-McCluer. 1994. "Changes in Family Finances from 1989 to 1992: Evidence from the Survey of Consumer Finances." *Federal Reserve Bulletin* (October): 861–82.

Kennickell, Arthur, and David Wilcox. 1992. "The Value and Distribution of Unrealized Capital Gains: Evidence from the 1989 Survey of Consumer Finances." Mimeo. Federal Reserve Board.

Laibson, David. 1995. "Golden Eggs and Hyperbolic Discounting." Mimeo. MIT.

Lucas, Robert E. 1976. "Econometric Policy Evaluation: A Critique." *Carnegie-Rochester Conference Series on Public Policy* 1: 19–46.

Mack, Phillip R. 1993. "Recent Trends in the Mutual Fund Industry." *Federal Reserve Bulletin* 79 (November): 1001–12.

Maki, Dean M. 1995. "Household Debt and the Tax Reform Act of 1986." Mimeo. Federal Reserve Board.

McGee, M. Kevin. 1989. "Alternative Transitions to a Consumption Tax." *National Tax Journal* 42 (June): 155–66.

Poterba, James, Steven Venti, and David Wise. 1996. "Do Retirement Saving Programs Increase Saving? Reconciling the Evidence." Working Paper 5599. Cambridge, Mass.: National Bureau of Economic Research (May).

Randolph, William C., and Diane Lim Rogers. 1995. "The Implications for Tax Policy of Uncertainty about Labor-Supply and Savings Responses." *National Tax Journal* 48 (September): 429–46.

Reagan, Patricia B., and John A. Turner. 1995. "Youth, Taxes and Pension Coverage." Mimeo (January).

Rosen, Harvey S. 1985. "Housing Subsidies: Effects on Housing Decisions, Efficiency, and Equity." In *Handbook of Public Economics*, vol. 1, edited by Alan Auerbach and M. Feldstein, 375–420. New York: North-Holland.

Sabelhaus, John. 1996. "Public Policy and Saving Behavior in the U.S. and Canada." Mimeo. Congressional Budget Office.

Seidman, Laurence S. 1983. "Taxes in a Life-Cycle Growth Model with Bequests and Inheritances." *American Economic Review* 73 (June): 437–41.

———. 1984. "Conversion to a Consumption Tax: The Transition in a Life-Cycle Growth Model." *Journal of Political Economy* 92 (April): 247–67.

Shefrin, Hersh M., and Richard H. Thaler. 1988. "The Behavioral Life-Cycle Hypothesis." *Economic Inquiry* 26 (October): 609–43.

Shoven, John B. 1991. *Return on Investment: Pensions Are How America Saves.* Association of Private Pension and Welfare Plans (September).

Skinner, Jonathan. 1988. "Risky Income, Life-Cycle Consumption, and Precautionary Savings." *Journal of Monetary Economics* 22 (September): 237–55.

———. 1994. "Housing and Saving in the U.S." In *Housing Markets in the United States and Japan*, edited by Yukio Noguchi and James Poterba. University of Chicago Press.

Starrett, David A. 1988. "Effects of Taxes on Saving." In *Uneasy Compromise: Problems of a Hybrid Income-Consumption Tax*, edited by Henry J. Aaron, Harvey Galper, and Joseph A. Pechman, 237–59. Brookings.

Steuerle, C. Eugene. 1985. *Taxes, Loans, and Inflation.* Brookings.

Summers, Lawrence H. 1981. "Capital Taxation and Accumulation in a Life Cycle Growth Model." *American Economic Review* 71(September): 533–44.

Thaler, Richard H., and Hersh M. Shefrin. 1981. "An Economic Theory of Self-Control." *Journal of Political Economy* 89 (April): 392–405.

U.S. Department of the Treasury. 1992. "Integration of the Individual and Corporate Tax Systems."

Wright, Colin. 1967. "Some Evidence on the Interest Elasticity of Consumption." *American Economic Review* 57 (September): 850–54.

———. 1969. "Saving and the Rate of Interest." In *The Taxation of Income from Capital*, edited by Arnold C. Harberger and Martin J. Bailey, 275–95. Brookings.

Zeldes, Stephen P. 1989. "Optimal Consumption with Stochastic Income: Deviations from Certainty Equivalence." *Quarterly Journal of Economics* 104 (May): 275–98.

PART TWO

Behavioral Effects

CHAPTER 4

Fundamental Tax Reform and Employer-Provided Health Insurance

Jonathan Gruber and James Poterba

T HE FEDERAL income tax currently excludes most fringe benefits from taxation. The two most important are employer-financed health insurance and pension plans. Each reduces federal income tax revenues by nearly $60 billion a year. Most current tax reform proposals would end the exclusion of employer-provided health insurance benefits but retain the exemption of employer contributions to pension plans.

Ending the exclusion of employer-provided health insurance could have important effects. Several studies indicate that current tax subsidies to health insurance lead to overinsurance.[1] This overinsurance, in turn, may have contributed to the rise in medical costs that caused the medical sector to consume twice as large a share of gross national product in 1996 as it did twenty-five years earlier. Although the tax system may encourage some households to overinsure, nearly 40 million Americans remain without health insurance. Since several recent studies have suggested that the decision to buy insurance is sensitive to the price of insurance, reducing the tax subsidy to health insurance could increase the ranks of the uninsured.

This chapter examines the effect of fundamental tax reform on the market for employer-provided health insurance.[2] We examine three issues. First, how would tax reform affect the demand for employer-

We are grateful to Sue Dynarski, Sam Liu, and Todd Sinai for excellent research assistance, to Len Burman, Peter Diamond, Victor Fuchs, and Mark Pauly for helpful discussions, and to the National Science Foundation and the National Institute of Aging for research support. The views expressed here are the authors' and do not necessarily reflect those of the agencies noted.
    1. See, for example, Feldstein (1973), Feldstein and Friedman (1977), and Pauly (1986).
    2. Much of our analysis can be applied to other employer-provided benefits, such as group life insurance or disability insurance.

sponsored insurance and employer-financed insurance coverage? We use a simulation model that combines information on insurance status from the 1987 National Medical Expenditure Survey with marginal tax rate information from the TAXSIM program of the National Bureau of Economic Research (NBER). We modify the TAXSIM program to estimate household tax rates under several tax reform proposals. We then compare the after-tax price of employer-provided health insurance under the current tax code with those under several reform proposals. We combine these estimates of the after-tax price of health insurance under various tax proposals with demand elasticities to estimate how these tax reforms might affect health insurance coverage and spending.

We recognize that changes in the tax subsidy to employer-provided insurance could affect decisions at several different margins of insurance demand. Some workers might drop coverage. Others might opt for "less insurance" by selecting higher copayment rates or deductibles. Others might choose different health care provider arrangements, such as managed care, rather than fee-for-service provision. Unfortunately, the empirical basis for allocating any changes in insurance spending across these various margins is weak. We describe the available evidence and present some illustrative calculations.

Second, we speculate on how the private health insurance market might respond to a reduction in the tax subsidy to employer-provided insurance. The most important issue is whether tax reform would reduce workplace pooling in insurance purchases. Again, little empirical evidence bears on this question. Two considerations suggest that income tax changes are not likely to change the current reliance on workplace groups in purchasing health insurance: workplaces enjoy inherent advantages as a site for pooling, and most reform proposals would leave the substantial payroll tax subsidy to employer-provided insurance intact. Raising the after-tax cost of employer-provided health insurance could, however, induce changes in the structure of this insurance. For example, it might accelerate the current trend away from expensive fee-for-service insurance and toward coverage by health maintenance organizations (HMOs).

Finally, we consider how increases in the after-tax price of employer-provided health insurance might affect the health care sector and the labor market. We show how changes in insurance demand might affect health care costs and conclude that limiting the insurance subsidy will not significantly slow the growth of health care costs. With respect to the labor market, we consider how wages would respond to changes in the

Table 4-1. *Composition of Employee Compensation, 1960, 1980, 1993*

Billions of current dollars

Category	1960	1980	1993
Employer payments			
Wages and salaries	272.8	1,376.6	3,100.8
All benefits	23.7	265.8	673.6
Group health insurance	3.4	61.0	235.6
OASDHI and UI[a]	8.6	83.6	222.9
Pensions	8.6	96.0	154.8
Other	3.1	25.2	60.3
Total compensation	296.7	1,644.4	3,774.4
Employee payments for group health insurance	1.8	12.8	46.2

Source: National income and product accounts and authors' calculations.
a. Old age, survivors', disability, and health insurance and unemployment insurance.

level of employer-provided insurance and also examine how tax-induced changes in insurance demand might affect labor market mobility. Our analysis of both the health care market and the labor market effects of tax reform is necessarily more tentative than our examination of demand effects, because many of the key influences have not been studied much.

Employer-Provided Health Insurance: The Current Situation

Employer-provided benefits are a substantial and rising share of employee compensation in the United States. The share of benefits in total compensation has increased two and one half times, and the share of health care benefits has increased fivefold since 1960 (table 4-1). A. Foster Higgins's recent survey of large employers reports that the average medical plan cost per employee in 1993 was $3,781.[3] Employees contribute substantially to the cost of employer-provided health insurance (table 4-1, line 6). Monthly contributions of employees at large companies averaged $31.55 for individual health insurance coverage and $107.42 for family coverage in 1993.[4] In 1992, when small businesses were surveyed, the analogous employee costs were $36.51 for individual coverage and $150.54 for family coverage. The higher premium at small companies may reflect lower employer contributions at these firms as well as higher insurance costs, because insurers demand higher premiums to cover smaller, generally less diversified, groups. In 1980, 74 percent of

3. A. Foster Higgins (1994).
4. EBRI (1995, p. 307).

full-time employees with employer-provided individual health insurance had coverage that was fully paid by the employer; the comparable fraction in 1993 was only 37 percent. For family coverage, 54 percent of employers paid the full cost in 1980, compared with 21 percent in 1993.[5]

In 1993, 69.7 percent of the population under the age of 65 had private health insurance coverage, with 60.8 percent covered through an employer-provided health insurance plan.[6] Another 16.1 percent had public health insurance, while 18.1 percent reported no health insurance.[7] Medicare was the primary insurance coverage for 95.5 percent of people over age 65, but 32.3 percent of this group also had employer-provided health insurance.[8]

Large companies are more likely than small companies to provide health insurance. In 1993, 75 percent of full-time employees at companies with more than 100 employees, and 44 percent of workers at companies with fewer than 100 workers, were covered by group health insurance plans at their jobs.[9]

Employer insurance contributions by private business, the federal government, and state and local governments account for $192.2 billion, or 26.4 percent of total health care spending in 1991 (table 4-2). Adding individual contributions raises the total employer-provided health insurance share to 33.5 percent of the health care marketplace. Out-of-pocket spending by households is roughly equal to the value of employer contributions to group health insurance. Changes in the tax treatment of employer-provided health insurance could substantially affect total health care spending. Absent spillover effects on the spending of individuals with other health care financing arrangements, however, there is an upper bound on the effect of such tax changes.

Insurance coverage varies widely for different procedures (table 4-3). Virtually all employer-provided health insurance covers hospitalization and related medical procedures. Coverage for dental or vision care is much less common. Accordingly, changes in the after-tax cost of health insurance would affect insured procedures quite differently.

5. EBRI (1995, p. 306).

6. Tabulations for 1993 from the March 1994 Current Population Survey (CPS), reported in EBRI (1995, p. 239).

7. These population shares can add to more than 100 percent, because some people have multiple forms of insurance coverage.

8. EBRI (1995, p. 390).

9. Data from the CPS Employee Benefit Survey (EBS), reported in EBRI (1995, p. 43). The levels of coverage appear to differ between the EBS and the CPS.

Table 4-2. *Expenditures for Health Services and Supplies,*
by Type of Payer, 1991

Type of payer	Amount (billions of 1991 dollars)	Percent of total
Private business		
Employer insurance contributions	152.7	21.0
Employer HI contributions	32.8	4.5
Workers' comepnsation and DI	17.5	2.4
In-plant health services	2.4	0.3
Households		
Contributions to employer-provided health insurance	52.2	7.2
HI contributions	39.9	5.5
Medicare supplementary medical insurance	10.7	1.4
Out-of-pocket spending	144.3	19.8
Nonpatient revenue	21.7	2.9
Federal government		
Employer contributions to private health insurance	9.8	1.3
Net medicare	34.8	4.8
Medicaid	55.9	7.7
Other programs	33.3	4.6
State and local government		
Employer contributions to private health insurance	29.7	4.1
Medicaid	44.6	6.1
Other	46.4	6.4
Total	728.6	100.0

Source: Cowan and McDonnell (1993, p. 228).

Insurance payment arrangements differ widely among employers and have been changing fast. Traditional fee-for-service care with corresponding insurance reimbursement was available to only half the workers at large or medium-size establishments in 1993, down from 74 percent in 1988.[10] The sharp decline in fee-for-service coverage during only a five-year period reflects the growth of cost containment in group health insurance coverage. Conditional on offering insurance, small companies are more likely than large companies to provide fee-for-service coverage, because small companies have a harder time striking attractive bargains with health care providers through preferred provider organizations.[11]

10. For 1988, CPS (1993).
11. EBRI (1995, p. 294).

Table 4-3. *Covered Benefits in Group Health Plans, 1992–93*

Percent

| | Private firms | | State and local |
Benefit type	Medium and large	Small	government
Hospital room and board	100	100	100
Inpatient surgery	100	100	100
X-rays and laboratory	100	100	100
Outpatient mental health	97	95	93
Prescription drugs	98	95	88
Extended care facility	82	84	84
Hospice	65	57	54
Dental	62	33	65
Vision	26	10	. . .

Source: EBRI (1995, pp. 323–24).

Modeling the Effect of Tax Rules on Health Insurance Demand

Employer contributions for health insurance have always been excluded from individual taxable income, first by administrative practice and, after 1943, by court ruling.[12] Employer payments for health insurance are also excluded from payroll and from state income tax as well.

The Tax Subsidy to Employer-Provided Insurance

We measure the after-tax price of employer provided health insurance relative to the after-tax cost of out-of-pocket medical spending.[13] The tax subsidy to employer-provided health insurance equals the difference between its price in terms of other consumption goods under current tax rules and the analogous relative price in a no-tax world, assuming coverage of the same people and the same price of medical services. We perform similar calculations for the reform proposals. Appendix A explains the specific formulas for the tax subsidy to employer-provided insurance. Three tax variables affect the tax subsidy: the marginal individual federal income tax rate, the marginal state income tax rate net of

12. U.S. Congressional Budget Office (1994). Hereafter CBO.

13. Even without taxes, these two methods of purchasing medical care would not have the same cost. Insurance companies typically charge a load on their policies, so the cost of the insurance policy exceeds the expected medical care payments of the insured. The expected *utility* of buying insurance may be much greater than the expected utility of paying for health care out-of-pocket, even though the expected payouts are smaller under the insurance policy.

federal deductibility, and the marginal payroll tax rate. Each tax is levied on wage income but not on the value of employer-provided health insurance. One complication that arises in measuring the payroll tax rate concerns the degree to which changes in employer-provided health insurance benefits affect not just current payroll tax payments but also future social security benefits. If reductions in employer-provided benefits translated into higher wages, these wages would in turn lead to higher lifetime earnings and potentially higher social security benefits. This "tax-benefit linkage" reduces the effective marginal payroll tax rate to less than its statutory rate. It also implies that the present discounted value of revenues raised by including health insurance in the payroll tax base is lower than the statutory tax rates would imply, since current tax collections imply future payment obligations.[14]

In measuring the after-tax cost of employer-provided health insurance, we recognize that not all employer-sponsored insurance is paid for with pre-tax dollars. Employees currently pay about one-quarter of the cost of employer-sponsored insurance, and roughly three-quarters of workers make these contributions from post-tax dollars. This reduces the average tax subsidy to employer-provided insurance.

We also recognize that the current tax system permits people to deduct spending on medical care and health insurance in excess of 7.5 percent of adjusted gross income. Such outlays also receive a tax subsidy. This tax provision partly offsets the current tax subsidy to employer-provided health insurance by subsidizing self-insurance. An uninsured taxpayer is more likely to incur large health care bills than is a similar person with employer-provided, or self-purchased, health insurance.

Calibration and Measurement of Tax Subsidies

To evaluate the after-tax price of health insurance, we develop a database with information on marginal tax rates and the probability that medical expenditures are deductible from income taxes. We use the U.S. Treasury Individual Tax Model and the NBER TAXSIM program to impute tax rates to family units in the 1987 National Medical Expendi-

14. We account for tax-benefit linkage using Feldstein and Samwick's (1992) estimates of the net effective marginal OASI tax rates for different types of individuals. These authors present net tax rates by type of family, income class, and age; we use these characteristics to impute these tax rates to our NMES sample. We also assume that their calculations, which apply only to old age and survivors' insurance, can be applied to disability insurance as well.

ture Survey (NMES). We then use these data on health insurance and health care spending to estimate the tax subsidy to employer-provided health insurance under the current tax code and various alternative proposals.

The NMES is a nationally representative household survey of about 20,000 families that gathered information about demographic and economic characteristics, insurance coverage, and medical spending for 1987. We aggregate individual NMES respondents into "health insurance units": the family head, his or her spouse, any children under age 19, and full-time students until they reach age 23. We limit our sample to employed individuals in households with no member over the age of 65. We also exclude families in which anyone is covered by medicaid, and families with missing information on insurance status. Since family heads and spouses are the only relevant decisionmakers for insurance purchases, we use only their sample weights in making our calculations.[15]

Our final sample has 5,961 health insurance units (HIUs), representing a total of 71.1 million household heads and spouses. Of this sample, 1,936 HIUs (representing 24.8 million households) report only employer-paid health insurance, 228 (3.0 million households) report only individual premium payments for health insurance, and 2,360 (30.6 million households) report both employer and individual premiums. In our sample, 1,437 HIUs, corresponding to 12.7 million households, reported that they were uninsured.[16]

Employer and total spending per household differs widely (table 4-4). While the NMES figures are measured in 1987 dollars, all results in this paper have been inflated to 1994 dollars by using the growth in personal health spending over the 1987–94 period.[17] Mean employer spending is

15. One difficulty with the NMES database is its age. During the nine years since the NMES data were collected, the incidence of employer-provided health insurance has fallen, and the share of the cost of such insurance paid by employers has decreased. Though dated, the NMES remains the best, and most recent, data base for analyzing employer-provided health insurance in the population at large.

16. This is a relatively high uninsurance rate for employed individuals. We have disproportionately few insured households, because we required information on the structure of the family's insurance plan for them to be in our insured sample, and this information is collected only for a subset of NMES households.

17. CBO (1993) presents data on private health insurance expenditures in 1987 ($155 billion), along with forecasts for 1993 ($289 billion) and 1995 ($343 billion). We estimate 1994 expenditures by interpolating between the 1993 and 1995 forecasts; this yields $316 billion. We then use the ratio of 1994 to 1987 spending, $316/$155, or 2.039, to impute the distribution of 1987 spending to 1994. Because the number of individuals with

Table 4-4. *Distribution of Estimated Expenditures on Employer-Provided Health Insurance for Sample Households, 1994*

Percentile	Employer spending	Employer plus pre-tax employee spending
5	0	602
10	1,020	1,250
25	1,877	2,044
50	3,816	4,130
75	5,872	6,021
90	7,950	8,130
95	9,920	10,159
Mean	4,249	4,483

Source: Authors' tabulations using 1987 National Medical Expenditure Survey data. Estimates for 1994 are based on the ratio of total private health insurance spending in 1994 to 1987, as projected in U.S. Congressional Budget Office (1993a).

$4,249, and mean employer and pre-tax employee spending is $4,483. The distribution of this tax-subsidized spending is somewhat skewed, as is revealed by the lower median value. Nearly 10 percent of the sample reports employer contributions worth more than $8,000 a year, and more than 25 percent report values of less than $2,000.

We impute tax rates to HIUs using the NBER TAXSIM model. We apply the federal income tax code to the income data in the NMES and use self-reported itemization status to determine taxpayer eligibility for various deductions. To apply 1994 tax law to these 1987 data, we "age" each family's adjusted gross income by assuming that it grows in proportion to aggregate AGI. The NMES reports in which census region, but not in which state, each respondent lived. We impute state tax rates by using a population-weighted average of state tax rates for families of different income levels and family structures within each census region.

The exclusion of employer-provided health insurance from the payroll tax base is an important source of current subsidy to this insurance. The exclusion from the OASDI (old age, survivors', and disability insurance) payroll tax provides a subsidy only to those with earnings below the OASDI taxable maximum of $60,600, while the exclusion from the HI (health insurance) payroll tax subsidizes all wage earners.

---

employer-provided insurance changed little between 1987 and 1994, an imputation based on per capita spending for those with such insurance in 1987 and 1994 would yield very similar results.

Sample Limitations

Our analysis is limited to employed individuals and does not consider two additional groups whose insurance coverage may be affected by tax incentives: the self-employed and retirees who receive retiree health insurance from their previous employers. For the self-employed, the current income tax system offers a deduction for 25 percent of health outlays.[18] We do not model the response of self-employed workers to tax reform, because the NMES database contains relatively few self-employed people with insurance information.

Many retirees have employer-provided health insurance coverage. Of 30.7 million Americans over the age of 65 in 1993, 9.9 million reported some employer-provided coverage.[19] Health insurance plans for 41.4 percent of the 23.7 million employed workers over age 45 promised retiree health insurance.[20] It is not clear how the cost of employer-provided insurance should be modeled for the retiree population. Many employers have committed to a stream of benefits for their current workers, and it may be difficult to abrogate these commitments in the near term.

The Tax Subsidy to Employer-Provided Insurance: 1994 Tax Law

Table 4-5 summarizes our analysis of the tax subsidy to employer-provided health insurance. The first four rows show our estimates of the various marginal tax rates that enter the calculation of the after-tax price of health insurance.[21] For the employed insured, shown in the first column, the weighted average marginal federal income tax rate in 1994 was

18. The tax subsidy may actually be somewhat higher, since a self-employed person who buys very expensive insurance can deduct the excess of the cost of the insurance above the income floor from her taxes. If this exceeds 25 percent of the cost of the insurance, then the numerator of the tax price expression will be even lower.

19. EBRI (1995, p. 387).

20. EBRI (1995, p. 392). For 1.4 million (6 percent of the employed total), the employer paid all of the post-retirement premiums; for another 4.1 million (17.3 percent), the employer paid part of the premiums. Thus for more than half of those who were eligible for retiree health insurance, the employer pays at least part of the cost.

21. We weight marginal tax rates and after-tax prices for the insured by total insurance spending per HIU, to reflect the dollar-weighted incentives under the tax code. For the uninsured, who have no insurance spending, we use population weights.

Table 4-5. *Tax Subsidies to Employer-Provided Health Insurance*

Item	Calculations assuming payroll tax–benefit linkage		Calculations without payroll tax–benefit linkage	
	Employed, insured (1)	Employed, uninsured (2)	Employed, insured (3)	Employed, uninsured (4)
Average marginal tax rate				
(1) Federal income	0.219	0.117	0.219	0.117
(2) State income	0.035	0.017	0.035	0.017
(3) Payroll (employee and employer shares)	0.148	0.152	0.148	0.152
(4) Payroll tax–benefit offset	−0.064	−0.101	0.000	0.000
(5) Average after-tax wage cost of employer-provided health insurance (1994 law)	0.684	0.829	0.624	0.734
(6) Average after-tax price of employer-provided health insurance (1994 law)	0.839	0.946	0.780	0.859
Average marginal after-tax price of employer-provided health insurance				
(7) No-tax world	1.101	1.101	1.101	1.101
(8) 1994 law	0.806	0.941	0.750	0.854
(9) Armey-Shelby, Gephardt, and retail sales tax plans	0.972	1.031	0.916	0.929
(10) USA tax plan	1.111	1.188	1.053	1.081

Source: Authors' calculations. Prices are weighted by total insurance spending for the insured, and by population weights for the uninsured. Employed insured (uninsured) account for 82.1 (17.9) percent of the sample, corresponding to 58.4 (12.7) million people.

21.9 percent; state taxes contributed an additional 3.5 percent. The statutory combined payroll tax rate on both employers and employees totaled 14.8 percent, slightly less than the statutory rate of 15.3 percent because some people earn more than the taxable earnings maximum for OASDI. Combining the employer and employee shares, the payroll tax is roughly two-thirds as important as the income tax in contributing to the tax subsidy to employer-provided health insurance. The tax-benefit offset implied by Martin Feldstein and Andrew Samwick's calculations, however, averages 43 percent of the combined employer and employee payroll tax,[22] so allowing for such linkage substantially reduces the insurance subsidy due to the payroll tax.

The after-tax wage cost of employer-provided health insurance is 0.684, meaning that an employee would have to forgo 68.4 cents of post-

22. Feldstein and Samwick (1992).

tax wage income, after federal and state income taxes and payroll taxes, if an employer increased health insurance spending by one dollar and held total compensation costs unchanged (table 4-5, row 5, col. 1). The true after-tax price of health insurance also includes the load factor of about 10 percent, employee premium-sharing, and the availability of the self-insurance option. These factors are included in the next row, and we find that the after-tax marginal price of employer-provided health insurance (0.839) is roughly 23 percent higher than would be implied by the change in wages alone. In a no-tax world, the relative price of employer-provided health insurance and self-insurance would be 1.101, because of the load factor. Thus the current system of income and payroll taxes reduces the marginal after-tax price of employer-provided health insurance, relative to self-insurance, approximately 27 percent (1 − 0.806/1.101 = 0.268). The average after-tax price is somewhat higher than the marginal price, because self-insurance is much less important on the margin than on average.

For the uninsured employed tax distortions are smaller than those for employed insured workers, largely because the marginal federal income tax of the employed insured group is lower than that of the insured employed (table 4-5, col. 2). Tax provisions reduce the marginal price of employer-provided health insurance for this group by 14 percent (1 − 0.941/1.101 = 0.145).

The linkage between payroll taxes and social security benefits is an important determinant of these after-tax prices. Feldstein and Samwick examined this linkage, and their work is the most comprehensive available study.[23] But their results are sensitive to assumptions about discount rates, life expectancies, and individual understanding and expectations of future benefit calculations. Calculations that ignore the tax-benefit linkage yield significantly higher estimates of the tax distortion (table 4-5, cols. 3 and 4). Under these assumptions, taxes lower the marginal price of insurance by nearly 32 percent for the employed insured.

Tax Incentives and Insurance Demand

Major tax reform proposals would dramatically change the tax treatment of employer-sponsored and -financed health insurance (table 4-5, rows 9 and 10). The value-added tax (VAT), the Armey-Shelby flat tax, Senator

23. Feldstein and Samwick (1992).

Richard Lugar's national retail sales tax, and Representative Richard Gephardt's modified income tax all would eliminate the income tax wedge between employer-provided health insurance and wage income, but not the payroll tax advantage.[24] These three plans therefore have similar effects on the after-tax price of employer-provided health insurance. The Gephardt plan would be substantially more complex to administer than either the Armey-Shelby flat tax or the national retail sales tax, because it preserves individual filing and would require an imputation for the value of employer-provided health insurance benefits to each worker.[25]

The USA tax, advanced by Senators Sam Nunn and Pete Domenici, differs from the other proposals because it not only eliminates the income tax subsidy but also curbs the payroll tax subsidy by allowing a refundable credit for the HI tax and for the OASDI tax, up to the wage limit on the OASDI payroll tax. The USA tax, like the Gephardt proposal, would require imputations to individual taxpayers for the value of employer-provided insurance.

Imputation raises difficult problems. If the same share of the cost of all employer-provided insurance is imputed to workers, then employees with identical insurance policies who work at different companies that pay different amounts for their group policies would have different imputations for the same insurance coverage.[26] In addition, the fact that actuarially fair prices of health insurance coverage vary widely for workers of different ages might also be omitted from the imputation. Under the current tax rules employers and employees never explicitly confront the subsidies that result from community rating within firms. If imputations were precise, these cross-subsidies would become obvious and, in all likelihood, controversial.

The Armey-Shelby flat tax sidesteps the problems of imputation by denying employers a deduction for health insurance. By raising the net cost of insurance to employers, this change would increase incentives for

---

24. The Armey-Shelby flat-tax proposal and the national retail sales tax are more likely than either the USA tax or the Gephardt plan to lead to substantial changes in state tax rules, because the former plan would radically alter or eliminate the current federal income tax framework on which many state income taxes are based.

25. If a national retail sales tax requires employers to pay tax on their purchases of health insurance, it would not be necessary to impute outlays to individuals.

26. The per-employee share of the cost of identical insurance plans could differ, for example, based on the underlying health of an employee's coworkers, given that the cost of insurance is experience rated at most companies.

employers to discriminate in hiring against workers expected to generate above-average medical costs unless such costs are shifted on a worker-by-worker basis. In fact, the Armey-Shelby plan discourages companies from financing insurance to the extent that they employ workers who earn less than the rather generous exempt earnings levels. Low-wage workers would pay no tax on their wage income, since the Armey-Shelby plan incorporates high individual exemptions. Yet health insurance costs would be fully taxed at the business level. Businesses could cut taxes by canceling insurance and raising wages by the amount saved on premiums.

The Health Insurance Market after Fundamental Tax Reform

Eliminating the income tax deductibility of both employer spending and out-of-pocket spending, but not the payroll tax exclusion, as under the Armey-Shelby, Gephardt, and Lugar tax reform proposals, puts the marginal after-tax cost of insurance at an average of 0.972 for currently employed insured workers, a 12 percent subsidy relative to the no-tax cost of 1.101 (table 4-5, lines 7 and 9). For employed uninsured workers, the after-tax price of employer-provided health insurance rises to 1.031, a net tax subsidy of 6.2 percent.

The continued exclusion of employer-provided health insurance from the payroll tax and from state income taxes preserves a substantial tax subsidy to employer-provided health insurance under each of the tax reform proposals.[27] The current average of state marginal income tax rates is 3.5 percent, net of federal tax deductions for itemizers. Eliminating this tax subsidy would raise the after-tax price of employer-provided health insurance by approximately 3 percent.[28]

The foregoing calculations do *not* apply to the USA tax, which also reduces the effective payroll tax rate through a credit system. The payroll tax credit raises the after-tax price of employer-provided health insurance to 1.111 for employees (table 4-5, row 10). That is, the USA tax would replace the current tax subsidy with a tax penalty on employer-provided

27. It is possible that federal income tax reform might trigger changes in the definition of the payroll tax base, leading ultimately to the reduction or elimination of the payroll tax subsidy to health insurance as well. Since there are no currently active proposals for such changes, however, we consider the maintenance of the current payroll tax structure the most likely scenario.

28. Because the various reform proposals would eliminate the federal income tax deduction for state and local income taxes, however, the effective rate of these income taxes rises by the amount of the current federal marginal tax rate.

health insurance relative to self-insurance, because the provision of health insurance saves no current taxes but reduces subsequent social security benefits. For the employed uninsured, this net tax is even more sizable.

If people disregard the effects of employer-financed health insurance on future social security benefits, the implicit subsidy to health insurance under current law is increased, but the relative effect of removing the income tax subsidy of insurance changes little (table 4-5, cols. 3 and 4, lines 7 to 10). For the Armey-Shelby, Gephardt, and Lugar cases, even after reform there remains a 17 percent subsidy $(1 - 0.916/1.101 = 0.083)$ to insurance purchase. Under the USA tax, the remaining tax wedge from state income taxation produces a small net subsidy to insurance purchase.

Tax Reform and the Demand for Employer-Provided Health Insurance

The calculations reported in table 4-5 suggest that any of the current tax reform proposals we consider will substantially reduce the tax subsidy to employer-provided health insurance. While price effects are of interest, the more important question concerns how these changes in tax subsidies would affect the demand for employer-provided health insurance.

To answer this question, we must make some assumptions about how health insurance spending responds to changes in the price of insurance. Either insurance spending per insured person or the number of people with employer-provided insurance can change. The current tax subsidy affects both quantities.

These two adjustments should be distinguished for several reasons. First, a reduction in the number of insured people may affect other participants in the medical marketplace; for example, if uninsured individuals rely on uncompensated care. Second, the welfare effects of changes in per-employee insurance spending, through narrowed provider coverage or higher deductibles, may differ from the effects of a decline in the number of people with insurance coverage.[29] A final reason is political. Apparent public concern with the large and rising number of

---

29. For example, while the RAND Health Insurance Experiment found that changes in the cost-sharing structure of insurance had little effect on health status (Manning and others, 1987), there is evidence that losing insurance altogether may have important health implications (Lurie, 1984; Currie and Gruber, 1994, 1996).

uninsured people sparked the recent debate on national health insurance. Some people might view an induced increase in the number of uninsured as a disadvantage of fundamental tax reform.

Unfortunately, little empirical evidence is available to help one distinguish coverage effects from spending-given-coverage effects. Many studies have estimated the elasticity of demand for total insurance spending, and for insurance coverage, but we are not aware of any study that has considered both effects simultaneously. Moreover, the existing estimates from previous studies vary widely and do not provide much guidance in finding a "consensus" figure to use for our computations. Appendix B reviews these studies.

Previous studies on total insurance demand and on the demand for insurance coverage yield a broad range of estimates for our key parameter. None of these studies yields any guidance about how the quantity and coverage margins should be combined to yield an overall elasticity estimate. Moreover, previous work has not considered the possibility that the margin of adjustment differs at different points in the income distribution.[30] In particular, it is possible that for low-income persons with less generous insurance plans, the critical choice is whether to be insured or not, whereas for high-income persons the operative margin is the amount of insurance conditional on being insured. Explicit public insurance (medicaid) and implicit public insurance (care at public hospitals) may be more relevant alternatives for low-income persons than for those in higher-income brackets.

We present estimates of the effects on demand for health insurance based on four sets of elasticity parameters selected to span the range of empirical estimates (table 4-6). For two cases, we assume that family income does not affect demand elasticity. We consider one case with an overall elasticity of demand of -0.5 and an associated coverage elasticity of -0.3 (col. 1), and a second case with an overall elasticity of -1.0 and an associated coverage elasticity of -0.5 (col. 3). We also consider two cases in which the coverage elasticity, but not the overall expenditure elasticity, varies over the income distribution. One case allows for an overall expenditure elasticity of -0.5, with an elasticity of coverage of -0.5 below the median income level and -0.1 above the median income level (col. 2). Another allows for an overall elasticity of demand of -1.0, with an elasticity of coverage of -0.9 below the median income level and -0.1 above.

---

30. We are grateful to David Cutler for suggesting this issue.

On average, the elasticities underlying results shown in columns 1 and 2 are the same, as are the elasticities underlying the results shown in columns 3 and 4, but within each pair the latter results differ above and below median income. The assumptions in columns 2 and 4 implicitly allow the elasticity of demand for insurance, conditional on coverage, to rise with income. We should emphasize that there is no empirical evidence that directly bears on the pattern of elasticities at different income levels.

If the price elasticity of insurance demand is -0.5, the three tax reform proposals that eliminate only the federal income tax component of the tax subsidy to employer-provided insurance reduce insurance demand by $614 per insured employee, or 11.7 percent. The USA tax would lower insurance demand by 19.1 percent, since it raises the after-tax price of such insurance by more than the other proposals. These effects double if the elasticity of demand is -1.0.

The estimates also show that fundamental tax reform could reduce the insured population substantially.[31] For the Armey-Shelby, Gephardt, or retail sales tax proposals, the estimated decline in insurance coverage ranges from 5.7 million to 14.7 million people, 4.1 percent to 10.7 percent of the currently insured population. These changes may be compared to the uninsured population of 40.9 million in 1993. Under the USA tax, the estimated reduction in the privately insured population ranges from 10.3 million to 24.8 million people, or 8 to 18 percent of the currently insured population. In all the cases, the response is larger if the coverage elasticity is assumed constant over the income distribution than if the elasticity is assumed to fall with income. This difference arises because tax reform affects the after-tax price of insurance more for high- than for low-income households.

The relative effects of tax reform on health insurance coverage and spending is acutely sensitive to the elasticity of demand and to whether it varies with income (table 4-7). We consider five income groups, and for each group we show the percent change in the marginal price, in total insurance demand, and in coverage, for cases shown in columns 1 and 4 of table 4-6. As we noted, changes in price and demand for insurance are much larger for high- than for low-income households. Whether these

---

31. We calculate the change in the number of insured individuals by first computing the percent change in insurance coverage in our NMES sample, given our estimate of the price elasticity of demand for insurance coverage, and then applying this percent change to the aggregate total of 137.4 million individuals with employer-based insurance coverage in 1993 (EBRI, 1995, p. 249).

Table 4-6. *Effect of Fundamental Tax Reform on Demand for Employer-Provided Health Insurance*

	Overall price elasticity			
	-0.5		-1.0	
	Coverage price elasticity			
Item	-0.3 (1)	-0.5 (low Y) -0.1 (high Y) (2)	-0.5 (3)	-0.9 (low Y) -0.1 (high Y) (4)
Armey, Gephardt, retail sales tax plans				
Change in insurance spending (dollars)	-614	-614	-1,227	-1,227
Percent change	-11.7	-11.7	-23.4	-23.4
Change in insurance coverage (millions of people)	-8.6	-5.5	-14.3	-9.5
Percent change	-6.4	-4.1	-10.7	-7.1
USA tax plan				
Change in insurance spending (dollars)	-1,003	-1,003	-2,006	-2,006
Percent change	-19.1	-19.1	-38.3	-38.3
Change in insurance coverage (millions of dollars)	-14.4	-10.0	-24.1	-15.2
Percent change	-10.8	-7.5	-18.0	-11.4

Source: Authors' calculations. Tabulations weighted by NMES population weights.

effects translate to larger changes in insurance coverage as well depends on the level of the total elasticity and whether the elasticity of coverage with respect to price is lower for higher-income groups. If this elasticity falls with income, coverage of the wealthy is not much affected. In any case, for those with incomes above $100,000, the decline in insurance demand ranges from 18.3 percent under the various flat-tax plans and the low-elasticity values, to 22.6 percent under the USA tax with these elasticities. With the higher-elasticity assumption, the percent decline in insurance spending by the top income group ranges from 37 to 45 percent under the flat tax and USA tax.

Tax Reform and Public Spending

We have shown that tax reform could reduce private insurance demand, but it could also *raise* the demand for government-provided insurance. Some people who now have employer-provided health insurance are eligible for free public insurance coverage under the medicaid program. Congress dramatically expanded medicaid eligibility for children and pregnant women over the mid-1980s to early 1990s. Approximately

Table 4-7. *Distributional Analysis of Fundamental Tax Reform and the Demand for Employer-Provided Health Insurance*
Percent change; income in dollars

Item	Armey, Gephardt, retail sales tax		USA tax	
	Overall price elasticity			
	−0.5	−1	−0.5	−1
	Coverage elasticity			
	−0.3	−0.9 (low Y) −0.1 (high Y)	−0.3	−0.9 (low Y) −0.1 high Y)
Income <20,000				
After-tax price	13.5	13.5	31.3	31.3
Insurance spending	−5.6	−11.2	−12.9	−25.9
Insurance coverage	−3.5	−10.4	−7.8	−23.5
Income = 20,000–40,000				
After-tax price	17.1	17.1	36.0	36.0
Insurance spending	−8.6	−17.2	−16.8	−33.6
Insurance coverage	−5.1	−11.9	−10.0	−23.2
Income = 40,000–60,000				
After-tax price	21.9	21.9	41.5	41.5
Insurance spending	−10.3	−20.6	−18.9	−37.7
Insurance coverage	−5.7	−1.9	−10.7	−3.57
Income = 60,000–100,000				
After-tax price	30.4	30.4	47.1	47.1
Insurance spending	−14.5	−28.9	−21.5	−43.1
Insurance coverge	−8.0	−2.6	−12.1	−4.02
Income = 100,000 +				
After-tax price	38.5	38.5	47.6	47.6
Insurance spending	−18.3	−36.6	−22.6	−45.2
Insurance coverage	−11.1	−3.7	−13.6	−4.54

Source: Authors' calculations. After-tax price denotes the marginal after-tax price of employer-provided health insurance. Changes in prices are weighted by total insurance spending for insured, and by population weights for uninsured. Changes in quantities are weighted by population weights.

two-thirds of those made eligible for public coverage by these expansions had private insurance before the expansions took place.[32] For every two people who joined the medicaid program over this period, David Cutler and Gruber estimate, one dropped private insurance. People giving up tax-subsidized employer-based coverage to take up medicaid were largely responsible for the 50 percent crowd-out estimate. Even in this world workers typically pay roughly one-third of the cost of their total medical spending, insurance plus out-of-pocket costs, during the year. If the tax

32. Cutler and Gruber (1996).

subsidy to insurance is removed, then presumably even more people will find the free medicaid coverage attractive. The resulting increase in government expenditures would offset and might even exceed any revenue gains from taxing insurance expenditures.

Government rules do not permit people to use medicaid benefits to "top off" private insurance. How tax reform affects private insurance coverage is therefore critical for assessing potential medicaid effects. To estimate how a tax-reform-induced reduction in private insurance coverage would translate into an increase in medicaid spending, we impute to each family in our NMES sample the share of their medical spending that would be eligible for medicaid coverage.[33] We then use this imputed share to estimate the odds that each family drops private coverage, the share of that family's medical spending that will migrate to the medicaid program because the family lost private coverage, and the expected cost to medicaid of providing insurance. We assume everyone eligible for medicaid takes it, although many do not. These assumptions, in combination, probably lead to excessively high estimates of medicaid costs.

Even so, our calculation suggests that increases in medicaid program costs are not an important consideration in evaluating the tax treatment of employer-provided insurance. For the Armey-Shelby, Gephardt, and Lugar plans, we estimate that removing the income tax subsidy increases medicaid outlays by only $251 million to $748 million; for the USA tax, the cost increase is $648 million to $1,933 million. These effects are small even though many medicaid eligibles have private insurance, because the share of the total privately insured population eligible for medicaid remains small. Moreover, the share of costs is low because medicaid covers low-cost children more generously than it does higher-cost adults.

Two other effects on public sector budgets from tax reform are potentially important. First, a reduction in private insurance demand might cause an indeterminate increase in the use of uncompensated hospital care, particularly that delivered by public hospitals. Second, tax-induced changes in private insurance coverage might also affect medicare outlays. Employers may reduce the generosity of insurance for older workers and retirees, with some spillover to the medicare budget. Medicare is the secondary payer of health insurance bills for people over age 65 who are working. Reductions in private insurance generosity for these people would raise medicare costs. Medicare is the primary payer for retirees.

---

33. The higher of these figures comes from calculations with the overall elasticity of − 1.0, and the coverage elasticity set to − 0.9 below the median and − 0.1 above.

Private insurance often covers medicare copayments, thereby inducing increased expenditures, most of which are borne by medicare. Reductions in employer-sponsored retiree health insurance would therefore lower medicare expenditures. Thus the net effect of tax-induced changes in health insurance demand on medicare spending is unclear.

Tax Reform and the Health Insurance Marketplace

In addition to its effects on health insurance coverage and on the quantity of insurance purchased conditional on coverage, the tax laws influence the health insurance marketplace in other important ways. Health insurance is a heterogeneous product, with many distinct features that might respond to changes in the tax subsidy. One of the central issues that arises in this regard is whether the workplace would remain the predominant source of health insurance risk pooling in the absence of a tax incentive for employer provision of health insurance.[34] What follows is speculative, because almost no empirical evidence exists on how changes in the after-tax price of health insurance might affect many characteristics of health insurance and the viability of the workplace as the locus for most private health insurance.

Tax Reform and the Characteristics of Employer-Provided Insurance Policies

Tax reform could affect at least three attributes of employer-provided health insurance policies: health benefits covered, out-of-pocket costs to enrollees through copayments and deductibles, and the use of managed care. Adjustments on each of these margins are likely, but difficult to predict or quantify.

First, raising the after-tax price of employer-provided health insurance would probably reduce demand for some "auxiliary care coverage," such as dental coverage and vision coverage, which many employer health plans now include. Two factors suggest that such benefits may be curtailed if marginal tax subsidies are reduced. One, higher-income households that typically purchase such insurance will see the largest increases in their after-tax costs of insurance. Two, insurance against these risks is less valuable than, for example, insurance against major hospitalization.

---

34. Pauly (1986) discusses these issues and related questions in greater detail.

These benefits resemble tax-favored savings plans more than insurance against major medical risks, because the risk of financially ruinous charges is small.

Second, tax reform may cause increases in out-of-pocket payments by enrollees, through either increased copayment rates or deductibles. At present, tax laws encourage policies that minimize out-of-pocket spending by the insured, because such spending is typically paid for with after-tax dollars, while insurance is purchased with before-tax dollars. If the tax distortion along this margin is removed, policies might shift toward higher copayment rates or deductibles, to hold down policy cost. Evidence is plentiful that demand for medical care is price elastic. Moreover, according to Feldstein and Gruber, increasing copayments, while capping out-of-pocket expenses as a share of income, can both reduce the excess burden of health insurance and increase individual welfare, through limiting out-of-pocket risk more than many current fee-for-service plans.[35] They suggest the reason is that the current tax subsidy has discouraged such plans. But we are not aware of any evidence on what increases in copayment rates or deductibles tax reform might induce.

Third, elimination of the tax subsidy would probably accelerate the trend of employer-provided health insurance toward managed care and direct employer provision of health care. Insurance plans have moved a long way in recent years, from traditional fee-for-service insurance toward HMOs and other managed care arrangements. As the per-unit cost of employer-provided health insurance increased, employers sought to reduce their health care outlays. Shifting to managed care helps, as the costs of HMOs are significantly lower than those of fee-for-service providers.[36] Fundamental tax reform would intensify pressures for business to shift company plans to HMOs, either by restricting employee choices to managed care plans only, or by increasing the employee share of health insurance premiums, inducing employees to choose the lowest-cost option. Currently the tax subsidization of employer payments, but typically not employee payments, penalizes the use of this incentive mechanism. If the tax subsidy is limited, employers may follow this course more often than they now do.

35. Feldstein and Gruber (1995).
36. Manning and others (1987).

Incentives for Employers to Provide Medical Care Rather Than Medical Insurance

Tax reform could bring back the "company doctor" or "company hospital" that was not uncommon in U.S. industry at the turn of the twentieth century.[37] Although the details will depend on legislative language, many proposals would provide an incentive for employers to hire doctors directly and to deliver health care at the workplace. It is unlikely that services a workplace physician provides to a worker or even the worker's family would be included in the employee's tax base. However, the employer's spending on the doctor's salary would probably be deductible from the business tax.

This same incentive may cause companies searching for low-cost providers to switch from externally managed preferred provider organizations to internal, tax-deductible staff. The extent of in-house medical service delivery is likely to vary substantially across different types of care.

Whither Workplace Pooling?

One of the central issues associated with tax reform and the health insurance marketplace is whether reducing the tax subsidy to employer-provided insurance would lead to a systematic shift from workplace pooling of health insurance risks.[38] Such a shift would have far-reaching implications for health insurance more generally, ranging from changes in the cost of some employer-provided benefit plans to an increase in market segmentation and potentially in the number of people who are unable to obtain insurance.

Pooling health insurance risks through the workplace is attractive for several reasons. The tax subsidy may be the most important motivation, but it is not the only one. Workplace pools also permit people to purchase insurance on more favorable terms than they would find in the market for individual insurance. Group insurance holds down administrative costs, in part by using payroll systems to process individual contributions to group health insurance policies. And it lowers the adverse selection

37. Businesses would not need to restrict employees to using company providers. As with current point-of-service plans, employees could use other providers, but at the cost of paying a higher copayment rate.

38. We are grateful to Mark Pauly for detailed comments and suggestions on these issues. Pauly (1996) discusses related issues in substantial detail.

premium that insurers add to the price of individual policies. Workplace groupings are largely determined by factors other than health status. Consequently, workplace groups consist of a more or less random mix of those with high- and low-expected future outlays. As a result of the factors, the cost of insurance for groups with fewer than five persons is an estimated 35 percent higher than the cost for groups with ten thousand or more members.[39]

Whether workplace pooling is attractive to each person depends on whether he or she can pool through other groups. Within workplace pools, employees are charged some proportion of the average cost of insurance for employees purchasing their policy. These premiums can involve substantial cross-subsidies within the workplace. One important feature of community rating of health insurance costs within the workplace is that it increases the after-tax burden on healthy workers. Excluding the tax subsidy, insurance provides net benefits of $539 (in 1987 dollars) to those families with a member in fair or poor health, and imposes a net cost of $950 on families with a member in excellent or good health.[40] The net-of-tax benefit to the families in poor health is $1,059, while the net-of-tax cost to the families in good health is $437.

Some insurance that is now less costly at the workplace than elsewhere might become less costly, for at least some employees, when purchased elsewhere if tax reform ends the workplace tax subsidy.[41] As a result, some employers might drop insurance coverage, and some employees might opt not to participate in such coverage when they have a choice. We cannot forecast confidently whether enough people would choose nonemployer coverage to start a vicious cycle in which workplace pooling unravels as those who remain in the workplace pool become more and more expensive to insure. But we do not consider a major shift from employer-provided insurance as likely, because most of the tax reform proposals preserve a substantial subsidy to employer-provided insurance through the payroll tax and state income taxes. Moreover, as Mark Pauly

39. Congressional Research Service (1988). The relative costs of insurance purchased through small and large groups can be affected by various institutions that impinge on the health insurance marketplace. For example, proposals that would require businesses to insure new employees without exclusions for pre-existing conditions might reduce the administrative costs of policies currently offered to small companies.

40. Monheit, Nichols, and Selden (1995).

41. David Cutler has pointed out that this pattern may hold for the median worker at the firm, who may play a central role in determining the firm's benefit policies.

observes, many of the factors that lead to workplace pooling at present are unaffected by fundamental tax reform.[42]

Even if the workplace remains the source of most health insurance purchases, removing the tax subsidy might cause changes in employer-provided insurance. On the one hand, without the tax subsidy, employees may be more attuned to the cost of their health insurance policies, particularly if employers increase employee premium-sharing. Such developments would strengthen incentives for healthy or young workers within a workplace to form their own employment-based but selective insurance pool. Increased segmentation of the workplace pool could result. On the other hand, part of the attractiveness of this community-rated pool is that it minimizes administrative costs. At present, these administrative costs are tax subsidized, and employees do not bear their full cost. Without the tax subsidy, the after-tax cost of administration would rise, potentially creating stronger pressures for workplace-wide community rating.

The current tax subsidy to employer-provided insurance encourages the formation of employer-based risk pools. It thereby reduces the market failure that results from adverse selection in the individual health insurance market. The tax subsidy achieves this end at the cost of distorting marginal decisions about how much insurance to purchase, and it is a regressive subsidy that is worth more to high-marginal-tax-rate—and, therefore, high-income—taxpayers than to lower-wage-rate taxpayers. A complete evaluation of the tax subsidy requires comparing it with other policies that might achieve the same risk-pooling objectives.

Tax Reform and Health Insurance: Effects on Health Care Costs and Labor Markets

It is difficult to draw precise conclusions about the effect of fundamental tax reform on the demand for health insurance and the structure of the health insurance marketplace. We believe that employer-provided insurance would continue to predominate even if the income tax subsidy to employer provision was removed. But tax reform could cause, intensify,

42. Pauly (1986).

or accelerate substantial changes in the insurance market, which might affect the markets for health care and labor more broadly.

Health Care Costs

Many analysts have pointed to the current tax treatment of employer-provided health insurance as a major cause of the recent rise in U.S. health care spending. The essential argument is that the tax subsidy increases insurance coverage, which in turn increases the demand for medical care, which ultimately leads to a rise in the cost of this care.[43] On this logic, reductions in the tax subsidy could lower medical care costs.

This argument contains three steps. Our analysis strongly supports the first—the link between tax subsidies and the demand for health insurance. The other two steps are more suspect. The next involves the sensitivity of the demand for medical care to the price of such care at the time of service. Insurance reduces this price to individuals receiving medical treatment. The most widely cited estimates, drawn from the RAND Health Insurance Experiment, put this elasticity at about -0.2. This elasticity suggests that increases in copayment rates, higher deductibles, and reduced insurance coverage will reduce the demand for medical care, but that the effect will be small.[44] Also, recall that employer-provided health insurance accounts for roughly one-third of health care spending. This fact means that the potential of tax reforms to affect overall health care costs is limited. Even if reduced demand for insurance translated into a proportional reduction in the demand for medical care—a far more generous assumption than is warranted by the RAND evidence— the estimates we report in table 4-6 would indicate that total demand for medical care would fall between 4.0 percent and 9.5 percent.[45]

---

43. Pauly (1986).

44. It may be misleading to apply the RAND elasticity of demand to evaluate how changes in the insurance market may affect the demand for medical care, for at least two reasons. First, if reduced tax subsidies lead individuals to shift into managed care plans or similar arrangements, then local analysis of changes in the current price of medical care do not apply. Second, a more widespread change in insurance arrangements than was possible through the small-scale RAND study may feed into average practice patterns and have larger effects on the extent of medical care delivered.

45. On the other hand, if private health insurance plans exert a leadership role in the medical marketplace in determining acceptable treatment regimens and thus average practice styles, then changes in what these plans cover or reimburse might have spillover effects

The link between the demand for medical care and total spending on this care is also more complex than it might be in a market for another product. Changes in the average age of the population, increased incomes, and increased insurance coverage can explain less than one-half of the increase in U.S. medical spending between 1960 and 1990, according to Joseph Newhouse; he attributes the remainder to advances in medical technology.[46] These findings suggest that understanding how changes in the tax subsidy to employer-provided health insurance will affect technology is key to understanding how these changes will affect aggregate health care costs.

The available evidence on the link between financial incentives and technological change in medicine is inconclusive. Some studies do suggest substantial effects. One study found that payer mix was an important determinant of adoption and frequency of five surgical technologies in hospitals.[47] Several studies found some evidence that reimbursement rates affect technological diffusion.[48] On the other hand, there is little evidence that changes in the structure of insurance have slowed the diffusion of expensive technologies. For example, although managed care insurance plans have lower costs at any time than fee-for-service plans, even after controlling for differences in the underlying patient base, their costs have grown as quickly as those of fee-for-service plans.[49] Thus we find little basis for concluding that fundamental tax reform is likely to have substantial effects on the growth of health care costs. Even if there are such effects, they are unlikely to be evident in the short term, since much of the medical technology that is likely to become available in the near future is already in the development process.

Labor Market Effects

It is more likely that changes in the tax treatment of employer-provided health insurance will have significant effects on the wage dis-

---

on outlays by the medical patients who are insured through other means, such as medicare, as well.

46. Newhouse (1992). Cutler and McClellan (1996), Aaron (1991), and Weisbrod (1991) draw similar conclusions.

47. Sloan and others (1986).

48. Sloan, Morrisey, and Valvona (1988); Romeo, Wagner, and Lee (1984); Lee and Waldman (1985); Cutler and McClellan (1996); Gruber and Owings (1996).

49. Newhouse (1992).

tribution, work force mobility, and the sorting of workers among companies.

The wage effects of reducing the tax subsidy to employer-provided health insurance depend on whether the workplace remains the locus of insurance provision. Since group health insurance currently represents 7.6 percent of wage and salary payments, and these benefits are distributed progressively, a shift toward less employer-provided insurance would affect the measured wage distribution. Several empirical studies find that workplace fringe costs are fully passed back to workers in the form of lower wages.[50] An 11.7 percent decline in employer-provided health insurance, which we view as our baseline case for the Armey-Shelby, Lugar, and Gephardt tax reform plans, would therefore raise aggregate wages by 0.9 percent.

How the increase in wage payments would be distributed across workers is difficult to assess. Although Gruber and Louise Sheiner show that the cost of benefits can be shifted to broad demographic groups within the workplace, it is not clear how finely such groups can be drawn.[51] This issue is central for determining whether particular workers who refuse employer-provided insurance will be compensated with higher wages or whether the employer will reap the savings. In addition, if wages do not adjust fully to compensate for intergroup differences in employer costs, then employers will be under increased pressure to adjust their work forces toward groups with homogeneous tastes for insurance. The result could be increased attention to health issues in hiring decisions.[52]

If fundamental tax reform leads to a shift from employer-provided insurance to other groupings for creating risk pools, labor market mobility could increase. The current system of employment-linked health insurance may greatly reduce labor market mobility among workers with substantial health care needs.[53] If people bought insurance outside the workplace, these disincentives to mobility would be eliminated. Estimating this effect is virtually impossible. We cannot judge precisely how many people would drop employer-provided insurance under various tax

---

50. Gruber and Krueger (1991); Gruber (1994); Sheiner (1995).

51. Gruber (1994); Sheiner (1995).

52. These pressures already exist under the current system. The removal of the tax subsidy to employer-provided insurance would, however, increase the financial incentive to pursue health-conscious hiring policies.

53. Madrian (1994).

reform proposals, and the effect of health insurance on labor market mobility is also a subject of some controversy.[54]

Conclusion

We have used data from the 1987 National Medical Expenditure Survey and the Treasury Tax Model data files to estimate the effect of fundamental tax reform on the tax subsidy to employer-provided health insurance. Three of the reform proposals currently under discussion, the Armey-Shelby flat tax, the Gephardt "modified income tax," and the Lugar retail sales tax would reduce the current tax subsidy to employer-provided health insurance by slightly more than one-half. These plans leave in place part or all of the current payroll tax subsidy to this insurance. The combined employer and employee payroll tax rate of 15.3 percent, less any tax-benefit offsets, represents a substantial subsidy and one that would support the present system of employer-provided insurance even after fundamental tax reform. State income taxes now follow the federal income tax treatment of employer-provided insurance benefits. If they remained in effect, they would continue to encourage employer-provided insurance even after modification of the federal income tax code.

The USA tax would reduce the tax subsidy even more than the other three plans, because it eliminates the federal income tax incentive and reduces the payroll tax subsidy for employer-provided health insurance. Under this proposal, the tax subsidy to insurance essentially disappears.

Our baseline analysis suggests that the flat tax, the modified income tax, and the national retail sales tax would reduce the overall demand for insurance by between 12 and 23 percent, depending on the price elasticity. Under the USA tax, the demand reduction would be larger, ranging from 19 percent to 38 percent, again depending on the elasticity of insurance demand. Under plausible assumptions, each of these tax reform plans substantially increases the ranks of the uninsured—by 6 million to 14 million under the Armey-Shelby, Gephardt, and retail sales tax reforms, and 10 million to 24 million under the USA tax.

Although our discussion has been limited to analyzing the potential effects of fundamental tax reform, we should note in closing that other modifications to the current tax treatment of employer-provided health

54. Cutler (1996).

insurance could reduce the incentive for excessive insurance with smaller effects on the number of uninsured persons. One approach would be to allow a tax exemption for employer-provided health insurance premiums up to some ceiling, while taxing spending above this level.[55] At the median insurance expenditure in 1994 such a tax cap would achieve two-thirds or more of the reduction in insurance spending that obtains with the elimination of the tax subsidy, but it would have a much smaller effect on the insurance coverage decision.[56] A general concern that might arise if the tax subsidy to employer-provided health insurance were reduced involves individuals who may no longer have access to group health insurance but who find it difficult or expensive to obtain coverage in the individual insurance market. If this group of individuals proves to be large, there may be political pressure for various policies designed to alter the functioning of the individual insurance marketplace.

Appendix A
Derivation of the Tax Price of Health Insurance

In this appendix we describe our methodology for computing the average after-tax price of employer-provided health insurance.[57] We consider an individual with a federal marginal income tax rate on earned income of τ, a net-of-federal-tax state income tax rate of τ_s, and statutory employer and employee rates of payroll tax each equal to τ_{ss}. We assume that labor income taxes and payroll taxes are fully borne by labor, so that when an employer purchases insurance for E dollars, the employee's wage is reduced by $E/(1 + \tau_{ss})$. The change in the employee's after-tax wage income per dollar of employer-provided insurance, dw_{AT}/dE, is, therefore,[58]

---

55. Such tax caps have been analyzed extensively for the current tax code by CBO (1994).
56. Gruber and Poterba (1996).
57. Our framework draws heavily on Gruber and Poterba (1996).
58. Many previous studies of how tax rules affect the demand for fringe benefits, or health insurance in particular, have used dw_{AT}/dE as their primary measure of the tax subsidy. Woodbury and Hamermesh's (1992) study of how the Tax Reform Act of 1986 affected the demand for fringe benefits versus wage income at universities is a recent example in this tradition. Earlier studies that adopt similar approaches, in many cases omitting either the state tax or payroll tax terms in equation 1, include Feldstein and Allison (1974), Long and Scott (1982), Taylor and Wilensky (1983, pp. 163–84), Holmer (1984), Sloan and Adamche (1986), and Burman and Williams (1994).

(1)
$$\frac{dw_{AT}}{dE} = \frac{1 - \tau - \tau_s - \tau_{ss}}{1 + \tau_{ss}}.$$

The after-tax price of health insurance depends on the after-tax wage cost per dollar of insurance as well as on other factors, including the load factor in insurance policy prices.[59] We denote this load factor by λ. It reflects costs of administering an insurance plan, the profits of the insurer, and any other expenses incurred in minimizing the health risk of a given group to the insurer. The load factor raises the after-tax cost of employer-provided insurance relative to that of self-insurance.[60]

Another component of the after-tax price of health insurance is the fraction of health insurance premiums that is paid for by employees. Approximately three-quarters of these employee premiums are paid after tax, and paying them is a requirement of taking advantage of the favorable tax treatment of employer-provided insurance.[61] Because those employees who must make post-tax contributions to their employer-provided insurance receive favorable tax treatment of a smaller fraction of their health insurance than those employees whose insurance is fully provided by the employer, the presence of employee contributions raises the after-tax price of employer-provided health insurance.

In defining the after-tax price of insurance, we use G to denote employee payments for employer-provided insurance and E to denote em-

59. The load represents the fact that the expected value of medical care outlays from one dollar of spending on medical insurance is less than one. This results from administrative and other costs. It may also be appropriate to include the distortion in spending patterns that results from moral hazard in medical care demand as part of the load factor.

60. Part of what we denote as the load factor may reflect administrative costs that would have to be paid by a self-insured individual as well as by someone with employer-provided insurance. The load factor may also include insurer spending to achieve cost economies; in either of these cases, calling the load factor a pure cost of insurance overstates the price differential between insurance and self-insurance. It is particularly difficult to measure the *marginal* load factor on insurance; our data refer to average loads. Fortunately, in light of these difficulties, our central findings on tax subsidy to employer-provided insurance and the effect of tax reform on health insurance demand are not particularly sensitive to our assumption about the load factor.

61. The U.S. Bureau of Labor Statistics (1993) reports that approximately 33 percent of employees of firms with more than 100 employees, and 20 percent of employees of firms with fewer than 100 employees, can deduct their own premium payments from taxes. These are employees who can pay their premiums through cafeteria plans provided by their employers. We are not able to identify which employees can make pre-tax premium payments in the data we use, so we randomly assign individuals with employee premiums between the pre-tax and post-tax groups with a probability of 0.25 for the first group.

ployer payments, and we assume that a fraction δ of employee premiums can be paid for on a pre-tax basis. Recognizing both the load factor on employer-provided insurance and the existence of employee contributions to such insurance yields the following expression for the after-tax price of employer-provided insurance:

(2)
$$P_{Health\ Insurance} = \left(\left[\frac{1 - \tau - \tau_s - \tau_{ss}}{1 + \tau_{ss}} \right] * \left(\frac{E + \delta * G}{E + G} \right) + \frac{(1 - \delta) * G}{E + G} \right) * (1 + \lambda).$$

We define the tax subsidy to employer-provided insurance by comparing this after-tax price with the after-tax cost of self-insurance. This cost is affected by the possibility of claiming an itemized deduction for medical expenses in excess of 7.5 percent of adjusted gross income. This provision discourages insurance purchase by reducing the after-tax cost of out-of-pocket medical spending. For a nonitemizer, this deduction is irrelevant, so the after-tax cost of such spending is one dollar. For itemizers, however, the after-tax cost of the marginal dollar of out-of-pocket medical spending is $(1 - \alpha\tau)$, where τ is the federal marginal tax rate and $\alpha = 1$ if the marginal dollar of spending exceeds the AGI floor and zero otherwise.

The parameter α, which denotes the probability that the marginal dollar of health care costs that is covered by employer-provided insurance would have been deductible if it had been incurred on own account, is difficult to measure. A person considering an insurance purchase may have expectations regarding α, but the true value of α will not be known until actual health expenses during the year are known. In our calculations below, we assume that individuals have perfect foresight, and we use actual, *ex post* values of α in place of expected values to evaluate the after-tax price of insurance.[62]

---

62. Individuals with health insurance typically face lower marginal costs of health care services at the time of consumption than individuals without such insurance, and this may affect their demand for medical services. We do not allow for this factor in our current analysis; see Gruber and Poterba (1996) for evidence that the estimated tax subsidy to employer-provided health insurance is insensitive to this assumption.

(3) $P_{relative} =$

$$\frac{\left(\left[\dfrac{1 - \tau - \tau_s - \tau_{ss}}{1 + \tau_{ss}}\right] * \left(\dfrac{E + \delta * G}{E + G}\right) + \dfrac{(1 - \delta) * G}{E + G}\right) * (1 + \lambda)}{1 - \alpha * \tau}.$$

We define the relative after-tax price of employer-provided insurance as the ratio of the after-tax price of this insurance and the after-tax cost of out-of-pocket medical spending: if the tax code treated insurance premiums and medical expenditures symmetrically—for example, if neither was deductible from taxable income, or if both could be excluded from federal and state taxable income as well as from the payroll tax wage base—then the cost of insurance relative to the direct outlays on medical care would be $P_{relative} = 1 + \lambda$. The tax-induced distortion in the relative price of insurance is therefore $[P_{relative}/(1 + \lambda) - 1]$, where $P_{relative}$ is given by equation 3.

Our measures of the after-tax price of health insurance and the relative price of insurance suffer from several limitations. First, we fail to distinguish between marginal purchases of incremental employer-provided insurance and the discrete decision to purchase such insurance. The load factors on marginal insurance purchases may be lower than average load factors if these factors in part reflect administrative costs that do not rise when a policy becomes more extensive.

Second, we assume that when expenditures on employer-provided insurance fall, both G and E are reduced proportionally. If employers contribute a fixed amount to their group health insurance plans, and employees make nondeductible contributions equal to the cost differential between the plan they choose and the lowest-cost option, then there is no tax subsidy to insurance on the margin. In this case our analysis overstates the average tax subsidy to workplace insurance.

Third, our formulation also ignores the fact that under some cafeteria plans individuals can pay for their out-of-pocket medical costs with pre-tax dollars. This will also lead us to overstate the tax subsidy to insurance because we understate the increased tax benefit of self-insurance when this option is available. Unfortunately, we have no data on the structure of employer contributions or the availability of such pre-tax out-of-pocket arrangements.

One final point, concerning tax-benefit linkage, deserves discussion. We subtract from the statutory individual payroll tax rate in the numerator of equation 3 the extent of the tax-benefit offset, τ_{ss}^*. In some cases,

$\tau_{ss}{}^*$ (a negtive number) can be greater in absolute value than τ_{ss}, if the net increment to the present discounted value of benefits from another dollar of earnings is greater than the employee share of the payroll tax.[63] Thus the expression that we use to evaluate the after-tax relative price of employer-provided insurance in the case with tax-benefit linkage is:

(4)
$$P_{relative} = \frac{\left(\left[\dfrac{1 - \tau - \tau_s - \tau_{ss} - \tau_{ss}{}^*}{1 + \tau_{ss}}\right] * \left(\dfrac{E + \delta * G}{E + G}\right) + \left(\dfrac{(1 - \delta) * G}{E + G}\right) * (1 + \lambda)\right)}{1 - \alpha * \tau}.$$

The Armey-Shelby flat tax, the Gephardt modified income tax, and the Lugar retail sales tax all have exactly the same effect: they set $\alpha = \tau = 0$. To compute our tax prices, we further assume that fundamental tax reform would not affect current state tax rules. Thus each of these tax plans changes the after-tax price of employer-provided insurance to

(5)
$$P_{relative,\ Armey} = \left(\left[\dfrac{1 - \tau_s - \tau_{ss} - \tau_{ss}{}^*}{1 + \tau_{ss}}\right] * \left(\dfrac{E + \delta * G}{E + G}\right) + \dfrac{(1 - \delta) * G}{E + G}\right) * (1 + \lambda).$$

Evaluating this expression for each of the health insurance units in the NMES data base is straightforward, given the information on each household that we have used to compute the after-tax price of health insurance under the current income tax.

There is an important difference, however, between these proposals and the USA tax, because of the payroll tax credit that is available under the USA tax. The payroll tax credit affects the after-tax price of health insurance, since it further reduces the tax subsidization of employer-provided insurance. That is, the relative price becomes

63. Our analysis has also ignored the nontrivial payroll taxes, which support the unemployment insurance, and workers' compensation programs, which may provide a further wedge between cash compensation and health insurance. We exclude these taxes, since previous research suggests that employer payments are fully valued by employees, so that there is no perceived net tax. See Gruber and Krueger (1991) for supportive evidence for workers' compensation, and Anderson and Meyer (1995) for the case of unemployment insurance.

(6)
$$P_{relative,\ USA} = \left(\left[\frac{1 - \tau_s - \tau_{ss}^*}{1 + \tau_{ss}}\right] * \left(\frac{E + \delta * G}{E + G}\right)\right.$$
$$\left. + \left(\frac{(1 - \delta) * G}{E + G}\right) * (1 + \lambda)\right).$$

Since τ_{ss}^* is less than zero, the OASDI system actually induces an *increase* in the relative price of insurance under the USA tax. That is, since the USA tax gives a credit for statutory tax payments, but the effective tax payment by the individual is net of-tax-benefit offset, there is actually a net subsidy to earned income, and a net tax on health insurance purchase, from OASDI taxes.

Appendix B
Estimates of Response of Insurance Purchase to Price

Estimates of the response of overall insurance spending to after-tax prices come from four types of studies: time-series studies that use changes in the average price of health insurance, or the tax system, to identify the demand elasticity; cross-sectional studies that use differences in marginal tax rates across households to identify the demand elasticity; experimental studies that use information on experimentally induced variation in insurance costs to explore insurance demand effects; and "natural experiment" studies that use variation from legislated differences in tax prices to identify elasticities. Time-series evidence on how total spending on employer-provided health insurance responds to tax incentives is presented in several studies.[64] These studies, which suffer from the standard difficulties of interpreting aggregate time-series correlations in the presence of multiple shocks, typically yield estimates of the price elasticity of demand between 0 and -0.5.

A second set of studies analyzes cross-sectional data on individuals or firms and asks whether those with higher tax-related subsidies to insurance purchase spend more on insurance coverage.[65] These studies are potentially contaminated by the fact that cross-sectional differences in tax rates arise in part from differences in the underlying behavior of individuals or firms, such as differences in labor supply, family structure,

64. Long and Scott (1982); Vroman and Anderson (1984); Turner (1987).
65. These include Phelps (1973); Taylor and Wilensky (1983); Woodbury (1983); Sloan and Adamche (1986).

or the nature of the work force. It is impossible to tell whether differences in observed insurance coverage are due to taxes or these behavioral differences. These studies also suffer from difficulty in specifying "the" marginal tax rate that applies to the insurance purchase decision of firms, which are composed of many workers facing different tax rates. A wide range of estimates emerges from these studies; Pauly summarizes the consensus range as -0.2 to in excess of -1.0.

A third and notable line of research, which avoids the problems with cross-sectional or time-series variation in after-tax insurance prices, is the "experimental" approach, used for example by M. Susan Marquis and Charles Phelps.[66] They use evidence from the RAND Health Insurance Experiment to estimate a price elasticity of demand for supplementary insurance of -0.6. It is not clear, however, whether such experimental evidence generalizes to evaluating the design of broad-based tax policies toward health insurance. Individual demand behavior may be affected by the explicitly short-lived nature of the health insurance experiment. In addition, there could be general equilibrium effects on the health insurance marketplace that influence demand responses when tax reform affects all participants in the insurance market, but that are not observed when an experimental program affects only a small fraction of these market participants.

The final approach, which attempts to overcome the problems inherent in the previous cross-sectional literature, examines how demand for insurance responds to plausibly exogenous legislated tax differences. Stephen Woodbury and Daniel Hamermesh analyze fringe benefit expenditures at the time of the Tax Reform Act of 1986 in a panel data set of colleges and universities. They conclude that tax reform substantially reduced the demand for fringes, with an estimated elasticity in excess of -2, but it is difficult to disentangle the income and price effects of tax reform from the authors' evidence. It is also once again difficult to determine what tax rate should be used in modeling insurance demand, since individuals within the workplace exhibit different tax rates. In light of the range of existing estimates of the price elasticity of demand for insurance, we consider a range of elasticity values in our calculations.

The elasticity of the insurance coverage decision with respect to the after-tax price of insurance has attracted less research attention than the price elasticity of demand for insurance spending. Two strands of literature bear on this question. The first views firms as the units of choice

---

66. Marquis and Phelps (1987).

and studies how the decision to make group health insurance available to workers is affected by its price. Arleen Leibowitz and Michael Chernew analyze a cross section of firms with fifty or fewer employees.[67] They use cross-state differences in state marginal income tax rates and in the prices of a standardized group health insurance policy to estimate the effect of after-tax costs on the decision to offer insurance to workers. Because some of the variation in costs across states may not be exogenous, the interpretation of the resulting estimates is open to question. Nevertheless, their results imply a substantial price elasticity of demand. They estimate that providing a 10 percent price subsidy to insurance purchases by small employers would raise the fraction of employers offering health insurance from 41 percent to 53 percent; this is a price elasticity of demand for coverage of approximately −2.7. William Gentry and Eric Peress study cross-city differences in the average share of workers offered health insurance benefits, as a function of cross-state differences in after-tax prices of insurance.[68] They find that for each percentage point increase in the price of health insurance, the percentage of workers covered by employer-provided insurance declines by 1.8 percent, which implies a price elasticity of demand of −1.8. A different approach is taken by Kenneth Thorpe and his colleagues, who identify the price elasticity of demand by using insurance cost variation that resulted from a New York state pilot program to subsidize small-firm purchases of health insurance.[69] This study suggests that if all firms were aware of the price subsidy, an upper-bound estimate of the price elasticity of coverage demand would be −0.33. These estimates are an order of magnitude smaller than those in Leibowitz and Chernew or Gentry and Peress.

A second source of evidence on the price elasticity of demand for insurance is household-level analysis. Our 1994 study of how the self-employed responded to the Tax Reform Act of 1986 illustrates this approach.[70] TRA86 introduced a subsidy to insurance purchases by self-employed workers, with the subsidy potentially equal to one-quarter of the individual's federal marginal tax rate. We analyzed Current Population Survey data from 1985 through 1989. The percentage of self-employed persons who reported that they had health insurance coverage

67. Leibowitz and Chernew (1992).
68. Gentry and Peress (1994).
69. Thorpe and others (1992).
70. Gruber and Poterba (1994).

rose from 69.4 percent in 1985–86 to 73.3 percent in 1988–89, while the percentage of non-self-employed workers with insurance actually fell. Our analysis suggests a price elasticity of approximately −1.8 of insurance coverage with respect to the after-tax price of such insurance. We suspect that this demand elasticity may be greater for the self-employed than for employed workers, but this issue requires further empirical study.

In a related study Marquis and Steven Long use locational differences in insurance costs to estimate an insurance purchase equation.[71] They find that a 1.0 percent increase in insurance prices results in a 0.6 percent decline in health insurance coverage. Their analysis is limited to the individual insurance market rather than the market for group policies.

Comment by David Cutler

Jonathan Gruber and James Poterba have written an interesting essay on the implications of tax reform for the provision of health insurance. Changes in the taxation of fringe benefits are one of the frequently omitted implications of fundamental tax reform. But these changes may be among the most important effects of tax reform. For every study showing that saving is unresponsive to taxation, another study shows that the demand for fringe benefits is responsive to taxation. For better or worse, fundamental tax reform will have large effects on the provision and financing of fringe benefits, and it is important to analyze those responses.

Gruber and Poterba show that tax reform will increase the cost of employer-provided health insurance by about 20 percent. They talk about the fact that insurance coverage is likely to fall. They do not offer many specifics on what this means, however, and they leave aside the welfare analysis of the changes. What I want to do is try to interpret the results a bit: first, to ask whether the policies under consideration can even be implemented; second, to ask whether the changes that would result from tax reform are large; and third, to examine the implications of these changes for tax reform.

Implementing Tax Reform

I want to start off with an important issue—the implementation of these different policies. "Taxing health insurance" means one of two

71. Marquis and Long (1995).

things: either including the value of employer payments for health insurance in individual income, or eliminating the deductibility of employer payments for health insurance. The first way is conceptually simpler; one just counts as income what employers are paying for workers. But a moment's thought reveals the difficulty. If one firm spends more on insurance than another firm because its workers are less healthy, are the employees really being compensated more? What if one firm has older workers and another has younger workers? These questions have no clear theoretical answer.

There are two ways of treating these issues. The first is to say that what one wants to measure is *not* the dollars of spending, but the generosity of the insurance offered—that is, how much the average person would receive in the way of insurance payments if he or she was insured under that policy. This is a concept known as the actuarial value of the insurance policy. Conceptually, that is what most people mean when they talk about valuing health insurance for workers. In the late 1980s there was a brief experiment in which firms were required to measure actuarial values. The system proved unworkable, however, and it is unlikely it can be reinstituted in an acceptable way. So the actuarial value approach is probably not feasible.

That leaves the second approach to imputing health insurance to workers: using something like average health insurance payments per worker. This approach has large inequities. In a cross section, less than 10 percent of the variation in insurance premiums can be explained by the generosity of the benefits offered. Much more has to do with location (area-specific medical costs), the demographics of the work force, and particularly average health status. For some, taxing along these margins is an unacceptable distribution of the tax burden. It is certainly something to be kept in mind in advocating taxation of health insurance benefits.

If health insurance is not to be counted as income to workers, a second approach is to disallow the business deduction for health insurance payments. This is administratively simpler than including insurance in workers' income, since one has to deal only with employers, not individuals. But this proposal has a particularly pernicious effect on low-wage workers. Consider the version of the flat tax proposed by Steve Forbes—in which a family of four pays no tax on income up to $36,000. Income above $36,000 is taxed at 17 percent, as are corporate profits. Suppose that a family of four has one worker, who earns $25,000 in total compensation. If the firm pays the $25,000 entirely as wages, there is no tax. If $5,000 is paid as health insurance, however, there is a tax at the corporate level of $850 ($5,000 × 0.17). For a high-wage worker (above $36,000), in contrast, the $5,000 would be taxed at a 17 percent rate regardless of whether it is paid as health insurance or wages.

Disallowing the corporate deduction thus leaves the high-wage worker indifferent between receiving income in the form of health insurance or wages. There would be a substantial *disincentive* to low-wage workers, however, if the firm is providing health benefits. The tax on low-wage workers would be $850—not a small amount. Today low-wage workers have a hard time finding employment in firms that provide health insurance, even with the tax subsidy. I don't think one wants to compound that by taxing the provision of health insurance, particularly for these workers.

One could try to ameliorate these effects with a credit for firms that provide health insurance to low-wage workers, but this just gets back to the problems noted above of imputing health benefits to particular workers. Disallowing the deductibility of employer-provided health insurance thus seems to me to be a nonstarter.

In short, there is no ideal way to level the playing field between health insurance and wages. One can't do the policy that one would want to do (imputing the actuarial value of health insurance to workers), and one almost certainly doesn't want to do the policy that is easiest (disallowing the deductibility of employer payments). One could impute average spending to workers, but that would create substantial inequities.

Evaluating Changes in Employer-Provided Insurance

Let me put aside the question about how tax reform would be implemented to consider some of its economic effects. Perhaps the most troubling issue of tax reform is how it will affect employer-sponsored insurance coverage. Start with the following simple computation. Tax reform would increase the price of health insurance by about 20 percent. The elasticity of demand for employer-provided insurance is usually estimated as being between 0 and −2.0, with a consensus estimate of between −0.5 and −1.0. Therefore, tax reform would lower the share of the working-age population with employer-provided insurance by between 10 and 20 percentage points. Since about 60 percent of the non-elderly population now has employer-based health insurance, the reduction in employer-sponsored insurance would be about 15 to 30 percent of current levels.

That is very large. The "fundamental" reduction in employer coverage over the 1980s that gets politicians agitated was only about a 5 percentage point decrease in insurance coverage. So the result of tax reform would be like compressing four or five decades of historical experience into one event.

Is this analysis right? Maybe. There are biases both ways. I suspect that as an average demand elasticity the -0.5 to -1.0 is overstated. Most of the data used in estimating elasticities of demand for health insurance are from low-income groups (for example, workers in small firms and the self-employed). Insurance is a very different product for low-income people than it is for high-income people. The reason why lies in the alternative to employer-provided insurance. Gruber and Poterba suggest that the alternative to employer insurance is "self-insurance." That is a euphemism. For the rich, the alternative is purchasing insurance in the nongroup market; for the poor, the alternative is being uninsured.

Being uninsured is a form of insurance. The uninsured generally do get care; they get it when they are very sick, and if they have any wealth they must use it to pay for care. In economic terms, being uninsured is like a catastrophic insurance policy with a deductible equal to one's wealth. What purchasing insurance does is to allow a person to see a greater choice of providers than the uninsured get to see and to provide a form of wealth insurance.

For the low-income population, wealth insurance is not worth that much; and since the demand for medical care is low at low incomes, having a broader choice of providers is not worth the high price. The result is that the elasticity of demand for insurance is high. Higher up in the income distribution, wealth insurance and choice of providers are both valuable, so the elasticity of demand for insurance is smaller. The studies that find a high elasticity of demand for insurance, I suspect, overstate the average elasticity because they focus on the highly elastic group. Hence the 10 to 20 percent estimate of a reduction in employer-provided coverage may be too high.

There are several countervailing issues, however. One issue, noted by Gruber and Poterba, is that the tax subsidy keeps employer groups together when otherwise people might look harder at exactly how much they are paying and receiving for being in the employer group. Because health spending is so skewed, the *median* worker in any year almost certainly receives less in the way of health benefits than he or she pays in the *average* cost of insurance. Thus if there was no tax subsidy to health insurance, the median worker in most firms might well feel that health insurance through the firm was not a good deal. That would be true even if everybody at the firm wanted to purchase health insurance at his or her actuarially fair price.

In addition, demand elasticities are often estimated at the firm level, and the issue of what is a firm is quite elastic. Under current nondiscrimination rules, if a firm provides health insurance to any full-time employees, it must provide it to all full-time employees. One way that firms have cut back on health insurance is to contract out the services of workers for whom health insurance is very expensive (for example, janitorial supply companies, temporary secretaries, and so forth). This type of response is not picked up in the models that have been estimated, suggesting an even larger demand elasticity.

My sense is that, on net, tax reform of the type being considered will lead to a large decline in employer-sponsored insurance. The response will be particularly large for the low-income population, but there may be dramatic changes for the higher-income population as well.

What are the implications of this decline in coverage? Some people who lose employer-sponsored insurance will join other pools to buy insurance. These groups will be decidedly nonrandom: healthy people will want to pool with other healthy people, and sick people will have to pool with other sick people. That is an unhappy prospect.

Others will buy insurance in the nongroup market. That too is less than ideal. In the nongroup market, coverage is bad, premiums are high, and there is no guarantee that people who get sick can retain their coverage at reasonable rates. As a policy matter, if there is ever to be this type of policy change (and even if there isn't), it will be necessary to couple it with restructuring the nongroup insurance market

And some of those who lose employer coverage are likely to wind up uninsured. This is where the big financial and social consequences are. Traditionally, some of the bills for the uninsured were paid by private insurers in the form of "cost shifting"—providers marked up the costs for those who were insured to pay for those who were not. That is not a viable long-run option. Even in the absence of tax reform, markets are getting more competitive, and competitive markets do not usually have that sort of transfer. Tax reform will only hasten the phaseout of this practice.

Thus many of these people will wind up in providers of last resort—largely public hospitals. That will be a significant cost to the public sector. I suspect it will also have more profound social implications. Currently the uninsured—even those in public hospitals—fare reasonably well. Their care is roughly comparable to that of the insured even if they receive it at different times and have to wait longer for it. If the uninsured population increases significantly, however, care in public institutions will almost surely decline. I see no evidence that the public sector has the ability or desire to keep the standard of care in public hospitals at the same level as that in private hospitals. If tax reform of this magnitude passes, the disparity between care for the insured and care for the uninsured will certainly grow.

Implications for Tax Reform

If that is the future, is it worth it? Gruber and Poterba spend little time discussing whether it is good or bad to eliminate the favorable income tax treatment of health insurance. This is unfortunate, because it is something they should discuss.

Uncompensated care and programs like medicaid subsidize being uninsured. In the absence of cutting off such care, it is natural for tax policy to offset that subsidy with a subsidy for insurance coverage. For incentive reasons it is good that people pay for the cost of their health insurance choices *at the margin*. To encourage insurance purchase overall, however, it may be worthwhile to consider an *inframarginal* subsidy for health insurance—for example, by allowing a tax exclusion for health insurance but capping it at a level below the cost of most health plans. Alternatively, health insurance payments could be included in income, but refundable credits could be provided for the purchase of health insurance. Both methods subsidize insurance coverage without providing a large marginal subsidy. With the potential for such dramatic changes in health insurance coverage resulting from tax reform, it will be essential to think much more deeply about the goals of the tax system before engaging in that type of reform.

References

Aaron, Henry J. 1991. *Serious and Unstable Condition: Financing America's Health Care.* Brookings.

Anderson, Patricia U., and Bruce D. Meyer. 1995. "The Incidence of a Firm-Varying Payroll Tax: The Case of Unemployment Insurance." Working Paper 5201. Cambridge, Mass.: National Bureau of Economic Research.

Burman, Leonard E., and Roberton Williams. 1994. "Tax Caps on Employment-Based Health Insurance." *National Tax Journal* 47 (September): 529–45.

Congressional Research Service. 1988. *Costs and Effects of Extending Health Insurance Coverage.*

Cowan, Cathy A., and Patricia A. McDonnell. 1993. "Business, Households, and Governments: Health Spending, 1991." *Health Care Financing Review* 14 (Spring): 227–48.

Currie, Janet, and Jonathan Gruber. 1994. "Saving Babies: The Efficacy and Cost of Recent Expansions of Medicaid Eligibility for Pregnant Women." NBER Working Paper 4644. *Journal of Political Economy* (forthcoming).

———. 1996. "Health Insurance Eligibility, Utilization of Medical Care, and Child Health." *Quarterly Journal of Economics* 111 (May): 421–66.

Cutler, David M. 1996. "Public Policy for Health Care." *Fiscal Policy: Lessons from Economic Research,* edited by Alan Auerbach. MIT Press (forthcoming).

Cutler, David M., and Jonathan Gruber. 1996. "Does Public Insurance Crowd Out Private Insurance?" *Quarterly Journal of Economics* 111 (May): 391–430.

Cutler, David M., and Mark McClellan. 1996. "The Determinants of Technological Change in Heart Attack Treatment." Harvard University.

Employee Benefit Research Institute. 1995. *EBRI Databook on Employee Benefits: Third Edition.* Washington.

Feldstein, Martin S. 1973. "The Welfare Loss of Excess Health Insurance." *Journal of Political Economy* 81 (March-April): 251–80.

Feldstein, Martin S., and Elisabeth Allison. 1974. "Tax Subsidies of Private Health Insurance: Distribution, Revenue Loss, and Effects." In U.S. Congress, Joint Economic Committee, *The Economics of Federal Subsidy Programs,* 997-94. 93 Cong. 2 sess. Government Printing Office.

Feldstein, Martin S., and Bernard Friedman. 1977. "Tax Subsidies, the Rational Demand for Insurance, and the Health Care Crisis." *Journal of Public Economics* 7 (April): 155–78.

Feldstein, Martin S., and Jonathan Gruber. 1995. "A Major Risk Approach to Health Insurance Reform." In *Tax Policy and the Economy,* vol. 9, edited by James Poterba, 103–30. MIT Press.

Feldstein, Martin S., and Andrew Samwick. 1992. "Social Security Rules and Marginal Tax Rates." *National Tax Journal* 45 (March): 1–22.

Gentry, William, and Eric Peress. 1994. "Taxes and Fringe Benefits Offered by Employers." Working Paper 4764. Cambridge, Mass.: National Bureau of Economic Research.

Gruber, Jonathan. 1994. "The Incidence of Mandated Maternity Benefits." *American Economic Review* 84 (June): 622–41.

Gruber, Jonathan, and Alan B. Krueger. 1991. "The Incidence of Mandated Employer-Provided Insurance: Lessons from Workers' Compensation Insurance." In *Tax Policy and the Economy,* vol. 5, edited by David Bradford, 111–43. MIT Press.

Gruber, Jonathan, and Maria Owings. 1996. "Physician Financial Incentives and the Diffusion of Cesarean Section Delivery," *RAND Journal of Economics* (forthcoming).

Gruber, Jonathan, and James M. Poterba. 1994. "Tax Incentives and the Decision to Purchase Health Insurance: Evidence from the Self-Employed." *Quarterly Journal of Economics* 109 (August): 701–33.

———. 1996. "Tax Subsidies to Employer Provided Health Insurance." In *Empirical Foundations of Household Taxation,* edited by Martin S. Feldstein and James Poterba, 135–64. University of Chicago Press.

A. Foster Higgins and Co. 1994. *National Survey of Employer-Sponsored Health Plans, 1993.* Princeton, N.J.

Holmer, Martin. 1984. "Tax Policy and the Demand for Health Insurance." *Journal of Health Economics* 3 (December): 203–21.

Lee, Robert H., and Waldman, Donald. M. 1985. "The Diffusion of Innovations in Hospitals: Some Econometric Considerations." *Journal of Health Economics* 4 (December): 373–80.

Leibowitz, Arleen, and Michael Chernew. 1992. "The Firms' Demand for Health Insurance." In U.S. Department of Labor, *Health Benefits and the Workforce,* 77–83.

Long, James E., and Frank A. Scott. 1982. "The Income Tax and Nonwage Compensation." *Review of Economics and Statistics* 64 (May): 211–19.

Lurie, Nicole, and others. 1984. "Termination from Medi-Cal: Does It Affect Health?" *New England Journal of Medicine* 311 (August): 480–84.

Madrian, Brigitte C. 1994. "Employment-Based Health Insurance and Job Mobility: Is There Evidence of Job-Lock?" *Quarterly Journal of Economics* 109 (February): 27–51.

Manning, Williard G. 1987. "Health Insurance and the Demand for Medical Care: Evidence from a Randomized Experiment." *American Economic Review* 77 (June): 251–77.

Marquis, M. Susan, and Steven H. Long. 1995. "Worker Demand for Health Insurance in the Non-Group Market." *Journal of Human Resources* 14 (May): 47–63.

Marquis, M. Susan, and Charles E. Phelps. 1987. "Price Elasticity and Adverse Selection in the Demand for Supplementary Health Insurance." *Economic Inquiry* 25 (April): 299–313.

Monheit, Alan C., Len M. Nichols, and Thomas M. Selden. 1995. "How Are Net Health Insurance Benefits Distributed in the Employment-Related Insurance Market? " Rockville, Md.: Agency for Health Care Policy and Research.

Newhouse, Joseph P. 1992. "Medical Care Costs: How Much Welfare Loss?" *Journal of Economic Perspectives* 6 (Summer): 3–21.

Pauly, Mark. 1986. "Taxation, Health Insurance, and Market Failure in the Medical Economy." *Journal of Economic Literature* 24 (June): 629–75.

Pauly, Mark. 1996. "An Efficient and Equitable Approach to Health Reform." University of Pennsylvania, Wharton School.

Phelps, Charles E. 1973. "Demand for Health Insurance: A Theoretical and Empirical Investigation." Santa Monica, Calif.: Rand Corporation.

Romeo, Anthony A., Judith Wagner, and Robert H. Lee. 1984. "Prospective Reimbursement and the Diffusion of New Technologies in Hospitals." *Journal of Health Economics* 3 (April): 1–24.

Sheiner, Louise. 1995. "Health Care Costs, Wages and Aging: Assessing the Impact of Community Rating." Federal Reserve Board.

Sloan, Frank A., and Killard Adamache. 1986. "Taxation and the Growth of Nonwage Benefits." *Public Finance Quarterly* 14 (April): 115–39.

Sloan, Frank A., and others. 1986. "Diffusion of Surgical Technology: An Exploratory Study." *Journal of Health Economics* 5 (March): 31–61.

Sloan, Frank A., Michael A. Morrisey, and Joseph Valvona. 1988. "Medicare Prospective Payment and the Use of Medical Technologies in Hospitals." *Medical Care* 26 (9): 837–53.

Taylor, Amy, and Gail Wilensky. 1983. "The Effect of Tax Policies on Expenditures for Private Health Insurance." In *Market Reforms in Health Care: Current Issues, New Directions, Strategic Decisions*, edited by Jack Meyer, 163–84. Washington: American Enterprise Institute.

Thorpe, Kenneth L, and others. 1992. "Reducing the Number of Uninsured by Subsidizing Employment-Based Health Insurance: Results from a Pilot Study." *Journal of the American Medical Association* 267 (February 19): 945–48.

Turner, Robert. 1987. "Are Taxes Responsible for the Growth of Fringe Benefits?" *National Tax Journal* 40 (June): 205–20.

U.S. Bureau of Labor Statistics. 1993. *Employee Benefits in Medium and Large Private Establishments: 1991.* Bulletin 2422. Department of Labor.

U.S. Congressional Budget Office. 1993. *Projections of National Health Expenditures, 1993 Update.*

———. 1994. *The Tax Treatment of Employment-Based Health Insurance.*

Vroman, Susan, and Gerard Anderson. 1984. "The Effect of Income Taxation on the Demand for Employer-Provided Health Insurance." *Applied Economics* 16 (February): 33–43.

Weisbrod, Burton. 1991. "The Health Care Quadrilemma: An Essay on Technological Change, Insurance, Quality of Care, and Cost Containment." *Journal of Economic Literature* 29 (June): 523–52.

Woodbury, Stephen A. 1983. "Substitution between Wage and Nonwage Benefits." *American Economic Review* 73 (March): 166–82.

Woodbury, Stephen A., and Daniel S. Hamermesh. 1992. "Taxes, Fringe Benefits, and Faculty." *Review of Economics and Statistics* 74 (May): 287–96.

CHAPTER 5

Taxes, Mortgage Borrowing, and Residential Land Prices

Dennis R. Capozza, Richard K. Green, and Patric H. Hendershott

MEASURING income from owner-occupied housing is difficult because the owner receives imputed rents, not cash. Even when the house is sold and cash changes hands, the true capital gain is sometimes hard to measure because the basis has changed owing to economic depreciation and major improvements. These circumstances make it hard to measure, and therefore to tax, income from housing.[1] A solution often adopted is to tax housing lightly, if at all.

Although lightly taxing owner-occupied housing simplifies the tax code, it has major revenue implications because owner-occupied housing constitutes 40 percent of the capital stock.[2] Thus the taxation (or nontaxation) of the income from housing affects tax rates applied to economic activity generally. Moreover, because housing is the largest single component of the capital stock, its relative taxation could have an enormous impact on the efficient allocation of the total capital stock.[3] To illustrate, the Tax Reform Act of 1986 sharply lowered marginal tax rates; on this score it lowered the *absolute* tax advantage to owner-occupied housing. The act also sharply reduced differences among tax rates on various components of business capital, increasing the efficiency within business capital. However, this gain in efficiency was achieved by sharply increasing the taxation of business capital by removing investment tax credits and lengthening tax depreciation lives. It thereby wors-

---

1. One of the arguments advanced for taxing consumption instead of income is the difficulty of accounting for depreciation and inflation. Capital income generally is difficult to measure, and revenues raised from taxing it may be low; Gordon and Slemrod (1988).
2. Musgrave (1990).
3. Rosen (1985); Smith, Rosen, and Fallis (1988).

ened the overall allocation of capital by increasing the *relative* tax advantage of owner-occupied housing.[4]

Although the tax bias favoring owner-occupied housing over rental housing and other real capital investment is widely recognized, the source of the tax advantage is not well understood and, as a result, neither is the role of the home mortgage interest deduction.[5] Like many investments, owner-occupied housing provides both a periodic imputed cash flow (the rent that owners avoid paying to other landlords, they implicitly pay to themselves) and a generally positive capital gain upon sale. In the current income tax system, the fundamental tax advantages to owner-occupied housing are the exclusion of the imputed cash flow from the house, the particularly light taxation of capital gains caused by generous rollover provisions, and the one-time $125,000 capital gains exclusion.[6] If someone other than the owner occupied the house, the rent actually paid would be taxed; and the income from other assets—bonds or stocks, for example—would be taxed.

Note that we have not mentioned the mortgage interest deduction. The tax advantage from owner-occupied housing accrues as fully to homeowners who have no mortgage as to those who do. Forty percent of U.S. homeowners do not have a mortgage because they have sufficient wealth to finance their house entirely with equity. If they borrowed, say, $100,000 and invested it in comparable-risk Ginnie Mae mortgage-backed securities, their tax position would not be improved. Although the interest paid on the mortgage is deductible, the interest earned on the Ginnie Maes is taxed.

So what is the role of the mortgage interest deduction? It extends the tax advantage received by wealthier, mostly older, households, who carry no mortgages, to less wealthy, mostly younger, households who borrow to finance their houses. The deduction creates a small bias in favor of mortgage financing, but only for homeowners who itemize their deductions, especially those subject to high rates, who can use the loan proceeds to buy fully or partly tax-sheltered assets. For the most part, the cost of equity financing one's house is the after-tax yield that would be earned

---

4. Hendershott (1987).

5. The rationale for this bias is the positive externalities attributed to homeownership. For example, Green and White (1996) show that children of owners are more likely to finish high school and less likely to have children or be arrested while they are teenagers (holding constant parent income, education, race, age, and marital status and correcting for selectivity bias).

6. Aaron (1972); Laidler (1969); Hendershott (1983).

if the funds were invested elsewhere, while the cost of debt financing is the *after-tax* debt rate.

A tax law change that treats equity and debt financing differently will dramatically alter financing behavior because this behavior is easy to alter.[7] More specifically, removing the mortgage interest deduction would accelerate the buildup of home equity as households age and accumulate wealth. Adoption of the USA (unlimited savings allowance) tax, which favors debt finance, would encourage initial loans to cluster at around 80 percent of value, the ratio at which the marginal cost of borrowing increases significantly, and to remain at that ratio. Given the size of the housing stock, these debt shifts would significantly cut tax revenue.

Changes in the taxation of owner-occupied housing will primarily affect prices of prime residential land, not housing consumption. We present theoretical arguments and empirical evidence to support this belief. Although estimates of the supply elasticity of housing structures with respect to shifts in demand are reasonably high, the supply elasticity is low for prime residential land—that is, land not on a city's outer fringe. Just as the removal of the tax exemption on interest earned on existing long-term municipal bonds would cause prices of such bonds to plummet, removal of the tax advantage of owner-occupied housing would cause prime residential land prices to plummet. Because we expect primarily price rather than quantity responses, we believe that earlier estimates that the tax advantages of owner-occupied housing cause large efficiency losses by inducing excess housing consumption are overstated. All major tax reform proposals now under discussion would reduce the relative tax advantage of owner-occupied housing. We measure their effects in terms of the percentage decline in house prices in sixty-three metropolitan statistical areas.

We begin with estimates of how three proposals would affect mortgage borrowing. The three proposals are elimination of the mortgage interest deduction (and using the revenues to lower current income tax rates); the Armey-Shelby flat tax;[8] and the USA tax sponsored by Senators Sam Nunn and Pete Domenici. We conclude that the effects would be large. The flat tax would halve the volume of mortgages outstanding and orig-

---

7. Slemrod (1990). Bourassa and Hendershott (1994) note that a national property tax would reduce the tax preference for owner-occupied housing without distorting the financing of it. If net rents were 6 percent of property value and the average income tax rate were 25 percent, then a 1.5 percent property tax (over and above that required to pay for local services) would be equivalent to taxing net rents fully.

8. Based on Hall and Rabushka (1995).

inated, while the USA tax would double mortgage volume. The corresponding effects on the mortgage banking, insuring, and securitizing industries would also be large. We then calculate declines in house prices—the land component—and find substantial declines, particularly for the flat tax. These declines could cause significant default problems for private mortgage insurers and the Federal Housing Administration, both of which specialize in high loan-to-value (LTV) loans.

Removal of the Home Mortgage Interest Deduction

Removing the mortgage interest deduction would penalize mortgages relative to other borrowing by raising mortgage costs to the pre-tax debt rate. Moreover, removing the deduction and using added revenue to cut tax rates proportionately would significantly redistribute the U.S. tax burden. The redistribution would not be primarily by income class.[9] The loss of deductions would hurt higher-income households, but they would also gain a lot from the tax cut because they pay a disproportionate share of taxes. Lower-income households would lose less from repeal of the deduction but would also gain less from the rate cut.

The primary redistribution would instead be among age classes. Older households would gain more from a rate cut than they would lose from denial of deductions for mortgage interest, while young households would lose more from the removal of the deduction than they would gain from the tax cut. The magnitude of the redistribution is shown in table 5-1 (panel A). It shows observed LTVs for households in four age classes and three income ranges based on the 1989 Survey of Consumer Finance (SCF). The LTV declines from 0.57 for households under age 35 to 0.04 for those over age 65.

LTVs vary considerably by income, holding age constant. For households between ages 35 and 65, the average LTV for those with income over $75,000 (the top tenth of owner income distribution) is 0.12 greater than it is for households with income under $50,000 (the bottom three-quarters). One would expect households with relatively high income or wealth to be more likely to engage in "tax arbitrage," the practice of negotiating loans with fully deductible interest and investing in assets, such as common stocks, with at least partially tax-sheltered returns. These data show that the benefits of the mortgage interest deduction

9. Follain, Ling, and McGill (1993).

Table 5-1. *Loan-to-Value Ratios, by Household Income and Age of Household Head*

| Age of household head | Household income[a] | | | |
	Under $50,000	$50,000–$75,000	Over $75,000	All income classes
Panel A: Current loan-to-value ratios for owner-occupiers				
Under 35	0.56	0.58	0.58	0.57
35–54	0.31	0.40	0.43	0.35
55–64	0.11	0.14	0.23	0.14
65 and over	0.04	0.04	0.05	0.04
All ages	0.23	0.39	0.36	0.27
Panel B: Maximum loan payoff as percentage of house value, using liquid assets				
Under 35	0.08	0.13	0.25	0.10
35–54	0.07	0.16	0.19	0.11
55–64	0.03	0.06	0.18	0.06
65 and over	0.01	0.04	0.02	0.01
All ages	0.05	0.14	0.18	0.08

Source: 1989 Survey of Consumer Finance.

a. Response to question put to Survey of Consumer Finance participants asking for total household income. $50,000 is the seventy-fifth income percentile for owner-occupiers in the Survey of Consumer Finance; $75,000 is the ninetieth percentile.

accrue overwhelmingly to the young, whose limited wealth forces them to borrow, but also disproportionately to those with higher incomes and greater incentives to engage in tax arbitrage.

Because removal of the deduction would penalize debt, households with marketable financial assets would shift to greater equity financing of their homes. Panel B of table 5-1 shows the decline in LTVs that would result if households in the 1989 SCF liquidated all marketable assets (but did not change business asset holdings) and used the proceeds to repay debt. Because older households already have low LTVs, the decline is greater for younger households—0.11 for those under age 55, half that for those between 55 and 64, and negligible for those over age 64. Because higher-income households also have more financial assets, the reduction is greater for them. In fact, the "adjusted" LTVs (the number in panel A less the corresponding number in panel B) vary with income only for households under age 35. Higher-income people are clearly choosing higher LTVs, probably to engage in tax arbitrage.

We estimate the loss of tax revenue from this behavioral shift in two steps. First, we estimate the tax revenue gained in the absence of a behavior shift and then we compute the loss caused by the shift. The average

Table 5-2. *House Values, by Household Income and Age of Household Head*

Household values in dollars

Age of household head	Household income[a]			
	Under $50,000 (federal tax rate 16%)[b]	$50,000– $75,000 (federal tax rate 28%)[b]	Over $75,000 (federal tax rate 31%)[b]	All income classes (federal tax rate 23%)[b]
Under 35	68,896	117,838	193,734	84,649
35–54	78,789	114,168	219,832	107,354
55–64	70,533	131,314	253,407	102,130
65 and over	70,288	193,702	328,523	85,008
All ages	73,072	119,505	238,156	96,985

Source: 1989 Survey of Consumer Finance.

a. Response to question put to Survey of Consumer Finance participants asking for total household income. $50,000 is the seventy-fifth income percentile for owner-occupiers in the Survey of Consumer Finance; $75,000 is the ninetieth percentile.

b. Marginal tax rates assume 1990 brackets.

gain for each cell is the product of the original LTV in table 5-1, the average house values of the households in the cell, the average tax rates of the household cell, and the average mortgage rate paid. Table 5-2 shows the mean house values and the average marginal tax rates. We assume a 10 percent mortgage rate. The total gain is the sum of each of these products weighted by the number of households in the cells. The reduction in tax revenue caused by the paydown of debt by an individual household is the product of the paydown, the tax rate paid on the income from the financial assets used to make the paydown, and the yield earned on these assets. With a decline in LTV from 0.4 to 0.25, the paydown is three-eighths the initial debt level. The tax rate on the paid-down financial assets is less than that at which the mortgage is deducted because such assets as corporate equities are partially tax sheltered; also, the pre-tax yield on such assets as bank deposits can be lower than the mortgage rate, while the yield on such assets as corporate equities can be higher. Taking these considerations into account, our best estimate is that the shift to lower LTVs would cost about one-quarter of the revenue otherwise to be obtained.

While the data in panel B of table 5-1 are hypothetical, such a behavioral shift is both logical and consistent with data from Australia.[10] Aus-

10. Canada also does not allow mortgage interest deductibility, but Canadian data are not readily available. We have, however, obtained some average data from Statistics Canada based on their Survey of Family Expenditures. For households aged 35–44, the average Canadian ratio is 36 percent, or only two-thirds of the comparable U.S. 53 percent. For

Table 5-3. *Regressions Explaining Loan-to-Value Ratios, Australia and United States*

Variable	Australia	United States
Intercept	−0.053	0.033
	(0.032)	(0.018)
Age of household head		
18–20	0.639	−0.058
	(0.092)	(0.113)
21–24	0.489	0.406
	(0.021)	(0.034)
25–29	0.432	0.501
	(0.011)	(0.014)
30–34	0.332	0.469
	(0.009)	(0.010)
35–39	0.222	0.363
	(0.009)	(0.009)
40–44	0.136	0.284
	(0.009)	(0.008)
45–50	0.104	0.209
	(0.010)	(0.008)
50–54	0.058	0.145
	(0.010)	(0.008)
55–59	0.023	0.106
	(0.009)	(0.008)
Natural log of income	0.0070	0.0023
	(0.0040)	(0.0016)
N	4,000	11,784
R^2	0.40	0.29

Sources: Bourassa & Hendershott (1994); authors' estimates based on data in 1989 Survey of Consumer Finance.

tralia does not have the mortgage interest deduction and had a national aggregate LTV of 0.14 in 1986. The comparable U.S. number was 0.32, and it has since risen to 0.41 owing to the limitation on nonmortgage deductibility imposed in the 1986 tax act.[11] The first column of table 5-3 contains the regression coefficients on income and age dummies based on a regression of LTVs of just over 4,000 Australian households in 1986.[12] Column 2 gives the same coefficients for the United States, using data on nearly 12,000 households in the 1989 SCF.

---

older households, the Canadian ratio is about three-quarters of that in the United States, but these households are able to deduct mortgage interest on debt used to purchase retirement accounts before 1981. For a comparison of U.S. and Canadian borrowing, see Jones (1993).

11. Federal Reserve System (1995).
12. Bourassa and Hendershott (1994).

Table 5-4. *Homeownership Rate, by Household Income and Age of Household Head*

Percent

	Household income[a]			
Age of household head	Under $50,000	$50,000–$75,000	Over $75,000	All income classes
Under 35	34	85	92	43
35–54	66	88	95	79
55–64	78	91	98	87
65 and over	77	88	95	82

Source: 1989 Survey of Consumer Finance.
a. Response to question put to Survey of Consumer Finance participants asking for total household income. $50,000 is the seventy-fifth income percentile for owner-occupiers in the Survey of Consumer Finance; $75,000 is the ninetieth percentile.

The mean LTVs implied by the U.S. regression for households aged 25–29, 40–44, and 55–59 are 0.56, 0.34, and 0.16. These values are obtained using the mean incomes of households under age 35, ages 35–55, and ages 55–64 ($25,318, $44,390, and $37,106). Comparable estimates based on the Australian regression are 0.42, 0.12, and 0.01. That is, the Australian LTVs start off a bit lower than U.S. LTVs and decline much more rapidly, from 80 percent of U.S. ratios at age 25–29 to 35 percent at age 40–44 and 10 percent at age 55–59.

One final point: although young homeowners would lose relative to old homeowners if the mortgage interest deduction were removed and used to lower tax rates, many more young households are renters than are older households. Table 5-4 gives the ownership rate by household age and income class. Only 43 percent of households under age 35 own, compared with 87 percent of households between the ages of 55 and 64. (For all ages, ownership rises significantly with income.) All taxpaying renters would gain from the removal of the interest deduction and the cut in tax rates. Taking account of ownership rates as well as age-related differences in LTVs reduces the age redistribution, but those under age 55 still lose relative to older households, especially those over age 64.

The Flat Tax, the USA Tax, and Home Mortgage Borrowing

The two fundamental reforms being proposed, the Armey-Shelby flat tax and the USA (unlimited savings allowance) tax, are both consumption taxes. The personal component of the flat tax is a wage tax that explicitly exempts the taxation of returns to capital. It is like an unlimited "back-loaded" individual retirement account, which provides no deduction for saving and no taxation of distributions. It also repeals the deduction of interest generally and of mortgage interest specifically. The USA tax includes capital income in the tax base but allows deductions for asset purchases financed by saving but not by borrowing. It is like an unlimited "front-loaded" IRA, with deductions for contributions and taxation of distributions. In principle, neither tax contains a bias for or against mortgage financing of owner-occupied housing. Under the flat tax, both the opportunity cost to owner equity and the cost of borrowing would be the pre-tax interest rate. Under the USA tax, both the opportunity cost and the borrowing rate would be the after-tax interest rate. The former would remove the tax preference for housing, although any decline in pre-tax interest rates that might result would mitigate the removal. The latter would maintain the tax preference largely as it is.

In practice, the USA tax treats real assets differently from financial assets and owner-occupied housing differently from other real investments. First, only saving in financial assets is deductible. Thus drawing down financial assets to purchase a house would increase one's taxable income dollar for dollar. Second, increases in mortgage debt, including that on an existing house, could be used to offset taxable income dollar for dollar. In effect, the tax preference for debt-financing would remain, while the tax preference for own-equity financing would be substantially reduced.[13] The result would be a surge in borrowing.[14]

In the calculations below, we assume that all households would raise their LTVs to 80 percent. Currently the secondary market institutions require private mortgage insurance on loans with LTVs above 0.8, and the cost of this insurance is high. For the typical default insurance on 90 percent LTV loans, the cost is about a third of a percentage point per year, and this cost is paid on the entire loan balance, not just the amount above 80 percent. If the mortgage rate is 8 percent, this insurance raises to 11 percent the interest rate on the increase from an 80 percent LTV

13. The preference is not eliminated, because when the debt is retired taxable income rises by an equivalent amount. The present value of tax liability deferred ten, twenty, thirty, and forty years, assuming a 7 percent discount rate, is 0.51, 0.26, 0.13, and 0.07, respectively.

14. Another $35,000 in nonmortgage debt is permitted without raising taxable income, which would lead to greater debt finance of consumer durables and lost tax revenue (see below). If households borrow to invest in financial assets, there is no reason to think the general level of interest rates will change. The existence of an active secondary market for loans means that mortgage rates should not rise relative to other rates, except perhaps briefly.

Table 5-5. *Average Increase in Mortgage Debt among Homeowners,*
Arising from USA Tax, by Household Income and Age of Household
Head[a]

Mortgage debt in dollars

| | Household income | | | |
Age of household head	Under $50,000	$50,000–$75,000	Over $75,000	All income classes
Under 35	16,535	25,924	43,622	19,469
35–54	38,611	45,667	81,337	48,309
55–64	48,667	86,667	144,442	67,405
65 and over	53,418	147,213	246,392	64,606
All ages	41,651	48,997	104,788	51,402

Source: 1989 Survey of Consumer Finance.
a. We assume USA tax would induce households to raise LTVs to 0.8. We do not take payment constraints into account in these calculations. The table also assumes that housing prices are held constant.

to a 90 percent LTV.[15] Of course, we might expect lenders to bid aggressively for the new business if the USA tax were introduced, and many borrowers might be able to obtain, say, 85 percent loans at little additional cost.

The rise in debt finance would cause both one-time and continuing losses of tax revenue. Table 5-5 shows how much income could be sheltered by a one-time increase in debt. These data are computed as the product of the household's house value and the difference between 0.8 and its observed LTV. The rise in mortgage debt increases with age, because older households have lower observed LTVs, and with income, because higher-income households have more costly houses.

The revenue loss from the increase in debt can be computed as the sum over all households of the product of the household's debt increase, its tax rate, and the number of households each SCF observation represents. The total loss would be $50 billion, most of which would probably be realized in the first three years because few households have annual taxable income of more than triple the assumed increase in debt finance, and this loss would have to be offset by high transition tax rates. Moreover, in an environment where house prices are rising continuously the personal income tax base would shrink annually by the product of the house price inflation rate, the initial house value, and the LTV. Assuming 2.5 percent inflation, an average house value equal to 2.5 times wage income, and an 80 percent LTV, the annual shrinkage would be 5 percent

15. The incremental rate, x, comes from the solution to the equation $8(0.8) + x(0.1) = 8.33(0.9)$.

of current wage income. If inflation should accelerate to 5 percent, the shrinkage would double, and at 10 percent it would quadruple. Eventually, repayment of debt by the elderly moving out of owner-occupied housing would act to offset this shrinkage.

Finally, mortgage interest deductibility could be appended to the flat tax, retaining the current tax preference for debt-financed owner-occupied housing but eliminating the preference for equity-financed purchases. Because households could borrow at the after-tax interest rate and invest in Ginnie Mae securities at the pre-tax rate, we anticipate that debt financing would increase greatly and that it would cushion the house price decline. And again, a one-time borrowing surge on existing homes would be expected, requiring higher transitional tax rates and an even higher long-run tax rate. That is, the borrowing effects would be very similar to those of the USA tax. Transition rules, such as no deductible debt increases without a move or house renovation, could extend the duration of the transition loss, under either the flat tax or the USA tax.

Effects of Tax Changes on Aggregate House Prices

In equilibrium, the risk-adjusted expected annual yields on the last unit of all assets must be equal. In the case of owner-occupied housing under current law, the cash-flow yield (that is, the ratio of implicit rents not paid to a landlord to the price of a unit of housing), f, and the expected appreciation yield, g, are generally untaxed, but interest income earned is taxed. Thus we write the equilibrium relation as:

$$(1) \qquad\qquad f + g = (1 - t_y)\, i,$$

where t_y is the relevant marginal income tax rate and i is the relevant (equal-risk) taxable yield. We specify f as the gross rent-price ratio (R/P) on the last unit of housing purchased less the tax deductible property tax rate (t_p) and the nondeductible maintenance expense rate (m).[16] Substituting these three terms into equation 1 and solving for R, we have

16. There is a long-standing debate over whether the net property tax rate should appear on the right side of equation 2 while adding the benefits provided by these taxes to the left side (and then canceling the two under the assumption that they are equal). Hendershott and Hu (1981) argue that the rate alone ought to appear when one is considering the marginal cost of purchasing another square foot of housing (negligible benefits are obtained from the additional property taxes paid), but that services of value approximately equal to the property taxes paid should be included when one is considering a household's tenure decision.

(2) $R = [(1 - t_y) i + (1 - t_y) t_p - g + m] P.$

This equation indicates that a household will invest in owner-occupied housing until the value of the implicit rents earned on an additional unit of housing purchased declines to the user cost of capital, given by the expression on the right.[17] Given a constant price of housing, high-income (high t_y) homeowners will purchase sufficient housing to drive implicit rents on the last unit purchased down further than will low-income homeowners (that is, the former "overinvest" in housing). Moreover, an increase in the marginal income tax rate of a household, holding its average rate constant, will increase its demand for housing services, driving down implicit rents on the last unit purchased.

In the conventional view, housing is an investment good produced by highly competitive builders who take orders for new houses and subsequently construct the houses over the next three to six months. Small changes in house prices will elicit a large supply response from builders and prevent large changes in prices. Estimates of the supply elasticity for housing are large and are consistent with the conventional approach. The large annual fluctuations in real housing prices observed in metropolitan areas seem at odds with this view.[18]

We say "seem" because house prices and structure prices are not the same thing. House prices include the land on which the houses are located, as well as the structures: housing is bound to the land on which it rests. And in the United States, land constitutes 40 percent of value, on average.[19] Although the supply of structures may respond elastically to small changes in the price of structures, the supply of prime residential land cannot. At any given location, land is in completely inelastic supply.[20] Because our model incorporates this inelastic land supply, we conclude that an increase in individual marginal income tax rates, holding average tax rates constant, will be capitalized into housing prices with little change in implicit rents or in the allocative efficiency of housing

17. Hendershott and Hu (1981); Poterba (1984).
18. Abraham and Hendershott (1994).
19. Federal Reserve System (1995).
20. Empirical estimates of large supply elasticity apply to new houses built on the (moving) periphery where land is available for new construction. To evaluate tax impacts we need the response of an existing home at a given location to changes in the tax. Mayer and Somerville (1996) estimate the stock elasticity using repeat sale data that hold location constant and find a minuscule elasticity (0.1).

investment.[21] Simply put, one should not assume that elasticity in the supply of structures means that house prices are fixed.

Consider a small open city with two housing zones, rental and owner-occupied. The city is part of a system of cities among which migration occurs freely. In equilibrium, the well-being of households is similar among urban areas. Corporations are the marginal owners of rental housing and pay tax at rate t. Net rent in the rental zone is given by R^r. The pre-tax required rate of return on rental housing is also i, so that the equilibrium relationship for rental housing is given by

$$(3) \quad (1 - t)\, R^r = [(1 - t)\, i + (1 - t)\, t_p - g + (1 - t)\, m]\, P^r$$

or

$$R^r = [i + t_p - g/(1 - t) + m]\, P^r,$$

where P^r is the price of the rental structure plus land and, for simplicity, capital gains are assumed to be untaxed.

Equation 3 determines the R^r/P^r ratio for each rental market. R^r itself is determined from internal spatial equilibrium in each market. That is, rents must allocate households over the existing space. Spatial equilibrium includes allocating households both within metro areas and among metro areas through intercity migration. Theoretically and empirically, real rents in a metropolitan area should be related to metropolitan variables such as real income, population, and real construction costs.[22] This rent equation and equation 3 determine P^r.[23]

The marginal homeowner in a particular geographic market is indifferent between renting and owning. For this household, equation 2 holds, with market rents for a unit of housing replacing implicit rents. With a graduated income tax and no differences among households except income, all households in tax brackets equal to or above that of the mar-

21. In general, there will be some quite involved real general equilibrium effects of a secondary nature.

22. Capozza and Helsey (1989, 1990); Capozza and Schwann (1989, 1990).

23. For simplicity, we have ignored complications like depreciation tax rules and capital gains taxation. With current long tax lives and low inflation, these complications are probably of little importance. Note, however, that both these and the corporate tax rate affect the price of land in rental housing.

ginal household will own, while those in lower brackets will rent.[24] This marginal tax rate, along with the other variables in equation 2, determines owner-occupied house prices in the particular geographic market.

If all houses could be moved and lot lines redrawn at no cost, land could be freely converted from lower-price use to higher-price use. An increased tax preference would enlarge owner-occupied housing lots at the expense of rental housing lots, cushioning the impact of the greater preference on owner-occupied housing land prices and generating greater structure demand—the overinvestment discussed above. Because houses are generally not mobile and costs of redrawing lot lines are large, neither the land response nor the structure response occurs.

If marginal, but not average, individual income tax rates decline, land prices in the owner-occupied sector will fall, while land prices in the rental sector and rents in both sectors will be unchanged. There are no real effects because both actual and implied rents are constant. Because the owner-occupied tax preference is fully capitalized into owner-occupied house prices, a reduction in the preference lowers house prices (the land component).

Estimates of the Model and Their Interpretation

We have previously estimated a regional equilibrium relationship for owner-occupied housing on the basis of data from sixty-three metropolitan statistical areas (MSAs) for 1970, 1980, and 1990.[25] We rewrote equation 2 as

$$(2') \qquad R^r/P = a\,(1 - t_y)\,i + b\,(1 - t_y)\,t_p - g + m.$$

That is, we replaced implicit rents by market rents, divided through by P to make the ratio of median rent to median house price the left-hand variable, and allowed the net-of-tax interest and property tax rates to have coefficients, a and b, different from the theoretically expected value of one. We also included a crude estimate of expected house price appre-

---

24. Titman (1982). For a variety of reasons, not all households in the same tax bracket wish or are able to become owners. Some young households with low wealth are constrained from owning by the capital market. Some older households find maintenance too onerous. Mobile households find transactions cost of owning too high, and so on. With a single tax rate system, characteristics other than income, such as expected mobility, would partition households between renting and owning.

25. Capozza, Green, and Hendershott (1995).

Table 5-6. *Metropolitan Statistical Areas with Highest and Lowest Average Marginal Tax Rates, 1970, 1980, and 1990*

MSA	Tax rate		
	1970	1980	1990
Highest			
Anaheim	29	32	27
Honolulu	30	28	28
Milwaukee	29	29	24
Minneapolis	30	32	26
Rochester	29	28	25
San Francisco	29	29	26
San Jose	30	31	28
Washington, D.C.	n.a.	30	28
Mean of highest five	30	30	27
Lowest			
Birmingham	20	22	21
El Paso	21	17	15
Knoxville	20	17	17
Memphis	21	19	18
Miami	21	19	18
Pittsburgh	20	23	20
San Antonio	20	18	17
Tampa–St. Petersburg	20	18	18
West Palm Beach	22	17	20
Mean of lowest five	20	17	17

Source: Authors' calculations based on 1970, 1980, and 1990 Public Use Microsample from U.S. Bureau of the Census; and federal and state tax tables. The authors thank Wenzel Hoberg for his assistance in these calculations.
n.a Not available.

ciation and a constant term to reflect m.[26] For the MSA-specific income tax rate, we used an instrument for the average marginal income tax rate (federal and state) t_y for all households in the relevant MSA.[27]

The estimated average marginal income tax rates vary widely across MSAs. Table 5-6 lists MSAs that were among the five highest and lowest in any of the three census years. Three of the eight highest tax rate MSAs

26. All data except the income tax rates are described in Capozza and Seguin (1996).

27. A good instrument is a rate that is highly correlated with the variable being instrumented, the accurately measured average marginal tax rate, without being influenced by the variable being explained, the rent-price ratio. Of course, households in high rent-price areas are more likely to be owners, but owners in such areas are less likely to be itemizers (high R/P areas are really low house price areas). Instrumented individual household combined federal and state marginal tax rates are computed based on two assumptions: the number of dependents equals all related individuals under age 18 in the household, and households do not itemize. While treating owners as nonitemizers sets marginal tax rates at their maximum possible level, the use of renting and owning households acts to offset the upward bias in tax rates.

are found in California, and the nine lowest tax localities are all in the South. The cross-sectional differences are large. The average tax rate in the five highest tax MSAs is 50 percent to 75 percent above the average of those in the five lowest in each of the three years. In addition, property tax rates vary considerably, with six MSAs having rates above 2.5 percent and five having rates below 0.8 percent.

Income tax rates reflect MSA differences in both nominal income, which causes federal taxes to differ, and in state tax rate schedules and incomes. To illustrate, the average federal (average marginal) tax rate in the five highest tax rate MSAs in 1990 was 40 percent higher than that in the five lowest (0.234 versus 0.165). The average state tax rate in the highest five MSAs was 0.058 versus 0.0 in the five lowest (Florida, Tennessee, and Texas have no state income tax).

With these data, we estimated the a and b coefficients on the net-of-tax interest rate and property tax variables in equation 2'. The coefficients, 1.14 for the net interest rate and 1.09 for the net property tax rate, do not differ from 1 with statistical significance.[28] Because we use panel data for three census years and sixty-three metropolitan areas, most of the variation is across metropolitan areas. These intermetropolitan area results would normally be interpreted as long-run or even very long-run results.

Our theory suggests that these estimates reflect price effects—that is, capitalization effects—rather than rent adjustments. The raw data are consistent; the coefficient of variation in prices in our sample is twenty times larger than that in rents. Prices vary far more geographically than rents do. Moreover, when we regress the percentage change in real house prices on the percentage changes in the determinants of real rents—real income, population, and construction costs—and the change in the after-tax interest rate, the coefficient on the interest rate is -12.1. In terms of the model, this coefficient should be minus unity divided by the mean value of R^r/P (0.065), that is, $-1/0.065 = -15.4$.[29] The estimated coefficient is not statistically different from this expectation.[30]

Because empirical findings support our theoretical assertion that changes in the taxation of owner-occupied housing largely affect land

---

28. The standard errors of estimate for the coefficients are 0.24 and 0.14, respectively.

29. To obtain the expected percentage change in house prices, we begin with $R/P = Z$, where Z is the after-tax interest rate. Taking the total derivative and solving for dP/P, the coefficient on Z is $-1/(R/P)$.

30. The standard error of estimate is 0.555, so we can be confident that the coefficient is not zero. Moreover, the coefficient is not significantly different from the expected -15.4.

values, tax changes should not be expected to have significant effects on either the quantity of housing demanded or the homeownership rate. This indicates that previous estimates of efficiency losses from the tax advantage to owner-occupied housing are much too high.[31] To be more specific, if taxes were uniform and the supply of housing were fixed, nontaxation of housing would have no efficiency costs. Investors in owner-occupied housing would push the full benefit of the subsidy into higher real house prices. With a progressive tax, some inefficiencies will exist because the housing stock will be misallocated among households in different tax brackets. Households in higher tax brackets would "over-invest" in owner-occupied housing, driving down implicit rents, while households in lower tax brackets would underinvest (although most such households would be renters). However, even some of these inefficiencies might be eliminated; one could envision higher-income homeowners in a given MSA concentrating in particular areas and bidding up land values by more than average, while prices would be bid up by less than average where lower-income owners concentrate.

If the stock of housing were given, tax-reform-induced increases in the after-tax financing rate would be offset by house price declines, and the price of housing services would be largely unchanged. A renting household considering owning would quickly see the offset. Although the offset would not be so apparent to households who could no longer deduct mortgage interest, households that moved within the same area and compared the cost of owning with renting would find that the lower cost of the housing purchase offset the higher net interest cost. Thus, in the absence of significant changes in market rents, home ownership should not be greatly affected by the tax changes.

We will not analyze how the tax changes might affect market rents owing to changes in the user cost of rental housing, but it is unlikely that large changes would occur. Consider the flat tax. Although it eliminates the deductibility of interest, it allows the immediate write-off of land and structure, not just the depreciation of the structure over 27.5 years. Crude calculations suggest a rise of less than 10 percent in the equilibrium rent-price ratio with constant interest rates, and a decline of less than 5 percent with a 1 percentage point decline in interest rates. Again, we would expect the impact to be on the price of rental properties, not the rent level.[32]

31. See Rosen (1985) and Smith, Rosen, and Fallis (1988) for summaries of research on the efficiency costs of these tax advantages.
32. Blackley and Follain (1996) find extremely slow adjustment of nationwide rents on

Aggregate House Price Effects

We use the asset-equilibrium model to infer house price responses to four possible tax changes: the elimination of the property tax deduction, elimination of the property and mortgage interest deductions, the flat tax, and the USA tax. We calculate price changes for all sixty-three MSAs based on straightforward manipulations of the asset-equilibrium model. We assume the user cost—the right-hand side of equation 2—is the same before and after the tax change. Solving this equality for the ratio of the post-tax-change price to the pre-tax-change price yields

$$\frac{P_1}{P_0} = \frac{(R/P)_0}{(R/P)_0 + [(1 - \theta t_1)i_1 - (1 - t_0)i_0] + [(1 - \gamma t_1) - (1 - t_0)]t_p},$$

where θ and γ represent the fractions of the financing cost and the property tax that would be deductible under the tax changes analyzed; θ and γ equal 1 under current law. Note that the equation allows for changes in interest rates as well as the income tax rate.

To allow for both state and federal income taxes, the tax rate, t_y, is measured as $t_y = t_f + (1 - t_f) t_s$, where t_f and t_s are the federal and state average marginal tax rates.

We assume federal revenues are held constant by offsetting and proportional changes in tax rates. Personal federal income tax revenues in 1994 were roughly $550 billion. Removal of the property tax deduction would raise revenues $14 billion or 2.5 percent. The average of the marginal income tax rates across the sixty-three MSAs is 0.22. Loss of the property tax deduction would allow this rate to be lowered from 0.22 to 0.214. Removal of both the property tax and interest deductions would raise revenue $65 billion, or 12 percent, assuming no shift in LTVs. This revenue would permit the tax rate to be lowered to 0.194. With a decrease in LTV to 0.25, the tax revenue gain falls to $40 billion, and we set the tax rate at 0.205. With the flat tax, the new tax rate is irrelevant to the calculations of house price decline because both θ and γ are zero. With the USA tax, we have calculated average marginal tax rates for each MSA using the rate schedule in the current proposal and

---

rental housing in response to large shifts in the real after-tax required returns to rental housing investment during the 1970s and 1980s. The large transactions costs associated with converting land from one use to another, including zoning regulations, and the uncertainty about future discount rates, including tax law, substantially delayed conversions among land uses.

the assumptions we used for calculating current tax rates. The average of the MSA rates is 0.217, a 0.003 reduction from current law.

Some analysts anticipate significant interest rate declines in response to some of the proposals. For example, Alan Auerbach estimates that both the flat tax and the USA tax would lower interest rates about one percentage point.[33] Robert Hall and Alvin Rabushka claim rates would fall two percentage points in response to their flat tax.[34] On the other hand, William Gentry and Glenn Hubbard argue that interest rates could actually rise.[35] We first report estimated effects on house prices if interest rates do not change and then indicate, for the flat tax, the cushioning impact of interest rate declines. We believe that interest rates would decline under the flat tax because interest would be neither deductible nor taxed.

Our latest MSA-level data are for 1990, and the SCF data we analyze are from 1989. We therefore base our sample calculations on average 1990 data. We discuss below the effect of different initial data values. The 1990 mortgage rate and mean values of the MSA property tax rates, the combined federal and state average-marginal income tax rate, and the R^r/P ratios, respectively, are 0.105, 0.014, 0.22, and 0.065.

ELIMINATION OF THE PROPERTY TAX AND MORTGAGE INTEREST DEDUCTIONS. Eliminating the property tax deduction alone means that θ remains at unity (the interest rate terms in the denominator cancel with constant interest rates), while γ becomes zero. The result is a 5 percent decline in house prices. With revenue neutrality imposed on local governments—they raise property rax rates when house prices fall—the decline is 7 percent.[36] Elimination of both the mortgage interest and property tax deductions would lower prices further. With no change in LTV from its current value of 0.4, γ falls to 0.6 (the equity share of the financing cost remains deductible). With the new tax rate of 19.4 percent, house prices fall 17 percent. If households responded by paying down debt and cut the LTV to 0.25, as we fully expect, house prices would fall an estimated 13 percent (15 percent with local government revenue neutrality).

33. See chapter 2 by Alan J. Auerbach in this volume.
34. Hall and Rabushka (1995).
35. Gentry and Hubbard (1995).
36. Work from Inman (1979) suggests that local governments would attempt to recapture a substantial part (although not all) of the revenue lost from declining values.

USA TAX. The USA tax would raise the property tax and own-equity financing costs to their pre-tax costs. Further, a cut in the income tax rate would reduce the value of interest deductibility. With an LTV and γ of 0.4 and an average marginal tax rate of 21.7 percent, the price decline is 20 percent. With the expected sharp rise in borrowing pushing γ to 0.8 and no decline in the income tax rate, the price decline is 10 percent (13 percent with revenue neutrality).

THE FLAT TAX. The flat tax would raise the costs of financing and property taxes to their full pre-tax costs (lower θ and γ to zero). With declines in the interest rate of 0, 1, and 2 percentage points, the respective price declines are 29 percent, 20 percent, and 9 percent. With local government revenue neutrality, the 29 percent decline increases to 34 percent.

EFFECTS WITH DIFFERENT INITIAL CONDITIONS. The response of house prices to a given negative change in the tax treatment of financing and property tax costs of owner-occupied housing depends directly on the initial levels of interest rates and property taxes. The higher these are, the greater will be the percentage decline in house prices.[37] The response also depends on the initial rent-price ratio. The higher the ratio, the smaller the percentage decline in house prices. The dominant determinant of this ratio is the real after-tax interest rate.

Changes in House Prices at the MSA Level

The previous calculations were based on national averaged data. But our analysis suggests that the effects will vary considerably by metropolitan area because the value of the current tax preference is greater in high tax areas and has boosted prices more in such areas. Here we report estimated price effects for sixty-three MSAs based on MSA-specific variable values in 1990. We use the 1990 mortgage rate, average marginal tax rates, the Capozza-Seguin property tax rates, and rent-price ratios after

37. A consideration with the flax tax is its likely effect on the level of interest rates. Recall that this tax is expected to lower the level of interest rates because interest would no longer be taxed or deductible. The higher the initial level of interest rates, the larger will be the decline in rates, which offsets the tendency of the high initial interest rate level to trigger an especially large decline in house prices.

adjustment.[38] The adjustment is based on evidence in Abraham and Hendershott, who suggest that both the Northeast and California were in the beginning stages of unraveling house price bubbles in the early 1990s.[39] More specifically, they estimated that actual prices exceeded equilibrium prices by 30 percent in their three New England cities and by 20 percent in their eleven western cities. With 20 to 30 percent lower initial prices (25 to 40 percent higher R^r/P ratios in equation 2'), the effect of tax reforms on house prices would be dampened by 25 to 40 percent. To limit the possibility that we are overstating that effect, we raise the observed R^r/P ratios by 30 percent in New England and 20 percent in California when doing the price-decline calculations.

We begin with removal of deductions within the context of the current U.S. income tax and then turn to the USA and flat taxes. We conclude with implications for the mortgage industry.

Elimination of Property Tax and Mortgage Interest Deductions

Elimination of the property tax deduction is estimated to lower prices by 5 percent, on average, in the sixty-three MSAs, but the declines range from 2 percent to 13 percent. The seven MSAs with the largest declines, shown in table 5-7 (panel A), are all East Coast cities with high property tax rates as well as low rent-price ratios. All of these MSAs have property tax rates above 2 percent and substantially above the 1.4 percent sample average.[40]

The eleven MSAs with the smallest declines in prices appear in the first column of panel B of table 5-7. These cities are all in the South and have low income tax rates: all except New Orleans and Birmingham have no state income tax, and these two have property tax rates less than half the national average.

A simple example illustrates why the percentage decline is greater in areas with high tax rates and house prices. Say that house prices would be 100 in the absence of a tax preference. With a preference, prices rise by 33 percent in high-tax areas and 20 percent in low-tax areas. Removing the tax preference would then lower house prices by one-quarter in the high-tax areas versus only one-sixth in the low-tax areas.

38. See Capozza and Seguin (1996).
39. Abraham and Hendershott (1994).
40. Only three of the MSAs not listed in column 1 of table 5-7 had property tax rates in 1980 above 2 percent: Detroit, Grand Rapids, and Lansing. Michigan property tax rates have been cut sharply in recent years.

Table 5-7. *Effect on Housing Prices of Eliminating Property Tax and Mortgage Interest Deductions, by Metropolitan Statistical Area*
Percent

	Eliminate property tax deduction	Eliminate mortgage interest and property tax deductions	
MSA		0.4 loan-to-value ratio	0.25 loan-to-value ratio
Panel A: Largest percentage price decline			
Honolulu	−7	−34	−27
Boston	−13	−26	−22
San Jose	−7	−28	−22
Hartford	−10	−26	−21
San Francisco	−7	−28	−22
Washington	−9	−27	−21
Albany	−12	−25	−21
Los Angeles	−6	−25	−19
Providence	−10	−22	−18
Buffalo	−10	−21	−17
Syracuse	−10	−21	−17
Anaheim	−6	−25	−19
Rochester	−10	−22	−18
Philadelphia	−8	−20	−16
Panel B: Smallest percentage price decline			
El Paso	−4	−11	−8
Chattanooga	−3	−12	−9
Tampa	−3	−12	−9
San Antonio	−4	−17	−9
Jacksonville	−3	−12	−9
Fort Lauderdale	−3	−13	−10
Birmingham	−3	−13	−10
Nashville	−4	−14	−10
W. Palm Beach	−3	−14	−10
Orlando	−4	−13	−10
New Orleans	−2	−13	−11
Mean change	−6	−17	−13

Elimination of both the mortgage and property tax deductions cuts house prices by an average of 17 percent, but the drops range from 11 percent to 34 percent (column 2 of table 5-7). The largest price declines are in the same cities as in column 1, although the ranking changes because the importance of the property tax rate is reduced. But households will cushion the negative price impact of removal of the mortgage interest deduction by switching from debt finance to own-equity financing. The results for the fourteen MSAs with the largest declines and the

Table 5-8. *Effect of USA Tax on Housing Prices, by Metropolitan Statistical Area*

MSA	0.4 loan-to-value ratio	0.8 loan-to-value ratio
Panel A: Largest percentage price decline		
Honolulu	−40	−21
San Jose	−34	−18
San Francisco	−31	−13
Washington	−31	−18
Boston	−29	−18
Anaheim	−29	−13
Albany	−29	−17
Rochester	−26	−16
Syracuse	−24	−15
Lansing	−21	−13
Panel B: Smallest percentage price decline		
Fort Lauderdale	−15	−4
Jacksonville	−13	−4
Charleston	−17	−5
Tampa	−14	−6
New Orleans	−16	−6
Miami	−16	−6
Orlando	−16	−7
Chattanooga	−15	−7
San Antonio	−14	−7
Oklahoma City	−16	−7
Knoxville	−16	−7
El Paso	−14	−8
Mean change	−20	−10

eleven with the smallest declines are shown in column 3. The average price decline shrinks from 17 percent to 13 percent.

The Flat Tax and USA Tax

The effects of the USA tax are shown in table 5-8. Two sets of estimates assume either no change in the LTV (remaining at 0.4) or an increase from 0.4 to 0.8. Not surprisingly, the results look much like those for the removal of the property tax and mortgage interest deduction. Without a financing response, the tax preference is less under the USA tax than with removal of the deductions because the 40 percent of value that is debt-financed and would still be given tax preference under the USA tax is less than the 60 percent of equity that would still be given

Table 5-9. *Effect of Flat Tax on Housing Prices, by Metropolitan Statistical Area*[a]

MSA	No interest rate cut	2 percent interest rate cut
Panel A: Largest percentage price decline		
Honolulu	−52	−27
San Jose	−44	−22
San Francisco	−44	−20
Washington	−41	−21
Anaheim	−40	−19
Los Angeles	−40	−14
Boston	−40	−22
Albany	−37	−17
Providence	−34	−13
Rochester	−33	−16
Hartford	−33	−11
Panel B: Smallest percentage price decline		
El Paso	−19	3
San Antonio	−20	0
Chattanooga	−21	−2
Miami	−21	−1
Tampa	−21	−1
Knoxville	−22	0
Memphis	−23	−1
New Orleans	−23	−1
Orlando	−23	−3
Nashville	−23	−2
Fort Lauderdale	−23	−3
Jacksonville	−24	−1
Mean change	−29	−9

a. All cities listed are among the top ten for at least one calculation.

tax preference under an income tax even without the mortgage interest deduction. Thus the mean price decline is greater with the USA tax (20 percent versus 17 percent). However, we believe that both tax changes would induce a behavioral response. Specifically, we estimate that the average LTV would fall to 0.25 if the mortgage interest deduction were repealed and would rise to 0.8 if the USA tax became law. The 75 percent equity that would still receive tax preference with repeal of the deduction would be less than the 80 percent debt receiving tax preference under the USA tax. Thus the mean price decline with the USA tax is less (10 percent versus 13 percent).

The effects of the flat tax are shown in table 5-9, under alternative assumptions regarding interest rate declines. Average price declines when interest rates are unchanged are greater under the flat tax (29 percent) than with removal of the mortgage interest and property tax deduction

(13 percent with the LTV shift) or the USA tax (10 percent) because the flat tax removes the entire tax preference for financing. But the range of price declines under the flat tax is enormous—from 19 to 52 percent with no decline in interest rates, and from 10 to 27 percent if interest rates fall two percentage points. Once again, the high-priced California MSAs and Honolulu are the most adversely affected and the same low-income tax, low-house price southern MSAs are least affected.

Are 25 Percent Real Declines in House Prices Believable?

One reality check on the results is whether price changes as large as our estimates have ever been experienced. Of course, the total removal of an important tax preference may be a larger change in conditions affecting housing prices than any previous disturbance to the housing market, so the historical comparison may be an unduly demanding test.

Jesse Abraham and Patric Hendershott report numerous large changes in real house prices in broad areas of the United States during the past twenty years.[41] Real house prices in both the Midwest and West increased about 20 percent in the late 1970s and then fell substantially in the early 1980s. Real house prices rose over 50 percent in the West and Northeast and 24 percent in the Southeast in the middle and late 1980s. Subsequently, real prices fell about 25 percent.

One could argue that these changes are not relevant because they reflect local, rather than national, shocks. But we do not believe one would want to push that argument too hard. After all, the large real price increases in the middle and late 1980s occurred simultaneously in several areas of the country. Moreover, both these increases and the earlier decreases understate real changes in house prices. When real and nominal interest rates soared in the early 1980s, seller financing became extremely popular. According to the National Association of Realtors survey of home financing transactions, more than one-third of transactions in the early 1980s were seller-financed, and still more involved assuming mortgages with below-market interest rates Because most of these transactions carried interest rates well below market rates, the transaction price substantially overstated the actual market value of houses because it reflected both the house value and the value of the below-market financing. Despite this fact, Joe Peek and James Wilcox estimate that real house prices nationally fell by more than 15 percent between 1979 and 1983.[42]

---

41. Abraham and Hendershott (1994).
42. Peek and Wilcox (1991). Roger Gordon pointed out a general difficulty with mea-

Eliminating a large tax preference will not be costless to the holders of the previously tax-preferenced asset. While a supply response will cushion the decline in structure value, houses do not float in the air. They are located on prime residential land that is very inelastically supplied except in the very long run.

Implications for Mortgage Originators, Securitizers, and Insurers

The effects of major tax change on the mortgage market would be substantial. Removing the mortgage interest deduction would lower the average LTV by just over a third. In combination with a fall in average housing prices of 10 percent, the market for mortgage loans would fall by about 40 percent. The effect on the main secondary market operators, Fannie Mae and Freddie Mac, and the mortgage banking industry would be large. On the other hand, the USA tax could double the average LTV and, even with a 10 percent drop in house prices, would nearly double the size of the mortgage market.

A fall in house prices could significantly increase mortgage defaults, which would have particularly severe effects on private mortgage insurers and the Federal Housing Administration's Mutual Mortgage Insurance Fund. Even if interest rates fell 1 percentage point, we estimate that the flat tax would lower house prices by 20 percent on average and by more than 10 percent in fifty-one of the sixty-three MSAs. Removing the mortgage interest and property tax deductions and enacting the USA tax are likely to lower house prices by about 10 percent on average.

It is hard to know exactly how much such price declines would increase defaults, but the following calculations give some sense of the range. According to the 1989 SCF, 12 percent of mortgage borrowers have LTVs above 80 percent and 6 percent have LTVs over 90 percent. At least these proportions of mortgagees would have negative equity were house prices to decline by 20 and 10 percent, respectively. And these estimates may be low because respondents in the survey tend to overestimate house prices and, therefore, to underestimate LTVs.

Because normal default rates are low—less than 2 percent for conventional mortgages and 5 percent for FHA-insured mortgages—a doubling

---

suring price declines in poor housing markets: potential sellers with the sharpest price declines effectively remove their houses from the market rather than sell them at a low price. The lengthy time-on-market statistics from many markets in the early 1980s support this view.

or tripling of default rates is possible. Given the house price limits on FHA home mortgage insurance and the likelihood of greater percentage declines in higher-price MSAs, the private mortgage insurers would face the largest risks, but even Fannie Mae and Freddie Mac, with their billions of outstanding default-guaranteed, mortgage-backed securities, could face serious losses.

Summary and Conclusion

We have reported estimates of effects on housing prices of three tax reforms: removal of the property tax and mortgage interest deductions and replacement of the current tax system with either a flat tax or the USA tax. All three changes would eliminate the tax preference for property taxes. Elimination of the mortgage interest deduction, the tax preference for debt financing, would lower borrowing. The USA tax would remove the preference for equity financing and increase borrowing. The flat tax would remove the preference for both types of financing. We conclude that the first two of these tax law changes would have large effects on mortgage borrowing and that all would significantly lower house prices. We believe the impact will be on house prices because the existing tax preference has been capitalized into residential land prices.

We expect households to limit the negative effect of tax changes on their after-tax income by choosing the most tax-favored method of finance that remains available. This behavior is important for two reasons: it will mitigate the negative effect of tax changes on house prices, and it will reduce tax revenue and thereby lessen any cut in tax rates that broadening the tax base would otherwise make possible. The mortgage preference under the USA tax could severely erode revenue, particularly in the short run as households rush to raise their LTVs.

The changes in house prices depend on the size of the tax preferences removed and the decline in interest rates the reform causes. Holding interest rates constant, prices would fall the most with the flat tax, as it ends all financing preferences. Prices would fall significantly with repeal of the mortgage interest deduction, a step that would end tax preference on 25 percent of financing after households adjust their LTVs, on average, and with implementation of the USA tax, which would end tax preference for 20 percent of financing. However, the flat tax is likely to lower interest rates, given that interest would no longer be either taxed or deductible. Allowing for a 1 percentage point rate decline, our best estimates of the average price declines are 20 percent with the flat tax, 13 percent with the removal of the deductions, and 10 percent with the USA tax.

The price effects would vary widely across regions. They would be largest in regions with high property taxes—largely the Northeast—and high house prices—largely the Northeast and California. The range of percentage price declines across the sixty-three MSAs associated with the above averages are 8 to 40 (the flat tax), 8 to 27 (removal of the property tax and mortgage interest deductions), and 4 to 21 (the USA tax).

The effects of price declines on households vary by age and income class. For renters who will become owners, there is no effect. Although the after-tax interest rate and property tax rate rise, real house prices fall, so that the total annual cost of owner-occupied housing is roughly unchanged. Removal of the mortgage interest deduction and changing to the USA tax benefit older households relative to younger ones because older households have lower LTVs. On the removal of the deduction, these households lose less of a tax preference. With the USA tax, these households can shield greater amounts of income from taxation by increasing mortgage debt, again because of their low LTVs.

Comment by Douglas Holtz-Eakin

The treatment of owner-occupied housing is perhaps the most vexing tax policy problem. The durability of the deduction for mortgage interest in the face of continuous assault from academics and analysts of all stripes is living testimony to the political and economic stakes. The current wave of reforms, whose broad goal is to tax comprehensively nonhousing and housing consumption, takes direct aim at the tax-preferred treatment. In light of history, there is no reason to expect a quick surrender. Hence, before all else, the authors should be congratulated for entering the combat zone.

The chapter by Dennis R. Capozza, Richard K. Green, and Patric H. Hendershott begins with a general discussion of the role of the mortgage interest deduction. It then turns to the consequences of three potential reforms—removal of the mortgage interest deduction, the USA (unlimited saving allowance) tax of Nunn and Domenici, and the Armey-Shelby flat tax—for debt-equity mix of housing finance, the aggregate change in

I thank Donald Bruce for superb research assistance.

housing and land values, and the distribution of price changes across sixty-three metropolitan areas.

In doing so, the authors make four main points. First, the primary tax advantage to owner-occupied housing is not the mortgage interest deduction but rather the nontaxation of the imputed rent. Instead, the mortgage interest deduction serves to eliminate arbitrage opportunities by equating the after-tax cost of borrowing with the after-tax return on investing. Second, households are likely to be quite sensitive to these relative costs; any reform that disrupts this equality should be expected to result in a substantial shift in the financial underpinnings of the real stock of owner-occupied housing. Concomitantly, the tax revenue to be gained by eliminating the mortgage interest deduction will be limited substantially by the ability to equity-finance homes. As far as the pricing of the housing stock, the authors' main message is that the (very) low elasticity of supply of residential land will preclude large quantity shifts. Instead, declines in asset prices will serve to equilibrate the housing market by capitalizing the value of the tax reform. Finally, a national tax reform will have far from uniform effects as price declines will differ greatly across the metropolitan landscape.

On the whole, I agree with at least the spirit of much of the discussion. Nevertheless, let us revisit some of the issues, beginning with the character of the mortgage interest deduction. The nontaxation of imputed rent has long been recognized as the fundamental tax preference toward owner-occupied housing.[43] In contrast, the deductibility of mortgage interest is simply correct treatment under an income tax. The authors note that it accrues "disproportionately to those with higher incomes and greater incentives to engage in tax arbitrage." But a distributional analysis of the "benefits" of the mortgage interest deduction strikes me as odd. Arbitrage opportunities provided by the mortgage interest deduction are just the flip side of the same coin as the fact that we do not tax equally all capital earnings. It would be equally appropriate, and perhaps more on target, to argue that the benefits of incomplete taxation of capital earnings accrue disproportionately to these groups.

A corollary to this point is that reforms that simply eliminate the mortgage interest deduction do not correspond to any particular "fundamental" tax system. Under an income tax, interest earnings should be taxable; interest costs, deductible. Adopting a consumption-based tax would result in both nontaxation of earnings and nondeductibility of

43. See, for example, the survey provided by Rosen (1985).

interest costs. Eliminating the mortgage interest deduction in isolation is simply an unprincipled money grab. For this reason, the unequal treatment of debt and equity finance is an unappealing aspect of the USA tax; equally undesirable are moves to append a mortgage interest deduction to the flat tax. It is not the authors' fault that not all tax plans are built on sound principles, but analyzing the mortgage interest deduction in isolation does not further the goal of clear thinking about the implications and objectives of tax reforms.

One of the chapter's central themes is that housing finance will respond elastically and quickly to changes in tax incentives. In particular, the authors argue that the tax preferences for mortgage debt in the USA tax would lead to a surge in debt finance. To gauge the potential size of these effects, the authors assume that all owners would raise their mortgage debt to 80 percent of their house value. Of course, this is a deliberately extreme case: perfectly elastic behavior up to a maximum response. As such, it provides a useful upper bound. It does not, however, give the reader much guidance about the most likely response, nor does it explain the sensitivity of the results to the range of possible behaviors.

Thus, despite the fact that I think the spirit is right, it remains useful to push further, to explore the likely responses and their implications. Getting a handle on the implications strikes me as especially important. Despite the authors' concern over the possibility of increased defaults and pressures on housing market financial institutions, the only metric offered by which to evaluate the shifts in financing is the revenue implications. Evaluating tax policy by the revenue effects alone is, in the extreme, a recipe for disaster. Instead, the usual objective is to compare equal-yield policies on the basis of their efficiency costs and equity implications, thus giving policymakers the means to compare the effects of alternative policies.

What have we learned about these efficiency and equity issues? The primary evidence consists of comparisons between the life-cycle profile of loan-to-value ratios in the United States and the corresponding profile in Australia. Since Australia does not have a mortgage interest deduction, the implication is that one may view this situation as the "no-tax" profile, with deviations from it in the United States capturing the behavioral response to the tax system. If so, these behavioral responses are at the heart of the efficiency consequences. But these comparisons are at best suggestive. And even if taken to be correct, one needs to push much further to provide the types of measures (deadweight losses and so on) that typically form the basis for policy evaluation.

In the same way, it seems possible to push further on the equity consequences too. For example, the notion that removal of the mortgage interest deduction would hurt the young and aid the old seems incomplete. To some extent, the age effects strike me as a type of transition effect; in a fully implemented system the new generations would first be young (hurt) and then old (helped). What is the net effect over the lifetime? In general, economists have moved away from strict reliance on single-year distributional analysis in favor of lifetime computations of benefits and costs. The use of a multiyear lens seems especially useful here.

Deadweight losses, behavioral responses, equal-yield tax, and the like are the domain of analysts. The public (and policymakers) care about housing prices. And the prospect of fundamental tax reform has raised the specter of an apocalyptic fall in housing values. A prominent study by DRI suggested that the flat tax would result in an aggregate decline of 15 percent in housing values, for a total loss of $1.7 trillion in housing equity.[44] Read superficially, the authors' results would seem to buttress this view. The authors, ignoring any reform-induced decline in interest rates but incorporating incentives to alter the financing mix, estimate that the aggregate effect of removing the deductions for mortgage interest and property taxes would result in a decline in house values of roughly 13 percent. The USA tax would lead to a fall in values of 10 percent, while the flat tax would generate a whopping 29 percent fall in house values if interest rates are unchanged.

Read a bit closer, the numbers are not quite so scary. The bulk of the calculations are based on 1990 data; the authors indicate that using more recent data (and any real reform will be *quite* recent) gives results for price declines that would be up to 5 percentage points smaller (hence 8 percent for eliminating deductibility and 5 percent for the USA tax) except for the flat tax, where the fall would be 14 percentage points smaller (that is, a decline of 15 percent). Further, recall that the computations embody the logic that the *entire* market response to reform will take the form of declines in residential land and housing values.[45]

<hr />

44. See Martin Sullivan, "Housing and the Flat Tax: Visible Pain, Subtle Benefits," *Tax Notes*, vol. 70, January 22, 1996, pp. 340–45.

45. The absence of a quantity response stands on its head the substantial body of research documenting the deadweight cost of tax subsidies to owner-occupied housing. It is similarly at odds with the view that nontaxation of imputed rent leads to a sectoral misallocation of capital, undercutting a key virtue of consumption-based reform. Ironically, then, the authors' approach to modeling fundamental reform is in itself an argument against the need for reform.

As a qualitative matter, price effects from tax reform should not be surprising. By their very nature, consumption taxes are designed to tax housing services. Since owner-occupied housing is currently tax subsidized, the reform must make residential housing consumption more expensive and reduce the demand for these services (other things equal). Unless the supply of these services is perfectly elastic, the decline in demand will be reflected in part by lower prices.

But the quantitative aspects are a bit trickier. The computations in this chapter hinge on a long-run analysis in which "housing" is produced by using a single input—residential land—that is fixed in supply. Although the authors provide a vigorous analytic and empirical defense of this assumption, other views are possible. To get a sense of the importance of the assumptions, consider the opposite extreme by focusing instead on the transitional dynamics (rather than the long run) and ignoring for the moment the role of land in favor of the impact on reproducible structures (capital).

Specifically, suppose that there are H identical "houses," each of which yields an implicit service-flow (imputed rent) of S/H per year. Let V/H be the market value per house, so V is aggregate housing value. Abstract from financing issues by assuming a single interest rate, i, so mortgage and opportunity cost are given by iV/H, property taxes by $t_p V/H$, and maintenance/depreciation by mV/H.

For purposes of exposition, suppose that there is no tax system in place. The user cost is given by

$$\frac{S/H}{V/H} = \frac{S}{V} = \left\{ i + t_p + m - \frac{\dot{V}}{V} \right\},$$

where the "$\cdot$" denotes a derivative with respect to time. As in the authors' equilibrium, owners would be indifferent between owning the house and renting at an annual rental cost of S/H, or investing in an alternative financial asset. The user-cost can be rearranged to yield the housing-value appreciation necessary to maintain this indifference:

$$\dot{V} = \{ i + t_p + m \} V - S.$$

Houses will appreciate in equilibrium only to compensate owners for the excess of costs over the imputed rent.

On the supply side, let construction of new houses, C, be driven by the ratio of market value (V) to replacement cost (H), with the latter normalized at 1 per house. Thus,

$$C = \dot{H} = C\left(\frac{V}{H}\right)H.$$

In direct analogy to the corporate investment literature, let q be the ratio of market value to replacement cost. We can write the supply side of the residential market as a function of H and q

(1) $$\dot{H} = C(q)H.$$

Similarly, we can rewrite the demand (user-cost) in terms of H and q as well by noting that

$$\dot{q} = \frac{\dot{V}}{H} - q\frac{\dot{H}}{H} = \frac{\dot{V}}{H} - qC(q),$$

yielding:

(2) $$\dot{q} = \{i + t_p + m\}q - \frac{S}{H} - qC(q).$$

Equations 1 and 2 describe the transitional dynamics of the housing market, and may be examined by using the phase-diagram in figure 5-1. The steady state is at H^* and $q^* = 1$ (that is, $V = H$). In itself, the steady state is not very interesting as the long-run price of houses is dictated by the exogenous replacement cost. The transition to the steady state, however, is shown by the saddle path marked with arrows and permits short-run fluctuations in the asset price of houses.

Suppose now that one enacts a consumption tax through use of the flat tax. The key feature of this reform is that the tax on residential housing is imposed solely via the entity-level tax on new construction. Thus the tax is not imposed on existing housing but enters only the computation of the desirability of new houses. Specifically, it raises the "break-even" V from H to $H(1 + \theta)$, where θ is the consumption tax rate (for example, the 17 percent entity-level tax). Thus the long-run value of q rises from $q^* = 1$ to $q' = 1 + \theta$. As shown in figure 5-1 the steady state level of H declines to H'; exactly what one would expect when housing is taxed more heavily (that is, at all). However, the tran-

Figure 5-1. *Housing Market Transitional Dynamics*

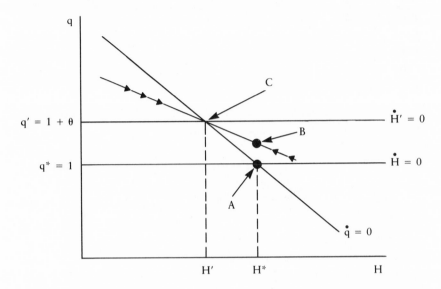

sition to the new steady state takes place in two steps. Instantaneously, the value of *H* is fixed; the market adjusts to the need for making the transition by having *V* (and *q*) jump *up* at the existing housing stock (from A to B). Intuitively, old houses are more valuable because they do not face the consumption tax; people will bid up the price of such houses until they are indifferent between the existing stock and the new, taxed housing. In the aftermath, housing prices evolve to the long-run equilibrium, and the size of the residential sector shrinks as the market evolves toward the new steady state (B to C).

In short, the transition from nontaxation to consumption taxation, combined with the exemption of old housing from the tax base, leads to a short-run *rise* in house values, a result constructed deliberately to contrast with the authors' conclusions. But the example is not empirically irrelevant, as it mimics precisely the situation for any homeowner who is not currently itemizing deductions, a population placed by the authors at roughly 40 percent of homeowners.

Clearly, to the extent that itemizers are deducting interest payments and property taxes, the evolution of housing values must reflect this fact,

$$\dot{V} = \{i(1 - \tau) + t_p(1 - \tau) + m\}V - S,$$

and the analysis could follow as outlined above. The major difference is that removing deductibility applies to both new and old houses. As a result, removing deductibility alone results in a downward shift in the $\dot{q} = 0$ locus in figure 5-1. Thus, in contrast to the example above, removing deductibility results in an immediate fall in housing values and a subsequent transition to a new steady state that has lower quantities of housing and a recovery of housing values to $q = 1$.

The proposed tax reforms combine elements of both changes; only an empirical assessment can clearly lay out the consequences. But to do so requires an explicit analysis of short-run dynamics and incorporating the entity-level taxes present in both the USA tax system and the flat tax.

By design, I have ignored land and shifted the discussion away from the authors' focus. What happens if one expands the exercise to recognize that housing is produced by both land and structures? Handling the transitional dynamics in a setting with both land and structural assets is quite demanding, but we can get some idea of the long-run effects. Suppose, as in the analysis by James Poterba, there is a constant-elasticity demand for housing services (h) that are produced by using a Cobb-Douglas production function from inputs of housing structures (H) and land (L)[46]

$$h = H^\alpha L^{1-\alpha}.$$

The user costs for structures and land, respectively, that satisfy the steady-state asset market equilibrium conditions are

$$R_H = [i(1 - (1 - \beta(1 - \theta))\tau) + (1 - \gamma\tau)t_p + \delta - m - g]Q_H$$

and

$$R_L = [i(1 - (1 - \beta(1 - \theta))\tau) + (1 - \gamma\tau)t_p]Q_L,$$

where β is the loan-to-value ratio, θ is the portion of financing costs that are deductible, τ is the income tax rate, i is the interest rate, γ is the fraction of property tax costs that are deductible, t_p is the property tax rate, δ and m are depreciation and maintenance costs, and g is the capital gain. In each case, R and Q represent prices and quantities, respectively. Note that land is assumed not to depreciate, require maintenance costs, or involve a capital gain.

46. See Poterba (1984).

Taxes affect the user costs of land and structures, hence the demand for each component. Supply of both land and structures is assumed to be a constant-elasticity function of the prices of each input into housing services. Thus in the long run, supply considerations are permitted to influence the net price of housing.

To gain a feel for the magnitude of price changes introduced by tax reform in this setting, I employ the authors' assumptions and a log-linearized version of the model to estimate the effects on the asset prices for land, structures, and the produced good, housing.[47]

To begin, assume that the share of land in housing services is exactly 1.0 and that land is completely inelastic in supply. That is, adopt the authors' assumptions. Simulating the impact of the flat tax under the assumption of fixed interest rates implies that housing (land plus structure) prices fall by roughly 20 percent, similar to the authors' estimates. But this is in part an artifact of the assumptions. For purposes of illustration alone, suppose instead that each factor enters with equal shares into the production function and that structures are supplied with unitary elasticity. (Land remains fixed in supply.) Permitting this richer economic environment indicates that the price of housing falls by a more modest 13 percent.

Of course, even these parameter estimates are not especially realistic. As a modest move toward realism, permit structures to constitute 80 percent of the house value (with land having the remainder). Further, permit the supply of structures to be quite elastic (2.0), an assumption consistent with the partial-equilibrium nature of the paper (that is, the supply of capital to this single sector is quite elastic). Next, allow the elasticity of supply of land to be nonzero (because residential boundaries do change) but extremely limited (0.1). In these circumstances, the flat tax produces a decline of only 7 percent in housing values. Finally, accommodate the authors' observation that roughly 40 percent of homeowners do not itemize their deductions by introducing a weighted average user cost in which only 60 percent itemize (that is, I set $\theta = \gamma = 0.6$). In this setting, the flat tax results in a 4.5 percent decline in housing values.

Not surprisingly, the effects of other reforms are correspondingly more modest under the same scenario. The USA tax (assuming the authors' estimated response in loan-to-value ratios) introduces a 2.5 percent decline; the elimination of mortgage and property tax deductibility leads to a 2 percent falloff in values. Thus, even in the long run, allowing even

47. Details of the numerical simulations are available upon request.

a very small elasticity of supply of land has the potential for substantially altering the quantitative implications of fundamental tax reform.

In the end, these exercises highlight the need for caution about the magnitude and timing of the estimated price effects, effects that will be central to the debate in any such sweeping reform. First, while the authors have done us a service by beginning the process of estimating the impacts of tax reform, much work remains to be done to lay out the sensitivity of the estimates to the underlying conceptual framework.

In particular, the estimates in the chapter are derived on the basis of long-run behavior in a model focusing on residential land alone, an approach consistent with the authors' focus on spatial equilibrium in a stationary setting. But the construction component of housing is an important part of the economy, and the vagaries of the construction industry are testament to the need to accommodate short-run deviations from equilibrium.

In the same spirit, it would also be useful to bring into the analysis an explicit consideration of changes in the rental market as well. A central aspect of the USA tax and flat tax plans is the move to a value-added-style tax at the business level, eliminating the double taxation of corporate income and altering dramatically the tax environment facing landlords. How will rental market adjustments spill over into the residential housing market? In a framework with a fixed supply of residential housing, the only possible answer is a more refined estimate of the price impacts. But the discussion above suggests that a more subtle and complicated set of responses may ensue.

A second major point is that timing issues appear especially important in this context. To a great degree the politics of tax reform *is* the nature of the transition. Who wins and loses this year? Next year? For example, the authors note that under the USA tax the shift to mortgage finance would have "to be offset by high transition tax rates." But a sequence of falling tax rates over a known horizon offers very different incentives for housing sale, purchase, and finance decisions than does a one-time, permanent reform. Without modeling the transition explicitly, it is simply not possible to address short-term incidence and efficiency issues, and hence difficult to inform the political debate.

Finally, and as noted earlier, it would be useful to permit an explicit analysis of the dynamics to enter the distributional analyses as well. Economists have in general moved away from single-year, snapshot distributional analysis in favor of lifetime incidence analyses. In the context of residential housing, with its dramatic life-cycle patterns, it would seem that one should be especially careful in using either the income-distribution effects or the age-distribution effects derived from a cross-section of the population.

The concluding analyses in the chapter are devoted to documenting the regional variations in price effects by using data for sixty-three metropolitan areas. Because these computations share the same conceptual basis as the aggregate analyses, further discussion is largely redundant. It is not surprising that one would find regional variation in the impacts. However, if the assumption is that these derive exclusively from demand shifts, it would be comforting to document a regional correlation between tightness in the residential housing market and the magnitudes of the estimated price effects.

To summarize, the authors are to be congratulated for a detailed analysis of the price impacts of fundamental tax reform, especially the impressive, rich geographic distribution of the estimated impacts on land price. They have set the benchmark by which other studies will be judged. With respect to the qualitative nature of the results, they simply cannot be far wrong; consumption-based reforms by their nature aim directly at residential housing. However, the timing and magnitudes will be crucial to the debate over tax reform, and the central message of this note is simply that even these carefully constructed estimates will not suffice. Instead, it will be essential to uncover the sensitivity of these findings with respect to the particular parameters employed, the nature of the modeling environment, and the degree to which transitional issues are explicitly evaluated.

References

Aaron, Henry J. 1972. *Shelter and Subsidies: Who Benefits from Federal Housing Policies?* Brookings.

Abraham, Jesse M., and Patric H. Hendershott. 1994. "Bubbles in Metropolitan Housing Markets." Working Paper 4774. Cambridge, Mass.: National Bureau of Economic Research (June).

Blackley, Dixie, and James R. Follain. 1996. "In Search of Empirical Evidence That Links Rent and User Cost." *Regional Science and Urban Economics* 26 (June): 404–22.

Bourassa, Steven, and Patric H. Hendershott. 1994. "On the Equity Effects of Taxing Imputed Rent: Evidence from Australia." *Housing Policy Debate* 5 (1): 73–95.

Capozza, Dennis R., and Robert Helsley. 1989. "The Fundamentals of Land Prices and Urban Growth." *Journal of Urban Economics* 26 (November): 295–306.

———. 1990. "The Stochastic City." *Journal of Urban Economics* 28 (September): 187–203.

Capozza, Dennis R., Richard K. Green, and Patric H. Hendershott. 1995. "Taxes, House Prices and Housing Consumption." Ohio State University Working Paper (December).

Capozza, Dennis R., and Gregory Schwann. 1989. "The Asset Approach to Pricing Urban Land: Empirical Evidence." *Journal of the American Real Estate and Urban Economics Association* 17 (Summer): 161–74.

———. 1990. "The Value of Risk in Real Estate Markets." *Journal of Real Estate Finance and Economics* 3 (June): 117–40.

Capozza, Dennis R., and Paul J. Seguin. 1996. "Expectations, Efficiency, and Euphoria in the Housing Market." *Regional Science and Urban Economics* 26 (June): 369–86.

Federal Reserve System, Board of Governors. 1995. "Balance Sheets for the U.S. Economy, 1945–94." Flow of Funds.

Follain, James, R., David C. Ling, and Gary A. McGill. 1993. "The Preferential Income Tax Treatment of Owner-Occupied Housing: Who Really Benefits?" *Housing Policy Debate* 4 (1): 1–24.

Gentry, William M., and R. Glenn Hubbard. 1995. "Distributional Implications of Introducing a Broad-Based Consumption Tax." Paper prepared for Stanford University Tax Conference (December).

Gordon, Roger H., and Joel Slemrod. 1988. "Do We Collect Any Revenue from Taxing Capital Income?" edited by Lawrence H. Summers, 89–130. Cambridge, Mass.: MIT Press and National Bureau of Economic Research.

Green, Richard K., and Michelle J. White. 1996. "Measuring the Benefits of Homeowning: Effects on Children." *Journal of Urban Economics* (forthcoming).

Hall, Robert, and Alvin Rabushka. 1995. *The Flat Tax*, 2d ed. Stanford, Calif.: Hoover Institution Press.

Hendershott, Patric H. 1983. "Government Policy and the Allocation of Capital between Residential and Industrial Uses." *Financial Analysts Journal* 39 (July–August): 37–43.

———. 1987. "Tax Changes and Capital Allocation in the 1980s." In *The Effects of Taxation on Capital Formation*, edited by Martin Feldstein, 259–90. University of Chicago Press.

Hendershott, Patric H., and Sheng Cheng Hu. 1981. "Inflation and Extraordinary Returns on Owner-Occupied Housing: Some Implications for Capital Allocation and Productivity Growth." *Journal of Macroeconomics* 3 (Spring): 177–203.

Inman, Robert P. 1979. "The Fiscal Performance of Local Governments: An Interpretive Review." In *Current Issues in Urban Economics*, edited by Peter Mieszkowski and Mahlon Straszheim, 270–321. Johns Hopkins University Press.

Jones, Lawrence D. 1993. "The Demand for Home Mortgage Debt." *Journal of Urban Economics* 33 (January): 10–28.

Laidler, David. 1969. "Income Tax Incentives for Owner-Occupied Housing." In *The Taxation of Income from Capital*, edited by Arnold C. Harberger and Martin J. Bailey, 50–76. Brookings.

Mayer, Christopher J., and Tsur Somerville. 1996. "Testing Alternative Paradigms of the Supply of Owner-Occupied Housing." Paper prepared for annual meeting of Allied Social Sciences Association.

Musgrave, John C. 1990. "Fixed Reproducible Tangible Wealth in the United States, 1986–1989." *Survey of Current Business* 70 (August): 99–102 .

Peek, Joe, and James Wilcox. 1991. "The Measurement and Determinants of Single-Family House Prices." *American Real Estate and Urban Economics Association Journal* 19 (Fall): 353–82.

Poterba, James M. 1984. "Tax Subsidies to Owner-Occupied Housing: An Asset-Market Approach." *Quarterly Journal of Economics* 99 (November): 729–52.

Rosen, Harvey S. 1985. "Housing Subsidies: Effects on Housing Decisions, Efficiency, and Equity." In *Handbook of Public Economics*, edited by Alan Auerbach and Martin Feldstein, 375–420. Vol. 1. North-Holland.

Slemrod, Joel. 1990. "The Economic Impact of the Tax Reform Act of 1986." In *Do Taxes Matter? The Impact of the Tax Reform Act of 1986*, edited by Joel Slemrod, 1–12. MIT Press.

Smith, Lawrence B., Kenneth T. Rosen, and George Fallis. 1988. "Recent Developments in Economic Models of Housing Markets." *Journal of Economic Literature* 26 (March): 29–64.

Summers, L. 1983. "The Asset Price Approach to the Analysis of Capital Income Taxation." *Proceedings of the National Tax Association*, 112–20.

Titman, Sheridan. 1982. "The Effects of Anticipated Inflation on Housing Market Equilibrium." *Journal of Finance* 37 (June): 827–42.

CHAPTER 6

The Impact of Fundamental Tax Reform on Nonprofit Organizations

Charles T. Clotfelter and Richard L. Schmalbeck

T O A remarkable degree, the nonprofit sector of the economy is shaped by the tax code, from which it is largely exempt. Although nonprofit organizations are not targets of the tax reform movement, they are nevertheless likely to be profoundly affected by any major changes in the tax system. We assess what effect tax changes now under discussion might have on nonprofit organizations and the charitable contributions that support them.

Overview of the Nonprofit Sector and Charitable Giving

The nonprofit sector is a vast and heterogeneous collection of religious groups, schools, hospitals, associations, and other nongovernmental organizations that fulfill a host of important functions. They range from the tiniest churches and fraternal associations to giant research universities and international relief agencies. Some exist entirely for the benefit of their members. Others devote themselves exclusively to helping the indigent or homeless. Many operate independently of government. Others are wholly dependent on government funding and act as virtual extensions of government programs. The size and significance of this sector make it impossible to ignore. The United States relies more than most countries on such nongovernmental, nonprofit entities to carry out vital social functions and also provides them more favorable tax treatment.

We are grateful to Gerald Auten and Steven R. Smith for helpful comments and to Eric Crutchfield for sharing unpublished Form 990 data with them.

Table 6-1. *Estimated Number of Tax-Exempt Nonprofit Organizations,*
1990

Thousands

Type of organization	Number
Charitable[a]	
Churches	351
Foundations	40
Other[b]	450
Noncharitable[c]	534
Total	1,375

Sources: Hodgkinson and others (1992, tables 1.1, 1.2; Meckstroth (1993–94, table 1).
a. All 501(c)(3) organizations.
b. Includes, for example, colleges, universities, hospitals, arts and cultural organizations, and social service charities. Hodgkinson and others (1992, table 1.2) shows a total of 490,000 501(c)(3) organizations. Subtracting foundations yields this total; because churches are not required to file for 501(c)(3) status, we assume this total includes no churches.
c. 501(c)(4) and other nonprofit organizations exempt from federal income tax. Includes, for example, civic leagues, labor organizations, social and recreational clubs, and fraternal organizations.

The nonprofit sector in the U.S. defies precise measurement. Reporting requirements are not universal and vary in frequency and detail, depending on the type of organization.[1] However, reasonable estimates of the number of organizations exist, as do partial reports of their revenues. Nearly 1.4 million nonprofit organizations were operating in 1990 (table 6-1).

The total revenue of a small subset of these organizations exceeded $600 billion in 1991 (table 6-2), accounting for roughly one-tenth of the gross domestic product. This figure, though large, almost certainly understates the economic importance of these organizations, as they receive the services of numerous volunteers, the value of which is not included in table 6-2. In contrast, governments and private businesses receive comparatively little volunteer labor. Some nonprofit enterprises—referred to here as "charitable" organizations—are eligible to receive deductible contributions, while others are not. Charities—including

---

1. Generally, exempt organizations must apply for exempt status and file annual financial returns of varying detail, depending on the size and other characteristics of the organization. Churches and most other religious organizations are exempt from these requirements. Organizations that normally receive less than $25,000 of revenue each year are exempt from the annual reporting requirement. In addition, many organizations lawfully operate as exempt organizations while their applications for recognition of that status are pending with the Internal Revenue Service. Finally, many exempt organizations are for all practical purposes defunct, but have failed to formally terminate their exempt status. Because annual reporting is not universal, this situation can continue indefinitely.

Table 6-2. *Revenues of Large Nonprofit Organizations, 1991*[a]

Type of organization	Number	Revenue (millions of dollars)
Charitable	189,885	515,716
Private foundations	40,341	24,610
Public charities	149,544	491,106
Other[b]	100,089	124,320
Total	289,974	640,036

Sources: Hilgert (1995, figures B, J); SOI Data Release (1995, table 1).

a. Because the sources base their estimates on samples of Form 990 reporting, the figures do not include data for most churches or religious organizations, nor do they include data for organizations that normally receive revenue of less than $25,000 a year.

b. Organizations covered by paragraphs 501(c)(4) through 501(c)(9), including, for example, civic leagues, labor organizations, social and recreational clubs, and fraternal organizations.

churches, private universities, cultural organizations, and nonprofit hospitals—represent more than 65 percent of nonprofit organizations and receive more than 80 percent of total revenues. However, the noncharitable nonprofit sector—which includes social clubs, labor unions, and civic and business leagues—is also large. All nonprofit organizations are currently exempt from income taxation and have reason to be concerned about reforms that may affect their tax-exempt status. Charities will also be concerned about proposals that may affect their contributions.

Although churches and other religious organizations enjoy a special status under the First Amendment to our Constitution, which effectively insulates them from taxation, Congress has subjected private foundations to special restrictions and scrutiny to curb their use for tax avoidance.[2] More than 90 percent of private foundations are "nonoperating" foundations that act merely as conduits of funds from donors to ultimate beneficiaries.[3] Having little or no operating income, they may be relatively unaffected by transactions taxes that would be burdensome to an organization with substantial program service revenue, such as admission charges, tuition, or other fees.

The charitable sector as a whole relies on contributions for little more than 10 percent of its revenue (table 6-3). The importance of contribu-

2. For example, private foundations must pay a 2 percent excise tax on their investment income and distribute at least 5 percent of their net assets each year. They are also subject to greater scrutiny, particularly with respect to possible self-dealing. Their donors are subject to lower caps on the proportion of their income that may be deducted for gifts to the private foundation in any year than are donors to other charitable organizations, and they may lose the advantages of full-market-value deductions for gifts of appreciated property.

3. Meckstroth (1993–94, table 1, p. 60).

Table 6-3. *Sources of Revenue of Charitable Organizations, by Subsector, 1992*[a]

Billions of dollars

Category	Total revenue	Contributions	Government grants	Program service	Other[b]
Cultural	11.8	4.3	1.6	3.0	2.8
Education and research	109.1	15.5	14.8	62.3	16.4
Hospitals and health	289.9	9.1	6.8	268.3	14.6
Social service[c]	76.9	20.8	16.8	29.7	9.6
Other and unclassified[d]	25.5	2.9	1.4	11.1	10.1
Total	522.2	52.7	41.5	374.4	53.6

Source: Unpublished data from Form 990 filings by section 501(c)(3) organizations.

a. Filing Form 990 is not required of churches and other religious organizations, public schools and universities, and organizations normally having revenues of less than $25,000 a year. Figures do not necesarily sum to totals due to rounding.

b. Includes dues, investment income, and net income from sales.

c. Includes organizations concerned with environment, animals, crime and legal issues, employment, food and nutrition, housing, public safety and disaster preparedness, recreation and sports, youth development, human services, international affairs, civil rights, and community improvement.

d. Includes religion-related, mutual/membership benefit, and unidentified organizations.

tions varies widely among types of organizations, however. Contributions amount to less than 3 percent of the revenue of hospitals and other health organizations, but represent nearly 37 percent of the revenue of cultural organizations. Organizations that depend heavily on program service revenue may be somewhat affected by tax changes that reduce contributions, but they are more concerned about increases in transaction taxes. Of course, even these categories conceal important differences within each category. For example, cultural organizations include both nonprofit radio stations that are wholly dependent on contributions and cinema societies whose box office receipts provide all their revenue.

Charitable organizations also differ from one another in their dependence on donors in various income classes. High-income donors are more likely to itemize deductions than are low-income donors. Some proposals would primarily dampen the contribution incentives of high-income itemizers but have little or no effect on moderate-income nonitemizers. Unfortunately, little up-to-date information exists on the characteristics of donors by categories of recipients. We report some estimates below, but this area is one in which further research is surely needed.

Charitable contributions come from three sources: living individuals, estates, and corporations. Individuals contributed $105 billion in 1994, far more than the $8.8 billion in charitable bequests and the $6.1 billion in corporate donations.[4] Tax return data are excellent on corporate con-

4. *Giving USA* (1995, p. 12).

tributions and fair on charitable bequests, as most bequests come from the largest estates, which are subject to taxation. We have estimated contributions by nonitemizers by income class (see the appendix). Patterns of giving differ markedly by income level (table 6-4). Average contributions rise with income. Although few in number, high-income taxpayers account for a large share of total contributions (table 6-4, column 11). As a percentage of income, contributions are highest among those in the lowest and highest income classes.[5] The percentage of taxpayers who itemize rises markedly with income, reaching nearly 90 percent in the $75,000 to $100,000 income class and remaining above 90 percent at even higher income levels. Itemizers contribute more than nonitemizers at each income level.

The table also presents estimates of the kinds of organizations supported at various income levels. Contributions to religious organizations constituted over three-fourths of contributions from taxpayers with incomes below $40,000. At the highest income levels, gifts to colleges and universities, hospitals, and arts and cultural organizations account for a much larger share of gifts.[6] The relative impact of tax reform on contributions to religious and nonreligious charitable organizations is likely to depend on how the reforms change the incentives of different income classes to give.

Current Treatment of Exempt Organizations

Nonprofit organizations in the United States qualify for exemption from income taxes under one or more of the several paragraphs of section 501(c) of the Internal Revenue Code. The value of exempt status is considerable but not easily quantified. If they were taxable, many nonprofits could arrange their affairs to produce enough deductible expense to leave little or no taxable income in normal years. After all, "nonprofit" organizations should be expected normally to not generate profits. Even so, nonprofit status relieves qualifying organizations from the burden of closely matching income and expense items, protects them from having to pay tax when they accidentally are "profitable," and allows them to expand by returning to operations profits that would otherwise be taxed.

5. The data on contributions as a share of income for low-income groups are somewhat suspect, as some filers have low incomes because they have earnings offset by business losses.

6. Charles Clotfelter, "Tax Reform and Charitable Giving in 1985," *Tax Notes*, vol. 26, February 4, 1985, p. 485.

Table 6-4. Selected Information on Taxpayers, by Adjusted Gross Income Class, 1992

Adjusted gross income (dollars)[a]	Number of returns (millions) (1)	Average AGI (dollars) (2)	Average giving (dollars) (3)	Giving as percent of AGI (4)	Average giving — Itemizers (dollars) (5)	Average giving — Non-itemizers (dollars) (6)	Estimated percentage of contributions, by type of recipient — Religion (7)	Estimated percentage of contributions, by type of recipient — Higher education (8)	Estimated percentage of contributions, by type of recipient — Other (9)	Percentage itemizers (10)	Percentage of all contributions (11)
5,000–10,000	14.87	7,505	327	4.4	689	311	72.4	1.4	26.2	4.1	3.1
10,000–15,000	13.24	12,438	428	3.4	838	397	76.2	0.8	23.0	7.1	4.5
15,000–20,000	11.49	17,413	553	3.2	1,084	475	76.4	0.7	22.9	12.8	5.5
20,000–25,000	9.55	22,411	621	2.8	963	550	75.6	0.7	23.7	17.1	5.9
25,000–30,000	7.59	27,434	752	2.7	1,149	603	74.3	0.8	24.9	27.3	5.7
30,000–40,000	12.32	34,765	914	2.6	1,281	696	72.1	0.9	27.0	37.4	11.8
40,000–50,000	9.01	44,746	1,107	2.5	1,333	818	68.5	1.1	30.3	56.1	11.1
50,000–75,000	11.80	60,381	1,496	2.5	1,660	1,010	62.4	1.5	36.1	74.8	19.6
75,000–100,000	3.99	85,410	2,139	2.5	2,229	1,341	52.6	2.3	45.1	89.8	9.4
100,000–200,000	2.81	131,066	3,303	2.5	3,375	2,001	37.8	4.0	58.2	94.7	10.1
200,000–500,000	0.75	292,900	7,147	2.4	7,323	4,418	15.2	11.2	73.6	93.9	6.0
500,000–1,000,000	0.14	675,591	17,301	2.6	17,811	10,604	6.1	23.1	70.8	92.9	2.6
1,000,000 or more	0.07	2,631,348	81,122	3.1	84,672	33,811	6.3	20.5	73.3	93.0	4.9

Sources: U.S. Internal Revenue Service (1995); and authors' calculations. Details underlying the calculations are given in the appendix.

a. Categories exclude upper-bound amount.

Nonprofit organizations are frequently exempt from state and local income, sales, and property taxes. The latter exemptions lower the cost of purchased inputs and physical capital. State and local governments, which have become concerned about erosion of revenue bases, have restricted eligibility for these exemptions, but most organizations exempt from federal taxes continue to be exempt from state and local taxes as well.

Nonprofit entities that engage in business activities unrelated to the purpose that justifies their exemption are subject to a federal tax, at ordinary corporate rates, on their "unrelated business taxable income." The threat of this tax no doubt narrows the activities of nonprofit organizations, but it generates little revenue. Nonprofit organizations paid only $116 million in unrelated business income tax in 1991—less than three-hundredths of 1 percent of their half a trillion dollars in revenue.[7]

Deductibility of Contributions

The largest benefit most charitable organizations enjoy is the ability of their donors to deduct contributions in calculating taxable income. Deductibility reduces the net cost of making charitable donations, which is measured by the current consumption forgone by the donor per dollar of contributions received by the charity. Without deductibility, each dollar of contribution revenue reduces potential donor consumption by a dollar. If contributions are deductible, each dollar of contributions by a taxpayer with a marginal tax rate of m costs that taxpayer $(1 - m)$ dollars of consumption. Gifts of appreciated property cost even less. Subject to some limitations, donors may deduct the full market value of such property, even if they have paid no tax on the appreciation. The price of giving such appreciated property depends on both the marginal tax rate on ordinary income and the tax rate on capital gains income (n), the gain-to-value ratio of the asset (g^*), and what otherwise would have been done with the asset. If the asset would otherwise have been sold immediately, the consumption cost of donating one dollar of appreciated property is $P = 1 - m - g^* n$. This equation means that a person who donates one dollar of appreciated property saves tax that would otherwise have been paid on the capital gain and also enjoys a reduction of taxes otherwise due on other income.

7. Riley (1995, figure C, p. 39, and table 2).

The corporation income tax and the estate and gift tax allow similar deductions. The double taxation of corporate earnings means that both the marginal corporate tax rate and the individual's marginal personal tax rate affect the reduction in consumption from a corporation's contributions. If corporate contributions have no effect on profits or compensation, a dollar of corporate contributions has a price in terms of forgone consumption of immediate dividends equal to $(1 - t)(1 - m)$, where t is the marginal corporate tax rate.

The charitable deduction also reduces the amount of noncharitable bequests that must be given up per dollar of charitable bequests. The price of testamentary gifts is $1 - e$, where e is the marginal tax rate on a decedent's estate. The estate tax also encourages contributions by living donors, because such contributions not only reduce the size of the estate but also generate current income tax deductions. Because of this double effect, a gift of cash by a donor in the last year of that person's life has a tax price of $(1 - m - e + em)$.[8] Thus elimination of the estate tax would reduce incentives for lifetime giving as well as charitable bequests.

Nonprofit organizations, particularly in the charitable sector, make extensive use of volunteer labor. Volunteer labor causes neither imputed taxable income for the volunteer nor a deduction for the contribution of time and effort.[9]

Below-Market-Rate Financing

Charitable organizations may have up to $150 million of "qualified 501(c)(3) bonds" outstanding at any time. The $150 million cap applies collectively to affiliated organizations, but not to hospitals.[10] Not all charitable organizations are equally able to sell bonds. Smaller organizations are likely to find underwriting costs prohibitive, or they may lack creditworthiness. Furthermore, the general limitations on arbitrage bonds apply to these offerings.[11] For that reason, they are usually appro-

---

8. A donation of $1 saves m in the personal income tax, reducing the taxable estate by $(1 - m)$, which in turn reduces the estate tax by $e(1 - m)$. All told, the tax saving is $m + e(1 - m) = m + e - em$.

9. Volunteers are allowed to deduct as a charitable contribution expenses—such as automobile mileage—incurred in providing services to a charitable organization.

10. Internal Revenue Code, section 145.

11. Generally speaking, "arbitrage bonds" under Internal Revenue Code, section 103, are bonds whose proceeds are invested in taxable securities.

priate only for large investments in tangible assets, which not every organization needs. The license to issue such bonds can be quite valuable for large universities and nonprofit hospitals, which typically rely heavily on tax-exempt bonds to finance capital improvements, especially buildings. Yield spreads between tax-exempt bonds and comparable nonexempt bonds vary widely over time, depending on the relative supplies of the respective bonds, the marginal tax rates of investors, and the general levels of nominal interest rates. The interest rate spread between exempt and comparable nonexempt bonds has run between one and one-half and two percentage points in recent years.[12] This would have been sufficient to save more than $2 million annually for an organization that had its maximum of $150 million of bonds outstanding. Because they are not subject to the $150 million cap, hospitals may reap even larger savings.

Behavioral Models of Charitable Giving by Individuals

Because of the overwhelming importance of individual giving, estimates of how taxes affect individual giving are central to assessing the effects of tax reform on charitable giving. Although few people argue that donors give principally because of tax provisions, it is now widely accepted that the income tax does affect the amount that people give, in two ways. Changes in taxes alter net income after taxes. Since giving rises with income, tax cuts raise contributions. In addition, the marginal income tax rate affects the net cost, or price, of giving.

Elasticity Assumptions

Because tax reform schemes often propose either reducing marginal tax rates or eliminating the charitable deduction, the price effect is especially important.[13] Some observers have dismissed such price effects, citing the continual rise in aggregate contributions during the 1980s, when marginal tax rates were cut significantly in upper income classes.[14]

---

12. Compare, for example, the Moody's Aaa corporate bond rate and Standard and Poor's high-grade municipal bond rate. U.S. Council of Economic Advisers (1994, table B-72, p. 352).

13. For a review of this literature, see, for example, Clotfelter (1985) and Andreoni, Gale, and Scholz (1995).

14. For example, see Hall and Rabushka (1995, pp. 99–101).

But many other factors that also affect giving changed over this same period and could explain increased giving. Most economists agree that the tax rate, as well as after-tax income, affects giving, although disagreement remains about the size of these effects. Until recently most studies found that the absolute value of the elasticity of giving with respect to the price of giving was more than 1. These studies also reported a statistically significant income elasticity of somewhat less than 1. We present one set of simulations, deriving from this line of research, based on a price elasticity of − 1.3 and an income elasticity of 0.8.[15] Another line of research finds smaller elasticities. William Randolph argues that the income elasticities implied by conventional models of charitable giving include the effects of transitory as well as permanent income and tax price. He estimates the permanent price elasticity at − 0.51 and the permanent income elasticity at 1.14.[16]

To get a sense of how consistent these models are with recent trends in giving, table 6-5 presents two sets of estimates of how the changes in tax rates in the Tax Reform Act of 1986 would affect giving by five economic classes. One set is based on the larger price elasticity, one on the smaller. The projections refer to the predicted change in giving over two periods: 1985–88 and 1985–89. Three- and four-year spans may be too short to accommodate all desired changes in giving behavior to be realized. To this extent it is not fair to expect long-run parameters to predict patterns of giving exactly. Neither set of elasticity assumptions yields clearly superior predictions. The high-income-elasticity, low-price-elasticity estimates perform better for income classes below $100,000 but worse for the top income classes. These comparisons are far from definitive. They ignore changes in other variables affecting contributions, and they span a period too brief to allow long-run changes in behavior to be reflected in full. Nevertheless, they suggest caution in choosing a preferred set of behavioral parameters. In the simulations reported below, we use the high-income-elasticity, low-price-elasticity assumptions for the baseline estimates and report alternate estimates based on the high-price-elasticity, low-income-elasticity assumption.

15. For summaries of the research underlying these values see Clotfelter (1985, 1990).

16. Randolph (1995). Another recent study, by Andreoni, Gale, and Scholz (1995), implies small values of both parameters, − 0.35 for price and 0.28 for income. The equation in which they estimate the (permanent) income elasticity also has education in it. If this education variable is in fact a better measure of permanent income than the one included in the equation—that is, if there is noise in the permanent income measure—the coefficient of the latter will tend to be biased toward zero. Therefore the income elasticity derived in that study may be biased downward.

Table 6-5. *Actual and Predicted Changes in Itemized Charitable Giving after the 1986 Tax Act, by Sample and Selected Income Group*
Amounts in December 1991 dollars

Sample and adjusted gross income (dollars)[a]	Actual contributions	Mean after-tax income	Mean tax price	Actual percentage change in contibutions	Predicted precentage change in different models[b]	
					Baseline	Larger behavioral response
Panel sample						
20,000–50,000						
1985	1,449	36,188	0.79	. . .	. . .	. . .
1988	1,617	37,566	0.81	0.12	0.03	−0.00
50,000–100,000						
1985	2,311	58,481	0.69	. . .	. . .	. . .
1988	2,483	64,842	0.73	0.07	0.09	0.01
100,000–200,000						
1985	5,278	105,179	0.59	. . .	. . .	. . .
1988	6,043	146,124	0.69	0.14	0.34	0.06
200,000–1,000,000						
1985	23,322	229,717	0.52	. . .	. . .	. . .
1988	19,907	415,999	0.70	−0.15	0.69	0.09
1,000,000 or more						
1985	167,361	1,279,731	0.49	. . .	. . .	. . .
1988	217,779	2,993,607	0.69	0.30	1.21	0.26
Cross-section sample						
20,000–50,000						
1985	1,158	33,070	0.80	. . .	. . .	. . .
1989	1,210	32,626	0.82	0.04	−0.03	−0.04
50,000–100,000						
1985	1,691	57,830	0.69	. . .	. . .	. . .
1989	1,728	58,321	0.73	0.02	−0.02	−0.06
100,000–200,000						
1985	3,406	104,678	0.60	. . .	. . .	. . .
1989	3,310	105,451	0.68	−0.03	−0.05	−0.15
200,000–1,000,000						
1985	13,759	255,702	0.56	. . .	. . .	. . .
1989	8,476	274,348	0.69	−0.38	−0.03	−0.19
1,000,000 or more						
1985	105,129	1,969,845	0.56	. . .	. . .	. . .
1989	82,113	1,964,988	0.69	−0.22	−0.10	−0.24

Source: Data taken from Auten, Cilke, and Randolph (1992, tables 7, 9).
a. Categories exclude upper-bound amounts.
b. Predicted percent change: $(P_2/P_1)^\beta (Y_2/Y_1)^\alpha - 1$ where β is price elasticity and α is income elasticity. The baseline model, based on Randolph (1995), uses an income elasticity of 1.14 and a price elasticity of −0.51. In the alternative model, which is based on conventional estimates, the comparable parameters are 0.80 and −1.3.

Other Issues

Beyond the uncertainty over the price and income elasticities, existing models leave unanswered some questions regarding individual giving.

ESTATE AND GIFT TAXES. The estate and gift tax affects giving during life because such giving reduces taxable income in the personal income tax as well as the size of the taxable estate at death. However, there has been virtually no empirical modeling on how the estate and gift tax affects lifetime giving. Only Gerald Auten and David Joulfaian address this issue, estimating models for parents that suggest that higher estate taxes are indeed associated with higher lifetime contributions. Their model implies that the elimination of bequest taxes would reduce lifetime giving of parents by 12 percent.[17]

SAVING VERSUS GIVING. Empirical work is also lacking on the interconnection among contributions, current consumption, and future consumption. Conventional analysis of tax incentives for charitable giving focuses on the price of giving in terms of forgone *current* consumption. But taxpayers may also save for some future use. Taxation of income may affect the trade-off between giving and current consumption differently from that between giving and future use.[18] Because it ignores this complication, current analysis may be a poor guide to the effects on charitable giving of an unlimited savings deduction, which changes the trade-off between current consumption and saving for future consumption, as well as between giving and current consumption.

PRICE EFFECTS. Some tax proposals would reduce the relative price of goods and services in the charitable sector. A value-added tax might exempt such goods. No definitive evidence exists on whether the effect of such an exemption would be larger, smaller, or similar to the effect on giving of a change in the contributions deduction that had a similar effect on the relative price of charitable goods and services.

17. Auten and Joulfaian (1996, p. 64).
18. Of course, this generalization is subject to many exceptions under current law, including, for example, contributions to individual retirement accounts, cash or deferred arrangements, Keogh plans, and the like.

How Structural Tax Reform Would Affect Nonprofit Organizations

We discuss four tax reform proposals: a business-transactions tax, such as a value-added or retail sales tax; a consumed-income tax, with a general deduction for net savings; a "flat tax" in which wages are taxed at the individual level; and an income tax system with flat rates in all but the upper income ranges, fewer deductions, and none at all for charitable contributions. We are able to apply conventional empirical models of giving to all but the first of these proposals.

A business-transactions tax is levied on sales of goods and services rather than on people, who are taxed by the income tax. The tax can be confined to retail sales, as proposed by Senator Richard Lugar (Republican of Indiana) or levied on value added at each stage of production (a value-added tax), such as Representative Sam Gibbons (Democrat of Florida) has proposed as the primary federal revenue source. Senators Sam Nunn (Democrat of Georgia) and Pete Domenici (Republican of New Mexico), in their USA (unlimited savings allowance) tax, have proposed a business transfer tax (BTT) to function in tandem with individual income taxes.

The individual tax in the Nunn-Domenici plan is a consumed-income tax. The flat tax consists of a cash-flow tax on business, levied on value added less wages and pension contributions, and a tax on employees levied against wages less personal exemptions and a standard deduction. The flat tax proposed by House Majority Leader Dick Armey (Republican of Texas) and Senator Richard C. Shelby (Republican of Alabama) allows a standard deduction plus dependency allowances that would total $31,400 for a family of four. The permanent rates would be 17 percent on both businesses and individuals. This proposal would repeal the federal estate and gifts taxes and personal and business deductions for charitable contributions. Other versions of the flat tax would not repeal the federal estate and gift taxes and would allow deduction of some charitable contributions.

Representative Richard A. Gephardt (Democrat of Missouri) has proposed to eliminate all deductions (including those for charitable contributions) except home mortgage interest and to include fringe benefits in gross income. He would apply the added revenue from these provisions to reduce the rate on taxable incomes below $40,200 to 10 percent. Rates of 20 percent through 34 percent would apply to higher incomes.

Exempt Status Issues

All tax proposals discussed here could exempt nonprofit entities, and most do so.[19] They would continue the current tax on unrelated business income.[20]

BUSINESS TRANSFER TAX. Exemption from business transfer taxes can be quite problematic, depending on the precise form of the tax. Some definitions of the tax base would not exempt all activities of nonprofit entities.[21] Because they wish to use the BTT as the sole or primary federal revenue source, exemptions threaten to raise excessively the rate required to sustain revenues.

A comprehensive transactions tax that provides no exemption presents nonprofit organizations with something of a worst-case scenario. Such payments as university tuition, hospital bills, and museum admissions would generate significant tax liability, raising the effective price and curtailing the amounts demanded of such services. Churches would probably remain exempt. Organizations that do not directly conduct charitable activities, such as most private foundations, would not be directly burdened by the tax but would find that their gifts bought less than before, because of the burdens imposed on operating charitable organizations. Other, more difficult questions arise when a nonprofit organization provides a service without explicit charge to the users. For example, if neighbors form an organization that collects contributions and uses them to construct a swimming pool that is available to members without explicit use charges, should the flow of services be subject to

19. Many of the proposals, especially those of the flat-tax variety, are extremely skeletal outlines, rather than the detailed draft legislation they will no doubt become if they are subject to serious committee consideration. For example, the proposal of Senator Arlen Specter (Republican of Pennsylvania), S. 488, is printed on a single page in the Congressional Record (S. 3422, March 2, 1995). It contains no provisions explicitly exempting nonprofit organizations; however, it also does not repeal the provisions of the current section 501(c) that provide exempt status. It may be helpful in this regard to note that Hall and Rabushka declare that nonprofit organizations would continue to be exempt from the business tax. Hall and Rabushka (1995, p. 126.)

20. See, for example, paragraph 301 of the USA tax (S.722). Again, this generalization only holds for the more detailed plans. Any bill that ultimately emerges from Congress would probably retain the unrelated business tax concept as well. This provision is extremely popular among owners of small businesses, who fear that without it they would face unfair competition.

21. See, for example, Congressional Budget Office (1995, table 5-3, p. 394).

tax? What if instead the organization operated a soup kitchen to provide meals to the poor?

If Congress wished to exempt all or some nonprofit corporations from the BTT, it could do so, but the mechanism would vary depending on the form of the tax. Under a national sales tax, a simple exemption of sales by nonprofit entities would relieve them from its burdens. Relief for nonprofit entities under a value-added tax is a good deal more complex. Simple exemption is not enough, because the VAT would fall on the services of nonprofit entities to the extent that they used commodities purchased from taxable companies.[22] Exempting both sales and purchases of nonprofits complicates administration, as suppliers would need to verify the status of the nonprofit organization—something they would not otherwise need to do. More important, if the tax is a credit-method VAT,[23] the suppliers need at least partial payment of a VAT by their buyers to offset the VAT they will have paid on their own inputs.[24] Requiring payment of the tax on inputs but allowing nonprofit organizations to obtain refunds on all of their taxable purchases achieves the goal of exemption, but it also increases administrative and compliance burdens by forcing nonprofits to pay taxes, keep records, file returns, and verify returns. In addition, it results in possibly substantial government refund payments to private entities.[25]

CONSUMED-INCOME TAX. A consumed-income tax could simply replace the current individual income tax without significant changes in other parts of the Internal Revenue Code. That approach would have

22. It is not absolutely clear that this is a problem; after all, nonprofit organizations may bear part of the burden of the corporate income taxes paid by their suppliers under the present system. The assumption seems to be, however, that the direct assessment of a VAT permits greater and more reliable shifting to customers, including previously exempt customers.

23. Under a credit-method VAT, each business computes a tentative tax on its total sales but then subtracts a credit based on its purchases, so that the net tax represents an assessment only on the increase in value produced by that business. A subtraction-method VAT allows a deduction for purchases from gross sales and then applies the VAT rate to that net amount. For more detailed descriptions, see McLure (1987).

24. For example, if a hospital spent $700 on a particular input and the supplier itself spent $300 on its inputs, it will have paid a tax on the $300 and will effectively reimburse itself by reporting a $700 sale, collecting a tax on that gross amount but then taking a credit for 3/7ths of that amount for the tax it paid on inputs. If it collects no VAT, it loses the wherewithal to recoup its prior VAT payments. This example is drawn from similar ones in McLure (1987, pp. 71–79).

25. McLure (1987, pp. 140–42).

little effect on the accessibility or value of exempt status for nonprofit organizations. Section 501 of the present code could be kept intact, and those provisions would protect qualifying nonprofit organizations from exposure to the corporate income tax. However, the most prominent consumed-income tax proposal—the USA tax—contains as one of its important features a subtraction-method VAT. That bill would continue the exemption for most organizations currently exempt under section 501(c)(3) but would end exemptions for labor unions, social welfare organizations, social clubs, and other organizations covered by other paragraphs of section 501(c). Organizations that lose exempt status and have taxable gross profit would be adversely affected. The USA tax would also reduce the value of exempt status for nonprofit entities if the business tax falls on them.

FLAT TAX. Reform plans can exempt nonprofit organizations from the business portion of the flat tax. The Armey-Shelby proposal does so.[26] As with the BTT, nonprofit entities would probably bear some of the business tax burden indirectly, because prices of their purchases from taxable businesses are likely to rise to cover the business tax those vendors face.

MODIFIED INCOME TAX. The federal tax system has long exempted a broad range of nonprofit organizations, and there is no indication in the Gephardt proposal of any intention to repeal any part of the current exemption rules regarding nonprofit organizations.

Individual Contributions

The various tax reform proposals described in this paper are likely to have both price and income effects, along the lines set forth above.

BUSINESS-TRANSACTIONS TAX. No contribution deduction is feasible if a transactions tax is the primary revenue source. The price of giving a dollar to a charitable organization, in terms of forgone consumption opportunity, would still be less than 1. A 25 percent tax on all consumption that exempts expenditures by charitable nonprofits would raise the cost of all consumption while leaving unchanged the cost of financing

---

26. Paragraph 102 of that bill, H.R. 2060 (paragraph 11(c)(3) of the amended code).

charitable activities. Since 80 cents of consumption would generate a tax of 20 cents, the consumption cost of giving $1 would be 80 cents, for a price of 0.8.[27]

CONSUMED-INCOME TAX. A savings deduction need not affect the rules regarding charitable contributions deductions, and, indeed, the USA tax proposal leaves those provisions intact. It would also employ a graduated rate structure not unlike the current structure,[28] and therefore might not seem to alter significantly the price of giving compared with the current income tax. However, the USA tax also would reduce the price of future consumption as measured by the current consumption that must be forgone. This consequence creates some uncertainty about the actual price of giving that taxpayers would face under the USA tax.

The USA tax would continue to permit deductions for the full market value of property, even appreciated property. But this provision raises a serious issue: investment assets purchased after the USA tax is in effect will have a zero tax basis. Allowing any deduction at all for the contribution of such property would produce a double deduction—once when the funds to buy the asset were saved, and a second time when the asset was contributed to a charitable organization.

FLAT TAX. Proponents of the flat tax are not of one mind on whether to eliminate the deduction for charitable contributions. The central ideas behind these proposals—lowering rates and simplifying compliance burdens—militate against such deductions. The Armey-Shelby plan would eliminate such deductions, but the plan proposed by Senator Arlen

27. In general, the price of charitable giving in the presence of a transactions tax of rate t with an exemption for charitable activities is $1/(1 + t)$, as noted by U.S. Congress (1996, p. 80). This line of reasoning implies equivalence between exemption from tax of the charitable entity (under a transactions tax system) and deduction of contributions (under an individual income tax system). This inference involves assumptions that have not been empirically tested. For example, it assumes that the consumption tax will be passed through fully to consumers. We do not rely on this argument in performing any simulations.

28. The top marginal rate of 39.6 percent under the current tax, for example, appears very close to the top rate under the USA tax of 40 percent, though the latter applies at much lower income levels than the former. The current tax rates do not reach 39.6 percent until taxable income exceeds $250,000. The USA top rate applies by its terms to income on a joint return in excess of $24,000; however, because there is a credit for the employee's share of social security taxes on the first $62,700 of wages (for 1996), the actual rate for taxpayers who have only earned income of less than $62,700 would not exceed 32.35 percent.

Specter would allow up to $2,500 per return in deductions for cash contributions to charities.

Elimination of the deduction would increase the price of giving to 1. Gifts of the roughly 70 percent of taxpayers who do not itemize their deductions would presumably be unaffected. Since itemization rises with income and lower-bracket taxpayers tend to favor religious organizations in making charitable contributions, these plans would erode support of religious organizations less than support of organizations traditionally favored by higher-bracket taxpayers.[29]

MODIFIED INCOME TAX. The Gephardt plan would lower marginal rates somewhat and eliminate most deductions, including charitable contributions. The latter change effectively raises the price of giving to unity, which would produce a full-bore price effect. There would also be modest income effects, variously positive and negative, as the rates shifted slightly within the existing tax brackets.

Simulations of Effects of Reform

We now turn to quantitative estimates of the effects of tax reform on individual gifts by living donors, corporate contributions, and testamentary gifts.

Individual Giving

Table 6-6 summarizes the simulations for individual contributors. The simulations employ two sets of parameters, reflecting the range of esti-

---

29. The Specter plan would preserve deductibility of up to $2,500 in cash contributions. This plan is unlikely to ameliorate significantly the unfavorable effects of the flat tax on charitable organizations favored by the wealthy. The maximum deduction is well below the amounts typically contributed by high-bracket taxpayers. In 1993 the roughly 4 million taxpayers who reported adjusted gross incomes above $100,000 took deductions for charitable contributions of nearly $25 billion—about $6,000 per return. Cruciano (1995, p. 26). On the other hand, the Specter plan would extend charitable contribution deduction to all taxpayers, including those who currently do not itemize deductions. As such, it would lower the cost of giving for low- and moderate-income taxpayers, few of whom currently itemize.

Table 6-6. *Calculations of Tax Revenue and Contributions under Different Tax Plans and Behavioral Assumptions, 1996*[a]
Dollars unless otherwise indicated

Behavioral assumption and tax regime	Total	Percentage change from baseline	Type of recipient			High-income taxpayers[b]	
			Religion	Higher education	Other	Total	Percent of total
Estimated actual values under current law, indexed	115.8	. . .	66.7	4.2	44.9	26.5	22.9
Calculated hypothetical values							
Baseline behavioral assumption[c]							
Armey-Shelby	104.5	−10	60.6	3.9	40.2	23.8	22.8
Gephardt	103.8	−10	62.0	3.3	38.6	20.2	19.5
USA	128.0	11	75.4	4.3	48.3	26.2	20.5
Larger behavioral response[d]							
Armey-Shelby	90.1	−22	54.3	2.9	32.8	16.9	18.8
Gephardt	89.9	−22	55.2	2.6	32.1	15.0	16.7
USA	151.9	31	90.4	4.9	56.7	29.3	19.3

Source: Authors' calculations.

a. Calculations are based on 1992 figures, adjusted for forecasted growth in per capita income (18 percent) and number of taxpayers (5 percent). Actual contributions are estimated 1992 figures, expressed in 1996 dollars.

b. Taxpayers with incomes of $100,000 or more in 1992 dollars.

c. Price elasticity of −0.51; income elasticity of 1.14.

c. Price elasticity of −1.3; income elasticity of 0.8.

mates produced in empirical studies. Both sets embody a price effect arising from the deductibility of contributions and an income effect based on after-tax income. We do not allow for effects of the estate and gift tax, other than its impact on tax liability and net income, or for the deductibility of saving. We simulate effects on individual giving by both itemizers and nonitemizers and calculate the distribution of contributions under different hypothetical tax regimes, all for 1996. In addition, we estimate the distribution of these contributions among three broad categories of recipient organizations (see appendix for additional details).

The first row of table 6-6 shows the baseline estimate of contributions in 1996, based on the actual 1992 levels, inflated by the consumer price index to 1996 levels. The assumed distribution of gifts by type of recipient is based on data in table 6-4. Two-thirds of individual contributions of $116 billion go to religious organizations. Institutions of higher education are estimated to receive about $4 billion from living donors. High-income taxpayers (defined as those with incomes over $100,000 in 1992), who represented 3.9 percent of all taxpayers with incomes over $5,000, accounted for an estimated 22.9 percent of total giving, slightly less than their 23.6 percent share of adjusted gross income.[30]

The remainder of the table shows the results of applying the two sets of behavioral parameters to the changes in income and price of giving implied by three proposals. For each proposal, we calculated for each taxpayer group (arranged by filing and itemization status) at each income level the taxes, after-tax income, tax rates, and price of giving that would apply. The tax rates were adjusted so that each proposal would raise the same revenue as the 1996 actual tax law. We then applied elasticities from a behavioral model of charitable giving to estimate the long-run level of contributions under the various tax regimes.[31]

The baseline calculations imply a 10 percent reduction in total giving by individuals under both the Armey-Shelby and Gephardt proposals, because both eliminate the charitable deduction. The more progressive Gephardt proposal reduces after-tax income of the affluent, and the Armey-Shelby plan increases it. For that reason, the Gephardt plan reduces giving to religious organizations slightly less and giving to higher education and other charities slightly more than the Armey-Shelby plan does. By contrast, the USA tax, featuring a charitable deduction for all taxpayers and increased marginal rates for many, would increase giving by an estimated 11 percent.

The larger price elasticity of the alternative model accentuates all effects. The Armey-Shelby and Gephardt plans cut giving by an estimated 22 percent while the USA tax increases giving by more than 30 percent. To reiterate, these calculations should be treated as no more than illustrations of the sorts of magnitudes one would expect in comparing one tax regime with another in the long run and assuming that nothing but the tax regime changed. As expected, proposals that eliminate the charitable deduction are likely to cause contributions to be less than they otherwise would have been.

In addition, some of the flat-tax bills—including the Armey-Shelby proposal—would repeal the entire estate and gift tax, and, with it, the

---

30. Because their average adjusted gross income was negative, taxpayers whose incomes are less than $5,000 in 1992 are excluded from these calculations.

31. We applied the assumed income elasticity a and price elasticity b for the model being used. Where G_1 is a taxpayer's actual contributions, Y_1 and P_1 are the taxpayer's after-tax income and tax price under the existing tax law and Y_2 and P_2 are the corresponding values under an alternative plan. The calculated hypothetical level of contributions under the alternative plan, other things being equal, is: $G_2{}^* = G_1(Y_2/Y_1)^a (P_2/P_1)^b$. The two parts of the remainder of the table correspond to the two sets of behavioral parameters used in the calculations. Details of the tax calculation are given in the appendix.

tax incentive to leave bequests to charitable organizations.[32] Although information on testamentary gifts is sparse, charitable organizations that high-bracket taxpayers favor—colleges, universities, hospitals, and cultural organizations—are probably also principal beneficiaries of charitable bequests and corporate gifts. In the case of testamentary gifts, this inference is plausible because such gifts come from the estates of individuals who generally had been high-bracket taxpayers. In the case of corporations, virtually no contributions are given to religious organizations; instead, the bulk of corporate gifts go to education, health and welfare, civic, and cultural organizations.[33]

Corporate Contributions

Most of the proposals—including the USA tax, the various flat taxes, and several of the VAT proposals—would eliminate deductions for corporate gifts. As is the case for individuals, the deduction for charitable contributions under the corporate income tax reduces the corporation's net-of-tax cost of making charitable gifts.[34] Models of corporate charitable giving focus on the effect of the net-of-tax price of contributions and after-tax net income. Two studies suggest that the price elasticity ranges from -0.6 to -0.4 and the net income elasticity is about 0.5.[35] These models suggest that repealing either the charitable deduction or the corporate tax would reduce corporate giving. We believe that these models should be used cautiously in assessing the effect of eliminating the charitable deduction for corporations. These models are estimated for a regime in which both contributions and "ordinary and necessary" business expenses are deductible. It is not clear that these elasticities would apply to a situation in which contributions lose their deductibility while other expenses do not. Some expenditures currently deducted as charitable contributions could qualify as business deductions for adver-

---

32. See paragraph 106 of H.R. 2060. Paragraph 106 of S.1038, the flat-tax bill introduced by Senator Jesse Helms, would also repeal the estate and gift taxes; Senator Specter's plan, however, would apparently retain these taxes.

33. See, for example, Clotfelter (1985, p. 181).

34. Although the mechanisms governing corporate contributions are not well understood, more than one model of corporate behavior suggests reasons why the existence of the deduction might lead corporations to contribute more than they would in the absence of the deduction. See Clotfelter (1985, chap. 5) for a discussion of models of corporate giving.

35. Carroll and Joulfaian (1995); Clotfelter (1985). See notes to table 6-7 for details.

Table 6-7. *Actual and Simulated Corporate Contributions under Elimination of the Charitable Deduction, 1991*
Millions of dollars

	Actual	Simulated values[a]		
Item	values	A	B	C
Corporate tax	91,682	91,682	91,682	110,019
Charitable contributions	4,592	3,608	3,909	3,822
Percentage change from baseline	...	−21	−15	−17

Source: Data taken from U.S. Internal Revenue Service (1993, table 3, pp. 35–36), for returns with net income.
a. Simulations A and B assume no change in corporate income collected. Simulation A assumes price elasticity of −0.6 (see Carroll and Joulfaian, 1995, p. 14). Simulation B assumes −0.4 (see Clotfelter, 1985a). Simulation C assumes a 20 percent increase in corporate tax liability, a price elasticity of −0.4, and an income elasticity of 0.5 (see Clotfelter, 1985a, table 5.13, p. 212).

tising or promotion,[36] thus mitigating the impact of loss of deductibility for contributions.[37]

We estimate the effects of tax reform on corporate giving with data from corporate tax returns for 1991. The marginal tax rate in that year for the largest corporations was 34 percent. Elimination of the deduction for these firms would have raised the cost of corporate gifts by more than 50 percent.[38] We aggregated information on corporate income, income tax, and charitable gifts for corporations arrayed by asset-size classes and applied two sets of elasticity values to reflect uncertainty about the size of the price elasticity.[39]

Table 6-7 summarizes the simulations. Simulation A, employing a larger elasticity, suggests that eliminating the corporate charitable deduction would reduce corporate giving by about 21 percent. The smaller

36. Washington lawyers observed a similar phenomenon in the partnership context in 1991 when the limit on income subject to the hospital insurance portion of the Self-Employment Contributions Act (SECA) tax was more than doubled. Some charitable contributions previously deducted by individual partners were determined to be items that could be characterized in the future as business expenses of the partnership, a choice that meant, in effect, that those items were deductible for SECA as well as for income tax purposes.

37. The case of travel and entertainment expenditure illustrates the difficulty in assessing the effect of loss of deductibility of one item at the same time that others retain deductibility. Clotfelter (1983).

38. At a marginal tax rate of 34 percent, the initial price is 0.66. With no deductibility, it is 1.00. The change in price as a percentage of the initial price is (1.00 − 0.66)/0.66.

39. To calculate the hypothetical level of corporate giving under a regime of no deduction, elasticity values were applied to the marginal tax rate applying to the class's average taxable net income as well as to average values of corporate contributions and after-tax net income and then summed by multiplying by the number of tax returns in each class. Summary data from this information are shown in appendix table 6-A1.

elasticity indicates giving would fall 15 percent. Taxes on businesses might have to increase to make up for cuts in individual rates. A third simulation, based on the assumption that the charitable deduction is repealed and corporate tax rates are cut by one-fifth, indicates a further dampening effect on giving.

Charitable Bequests

The estate and gift tax applies to few people because a credit spares from taxation individuals' estates smaller than $600,000 and, with a modicum of planning, couples' estates smaller than $1.2 million. The tax applies to only about 2.5 percent of all decedents.[40] However, the stimulus to charitable giving by the small proportion of decedents subject to the tax is powerful, because the initial rate is 37 percent and rises to a top rate of 55 percent. For an estate subject to the 55 percent rate, the net cost of bequeathing $1,000 to a charitable organization would be $450 that could otherwise have been left, net of tax, to a family member or other individual. Although rates are high and the presumed stimulus to giving large, few studies have been done on how much testamentary giving the tax system induces.[41]

We estimated the effect of eliminating the estate and gift tax on testamentary gifts, based on representative parameters from previous studies and on information about the size of the after-tax, disposable estate. For estates subject to tax, repeal would increase the price of giving, which would tend to reduce bequests, but it would also increase the estate that could be bequeathed, which would tend to increase bequests.[42]

We took data on charitable bequests from published summaries of tax returns, calculated average values for various classes of returns, and divided by the size of the estate. For each class, we calculated actual and hypothetical values for average charitable bequests, the price of making charitable bequests (1 minus the marginal tax rate for taxable returns), and the net disposable estate (gross estate minus estate and gift tax after

40. In 1991 there were 2,169,518 deaths. U.S. Bureau of the Census (1994, table 127, p. 95). In that year, 53,576 estate tax returns were filed. Johnson (1993, table 1, p. 88).
41. For a summary of studies of charitable bequests, see Clotfelter (1985, chap. 6).
42. Those bills that do not eliminate the estate and gift taxes may provide a modest boost to the private foundation sector of the nonprofit universe: if unlimited savings allowances or a VAT encourage saving for other than life-cycle purposes, they may plausibly increase taxable estates, resulting in a larger stock from which bequests could be made.

Table 6-8. *Actual and Simulated Charitable Bequests under Elimination of the Estate Tax: 1993*[a]

Millions of dollars

Item	Actual values	Simulated values	
		A	B
Estate and gift tax revenues	10,335	0	0
Charitable bequests	7,292	5,565	4,073
Percentage change from baseline	...	− 24	− 44

Source: Data taken from "Estate Tax Returns, 1992–1993," *SOI Bulletin* 14 (Spring 1995), table 2, pp. 109–13.
a. Elasticities with respect to price and net disposable estate based on Clotfelter (1985a, p. 250). For gross estates less than $1 million in 1976 dollars the elasticities were − 1.6 and 0.4, respectively. For larger estates the elasticities were: A: − 1.0 and 0.4; B: − 2.4 and 1.3. The GDP price deflator was used to adjust dollar amounts for inflation. For details of the calculation, see text and table 6A-2.

credits). We used two sets of parameters to reflect the uncertainty about behavioral responses to the charitable deduction.[43]

Our estimates of the effect on the level of charitable bequests of eliminating the estate and gift tax are shown in table 6-8. Charitable bequests in 1993 totaled $7.3 billion. The results of two simulations are shown; the second one's parameters imply that tax policy has a greater effect on behavior.[44] Simulation A indicates that repeal of the estate and gift tax would lower total charitable bequests by 24 percent, to $5.6 billion, in the long run. Simulation B indicates a much larger reduction in charitable bequests, by 44 percent, to $4.1 billion. These estimates imply very large reductions from the elimination of the estate tax. As with corporate giving, these estimates are quite uncertain, as they are based on parameters estimated on data that do not include the policy change being contemplated. The calculations presented here simply extrapolate observed behavior and may be too large or too small.

Another consideration suggests that the total effect of repealing the estate and gift tax may be considerably larger than these estimates. The elderly account for a sizable fraction of gifts made by living donors. These gifts dwarf testamentary gifts in size. As noted, a prudent taxpayer, realizing that death is not far off, can enjoy income tax benefits as well

43. The range of parameters follows the summary of estimated models in Clotfelter (1985). See table 6-8 for a detailed description of the elasticities used.

44. To illustrate the data on which the simulations are based, appendix table 6A-2 presents summary data for 1993, including the number of estate and gift tax returns by asset class, the average values for estate size, tax, and charitable bequests, and the actual marginal tax rate applying to the average taxable estate for each class under the 1993 law. The data reveal tremendous variation in estate size and amount of charitable bequests, with the average charitable bequest in the top asset class being some $13 million.

as estate tax benefits by making gifts before death. Development officers at universities and hospitals emphasize these advantages in soliciting gifts.

Volunteer Effort

People can support a charitable organization with either money or time in the form of volunteer effort. None of the reforms would directly affect treatment of volunteer labor. However, household surveys consistently show that those who volunteer more also tend to give more in money donations. This finding suggests that a tax reform that reduces cash gifts may also lower volunteering. The finding does not establish complementarity, however. Some people may simply be much more charitably inclined than others. Studies that allow for this linkage still suggest that volunteering is complementary with monetary donations, but that the effect is small.[45] For this reason, we do not include any explicit estimate of the likely effects of tax reform on volunteering.

Transitional Problems and Avoidance Devices

All of the reform proposals under discussion require discussion of provisions to ease the transition from the current tax system to the new one.[46] For example, the flat-tax plans and a BTT would dramatically lower marginal tax rates, creating powerful incentives to move taxable income from the last accounting period of the old system to a later accounting period under the new regime. There are clear implications for charitable organizations, especially ones that depend on high-bracket taxpayers for support, because charitable gifts are one of the most flexible and reliable sources of immediate deductions under the present tax system. Taxpayers with ample liquid assets can accelerate charitable contri-

---

45. See, for example, Clotfelter (1985, chap. 4) or Andreoni, Gale, and Scholz (1995).

46. For example, if one of the goals of tax reform is to stimulate saving, the tax system might be structured to provide deductions only for new saving. Such a provision would be difficult to enforce, however, because taxpayers could easily convert assets to cash before the new law takes effect and then deposit it as "new saving" after the effective date of the new law. William G. Gale, "Building a Better Tax System: Can a Consumption Tax Deliver the Goods?" *Tax Notes*, vol. 69, November 6, 1995, p. 785. Similar problems would arise with respect to homeowners if mortgage interest deductions are curtailed (see chapter 5 by Capozza, Green, and Hendershott in this volume). For a general discussion of transition issues, see chapter 11 by Pearlman in this volume.

butions by making what would otherwise be future contributions during the last year of the current tax system.

Informal review of past changes gives some sense of the dimensions of the possibilities. For example, taxpayers having adjusted gross incomes exceeding $1,000,000 took deductions for charitable contributions equal to 9.1 percent of their adjusted gross incomes in 1986, the last year in which they were exposed to a 50 percent marginal tax rate; in the following year, after their marginal rate had fallen to 28 percent, their charitable contributions accounted for only 3.9 percent of their adjusted gross incomes.[47] Illiquid but wealthy taxpayers may use charitable remainder trusts, which allow current deductions of the present value of interests that may not pass to their charitable recipients for many years. Creditworthy taxpayers can simply borrow funds to finance current contributions that generate current deductions and spread the repayments into the future.[48]

These opportunities are not unlimited, however. Section 170(b) of the Internal Revenue Code generally limits deductions for contributions to no more than 50 percent of the taxpayer's "contribution base"—roughly, adjusted gross income—and lower percentages apply to certain gifts and recipients. Gifts over these limits may be carried over to returns covering up to five subsequent tax years. However, several of the proposals under consideration raise doubts about the fate of carryover deductions.[49] Still, significant opportunities exist to accelerate donations.

47. Authors' calculations based on table 2.1 in the 1986 and 1987 SOI Individual Income Tax Returns series.

48. Transfers of this sort must be done with care. The IRS has successfully challenged one contribution financed with borrowed money, in a situation where the borrowing was not at arm's length. See *Allen* v. *Comm'r*, 92 T.C. 1 (1989). However, the IRS has held that a contribution charged to a credit card is made when charged, regardless of when the debt is paid. Rev. Rul. 78-38, 1978-1 C.B. 67. One might think that the easiest way to use debt to make a deferred contribution would be simply to deliver a donor's note to the charitable organization. However, the Supreme Court has held, in the context of pension contributions, that delivery of a note is insufficient to generate a current deduction. *Williams* v. *Comm'r*, 429 U.S. 569 (1977). The IRS has held that the same rationale applies to charitable contributions. Rev. Rul. 68-174, 1968-1 C.B. 81.

49. Section 201 of the USA tax, which adds section 11(b)(2) to the code (as expressed in S. 722), would preserve carryovers for up to five years. Section 2(b)(3) of Specter's flat tax proposal (S. 488) would specifically repeal the current provisions of section 170(d) that authorize deduction of carried-over gifts. Most of the other bills are silent on this question, but those that do not allow a charitable contribution deduction by implication would presumably deny deductions for carryovers from pre-enactment years. This is hardly a trivial matter; in 1992, more than $4 billion of charitable contribution deductions were in the form of carry-overs from prior years. SOI, Individual Income Tax Returns 1992, table 2.1, col. 85.

Conclusion

The tax reform plans we examine do not appear to have nonprofit organizations as intended targets. However, like bystanders at a gunfight, nonprofits have a good chance of being hit. Our analysis indicates that at least some plans will harm nonprofit organizations. Nonprofits generally would be badly damaged by any business-transactions tax that does not explicitly exempt their provision of goods and services. In addition, the various flat-tax proposals, especially those that make no provision for deductibility of cash gifts, reduce incentives to make such gifts to charitable organizations. The size of these effects, though uncertain, may be large. The details of many current tax proposals are missing, and knowledge about likely behavioral responses is also quite imperfect.

Nonprofit organizations, charitable and otherwise, will no doubt continue to play an important role in American society regardless of the outcome of the current wave of tax reform proposals. However, the ability of nonprofits to perform at the levels of the recent past may be in jeopardy unless special provisions on their behalf are added to the bills under consideration. The problem with such special provisions, of course, is that by narrowing the tax base they make it more difficult to lower marginal tax rates, one of the principal motivations of the whole tax reform effort.

Appendix: Methodology Used in Simulations of Charitable Giving by Individuals

The purpose of devising a simulation model of individual contributions is to provide calculations suggesting the likely magnitudes of various tax reform proposals. Because the giving behavior as well as the size of the likely changes in relevant tax characteristics differs markedly by income level, it is important that any model distinguish among taxpayers by income level. The data used in the present study are aggregated by adjusted gross income (AGI) class and are taken from the published *Statistics of Income* reports based on tax return data. The basic data, including numbers of taxpayers by income class, the percentage of taxpayers at each income level who itemized their deductions, the components of taxable income that enter into the calculation of tax liability and marginal tax rates, and the charitable deductions reported on the tax returns for itemizers, are from the tax year 1992.[50] Data based on all other years are adjusted so as to make them comparable to the 1992 data. For the simulations, incomes and other components of taxable income such as wages and mortgage interest deductions were increased to reflect 1996 levels by the projected growth in per capita personal income (18 percent for the four-year period).[51] To reflect the projected growth in number of taxpayers, the number of returns was increased at 1.25 percent per year, the rate of growth of the work force between 1985 and 1993, or 5 percent for the period.[52]

In order to estimate total giving by individuals, it was necessary to estimate the amount that nonitemizers contributed, information that is not ordinarily available because it does not appear on the tax returns of nonitemizers. To obtain an estimate for nonitemizers' giving, we turned to data for the year 1986, a unique year in which nonitemizers were allowed a deduction for all of their charitable contributions.[53] Average contributions by nonitemizers in each income class were regressed on average AGI, its square, and its cube, where these 1986 quantities were expressed in 1992 dollars.[54] Then this estimated regression was used to calculate fitted values for each income class in 1992 using each class's average AGI. One can certainly question the accuracy of the deductions claimed by nonitemizers in 1986 as a basis for estimating actual contributions by nonitemizers. Nonitemizers may have overstated actual contributions due to poor recordkeeping or in the belief that returns would not be carefully audited. Another reason the 1986 figures may overstate typical nonitemizer giving is that apparently a few large contributors, who normally would have itemized because of their large donations,

50. U.S. Internal Revenue Service (1995).

51. For 1996, OMB's assumption for the CPI is 157.8 and for personal income it is $6,366 billion (U.S. Office of Management and Budget, 1996, table 1-1, p. 4). U.S. Council of Economic Advisers (1994) gives corresponding values for 1992 of 157.8 (p. 335) and $5,145 billion (p. 300). Population was taken from U.S. Bureau of the Census (1994, table 4, p. 9).

52. The labor force grew from 117.2 million in 1985 to 129.5 million in 1993 (U.S. Bureau of the Census, 1994, table 614, p. 395), implying an exponential annual growth rate of 1.25 percent.

53. The 1981 tax act provided for the gradual phasing-in of an "above-the-line" deduction for charitable contributions by nonitemizers, in addition to the deduction for contributions used by those taxpayers choosing to itemize their deductions, culminating with a deduction of half of contributions without limit in 1985 and all of contributions in 1986, after which the provision would expire if not reenacted, as it in fact was not.

54. The GDP implicit price deflator was used throughout to adjust dollar quantities for inflation. See U.S. Council of Economic Advisers (1994, p. 272.)

found it advantageous in 1986 to use the nonitemizer deduction, thus increasing average giving by nonitemizers in that year. Still another reason the 1986 figures could overstate nonitemizer giving is that AGI in 1986 excluded a portion of long-term capital gains.[55] Operating in the opposite direction is the possibility that nonitemizers in 1986 may have understated actual contributions out of ignorance of this newly introduced provision.[56] We chose not to make any adjustments, in part because the resulting estimates, shown in table 6A-1, do not appear to be unreasonable. The calculated aggregate level of contributions for all individuals resulting from this procedure, some $94 billion for the year 1992, is rather close to the $102 billion estimate for the same year presented in the widely cited *Giving USA*.[57] In the simulations of contribution levels for 1996, 1992 levels of giving are inflated using the CPI to 1996 levels for use as the baseline level.

Much more problematic was the task of obtaining accurate information on the types of organizations to which these contributions were directed, owing to the paucity of data. Previous work, based on information taken from an analysis of tax returns in 1962 and a national household survey in 1973, suggests strongly that giving patterns do differ markedly by income level.[58] The only information on patterns of giving by type of organization that is more recent is a series of national surveys on giving and volunteering conducted by the Gallup organization.[59] However, the data obtained in these surveys have limited usefulness, for two reasons: the small samples used in these surveys include very few high-income households, and they provide only a two-way breakdown, between religious and other organizations, in which the religious category includes organizations normally classified elsewhere (for example, the Salvation Army and parochial schools).

For these reasons, we constructed an estimated distribution of gifts beginning with the 1973 data, updated to 1982 dollars and modified to conform to 1992. For gifts to religious organizations and institutions of higher education, the logarithm of the ratio of the percentage of gifts

55. We are grateful to Gerald Auten for pointing out these possibilities.
56. One might also question the accuracy of the claimed deductions by itemizers, but most researchers accept these claims as essentially correct.
57. See *Giving USA*, 1993 edition, p. 21.
58. A table showing the distribution of gifts by type of organization and income class, using 1982 income classes, is given in Clotfelter, "Tax Reform," p. 485, table A-6.
59. Surveys covered the years 1987 and 1989. See Hodgkinson and others (1992, table 2.9, p. 68).

Table 6A-1. Basic Data Used in Calculations of Corporate Contributions

| Size of total assets (millions of dollars) | Number of returns | Average values | | | Marginal tax rate | Total charitable contributions (thousands of dollars) |
		Net income (dollars)	Corporate tax (dollars)	Contributions (dollars)		
0	69,803	141,969	15,702	312	0.15	21,746
Under 0.1	939,422	14,970	331	35	0.15	32,582
0.1–0.25	343,597	29,968	1,579	143	0.15	49,061
0.25–0.5	214,757	45,658	3,471	293	0.15	62,975
0.5–1.0	155,290	70,312	6,251	503	0.15	78,169
1.0–5.0	160,607	188,135	21,213	1,241	0.34	199,277
5.0–10.0	22,779	610,711	84,400	3,155	0.39	71,877
10.0–25.0	15,566	1,206,896	181,837	7,805	0.34	121,496
25.0–50.0	7,467	2,315,152	449,521	18,136	0.34	135,420
50.0–100.0	5,400	3,127,707	600,670	26,202	0.34	141,492
100.0–250.0	4,392	7,070,810	1,336,984	58,817	0.34	258,324
250 or more	4,370	80,707,439	15,419,848	782,554	0.34	3,419,759
Total	1,942,450	. . .	. . .	. . .	. . .	4,592,178

Sources: Data taken from U.S. Internal Revenue Service (1993, pp. 35–36, table 3); for returns with net income; Internal Revenue Code, Sec. 5(b)(2).

made to that category divided by 100 minus that percentage was regressed on the logarithm of the average AGI in 1992 dollars, its square, and its cube, with the fitted values using average AGI for the 1992 classes translated back into a proportion. The resulting proportions, when applied to the 1992 data, produced a total for religious giving that was markedly higher than the total estimated by *Giving USA*. We therefore reduced all the proportions by multiplying them by the ratio of *Giving USA*'s total for religious giving to our initial total. No change was made to the estimates for giving to higher education because the resulting estimate of total contributions by individuals is not unreasonable in light of totals for giving to higher education that include bequests and corporate gifts. The resulting assumed distribution is shown in table 6-4. It should be clear, though, that this assumed distribution must be taken as no more than an illustration of how contributions are in fact distributed among types of recipient, since it is based on a survey taken in 1973. Our use of these proportions assumes that the distribution of contributions by recipient group is a function of income only and is independent of itemization status or other aspects of tax incentives to make contributions.

The simulations themselves are based on calculations of hypothetical contributions, using prospective values of taxes and marginal tax rates and applying both sets of parameters, for six representative taxpayers in each of thirteen income classes. In each class the six representative taxpayers are single itemizers, married itemizers, itemizing heads of households, single nonitemizers, married nonitemizers, and nonitemizing heads of households. For the purpose of these simulations, we assigned all taxpayers to be single, married filing jointly, or heads of households. The filing status of married filing separately is ignored.

For the base year of 1992, the price of giving reflects the favorable treatment of gifts of appreciated assets. Following the approach conventionally taken in this literature, the price of giving that is faced by an itemizer is a weighted average of the price of giving cash and the price of giving appreciated property, where the weights are based on the actual distribution in each income class of gifts between cash and noncash gifts. Where m is a taxpayer's marginal tax rate on ordinary income and n is the marginal tax rate on capital gains income, R is a dichotomous variable taking on the value of 1 if the asset's alternative disposition would have been immediate realization and 0 if it would never have been sold, g^* is the gain-to-value ratio for the asset in question, and C is the proportion of contributions made in the form of cash, the weighted average of price in the base year, that is under the current tax regime, is $[C(1 - m) + (1 - C)(1 - m - Rg^*n)]$. In these simulations, we assume $Rg^* = 0.5$, which is in line with the assumption in previous studies.

For purposes of calculating after-tax income and the price of giving, it was necessary to calculate the tax liability for all actual and proposed tax regimes and the marginal tax rate for regimes that allow a deduction for charitable contributions. Although the calculations were necessarily rough ones, as tax return data were aggregated into thirteen income classes and six types of taxpayers within each class, the calculated tax revenue for 1992 ($503 billion) was close to the actual amount ($476 billion).[60] For 1996 the projected revenue from the current tax regime— accounting for the growth in income, the number of taxpayers, and the indexation of the tax schedule—was $960 billion. To assure that alternative plans were revenue-neutral, the rates of the other simulated plans were adjusted to achieve that level. This adjustment is important for simulating the effects of tax changes on charitable contributions because of the positive income elasticity implied in the behavioral models. In calculating the tax prices applying to the USA tax, however, we used the fully phased-in marginal tax rates (8 percent, 19 percent, and 40 percent) as the basis for calculating the tax price, not the rates as adjusted for revenue-neutrality.

We used several assumptions in calculating the various taxes. Fringe benefits, which are taxed in the Gephardt plan, were estimated as the sum of health insurance and pensions as a percentage of AGI, where the percentage for health insurance is based on data from the Congressional Budget Office and that for pensions is the ratio of pensions, profit sharing, stock, and annuities for corporations in 1992 ($46.5 billion) to wages and salaries ($2,674.3 billion).[61] For the USA tax, the average propensity to save is based on a tabulation from the Survey of Consumer Finances. This average propensity to save rises to 11.3 percent for taxpayers with incomes above $200,000 in 1996. The USA tax also allows a deduction for educational costs up to $2,000 per student; we assume this averages out to $500 per dependent.

---

60. U.S. Internal Revenue Service (1995, table 1.2, p. 31).
61. Congressional Budget Office (1994, table 1, p. xiii); Internal Revenue Service (1994, p. 8).

Table 6A-2. Basic Data Used in Calculations of Charitable Bequests

Asset class (millions of dollars)	Number of returns	Average values			Marginal tax rate	Total charitable bequests (thousands of dollars)
		Gross estate (dollars)	Estate tax (dollars)	Charitable bequests (dollars)		
Taxable returns						
0.6–1.0	12,054	811,105	46,060	4,010	0.39	48.339
1.0–2.5	11,222	1,479,395	234,990	27,457	0.43	308,124
2.5–5.0	2,646	3,416,358	838,961	93,984	0.53	248,681
5.0–10.0	1,014	6,854,701	1,734,208	402,118	0.55	407,748
10.0–20.0	364	13,832,462	3,431,140	1,006,907	0.55	366,514
20 or more	205	57,331,078	9,343,829	13,300,463	0.55	2,726,595
Nontaxable returns						
0.6–1	19,901	741,315	0	36,161	1	719,633
1.0–2.5	10,329	1,446,358	0	98,737	1	1,019,857
2.5–5.0	1,744	3,397,088	0	298,140	1	519,957
5.0–10	537	6,661,929	0	559,194	1	300,287
10.0–20.0	143	13,083,224	0	1,369,706	1	195,868
20 or more	52	66,792,558	0	8,278,173	1	430,465
Total	60,211	...	...	...	...	7,292,068

Sources: Data taken from "Estate Tax Returns, 1992–1993," *SOI Bulletin* 14 (Spring 1995), pp. 109–13, table 2; Internal Revenue Code, Sec. 2001(c).

Comment by Bruce K. MacLaury

The authors begin their interesting chapter with the accurate but not very surprising observation, "To a remarkable degree, the nonprofit sector of the economy is shaped by the tax code from which it is largely exempt." To a greater or lesser degree, could not the same be said about oil drilling, feed lots, or commercial real estate investments? Yet, in these instances, earlier tax reforms have diminished if not eliminated special tax benefits, and helped reshape those industries as a result. Is the same in store for nonprofits?

My guess is probably not. As the authors point out, few of the current crop of reform proposals have nonprofit organizations as their intended target, in contrast, say, to commercial real estate a decade ago. Moreover, they note that all the tax proposals they discuss "could exempt nonprofit organizations and most do so." Finally, the largest category of beneficiaries of charitable contributions—religious organizations—is virtually certain to remain exempt and retain deductibility of contributions. And this category may well provide shelter, literally and figuratively, for other types of nonprofit organizations in the process.

That said, the authors quite rightly conclude that "like bystanders at a gunfight, nonprofit organizations have a good chance of being hit." And for that reason alone, their careful dissection of the distinctions among nonprofits and their taxonomy of the potential effects of differing reform proposals on different types of organizations provide a very useful map of the minefields for those proposing or opposing structural tax reform.

One of the most novel ideas, at least for me, was their argument that in pursuing the laudable objective of encouraging saving, proponents of a consumed-income tax or a business-transactions tax are providing a new tax-favored competitor for contributions, namely, saving itself. I share their regret about the lack of empirical studies that try to measure the potential effect on individual contributions of such a savings deduction.

Another eye-opener for me was the thought that in a world where saving is not taxed, gifts of assets as charitable contributions would result in double deductibility—once when income was saved and once when the resulting asset was given. I doubt that this type of tax generosity could withstand scrutiny.

Finally, I had not focused on the fact that most of the proposals would eliminate deductions for corporate charitable contributions, and that some of the flat tax proposals would eliminate estate and gift taxes. As the authors point out, these changes would have far greater effects on those organizations and activities to which high-income/high-wealth individuals and corporations contribute, than on nonprofit organizations in general and religious organizations in particular.

When the authors try to quantify the likely impact of the various types of reform proposals, they are handicapped by the wide range of estimates of income and price elasticities cited in various studies. Nevertheless, as they say, the evidence summarized in tables 6-6 and 6-7 is illustrative that structural tax reform—as one would have suspected—carries major implications for nonprofits. (Incidentally, if their estimates of the likely revenue to be derived from the USA tax—a major increase from current levels—are even close to correct, one has to wonder about its political feasibility, quite apart from any distributional effects.)

In the end, the message for nonprofit organizations is that structural tax reform, if ever enacted, is likely to be painful, and for some activities—like private higher education and the arts—could be calamitous. At the same time, it has always been difficult to defend high marginal tax rates on the grounds that they provide incentives for charitable gifts and enhance the value of nonprofit exemptions. The lesson, then, is not that tax reform is doomed because it threatens a valued segment of the economy and of society—the nonprofit sector—but that the law of unintended consequences is in play in full force. We should be grateful to the authors for highlighting many of the potential booby traps.

References

Andreoni, James, William G. Gale, and John Karl Scholz. 1995. "Charitable Contributions of Time and Money." Unpublished paper.

Auten, Gerald E., James M. Cilke, and William C. Randolph. 1992. "The Effects of Tax Reforms on Charitable Contributions." *National Tax Journal* 45 (September): 267–90.

Auten, Gerald, and David Joulfaian. 1996. "Charitable Contributions and Intergenerational Transfers." *Journal of Public Economics* 59 (March): 55–68.

Carroll, Robert, and David Joulfaian. 1995. "Taxes and Corporate Giving to Charity." Office of Tax Analysis (December).

Clotfelter, Charles T. 1983. "Tax-Induced Distortions and the Business-Pleasure Borderline: The Case of Travel and Entertainment." *American Economic Review* 73 (December): 1053–65.

———. 1985. *Federal Tax Policy and Charitable Giving.* University of Chicago Press.

———. 1990. "The Impact of Tax Reform on Charitable Giving: A 1989 Perspective." In *Do Taxes Matter? The Impact of the Tax Reform Act of 1986,* edited by Joel Slemrod, 203–35. MIT Press.

Cruciano, Therese M. 1995. "Individual Income Tax Returns, Preliminary Data, 1993." *Statistics of Income Bulletin* 14 (Spring): 9–27.

Giving USA. 1993, 1995. American Association of Fund-Raising Counsel Trust for Philanthropy. New York.

Hall, Robert E., and Alvin Rabushka. 1995. *The Flat Tax,* 2d ed. Stanford, Calif.: Hoover Institution Press.

Hilgert, Cecelia. 1995. "Charities and Other Tax-Exempt Organizations, 1991." *Statistics of Income Bulletin* 15 (Summer): 26–45.

Hodgkinson, Virginia Ann, and others. 1992. *Nonprofit Almanac 1992–1993: Dimensions of the Independent Sector.* Jossey-Bass.

Johnson, Barry W. 1993. "Estate Tax Returns, 1989–1991." *Statistics of Income Bulletin* 12 (4): 76–104.

McLure, Charles E. Jr. 1987. *The Value-Added Tax: Key to Deficit Reduction?* Washington: American Enterprise Institute.

Meckstroth, Alicia. 1993–94. "Private Foundations and Charitable Trusts, 1990." *Statistics of Income Bulletin* 13 (3): 32–79.

Randolph, William C. 1995. "Dynamic Income, Progressive Taxes, and the Timing of Charitable Contributions." *Journal of Political Economy* 103 (August): 709–38.

Riley, Margaret. 1995. "Exempt Organization Business Income Tax Returns, 1991." *Statistics of Income Bulletin* 14 (Spring): 38–63.

U.S. Bureau of the Census. 1994. *Statistical Abstract of the United States, 1994.*

U.S. Congress. Joint Committee on Taxation. 1996. *Impact on State and Local Governments and Tax-Exempt Organizations of Replacing the Federal Income Tax.* JCS-4-96. April 30.

U.S. Congressional Budget Office. 1994. *The Tax Treatment of Employment-Based Health Insurance.*

———. 1995. *Reducing the Deficit: Spending and Revenue Options.* February.

U.S. Council of Economic Advisers. 1994. *Economic Report of the President.*

U.S. Internal Revenue Service. 1993. *Statistics of Income—Corporation Income Tax Returns, 1991.*

———. 1994. *Corporation Source Book of Statistics of Income, July 1991–June 1992.* Department of the Treasury.

———. 1995. *Statistics of Income—Individual Income Tax Returns, 1992.*

U.S. Office of Management and Budget. 1996. *Budget of the United States Government, Fiscal Year 1996: Analytical Perspectives.*

CHAPTER 7

Fundamental Tax Reform and Labor Supply

Robert K. Triest

S EVERAL RECENTLY PROPOSED TAX REFORMS would dramatically change the structure of the U.S. tax system. Some would flatten the rate structure and change the tax base. In this chapter, I examine how these reforms would affect labor supply. Despite extensive study of the effects of taxes on labor supply, this task is difficult because nearly all previous research has dealt with the effect of tax *rates* on work effort and has largely ignored the effect of the tax *base*. In addition, the complexity of the tax structure makes it difficult to sort out how the various tax and transfer programs interact to affect labor supply. Despite these problems, it is possible to provide "ballpark" estimates of how labor supply would probably respond to the proposed reforms.

The Current Tax System

The current U.S. tax and transfer system results in a nonlinear net wage schedule for most workers. The basic federal income tax has six statutory rates (including the zero bracket), but the overall structure is much more complicated because of phaseouts within the income tax, social insurance payroll taxes, the earned income tax credit (EITC), and the high marginal tax rates implicit in the benefit reduction rules for many transfer programs.

The views expressed in this paper are not necessarily shared by the Federal Reserve Bank of Boston or its staff. I thank Rachel Deyette for excellent research assistance and conference participants and colleagues at the Boston Fed for helpful comments and suggestions.

Figure 7-1. *Budget Constraint for Individual with Two-Bracket Tax on Earnings*

Consumption

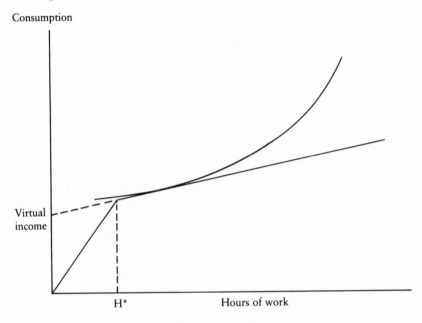

A tax system with marginal tax rates that vary with income confronts workers with a nonlinear budget constraint. Figure 7-1 shows the single-period budget constraint of an individual with no unearned income who faces a two-bracket earnings tax. The slope of each segment of the budget constraint is equal to the net of tax wage rate, $(1 - t)w$, where w is the gross wage rate and t is the marginal tax rate. The figure is drawn for a marginal tax rate that is higher in the second tax bracket than in the first. People are in the first tax bracket if they work fewer than H^* hours and in the second bracket if they work more than H^* hours. People who maximize utility by working more than H^* hours select the same point on their budget constraints as they would select if they faced a single-bracket tax rate with a constant marginal tax rate (equal to the rate they face in the second bracket) and received lump-sum subsidies equal to the differences between what they would owe if they faced only the higher marginal tax rate on all taxable income and the amounts they actually owe. Graphically, these subsidies equal the height of the vertical (consumption) axis intercept of the linear extension of the second segment of the budget constraint. Gary Burtless and Jerry Hausman called the sum of actual unearned income and the lump-sum subsidy implicit in the tax

Table 7-1. *U.S. Federal Individual Income Tax Schedule, 1995*[a]

Gross income range (dollars)	Marginal tax rate (percent)	Implicit lump sum transfer (dollars)	Average tax rate at start of bracket (percent)
0–14,050	0	0	0
14,500–53,050	15	2,108	0
53,050–108,300	28	9,004	11.0
108,300–157,650	31	12,253	19.7
157,650–270,550	36	20,136	23.2
Over 270,550	39.6	29,875	28.6

a. Based on the tax schedule for married couples filing jointly who are eligible for three exemptions and who do not itemize deductions or have other adjustments to income. The effects of the earned income tax credit, the social security and medicare payroll taxes, and the phaseout of personal exemptions are not shown.

system "virtual income," since individuals act as though they had unearned income equal to this amount.[1] A progressive tax system affects labor supply through both the reduction in the net wage rate and the implicit lump-sum subsidy for those locating in higher brackets. Table 7-1 shows the values of the virtual income adjustments (implicit lump-sum subsidies) for each bracket of the current U.S. income tax system. The implicit lump-sum subsidies are quite large, reflecting the fact that average tax rates are far below marginal tax rates.

Effective tax rates become much more complicated when the EITC and social security and medicare payroll taxes are incorporated into the tax schedule.[2] Figure 7-2 shows how the marginal tax rate on earnings varies with income for married couples filing jointly, single heads of households, and single filers. The EITC creates an initial tax bracket with a negative marginal tax rate for taxpayers with a qualifying child. The marginal tax rate rises quickly with income as the EITC hits its maximum value and is then "clawed back," and also rises as taxpayers enter the 15 percent income tax bracket when income exceeds personal exemptions and the standard deduction or itemized deductions. As income rises further, the marginal tax rate follows an erratic pattern. The tax rate falls where the EITC has been reduced to zero, rises as taxpayers enter the 28 percent income tax bracket, falls as earnings exceed the maximum amount taxable under the social security payroll tax, and rises as taxpayers enter higher income tax brackets. Figure 7-2 also shows the small temporary increase in the marginal tax rate caused by the phasing out of

1. Burtless and Hausman (1978).
2. As discussed below, the tax calculations include both the employee-paid portion and 65 percent of the employer-paid portion of the payroll taxes.

Figure 7-2. *Federal Marginal Tax Rates on Earned Income*[a]

Single filers

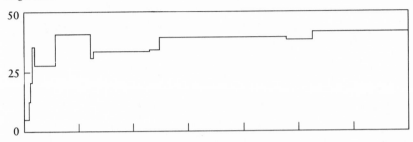

Heads of household

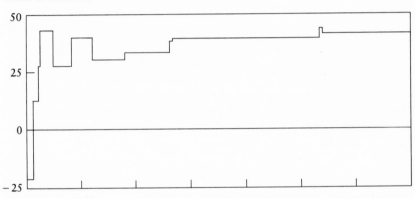

Joint filers

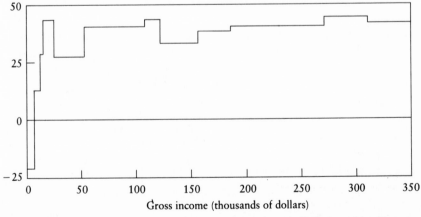

Gross income (thousands of dollars)

a. The calculations underlying this figure assume that taxpayers take the standard deduction, and that all income is from wages and salaries (half of which comes from each spouse in the case of joint filers). The joint filers and heads of household are both assumed to have one child (who qualifies under the EITC rules). The payroll tax component of the marginal tax rate is equal to the employee-paid portion plus 65 percent of the employer-paid portion.

Figure 7-3. *Budget Constraint for Individual with Three-Bracket Tax on Earnings*

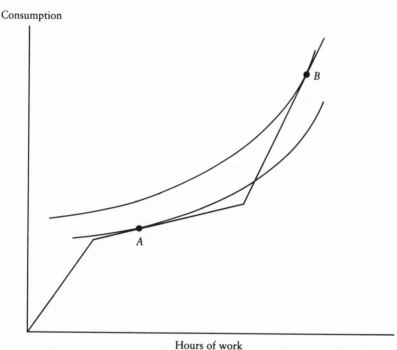

Hours of work

personal exemptions for high-income taxpayers, although it does not reflect similar rate increases caused by limitations on the use of other credits and deductions.

When payroll taxes, the EITC, and the phaseout of the value of personal exemptions are taken into account, the marginal tax rate sometimes decreases as earnings increase. In this situation, nonconvex kinks are created in workers' budget constraints,[3] and there may be multiple tangencies between indifference curves and the budget constraint, indicating multiple local equilibria (see figure 7-3). These equilibria are better than any other in the immediate neighborhood, and one of these equilibria is better than any of the others. In figure 7-3, the equilibrium associated with the most hours of work (point *B*) results in the highest utility. However, an increase in the marginal tax rate applicable in the segment

3. This problem was first dealt with by Burtless and Hausman (1978), who developed an econometric method for modeling behavior in the presence of nonconvex budget sets.

farthest to the right might cause the other tangency (point A) to become most preferred. Thus small changes in tax policy may cause large changes in an individual's desired hours of work. It is important to incorporate the nonlinearities in the budget constraint when simulating tax reforms.[4] The simulations described below include the complications resulting from the nonconvex budget constraints.

Figure 7-2 shows that people with moderate incomes as well as the rich face high marginal tax rates, and, because of benefit reduction rates under transfer programs, some of the poor confront implicit marginal tax rates that exceed any explicit tax rates facing the rich. Aid to families with dependent children (AFDC) taxes earnings at a rate of approximately 70 percent.[5] Food stamp benefits are reduced 30 cents for every additional dollar of income (including AFDC).

Descriptive statistics for the data I use in simulating the effects of the reform proposals are shown in table 7-2 (I discuss construction of the data set later in this chapter). The first column, showing the mean marginal tax rate calculated over all members of the income decile, reveals that the average marginal tax rate varies remarkably little over the income distribution. However, the average marginal tax rate for low-income families masks considerable heterogeneity. Some low-income workers face marginal tax rates approaching 100 percent from high benefit reduction rates, while other low-income workers who do not participate in the AFDC or food stamp programs face a negative marginal tax rate because of the EITC.

Will the Real Marginal Tax Rate Please Stand Up?

Pinning down the actual effective marginal tax rates on earned income is tricky. The marginal tax rates shown in figure 7-2 may be higher than taxpayers actually face because of tax avoidance or evasion. Upper-income taxpayers may shelter income in defined-contribution pension plans or IRAs and may spend an increasing portion of their income on tax-deductible items such as mortgage interest payments and charitable contributions. Workers can increase their remuneration by switching to

4. Moffitt (1990) provides an exposition of comparative statics with piecewise-linear budget constraints.

5. The statutory benefit reduction rate is as high as 100 percent, but work expense allowances and other factors lower the effective rate (Burtless, 1990).

Table 7-2. *Sample Characteristics, by Income Group*[a]

Income decile	Income range (1995 dollars)	Marginal tax rate	Proportion itemizing deductions (percent)	Hours of work per year (conditional on participation)		Wages (1995 dollars per hour)	
				Male	Female	Male	Female
1	0–11,680	33	4	1,067	803	8.15	6.74
2	11,696–17,563	39	16	1,766	1,413	6.52	5.95
3	17,571–22,074	38	36	1,879	1,206	7.40	7.43
4	22,089–27,485	34	43	2,069	1,186	8.36	8.01
5	27,492–31,745	38	57	2,206	1,244	9.42	8.66
6	31,748–36,626	39	79	2,265	1,142	10.54	7.97
7	36,630–42,125	39	76	2,185	1,357	11.96	8.01
8	42,157–51,278	38	86	2,277	1,393	13.53	8.92
9	51,291–66,246	39	90	2,391	1,362	15.72	10.29
10	66,382–235,851	40	95	2,475	1,357	25.28	13.35
Overall		38	58	2,159	1,256	12.77	8.64

Source: Author's calculations.
a. Means from sample used in simulation.

jobs that offer a rising proportion of total compensation as untaxed fringe benefits and job amenities. The proportion of people who itemize deductions increases strongly with income (table 7-2).

Although theorists have recognized the potential importance of tax avoidance, empirical labor supply research has all but ignored it.[6] Empirical studies treat the statutory marginal tax rate as the effective tax rate.

In previous work, I estimated a model of labor supply that allows for the possibility that consumption of tax-deductible goods and the decision to itemize deductions are subject to taxpayer control and are influenced by the tax rate.[7] In this model, taxes affect not only the price of leisure relative to ordinary consumption but also the price of deductible consumption relative to nondeductible consumption (for those who choose to itemize).[8] My empirical estimates suggest that deductibility of some consumption goods increases labor supply relative to a tax system without such deductibility. However, the estimates refer to deductible goods as a composite and do not allow estimates of how labor supply would respond to changes in the tax treatment of particular goods.

Because of the lack of research on how the tax base and possibilities for tax avoidance influence labor supply, caution is in order in predicting the effect of tax reforms that change the tax base or the scope for avoidance. Existing estimates of responses to tax rates are based on rate changes when the base and avoidance opportunities are fixed. Even when such models accurately predict how changes in tax rates affect hours of work, they may miss badly in predicting labor supply responses to tax reforms that change not only tax rates but also the tax base. This problem is likely to be particularly acute in predicting the response of upper-income taxpayers, as this group generally has the largest scope and motivation for tax avoidance.

Most of the reform proposals would reduce the scope for tax avoidance in two ways. They would simplify the tax base and they would lower rates, thereby reducing the payoff to tax avoidance. Furthermore, the reduction in avoidance activity is likely to increase with income. The simulation results I present below, like those of other traditional models, do not allow for this reduction in tax avoidance possibilities. Accordingly, they may overstate the effects of the reforms on hours of work.

---

6. Theorists include Heckman (1983); Slemrod (1994).

7. Triest (1992).

8. Other models (Slemrod, 1994) also suggest that the tax rate affects labor supply in ways outside of the usual net wage and virtual income channels.

They may also overstate the reduction in progressivity and understate gains in efficiency from the reforms.

The payroll tax is another source of uncertainty regarding the true marginal tax rate. Earnings on which payroll taxes are levied help determine future social security benefits.[9] It is not clear whether workers regard current payroll taxes as the price of future benefits—and, hence, no more relevant to labor supply than any other price—or as a real tax. Although some workers may see a connection between current payroll taxes and future benefits, I treat the entire social security payroll tax as a real tax. Even if workers understand how the payroll tax–benefit relationship worked for earlier cohorts, public opinion polls document widespread skepticism among today's workers that they will receive benefits. Proposals to curtail or privatize social security are being widely discussed. The payroll tax rates incorporated into figure 7-2 are equal to the sum of the employee contribution and 65 percent of the employer contribution (assuming that the employer deducts the employer part of the tax at a 35 percent marginal rate).

Hours of Work

The tax reform proposals reviewed in the introduction to this volume would alter work incentives in two ways.[10] Most obviously, they would change marginal tax rates on earned income. They would also redistribute tax burdens and, possibly, wealth. Some taxpayers would pay more taxes after reform, while others would pay less. Those with reduced expected lifetime tax liability would tend to reduce labor supply, while those who expect to have a higher lifetime tax burden would tend to increase it. Since many of the tax reform proposals would lower both marginal tax rates and the lifetime tax burdens for those with high incomes, the wealth effect and the marginal tax rate effect are likely to work in conflicting directions. A switch to consumption taxation produces another wealth effect. Such a transition penalizes existing wealth holdings, unless the proposal contains transition rules that protect existing

9. See Feldstein and Samwick (1992) for an analysis of social security tax rates assuming that workers are fully cognizant of the way in which their current earnings affect future benefits.

10. Many of the reform proposals would also reduce the relative price of future consumption, although the effect of this on hours of work is not modeled in this chapter. As Metcalf (1996) points out, there is little empirical evidence on the size of this effect.

wealth, such as those in the USA tax proposal. A consumption tax without transition relief would increase the labor supply of wealth holders.

Results from Empirical Research

Most recent research has found that taxes have relatively small effects on labor supply. Male labor supply appears to be particularly unresponsive to tax incentives. Female labor supply generally exhibits greater response, perhaps because women are more likely than men to be on the margin of deciding whether or not to work at all.[11] Studies based on data from the income maintenance experiments of the late 1960s through early 1980s report that male uncompensated wage elasticities are clustered tightly around zero, and compensated elasticities average only about 0.08.[12] For wives, the experimental studies produce uncompensated wage elasticities averaging (weighting by sample size) approximately 0.07.[13] Studies examining the labor supply response of single mothers produce uncompensated wage elasticities averaging about −0.04.

The major federal tax reforms of the 1980s constitute a natural experiment of the effects of taxes on labor supply. These tax laws reduced marginal taxes more for upper-income filers than for lower-income ones. Accordingly, labor supply effects should be particularly evident for upper-income groups. In fact, the tax reforms seem to have increased hours of work of upper-income women but had, at best, only a small effect on labor supply of upper-income men.[14]

Analysis of nonexperimental data provides additional evidence on how taxes affect labor supply. While some older studies found large effects, most recent studies have found that taxes have small effects on hours of work of prime-aged males. Results of studies of the effect of taxes on female labor supply have varied quite a bit. They have found

11. Heckman (1993) provides a recent summary and interpretation of the empirical labor supply literature.

12. My summary of labor supply results from the income maintenance experiments is based on Burtless (1987).

13. The nonexperimental studies tend to produce much larger estimates.

14. These conclusions are based on empirical work reported in Bosworth and Burtless (1992) and Eissa (1995, 1996). Eissa attributes much of the labor supply response of women to changes in labor force participation. Mariger (1995), using panel data spanning the period surrounding the Tax Reform Act of 1986, finds little evidence of a labor supply response by men or women. However, he restricts his sample to married men and women who worked at least ten hours per week in each year between 1985 and 1988. Thus his results are consistent with responsiveness of female labor supply to tax incentives at the participation margin.

that taxes strongly affect female labor force participation, but, given participation, taxes have little effect on hours of work.[15]

Simulating Labor Supply Responses

In order to quantify how labor supply is likely to respond to tax reform, I simulate the effect of introducing several different tax reforms. I assume that desired hours of work *(h)* of household heads and spouses are linear functions of the net hourly wage *(w)* and virtual annual income *(y)*: $h = \gamma + \alpha w + \beta y$. The wage coefficient, α, indicates how many additional hours of work would be desired if the individual's net wage rate increased by one dollar, while the virtual income coefficient, β, indicates the change in desired hours caused by a one-dollar increase in virtual income. Specific values are assigned to α and β in performing the simulations.

The linear labor supply specification has two main advantages. It has been often estimated, which facilitates the choice of empirically based parameter values. And the indirect and direct utility functions underlying this functional form are known and can be expressed in closed form.[16] On the other hand, the specification is static and not well suited to analyzing tax reforms that have a strong effect on intertemporal decision-making.[17]

I used three sets of wage and income coefficients (α and β) in the simulations in order to gauge the sensitivity of the results to the choice of parameters (table 7-3). Parameter set 1 is based on estimates from an empirical study that estimated the linear labor supply specification. I take this set of parameters as the base case.

In parameter set 2, I set both the net wage and virtual income coefficients to zero for men and to one-half the values they take in parameter set 1 for women. I regard parameter set 2 as a lower bound to the likely responsiveness of labor supply to economic incentives.[18]

15. Mroz (1987); Zabel (1993).

16. Hausman (1981) shows the functional form for utility that underlies this specification. The utility function is needed in order to predict desired hours of work when the budget constraint has nonconvex kinks.

17. MaCurdy (1983) provides a framework for adapting similar models with consistent life-cycle decisionmaking by replacing unearned income with (endogenous) net dissaving. However, determining how savings responds to the tax reform greatly complicates the simulations, and I have not used that approach here.

18. MaCurdy, Green, and Paarsch (1990) estimate the linear labor supply model for prime-aged males using the methodology of Hausman (1981) and find that their estimates for both the wage and income coefficients are driven to zero.

Table 7-3. Behavioral Parameters Used in Simulations of Hours of Work

Coefficient	Parameter set 1[a]	Parameter set 2[b]	Parameter set 3[c]
Male net wage (α)	9.2	0	9.2
Male virtual income (β)	0	0	0
Female net wage (α)	47.6	23.8	153.3
Female virtual income (β)	−0.0072	−0.0036	−0.0144

a. Parameters based on the "dual additive errors" estimates in table 3 (for men) and table 5 (for women) of Triest (1990); all values have been adjusted for changes in consumer prices.

b. Parameters for women equal to one-half of their values in parameter set 1.

c. Parameters for women based on the "dual additive errors" estimates in table 4 of Triest (1990).

The female labor supply coefficients in parameter set 1 are based on an econometric specification that uses data only for women with positive hours of work. In that study, I also used data on both labor force participants and nonparticipants and estimated parameters indicating that female labor supply is considerably more responsive to economic incentives.[19] Parameter set 3 uses these parameters for women, while parameters for men are the same as those in parameter set 1. I regard the female labor supply coefficients in parameter set 3 as plausible but less likely to be true than those in parameter set 1. Because of the accumulating empirical evidence that the participation decision of women is more elastic than the choice of hours of work, given participation, I build into the model fixed monetary costs of working.[20] The existence of fixed costs of work is consistent with the participation decision's greater responsiveness to economic incentives. The fixed costs vary by marital status, number of children, and family size. This procedure implicitly conditions the responsiveness of the participation decision to economic incentives on these variables.

This behavioral model incorporates a standard, although increasingly unrealistic, model of the family decisionmaking process. Husbands are assumed to decide how many hours to work without considering their wives' labor supply decisions or earnings. Wives are assumed to regard their husbands' hours of work as fixed in making their own decisions and to treat husbands' earnings as exogenous income. Most empirical labor supply models make similar assumptions, but recognition of the joint character of labor supply decisions by husbands and wives is clearly needed.

19. Triest (1990). The specification estimated using data on both labor market participants and nonparticipants employed a censored tobit-like specification.

20. Based on estimates of Hausman (1981).

I use an extract from the Panel Study of Income Dynamics (PSID) data in my simulations. The PSID is particularly well suited for tax reform simulations since it contains data on wealth holdings in 1984 and 1989, as well as information on annual labor supply and earnings and demographic characteristics. The information on wealth can be used to calculate savings and consumption, which are useful in the simulations. The main labor supply, income, and demographic variables were taken from the 1988 wave (which collects income information for 1987), which was matched to the wealth information collected in 1984 and 1989. I included only prime-aged people who are household heads (including single heads) or the spouse of a household head in the simulations.[21]

The linear labor supply specification I employ might overstate labor supply response. The linear functional form implies that the net wage and virtual income elasticities increase with the net wage and virtual income.[22] Since average wage rates increase sharply with income (table 7-2), elasticities will be largest for upper-income taxpayers, whose marginal tax rates fall most under tax reform.

I first calibrate the model to the data by finding, for each sample member, the value of the constant term (γ) for each person that causes the model to predict the number of hours of work actually observed. Following the calibration exercise, I compute "base case" values for hours of work by simulating what the model predicts hours would be under the 1995 tax system. In doing the calibration and simulations, I take full account of the federal income tax, the earned income tax credit, the social security and medicare payroll taxes, and the benefit reduction rates faced by recipients of food stamps and AFDC. The simulations also allow people to change labor force participation status in response to tax changes. The appendix contains a more detailed description of the sample selection, variable construction, and simulation procedures.

I first consider the effects of replacing the federal corporate and individual income taxes with a single-rate value-added tax. According to Eric Toder, a 14.3 percent VAT (applied on a tax-inclusive basis) would raise approximately the same revenue as the current individual and corporate

---

21. My simulations are restricted to household heads and spouses because data on other family members are limited and because relatively little is known about how taxes affect the hours of work of the other family members.

22. The net wage elasticity is equal to α times the ratio of the net wage to hours of work; the virtual income elasticity is equal to β times the ratio of virtual income to hours of work.

Table 7-4. *Simulation of Effects of Tax Reform on Hours Worked, Various Parameters*

Percent

Tax reform	Change in hours worked								
	Parameter set 1			Parameter set 2			Parameter set 3		
	Total	Male	Female	Total	Male	Female	Total	Male	Female
VAT	2.2	0.9	4.1	0.8	0.0	2.0	6.5	0.9	14.8
Flat tax	1.1	0.6	2.0	0.4	0.0	1.0	3.2	0.5	7.2

Source: Author's calculations.

income taxes.[23] Within the sample used for the simulations, the VAT yields considerably less revenue than does the income tax it replaces.[24] However, this is not necessarily inconsistent with overall revenue neutrality. A revenue-neutral VAT would tend to shift the tax burden toward groups of taxpayers who are not represented in the sample I use in the simulations. Elderly people are not represented in the simulations, and they would generally pay higher taxes under a VAT than they currently do. Younger people are also excluded from the sample if they are neither the head of a household nor the spouse of a head. Such individuals generally have relatively low incomes and would pay higher taxes if federal tax progressivity were reduced (as it would be under a VAT). Another factor is that my measure of consumption, the sum of pre-tax earnings and financial dissaving, does not include the value of fringe benefits. If this form of consumption were to be taxed under a VAT, my simulations would understate the revenue raised by the VAT.

I assume that the VAT is fully passed on to consumers and that nominal wage rates remain constant. Hours of work increase 2.2 percent, 0.8 percent, and 6.5 percent if the income tax is replaced by a 14.3 percent VAT under parameter sets 1, 2, and 3, respectively (table 7-4). The results are clearly quite sensitive to parameter values.[25]

Table 7-5 shows the effects of a VAT on labor supply by income deciles for parameter set 1. At all income levels, the percentage increase

23. Eric Toder, "Comments on Proposals for Fundamental Tax Reform," *Tax Notes*, vol. 66, March 27, 1995, pp. 2003–15.

24. Simulated total federal revenue (including the payroll tax) is 12 percent less with the 14.3 percent VAT than under the current income tax.

25. The results are also sensitive to the VAT tax rate assumed. In order to raise the same amount of revenue as the current income tax within the sample used in the simulations, the VAT tax rate must be set at 18.6 percent, rather than 14.3 percent. Under parameter set 1, the increase in hours of work associated with the tax reform is then 1.7 percent, rather than 2.2 percent.

Table 7-5. *Simulation of Effects of a VAT on Hours Worked, Parameter Set 1*

Percent

Income decile	Mean change in marginal tax rate	Change in hours worked		
		Total	Male	Female
1	13	−0.9	−0.2	−1.3
2	−2	1.4	0.1	2.1
3	−6	1.7	0.3	3.3
4	−4	1.1	0.2	2.4
5	−9	1.9	0.4	4.5
6	−10	2.0	0.6	4.8
7	−11	2.4	0.7	5.1
8	−11	2.1	1.0	4.1
9	−12	2.5	1.2	5.1
10	−17	4.4	2.7	7.6
Overall	−7	2.2	0.9	4.1

Source: Author's calculations.

in labor supply is greater for female workers. Labor supply responses increase with income. People in the bottom decile would actually work less under a VAT than they do under the current system. These workers now generally pay no personal income taxes and may receive a net payment under the earned income tax credit. Under the VAT, the EITC and the zero bracket both disappear. The average marginal tax rate goes up, and hours of work decrease. In contrast, labor supply rises most in the top decile. Members of this decile experience the largest declines in marginal tax rates. They also have the highest wage elasticities, an artifact of the linear labor supply function, which causes the wage elasticity to rise with the wage rate.

Although the VAT might raise labor supply, it is regressive. The flat tax is an appealing alternative to the VAT, as it results in a more progressive tax distribution. In the absence of personal exemptions and family allowances, the flat tax is identical to a VAT,[26] except for the administrative fact that workers pay tax on earnings under the flat tax, while employers pay tax on earnings at the same rate under the VAT. In either case, a critical question for incidence concerns transition rules. In simulating effects on labor supply of the flat tax, I assume that in addition to the earnings tax, the tax falls on consumption in excess of earnings (at the single positive rate applicable to earnings).

26. William G. Gale, "Building a Better Tax System: Can a Consumption Tax Deliver the Goods?" *Tax Notes*, vol. 69, November 6, 1995, pp. 781–86.

Table 7-6. *Simulation of Alternative Tax Reforms, Parameter Set 1*

Percent

	Change in hours worked		
Tax reform	Total	Male	Female
Flat tax retaining the EITC	0.9	0.5	1.5
Flat tax replacing income and payroll taxes	0.3	0.1	0.7
"Flat" tax with two positive marginal tax rate brackets	0.5	0.4	0.8
Gephardt tax proposal	0.9	0.5	1.5

Source: Author's calculations.

In the simulations, I constrain the flat tax to generate the same amount of revenue raised by the 14.3 percent VAT within the sample. Because the flat tax is more progressive than the VAT, this procedure might understate the marginal tax rate needed for the flat tax to be revenue neutral (relative to the current system). One would expect that the flat tax might shift the tax burden (relative to the VAT) away from individuals not represented in the sample and toward the prime-aged household heads and spouses included in the sample. If this is true, it would be more appropriate to require that the flat tax raise a larger amount of revenue in the simulations than does the VAT.

In simulating the flat tax, I used the values for the personal exemption for dependents ($4,500) and family allowance ($16,500 for married filing jointly, $9,500 for single filers, and $14,000 for single heads of household) proposed by Robert Hall and Alvin Rabushka,[27] and then solved for the tax rate that yields the same revenue as the VAT. Using parameter set 1, I find that a tax rate of 20.3 percent yields the same revenue as the VAT. Hours of work increase 1.1 percent relative to the current tax system, half the increase associated with the VAT. Simulations using parameter sets 2 and 3 also suggest that the increase in labor supply associated with the flat tax is half that associated with the VAT (table 7-4). Even these estimates may be on the high side, however, because of the avoidance possibilities under the current system, which are almost certainly larger than they would be under the flat tax. Accordingly, the reduction in effective rates and the increase in hours associated with the flat tax may be smaller than my simulations suggest.

The results of simulating three variants of the flat tax are shown in table 7-6. The first retains the earned income tax credit. To raise the same amount of revenue as would be raised without the EITC, the tax

27. Hall and Rabushka (1995).

rate must be increased to 20.8 percent.[28] The overall increase in hours is slightly less than when the flat tax is implemented without the EITC (0.9 versus 1.1). The EITC stimulates work effort in the lowest decile, but decreases it in higher deciles (relative to the results in table 7-5) because of the high marginal tax rate in the phaseout range of the EITC and the increase in the flat tax rate.[29]

Replacing both income *and* payroll taxes with a flat tax requires a rate of 38.9 percent to maintain revenues if family allowances and exemption levels are not changed from the previous simulations. Under this tax regime, hours of work rise a minuscule 0.3 percent, but this variant of the flat tax is more progressive than the other proposals. Simulations of a two-rate, "semi-flat" tax with rates of 18.5 percent for the first bracket and 23.5 percent for the second bracket reveal a general principle: as progressivity increases, labor supply diminishes.[30] In general, variants of the flat tax more progressive than the standard Hall-Rabushka proposal are likely to result in smaller increases in labor supply.

The last simulation is of a variant of Representative Richard Gephardt's 10 percent tax proposal. Values of the standard deduction, personal exemption, and tax bracket definitions were specified to be the same as in Gephardt's proposal. However, rather than fixing the first marginal tax rate at 10 percent, I set this rate to yield the same revenue as the other proposals. This resulted in the "10 percent tax" turning into the "13.9 percent tax." According to the simulation, Gephardt's proposal would increase hours of work slightly less than 1 percentage point, a shift that is comparable to the other proposals that produce a similar distribution of the tax burden.

28. It may not be fully appropriate to constrain this simulation to raise the same amount of revenue as the plans considered in the earlier simulations. Families that are eligible for the EITC are probably overrepresented in the sample. This may account for why I find that retaining the EITC requires that the flat tax marginal rate be increased by a slightly larger amount than Gale, Houser, and Scholz (chapter 8 in this volume) find is needed in their simulations.

29. Eissa and Liebman (1996) find that the expansion of the EITC in 1987 increased labor force participation among female household heads, but did not decrease hours for women who are already in the labor force. Their research suggests that my simulation may be understating the positive effect of the EITC on labor force participation and overstating the possible negative effect of the clawback provision of the EITC on hours of work. Simulation results broken down by income deciles are not shown, but are available from the author upon request.

30. In this simulation, I specified that the higher marginal tax rate be 5 percentage points higher than the lower rate. I then solved for the tax rates that resulted in identical simulated tax revenue under the two variants of the flat tax.

Two caveats apply to this simulation. First, one should note that although Gephardt's tax proposal has a graduated rate structure, I vary only the initial 10 percent rate in adjusting his proposal so that it raises the same amount of revenue as the other proposals I simulate. If I had instead increased all of the tax rates, the labor supply results could have been quite different. Second, Gephardt's proposal is fundamentally different from the other proposals simulated in this chapter, and it may not be appropriate to constrain it to produce the same amount of revenue within the sample used here. Unlike the other proposals, Gephardt's plan moves in the direction of a more comprehensive income tax. Income components that are not included in the current tax base, such as interest from municipal bonds and pension plan contributions, are taxed under Gephardt's plan. Since I do not have information about pension contributions and municipal bond interest in my data set, my calculations may understate the expansion of the tax base and overstate the tax rate needed for Gephardt's plan to produce the same revenue as the other proposals.

Timing Issues

The simulations give a rough measure of the likely changes in hours of work following fundamental tax reform, but they do not address issues of timing or incorporate general equilibrium effects. Most workers have little flexibility in how many hours they can work in their current job. A tax-induced change in desired hours may require a change in jobs in order to be implemented. Thus short-run changes in hours of work would probably be smaller than the simulations suggest.

The simulations are partial equilibrium in nature, and so do not reflect the probable effects of fundamental tax reform on pre-tax wages and rates of return. By increasing labor supply, tax reform would tend to initially decrease wages, attenuating the labor supply effect. In the long run, fundamental tax reform that raised saving would increase wages by expanding capital. The effects on labor supply, as always, include both the substitution effect, which would tend to boost work hours, and the wealth effect, which would reduce hours by increasing lifetime earnings.

Retirement

Retirement behavior is an important aspect of labor supply. Male retirement ages have been falling, a trend that concerns policymakers. Fundamental tax reform may have a major impact on retirement decisions in three ways: by generating wealth effects at the transition to the new tax system, by changing the rate structure, and by breaking the link between pensions and tax-preferred savings.

Transition Effects

Fundamental tax reform may generate wealth effects that affect the behavior of workers nearing retirement age. Economic theory suggests that increases in wealth promote retirement.[31] A reform that taxes wealth will discourage retirement because would-be retirees will find that their retirement savings cannot buy as much as they could under the old tax system. Depending on the transition rules and the nature of the reform, however, this effect could be reversed. A reform that protected "old wealth" and led to increases in real interest rates would encourage retirement.

The effect of tax reform on existing retirement savings will generally not be the same for all workers. Some assets may increase in value due to tax reform, while others may decrease.[32] Workers with assets, such as housing, that lose their tax-preferred status under at least some reforms could find themselves deferring retirement, particularly if they had intended to sell the assets and use the proceeds to finance their retirement consumption. Other workers might realize windfall gains or enjoy reduced taxes and retire earlier than they otherwise would have. While these effects could be important, they are virtually impossible to estimate with any precision.

Steady-State Effects

The most important long-run effect of the consumption tax on retirement behavior might be due to the severing of the link between tax-preferred savings and pension plans. The current tax code provides strong

31. Although theoretical models of retirement behavior suggest that an exogenous increase in wealth will result in individuals' choosing to retire earlier, the empirical literature suggests that this effect may be fairly small. For example, the wealth changes generated by the 1977 social security reform seem to have had relatively little effect on retirement behavior (Krueger and Pischke, 1992).

32. See chapter 2 by Alan J. Auerbach, chapter 5 by Dennis R. Capozza, Richard K. Green, and Patric H. Hendershott, and chapter 11 by Ronald A. Pearlman in this volume.

incentives to save for retirement within pension plans that have restrictions directly relevant to the retirement decision.

This would change under the tax reform proposals. Under the consumption tax proposals, normal returns to capital accumulate tax-free, eliminating a prime motivation for pension plans.[33] Under the Gephardt "10 percent tax" proposal, pension contributions made by employers are included in the tax base, which also reduces the attractiveness of saving through pension plans.

Many defined-benefit pension plans strongly encourage retirement within certain age windows and have probably contributed to the trend toward early retirement.[34] Although defined-contribution pension plans, such as 401(k) plans, are growing faster than traditional defined-benefit plans, both types of plan penalize withdrawal of funds except for approved purposes before age 59½, thus encouraging the accumulation of assets that can be used to finance retirement. Defined-benefit plans would probably further decrease in importance following implementation of a fundamental tax reform. Indeed, the reasons for mandatory savings plans of any kind would diminish, since they would enjoy no particular tax advantage. Although most of the reform proposals will increase overall incentives to save, withdrawal penalties would diminish or vanish. Pension plans provide workers a disciplined way to save voluntarily for retirement.[35] Reduced pension coverage would tend to cause workers to save less for retirement than they would under the current system and might delay their retirement as a result. In addition, nondiscrimination rules currently prompt employers to provide pension coverage to some workers who would not opt for coverage (or opt for less coverage) on their own. Without pension coverage, these workers would save less than they currently do through the pension system and would probably delay their retirement.

Human Capital

Tax policy can influence the level and distribution of wages by providing incentives for individuals to seek education and training. According to

---

33. Pension contributions might still have the advantage of being deductible from the social security and medicare payroll tax bases.

34. Kotlikoff and Wise (1988) document the retirement incentives created by many defined-benefit plans.

35. Shefrin and Thaler (1988).

some estimates, the value of human capital (measured as the present value of the increase in the stream of earnings due to education and training) substantially exceeds the value of physical capital.[36] Moreover, ownership of human capital is much less concentrated than that of physical capital, making human capital an especially important determinant of the distribution of economic well-being.

Current Tax Treatment

Current tax treatment of human capital closely resembles that under a consumption tax.[37] Most of the cost of human capital investment is earnings forgone by students and trainees while in school. Since forgone earnings are not taxed, this component of investment cost is immediately deducted from potential earnings, as it would be under a consumption tax. In the case of workers undergoing on-the-job training, earnings paid to the workers are deductible by their employers, and any forgone earnings—for example, because the workers receive a lower wage during training—are untaxed and so are implicitly expensed. Employers can deduct all tuition for job-related employee training and some tuition that is not directly job related.[38]

The only major human capital investment that does not currently receive favorable tax treatment is tuition payments paid by households. However, tuition at public institutions is usually much less than the full resource cost of the educational services. Private institutions often use endowment funds (which result from tax-deductible charitable gifts) and government grants to hold tuition below cost. Moreover, subsidized student loan programs and financial aid further reduce educational costs for many students.

Effects of Tax Reform

Tax reform could change incentives for human capital investment by flattening the rate structure and by changing the tax treatment of physical capital. Flattening the rate structure—that is, reducing progressivity—is likely to promote human capital acquisition. Under a graduated rate

36. Davies and Whalley (1991) review studies estimating the aggregate value of human capital.
37. Kaplow (1996) and Steuerle (1996) discuss the current tax treatment of human capital.
38. Dupor and others (1996).

structure, people typically face lower tax rates when in school or training than they do when they realize the gains from the investment. Little empirical work has been done on the importance of this effect. One recent study found "moderate to small" increases in human capital investment in a simulation of replacing the 1970 tax rate structure with a flat-rate income tax, although there is some evidence that the effect of a progressive rate structure may be large in some instances.[39] One factor not generally taken into account is that some students have limited financing options while in school and depend on earnings to finance their education. A tax system with a large exemption or a low initial rate reduces taxes on students' earnings relative to that under a proportional tax.

A shift to consumption taxation could also affect human capital investment indirectly. By increasing the net return on physical capital, a switch to consumption taxation would tend to reduce the relative attractiveness of human capital investment, at least in the short run.[40] Recent general equilibrium simulation models suggest that as the net return on physical capital returns to the pre-tax reform path, the effect on human capital is reduced. These models suggest that a change in the tax treatment of physical capital is likely to have little or no long-run effect on human capital.[41] However, again, there is a lack of direct empirical evidence.

Job Amenities and Occupational Choice

Taxation affects not only how many hours one chooses to work, but also what type of job one chooses to work at. Without incurring any tax liability, workers can forgo potential earnings in exchange for a pleasant work environment, a relaxed pace of work effort, reduced risk of financial or physical misfortune, and generous fringe benefits. All of these benefits are examples of job amenities favored by the tax code. Fringe benefits could be included in taxable income, but it is hard to see how such job attributes as an easy pace of work could be taxed.[42] However, reductions in tax rates reduce demand for all tax-favored items, including

---

39. Dupor and others (1996, p. 343).
40. Heckman (1976); Driffill and Rosen (1983).
41. See Dupor and others (1996); Trostel (1993); Davies and Whalley (1991).
42. This example illustrates the more general point that it is not possible to observe, or tax, potential earnings.

job amenities. Since the tax reform proposals would lower marginal tax rates for most workers, they could be expected to reduce the efficiency losses associated with tax-induced demand for job amenities.[43]

In addition to changing the allocation of labor supply over occupations, tax reform would also probably affect patterns of labor demand. If tax reform reduces incentives for tax avoidance and makes compliance easier than it now is, it will reduce demand for tax accountants in the long run. In the short run, however, tax reform is likely to raise demand for services of these professionals because of the complexities associated with the transition to the new tax regime.

One rationale for lowering marginal tax rates on high-income taxpayers is that high marginal tax rates may discourage entrepreneurial effort. Because self-employed entrepreneurs have greater flexibility in deciding how many hours to work than do most workers employed by firms, they may have labor supply that is more responsive to taxation. Empirical evidence on this question is scant.[44]

Tax avoidance considerations become paramount in considering how the self-employed are likely to respond to the tax reform proposals. Under current tax law, the self-employed have greater scope for tax avoidance than do most workers. Some tax-deductible business expenses (for example, home offices) have a strong consumption component, and with some effort and cost the self-employed can shelter large amounts of retirement savings in customized defined-benefit retirement plans. The wedge between the effective and statutory marginal tax rates is likely to be especially large for the self-employed. By lowering the statutory marginal tax rate, tax reform might have a stronger effect on tax avoidance activity by the self-employed than it does on hours of work.

Conclusion

Although a VAT would potentially have a relatively large effect on hours of work, the simulated effects of the more politically palatable proposals are small. The impossibility of taking tax avoidance into account may cause even these effects to be overstated. If tax rates higher than those I simulated were needed for revenue neutrality, this would also reduce the

43. There is a large literature in labor economics dealing with the implicit market for job amenities and characteristics. Rosen (1986) provides a survey and exposition.

44. One recent study estimates that self-employed male physicians have a larger wage elasticity than do physicians employed by hospitals or HMOs (Showalter and Thurston, 1996).

effect of the reforms on hours of work. The simulations described in this chapter have important limitations, but they do indicate that one should not expect tax reform proposals currently being considered to cause major changes in hours of work.

Appendix: Data Set Construction and Simulation Methodology

I selected family observations from the PSID data if both the family head and spouse (if present) were between 25 and 60 years old in 1988 and if there had been no change in the identity of the head or spouse between 1984 and 1989. I imposed the restriction that the identity of the head and spouse did not change to avoid problems in interpreting how much of the family's change in wealth between 1984 and 1989 was due to a change in family composition. The restriction that both the head and spouse were at least 25 in 1988 was partly motivated by the difficulty in modeling the effect of taxation on entry of youths into the labor force, and partly by the fact that younger families were very likely to have had a change in the identity of the head or spouse between 1984 and 1989. I dropped families with a head or spouse over 60 years old to avoid modeling retirement behavior. Imposing the selection restrictions resulted in a sample of 2,817 observations. Annual savings (which is used in constructing an estimate of consumption) is based on average annual financial savings between 1984 and 1989. Due to a number of outliers, annual savings was truncated to lie between −25 percent and 25 percent of total income in the simulations. Since wages are needed in the simulations for all potential workers, I imputed wages for nonworkers using a regression-based procedure.[45]

The intercept terms (γ) in the labor supply functions vary over individuals. As discussed in the text, they are calibrated to the data by finding, for each sample member, the γ value that would result in the observed value of hours of work being the desired value chosen by the model. I assumed that families that were AFDC or food stamps participants for 1987 were eligible for the programs, and that other families were ineligible. Since the budget sets created by the interaction of the welfare programs, fixed costs of working, and payroll and income taxes are generally not convex, the algorithm for picking γ for each observation determines which γ values are consistent with local optima, and then

45. See Triest (1994, p. 144) for a more detailed description of the imputation procedure.

picks the value within this set that yields the highest utility level. In the case of those observed to be nonworkers, the algorithm first finds the maximum value of γ that is consistent with labor force nonparticipation being utility maximizing. A draw from an assumed distribution for γ (truncated from above at the maximum value consistent with nonparticipation being optimal) is then generated, and used as the nonparticipant's γ value in the simulations.[46]

The γ values determined by this procedure will always result in the observed hours of work values being consistent with local utility maximization. However, in some cases they may not be global optima due to the existence of nonconvex regions of the budget set. In each of these cases, I solved for the utility-maximizing value of hours of work (given the values of γ, α, and β) and substituted this value for the observed value.

Comment by Hilary Williamson Hoynes

The single most important justification for fundamental tax reform is that it presumably increases efficiency, particularly by boosting labor supply. Accordingly, this chapter is essential reading for those interested in tax reform. Triest is well equipped to study this issue, as he has worked extensively on the effect of taxes on labor supply. The chapter reflects his command of the literature and his understanding of the complicated nature of the issue.

The first part of the chapter provides a discussion of the qualitative effects of tax reform on work effort, based on available evidence in the theoretical, and sometimes empirical, literature. This general discussion proceeds to consider a "generic" version of tax reform, manifested by a broadening of the tax base, a reduction in the tax rate, and a flattening of the tax rate schedule. Triest considers a wide range of issues critical for labor supply, including the effects of fundamental tax reform on tax avoidance, after-tax wealth holdings, hours worked, occupational choice, human capital investment, entrepreneurial activity, and retirement. One of the chapter's greatest strengths is the space devoted to the many dimensions of labor supply, leading to a more comprehensive analysis than the somewhat narrow issue of hours worked (the focus of most empirical

---

46. The distribution assumed for γ varies by sex, and is based on parameter estimates in Triest (1990).

studies). I find this discussion to be thorough, sensible, and intuitive. It is not, however, conclusive. Some aspects of tax reform are expected to lead to increases in work activity but others to decreases.

Triest tackles some of this ambiguity in the second part of the chapter by providing estimates of the effects of specific tax reform proposals (and variants thereof) on hours worked, using a simulation model developed in earlier work.[47] First, he adopts a linear labor supply equation that relates desired hours of work to net-of-tax wages and to virtual income. He borrows three sets of wage and income elasticities to create parameters for the labor supply equation. Second, he uses data from the Panel Study of Income Dynamics (PSID) to construct a sample of households that forms the basis for the simulation. Third, he predicts hours of work for each member in the sample. In order to do so, he needs to construct the individual's budget constraint, which is a function of gross wages, unearned income, tax filing status, and the particulars of the tax system being simulated. Last, he compares hours worked under current law with hours worked under various tax reforms. The results from these simulations show fairly modest overall increases in labor supply. Triest points out, correctly, that these overall estimates mask the larger increases that are concentrated among women and those in the highest income groups.

My main comments on the simulation model pertain to the specification of the labor supply equation and the choice of parameter values. First, the linear form for the labor supply equation implies that the wage and income elasticities increase in value as income increases. The importance of the assumption is striking. Triest has shown elsewhere that wage elasticities for men in the highest income decile are three times the size of the wage elasticity of those in the lowest income decile.[48] Although Feldstein provides evidence that elasticity of taxable income may be higher in higher income groups,[49] there is little evidence that labor supply sensitivity is positively related to income. In fact, quite large effects of taxes on labor supply have been found for low-income families who face high marginal tax rates because of the phaseout range in the earned income tax credit (EITC) and benefit reduction rates in means-tested transfer programs such as aid to families with dependent children

47. Triest (1994).
48. Triest (1994). Given the significant differences in the tax changes across income deciles, Triest should report the wage and income elasticities by income decile in the same way he did in his 1994 study.
49. Feldstein (1995).

(AFDC) and food stamps.[50] The tax reform proposals considered here generally tend to result in increases in marginal tax rates at the lowest income levels, contrasted with potentially large decreases in marginal tax rates at high income levels. Thus the relatively high elasticities at high income levels will tend to overstate the estimated increase in labor supply that results from tax reform. It is conceivable that the true reduction in labor supply experienced by the lowest income groups could completely offset the increase in labor supply of those at high income levels.

Second, Triest specifies separate wage and income elasticities for men and women for each parameter set. The labor supply literature has shown quite consistently that the overall responsiveness of men to changes in wages and income is smaller than the responsiveness of women (which is reflected in the parameter sets).[51] This literature has also shown that the elasticities of female heads of household are smaller than those of married women and much closer in magnitude to the elasticities of men. The estimates for women in Triest's analysis are based on studies of married women. Using lower elasticities for female heads of household will probably lead to lower estimates of the effect of tax reform on labor supply.[52] Since the estimates are readily available from the literature, the analysis would be greatly strengthened by using four sets of wage and income elasticities, allowing them to vary not only by sex but also by marital status.

Third, family labor supply for married couples is based on a second-ary-earner model, which assumes that decisions about labor supply for the husband and wife are made in ways that limit the possibility for substitution of leisure by the couple. It assumes that the husband makes a decision about hours of work, ignoring the wife's decision. The wife then decides how much to work, taking the husband's choice as given. The marginal tax rate for her first hour worked reflects the income that the husband is earning. The implication of this model is that each individual's labor supply decision depends on one's own wage, but not the wage of the spouse. The implication of this specification depends on the size of the own and cross-wage elasticities and whether the husband and wife's labor supply are substitutes or complements. One study has found

---

50. For example, see reviews of this evidence in Moffitt (1992) and Hoynes (1996).

51. For example, see the reviews by Pencavel (1986) and Killingsworth and Heckman (1986).

52. If female heads of household are heavily concentrated at the very lowest income levels, where labor supply actually decreases, then the opposite may be true.

that taking into account the joint nature of the labor supply decision results in labor supply responses about one-third the size of those that result from the secondary-earner model.[53]

Next, there is one aspect of the simulation results that warrants discussion. Triest considers implementing a version of the flat tax in which the EITC is either retained or eliminated. Retaining the EITC increases the returns to work for those out of the labor force (leading to increases in labor supply) but provides higher marginal tax rates for those in the flat and phaseout range of the credit (probably leading to decreases in labor supply). Triest's simulations show that, overall, keeping the EITC decreases hours worked for both men and women. This implies very large effects of the EITC in the phaseout range. This is contrary to studies that show positive effects of the EITC on hours worked.[54] This may be explained by the functional form relating higher elasticities to those in higher income groups (such as those in the phaseout range of the credit).

My last comments on the simulation results concern the choice and construction of the data set. Triest explains that the PSID is attractive for the analysis because it contains information on wealth (in addition to information on labor supply and family characteristics). The Survey of Income and Program Participation (SIPP) represents an alternative data set that, I think, provides many advantages over the PSID. The SIPP is a panel of approximately 20,000 families who are interviewed three times a year over a twenty-eight-month period. Each year since 1983 a new panel (with completely different samples) has been initiated. The first advantage of the SIPP is that since it is a much larger survey (collectively across panels), it has more coverage of families at the high end of the income range, which is very important for the purposes of the tax reforms being considered. Second, the difficulty in implementing these reforms is in measuring the changes in the tax base of the family.[55] The SIPP contains more information than the PSID on household tax status, which may be helpful for the purposes of accurately measuring the tax base and, consequently, the marginal tax rates. Last, it may be possible to use the SIPP data to examine the sensitivity to some of the other

53. Hausman and Ruud (1984).

54. Eissa and Liebman (1996); Dickert, Houser, and Scholz (1995).

55. Because of insufficient documentation of the data construction, it is not clear how well Triest measures the tax base using the PSID. Specifically, there is limited discussion of what information the PSID has on such questions as filing status and itemization status and how that information is used to construct estimates of household taxable income.

measures of work effort mentioned above (entrepreneurial effort, human capital investment) that are not covered in the empirical work.

I want to conclude my comments by broadening the discussion. The empirical results show that when one uses a narrow definition of work effort (hours of work), the efficiency gains are not likely to be large. However, at the same time Triest also presents a comprehensive discussion of the issues relevant for the debate on the effects of fundamental tax reform on work effort. This qualitative discussion suggests that issues such as the effect on tax avoidance, entrepreneurial effort, and retirement are of first-order importance and, in fact, may be more important than the effect on hours of work. Because these aspects are not addressed in the empirical analysis, the chapter whets the appetite for more. In sum, Triest's chapter is a solid first step toward a more comprehensive understanding of the effects of fundamental tax reform on labor supply. Moving beyond Triest's careful analysis, however, may require additional research to quantify the broader effects of taxes on work effort.

References

Bosworth, Barry, and Gary Burtless. 1992. "Effects of Tax Reform on Labor Supply, Investment, and Saving." *Journal of Economic Perspectives* 6 (Winter): 3–25.

Burtless, Gary. 1987. "The Work Response to a Guaranteed Income: A Survey of Experimental Evidence." In *Lessons from the Income Maintenance Experiments*, edited by Alicia H. Munnell, 22–52. Federal Reserve Bank of Boston and Brookings.

———. 1990. "The Economist's Lament: Public Assistance in America." *Journal of Economic Perspectives* 4 (Winter): 57–78.

Burtless, Gary, and Jerry A. Hausman. 1978. "The Effect of Taxation on Labor Supply: Evaluating the Gary Negative Income Tax Experiment." *Journal of Political Economy* 86 (December): 1103–30.

Davies, James, and John Whalley. 1991. "Taxes and Capital Formation: How Important Is Human Capital?" In *National Saving and Economic Performance*, edited by B. Douglas Bernheim and John B. Shoven, 163–97. University of Chicago Press.

Dickert, Stacy, Scott Houser, and John Karl Scholz. 1995. "The Earned Income Tax Credit and Transfer Programs: A Study of Labor Market and Program Participation." In *Tax Policy and the Economy*, edited by James Poterba, vol. 9, 1–49. MIT Press.

Driffill, E. John, and Harvey S. Rosen. 1983. "Taxation and Excess Burden: A Life-Cycle Perspective." *International Economic Review* 24 (October): 671–83.

Dupor, Bill, and others. 1996. "Some Effects of Taxes on Schooling and Training." *American Economic Review* 86 (May): 340–46.

Eissa, Nada. 1995. "Taxation and Labor Supply of Married Women: The Tax Reform Act of 1986 as a Natural Experiment." Working Paper 5023. Cambridge, Mass.: National Bureau of Economic Research.

———. 1996. "Tax Reforms and Labor Supply." In *Tax Policy and the Economy*, edited by James M. Poterba, vol. 10, 119–51. MIT Press and National Bureau of Economic Research.

Eissa, Nada, and Jeffrey B. Liebman. 1996. "Labor Supply Response to the Earned Income Tax Credit." *Quarterly Journal of Economics* 111 (May): 605–37.

Feldstein, Martin. 1995. "The Effect of Marginal Tax Rates on Taxable Income: A Panel Study of the 1986 Tax Reform Act." *Journal of Political Economy* 103 (June): 551–72.

Feldstein, Martin, and Andrew Samwick. 1992. "Social Security Rules and Marginal Tax Rates." *National Tax Journal* 45 (March): 1–22.

Hall, Robert E., and Alvin Rabushka. 1995. *The Flat Tax*, 2d ed. Stanford, Calif.: Hoover Institution Press.

Hausman, Jerry A. 1981. "Labor Supply." In *How Taxes Affect Economic Behavior*, edited by Henry J. Aaron and Joseph A. Pechman, 27–75. Brookings.

Hausman, Jerry, and Paul Ruud. 1984. "Family Labor Supply with Taxes." *American Economic Review* 74 (May): 242–48.

Heckman, James J. 1976. "A Life-Cycle Model of Earnings, Learning, and Consumption." *Journal of Political Economy* 84 (August): S11–S44.

———. 1983. "Comment on the Jerry A. Hausman Essay." In *Behavioral Simulation Methods in Tax Policy Analysis*, edited by Martin Feldstein, 70–82. University of Chicago Press.

———. 1993. "What Has Been Learned about Labor Supply in the Past Twenty Years?" *American Economic Review* 83 (May): 116–21.

Hoynes, Hilary. 1996. "Work, Welfare, and Family Structure: What Have We Learned?" Paper prepared for the Robert D. Burch Center for Tax Policy and Public Finance conference on Fiscal Policy: Lessons from Economic Research.

Kaplow, Louis. 1996. "On the Divergence Between 'Ideal' and Conventional Income-Tax Treatment of Human Capital." *American Economic Review* 86 (May): 347–52.

Killingsworth, Mark, and James Heckman. 1986. "Female Labor Supply: A Survey." In *Handbook of Labor Economics*, edited by Orley Ashenfelter and Richard Layard, vol. 1, 103–204. Amsterdam: North-Holland.

Kotlikoff, Laurence J., and David A. Wise. 1988. "Pension Backloading, Implicit Wage Taxes, and Work Disincentives." In *Tax Policy and the Economy*, edited by Lawrence H. Summers, vol. 2, 161–96. National Bureau of Economic Research and MIT Press.

Krueger, Alan B., and Jorn-Steffen Pischke. 1992. "The Effect of Social Security on Labor Supply: A Cohort Analysis of the Notch Generation." *Journal of Labor Economics* 10 (October): 412–37.

MaCurdy, Thomas E. 1983. "A Simple Scheme for Estimating an Intertemporal Model of Labor Supply and Consumption in the Presence of Taxes and Uncertainty." *International Economic Review* 24 (June): 265–89.

MaCurdy, Thomas, David Green, and Harry J. Paarsch. 1990. "Assessing Empirical Approaches for Analyzing Taxes and Labor Supply." *Journal of Human Resources* 25 (Summer): 415–90.

Mariger, Randall P. 1995. "Labor Supply and the Tax Reform Act of 1986: Evidence from Panel Data." Finance and Economics Discussion Series paper 95-34. Federal Reserve Board.

Metcalf, Gilbert E. 1996. "Labor Supply and Welfare Effects of a Shift from Income to Consumption Taxation." In *Empirical Foundations of Household Taxation*, edited by Martin Feldstein and James M. Poterba, 77–94. University of Chicago Press.

Moffitt, Robert. 1990. "The Econometrics of Kinked Budget Constraints." *Journal of Economic Perspectives* 4 (Spring): 119–39.

———. 1992. "Incentive Effects of the U.S. Welfare System: A Review." *Journal of Economic Literature* 30 (March): 1–61.

Mroz, Thomas A. 1987. "The Sensitivity of an Empirical Model of Married Women's Hours of Work to Economic and Statistical Assumptions." *Econometrica* 55 (July): 765–99.

Pencavel, John. 1986. "Labor Supply of Men: A Survey." In *Handbook of Labor Economics,* edited by Orley Ashenfelter and Richard Layard, vol. 1, 3–102. Amsterdam: North-Holland.

Rosen, Sherwin. 1986. "The Theory of Equalizing Differences." In *Handbook of Labor Economics*, vol. 1, edited by Orley Ashenfelter and Richard Layard, 641–92. New York: North-Holland.

Shefrin, Hersh M., and Richard H. Thaler. 1988. "The Behavioral Life-Cycle Hypothesis." *Economic Inquiry* 26 (October): 609–43.

Showalter, Mark H., and Norman K. Thurston. 1996. "Taxes and Labor Supply of High-Income Physicians." Brigham Young University, Department of Economics.

Slemrod, Joel. 1994. "A General Model of the Behavioral Response to Taxation." University of Michigan, Office of Tax Policy Research.

Steuerle, C. Eugene. 1996. "How Should Government Allocate Subsidies for Human Capital?" *American Economic Review* 86 (May): 353–57.

Triest, Robert K. 1990. "The Effect of Income Taxation on Labor Supply in the United States." *Journal of Human Resources* 25 (Summer): 491–516.

——. 1992. "The Effect of Income Taxation on Labor Supply When Deductions Are Endogenous." *Review of Economics and Statistics* 74 (February): 91–99.

——. 1994. "The Efficiency Cost of Increased Progressivity." In *Tax Progressivity and Income Inequality*, edited by Joel B. Slemrod, 137–69. Cambridge University Press.

Trostel, Philip A. 1993. "The Effect of Taxation on Human Capital." *Journal of Political Economy* 101 (April): 327–50.

Zabel, Jeffrey E. 1993. "The Relationship between Hours of Work and Labor Force Participation in Four Models of Labor Supply Behavior." *Journal of Labor Economics* 11 (April): 387–416.

PART THREE

Incidence

CHAPTER 8

Distributional Effects of Fundamental Tax Reform

William G. Gale, Scott Houser, and John Karl Scholz

FUNDAMENTAL tax reform would affect economic efficiency, the complexity of the tax system, and the distribution of tax burdens and income. This chapter examines the likely effects on the distribution of annual income among U.S. families. We apply standard assumptions about the incidence of specific taxes to household-level data, simulate the tax and transfer system, and estimate the distributional effects of the current system and various reforms.[1]

This approach has been criticized over the years for several reasons. First, some authors focus on lifetime rather than annual distributional analysis, with the view that tax burdens should be related to discounted lifetime income, not to annual incomes, which can fluctuate capriciously.[2] Both approaches provide useful information, but using annual income has important advantages. Because lifetime data are not available, styl-

We are grateful to Stacy Dickert for helping develop the microsimulation model used in this chapter, Phil Cross and Dale Knapp for their valuable comments and research assistance, and Jonathan Gruber for help with health insurance imputations. We also received valuable comments from Jerry Auten, Arik Levinson, Andy Reschovsky, conference participants, and members of the Public Affairs Workshop at the University of Wisconsin-Madison. Work on this project has been supported by grants from the Census Bureau, the National Institute on Aging, and the Office of the Assistant Secretary for Policy Evaluation at Health and Human Services through the Institute for Research on Poverty. Views expressed in this chapter are ours and do not necessary reflect those held by funding agencies.

1. See Pechman and Okner (1974) and Pechman (1985) for the most well-known incidence studies following this approach.

2. See, for example, Poterba (1989), Fullerton and Rogers (1993), and Lyon and Schwab (1995). Kotlikoff and various coauthors go beyond lifetime incidence and calculate the effects of various policies on tax burdens of different generations. See, for example, Kotlikoff (1992).

ized models of lifetime consumption and income are sometimes used. Other times annual consumption is used as a proxy for lifetime income. The stylized models may not accurately reflect behavior, however, and consumption in a given year may not be a good proxy for lifetime income.[3] In addition, analyses are most useful when they are understandable and considered relevant by those making policy. Thomas A. Barthold argues that politicians reject the lifetime view because they do not understand it and because it does not correspond to their view of political reality—tax systems change frequently and elections occur regularly.[4]

A second criticism of the methods we employ arises from the complexity of reactions that major tax reform would set in motion. Distributional effects of tax reform ultimately depend on accompanying changes in federal spending and borrowing, prices (including wages and interest rates), and the responses of individuals and businesses to these changes. Computational general equilibrium (CGE) models account for these changes rigorously, but they force analysts to specify household preferences and production functions, require strong simplifying assumptions about behavior, and demand parameters for which empirical estimates do not exist.[5] Furthermore, CGE models use highly aggregated data. For that reason, they typically do not capture the effects of detailed changes in tax policy, such as elimination of the home mortgage interest deduction, which will shift tax burdens from renters to homeowners and from older to younger households,[6] or changes in personal exemptions, which will redistribute taxes among families of different sizes. Effects of tax reform on such population groups are of interest to policymakers. In short, CGE analysis has advantages and disadvantages relative to our approach.

Thus, our approach complements lifetime and CGE analyses of tax reform. Even for those who believe general equilibrium effects are likely to be large, our static or "overnight" effects show how large general equilibrium effects would have to be to restore the existing distribution of tax burdens. Its usefulness is highlighted by the fact that the Joint

3. Bernheim (1994) discusses problems with stylized life-cycle models, and Attanasio and Browning (1995) examine consumption and income over the life-cycle. Consumption may not be a good proxy for lifetime income for households unable to borrow or lend freely in credit markets, among other reasons.

4. Barthold (1993).

5. See chapter 9 by Fullerton and Rogers in this volume and their citations for examples of this style of analysis and Whalley (1988) for discussion of the analytical difficulties.

6. See chapter 5 by Dennis R. Capozza, Richard K. Green, and Patric H. Hendershott in this volume.

Committee on Taxation (JCT), Congressional Budget Office (CBO), and Office of Tax Analysis (OTA) all use a similar approach in their distributional analyses of tax reform proposals.

Our analysis shows that the most prominent tax reform proposal—the flat tax—sharply lowers tax burdens on the top 1 percent of taxpayers. The rich pay less under the flat tax because its rate is well below the current average effective corporate and individual income tax rate for high-income families. The flat tax increases taxes on low-income families, largely because it eliminates the earned income tax credit. Taxes change little on average for families in the fiftieth to the ninety-ninth percentiles of the income distribution because elimination of deductions for charitable contributions and mortgage interest offset reduced rates and increased exemptions. Maintaining these deductions would exacerbate the shift of taxes to low-income from high-income families. If the earned income tax credit is retained, the flat tax fairly closely mirrors the existing distribution of tax burdens except at the very top of the income distribution. The USA tax and a base-broadening, rate-reducing reform to the income tax described below would maintain or slightly increase the progressivity of the existing tax system while at the same time achieving at least some of the objectives sought by proponents of fundamental tax reform.

The Microsimulation Model and the Distribution of Current Taxes

Our analysis is based on calculations from a detailed simulation model of the tax and transfer system.[7] The model uses data on income and demographic characteristics of families and individuals drawn from the Survey of Income and Program Participation (SIPP). Separate modules calculate state individual income taxes, federal individual and corporate income taxes, and the payroll tax.[8] The model determines household eligibility, participation, and benefits for the Aid to Families with Depen-

7. We provide a brief overview of the model in appendix A, and additional details are given in Dickert, Houser, and Scholz (1994, 1995). Detailed model documentation is available from the authors.

8. Throughout the analysis we assume that payments under state tax systems do not change in response to federal tax reform. States will undoubtedly alter their systems in response to federal changes, but the assumption that the distribution of tax revenue and its aggregate value stays constant strikes us as a good baseline.

dent Children, food stamps, and Supplemental Security Income programs.

Although tax burdens may fall on someone other than the person who pays the tax authorities, we assume those who pay state and federal individual income taxes bear the burdens of these taxes. Hence, once we calculate individual income taxes under the current and alternative tax systems, the distributional effects of changes to these taxes are immediately clear. We follow common practice in assuming that workers bear both the employee and employer portions of the payroll tax. This assumption means that in the absence of the payroll tax, gross wages would be higher by the tax paid by employers. Analysts have used a wide range of assumptions regarding the burden of corporation income taxes.[9] The JCT, CBO, and OTA allocate corporate tax payments in proportion to capital income.[10] We make the same assumption but describe results with alternative assumptions.[11]

Model Calibration

The model, without any adjustments, yields a distribution of federal income tax liabilities that differs from the actual distribution as reported by the Internal Revenue Service.[12] The differences result from two primary sources. First, the demographic structure of family units in SIPP

9. Pechman and Okner (1974), for example, use five: the corporate income tax is allocated in proportion to dividend receipts; to property income; half to dividends, half to property; half to dividends, one-fourth to consumption, one-fourth to labor earnings; and half to property income and half to consumption.

10. The CBO also uses a second variant where the corporate income tax is distributed half in proportion to labor income and half in proportion to capital ownership. If the United States is modeled as a small open economy, labor will bear the burden of changes in entity-level capital taxes such as the corporate income tax.

11. This assumption is consistent with the central specification of the seminal Harberger (1962) analysis of corporate tax incidence and is clearly plausible as shown by the more detailed general equilibrium analysis of Shoven (1976). Capital income comprises interest from saving accounts, money market funds, certificates of deposit, checking accounts, government securities, municipal and corporate bonds and other interest-bearing securities, stock and mutual fund dividends (including reinvested dividends), rental property income, mortgage income, royalty income, and income from other financial investments. Under our primary incidence assumption, capital income would be higher by the amount of corporate tax payments in the absence of the corporate income tax. Consequently, when calculating economic income for the subsequent distributional analyses, we increase household incomes by the imputed corporate tax payments and the employer share of payroll taxes paid on households' behalf.

12. Internal Revenue Service (1993).

differs somewhat from that of tax filers; to the extent we miscalculate filing status, our tax calculations will not match the distribution of reported tax burdens. Second, incomes reported on the SIPP differ from income reported to the Internal Revenue Service in part because of "top coding" of data items.[13]

As described in appendix A, we calibrate adjusted gross incomes (AGI) calculated from the model in 1990, the year of our baseline data, to match closely the distribution reported on income tax returns. The resulting data match income tax returns but retain the demographic and other features of the SIPP data. We then convert incomes to 1994 dollars using the Bureau of Labor Statistics series for average hourly earnings (for labor income) and the Consumer Price Index (for other income sources).

Baseline Distribution of Tax Burdens

Table 8-1 shows the baseline distribution of tax burdens from the model. We classify families by "expanded income," which we define as AGI plus the portions of interest, pension, and social security payments excluded from AGI, cash and near-cash transfer payments (AFDC, food stamps, and SSI), the employer portion of payroll taxes and corporate taxes, and an imputation of employer-provided health insurance.[14] We do not include employer-provided fringe benefits other than health insurance, the inside buildup of pensions, tax-deferred retirement accounts and life insurance, imputed rents on owner-occupied houses and other durable goods, the value of in-kind transfer benefits (beyond food stamps), and accrued capital gains or losses on other assets or liabilities. Although these items are clearly large in aggregate and should, in prin-

---

13. "Top coding" refers to the practice of statistical agencies of reporting broad, open-ended cells at the top of distributions to make sure that all cells contain enough households to preserve individual confidentiality.

14. AGI includes wage and salary income, interest and dividend income, alimony, business income, pension and annuity income, rents, royalties, income from partnerships, estates and trusts, taxable unemployment compensation and social security benefits, and other miscellaneous income. We add back the excluded portions of unemployment and the additional items mentioned in the text. Jonathan Gruber kindly provided the baseline regressions for the value of health insurance. He regressed the value of employer-provided health insurance for employees receiving benefits in the National Medical Care Expenditure Survey on the number of children, and dummies for marital status, unionization, four education groups, nine age groups, ten wage categories, ten industry groupings, and nine occupational categories. We use this regression and the equivalent variables in SIPP to impute the value of employer-provided health insurance to SIPP families.

Table 8-1. *The Distribution of Tax Liabilities and Transfer Payments, by Income Percentile, 1994*

Family expanded income percentiles[a]	Current law, average taxes[b]	Average tax rates (%)[c]	Average transfer payments[d]	Taxes paid minus transfers received	Average tax rates including transfers (%)
5–10	175	2.7	1,552	−1,376	−21.0
10–20	627	6.1	1,384	−757	−7.4
20–30	1,686	10.8	669	1,017	6.5
30–40	3,159	14.8	226	2,933	13.7
40–50	5,023	18.2	188	4,835	17.5
50–60	7,145	20.5	90	7,055	20.3
60–70	9,785	22.5	63	9,722	22.3
70–80	13,284	24.4	88	13,197	24.2
80–90	18,562	26.4	48	18,514	26.3
90–95	26,714	29.0	64	26,651	28.9
95–99	43,375	31.3	31	43,344	31.3
99–100	223,953	41.6	0	223,953	41.6
Total	11,834	25.8	376	11,457	24.9

Source: Data are from the 1990 Survey of Income and Program Participation, updated to 1994. Calculations are based on the microsimulation model described in the text.

a. Family expanded income is wage and salary income, taxable interest and dividend income, alimony, business income, taxable pensions and annuities, rents, royalties, income from partnerships, income from estates and trusts, unemployment compensation, taxable social security, other miscellaneous income, nontaxable interest income, nontaxable pension income, nontaxable social security income, Aid to Families with Dependent Children, food stamps, Supplemental Security Income, employer-provided health insurance, and the employer-paid portion of payroll taxes and corporate taxes.

b. Taxes under current law are federal individual and corporate income taxes; state income taxes; and payroll (OADSHI) taxes.

c. Average effective tax rates are taxes under current law divided by expanded family income multiplied by 100.

d. Transfer payments under current law, including AFDC, food stamps, and SSI.

ciple, be included in a comprehensive measure of income, there is no straightforward way to impute these items in SIPP.

We classify families, our unit of analysis, into income deciles, with additional detail in the top decile. We follow the common practice of dropping the bottom 5 percent of the income distribution.[15] Many of these families have large investment, business, or farm losses or other transitory variations in income that make current income a misleading categorizing variable.[16]

The first column of table 8-1 shows that the current distribution of tax payments is progressive—average effective tax rates rise with in-

15. See, for example, Pechman (1985).
16. The decile breakpoints of the calibrated income distribution in SIPP are $5,335 (fifth percentile), $7,820 (tenth percentile), $12,768, $18,415, $24,391, $30,981, $38,917, $48,471, $60,966, and $81,853. The breakpoint for the 95th income percentile is $106,057 and the ninety-ninth percentile is $207,740.

come.[17] The distribution of taxes paid and average effective tax rates, which range from 2.7 percent to 41.6 percent, are broadly comparable to distributions calculated at the CBO, JCT, and OTA.[18] Differences in definitions and included taxes alter the results in predictable directions. The OTA, for example, includes imputed rents in owner-occupied housing and a broader measure of fringe benefits in its income definition than we do. This difference lowers our estimates of average tax rates, for the general population and especially for the top income classes, below those of the CBO and JCT. The JCT's unit of analysis is taxpayers rather than families, and they measure tax liabilities over a five-year interval, which seems to have the practical effect of raising average tax burdens at the very bottom of the income distribution relative to our calculations. Each agency distributes federal excise tax payments and none distributes state income taxes. Relative to distributional estimates by CBO (which uses an income definition closest to ours), the distribution of average tax rates in table 8-1 should be lower in the lower income classes (because excise taxes are not included) and higher in the highest income classes (because of progressive state income taxes). This is the pattern we observe.[19]

Some scholars have argued that analyses of the distributional effects of tax policy should also include transfer payments.[20] It is not clear, however, why transfer programs should be singled out for inclusion. Taxes change independently of transfer programs, and many other government activities alter the distribution of market incomes.[21] Moreover, the *change* in tax burdens from a new tax policy is the same whether or not transfers are included. Nevertheless, the final three columns of table 8-1 treat AFDC, food stamp, and SSI benefits as negative taxes.[22] Average

17. These calculations omit state sales taxes and federal excise taxes, which would reduce progressivity.

18. Barthold, Nunns, and Toder (1995).

19. State individual income taxes are progressive, averaging 2.5 percent of income, but ranging from 0.1 percent in the lower-income classes to 4.4 percent in the highest-income percentile. Revenue from state sales and gross revenue taxes and from state income taxes are approximately equal—$107.8 billion and $104.4 billion, respectively, in 1992. Adding sales taxes to the model, therefore, would raise effective tax rates by a similar amount, though the distribution of sales taxes will be less progressive than state income taxes.

20. The largest transfer, social security taxes and payments, are included in our analysis.

21. Including only direct tax payments and federal transfers, for example, ignores exclusions from the tax base, such as that for state and local bonds, and direct subsidies, such as those for trade, agriculture, and research and development expenditures that disproportionately accrue to upper-income households. Consequently, our transfer-inclusive calculations overstate the progressivity of the distribution of the federal government's activities in the economy.

22. Phaseout rules from income transfer programs can lead to very high marginal tax

AFDC, food stamp, and SSI payments range from $1,552 for families in the lowest income group to $0 for families in the highest percentile.[23] The final column shows the transfer-inclusive average effective tax rate. Readers with the view that transfer payments should be included as negative taxes in distributional analyses of the type performed here can use the final column of table 8-1 to make the necessary adjustments to the subsequent analyses.

The Distributional Effects of the Flat Tax

The flat tax, originally described by Robert Hall and Alvin Rabushka, has been drafted into legislation by Representative Richard Armey (Republican of Texas) and Senator Richard Shelby (Republican of Alabama) and was a centerpiece of the Republican presidential campaign of Steve Forbes.[24] The flat tax consists of two pieces.

The first is a household-level tax on wages, salaries, and pension benefits of individuals. The most recent legislative proposal excludes from taxation the first $10,700 of labor income for individuals, $21,400 for couples, $14,000 for heads of households, and an additional $5,000 for each child. Tax would equal a constant fraction of income above the exclusion. The rules allow no deductions for home mortgage interest, property taxes, state and local taxes, charitable contributions, or major medical expenses. The second piece is a tax on gross revenues from sales, less wages, pension contributions, materials costs, and capital investments, levied on all businesses, whether incorporated or not, at the same flat rate of tax individuals pay.

The Armey-Shelby proposal calls for an initial rate of 20.8 percent to raise the same revenue as the current corporate and individual income tax, but the sponsors claim that a 17 percent rate would eventually suffice.[25] We use a flat tax rate of 20 percent in our simulations. The proposal contemplates a sharp change in the point of tax collection.

rates on transfer program recipients. See, for example, Dickert, Houser, and Scholz (1995). These high marginal rates should not be confused with the average tax rates reported in the table.

23. The small amount of SSI paid to individuals in families with substantial annual income accounts for the small but nonzero entries in the upper income percentiles.

24. Hall and Rabushka (1983, 1995).

25. Office of Tax Analysis, "'New' Armey-Shelby Flat Tax Would Still Lose Money, Treasury Finds," *Tax Notes*, vol. 70, January 22, 1996, pp. 451–61, estimates that the revenue neutral rate would be 20.8 percent.

Under current law the corporation income tax accounts for 22.3 percent of combined personal and corporation income taxes in our model. Under a flat tax, the business tax will collect 43 percent of total revenue.[26]

Table 8-2 shows the distribution of the flat tax if the wage tax is borne by workers and the business tax is borne by owners of capital (see appendix B). The top panel shows tax liabilities and the bottom panel shows effective tax rates. The first column repeats information given in table 8-1 on the distribution of tax burdens under current law. The second column shows tax liabilities and average effective tax rates under the flat tax.

The flat tax retains, but reduces, overall progressivity. Families in the fifth to tenth percentiles will see their average tax payments nearly double, going from $175 to $318, a 2.2 percentage point increase in average effective tax rates. Average tax payments would increase by $245 for those in the tenth to twentieth percentiles, a 2.4 percentage point increase in average effective tax rates. Despite the large exemptions incorporated into the flat tax, tax burdens on low-income families would rise. It is clear that no taxpayer with income below $10,700 would owe tax under the individual portion of the flat tax, and the large exemptions for couples and children will keep down taxes for low- and moderate-income families. The flat tax, however, eliminates the earned income tax credit (EITC), a credit available to families with low earnings. The EITC is refundable, which means that the taxpayer receives a check from the IRS if EITC benefits exceed income tax liabilities.[27] Because the flat tax eliminates the EITC, it increases taxes on low-income households relative to the current system.

The flat tax would also raise exemptions, reduce marginal tax rates for households whose rates are 28 percent or higher and raise them for others, and eliminate itemized deductions of disproportionate value to most middle- and upper-income households. The net effect of all these changes is to increase average effective tax rates by at least 2.2 percentage points for families in the bottom 40 percent of the income distribution, and by 1.3 percentage points or less for income groups above the 40th

26. The business tax base is similar to that reported in William G. Gale, "The Kemp Commission and the Future of Tax Reform," *Tax Notes*, vol. 70, February 5, 1996, pp. 717–30. Gale bases his calculations on Office of Tax Analysis, " 'New' Armey-Shelby Flat Tax Would Still Lose Money, Treasury Finds." Total 1994 tax collections in the simulation model are $640 billion.

27. See Scholz (1994) for a more detailed discussion of the EITC.

Table 8-2. *The Effect of the Flat Tax on the Distribution of Tax Liabilities, by Income Percentile*

Family expanded income percentiles[a]	Current law	Flat tax (FT)	Flat tax with EITC	Flat tax, itemized deductions	Flat tax, FICA deduction
		Average taxes[b]			
5–10	175	318	239	329	312
10–20	627	872	667	895	856
20–30	1,686	2,175	1,820	2,236	2,119
30–40	3,159	3,633	3,361	3,711	3,584
40–50	5,023	5,299	5,209	5,411	5,241
50–60	7,145	7,204	7,209	7,291	7,101
60–70	9,785	9,914	9,961	9,874	9,775
70–80	13,284	13,718	13,827	13,577	13,595
80–90	18,562	19,460	19,637	19,066	19,461
90–95	26,714	27,531	27,826	27,254	27,693
95–99	43,375	43,896	44,420	43,415	44,817
99–100	223,953	186,045	188,909	190,930	192,849
Total	11,834	11,825	11,826	11,819	11,886
		Average effective tax rates[c]			
5–10	2.7	4.9	3.7	5.0	4.8
10–20	6.1	8.5	6.5	8.8	8.4
20–30	10.8	14.0	11.7	14.3	13.6
30–40	14.8	17.0	15.7	17.3	16.7
40–50	18.2	19.2	18.9	19.6	19.0
50–60	20.5	20.7	20.7	20.9	20.4
60–70	22.5	22.8	22.9	22.7	22.5
70–80	24.4	25.2	25.4	24.9	25.0
80–90	26.4	27.7	27.9	27.1	27.7
90–95	29.0	29.8	30.2	29.5	30.0
95–99	31.3	31.7	32.1	31.4	32.4
99–100	41.6	34.5	35.1	35.4	35.8
Total	25.8	25.7	25.7	25.7	25.9

Source: Data are from the 1990 Survey of Income and Program Participation, updated to 1994. Calculations are based on the microsimulation model described in the text.

a. Family expanded income is wage and salary income, taxable interest and dividend income, alimony, business income, taxable pensions and annuities, rents, royalties, income from partnerships, income from estates and trusts, unemployment compensation, taxable social security, other miscellaneous income, nontaxable interest income, nontaxable pension income, nontaxable social security income, AFDC, food stamps, SSI, employer-provided health insurance, and the employer-paid portion of payroll taxes and corporate taxes.

b. Taxes under current law are federal individual and corporate income taxes; state income taxes; and payroll (OADSHI) taxes.

c. Average effective tax rates are taxes under current law divided by expanded family income multiplied by 100.

and below the top 1 percent of the income distribution. Families in the top 1 percent would receive tax cuts averaging $37,900, a 7.0 percentage point reduction in average effective rates.

We also examine the implications of an alternative incidence assumption sometimes used by the Congressional Budget Office. Under this assumption, business tax is distributed half to labor income and half to capital income (incidence assumptions are discussed in appendix B). This alternative assumption makes little difference in the qualitative distributional results, because the distribution of labor and capital income is quite similar across expanded household income groups and because the corporate income tax and the business portion of the flat tax collect less than one-quarter of the total taxes included in the analysis (see appendix table 8B-1).

Modifications to the Flat Tax

Political pressures might force modification of the pure form of the flat tax. These modifications could have some effect on the distribution of tax burdens.

RETAIN THE EITC. Retaining the EITC requires a 0.4 percentage point increase in the tax rate, to 20.4 percent, and would reduce tax burdens for families in the bottom 50 percent of the income distribution relative to the flat tax with no EITC.[28] Because the EITC is well-targeted toward low-income taxpayers, it reduces tax most (in percentage terms) in the fifth to the thirtieth percentiles of the income distribution, where average effective tax rates fall by 1.2 to 2.2 percentage points relative to the flat tax with no EITC. Even with the EITC, however, the flat tax imposes somewhat higher taxes on these families than does the current system. The EITC has very little effect on tax burdens for families above the fiftieth percentile of the income distribution. The flat tax with the EITC fairly closely mirrors the existing distribution of tax burdens except at the very top of the income distribution.

It may appear somewhat puzzling that taxes on low-income families still increase when the EITC is incorporated as part of the flat tax. After all, generous household-level exemptions keep most low-income families from paying the wage tax. The result occurs because business taxes increase. Because the corporation income tax under the existing tax system

28. The EITC delivers $13.1 billion to low-income taxpayers in the model. For two reasons, this total is considerably smaller than the $19.9 billion reported for 1994 in the Internal Revenue Service (1995). First, a significant fraction of EITC payments goes to families that are technically not eligible for the credit. See Yin and others (1994); Scholz (1996). There is no sensible way to allocate these overpayments in our model. Second, incomes of low-income families have grown more slowly than incomes of high-income families. Adjusting our 1990 data to 1994 dollars overstates income growth for low-income families and understates their EITC payments. The first explanation accounts for most of the discrepancy.

collects little revenue (and poor households typically do not owe taxes under the individual income tax), the increased reliance on the business tax under the flat tax would raise tax burdens for some low-income families (particularly the elderly) through their ownership of interest- and dividend-bearing assets.

RETAIN THE MORTGAGE INTEREST AND CHARITABLE CONTRIBUTIONS DEDUCTIONS. The conceptual basis for retaining the mortgage interest deduction in the flat tax is dubious. If interest receipts of households are untaxed, it makes little sense to allow taxpayers to deduct interest payments. Doing so gives taxpayers the opportunity to borrow at an after-tax rate and invest at the pre-tax rate of return. One goal of tax reform should be to eliminate these kinds of unproductive tax-arbitrage possibilities.[29]

However, the political incentive for retaining the mortgage interest and charitable contributions deductions is strong as these deductions are used heavily by middle-class families. Retaining them requires an increase in the flat rate by 1.5 percentage points to 21.5 percent. As shown in the fourth column of table 8-2, relative to the flat tax without deductions, retaining these deductions raises tax burdens for families in the bottom sixty percentiles of the income distribution and lowers tax burdens for families in the seventieth to ninety-ninth percentiles. Still, the distribution of flat tax burdens with these deductions closely resembles the distribution of burden without them.

ALLOW FULL DEDUCTIBILITY OF THE PAYROLL TAX. Currently employers can deduct their payroll tax payments from taxable income, but workers cannot. The Kemp Commission proposed that payroll taxes should also be deductible for workers. Most households now pay more in payroll taxes (when also counting the employer share) than in income taxes, so the justification for the proposal is twofold: to avoid having

---

29. Homeownership is tax preferred in the current system because the implicit rental value of the home is untaxed, not because mortgage interest is deductible. Thus, the current tax treatment of mortgages is consistent with a pure income tax in that interest income is taxable but the cost of borrowing is deductible. However, additional problems may arise under the current system because other forms of saving (for example, 401(k)s and pensions) accrue interest tax free but can be financed with tax-deductible debt, creating the same arbitrage problems discussed in the text. See Engen and Gale (1995). In contrast, the flat tax eliminates the mortgage interest deduction and taxation of interest income, that is, it provides symmetric treatment of borrowing and lending. See chapter 5 by Capozza, Green, and Hendershott in this volume for further discussion.

Figure 8-1. *Average Effective Tax Rates under Current Law and the Flat Tax*[a]

Average effective tax rate (percent)

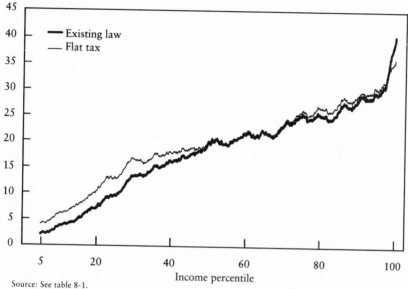

Source: See table 8-1.

a. Includes effects of the personal and corporation income taxes, payroll taxes, and state income taxes.

people pay taxes on top of other (payroll) taxes and to reduce the combined marginal tax rate imposed on the wages of middle-income households.

The distributional effect of this modification is shown in column 5 of table 8-2. Allowing self-employed and wage and salary workers to deduct payroll taxes increases the flat rate necessary to maintain revenues to 23.2 percent. Relative to the "pure" flat tax, this change lowers taxes by $140 or less in the bottom eight income deciles and raises taxes by an average of $921 in the ninety-fifth to ninety-ninth percentiles and $6,804 in the top percentile.

Further Distributional Effects of the Flat Tax

Figure 8-1 plots average tax rates under the current tax system and under the flat tax by income percentile.[30] The figure nicely summarizes

30. Tax rates are smoothed for families using a moving average of tax rates (the moving average is calculated from the adjacent 500 families). As in the tables, we drop families in the bottom 5 percent of the income distribution.

the distributional effects of the flat tax. It shows that the flat tax "tilts" the distribution of tax burdens from the very highest-income families to lower-income groups. Families in the bottom half of the income distribution pay higher taxes under the flat tax, while taxes increase slightly or are largely unchanged for all other families except those in the top 1 percent of the income distribution, who enjoy large gains.[31]

Table 8-3 indicates the size of income changes families experience in each income group. The dominant fact shown by table 8-3 is that moving to a flat tax would change taxes by less than 5 percent of income for most families. Overall, somewhat more families suffer tax increases than enjoy tax decreases. Not shown in the table is the fact that taxes for almost 6 percent of the population increase by more than 10 percent of income, while only 0.3 percent have tax reductions of that magnitude. Lower-income households are much more likely than others to have tax increases of more than 5 percent of income. Nearly 44 percent of households in the top income percentile would have tax decreases of more than 5 percent of income under the flat tax.

Because the flat tax changes so many aspects of the tax system, it would undoubtedly affect different demographic groups differently. Many allege that consumption taxes (like the flat tax) initially will shift tax burdens from younger to older households. Under an income tax, retirees whose past income exceeded consumption and who have accumulated assets by saving after-tax income can consume that wealth without facing further tax. When a consumption tax takes effect, these same retirees will confront consumption taxes they would not have faced if the income tax had stayed in effect. These effects are fairly obvious under a retail sales tax, but it is less clear that the flat tax will be overly burdensome to the elderly. The wage tax portion of the flat tax will not directly affect retirees. The increased reliance on the business tax may impose added burdens on elderly households, however, through their ownership of equity and interest-bearing assets.

Table 8-4 shows that tax changes by age groupings are fairly small.[32]

31. The flat tax raises roughly $20 billion additional taxes from families in the bottom half of the income distribution (primarily by eliminating the EITC). Families from the fiftieth to seventy-fifth percentile of the income distribution are left largely unaffected, while taxes increase on families with incomes in the seventy-fifth percentile to near the top of the income distribution. The highest-income families receive, in aggregate, more than a $40 billion reduction in taxes.

32. In chapter 9 in this volume Don Fullerton and Diane Lim Rogers examine the effects of tax reform on lifetime tax burdens, which addresses the point that the same person will be young, middle aged, and old over his or her lifetime.

Table 8-3. *Percentage of Families in Each Income Decile with Tax Changes of Various Magnitudes*[a]

Family expanded income percentiles[b]	Change in taxes as a percent of family income				
	Decrease exceeding 5 percent	*Decrease 1 to 5 percent*	*Change between −1 and 1 percent*	*Increase 1 to 5 percent*	*Increase exceeding 5 percent*
5–10	0.0	1.3	65.1	19.6	14.0
10–20	6.0	14.7	40.4	19.5	19.4
20–30	1.3	31.0	20.7	15.7	31.4
30–40	3.9	14.8	37.7	18.7	25.0
40–50	4.0	25.6	24.8	31.4	14.2
50–60	4.6	39.4	21.2	23.7	11.0
60–70	1.5	33.2	36.2	20.4	8.7
70–80	0.6	23.5	35.0	36.0	4.9
80–90	0.4	19.4	24.6	50.9	4.7
90–95	0.9	22.6	22.9	49.5	4.1
95–99	4.0	18.1	29.1	45.4	3.4
99–100	43.9	29.8	9.1	15.1	2.1
Total	3.0	23.6	31.3	28.5	13.7

Source: Data are from the 1990 Survey of Income and Program Participation, updated to 1994. Calculations are based on the microsimulation model described in the text.

a. Rows sum to 100.

b. Family expanded income is wage and salary income, taxable interest and dividend income, alimony, business income, taxable pensions and annuities, rents, royalties, income from partnerships, income from estates and trusts, unemployment compensation, taxable social security, other miscellaneous income, nontaxable interest income, nontaxable pension income, nontaxable social security income, AFDC, food stamps, SSI, employer-provided health insurance, and the employer-paid portion of payroll taxes and corporate taxes.

Table 8-4. Distributional Effects of the Flat Tax, by Age, Income Class, and Homeownership Status, 1994

Age and ownership status	Current taxes[a]	Average tax rate[b]	Flat tax	Flat tax average tax rate	Percentage point change
		All households			
Age of head					
<20	4,230	17.2	4,472	18.2	1.0
20–30	7,727	23.4	7,758	23.5	0.1
30–40	12,725	25.9	12,489	25.4	−0.5
40–50	17,941	28.1	17,366	27.2	−0.9
50–65	15,111	27.9	15,008	27.7	−0.2
>65	5,536	19.3	6,343	22.1	2.8
Total	11,834	25.8	11,825	25.7	0.0
		Owners who itemize			
Income quintiles					
5–20	766	7.4	1,032	9.9	2.6
20–40	2,526	12.7	3,374	17.0	4.3
40–60	5,941	18.4	6,616	20.5	2.1
60–80	11,317	22.5	12,231	24.4	1.8
80–95	20,865	26.5	22,391	28.5	1.9
95–99	42,910	30.9	44,033	31.7	0.8
99–100	222,484	41.3	186,536	34.7	−6.7
Total	25,737	29.6	25,593	29.4	−0.2
		Renters and owners who do not itemize			
Income quintiles					
5–20	475	5.3	685	7.6	2.3
20–40	2,416	13.1	2,878	15.6	2.5
40–60	6,108	19.7	6,193	20.0	0.3
60–80	11,669	24.2	11,558	24.0	−0.2
80–95	22,185	29.4	21,614	28.6	−0.8
95–99	46,761	34.7	42,901	31.9	−2.9
99–100	243,029	44.6	179,664	33.0	−11.6
Total	6,495	21.5	6,538	21.7	0.1

Source: Data are from the 1990 Survey of Income and Program Participation, updated to 1994. Calculations are based on the microsimulation model described in the text.

a. Taxes under current law are federal individual and corporate income taxes; state income taxes; and payroll (OADSHI) taxes.

b. Average effective tax rates are taxes under current law divided by expanded family income multiplied by 100.

c. Family expanded income is wage and salary income, taxable interest and dividend income, alimony, business income, taxable pensions and annuities, rents, royalties, income from partnerships, income from estates and trusts, unemployment compensation, taxable social security, other miscellaneous income, nontaxable interest income, nontaxable pension income, nontaxable social security income, AFDC, food stamps, SSI, employer-provided fringe benefits, and the employer-paid portion of payroll taxes and corporate taxes.

Taxes would increase slightly for the youngest households and a bit more—2.8 percentage points, or 14.6 percent of initial average taxes—for the elderly. Families with heads between 30 and 65 would enjoy modest tax reductions as, on average, the effect of lower rates and increased exemptions is larger than the effect of broadening the tax base.

The bottom panels of table 8-4 show the distributional effects of the flat tax for homeowners who itemize and homeowners who do not itemize (and all renters). Eliminating the deduction for home mortgage interest would slightly increase average tax burdens on homeowners with incomes below the top percentile of the income distribution. In contrast, tax liabilities for renters and owners who do not itemize fall in the top four deciles of the income distribution. When the two groups are compared, the flat tax redistributes some tax liability to itemizing homeowners from other taxpayers because in each income grouping, owners who itemize have larger tax increases (or smaller tax decreases) than renters and owners who do not itemize.

Distributional Results for a Particular Cohort

If annual income is a poor measure of long-term economic status, the calculations of economic burdens we have shown so far may be misleading. In particular, households with low annual income may be heavily weighted toward students and retirees who are not poor in any lifetime sense. Table 8-5 addresses this concern. It shows tax burdens of married families with heads between the ages of 40 and 50. Although families in this age bracket may be experiencing unusually good or bad years, income for this age group should reflect "permanent" income more closely than does income of the very young or the very old.[33] Table 8-5 shows the effects of the flat tax on the distribution of tax payments for this group. The shift of tax burdens from upper to lower income groups is even more pronounced for this age cohort than it is for the population at large. Tax burdens for families in the fifth to the thirtieth percentiles more than double, almost entirely from eliminating the EITC. Tax changes for families in the fortieth to ninety-ninth percentiles of the income distribution range from − 1.5 to 1.2 percentage points. The big gainers are families in the top percentile of the income distribution. Their effective tax rates fall by 7.9 percentage points, or $40,824.

---

33. King and Dicks-Mireaux (1982), for example, use normalized income at age 45 to measure permanent income.

Table 8-5. Distribution of Current Law and Flat Tax Burdens for Families, Age 40–50, 1994

Family expanded income percentiles[a]	Current law, average taxes[b]	Average tax rates (%)[c]	Flat tax	Average tax rates under flat tax	Flat tax with EITC	Average tax rates with flat tax and EITC
5–20	382	3.8	1,016	10.0	397	3.9
20–30	914	5.7	1,944	12.2	931	5.9
30–40	2,822	12.8	3,318	15.1	2,686	12.2
40–50	4,610	16.5	4,495	16.1	4,229	15.1
50–60	6,807	19.4	6,270	17.9	6,259	17.9
60–70	9,224	21.0	8,725	19.8	8,746	19.9
70–80	12,641	23.1	12,804	23.4	12,887	23.6
80–90	17,864	25.2	18,738	26.4	18,897	26.6
90–95	25,621	27.7	26,425	28.5	26,691	28.8
95–99	42,833	30.6	43,101	30.8	43,597	31.1
99–100	206,758	40.2	165,934	32.3	168,351	32.7
Total	22,443	28.4	21,488	27.2	21,625	27.4

Source: Data are from the 1990 Survey of Income and Program Participation, updated to 1994. Calculations are based on the microsimulation model described in the text.

a. Family expanded income is wage and salary income, taxable interest and dividend income, alimony, business income, taxable pensions and annuities, rents, royalties, income from partnerships, income from estates and trusts, unemployment compensation, taxable social security, other miscellaneous income, nontaxable interest income, nontaxable pension income, nontaxable social security income, AFDC, food stamps, SSI, employer-provided health insurance, and the employer-paid portion of payroll taxes and corporate taxes.

b. Taxes under current law are federal individual and corporate income taxes; state income taxes; and payroll (OADSHI) taxes.

c. Average effective tax rates are taxes under current law divided by expanded family income multiplied by 100.

The similarity of the overall pattern of effects in tables 8-2 and 8-5 suggests that the distributional results are not being driven by students and retirees or by others whose current incomes differ dramatically from their permanent incomes.

Alternative Reform Proposals: The VAT, the USA Tax, and Income Tax Reform

Table 8-6 shows the distributional effects of two other consumption taxes—the VAT and the USA tax—and of a particular income tax reform.

THE VALUE-ADDED TAX. The value-added tax removes the tax exemptions for children, taxpayers, and spouses contained in the flat tax. With these changes in the tax base, a tax rate of 13.1 percent maintains budget balance in our model. The VAT increases taxes on the bottom 90 percent of the income distribution, more than doubling taxes in the bottom two deciles. Taxes in the top percentile fall by more than one-third, or more than $80,000.

Many real-world VATs impose reduced rates on commodities consumed disproportionately by low-income households. Our model lacks detailed consumption data to permit examination of the effects of such plans. Using a computable general equilibrium model, Charles L. Ballard, John Karl Scholz, and John B. Shoven found that rate differentiation reduces regressivity but not very efficiently because high-income families also consume goods, such as food and clothing, that are typically granted reduced rates.[34] Furthermore, rate differentiation reduces the efficiency gains from the VAT by 25 to 40 percent.

THE USA TAX. The USA tax, sponsored by Senators Nunn and Domenici, assesses an 11 percent VAT on all businesses and places a graduated tax on households' consumed income, the difference between income and qualified net saving.[35] A family of four would receive exemptions totaling $17,600. Mortgage interest and charitable contributions would remain deductible. The exemption of municipal bond interest and the earned income tax credit would remain in effect. Households

---

34. Ballard, Scholz, and Shoven (1987).
35. We describe our saving imputations in appendix B. The mean imputed saving rate in the model is 6.3 percent.

Table 8-6. Distributional Effects of Alternative
Tax Reform Proposals

Family expanded income percentiles[a]	Current law	VAT	USA	Pechman Plan
		Average taxes[b]		
5–10	175	448	182	171
10–20	627	1,300	518	517
20–30	1,686	2,905	1,470	1,422
30–40	3,159	4,644	2,691	2,716
40–50	5,023	6,496	4,336	4,324
50–60	7,145	8,709	6,187	6,214
60–70	9,785	11,292	8,580	8,898
70–80	13,284	14,733	12,110	12,956
80–90	18,562	19,578	17,808	19,605
90–95	26,714	25,951	27,705	29,099
95–99	43,375	38,521	47,994	48,894
99–100	223,953	141,535	256,108	219,109
Total	11,834	11,831	11,832	11,865
		Average effective tax rates[c]		
5–10	2.7	6.8	2.8	2.6
10–20	6.1	12.7	5.1	5.1
20–30	10.8	18.6	9.4	9.1
30–40	14.8	21.7	12.6	12.7
40–50	18.2	23.5	15.7	15.7
50–60	20.5	25.0	17.8	17.9
60–70	22.5	25.9	19.7	20.4
70–80	24.4	27.0	22.2	23.8
80–90	26.4	27.8	25.3	27.9
90–95	29.0	28.1	30.0	31.5
95–99	31.3	27.8	34.7	35.3
99–100	41.6	26.3	47.5	40.7
Total	25.8	25.8	25.8	25.8

Source: Data are from the 1990 Survey of Income and Program Participation, updated to 1994. Calculations are based on the microsimulation model described in the text. Plan descriptions are also in the text.

a. Family expanded income is wage and salary income, taxable interest and dividend income, alimony, business income, taxable pensions and annuities, rents, royalties, income from partnerships, income from estates and trusts, unemployment compensation, taxable social security, other miscellaneous income, nontaxable interest income, nontaxable pension income, nontaxable social security income, AFDC, food stamps, SSI, employer-provided health insurance, and the employer-paid portion of payroll taxes and corporate taxes.

b. Taxes under current law are federal individual and corporate income taxes; state income taxes; and payroll (OADSHI) taxes.

c. Average effective tax rates are taxes under current law divided by expanded family income multiplied by 100.

and businesses would receive a full, refundable tax credit for payroll taxes. Consumed income less deductions would be taxed at rates starting at 8 percent and rising to 40 percent on amounts over $24,000 for married couples. The credit for payroll taxes lowers the effective tax rates 7.65 percentage points for the first $60,600 of earned income.[36]

36. To estimate the burdens of the USA tax we calculate AGI as under current law,

The third column of table 8-6 summarizes the distributional effects of the USA tax. Our calculations suggest the USA tax will keep tax liabilities nearly constant in the bottom decile of the income distribution and lower taxes by 1.1 to 3.2 percentage points for families in the tenth to seventieth percentiles of the income distribution. These tax reductions are financed by 3.4 to 5.9 percentage point tax increases in the top 5 percent of the income distribution.[37]

INCOME TAX REFORM. In the end tax reform may modify the existing system rather than replace it. To illustrate the distributional effects of one such plan, we present estimates of what we name the Pechman Plan after a proposed reform of Joseph A. Pechman.[38] We retain the generous family and child exemptions contemplated by the flat tax and the EITC to hold down tax burdens on low-income families. We also close tax "loopholes" by eliminating all itemized deductions as contemplated by the flat tax.[39] We impose two tax brackets on the broadened individual income tax base, at 15 percent on taxable income below $16,000 and 30 percent above this amount. This reform would extend changes made in the Tax Reform Act of 1986.

---

subtract the standard deduction, personal exemption, additional itemized deductions for mortgage interest and charitable contributions (we do not incorporate the deduction for educational expenses), and net saving. We apply the USA tax rates, incorporating the 8 percent bottom bracket that would be effective in the year 2000. The current law EITC is preserved, and we incorporate the refundable credit for the employee share of FICA taxes and half of the self-employment tax. The personal tax collects $306 billion in our model, while the business tax, distributed in proportion to capital ownership, collects $334 billion to maintain budget neutrality.

37. Our estimates differ from estimates presented in descriptions of the USA plan. These show smaller tax reductions at the bottom and smaller tax increases at the top, so the USA tax burdens come close to matching the existing distribution of tax liabilities. It is difficult to pinpoint the specific source of this discrepancy, but it is probably differences in assumptions about household saving. It is difficult to calculate household saving in existing data sets, and our procedures are likely to underpredict saving of very high-income families and hence overstate their tax liabilities under the USA tax. Differences in saving estimates cannot be the sole source of the discrepancy, however, because our procedures should result in quite accurate estimates for middle-income families. We calculate tax burdens on these families will be lower than estimates accompanying the USA plan.

38. Pechman (1990).

39. Pechman believed the deduction for major medical expenses should be retained and grudgingly admitted it would be politically impossible to repeal the home mortgage interest deduction. Thus, our Pechman Plan is somewhat more far reaching than Pechman (1990). He also advocated corporate tax reform, but we lack the ability to model detailed corporate tax provisions, and so we leave the corporate income tax as is.

Table 8-6 suggests the Pechman Plan would increase the progressivity of the current tax system, lowering tax payments for income groups through the eightieth percentile. The large increase in personal exemptions and standard deductions accounts for these reductions, which range from 1.0 to 2.6 percentage points for families from the tenth to the sixtieth percentiles. Average tax rates would rise by 1.5 to 4.0 percentage points for income groups ranging from the eightieth to the ninety-ninth percentiles, because the reform eliminates itemized deductions and slightly increases tax rates for some of these families. Families in the highest income class would receive a small, 0.9 percentage point, reduction in average tax rates, largely because of reductions in top bracket rates.

Transition and Capitalization Effects

Tax reform would change not only annual tax payments but possibly asset values as well. Some changes in asset values arise from transition effects of the various tax plans. Consider a retail store that purchases $10,000 of canned goods the day before a value-added tax is imposed and sells everything the day after.[40] The sale proceeds are taxed, but the store can take no deduction for the cost of inventory because it bought the goods before the new tax took effect. The effect is a one-time tax, at the value-added tax rate, on the entire stock of inventory at the time of the transition. In fact, a consumption tax with no transition rules imposes a one-time tax on the stock of wealth in the economy, which is frequently referred to as "old capital" or "old saving."[41]

The U.S. capital stock is roughly $24 trillion. Any significant changes in the value of existing assets (or "old capital") could have major distributional implications for tax reform. A 5 percent change in the value of existing equity would confer a one-time change in share values of $350 billion, which greatly exceeds the estimated redistribution of roughly $42 billion in annual income tax payments. In addition, upper-income house-

40. We take this example from Bradford (1995).
41. Bradford (1995, p. 20). Jane G. Gravelle, "The Flat Tax and Other Proposals: Who Will Bear the Tax Burden?" Tax Notes, vol. 69, December 18, 1995, pp. 1517–27, describes the same phenomenon through a simple numerical example. Suppose the pre-tax rate of return is 10 percent and the tax rate is 20 percent. A new investment will earn a 10 percent rate of return, but an existing one, where the flow of capital is subject to tax, will earn only 8 percent. Suppose a share of stock sells for $100. After tax, there will be an annual return of $8. The price of stock, therefore, must fall to $80 to earn a rate of return of 10 percent. Only with a drop in the value of the existing asset is it just as attractive as a new investment.

holds hold most equities. Table 8-7 shows the distribution of asset holdings of households in different income and age groups. U.S. households hold roughly $7 trillion in equity according to the Balance Sheets of the United States (Flow of Funds).[42] The richest 1 percent of households hold 18.9 percent of all equity and 28.9 percent of the wealth in privately held businesses. These figures show that if fundamental tax reform changes asset values significantly, the distributional effects could dwarf those associated with annual tax flows.

For a number of reasons, however, we question whether asset revaluation will be large. Tax reform that puts a consumption tax into effect entails not only imposing the new tax but also removing the existing income tax.[43] While a consumption tax without transition provisions imposes a one-time capital levy, repealing the income tax removes future capital gains taxes and corporate income taxes, which would be windfall gains to holders of existing assets. Of course, removal of the income tax also eliminates future depreciation deductions on previous investments, but since the existing tax system already grants accelerated depreciation, the proportion of depreciation deductions businesses have taken on capital investment at any time will exceed the proportion of total income to be earned on that investment.

Adjustment costs in investments are a second factor mitigating the effect of the capital levy on asset prices. If tax reform raises the value of new capital, but the capital stock adjusts sluggishly, old capital will earn rents during the transition, which will drive up its price. If Congress provides transition rules that attenuate the effects of the capital levy, the adverse effect of a consumption tax on the price of existing capital will be further reduced.[44]

Alan Auerbach estimates that the change in the value of existing assets is likely to be relatively small.[45] Without adjustment costs to investment, he estimates that asset values will change between −8.9 percent and 1.3 percent in the first two years after the reform proposal, depending on the particular proposal. The more plausible flat tax proposals with transitional relief involve asset price declines of 1.7 percent to 3.5 percent. With adjustment costs to investments, the range of asset price changes is −0.3 percent to 12.5 percent, with all estimates being positive except for the Armey plan with no transition.

42. Also see Gentry and Hubbard (1996) for a nice discussion of these issues.
43. Bradford (1995).
44. See chapter 11 by Ronald A. Pearlman in this volume.
45. See chapter 2 by Alan J. Auerbach in this volume.

Table 8-7. *Distribution of Asset and Liability Holdings in the U.S. Population, 1992 Survey of Consumer Finances*[a]

Income percentiles and age	Percent of home equity	Percent of mortgage debt	Percent of real estate wealth	Percent of businesses	Percent of equity	Percent of liquid, near-cash assets	Percent of bonds
Income							
0–20	7.4	2.2	2.4	3.5	4.4	4.5	5.8
20–40	9.7	4.9	4.7	3.4	2.4	11.5	5.8
40–60	12.7	12.4	11.2	7.1	10.7	13.1	9.6
60–80	21.5	26.4	11.8	8.3	16.3	19.9	11.7
80–90	17.2	23.6	11.1	7.5	11.4	14.8	15.4
90–95	14.3	14.6	12.1	10.7	13.6	11.1	8.8
95–99	12.6	12.4	20.3	30.6	22.4	15.0	20.7
99–100	4.4	3.5	26.4	28.9	18.9	10.1	22.2
Total (billions of dollars)	7,605	2,169	4,897	3,864	2,036	1,715	430
Age							
–30	3.4	6.2	1.4	3.0	2.1	2.7	2.2
30–45	31.5	55.4	23.9	30.7	14.4	16.2	15.5
45–60	32.6	31.7	41.5	41.6	33.0	26.5	31.0
60+	32.5	6.8	33.3	24.7	50.5	54.6	51.3

Source: Data are from the 1992 Survey of Consumer Finances.
a. Home equity is the gross value of owner-occupied housing. Real estate includes investment property and second homes. Business holdings combine active and passive holdings. Equity includes mutual funds as well as direct holdings. Near-cash assets are checking and saving accounts, money market accounts, and CDs. Bonds exclude tax-exempt bonds.

Estimates of capitalization effects should be treated with caution. They depend on how the overall price level responds to tax reform, but it is difficult to anticipate how prices will respond. If substitution of a consumption tax for an income tax raises the after-tax yield to wealth holders, that change would compensate at least in part for any wealth loss that occurs during transition. The degree of compensation depends on the consumption plans of wealth holders. Those planning long postponement of consumption will gain. Those planning near-term consumption will lose. If the after-tax rate of return does not increase, there is no compensating offset. The issue is further complicated by the fact that many existing assets are tax-preferred and hence already receive consumption tax treatment.

There is considerable uncertainty about whether the consumption tax will raise or lower the pre-tax rate of interest. Martin Feldstein argues that the pre-tax rate of interest is likely to increase; Robert Hall and Alan Auerbach think interest rates are likely to fall. The outcome depends critically on the saving response of families to the tax changes, which itself is a controversial issue.[46]

Conclusion

The flat tax will sharply lower tax burdens on the highest-income taxpayers. Tax rates on low-income families will rise, particularly if the EITC is repealed. On average, families in the fiftieth to ninety-ninth percentile of the income distribution will see small tax changes under the flat tax because the effect of eliminating the charitable contributions and home mortgage interest deductions is offset by lower rates and larger exemptions.

Retaining the EITC under the flat tax would require a 0.4 percentage point increase in the flat tax rate and would reduce some of the redistribution from lower- to very high-income families. Adding deductions for home mortgages and charitable contributions exacerbates the redistribution from lower- to high-income families. Other tax reform proposals, notably the USA tax and the Pechman Plan, would maintain or slightly increase the progressivity of the existing tax system while at the same

46. Feldstein (1995); Hall (1996); see chapter 2 by Auerbach and chapter 3 by Eric M. Engen and William G. Gale in this volume.

time achieving at least some of the objectives sought by proponents of the flat tax.

Besides the direct effects described in this chapter, the distributional effects of tax reform proposals depend on changes in interest rates, saving, and labor supply. Some evidence suggests that these effects will be small.[47] Even for those who believe these general equilibrium effects are likely to be large, our static or "overnight" effects provide a baseline for how large the general equilibrium effects need to be to restore the existing distribution of tax burdens.

The distributional effects of the flat tax on married couples from age 40 to 50 resemble those for the rest of the population. This finding suggests that annual and lifetime distributional measures of the flat tax would yield similar results. Don Fullerton and Diane Lim Rogers reach a similar conclusion when they find the lifetime distribution of tax burdens is quite similar to the annual measures presented by Joseph Pechman.[48]

Appendix A: The Microsimulation Model and Model Calibration

The microsimulation model includes modules for state individual income taxes, federal individual and corporate income taxes, and payroll taxes and modules for the three major cash or near-cash transfer programs (AFDC, food stamps, SSI) in the United States. The modules share a common structure. They first determine the underlying tax or transfer program unit based on SIPP data on family structure. Filing status is assessed for tax programs, and eligibility and participation are assessed for transfer programs making use of SIPP income, asset, and family structure data. Federal and state income taxes are calculated on the basis of the demographic structure of the household as of December, as the tax code requires. Annual tax payments and monthly transfer benefits are calculated for each program unit and then aggregated to annual family totals. Families with members in the sample for less than the full year are dropped owing to the complexity of imputing data for missing months. The model is coded in programming language C and runs on a personal computer.

47. See chapter 3 by Engen and Gale and chapter 7 by Robert K. Triest in this volume.
48. Fullerton and Rogers (1993); Pechman (1985).

The Tax Modules

Because the focus of this chapter is on the distributional effects of tax reform proposals, we provide additional detail for the tax modules.

FEDERAL INDIVIDUAL INCOME TAX MODULE. The first part of the federal tax module determines the appropriate tax filing status. All subfamilies, primary individuals, and secondary individuals are treated as potentially separate (from the primary family) tax filing units. After filing units are determined, the model generally follows the 1040 tax schedule. Exemptions are claimed for children and other adult dependents. We assume that adults living in the household who have gross income less than $2,450 are dependents. Total income includes wage and salary income, taxable interest and dividend income, alimony, business income, taxable pensions and annuities, rents, royalties, income from partnerships, estates and trusts, unemployment compensation, taxable social security, and other miscellaneous income. Adjusted gross income (AGI) in the model excludes adjustments to AGI (such as IRA contributions) because of data limitations. Taxable income is calculated by subtracting from AGI the standard or itemized deduction and exemptions.[49] Taxes before credits are calculated using the appropriate tax schedules for each filing unit. Tax liabilities are adjusted by nonrefundable credits for the elderly or disabled, child care, and the refundable EITC.

STATE INDIVIDUAL INCOME TAX MODULE. State tax liabilities are based on the tax laws of the household's state of residence in December 1990. We assume that the household's filing status for state income taxes is the same as for federal taxes.[50] States have different definitions of taxable income that are reflected in the model. Twenty-four states use federal AGI, nine use federal taxable income, nine calculate taxable income separately from the federal return, two base their income taxes on the federal tax liability, and seven have no income tax.

After the appropriate income measure is calculated, certain income sources are excluded. Most states, for example, exempt all social security benefits from taxation. Standard deductions and exemptions are then

49. We impute itemization status and amounts based on income, family characteristics, and home ownership status.

50. This assumption does not reflect the fact that eleven states allow couples to file combined separate returns to mitigate potential marriage penalties.

calculated and deducted by the model. Some states use a percentage of state AGI as the standard deduction, and many use the federal standard deduction. Tax liability is calculated using brackets and rates for each state and filing status.

Besides the tax liability, tax credits are calculated. The state tax module includes credits for low-income filers (nine states), the elderly and disabled (eight states), dependents (one state), and exemptions (six states). Credits vary among states with regard to eligibility, generosity, and whether the credits are refundable. New Mexico, for example, has a low-income credit that uses "modified AGI." Modified AGI includes AFDC, SSI, and food stamp benefits that we calculate in earlier modules. Using tax forms collected from the forty-four states, we calculate state income taxes (including the District of Columbia) with state income taxes in 1990. Average effective state income tax rates vary in the model from 0.0 percent (several states) to 5.5 percent in the District of Columbia and are strikingly similar to those reported in the Bureau of the Census.[51]

PAYROLL TAX MODULE. As mentioned in the text, we assume that both the employee and employer portions of the payroll tax are borne by workers. The assumption of full shifting implies that in the absence of the payroll tax, gross wages would be higher by the payroll taxes paid by employers. Hence the average effective payroll tax rate is 14.2 percent for taxpayers with incomes below the payroll tax ceiling.[52] Incomes above $60,600 are not subject to old-age, survivors' and disability taxes (a 6.2 percent payroll tax on both employers and employees), but the employer and employee both still pay a 1.45 percent health insurance payroll tax. Payroll taxes on the self-employed are computed according to the federal income tax schedule for self-employed taxpayers.

FEDERAL CORPORATE TAX MODULE. As described in the text, the corporate income tax module distributes corporate income tax payments to individuals based on pre-specified incidence assumptions. We allocate the corporate income tax according to capital ownership, but we also describe results with alternative assumptions. Corporate tax payments and payroll taxes paid by employers are added back to all definitions of

---

51. Bureau of the Census (1992, tables 463, 687). Dickert, Houser, and Scholz (1994) provide comparisons of the simulation model's output with administrative sources.

52. The average effective payroll tax rate is calculated as total payroll tax payments divided by gross income (.153/1.0765 per dollar of net-of-employer-share-of-payroll-tax compensation), or 14.2 percent.

economic income in this chapter since under our assumptions, household incomes would be higher by the amount of these tax payments in the absence of these taxes.

OTHER MODEL-RELATED ISSUES. The model does not calculate federal excise taxes (tobacco, alcohol, and gasoline taxes) because of the lack of consumption data of specific commodities in the SIPP,[53] and estate and gift taxes, because of a lack of detailed information on *inter-vivos* transfers and bequests in the SIPP. The federal individual income tax module also does not incorporate subtle provisions such as, for example, the alternative minimum tax (because of the lack of detailed information on tax preferences in the SIPP core data) and schedule C expenses for the self-employed.

MODEL CALIBRATION. The model, without any adjustments, yields a distribution of federal income tax liabilities that differs from their observed distribution as reported by the Internal Revenue Service.[54] The differences result from two primary sources. First, data in the SIPP are organized by families and households, while taxes are paid by taxpayers. In most cases it is straightforward to determine whether a family will file a single return, a joint return, or as a head of household. Puzzles still arise, however. We do not have a good way, for example, of determining whether couples will file married-filing-separate returns. A more perplexing problem is that there is some evidence that an unusually large number of head of household returns get filed, particularly where the single household head with children is male.[55] To the extent there are discrepancies in the underlying demographic structure of the SIPP and IRS data or to the extent we miscalculate the filing status of filing units, our tax calculations will differ from the distribution of reported tax burdens.

Second and more important, incomes recorded in SIPP differ from income reported to the Internal Revenue Service. The main reason for this is that the SIPP data are top-coded at a threshold of $8,333 per month for any income item. Hence, SIPP is missing the top tail of the distribution of income as reported on tax returns. In addition, there are

53. The OTA, JCT, and CBO incorporate federal excise taxes into their analyses.
54. Internal Revenue Service (1993).
55. Liebman (1995).

differences in income reports between SIPP and IRS data for less affluent households.[56]

The consequence of the data discrepancies is that we understate the number of taxpayers with AGI less than $20,000 in 1990,[57] overstate the number with AGI between $20,000 and $200,000, and understate the number of taxpayers with incomes exceeding $200,000. Because the distribution of tax liabilities is the central focus of this chapter, we take an additional step of calibrating the model. Specifically, we alter family income in a systematic way (including top-coded observations) to match the distribution of adjusted gross income reported on tax returns in 1990—the year of our data.[58] The resulting data set matches the distribution of AGI reported on income tax returns but retains the demographic and other features of the SIPP data. Our adjustments are similar to those made by CBO for their tax model. CBO starts with baseline data from the Current Population Survey, and then adjusts the CPS to match the observed distribution of income data as reported on tax returns.[59]

After our adjustments, aggregate adjusted gross income (AGI) is within 1.4 percent of the aggregate reported by the Internal Revenue Service.[60] Above the bottom 5 percent of the income distribution, the largest discrepancy by income class appears in the $8,000–$9,000 group, where aggregate AGI is 0.84 percent lower than the benchmark. Most other income classes are considerably closer than this. Because of differences in family composition and income sources between the IRS and SIPP data, our distribution of taxable income differs from the IRS data by a

56. Scholz (1990) presents tables documenting differences in income and reported family structure between SIPP and IRS data.

57. More precisely, we have too many taxpayers filing with zero tax liability because we assume that everyone files a return regardless of whether they owe taxes or will receive an EITC. It is straightforward to arbitrarily assume some taxpayers with no tax liability will not file returns. The unadjusted data underpredict the number of taxpayers with positive tax liabilities who have incomes under $20,000.

58. Internal Revenue Service (1993). Internal Revenue Service (1995) published preliminary income tax data for 1994. We calibrate to the 1990 IRS benchmark and then inflate dollar values to 1994 levels because very large revisions generally occur with the preliminary tax data. We first match the number of filers in each AGI category with the IRS *Statistics of Income* data for 1990. This was done preserving the AGI ranking of families in the simulation model. We then take a nonlinear transformation of family income within each AGI class to match mean incomes within a given class. Once the model is calibrated to the 1990 tax return data, we put all income amounts in 1994 dollars using the Bureau of Labor Statistics series for average hourly earnings and the CPI for other income and asset categories.

59. Kasten, Sammartino, and Toder (1994).

60. Internal Revenue Service (1993).

larger amount. Aggregate taxable income is very close, only 0.7 percent lower than the IRS data. The variation across income classes is 5.5 percent or less (in absolute value).

The calibrated model matches quite closely the distribution of tax before credits from the early release of the 1994 tax data.[61] In aggregate, we collect 1.7 percent less tax than indicated by the IRS, and no income class above $10,000 differs by more than 5.7 percent (and most are considerably closer).[62]

Appendix B: Alternative Incidence Assumptions

There are two principal ways in the literature of examining the distributional effects of consumption-based taxes. In recent years the JCT has allocated the burden of broad-based consumption taxes (such as the flat tax) as income is earned rather than when taxes are paid.[63] The approach makes use of the equivalence of a broad-based consumption tax to a tax on wages plus a tax on income from existing capital (but exempting income from new investments).[64] Because the quality of our income data is considerably higher than the quality of our consumption data, following the JCT convention leads to much more reliable distributional estimates than distributing the tax according to consumption. The practical implication of this modeling choice is that in our primary specifications we allocate the wage portion of the flat tax in proportion to wage and salary income. We allocate the business portion of the flat tax partly to labor earnings, through the inclusion of fringe benefits in the corporate tax base, and partly to all owners of capital in a manner equivalent to the way we distribute the burden of the existing corporate income tax.

The most common alternative assumption is to allocate consumption taxes in proportion to household consumption. This approach would be preferred if the flat tax (or any consumption tax) would cause a uniform increase in prices. The desirability of either approach depends in part on reactions by the Federal Reserve, which, of course, are difficult to antic-

61. Internal Revenue Service (1995).
62. We collect $11 more tax per family in the $0–$5,000 income class, which is 9.7 percent higher than the benchmark amount.
63. Joint Committee on Taxation (1993, pp. 51–59).
64. The equivalence does not necessarily hold when there are nonindexed government transfers.

Table 8B-1. *Distribution of Taxes under Alternative Incidence Assumptions*

Family expanded income percentiles[a]	Baseline assumptions (table 8-2)		Distribute flat tax by consumption		Distribute business tax half to labor, half to capital	
	Current law, average taxes[b]	Flat tax, average taxes	Current law, average taxes[b]	Flat tax, average taxes	Current law, average taxes[b]	Flat tax, average taxes
			Average taxes			
5–10	175	318	337	1,272	158	287
10–20	627	872	803	2,122	614	849
20–30	1,686	2,175	1,802	3,550	1,650	2,113
30–40	3,159	3,633	3,293	5,123	3,152	3,621
40–50	5,023	5,299	5,219	6,897	5,070	5,382
50–60	7,145	7,204	7,393	8,998	7,246	7,382
60–70	9,785	9,914	10,159	11,565	9,980	10,257
70–80	13,284	13,718	13,730	14,879	13,557	14,197
80–90	18,562	19,460	19,076	19,530	18,921	20,089
90–95	26,714	27,531	26,575	25,071	26,778	27,643
95–99	43,375	43,896	42,780	36,500	43,362	43,873
99–100	223,953	186,045	203,887	116,951	214,669	169,769
Total	11,834	11,825	11,831	11,802	11,835	11,827

Average effective tax rates[c]

5–10	2.7	4.9	5.1	19.4	2.4	4.4
10–20	6.1	8.5	7.9	20.8	6.0	8.3
20–30	10.8	14.0	11.6	22.8	10.6	13.6
30–40	14.8	17.0	15.4	23.9	14.7	16.9
40–50	18.2	19.2	18.9	25.0	18.4	19.5
50–60	20.5	20.7	21.2	25.8	20.8	21.2
60–70	22.5	22.8	23.3	26.6	22.9	23.6
70–80	24.4	25.2	25.2	27.3	24.9	26.1
80–90	26.4	27.7	27.1	27.8	26.9	28.6
90–95	29.0	29.8	28.8	27.2	29.0	30.0
95–99	31.3	31.7	30.9	26.4	31.3	31.7
99–100	41.6	34.5	37.8	21.7	39.8	31.5
Total	25.8	25.7	25.8	25.7	25.8	25.7

Source: Data are from the 1990 Survey of Income and Program Participation, updated to 1994. Calculations are based on the microsimulation model described in the text. Plan descriptions are also in the text.

a. Family expanded income is wage and salary income, taxable interest and dividend income, alimony, business income, taxable pensions and annuities, rents, royalties, income from partnerships, income from estates and trusts, unemployment compensation, taxable social security, other miscellaneous income, nontaxable interest income, nontaxable pension income, nontaxable social security income, AFDC, food stamps, SSI, employer-provided health insurance, and the employer-paid portion of payroll taxes and corporate taxes.

b. Taxes under current law are federal individual and corporate income taxes; state income taxes; and payroll (OADSHI) taxes.

c. Average effective tax rates are taxes under current law divided by expanded family income multiplied by 100.

ipate. While we focus primarily on the JCT's preferred approach, we also present sensitivity analysis for our incidence assumptions below.

In appendix table 8B-1 we distribute the flat tax in proportion to consumption under the assumption that upon adoption of the flat tax there would be a one-time increase in prices. We calculate saving for each household using an imputation based on detailed household-level saving data from the 1983–89 panel of the Survey of Consumer Finances. Saving in the SCF is constructed as an "income minus consumption" measure by computing the contribution for each asset and liability category needed to yield the second balance, given the first balance and an average rate of return for the asset or liability category. John Sabelhaus compares a similar measure of saving to one calculated directly from income and consumption data using the Consumer Expenditure Survey and concludes that the method adopted here yields a more accurate measure of household saving than using household income and consumption data directly.[65] We then run a median regression of SCF saving on a flexible function of age, education, household demographic characteristics, industry, and occupation.[66] The coefficients from this regression are then used to calculate saving for each family in the 1990 SIPP (in 1994 dollars).

Columns 3 and 4 of appendix table 8B-1 show the results of distributing the flat tax according to consumption.[67] Relative to the results in table 8-2 (reproduced in columns 1 and 2), taxes increase for the bottom nine deciles of the income distribution and increase sharply (by more than 20 percent) for families in the bottom six deciles. Taxes fall sharply for families in the top 5 percent. Thus the overall effect of using consumption to distribute the burden of the flat tax accentuates the previous conclusion. The flat tax is likely to raise tax burdens substantially on the lowest-income families, and reduce taxes substantially for the highest.

The CBO typically presents alternative incidence assumptions for the corporate income tax, where its burden is distributed half to capital and half to labor. This both alters the distribution of current law taxes and changes the distribution of taxes collected under the flat tax. This incidence assumption is compatible with plausible parameter choices in a well-specified computable general equilibrium model.

65. Sabelhaus (1993).
66. Outliers in the saving data make the results from a mean regression of saving nonsensical.
67. We compare this to the current tax system, where the existing corporate income tax is distributed according to consumption.

As shown in the final two columns of appendix table 8B-1, the alternative corporate tax incidence assumption has little effect on the results relative to the baseline results in table 8-2. We conclude that the business tax incidence assumption is unlikely to have a substantial effect on our results.

Comment by Louise Sheiner

Contemplating moving toward a flat tax involves contemplating certain trade-offs: the flat tax may have some efficiency advantages over our current tax system, but it also has some distributional costs. Determining whether we should change our tax system will involve evaluating each of the many different variants of the flat tax that have been proposed in order to determine which, if any, provide efficiency benefits that are worth their distributional cost.

This chapter is aimed at doing just that. It evaluates just how bad these distributional costs are and explores how variations on the flat tax scheme affect the distributional consequences. The other side of the equation—the potential efficiency effects—is left for other chapters in this book to explore. The authors find that a flat tax is quite a bit less progressive than the current tax structure. Some variations on the flat tax—such as maintaining the EITC, can help, while others—like retaining the deductibility of home mortgage interest and charitable contributions—hurt.

While I have a few comments on the methodology, which I will address in a moment, I would be very surprised if any changes in methodology affected the authors' basic conclusions. After all, the results of moving to a revenue neutral flat tax, without accounting for any growth effects, is simple mathematics: moving toward a flat tax from a progressive income tax lowers the rate on the top and raises it in the middle and possibly at the bottom. Broadening the base to include the value of employer-provided fringe benefits and mortgage interest deductions may help some, but these effects are swamped by the change in the rates, particularly at the top of the income distribution.

Of course, saying that a flat tax is less progressive than the current tax system is not enough. We need to know how much less progressive in order to evaluate whether the potential efficiency effects are large enough to outweigh the distributional costs. For this question, methodology is important.

I have one problem with the specific methodology used by the authors, and then I will comment on their general approach to distributing tax burdens. The data set chosen to do the analysis, the SIPP, presents a number of difficulties for analyzing changes in taxes that have large effects for those at the top of the income distribution. Not only are there relatively few observations on people with high income, but income is top-coded by income category. The authors try to account for this problem by doing a nonlinear adjustment to total income in a way that closely matches IRS income totals by income class while maintaining taxpayer ranking according to the truncated SIPP income. Unfortunately, the incidence of top-coding is probably not randomly distributed within the top income groups (for example, older taxpayers are more likely to have truncated capital income), so any adjustment made solely on the basis of reported total income is likely to be fairly crude. This shortcoming of the data set reduces its value for making comparisons of the effects of the flat tax along dimensions other than income—like age, number of children, or marital status. Also, because the ordering of the truncated SIPP data may bear little resemblance to the ordering of the untruncated data, the data set is not particularly useful for comparing the effects of the flat tax at the top of the income distribution (for example, comparing taxpayers in the ninety-fifth to ninety-ninth percentile with those in the top 1 percent).

Now I would like to comment on the general methodology. Most analyses of consumption taxes have shown them to be very regressive. A flat consumption tax often appears significantly more regressive than a flat income tax. This finding stems from the fact that, because of life-cycle saving patterns and consumption smoothing of transitory income fluctuations, consumption tends to be a small fraction of income when income is high, and a large fraction when income is low.

Previous analyses showing the regressivity of consumption taxes provided one of the motivations for researchers to evaluate the impact of consumption taxes on a lifetime basis, as these changes in income and consumption would be smoothed out. But another possible solution to this problem is to analyze consumption taxes like income taxes. That is, since we know that a consumption tax is equivalent to a tax on wages and existing assets, we can analyze the distributional consequences according to wages and capital income. The consumption taxes currently being discussed, except for the USA tax, generally are described in income tax terms—that is, businesses are taxed on the value of their revenues less costs, and workers are taxed on their wages. Thus, while we describe the flat tax as a consumption tax, the legal base of the tax is described in terms of income, making the choice of using an income-based methodology a natural one. With this method, the burden of the tax is distributed when the income is earned, rather than when the income is consumed. This makes sense when what you are dividing taxes by to determine progressivity is income.

The effect of this methodology can be seen clearly by comparing the authors' standard results with those in table 8B-1, which distributes the flat tax on the basis of consumption. A flat tax appears much more regressive under a consumption-based methodology. (Note that the chapter uses, by necessity, a consumption-based method to distribute the USA tax; a fair comparison of the distributional effects of the USA tax with the flat tax would use the consumption-based method in table 8B-1 for the flat tax as well.)

The authors' findings that the results of the analysis for middle-aged couples do not differ much from those for the population as a whole is not surprising—it is exactly what the income method is designed to produce. Under a consumption-based method, one would anticipate that the effects of the tax would vary more by age, since consumption as a fraction of income varies by age.

The income-based distribution methodology makes a lot of sense, but it is not without problems. In particular, the assumptions advocated by the Joint Tax Committee a few years ago, and followed by the authors, allocate the burden of current business taxes to current owners of capital. And, as the authors note, this method does not do a good job of accounting for capitalization effects. If everyone lived forever, then allocating the annual burden of capital income taxes to capital owners would be fine. But, of course, people do not live forever. The reduction in the value of the existing assets—which is roughly equal to the present value of the business taxes—will affect owners of capital intent on consuming those assets more than it will affect those intent on saving them. Thus this methodology is not particularly useful for looking at intergenerational issues—since it likely understates the burden actually borne by older taxpayers.

Would the capitalization effects undo the regressivity of the flat tax? That is a hard question to answer. What is the best way of allocating a one-time event and comparing it to a flow? (It is not clear from the chapter exactly how the business portion of the flat tax was distributed, how much of the revenue is permanent, and how much represents a one-time tax on old capital—through elimination of depreciation on existing assets, for example.) Should the entire value of the capitalized effect be accounted for in one year, or should the amount of capitalization take into account the expected lifetime of the owner, and the fraction that will be bequeathed. These issues should be explored.

The advantages of the relatively straightforward annual distribution of taxes used in this chapter is that no strong assumptions are necessary, and without huge behavioral changes, the results are likely to provide a pretty good description of the distributional effects of a flat tax. One of the main messages of the chapter is that, for anyone valuing the progressivity of our current tax system, the efficiency hurdle—the efficiency gain necessary to overcome the distributional costs—is high.

But what if we were to accept the findings of the flat tax's most ardent supporters—that economic growth could easily double, for example. If everyone's tax rates decreased, would there be any justification for distribution tables? The answer for that depends, of course, on the efficiency trade-offs. Clearly, a tax reform that could increase after-tax income for everyone is better than no tax reform at all—so reductions in the progressivity of the tax system should not preclude adopting a flat tax if the efficiency consequences are large enough. But these tables tell us is that, even in this optimistic case, the rich would probably still gain the most, and the lowest- or middle-income the least. If there were alternate tax systems that could provide a greater boost at the lower end of the income spectrum, even while having a slightly smaller efficiency effect, they would be worth considering.

References

Attanasio, Orazio, and Martin Browning. 1995. "Consumption over the Life-Cycle and over the Business Cycle." *American Economic Review* 85 (December): 1118–37.

Auerbach, Alan J., and Laurence J. Kotlikoff. 1987. *Dynamic Fiscal Policy*. Cambridge University Press

Ballard, Charles L., John Karl Scholz, and John B. Shoven. 1987. "The Value-Added Tax: A General Equilibrium Look at Its Efficiency and Incidence." In *The Effects of Taxation on Capital Accumulation*, edited by Martin Feldstein, 445–80. University of Chicago Press.

Barthold, Thomas A. 1993. "How Should We Measure Distribution?" *National Tax Journal* 46 (September): 291–99.

Barthold, Thomas A., James R. Nunns, and Eric Toder. 1995. "A Comparison of Distribution Methodologies." In *Distributional Analysis of Tax Policy*, edited by David F. Bradford, 96–110. Washington: American Enterprise Institute.

Bernheim, B. Douglas. 1994. "Comment on 'Do Saving Incentives Work?'" *Brookings Papers on Economic Activity* 1: 152–66.

Bradford, David F. 1995. "Consumption Taxes: Some Fundamental Transition Issues." In *Frontiers of Tax Reform*, edited by Michael J. Boskin, 123–50. Hoover Institution Press.

Bureau of the Census. 1992. *Statistical Abstract of the United States: 1992.* 112th ed. Washington.

Dickert, Stacy, Scott Houser, and John Karl Scholz. 1994. "Taxes and the Poor: A Microsimulation Study of Implicit and Explicit Taxes." *National Tax Journal* 47 (September): 621–38.

———. 1995. "The Earned Income Tax Credit and Transfer Programs: A Study of Labor Market and Program Participation." In *Tax Policy and the Economy*, edited by James M. Poterba, vol. 9, 1–50. National Bureau of Economic Research and MIT Press.

Engen, Eric, and William Gale. 1995. "Debt, Taxes, and the Effects of 401(k) Plans on Household Wealth Accumulation." Brookings (October).

Feldstein, Martin S. 1995. "The Effect of a Consumption Tax on the Rate of Interest." Working Paper 5397. Cambridge, Mass.: National Bureau of Economic Research (December).

Fullerton, Don, and Diane Lim Rogers. 1993. *Who Bears the Lifetime Tax Burden?* Brookings.

Gentry, William M., and R. Glenn Hubbard. 1996. "Distributional Implications of Introducing a Broad-Based Consumption Tax." Mimeo. Columbia University (May).

Graetz, Michael J. 1995. "Distributional Tables, Tax Legislation, and the Illusion of Precision." *Distributional Analysis of Tax Policy*, edited by David F. Bradford, 15–78. Washington: American Enterprise Institute.

Gravelle, Jane G. 1991. "Income, Consumption, and Wage Taxation in a Life-Cycle Model: Separating Efficiency from Redistribution." *American Economic Review* 81 (September): 985–95.

Hall, Robert E. 1996. "The Effects of Tax Reform on Prices and Asset Values." In *Tax Policy and the Economy—1995*, edited by James Poterba, vol. 10, 71–88. MIT Press.

Hall, Robert E., and Alvin Rabushka. 1983. *Low Tax, Simple Tax, Flat Tax.* McGraw-Hill.

———. 1995. *The Flat Tax*, 2d ed. Stanford: Hoover Institution Press.

Harberger, Arnold. 1962. "The Incidence of Corporation Income Tax." *Journal of Political Economy* 70 (June): 215–40.

Internal Revenue Service. 1993. *Statistics of Income-1990: Individual Income Tax Returns.* Washington.

——. 1995. *Statistics of Income Bulletin* 15 (Fall): 9–33. Washington.

Joint Committee on Taxation. 1993. "Methodology and Issues in Measuring Changes in the Distribution of Tax Burdens." JCS-7-93, June 14.

Kasten, Richard, Frank Sammartino, and Eric Toder. 1994. "Trends in Federal Tax Progressivity, 1980–93." In *Tax Progressivity and Income Inequality*, edited by Joel Slemrod, 9–50. Cambridge University Press.

King, Mervyn A., and Louis Dicks-Mireaux. 1982. "Asset Holdings and the Life-Cycle." *Economic Journal* 92 (June): 247–67.

Kotlikoff, Laurence J. 1992. *Generational Accounting: Knowing Who Pays, and When, for What We Spend*. Free Press.

Liebman, Jeffrey B. 1995. "Who Are the Ineligible EITC Recipients?" Mimeo. Harvard University (October).

Lyon, Andrew B., and Robert M. Schwab. 1995. "Consumption Taxes in a Life-Cycle Framework: Are Sin Taxes Regressive?" *Review of Economics and Statistics* 77 (August): 389–406.

Pechman, Joseph A. 1985. *Who Paid the Taxes, 1966–85?* Brookings.

——. 1990. "The Future of the Income Tax." *American Economic Review* 80 (March): 1–20.

Pechman, Joseph A., and Benjamin A. Okner. 1974. *Who Bears the Tax Burden?* Brookings.

Poterba, James. 1989. "Lifetime Incidence and the Distributional Burden of Excise Taxes."*American Economic Review* 79 (May): 325–30.

Sabelhaus, John. 1993. "What Is the Distributional Burden of Taxing Consumption?" *National Tax Journal* 46 (September): 331–44.

Scholz, John Karl. 1990. "The Participation Rate of the Earned Income Tax Credit." Institute for Research on Poverty Discussion Paper 28–90. University of Wisconsin-Madison (October).

——. 1994. "The Earned Income Tax Credit: Participation, Compliance, and Anti-Poverty Effectiveness." *National Tax Journal* 47 (March): 63–87.

——. 1996. "In-Work Benefits in the United States: The Earned Income Tax Credit." *Economic Journal* 106 (January): 156–69.

Shoven, John B. 1976. "The Incidence and Efficiency Effects of Taxes on Income from Capital." *Journal of Political Economy* 84 (December): 1261–83.

Whalley, John. 1988. "Lessons from General Equilibrium Models." In *Uneasy Compromise: Problems of a Hybrid Income-Consumption Tax*, edited by Henry J. Aaron, Harvey Galper, and Joseph A. Pechman, 15–49. Brookings.

Yin, George K., and others. 1994. "Improving the Delivery of Benefits to the Working Poor: Proposals to Reform the Earned Income Tax Credit Program." *American Journal of Tax Policy* 11 (Fall): 225–98.

CHAPTER 9

Lifetime Effects of Fundamental Tax Reform

Don Fullerton and Diane Lim Rogers

T HIS CHAPTER examines the effects of fundamental tax reform on the well-being of households in different generations and in different lifetime income categories. These matters are intricately linked to the effects of tax reform on economic efficiency and household decisions about saving and work effort.

The distinguishing feature of our analysis is the combination of general-equilibrium methodology and a lifetime horizon. The general-equilibrium approach allows us to examine how households and businesses respond to differential incentives created by tax reform. These responses matter because they affect relative prices, resource allocation, and incomes. The lifetime horizon allows us to classify households according to lifetime incomes as opposed to annual incomes and to add measures of lifetime incidence to the more traditional measures of annual incidence.

The lifetime perspective is valuable because annual income may not accurately reflect long-term ability to pay taxes. Over the life-cycle, many people migrate through the income distribution. Earnings generally start low, increase during prime working years, and eventually fall as workers retire. Thus the lowest income brackets in any year include some people who will eventually earn enough to put them in higher income brackets and some who once were in those higher brackets. Conversely, upper brackets each year include some people who once earned little or will earn little in the future. Annual data do not show the long-term economic

We are grateful for comments from Frank Sammartino and other participants at the Brookings conference. The views expressed here are ours and do not necessarily reflect the views of the Congressional Budget Office.

status of many taxpayers. We address this issue by sorting households according to lifetime income and by measuring tax burdens over entire lifetimes.

Studies of annual incidence indicate that, as a share of income, a proportional consumption tax places higher tax burdens on low-income households than on high-income households because the ratio of annual consumption to annual income falls as income increases. In contrast, James Poterba notes that a proportional consumption tax could be close to a proportional tax on lifetime income because the present value of lifetime consumption should equal the present value of lifetime income.[1] In an earlier study, however, we found that the incidence of a proportional consumption tax might not be proportional to lifetime income if income includes the full value of untaxed leisure, inheritances, and bequests.[2]

The lifetime perspective is also important in capturing how taxes distort decisions about whether to consume now or later. The consumption tax removes this intertemporal distortion, but at least initially it requires a higher tax rate that imposes a bigger distortion on decisions about how much to work. Thus the adoption of a consumption tax could increase or decrease economic efficiency depending on how much consumption people shift from one period to another by saving compared with how much they substitute leisure for work. A life-cycle model can account for both responses.

Our lifetime perspective also recognizes important differences among households of the same age and thus differs from a purely generational perspective. Several studies have found that the switch from an income tax to a consumption tax would increase burdens on the elderly because they must pay tax on all accumulated capital as it is subsequently consumed—in effect a tax on the principal as well as the interest.[3] In our lifetime perspective, people of the same age may have different saving patterns because their earnings may differ in amount or timing and because their inheritances and bequests may differ. Thus capital is held not just by the old more than the young, but also by the lifetime rich more than the lifetime poor. The consumption tax and its implicit capital levy

1. Poterba (1989).

2. Fullerton and Rogers (1993).

3. See, for example, Auerbach and Kotlikoff (1987) and Auerbach, Kotlikoff, and Skinner (1983).

redistribute wealth within as well as among generations. Both kinds of redistribution can affect economic growth and efficiency.

Major Features of Tax Reform Proposals

Proposals for fundamental tax reform combine many large and small changes that have complicated interactive effects. Rather than attempt to model each proposal specifically, we focus on four essential elements of such reforms.

First, the proposals would alter the tax base. The current income tax is actually a hybrid of a consumption tax and an income tax. A pure income tax would tax all sources of income, including items—such as municipal bonds, pension contributions, and the imputed income from home ownership—that are not taxed under the current system. In contrast, a pure consumption tax would allow deductions for all forms of saving, including items—such as saving in bank accounts, mutual funds, or other accounts—that are not deducted under the current system.

The compromise embodied in the current system creates different incentives to invest in various types of assets, and thus may be worse than either a broad-based consumption tax or a broad-based income tax.[4] The economy operates less efficiently if taxpayers shift investments from taxable stocks and bonds to tax-favored assets. Indeed, the economy is less efficient to the extent that any activity can be financed in a tax-favored manner. For example, if the income tax allows interest payments to be deducted, high-bracket taxpayers can borrow, deduct the interest paid, and use the borrowed funds to invest in tax-favored assets.

Consistent application of any comprehensive tax base prevents such misallocation of resources. Most proposals move toward a single base but differ on whether the base should be consumption or income. Other tax bases are also available: a wage tax is an often-cited alternative.

Second, the proposals would alter tax rates. The proposed rate structures vary from having one or two relatively low rates to having a full graduated rate structure. The rate levels would be lower in proposals that eliminate more exemptions or deductions, assuming revenues were held constant. Differences in the level and structure of tax rates imply differing economic incentives and effects.

4. Aaron, Galper, and Pechman (1988).

Third, the proposals may exempt various types of activities. For example, most proposals would eliminate the current extra level of tax on the corporate sector by integrating corporate and personal income tax or by instituting a cash-flow business tax with expensing of new investments. But the proposals differ in their treatment of financial assets, foreign assets, tax-exempt bonds, and mortgage interest.

Fourth, the proposals differ in their treatment of payroll taxes. One proposal—the USA (unlimited savings allowance) tax—allows a full tax credit at both the business and household level for payroll tax payments. This proposal would essentially eliminate the effect of the payroll tax. This feature could be incorporated in other plans as well.

Although our analysis focuses on these four essential elements of the proposals, other differences remain. Administrative arrangements can differ. Consumption taxes can be collected from retailers, from producers at every stage of production, or from households through personal filing. The reforms also may vary in costs of administration or compliance, or in their visibility to the public.

Modeling the Lifetime Effects of Tax Reform

We analyze the major features of tax reform with a computable general-equilibrium model. The appendix to this chapter provides a detailed description of the model and the parameters used.

Each household belongs to one of twelve lifetime income groups. Each group has its own estimated lifetime wage profile, inheritance received, and bequest left at the end of life. These features allow us to analyze the distributional effects of taxes. We assume that, in well-functioning markets and on the basis of good information about their lifetime resources, households make decisions about how much to save and work. The labor-supply response to a change in tax policy depends on the substitutability between consumption and leisure in the current period, and the saving response depends on the substitutability between current and future consumption. The size of these substitution parameters affects individuals' responses to tax reform.

Households also allocate their consumption among seventeen categories of consumer goods. Within each of these categories, they can substitute between versions of the good produced by corporate and noncorporate businesses. The imperfect substitutability of corporate and noncorporate goods explains their coexistence despite the higher tax burdens placed on corporate production under current tax law.[5] Thus the distribution of the tax burden can depend on how consumers spend as well as on how they earn their incomes.

The model allows for production of goods by corporate and noncorporate businesses, nineteen industries, five types of capital, and labor. Producers make profit-maximizing decisions on an annual basis and can substitute between capital and labor as well as among different types of capital. Resources can flow between the corporate and noncorporate sectors. The switch to a more neutral tax system boosts economic efficiency by reducing tax-induced substitutions.

We characterize the current tax system as a progressive system with constant marginal tax rates on corporate and personal income of 0.395 and 0.250, respectively, based on economywide weighted averages prevailing in 1993, our benchmark year. The values for depreciation allowances, tax credits, and other tax parameters also reflect 1993 tax law. We also allow for varying lump-sum grants in the personal income tax.[6]

We specify that consumption-based taxes are collected at the point of purchase, and wage taxes are collected from employers. We approximate the effect of exemptions by giving households a lump-sum grant equal to the tax rate times the exemption level. This allows very-low-income households to have negative tax liabilities. Our tax reforms with "exemptions" are therefore more generous to low-income households than a true exemption would be.

We assume the alternative taxes raise as much money as both the current personal and corporate income taxes on an annual basis.[7] The tax rates required for revenue neutrality depend on the tax base as well as on behavioral responses to tax reform.

Estimates of the Economic Effects of Tax Reform

We analyze the effects of the major features of tax reform on tax rates, aggregate economic variables, the distribution of income within and across generations, and economic efficiency.

5. Gravelle and Kotlikoff (1993) specify a similar imperfect substitutability of corporate and noncorporate outputs.

6. This procedure reproduces the current degree of progressivity, through average tax rates that rise with income, but it preserves the computational convenience of linear budget constraints.

7. This revenue neutrality accounts for changes in the price level, so that the real value of government purchases is held constant.

Tax Rates

Table 9-1 shows the tax rates that would be required under three replacement taxes, each of which has a proportional rate with no exemptions. The tax bases are, respectively, all consumption (the value-added tax, or VAT), all wages, and all income. The results of these simulations show the combined effect of changing the tax base and instituting proportional rates. The differences among the estimates show the effects of choosing different tax bases.

The table's stub shows initial statutory tax rates on capital income and effective rates on income from various types of capital under the current tax system. Columns 1 through 3 show statutory and effective rates if revenues are just maintained but the tax base is changed. These estimates are based on standard elasticity assumptions corresponding to the central case of Fullerton and Rogers, with intertemporal and leisure-consumption elasticities set at 0.50.[8] Columns 4 through 6 show the results with low-elasticity assumptions: both elasticities are set at 0.15.[9]

The rows under the heading "initial" correspond to an equilibrium immediately following the tax change. "Steady-state" results correspond to an equilibrium achieved one hundred years after the tax change. At that time prices have remained unchanged for thirty-five years and relatively stable for fifty-five years.

At any point in time the income base is larger than the consumption base. The difference is saving. Moreover, consumption can be financed with existing assets or with wage income. Thus, although perhaps less obvious, the consumption base turns out to be larger than the wage base. The difference is consumption of the return to existing capital less saving out of current earnings.

The initial replacement tax rates shown in the first row of table 9-1 reflect these size differences. The initial income tax rate is lowest, and the wage tax rate is highest. Under the low-elasticity assumptions the difference between the income and consumption bases narrows because personal saving responds less to the effective tax rate on capital income

---

8. Fullerton and Rogers (1993).

9. The econometric evidence on saving and labor-supply responses surveyed in Randolph and Rogers (1995) seems to be more consistent with the lower-elasticity assumptions. Because incidence patterns are not sensitive to these elasticities but efficiency and growth effects are, we show variants of elasticity assumptions for the efficiency and growth effects but not for the distributional effects.

Table 9-1. *Changes in Effective Tax Rates on Capital from Switching to Proportional Consumption (VAT), Wage, and Income Taxes*

Tax rates	Benchmark	Standard elasticity assumptions[a]			Low-elasticity assumptions[a]		
		VAT (1)	*Wage* (2)	*Income* (3)	*VAT* (4)	*Wage* (5)	*Income* (6)
Statutory rates							
Initial	0.25 and 0.395	0.179	0.206	0.157	0.148	0.182	0.144
Steady state	0.25 and 0.395	0.137	0.179	0.145	0.140	0.171	0.140
Effective rates on capital (initial)							
Corporate	0.529	0.121	0.102	0.227	0.124	0.106	0.221
Noncorporate	0.349	0.144	0.121	0.244	0.148	0.127	0.240
Owner-occupied housing	0.273	0.228	0.195	0.310	0.233	0.202	0.308
Effective rates (steady state)							
Corporate	0.529	0.167	0.140	0.241	0.134	0.121	0.226
Noncorporate	0.349	0.197	0.165	0.263	0.159	0.144	0.246
Owner-occupied housing	0.273	0.302	0.259	0.341	0.249	0.228	0.319

Sources: Authors' calculations based on data described in appendix.

a. The Fullerton and Rogers (1993) model is used to simulate the replacement of federal corporate and personal income taxes with flat-rate (single marginal rate) proportional taxes. "Standard elasticity assumptions" set intertemporal and leisure-consumption elasticities of substitution to 0.50; "low elasticity assumptions" set these at 0.15.

when the intertemporal elasticity is lower. However, the difference between the consumption base and the wage base widens. A low intertemporal elasticity implies that a larger share of the capital stock must be explained by intergenerational transfers of capital rather than life-cycle saving. As a result, more consumption is financed from the return to inherited capital. Thus, under low elasticities, the initial rates required for revenue neutrality are 14.8 percent for the consumption tax and 18.2 percent for the wage tax.

In the steady state, however, the tax rates necessary to sustain revenues depend on how the economy has responded to tax reform. These responses differ among the tax bases. With high ("standard") elasticities, adopting a consumption base enlarges the economy more than does switching to an income base. Accordingly, the revenue-neutral long-run consumption tax rate (13.7 percent) is lower than the revenue-neutral long-run income tax rate (14.5 percent). The higher the elasticities, the more attractive the consumption tax base.

Table 9-1 also shows how proportional taxes would affect the costs of capital for the corporate, noncorporate, and owner-occupied housing sectors. Under all tax reforms the effective tax rate falls more for corporate capital than for noncorporate or housing capital. All reforms reduce the personal marginal tax rate, and all would eliminate the extra layer of tax on the corporate sector. For both elasticity assumptions the effective tax rates fall more under the consumption tax and wage tax than under the income tax, since the income tax still applies to capital income.[10] Even the proportional income tax reduces the cost of corporate and noncorporate capital because it lowers marginal tax rates; but it increases the cost of owner-occupied housing because the pure income tax applies to imputed rent on owner-occupied housing.[11]

---

10. These effective tax rates are comparable across sectors and assets, but they are hard to compare across tax reforms because they depend on the level of the net rate of return relative to the wage rate. Our numeraire (nominal value held constant) is the net wage paid by firms, and the tax reforms are modeled as extra taxes paid by firms, so the gross wage increases. To maintain the relative costs of labor and capital for a company requires an increase in the nominal price of capital.

11. Under current tax law, owner-occupied housing is favored relative to rental housing and other forms of capital. Homeowners take mortgage interest deductions despite the fact that their imputed rental income is not taxed. The pure proportional income tax replacement does tax imputed rents. Even though all the proportional replacements remove the differential federal tax treatment of capital among sectors and asset types, a difference remains among corporate, noncorporate, and housing costs of capital because of the continued existence of property taxes.

Table 9-2. *Economic Effects of Switching to Proportional Consumption (VAT), Wage, and Income Taxes*
Percent

Effect	Standard elasticity assumptions[a]			Low-elasticity assumptions[a]		
	VAT	Wage	Income	VAT	Wage	Income
Change in saving rate						
Initial	334.0	275.0	201.0	62.3	75.8	60.6
Steady state	19.8	17.9	11.4	3.0	6.5	3.9
Change in capital ÷ labor						
Initial	−3.2	−2.6	−2.0	0.42	0.34	0.48
Steady state	21.2	19.3	13.3	5.67	8.91	5.75
Change in labor supply						
Initial	4.09	3.39	2.99	0.35	0.38	0.36
Steady state	0.52	0.30	0.71	0.00	−0.10	0.01
Change in output ÷ labor						
Initial	1.43	1.27	1.03	0.84	0.87	0.81
Steady state	4.53	4.22	3.13	1.53	2.09	1.53
Change in rate of return ÷ wages						
Initial	55.0	90.0	57.5	50.0	80.0	52.5
Steady state	7.5	32.5	22.5	37.5	55.0	40.0
Efficiency gains						
Share of lifetime income	0.97	0.86	0.70	−0.50	−0.20	−0.05
Share of revenue	6.85	2.96	2.44	−0.34	−0.73	−0.17

Sources: Authors' calculations based on data described in appendix.
a. "Standard elasticity assumptions" set intertemporal and leisure-consumption elasticities of substitution to 0.50; "low elasticity assumptions" set these at 0.15.

Aggregate Economic Effects

Table 9-2 shows the effects of adopting alternative proportional tax bases on five economic variables and one measure of efficiency gain. Although the choice of tax base affects economic variables differently, the differences are small. Under all three replacements, the net rate of return to capital increases sharply at first, as does saving. But eventually, growth of the capital stock causes the net rate of return to fall. This decrease is greater with the higher intertemporal elasticity because capital accumulates faster. All reforms boost labor productivity (output divided by labor) and efficiency by small but similar amounts. The small differences across the three bases indicate that all are broader and more neutral than the current income tax base. Any of these reforms would therefore contribute modestly to economic growth.

With high elasticities the percentage increases in steady-state capital-labor ratios, labor productivity, and efficiency are largest for the consumption tax and smallest for the income tax. Low elasticities sharply reduce both the size of these changes and the relative advantages of the consumption base. Under low elasticities, steady-state saving rates and initial and steady-state capital-labor ratios increase least for the consumption base. Efficiency improves little and may actually deteriorate, with no clear advantage to the consumption base.[12]

We no doubt overestimate initial responses because we do not let households build into current saving decisions the likelihood that the rate of return will fall in the future.[13] The steady-state increases are considerably smaller. Both the initial and steady-state changes in labor supply and productivity are smaller than the effects on saving.

One perhaps surprising feature of the results is that wage taxes increase saving more than consumption taxes do. In models that ignore intragenerational redistributions, one would expect the opposite result because the consumption tax places more burden on the old, who are dissaving, and redistributes toward the young, who save more. In our model, however, households differ not only by age but also by lifetime income, and saving propensities may vary with both characteristics. The consumption tax's levy on existing capital not only hits the old harder than the young, but also hits the lifetime rich harder than the lifetime poor.[14] If the capital levy hits the rich, and if the rich have higher pro-

12. Our efficiency measure is based on a calculation of present value of individual gains, added across all generations. We discount at a rate of 4 percent, which puts greater weight on the negative utility changes of older generations than on the positive changes for steady-state generations. A lower discount rate would thus increase the efficiency gain. This measure is somewhat arbitrary because it does not reflect a formally defined social welfare function, and it does not employ the "lump-sum redistribution authority" of Auerbach, Kotlikoff, and Skinner (1983). Instead, our model is meant to focus primarily on distributional measures. Our efficiency measure is perhaps most useful to compare across tax replacements, although this ranking also could vary with the choice of discount rate. At a more theoretical level, the proportional federal tax replacements are not necessarily less distortionary than the benchmark income tax system because of distortions that remain from pre-existing payroll, property, sales, and excise taxes.

13. With myopic expectations, people change their saving behavior based on the assumption that the net rate of return will forever equal the initial rate.

14. In the Fullerton-Rogers model the consumption and wage bases also differ because of bequests. The lifetime rich, who receive relatively large inheritances, can consume more

pensities to save, consumption taxes need not generate a larger saving response than wage taxes would.

Intergenerational Distribution of Burdens

In general, the reforms to the proportional tax rate hurt the old and help the young (left side of table 9-3). Our measure of welfare change for each age group is the percentage of lifetime income (added over all lifetime income categories) that each cohort would have to be granted to make it as well off under the new tax system as it would have been under the current one. This amount is called the "equivalent variation."

That a consumption tax would help the young at the expense of the elderly is not surprising, but adopting either a proportional wage or income tax produces similar effects. The usual explanation for this pattern of gains and losses from switching to a consumption tax focuses on the sources of income. A wage tax would seem to leave the old unaffected. But this ignores the distortions in the current income tax.

The elderly are actually made worse off by the adoption of a more neutral tax, even a wage tax, because reform changes the relative prices of consumer goods in a way that burdens the old more than the young. The elimination of preferential treatment of housing sharply raises its cost, especially of owner-occupied housing, and the incidence of home ownership increases with age.[15] In addition, the removal of capital taxation under either the wage tax or the consumption tax increases the relative price of health care, financial services, and other labor-intensive goods. Even with the adoption of a proportional income tax, these increases hold because of the removal of the double taxation of dividend income. Such changes in the relative prices of consumer goods cause intergenerational redistribution.

The elderly are only slightly worse off under the wage tax than under the current system because increases in the prices of labor-intensive goods are offset by the elimination of taxes on capital income, which accrues disproportionately to the elderly. Under the income tax replacement the elderly are relatively worse off than they would be under the wage tax because capital income is still taxed.[16]

---

than the present value of their labor income. This feature also makes the consumption tax more progressive than the wage tax, and it reinforces the intragenerational effect on total savings that occurs when those with high saving propensities are hit by the capital levy.

15. See chapter 5 in this volume by D. Capozza, R. Green, and P. Hendershott.

16. Because the old have more capital income than the young, however, and because

Table 9-3. *Distribution of Intergenerational Welfare Effects under Eight Tax Proposals, by Age*[a]

Equivalent variation as percent of lifetime income

Age at time of tax change	Proportional VAT	Proportional wage-income tax	Proportional income tax	VAT with exemption	Wage-income tax with exemption	Income tax with exemption	VAT with zero-rated goods	VAT replacing payroll taxes as well
79	-0.080	-0.048	-0.051	-0.088	-0.039	-0.046	-0.081	-0.095
69	-0.227	0.029	-0.058	-0.306	0.073	-0.059	-0.234	-0.337
59	0.230	0.581	0.407	0.077	0.577	0.333	0.085	0.085
49	1.122	1.389	1.174	0.904	1.236	0.973	0.833	1.015
39	2.309	2.203	2.033	2.115	1.844	1.700	2.004	2.353
29	3.252	2.549	2.512	3.285	2.132	2.181	2.754	3.538
9	3.501	1.995	2.037	4.018	1.800	1.910	3.122	4.216
-29	3.283	1.819	1.869	3.797	1.638	1.785	2.882	3.950

Sources: Authors' calculations based on data described in appendix.
a. Based on simulations from the Fullerton and Rogers (1993) model using 1993 benchmarks and assuming intertemporal and leisure-consumption elasticities of substitution of 0.50. Exemption levels are set equal to $10,000 per household per year (in 1993 dollars).

Consumption taxes entail the greatest intergenerational redistribution because of the tax on existing capital. Alternative elasticities do not change this conclusion. Making the taxes progressive by adding a personal exemption intensifies the generational effect of the consumption tax but not of the wage or income tax (middle of table 9-3). The exemption requires a higher tax rate to maintain revenue neutrality, which has the effect of raising prices more for goods purchased disproportionately by the elderly. The "zero-rating," or total exemption, of certain necessities (such as food, shelter, and utilities) does less to change the intergenerational pattern of burdens. Using the consumption tax to replace both income and payroll taxes (last column of table 9-3) intensifies intergenerational transfers because payroll taxes are relatively more burdensome for the young.

Lifetime Burdens by Lifetime Income Categories

We classify lifetime incomes of households in deciles and then subdivide the top and bottom deciles into the most extreme 2 percent and the next 8 percent. The result is twelve lifetime income categories, where category 1 is the poorest 2 percent. For each replacement plan, table 9-4 shows the intragenerational distributions of welfare effects, expressed as a percentage of lifetime income, across lifetime income categories for a generation alive in the steady state.[17]

In previous work we have shown that our income tax system is progressive on a lifetime basis.[18] Table 9-4 indicates that changing from the current income tax system to any of the proportional tax replacements results in greater welfare gains as a percentage of lifetime income for the lifetime rich than for the lifetime poor. The welfare of the lifetime poor deteriorates in absolute as well as relative terms, even in the steady state where overall welfare increases. From the lifetime perspective, wage taxes

---

capital taxes decrease more than labor taxes with the removal of the double taxation of dividend income, even a switch to a neutral income tax provides some relative gain for the old on the sources side.

17. If we showed absolute levels of equivalent variations, all replacements would appear relatively less favorable to the lifetime poor simply because lifetime income is much lower for the lifetime poor than for the lifetime rich. For example, the present value of lifetime income for a person in category 1 is about $200,000, while that of a person in category 12 exceeds $2 million. See chapter 3 in Fullerton and Rogers (1993) for a description of the lifetime income distribution and characteristics by lifetime income categories.

18. The personal income tax is progressive, but the corporate income tax is close to proportional measured from a lifetime perspective. See Fullerton and Rogers (1993).

Table 9-4. *Distribution of Intragenerational Welfare Effects under Eight Tax Proposals, by Income Category*[a]

Equivalent variation as percent of lifetime income in steady state

Lifetime income category	Proportional VAT	Proportional wage-income tax	Proportional income tax	VAT with exemption	Wage-income tax with exemption	Income tax with exemption	VAT with zero-rated goods	VAT replacing payroll taxes as well
1 (poorest)	-4.34	-5.91	-5.63	8.13	11.23	6.72	-1.66	-3.62
2	0.53	-0.91	-0.98	6.19	6.37	4.22	1.64	1.21
3	0.06	-1.61	-1.45	4.12	3.23	2.10	0.65	0.82
4	1.50	-0.15	-0.05	4.19	2.72	2.06	1.72	2.25
5	3.31	1.48	1.72	5.37	3.36	3.16	3.30	4.13
6	1.39	-0.39	-0.19	2.64	0.33	0.41	1.18	2.19
7	3.06	1.55	1.44	3.60	1.38	1.29	2.73	3.75
8	3.16	1.24	1.51	3.41	0.43	1.06	2.63	4.02
9	3.77	1.85	2.09	3.51	0.32	1.10	3.10	4.62
10	3.74	2.10	2.31	3.01	0.04	0.92	2.94	4.49
11	4.94	4.39	4.06	3.14	1.39	1.77	3.97	5.25
12 (richest)	9.98	9.95	9.28	7.17	5.77	5.99	8.79	10.10
Overall	3.32	1.85	1.90	3.85	1.69	1.81	2.93	4.00

Sources: Authors' calculations based on data described in appendix.
a. Based on simulations from the Fullerton and Rogers (1993) model using 1993 benchmarks, and assuming intertemporal and leisure-consumption elasticities of substitution of 0.50. The results are insensitive to elasticity assumptions.

are more regressive than consumption taxes because wage taxes exempt capital income, while consumption taxes impose a levy on accumulated capital. The proportional income tax is slightly less regressive than the proportional wage tax because the income base still includes capital income, although the integration of corporate and personal income taxes means that capital taxes fall more than labor taxes.

Table 9-4 also shows that exempting $10,000 of consumption, wages, or income per household goes far to maintain progressivity at the lower end of the lifetime income distribution. The lifetime poor enjoy larger welfare gains as a percentage of lifetime income compared with the proportional versions and compared with the average gains for all income groups. The exemption does not change regressivity at the upper end, however, because the lifetime rich still enjoy larger gains as a percentage of lifetime income than do households in the middle of the distribution. Thus the effect of the annual exemption on the distribution of lifetime income appears qualitatively similar to others' findings of the effect on the annual distribution—larger percentage gains to the richest and poorest, and smallest gains to the middle class. Exemptions with flat rates simply cannot maintain the current level of lifetime progressivity at the upper end of the lifetime income distribution.[19]

Zero rates for food, shelter, autos, fuel, and utilities reduce but do not eliminate the lifetime regressivity of a switch to a flat consumption tax.[20] Finally, the replacement of payroll as well as income taxes reduces regressivity because payroll taxes are lifetime regressive.[21]

Efficiency Gains

Table 9-5 shows the efficiency gains from the prototype tax replacements under various intertemporal and leisure-consumption elasticities. The eventual revenue-neutral tax rates appear in parentheses. The numbers suggest that if elasticities are high, a switch to any of the three broadbased taxes increases economic welfare, with a proportional consumption tax having the largest effect. The gains are modest, however—less than 1 percent of lifetime income, and the advantage of the consumption tax over a broad-based income tax disappears if the intertemporal elas-

19. An interesting extension would undertake a direct comparison of annual and lifetime incidence in the same model.

20. This result is similar to the conclusions from other studies that examine annual incidence. See, for example, Congressional Budget Office (1992).

21. Fullerton and Rogers (1993).

Table 9-5. *Efficiency Gains from Eight Tax Replacements under Various Assumptions about Intertemporal and Leisure-Consumption Elasticities*[a]

Percent of present value of lifetime incomes

Tax replacement	Intertemporal and leisure-consumption elasticities (ϵ_1, ϵ_2)			
	0.50, 0.50	0.50, 0.15	0.15, 0.50	0.15, 0.15
Proportional VAT	0.973	.818	.072	−.050
	(.137)	(.129)	(.151)	(.140)
Proportional wage-income tax	.861	.663	−.308	−.203
	(.179)	(.162)	(.192)	(.171)
Proportional income tax	.701	.573	.070	−.047
	(.145)	(.134)	(.151)	(.140)
VAT with exemption	.960	.847	.048	−.041
	(.202)	(.180)	(.224)	(.197)
Wage-income tax with exemption	.696	.671	−1.54	−.893
	(.309)	(.250)	(.326)	(.263)
Income tax with exemption	.606	.540	.073	−.056
	(.216)	(.189)	(.222)	(.195)
VAT with zero-rated goods	.791	.650	−.171	−.246
	(.344)	(.316)	(.388)	(.351)
VAT replacing payroll taxes as well	1.02	.858	.049	−.060
	(.205)	(.191)	(.221)	(.205)

Source: Efficiency gains are calculated as the present value of equivalent variation as a percentage of the present value of lifetime incomes, over all generations, based on the Fullerton and Rogers (1993) model and the 1993 benchmark.

a. Steady-state replacement tax rates are in parentheses.

ticity is low.[22] All these gains in efficiency are smaller than the increase in steady-state utility reported earlier because the losses of earlier generations are included, and indeed, given greater weight due to discounting. Moreover, if both elasticities are low, the switch to a consumption tax actually reduces economic efficiency relative to the current system, be-

22. The welfare gains of a switch from a progressive income tax to a proportional consumption tax are expected to be positively related to the magnitude of the intertemporal elasticity because gains from the proportionality and the change in base are positively related to this elasticity. However, the gains are ambiguous with respect to the magnitude of the consumption-leisure elasticity: although gains from proportionality are positively related to this elasticity, gains from the switch in base are inversely related to it. This is why the efficiency advantage of the consumption base is much more sensitive to the value of the intertemporal elasticity than to the value of the consumption-leisure elasticity.

Gravelle (1991) also finds that the efficiency gains associated with a consumption-tax replacement depend heavily on the intergenerational redistribution that takes place, and that the gains are more sensitive to the intertemporal elasticity than to the consumption-leisure elasticity. The Fullerton-Rogers model has been used to highlight these points as well. See Randolph and Rogers (1995) and Rogers (1996).

cause the losses to the elderly dominate gains to the young in present-value terms.

The smaller efficiency gain for a wage tax relative to a consumption tax indicates that the wealth component of the consumption base is important in contributing to whatever gains exist. Specifically, because the consumption base is larger than the wage base, the revenue-neutral consumption tax rate is lower and therefore less distorting than the revenue-neutral wage tax rate.

A gain in efficiency caused by a flattening of tax burdens is not surprising but may not be satisfactory either. If one role of taxation is redistributive, perhaps tax replacement designs that maintain the current level of progressivity and at the same time improve efficiency should be considered. Table 9-5 indicates that adding progressivity by sparing certain goods from a consumption tax reduces efficiency gains but that exemptions may not. One might expect that the higher rates necessary to maintain revenues as exemptions rise would increase distortions and reduce efficiency. But efficiency gains also depend on the intergenerational redistributions highlighted in table 9-3. Under a consumption tax base, the exemption level causes greater redistribution of income from the old to the young, which works to enhance efficiency. In fact, when the leisure-consumption elasticity is low, the net efficiency gains are higher under the exemption-level version of the consumption tax because the higher labor-supply distortion resulting from the higher marginal tax rate becomes less important than the effect of income redistribution. Finally, when the consumption tax is used to replace payroll taxes as well as income taxes (which also enhances progressivity slightly, as shown above in table 9-4), efficiency gains are larger with high values of the intertemporal elasticity but smaller with low values.

Three conclusions stand out from table 9-5. First, whether tax reform increases or decreases welfare depends on people's responses. Second, tax bases matter more than tax rates. Third, the efficiency gains are small. They are, in fact, smaller than some other economists have found.

We emphasize that the efficiency calculations depend on the specification of our model as well as on certain assumptions built into our present-value calculation of gains over all generations, both of which tend to produce low estimates. First, our benchmark income tax system did not include graduated marginal tax rates, but just increasing average tax rates. This assumption is likely to make us understate some of the gains from switching to flatter tax systems. Second, our treatment of exemptions may understate the gains from shifting to flat taxes with exemptions. We allow exemptions to generate negative taxes for low-decile households, necessitating higher marginal tax rates in our simulations than would be necessary if the minimum tax were zero. Third, we use a relatively high discount rate in our present-value calculation of efficiency gains. A lower rate would increase the weight on gains to later generations and thus raise the efficiency numbers. For these reasons our estimates of efficiency gains may be too low.

We have, however, used other assumptions that could cause our estimates to overstate efficiency gains. For example, Charles Ballard and Lawrence Goulder have shown that greater foresight on the part of consumers may lead to reduced efficiency gains associated with consumption-based taxation.[23] We have assumed that consumers are myopic. Also, in examining the various tax systems, we have ignored administrative costs and measurement problems. Under the comparison of proportional consumption and proportional income taxes, for example, we assume that capital income could be measured perfectly under the income tax. This is no doubt unrealistic. Our result that under low intertemporal elasticity the income tax is likely to be just as efficient as the alternatives holds only to the extent that truly neutral income taxation is possible.

Conclusion

Using our general-equilibrium model, we have explored the lifetime effects of fundamental tax reform on the distribution of intergenerational and intragenerational tax burdens and on economic efficiency. We have focused on prototype reforms that highlight some of the essential components of current tax reform proposals.

We find that the replacement of the current income tax system with any flatter and more neutral tax (consumption based, wage based, or income based) is likely to increase overall economic welfare. A consumption-based tax will outperform other broad-based taxes in efficiency and growth if the intertemporal substitution effects associated with capital taxation are strong.

An overall efficiency gain implies only that gains to some outweigh losses to others. We find significant intergenerational redistribution, especially under the consumption base. We also find that in moving to a

23. Ballard and Goulder (1985).

single marginal tax rate, even with exemptions, it is not possible to maintain the level of lifetime progressivity found in the current income tax system. Still, any enhancement of progressivity involves little apparent efficiency loss.

Consumption and wage bases have significantly different efficiency consequences, suggesting profound economic effects associated with the treatment of consumption financed from wealth existing at the time of the switch. Allowing exemptions for such consumption would move the proposal closer to a wage tax. According to our results, the tax on existing wealth is important in helping to add to lifetime progressivity and efficiency, although it might not increase saving.

Appendix: The Fullerton-Rogers General-Equilibrium Model

The Fullerton-Rogers model uses measures of lifetime income based on longitudinal data and classifies households according to lifetime income categories.[24] Through its specification of consumer utility and industry production functions, the model is able to calculate the general-equilibrium effects of tax changes on the prices and quantities of goods and factors and the subsequent effects on economic efficiency and the welfare of each income category.

Lifetime Incomes

The model incorporates data on lifetime incomes and requires longitudinal data for many individuals over many years. Although no data set spans the entire lifetimes of individuals, the University of Michigan's Panel Study of Income Dynamics (PSID) has been asking the same questions of the same individuals for more than twenty years. From the PSID, we drew a sample of 500 households that included 858 adults, with information on wages, taxes, transfers, and various demographic variables for 1970–87. We included heads of households and wives in the sample. For simplicity in defining the lifetime of a household, those whose marital status varied over the sample period were excluded. For heads of households and wives separately, we estimated the wage rate as a non-linear function of age, so that for each individual in the sample we were able to predict the wage rate for years that come after as well as before

---

24. See Fullerton and Rogers (1993).

the sample period. We then multiply the actual or estimated gross-of-tax wage rate by a total number of hours per year (for example, 4,000) to get the value of the endowment, and calculate the present value of this endowment for each person. Thus the level of well-being in the model is defined by *potential* earnings, including the value of leisure.

These levels are used to classify individuals into twelve groups according to lifetime ability to pay, in which lifetime income is defined as the average of the lifetime incomes of the head of household and the wife (if any). The groups are constructed by dividing the sample into deciles, then separating the poorest decile into two groups—the poorest 2 percent and the next poorest 8 percent—and the richest decile into the richest 2 percent and the next richest 8 percent.

For a given level of lifetime income, the timing of income matters because the shape of an individual's lifetime income profile helps determine savings and thus the composition of any year's annual income. Therefore we reestimated the nonlinear age-wage profile separately for each of the twelve groups. In addition, we estimated the time paths of personal income taxes paid and transfers received to set up consistent benchmark data with a path of consumer spending out of total available net-of-tax income.

Model Structure and Parameterization

The general-equilibrium approach to tax analysis accounts for behavioral effects and excess burdens caused by taxes. It can capture the important influences of taxes on household choices about labor supply, saving, and the consumption of various commodities. Utility maximization determines the demands for commodities and supplies of factors. The assumption of profit maximization on the part of producers determines the demands for factors and the effects of taxes on these demands. Solving for general-equilibrium prices captures the net impact of taxes when these behaviors are considered simultaneously.

In our model, consumer decisions are made according to the maximization of lifetime utility. To begin, the individual calculates the present value of potential lifetime earnings. These earnings are supplemented by government transfers, reduced by taxes, discounted at the after-tax interest rate, and augmented by a fixed initial inheritance. For computational simplicity the model assumes "myopic" expectations about future prices: the consumer expects the current interest rate to prevail in all future periods.

A person must save one part of the lifetime endowment for a bequest when he or she dies. We avoid the many possible motivations for individual bequests or the ways in which taxes might affect the size of those bequests. Instead, the model simply acknowledges that life-cycle saving by itself can only explain about half the observed capital stock. In the model, part of that stock is attributable to the fact that individuals receive inheritances. We then simply require them to leave comparable bequests at the end of life. Incidence results depend on the differences in these exogenous inheritances among groups. To achieve balanced growth, the members of each group must add some savings to their inheritance before they make their bequest.

The rest of the present value of income is available for spending. Decisions are made in stages. In the context of fundamental tax reform, the first two stages seem most important because they define the saving and labor-supply responses.

At the first stage the consumer chooses how much to spend each period. This choice depends on assumptions about the form of lifetime utility and the values of certain key parameters. Lifetime utility is specified as a constant-elasticity-of-substitution (CES) function,

$$U = \left[\sum_{t=1}^{T} a_t^{1/\epsilon_1} x_t^{(\epsilon_1 - 1)/\epsilon_1} \right]^{\epsilon_1/(\epsilon_1 - 1)},$$

where $T = 60$ (chronological age 79) is the individual's certain date of death, ϵ_1 is the intertemporal elasticity of substitution, and x_t is the amount of composite commodity (a combination of a composite consumption good and leisure) at economic age t. The weighting parameter, a_t, reflects the consumer's subjective rate of time preference, which is set at 0.005.

Although our 1993 study uses a central-case intertemporal elasticity equal to 0.5, that elasticity is varied from 0.15 to 0.5 in the present study's examination of efficiency gains. The consumer's choice about how much to spend each period is also affected by changes in the net rate of return (which is set at 0.04 in the central case).[25]

---

25. Chapter 8 of Fullerton and Rogers (1993) discusses the sensitivity of incidence calculations to these parameter values. The current chapter emphasizes the importance of

At the second stage, the consumer allocates one period's "spending" between leisure and other consumption goods, according to the CES subutility function

$$
x_t = \left[\alpha_t^{1/\epsilon_2} \, \bar{c}_t^{(\epsilon_2 - 1)/\epsilon_2} + (1 - \alpha_t)^{1/\epsilon_2} \, 1_t^{(\epsilon_2 - 1)/\epsilon_2} \right]^{\epsilon_2/(\epsilon_2 - 1)},
$$

where $\bar{c}_t$ is the amount of composite consumption good consumed at t, 1_t is the amount of leisure taken at t, and ϵ_2 is the elasticity of substitution between consumption and leisure. The decision about how much labor to supply depends on what is assumed about the value of this consumption-leisure elasticity of substitution. In our 1993 book we set this elasticity at 0.5 in the central case, but for the purposes of this study the elasticity is varied from 0.15 to 0.5 (just as the intertemporal elasticity is varied). In the general-equilibrium model, individuals can "buy" more leisure at a price equal to the forgone net-of-tax wage instead of buying other goods. This choice is affected by taxes, and it also depends on age. Individuals in this model never fully retire, but the weight on leisure increases with age after they reach 60 in a way that reflects actual choices.

In the third stage, individuals decide how to allocate current consumption spending among seventeen goods (food, alcohol, tobacco, utilities, housing, and so forth) according to the subutility function

$$
\bar{c}_t = \prod_{i=1}^{N} (c_{it} - b_{it})^{\beta_{it}},
$$

where N is the number of consumer goods (seventeen) and c_{it} is the amount of consumer good i consumed at age t. This decision function is of the Stone-Geary form, which means that a consumer at a given age has to buy a set of seventeen "minimum required purchase" amounts (b) and then allocates remaining spending according to a set of seventeen "marginal expenditure shares" (β). Using data from the Consumer Expenditure Survey, as described thoroughly in our 1993 book, we estimated these thirty-four parameters for each of twelve age categories. This Stone-Geary framework has several important implications. Making a part of spending nondiscretionary reduces the sensitivity of total consumption and saving to the net rate of return. In addition, because discretionary income may be spent in proportions different from minimum

---

the intertemporal elasticity in determining the efficiency gains from a switch to consumption-based taxation.

requirements, actual purchase proportions depend on total income. Required spending is relatively high for housing and gasoline, while discretionary spending is relatively high for clothing, services, and recreation. Thus the rich and the poor buy different bundles and bear different tax burdens on the uses side.[26]

In the fourth stage of the consumer's allocation process, the expenditure on each consumer good is divided by fixed coefficients among components drawn from a list of producer industries. No real decision is made here, but this step allows the matching up of consumption data using one definition of commodities with production data using a different definition. For example, expenditure on appliances is composed of portions from metals and machinery, transportation, and trade.

In the fifth and final stage of the decision tree, the consumer takes the spending on each industry output and allocates it between the corporate sector and the noncorporate sector, according to the CES subutility function

$$\overline{Q}_j = \left[\gamma_j^{1/\epsilon_3} (Q_j^c)^{(\epsilon_3 - 1)/\epsilon_3} + (1 - \gamma_j)^{1/\epsilon_3} (Q_j^{nc})^{(\epsilon_3 - 1)/\epsilon_3} \right]^{\epsilon_3/(\epsilon_3 - 1)},$$

where Q_j^c is the amount of corporate production of producer good j, Q_j^{nc} is the amount of noncorporate production of producer good j, and ϵ_3 is the elasticity of substitution between corporate and noncorporate outputs in consumption. Corporate output is assumed to be slightly different from noncorporate output in the same industry. Hand-carved furniture, for example, is not the same as manufactured furniture. The consumer chooses the amount of each, using a weighting parameter γ based on initial observed corporate and noncorporate shares of production within each industry and using another elasticity of substitution (ϵ_3, which is set to 5.0 in the central case). This specification is consistent

---

26. This framework also allows us to use the same utility function for everyone in the model. In previous efforts, rich and poor individuals spend in different proportions because they have different preferences. But then the rich and the poor differ in fundamental characteristics and not just by the amount of income they receive. With differences in utility functions, if the poor were to receive additional income, they would still spend it as if they were poor, according to their unchanged proportions. It seems more natural that a poor person with more money would begin to behave like a rich person. That is, the primary distinction between rich and poor is the amount of income they receive. Therefore, in our model everyone has the same preference parameters. The poor spend more on goods with high minimum required expenditures because they are poor, and the rich spend more on goods with relatively high marginal expenditure shares.

with the observed coexistence of both sectors within an industry, despite different tax treatments. If the outputs were identical, a higher tax rate would drive one sector out of production. The degree of similarity is reflected in the elasticity of substitution. The other purpose of this specification is to capture ways in which changes in corporate taxes affect relative product prices and quantities demanded of the outputs of each sector.

A similar process characterizes producer behavior in each sector of each industry. Each output is produced by many competitive companies in multistage production functions with constant returns to scale. Also, for computational simplicity, the model assumes no externalities, no adjustment costs, and no uncertainty.

In the first stage of production, output is composed of a fixed-coefficient combination of value-added and intermediate inputs. Each of the nineteen industries uses the outputs of all other industries in fixed proportions. Thus changes in one product price affect many other product prices. In the second stage, value added is a function of labor and composite capital, according to the function

$$VA = \varphi \left[\zeta^{1/\sigma_1} L^{(\sigma_1 - 1)/\sigma_1} + (1 - \zeta)^{1/\sigma_1} \overline{K}^{(\sigma_1 - 1)/\sigma_1} \right]^{\sigma_1/(\sigma_1 - 1)}.$$

The weighting parameters (ζ) are based on observed labor L and capital $\overline{K}$ in each industry, and the elasticity of substitution (σ_1) varies by industry (between 0.68 and 0.96 in the central case). Thus a tax on labor can induce the firm to substitute more capital, and vice versa. It also raises the cost of production, and thus output price, in any industry that uses a high proportion of the taxed factor.

In the third and final stage of production, composite capital is a CES function of five asset types (K_k)—equipment, structures, land, inventories, and intangibles:

$$\overline{K} = \left[\sum_{k=1}^{N_k} (\psi_k)^{1/\sigma_2} (K_k)^{(\sigma_2 - 1)/\sigma_2} \right]^{\sigma_2/(\sigma_2 - 1)}.$$

These types are defined by important tax differences such as the investment credit for equipment and the expensing of new intangible assets created through advertising or research and development. The weighting shares (ψ_k) are again based on observed use of assets in each industry, and the response to tax differentials is again specified by an elasticity of substitution ($\sigma_2 = 1.5$ in the central case).

Government in this model has several functions. It pays transfers to individuals according to the estimated lifetime transfer profiles discussed earlier. It produces an output for sale through an industry called government enterprises, and it also produces a free public good through a composite of its use of labor, capital, and purchases of each private industry output. The weights in this combination are based on observed government purchases, and the elasticity of substitution is one. The level of this public good is held fixed in all simulations because any tax change is accompanied by an adjustment that ensures equal-revenue yield. A final government function, of course, is to collect taxes.

Each tax instrument enters the model as a wedge between the producer's price and the consumer's price. The payroll tax, for example, applies at an ad valorem rate to each producer's use of labor, so the gross-of-tax wage paid by the producer is higher than the net-of-tax wage received by the worker. Similarly, sales and excise taxes appear as an ad valorem rate on each consumer good, so the gross-of-tax price paid by the consumer exceeds the net-of-tax price received by the seller.

The modeling of the personal income tax is a little more complicated in order to capture its progressive effect on tax burdens. The actual U.S. personal tax system imposes higher effective tax rates on higher incomes through a graduated rate structure with a changing marginal tax rate. Ideally, one would calculate the effects of individual choices at each different possible marginal tax rate to determine utility-maximizing behavior. For computational tractability, however, we use linear tax functions that approximate the U.S. system, with a negative intercept for each group and a single marginal tax rate (0.25 in the 1993 benchmark). Although all individuals face the same marginal tax rate, average tax rates still increase with income because of the negative intercepts. We do not model the many exemptions and deductions. These simpler, linear tax functions can replicate the observed data on personal taxes actually paid by each group.

The state and local property tax and the U.S. federal corporate income tax raise the producer's gross-of-tax cost of capital for each asset type relative to the investor's net-of-tax rate of return. The cost of capital corresponding to each type of asset depends on the statutory corporate tax rate (set at 0.395 to reflect federal and state taxes in the 1993 benchmark), depreciation allowances at historical cost, the way the real value of the allowances is eroded by a rate of inflation (set at 0.04), the rate of investment tax credit (set at zero after the Tax Reform Act of 1986), and the required net rate of return for the firm. This required rate of return depends on the going market rate and the personal taxation of interest (at rate 0.246), dividends (0.292), and capital gains (0.13). The simulations described in this chapter assume the old view of dividend taxation, in which the personal-level taxation of dividends affects the cost of capital for marginal investments.[27] A similar cost-of-capital formula applies to the noncorporate sector. This treatment allows the producer's choice among assets to depend on relative tax rules and the price of output in each industry to depend on the relative use of assets with different tax treatments.

Other assumptions help to close the model in a way that accounts for all flows and facilitates computation. The model ignores international mobility of labor and capital but allows for trade of industry outputs. Also, the value of imports must match the value of exports; the government's expenditures and transfer payments must match tax revenue; and the value of personal saving must match the value of investment expenditures. Producer investment is not the result of firms' intertemporal optimization but instead follows personal saving from consumers' optimization. The amount of personal saving is growing over time because consumers' labor earnings are growing through population growth and technical change. On the steady-state growth path the capital stock grows at exactly the same rate as the effective labor stock.

Data used in the Fullerton-Rogers model derive from many sources and are adjusted to represent 1993 as the base year.[28] In addition to the survey data used to estimate wage profiles and preference parameters, we use the National Income and Product Accounts for an input-output matrix, labor compensation by industry, government purchases, and international trade. These published data are combined with unpublished data on capital allocations and inheritances.

For some parameters, such as the elasticities of substitution, particular values are assumed. For others, such as the Stone-Geary preferences, econometric estimates are used. Finally, some remaining parameters are calibrated from data on actual allocations. Demand functions and all

---

27. See Fullerton and Rogers (1993), pp. 210–13, for discussion of how adopting the alternative "new view" affects the efficiency and distributional effects of the various U.S. taxes.

28. The benchmark specified in Fullerton-Rogers (1993) is based on 1984 data.

initial prices and observed quantities are used to solve backward for the value of the parameter that would make that quantity the desired one. This procedure establishes a benchmark equilibrium with existing tax rules and prices such that all consumers are buying the desired quantities and supplying the desired amounts of each factor, while producers are using their desired amounts of factors to produce the desired output.

Using all these parameters together, one can solve for an equilibrium with unchanged tax rules that replicates the benchmark-consistent data. This provides an important check on the solution procedure. From this benchmark any particular tax rule can be altered, and one can determine how much more or less consumers want to buy of each good. The solution algorithm then raises the price of any good in excess demand and lowers the price of any in excess supply until it finds a set of prices where the quantity supplied equals the quantity demanded for every good and factor. It simulates the effect of the tax change to calculate all new prices, quantities, and levels of consumer utility. The measure of the change in tax burden is the "equivalent variation," the dollar value of the change in utility measured in terms of benchmark prices. Efficiency gains associated with a tax change are calculated as the present value of equivalent variations added over all income groups and all generations, relative to the present value of lifetime incomes.

Comment by Laurence J. Kotlikoff

Don Fullerton and Diane Lim Rogers's chapter begins by reviewing many of the economic issues involved in tax reform. It then attempts to understand more fully the incidence and efficiency effects of fundamental reform using the Fullerton-Rogers model. I say "attempts" because I think the chapter has shortcomings that need to be addressed before the findings can be taken seriously. Unfortunately, many of these shortcomings can only be addressed by making basic improvements to the model. I will list these shortcomings in order of importance. I hope the authors will consider my criticism implicit praise. If I did not think their model was so close to getting at the truth, I would not be so frustrated by the imperfections in its current incarnation.

The model's transition is calculated based on myopic expectations in which individuals believe that all current economic variables, including current tax rates, will prevail in all future years. Because there is no reason to believe that people actually behave in this manner, there is no reason to believe the authors' findings with respect to the transitional incidence or the efficiency gains from tax reform.

Even if the model were solving for the economy's perfect foresight transition path, the approximation method used to calculate the efficiency gains from reform would be incorrect. This method involves discounting the equivalent dollar value of the change in the utility of initial and future generations. For very small tax changes, this method seems acceptable. But with extremely large tax changes, the approximation error could be huge; with a sizable tax reform one needs to integrate cohort-specific utility changes with respect to the degree to which one implements the reform. In other words, the integration must take into account the fact that the terms being integrated are not invariant with respect to the degree to which the reform is turned on.

One also needs to be aware that the rate of discount will not be constant; it will vary from period to period and to the extent that the reform is implemented. One cannot arbitrarily choose a discount rate and use it to make pure Harberger-type efficiency calculations. Of course, an alternative to calculating an intertemporal Harberger deadweight-loss formula in this manner is to use the procedure developed by Alan Auerbach and me, namely to use lump-sum taxes and transfers to compensate initial generations alive at the time of the reform for any utility changes and to redistribute across future generations in a lump-sum manner so as to produce a uniform level of utility for all future generations.[29] This method may actually be easier to implement than path integration, and it has the advantage that it is exact; that is, it entails no approximation error.

The chapter considers a benchmark case with constant marginal personal income tax rates as opposed to one in which the marginal rate increases with increases in income. This characterization of the current U.S. tax structure is likely to lead to a substantial understatement of the saving and efficiency gains from tax reform.

The chapter treats property tax as a tax on housing capital. I do not remember if this is the new view or the old view of property tax, but I think it is the wrong view. Property tax is used to finance local public goods. Homeowners who do not like the tax rate or the public goods they receive in one place can relocate to another with a different tax rate and a different bundle of goods. Because many of the results in the chapter seem influenced by the effective tax rate on owner-occupied

29. Auerbach and Kotlikoff (1987).

housing arising from local property taxes, it would behoove the authors to present their results under alternative assumptions about the size of this rate.

The chapter claims that wage taxation leads to larger saving increases than does consumption taxation because of intragenerational redistribution from the lifetime rich, with high propensities to save, to the lifetime poor, with low propensities to save. But this interpretation cannot be right. In the model the lifetime rich and the lifetime poor have exactly the same propensity to consume out of remaining lifetime resources because they have the same intertemporal consumption and leisure preferences and because bequests and inheritances are both treated as exogenous, that is, as equivalent to lump-sum taxes and transfers. The authors' suggestion that the lifetime rich have a higher propensity to save because they save a relatively high fraction of earnings (they have wage profiles that are more peaked and that peak earlier in life) confuses intertemporal consumption preferences with the shape of age-earnings profiles.

It is hard to understand why the steady-state increase in the capital-labor ratio under a wage tax is so similar to that under a consumption tax. The assumption of myopic expectations is not responsible because the authors are considering the steady state rather than the transition. It may have something to do with the level of bequests in the model, but I doubt it. So one is left not really understanding the authors' most interesting finding. They could easily, I think, help here by simulating their model without bequests and without a number of other features that differentiate it from the Auerbach-Kotlikoff model and then see if such a stripped-down version produces the same results for the steady state as the Auerbach-Kotlikoff model. If it does, they could add the additional features back in to see what is really causing wage and consumption taxation to produce such similar outcomes.

Some of the chapter's results appear to reflect Harberger-type modeling of the incidence of the corporate income tax. Specifically, when the corporate tax is eliminated, the model's relative prices change in a way that appears particularly detrimental to the elderly. I am not a big fan of the Harberger model as a model of the corporate income tax. I prefer the Gravelle-Kotlikoff model of the incidence of the corporate income tax, although I am not fully in love with it.[30] But if one were to use this model, there would be no reason to think that eliminating the corporate income tax would lead to changes in relative commodity prices. The reason is

---

30. See Gravelle and Kotlikoff (1993).

that in the Gravelle-Kotlikoff model the removal of the corporate income tax leads to more production of each good by corporations and less production of each good by noncorporations. Thus there is no reason for capital to shift among industries in response to the elimination of the corporate income tax and no reason for relative commodity prices to change.

The chapter fails to take into account initial government debt, the real value of which would likely be eroded through the increase in the price level that would arise from the introduction of a consumption tax in the form of, for example, a retail sales tax. This is a potentially sizable effect. If a 20 percent retail sales tax were implemented, for example, and if prices rose by 20 percent, the real value of federal debt would fall by one-fifth, or close to $1 trillion.

The authors also fail to consider capital adjustment costs. These costs could influence the size of initial capital levies arising from consumption taxation.

The chapter understates the progressivity of consumption taxation by focusing only on long-run steady-state progressivity. In so doing, it ignores the consumption tax's huge one-time taxation of initial wealth holdings. Because much of the inequality of wealth may reflect inheritances, the taxation of wealth under a consumption tax represents a substantial redistribution from those who receive inheritances to those who do not.

But the authors do not consider this matter at all. In addition, because of their special model of bequests, in which the distribution of inheritances over time is independent of changes in fiscal policy, there appears to be no feedback of tax reform on long-run inequality in intergenerational transfers. Other ways of modeling bequests might lead to the conclusion that taxing wealth in the present via a consumption tax reduces or increases the inequality of inheritances on a permanent basis, so that the short-run improvement in progressivity would also have long-run implications. For example, if inheritances reflect unintended bequests arising from imperfect annuitization, a one-time wealth tax that finances a permanently lower wage tax would reduce current intragenerational resource inequality but could well increase intragenerational inequality in the long run because unintended bequests arising in years after the reform would reflect saving out of higher after-tax wages.

The chapter sets up a straw man by choosing as its benchmark case a system in which there is a very large negative tax credit that is then eliminated under tax reform. In the conclusion the authors state that in moving to a single marginal tax rate, even with exemptions, it is not possible to maintain the level of lifetime progressivity found in the current income tax system. I think this conclusion is either wrong or too strong on two counts. First, I do not think the authors are actually modeling the current income tax system when they include their negative tax credit. Second, in table 9-4 they do not really compare tax progressivity before and after reform. Instead, they consider the steady-state welfare changes of different lifetime earnings groups. These welfare changes reflect factor price and commodity price changes as well as changes in tax rates. In mixing all these things together, they are, among other things, implicitly saying that any policy that makes the rich better off without hurting the poor is regressive.

The chapter treats the mortgage interest deduction as a subsidy to home ownership. I think this is wrong. It is the failure to impute rent on housing and include that rent as part of taxable income that represents the subsidy to home ownership under the personal income tax.

The chapter finds that with the assumption of a lower intertemporal elasticity the long-run increase in output associated with switching to a consumption tax is substantially reduced. This result does not arise in the Auerbach-Kotlikoff model, and I wonder why it arises here. The authors also find that the efficiency gain from moving to consumption taxation is highly sensitive to the choice of substitution elasticities. This finding is also at odds with that in Auerbach and Kotlikoff (1987).

The authors' statement in their conclusion that an overall efficiency gain implies only that gains to some outweigh losses to others suggests a misconception of efficiency gains. An efficiency gain means that there is the potential for a Pareto improvement. Indeed, any pure efficiency calculation must be predicated on a Pareto improvement.

References

Aaron, Henry J., Harvey Galper, and Joseph A. Pechman, eds. 1988. *Uneasy Compromise: Problems of a Hybrid Income-Consumption Tax*. Brookings.

Auerbach, Alan J., and Laurence J. Kotlikoff. 1987. *Dynamic Fiscal Policy*. Cambridge University Press.

Auerbach, Alan J., Laurence J. Kotlikoff, and Jonathan Skinner. 1983. "The Efficiency Gains from Dynamic Tax Reform," *International Economic Review* 24 (February): 81–100.

Ballard, Charles L., and Lawrence H. Goulder. 1985. "Consumption Taxes, Foresight, and Welfare: A Computable General Equilibrium Analysis." In *New Developments in Applied General Equilibrium Analysis,* edited by John Piggott and John Whalley, 253–82. Cambridge University Press.

Congressional Budget Office. 1992. *Effects of Adopting a Value-Added Tax.*

Fullerton, Don, and Diane Lim Rogers. 1993. *Who Bears the Lifetime Tax Burden?* Brookings.

Gravelle, Jane G. 1991. "Income, Consumption, and Wage Taxation in a Life-Cycle Model: Separating Efficiency from Redistribution." *American Economic Review* 81 (September): 985–95.

Gravelle, Jane G., and Laurence J. Kotlikoff. 1993. "Corporate Tax Incidence and Inefficiency When Corporate and Noncorporate Goods Are Close Substitutes." *Economic Inquiry* 31 (October): 501–16.

Poterba, James M. 1989. "Lifetime Incidence and the Distributional Burden of Excise Taxes." *American Economic Review* 79 (May): 325–30.

Randolph, William C., and Diane Lim Rogers. 1995. "The Implications for Tax Policy of Uncertainty about Labor-Supply and Savings Responses." *National Tax Journal* 48 (September): 429–46.

Rogers, Diane Lim. 1996. "Sorting Out the Efficiency Gains from a Consumption Tax." *Proceedings of the 87th Annual Conference of the National Tax Association.*

PART FOUR

Administrative and Transitional Issues

CHAPTER 10

Which Is the Simplest Tax System of Them All?

Joel Slemrod

$\mathbb{A}$ LUMP-SUM TAX. For many years I have yearned for the chance to write an academic paper whose title is in the form of a question, and which begins with a simple, one-sentence, verb-less answer to the question; the problem, as the reader will discover, is that no interesting question has a simple answer. Also known as a poll or capitation tax, the amount per period of the lump-sum tax is the same for everyone, at least for those above a certain age, but is definitely not dependent on any action of the taxpayer. In the United States poll taxes were usually tied to suffrage and were political rather than revenue tools. But poll taxes need not be repressive or even uniform. The notorious English poll tax of 1381 in fact differentiated by one's status.

What makes a poll tax simple? The base is clearly and easily defined, such as being a resident over the age of 21. The levy itself is clearly and easily defined. And the taxpayer cannot easily manipulate either the rate or base. In particular, the base does not depend on any economic decision of the taxpayer.[1]

The usual reason given for the modern rarity of poll taxes is that they do not assign taxes fairly among individuals. Although they might have been fair in primitive societies where there was a certain rough equality— leaving slaves aside—in personal status and abilities, most people find them inappropriate in modern societies where status and wealth are highly unequal.

I am grateful for comments by Edith Brashares, Brian Erard, and Michael Udell on an earlier version.

1. The absence of distortion is also the source of the argument that the lump-sum tax is the most efficient of all taxes.

Even the poll tax is not self-enforcing. The recent British experiment with replacing local property taxes with a "community charge" led to widespread protest and civil unrest. It almost certainly contributed to the downfall of the Thatcher government. Moreover, there was considerable nonpayment. In the first year of operation of the poll tax, administrative costs of collecting local taxes in England more than tripled.[2] In fact, John Major, Thatcher's successor, abandoned the poll tax because, he said, it had become "uncollectible."

It turns out that there are compliance issues lurking here: one-word answers are often wrong. First, to enforce a poll tax, individuals must be located. Second, something has to be done when people cannot or will not pay the tax, or when, most vexing of all, people who will not pay claim falsely that they cannot pay. Inability to pay was not a big issue in the United Kingdom, but it would be if the tax were large.

Noncompliance with the British poll tax raises a fundamental point. The simplicity of a tax system can be assessed only with respect to a standard of enforcement. Collecting a poll tax from only the duty-bound 70 percent of the population might be cheap and easy, if unfair, but achieving 99 percent compliance might require an expensive and highly intrusive enforcement bureaucracy. Should such a poll tax be regarded as cheap to collect and unintrusive to administer or as expensive and intrusive?

This difficult issue pervades the comparative analysis of tax systems' complexity. I shall not investigate a poll tax as a replacement for the income tax, as it has not (yet) become a live tax policy option. I shall, however, evaluate other tax systems: the retail sales tax, the value-added tax, the Hall-Rabushka flat tax, and the personal consumption tax. For each I shall draw on existing evidence and, in some cases, my own personal speculation to estimate collection cost and compare them with the collection cost of the current system. At the conclusion, I shall also comment on the potential savings of incremental changes in the current system.

I shall focus on the steady-state features of alternative tax systems, not the transitional costs of moving from the current system to another. Transitional costs for fundamental reform would be nontrivial, as both taxpayers and the collection agency would have to learn new rules and practices.

2. Smith (1991).

To minimize windfall gains and losses in transition, a proposal may contain provisions to grandfather the old tax treatment pertaining to existing conditions. These transition rules inevitably add complexity to any tax reform, although they diminish in importance over time.

This chapter focuses on aggregate compliance costs, and it neglects distribution of these costs among taxpayers. This distribution is of interest, however, because alternative tax plans bestow the benefits of promised simplification on different groups. My comments on the poll tax make clear that tax policy analysis should consider not only the relative simplicity of tax alternatives, but also their effects on such goals as equity and economic performance. The relationships and trade-offs among these three goals of tax policy are subtle.

Conceptual Issues in Measuring Complexity[3]

Nothing simplifies the tax system without also affecting equity and economic efficiency. Doubling the standard deduction, for example, would reduce the number of households that itemize deductions and lessen the attendant record-keeping requirements. It might be advocated as a simplifying measure. It would also reduce taxes of those households whose itemized deductions exceed the previous standard deduction but are below the new one. To maintain tax revenue, other households would have to pay increased taxes. In addition, the net after-tax price of the activities that give rise to itemizable deductions would be increased for those who no longer itemize and decreased for those who continue to itemize but now face a higher marginal tax rate.

Even tax changes narrowly addressed to simplification have such implications. A reform that simplifies instructions about how to receive a particular credit, but leaves the law unchanged, sounds like pure simplification, but it also redistributes disposable income. Households that did not receive the credit because the instructions were too complicated would now get it. To maintain revenue, some additional change in the system would be necessary. In the end, some households would gain, others would lose.

The ideal analysis would predict the change in welfare for all members of the society. If, as is likely, there are some winners and some losers,

3. These issues are discussed at greater length in Slemrod (1984).

one must apply standards of social justice to judge whether the changes are desirable. The total resource cost of collecting the revenue is a useful summary measure of the cost of tax complexity.[4] The cost of collection is the sum of the tax collection agency's budget, the value of the time and money spent by the taxpayers, and costs incurred in the collection process by third parties, such as employers who withhold tax for their employees. I shall refer to the budget of the Internal Revenue Service (IRS) as the administrative cost and to the costs borne directly by taxpayers and third parties as the compliance cost of taxation.

Certain characteristics of the total resource cost as an indicator of the cost of tax collection are worthy of note. First, this index does not distinguish on the taxpayer side between involuntary costs that are necessary to comply with the law and discretionary costs that are incurred to avoid or evade taxes. For many high-income individuals and businesses, the discretionary costs can currently be large, because the tax system encourages transactions that would not otherwise make sense. The degree to which a tax system encourages such behavior is often called "transactional complexity," and some tax systems would drastically reduce it. Administrative cost includes both the cost of running the tax collection process and the cost of minimizing evasion. Each of these costs of operating the tax system should be considered in assessing how simply it operates.

Second, the resource cost of tax collection refers to the social rather than the private cost of collection. Businesses and many individuals can deduct monetary costs of compliance in computing taxable income. Their private cost is less than the social cost. In addition, employers earn interest on withheld employee taxes because employers need not remit tax to the IRS immediately.

Although I believe that this is a useful measure, in some situations it may provide results that conflict with one's intuitive concept of simplicity. Suppose that the record-keeping and calculation requirements of a particular credit are relaxed so that only half as many resources as before are required to qualify for the deduction, that the number of households who apply for and receive the credit quadruples, and that measures to make up the lost revenue do not raise other collection costs. According to the cost-based measure, the tax system has become more complicated. I believe that, all things considered, this characterization of the change is

---

4. This measure is a natural complement to excess burden as an indicator of the efficiency cost of taxation.

accurate. The credit procedure itself has become simpler, but the system as a whole has become more complex. Whether this increased complexity is worthwhile depends on whether the value of the apparently improved equity of inducing households who "deserve" the credit to take it, plus any accompanying efficiency effects, exceeds the increase in total administrative and compliance costs. This example underscores why the complexity of a tax change, especially as measured by the change in the cost of collection, should be considered together with other implications of the policy.

The Cost of the Existing Tax System

Before turning to the cost-saving potential of alternative tax systems, a review of evidence about the collection cost of the current system is useful for two reasons. First, it brings up some of the difficult conceptual issues that plague all studies of the cost of collection. Second, the range of estimates has become so large that a critical review is now in order.

Most estimates of the compliance cost of the U.S. income tax system come from surveys I and coauthors have done and from a study commissioned by the IRS and carried out by Arthur D. Little (ADL).[5] James L. Payne and Arthur Hall have reinterpreted and reevaluated the data from these studies.[6] Table 10-1 summarizes the main conclusions of these studies. Before discussing the results, I first treat some important conceptual issues in survey-based measures of compliance cost.

Issues in Survey-Based Measures of Compliance Cost

The low response rate to marked questionnaires about tax compliance cost—often between 30 and 40 percent—raises concern about respondent bias. Many studies weight the responses to reflect observable differences in the demographic makeup of the respondent population. Nonetheless, questions remain about whether the compliance costs of the nonrespondents differ from those of respondents, because of differing attitudes or behavioral patterns. Alan Tait has argued that respondent

---

5. Because the administrative cost of the U.S. income tax system is not particularly controversial, I shall deal only with the compliance cost. The only issue in calculating administrative cost is what fraction of the total budget of the IRS, which oversees all federal taxes, should be allocated to the income tax system.

6. Payne (1993); Hall (1995).

Table 10-1. *Quantitative Estimates of the Compliance Cost of the U.S. Income Tax System*[a]

Type of filer	Slemrod and Sorum[b] (1982)	Arthur D. Little (1985)[c]	Blumenthal and Slemrod[b] (1989)	Slemrod and Blumenthal (1992)	Payne (1985)	Hall (1995)	"Best Guess"[d] (1995)
Individuals							
Hours (billions)	2.07	1.813	3.07	...	1.813	1.19	2.8
Average value per hour (dollars)	10.65	...	10.09	...	28.31	39.60	15.00
Value of hours (billions of dollars)	22.01	...	30.99	...	51.33	...	42.00
Monetary expenditure (billions of dollars)	4.21	...	8.64	...	5.78	...	8.00
Total resource cost (billions of dollars)	26.21 (41.44)	...	39.63 (48.71)	...	57.11 (80.89)	47.12	50.00
All business							
Hours (billions)	...	3.614	...	...	3.614	2.38	0.80
Average value per hour (dollars)	...	...	...	...	28.31	39.60	25.00
Total resource cost (billions of dollars)	...	...	...	...	102.31 (144.91)	94.25	20.00
Big business[e]							
Total resource cost (billions of dollars)	...	...	...	1.055 (1.146)	...	...	...

a. Dates in parentheses refer to the year studied. Number in parentheses are translated into 1995 dollars, using the consumer price index for urban consumers (CPI-U).
b. Refers to federal and (Minnesota) state individual income tax systems.
c. Estimates for 1985 were based on extrapolation from 1983 data.
d. See text for details of calculations.
e. Refers to Fortune 500.

bias will cause an overstatement of true costs. He argues that respondents are more likely to consider tax compliance to be a "vexatious cost" and to try to influence the perception of high costs in order to generate policy response to lower them.[7] Cedric Sandford counters that taxpayers who find tax forms particularly objectionable are also likely to object to completing complicated questionnaires about compliance costs.[8]

A second issue has to do with the difficulty of accurately measuring the incremental costs of the income tax system. Large corporations with separate tax departments can measure such costs straightforwardly if they note the costs of information gathering imposed on other departments. For smaller firms, it is much more difficult to identify accounting steps that could be forgone in the absence of income taxation.

The issue is much broader, though. If individuals did not have to file income tax returns, they would still need to keep some records. But which ones? What records, for example, would they have to provide mortgage lenders or college financial aid officers? Many federal transfer and other programs now rely on an annual measure of comprehensive income, for which labor income alone will not suffice. If many states continue to levy comprehensive income taxes, how much compliance cost would abolition of the federal income tax save?

These questions raise difficult conceptual issues and imply that any estimate of the collection cost of the income tax is subject to error. This warning is especially important for estimates of savings from fundamental reforms that would eliminate tax based on annual income.

Survey Studies of the Individual Income Tax

Nikki Sorum and I surveyed 2,000 Minnesota taxpayers in 1982, and Marsha Blumenthal and I did a similar study for 1989.[9] The objective of both surveys was to estimate the size and demographic patterns of the compliance cost to the entire country of filing federal and state individual income tax returns. The later study also sought to assess how the Tax Reform Act of 1986, which had been widely hailed as a step toward tax

7. Tait (1988, p. 352).

8. Sandford (1995). Allers (1995) offers some evidence for Sandford's view. In a survey of Dutch taxpayers, he included, with the final reminder, a single question on a prepaid postcard for those unwilling to complete the whole questionnaire, and he then compared their answers with those to an identical question completed by respondents. He found that nonrespondents perceive a significantly *higher* compliance burden than respondents do.

9. Slemrod and Sorum (1984); Blumenthal and Slemrod (1992).

simplification, affected compliance costs. Neither study tried to distinguish costs imposed by the federal and state systems.

For both studies, a professional sampling firm used telephone listings and voter registrations to randomly select households for the survey. For simplicity, the samples were not stratified. The respondents to both the surveys were not representative of the U.S. taxpayer population in terms of either income or itemization status. Low-income taxpayers were underrepresented, high-income taxpayers were overrepresented, and within income categories, nonitemizers were underrepresented. To obtain results that were representative of the taxpaying population, the authors used a weighting scheme that gave low-income, nonitemizing households heavier weights and middle- and upper-income, itemizing households lighter weights. This procedure generated a weighted sample that accurately reflected both the income distribution and the fraction of itemizers within each income class.

These surveys asked respondents to estimate separately the time spent on learning about tax rules, keeping receipts or records, looking up tax tables for deductions and tax liability, preparing the return, supplying a tax advisor with information, and, in the second survey, arranging financial affairs to minimize taxes.[10] Those respondents who received paid assistance were asked for the professional source of assistance and its cost. Finally, the surveys asked all respondents for information on such additional costs as the purchase of books, software, postage, or telephone calls.

An analysis of the weighted data for the two surveys suggested that in 1982 a Minnesota taxpayer devoted an average of 21.7 hours to federal and state income tax matters and an average of $44 on professional assistance and other expenses. The average total resource cost was $275 in 1982 dollars. The aggregate resource cost, based on 95.3 million taxpayers, comes to $26.2 billion in 1982 dollars, or $41.4 billion in 1995 dollars. In 1989 Minnesota taxpayers spent an average of 27.4 hours on tax matters, an increase of 5.7 hours. The real value of that

---

10. For each of these categories, respondents were given a blank line on which to write in their estimate. This procedure contrasts with the practice in other surveys (such as Vaillancourt, 1989) that confronted respondents with a choice of two or more ranges of time. Such a practice may bias responses. By offering the choice of, say, one, two, three, four, five, six, seven, or more than eight hours, as Vaillancourt did, the researcher implies that the respondent should have spent about that amount of time on that activity, (say, researching the tax laws). Such categories may lead a respondent who spent no time researching tax law to claim otherwise and another, who spent tens of hours on that activity, to report less.

time, however, had fallen by about 7 percent, because the average real after-tax wage rate of respondents declined almost 20 percent between 1982 and 1989. Changed wording of the wage question across the two surveys may explain part of this decline. An increase in the real value of fringe benefits, which rose about 12 percent faster than wages and salaries, may account for the remainder. Taxpayers spent an average of $66 on professional assistance in 1989, $21 more in real terms than in 1982. In real terms, the average total resource cost in 1989 of $353.70 per household was about the same as in 1982; the total, based on 112.1 million taxpayers, was $39.6 billion in 1989 dollars, or $48.7 billion in 1995 dollars.

In both surveys the distribution of compliance costs was highly skewed. The highest income classes spent the most time.[11] Both the percentage of taxpayers hiring professional advisors and average expenditures tended to rise with income.

Several studies have documented that tax compliance costs are considerably higher for the self-employed.[12] In the 1982 survey, self-employed taxpayers spent more than three times as much of their own time on taxes, were two times more likely to use professional assistance, and paid almost five times more in fees than did other taxpayers. Similarly, in the 1989 survey, those who were employed, retired, or homemakers spent an average of about twenty-one hours on taxes while the average among the self-employed was almost sixty hours. The self-employed were again almost twice as likely to hire a professional advisor and paid close to twice as much in fees.

Although these studies contain many possible sources of error, the resulting biases are partially offsetting. The studies extrapolate estimates to the United States from the experience of taxpayers in only one state. In 1982, but not 1989, Minnesota had a relatively complicated state tax form. On the other hand, Minnesotans are widely presumed to be more law-abiding than the typical state's residents. The troublesome U-shaped pattern of compliance costs by income suggests that the compliance costs of the lowest income groups are overestimated, perhaps to a large degree.

---

11. An anomaly of both surveys is the U-shaped pattern of average time spent by income class. However, since the weighting scheme (adjusting for income class and itemization status only) probably did not render the samples entirely representative, this pattern should be viewed with caution. In particular, even after weighting the low-income sample probably included too few households with small compliance costs and too many households with high compliance costs (where, for example, the head was self-employed).

12. Sandford (1995).

The survey provides no estimates of the incremental costs of federal and state income taxes. Finally, the sample size of each of these studies was fairly small, about 700 in both surveys.

The Compliance Cost of Big Business

Blumenthal and I estimate that the Fortune 500 companies spend $1.1 billion complying with the federal and state income tax systems.[13] The federal income tax accounts for about 70 percent of this cost. Compliance costs accounted for 2.6 percent of the federal income tax revenues for a similar group of businesses. Depreciation topped the list of federal tax code provisions corporate tax officers deemed most responsible for the cost of complying. The alternative minimum tax, uniform capitalization rules, and the foreign income provisions followed closely. However, respondents said that uniformity among state corporate tax systems and between the states and the federal system was the single change that would be most simplifying, followed by rules to conform taxable income with the measure of income used for financial accounting purposes.

Arthur D. Little Study

In 1982 the Internal Revenue Service contracted with the consulting firm Arthur D. Little to develop methods for estimating the paperwork burden of the federal tax reporting system, to gather the data necessary to produce the estimates, and to develop a model that would enable the IRS to easily update the estimates as the tax system changed over time. ADL conducted three surveys of taxpayers, two of individuals, and one of businesses. One survey asked approximately 750 people to keep track daily of the time they spent completing their 1983 federal income tax returns. A second survey of individuals, a questionnaire mailed in 1984 to a random sample of 6,200 taxpayers, requested information about the time taxpayers spent on various activities in preparing their 1983 federal income tax returns. The business survey sent a mail questionnaire to about 4,000 partnerships and corporations and to their tax preparers.[14]

13. Slemrod and Blumenthal (1996).
14. In addition to coming up with estimates for tax years 1983, 1984, and 1985, the ADL study provided a procedure for updating the burden estimates. An update done by Iocozzia and Shear (1989) calculated a slight 4 percent increase in hours between 1985 and 1987. They concur with the conclusion of Blumenthal and Slemrod (1992) that the Tax Reform Act of 1986 did not noticeably decrease the compliance cost of the U.S. income tax system.

ADL did not try to translate the estimates of time spent on tax compliance into dollar values.[15] Individuals in 1983 spent an estimated 1.6 billion hours; businesses, 2.7 billion hours; extrapolations to 1985 yielded 1.8 and 3.6 billion hours, respectively. This estimate for individuals is within the margin of error of the Slemrod and Sorum estimate for 1982 of 2.1 billion hours. The ADL business estimate was seven times higher than the official IRS estimates that it replaced. The IRS had considered only the burden associated with preparing forms and had ignored such activities as record keeping, which are now generally understood to constitute at least half of compliance cost. For reasons I indicate below, I believe that the ADL estimates for business are fundamentally flawed and substantially overestimate the true burden.

Revisionist Interpretations of Earlier Studies

In his book *Costly Returns:The Burden of the U.S. Tax System*, Payne estimated the dollar cost of compliance of the U.S. income tax system.[16] Payne's methods were simple enough; he began with an estimate of IRS's average hourly cost for administration—the IRS budget for tax administration divided by total employee hours worked, which comes to $21.14 for 1985. This estimate includes both direct labor and overhead costs associated with this function. Payne argued that the IRS average cost is understated because it excludes capital cost. Accordingly, he averaged the IRS cost with 1985 data for a private-sector accounting firm, Arthur Andersen. The estimate for tax processing work, $35.47 per hour, is total revenues per employee in 1985.[17] Payne applied the average of $21.14 and $35.47—$28.31 per hour—to the ADL 1985 estimates of taxpayer hours spent, generating an estimate of $153.6 billion. Including the Slemrod and Sorum estimate of the cost of individually hired professional assistance yields a total compliance cost of $159.4 billion for 1985, or $225.8 billion in 1995 dollars.[18]

15. This failure is glaring. The resource cost of the chief tax officer's time clearly differs greatly from that of a CPA fresh out of business school. The procedure is also questionable as it applies to the expense of professional advisors. The ADL report states that "the value of a hour does not depend upon the particular individual or individual's disposition in fulfilling an information requirement" (pp. II-3).

16. Payne (1993).

17. He actually calculates this figure for 1986 and extrapolates to real 1985 values.

18. Payne calculates the total cost of the tax system in 1985 to be $362.9 billion, but the great majority of the additional $203.5 billion cost is due to "disincentives to production," a concept akin to the excess burden caused by distortions in relative prices.

Hall uses similar methods to reach an estimate of $141.4 billion for the 1995 federal income tax compliance cost.[19] He begins with an estimate that taxpayers spent 5.1 billion hours complying with federal tax laws in 1995. This estimate comes from the official IRS estimate of total compliance hours, updated to 1995 with a modified version of the ADL burden model. He then assumes that the personal and corporation income taxes account for 70 percent of the total cost of federal tax compliance, or 3.6 billion hours. Next, he argues that business has borne about two-thirds of the compliance burden,[20] generating estimates of 2.4 billion hours for business and 1.2 billion hours for individuals. Using methods similar to Payne's, he averages labor costs in 1995 of the IRS and the accounting firm Price Waterhouse to reach an estimated hourly value of $39.60. This procedure yields an estimate of total annual compliance cost of $141.4 billion.[21]

I believe that Hall's $141.4 billion estimate and, especially, Payne's $225.8 billion estimate are both too high. Their estimates for individuals' time spent on compliance are clearly not a reason for their high estimates. Their estimates of time spent on compliance are lower than my own. But they place a much higher average value on that time. Recall that Blumenthal and I valued this time person by person based on a survey answer or estimate of that individual's wage rate per hour, after taxes. Payne argues that overhead costs justify a higher figure and that "it is unrealistic to value this frustrating, intellectual work at a wage rate established for a simpler, less demanding job that the taxpayer may happen to hold."[22]

In principle, both overhead costs and psychological costs should be included in the valuing of time spent in compliance. Researchers studying the cost of tax compliance cannot agree whether to use respondents' self-reported value of their time; that value or an hourly rate, if lower; the self-reported value of what taxpayers would pay to be rid of all tax matters; the before-tax wage rate; or the after-tax wage rate. Each of these methods has problems, even when data are available to estimate them. Because there are no such data to apply to the ADL hours estimates, a certain arbitrariness in valuing the estimates is inevitable.

---

19. Hall (1995).

20. The estimate of the proportion of compliance cost borne by business and households is based on the approximate breakdown in the Arthur D. Little study. Personal correspondence with the author.

21. Hall does not calculate a separate figure for the cost of professional tax assistance.

22. Payne (1993, p. 27).

My principal objection to the estimates of Payne and Hall is that both are based on flawed estimates of business compliance cost produced by ADL. The estimates are derived from implausibly simple models of the determinants of business compliance costs. They presume, for example, that this cost depends on the number of lines in the forms businesses submit to the IRS, regardless of the size, scale, or complexity of the business. Even more troubling, the ADL estimate of total hours is five times the weighted survey sample mean for hours presented in the ADL final report itself, with no explanation given for the discrepancy. I find the estimates based directly on survey responses much more likely to be accurate than the predicted hours generated by the model developed by ADL for the IRS.[23]

The Envelope, Please

Washington loves a number—*one* number. In the past I have offered $75 billion as my one number for the total collection cost of the U.S. income tax system. This estimate is a back-of-the-envelope calculation based on my impressions of the strengths and weaknesses of the empirical literature. It should be clear by now that such an estimate is shadowed by imperfect survey data and the need to make some rather arbitrary assumptions.

Here is the basis for my back-of-the-envelope calculation. For the individual income tax, I sense the Blumenthal-Slemrod estimate of hours is too high, primarily because of an overestimate for lower-income families with simple tax affairs. In addition, the estimate must be adjusted downward to isolate the fraction of total hours due to the federal income tax and upward to reflect the increase in complexity since 1989.[24] A reasonable estimate is 2.8 billion hours, to which I apply a valuation of $15 per hour, generating an estimate of $42 billion for the value of time. For monetary compliance expenditures, I lower the earlier estimate to eliminate the state portion and raise it to reflect the increase in use of tax preparers since 1982, resulting in an estimate of $8 billion. My estimate for the total compliance cost of the individual income tax is $50 billion.

23. The appendix describes the procedures ADL used and gives the reasons I believe they are flawed.

24. I have not tried to adjust for any bias arising from the fact that the sample is Minnesota taxpayers only or for the apparently anomalous estimates for the low-income groups. As indicated in the text, the bias could be in either direction.

As to businesses, I believe that the ADL survey averages, as calculated in table 10A-1 of this chapter, are closer to the truth than ADL's own model-based estimates.[25] Unfortunately, this survey is now thirteen years old and out of date. Since 1982 the number of businesses has increased. In addition, the feeling is nearly universal that the business tax system has grown much more complex in the last decade, in no small part due to the Tax Reform Act of 1986. The ADL study provides no guidance on how to value the hours spent on tax matters. A sensible estimate is 800 million hours valued at $25 per hour, totaling $20 billion. Adding the individual estimate ($50 billion), business estimate ($20 billion), and a $5 billion estimate for the IRS budget devoted to income tax yields $75 billion, which is about 10 percent of revenue collected.[26]

Estimating aggregate compliance cost requires making several somewhat arbitrary assumptions. More research would be helpful. Most needed is a careful study of the compliance cost of small and medium-sized businesses. However, even the most careful study will face the difficult problem of how to tell what accounting is done for tax purposes alone.

I now turn to estimates of the cost of collection of alternatives to the income tax. I shall draw on the experience of other countries with the VAT and of states with the retail sales tax. There is, alas, no experience to guide estimates for the Hall-Rabushka flat tax or a personal consumption tax such as the USA tax. I shall exploit similarities with related taxes and, ultimately, speculate. I shall estimate the implications for collection costs of incremental changes to the existing system.[27]

The Retail Sales Tax

Because forty-five states make use of a retail sales tax, it is reasonable to examine their experience to get a feel for the collection cost of a federal

---

25. The estimates for individual income tax include the self-employed and the individual income tax costs of partnerships. The ADL study excludes sole proprietorships but includes partnerships. This suggests that there may be some double counting of the compliance cost of business partnerships; how much is unknown.

26. In principle, the ADL business study includes big business, so it is not appropriate to separately add in an estimate for that sector. In practice, the ADL sample included only one company with assets greater than $250 million and only nine with assets over $10 million.

27. Hall (1995) also estimates the collection cost of the flat tax, USA tax, and retail sales tax.

sales tax. John F. Due and John L. Mikesell report that in 1991–93 the administrative cost as a percentage of revenue ranged from 0.4 to 1.0 percent in a sample of eight states.[28] Just as with the income tax, the administrative costs are only a small fraction of the total cost of collection. Compliance costs borne directly by the taxpayers—retailers in this case—account for the bulk of collection costs. A 1982 study of seven states found that compliance costs ranged from 2.0 to 3.8 percent of revenue. An important cost-increasing factor is the need to distinguish taxable from exempt items.[29] Adding these estimates suggests a range of collection costs between 2.4 and 4.8 percent of revenue collected, much lower than the 10 percent estimate for the income tax.

Unfortunately, these estimates are not directly comparable. The figures for the retail sales tax refer to state rather than federal taxes. Much more important, they refer to tax rates that typically range between 4 and 6 percent, while a revenue-neutral retail sales tax substitute for federal income tax rates would run to at least 20 percent and could easily exceed 30 percent.[30]

The cost to states of administering and enforcing a tax levied at 4 to 6 percent tells little about compliance costs of a federal tax five times that high. In a mechanical sense, collection costs less than double when rates double. But pressures to avoid tax (that is, use legal loopholes) and evade tax (that is, cheat) multiply as the tax rate rises, because the tax rate measures the gain from evasion or avoidance.[31] Maintaining administrative quality and enforcement becomes increasingly difficult as rates increase. Vexing issues of interpretation arise under the sales tax, as they do under the income tax. Americans typically never hear about these problems unless they run retail sales businesses.

One of these problems concerns classification. Suppose restaurant meals are taxable but other food sales are exempt. What is the appro-

---

28. Due and Mikesell (1994). Over a much larger sample of states in 1979–81, the average ratio was 0.73 percent.

29. A more recent study reported an overall average compliance cost of 3.2 percent. See Peat Marwick, Mitchell and Company cited in Due and Mikesell (1994, p. 12).

30. These totals are for a federal tax alone. Combined with existing state rates of between 4 percent and 6 percent, the total rate would go even higher. Furthermore, if the federal income tax were abolished, states would be under considerable pressure to abolish their own income taxes to avoid forcing individuals to keep records and file income tax returns. If states move away from the income tax, some of the revenue from income taxes would probably be made up by higher retail sales tax rates. In that event, the combined rate could easily reach 40 percent, depending on how broad a tax base is used.

31. Whether evasion rises with tax rates is not as clear when the penalty for detected evasion is proportional to the tax understatement. See Yitzhaki (1974).

priate tax treatment of salad bars in grocery stores or fast food restaurants, where the customer may eat in or take out?[32]

A second problem concerns the need under a retail sales tax to distinguish retail sales from sales to other companies. A well-functioning retail sales tax must restrict the tax to final sales to consumers. Most states give businesses a registration number that exempts them from sales tax liability when they purchase goods from other businesses. But many businesses end up paying tax on purchases used in their business. At high rates, the opposite problem arises with a vengeance. Final consumers make inappropriate use of business registration numbers to avoid the sales tax. This problem highlights the fact that under a retail sales tax the onus of tax enforcement is placed entirely on the retail sector.

These problems are difficult and contentious when the rate is 5 percent; they would be gravely serious at 25 percent. Worst of all, there is no historical precedent to indicate that these problems are manageable. Only five countries have ever operated retail sales taxes at rates over 10 percent. Two of them, Norway and Sweden, decided to switch to a value-added tax. At rates of 20 percent or more, enforcing equitable collection would be extremely challenging. Tait has written that "at 5 percent, the incentive to evade tax is probably not worth the penalties of prosecution; at 10 percent, evasion is more attractive, and at 15–20 percent, becomes extremely tempting."[33] Vito Tanzi concludes, based on a review of worldwide practice, that a retail sales tax of 10 percent is probably the maximum rate feasible.[34]

I conclude that whether the collection cost ratio for U.S. states is 2 percent or 4 percent is irrelevant for an analysis of its complexity as a replacement for the U.S. income tax. There is no reason to believe that such a tax is administrable at accepted standards of equity. Low collection cost ratios for the British poll tax undoubtedly offered little solace to either Margaret Thatcher or John Major.

Value-Added Tax

A VAT requires the involvement of many more businesses in the tax collection process than does a retail sales tax. All businesses, not just

32. One pervasive problem with state-level retail sales taxes, the difficulty of taxing interstate sales of goods and services, would vanish.
33. Tait (1988).
34. Tanzi (1995).

retailers, are subject to it. This proliferation of payers raises collection costs. More businesses must keep records, and more must be monitored by the IRS or its renamed successor agency. In return, the VAT adds a critical element of self-enforcement to the tax collection process under the standard credit-invoice type of VAT. Businesses can claim credits for taxes paid on purchased inputs only if their suppliers furnish evidence of having paid tax on those inputs. This self-enforcement feature is impossible at the retail level, as consumers have no incentive to show that they buy from compliant retail establishments.

If a VAT were to replace the income tax, individual income tax returns would be completely eliminated and business tax returns would require only information now collected in the normal course of business. Nevertheless, the new tax would not run itself. It would certainly require a bureaucracy to administer and enforce it. In 1984 the U.S. Treasury Department estimated that to run a relatively simple version of a VAT it would need 20,694 new staff positions, with a total administrative budget of $700 million when fully operational, assuming a 2.2 percent audit rate.[35] A 1993 study by the General Accounting Office estimated the annual administrative cost at $1.8 billion but assumed a 7.8 percent audit rate. The estimates are comparable because audits make up over 70 percent of the total cost in the GAO report.[36] The administrative cost depends in part on whether, and how many, small businesses are exempt from the VAT system. The GAO estimated that exempting all businesses with revenues below $100,000 would cut the cost from $1.8 billion to $1.2 billion.

Compliance costs are larger than administrative costs for the VAT, as for other taxes. The Congressional Budget Office estimated the total collection costs of raising $150 billion from a European-style VAT at between $5 billion and $8 billion, or between 3.33 and 5.33 percent of revenues collected.[37] They note, though, that these costs would be

---

35. U.S. Treasury Department (1984). These estimates, and those that follow, are based on the presumption that the VAT would be of the credit-invoice type, rather than the "subtraction" or "addition" type, and that a uniform rate would be applied to taxable goods. There is wide agreement that multiple-rate VATs are more costly to collect. The self-enforcement aspect of the VAT, alluded to earlier, applies only to the credit-invoice version of the VAT.

36. U.S. General Accounting Office (1993).The difference between the two estimates underscores the fact that one cannot evaluate the collection cost of a tax system without considering other criteria, especially the equity of the process. A poorly enforced, and therefore more inequitable, system is inevitably cheaper than a well-enforced system.

37. U.S. Congressional Budget Office (1992).

"largely independent" of the amount of revenue raised, suggesting that the cost-revenue ratio for a $700 billion VAT could be substantially lower. The CBO estimate suggests a large cost saving compared with the current system. But caution in accepting this conclusion is in order.

First, some of the saving stems from the assumed elimination of individual tax returns. Part of this saving would vanish if states retained personal income tax systems. Most of the information currently required to calculate income is used for both federal and state income tax purposes. Eliminating only the federal return would not spare most people the need to file returns and keep track of the requisite information.

Second, the cost estimates from CBO and others, summarized by Sijbren Cnossen, presume that businesses with low turnover will be exempt from VAT liability.[38] But small businesses have the highest cost-to-revenue ratio under an income tax as well as under a VAT. Exempting small businesses from tax would simplify the income tax, too. To put it another way, part of the estimated compliance and administrative cost savings from adopting a VAT comes from dropping hard-to-tax entities from the tax system, a feature that has nothing inherently to do with a VAT. The same kind of caution applies to replacing the current corporation income tax with a VAT. Some of the simplification would certainly reflect inherent structural features. Some simplification, though, is attributable to the elimination of current income tax provisions—such as the alternative minimum tax—that could be abolished or altered to simplify filing while retaining the basic income tax structure.

Third, the VAT poses some tricky administrative issues, such as how to tax financial institutions. The VAT base applies only to real flows—receipts for sales minus the cost of inputs—and not to the financial operations of a firm. But real and financial transactions are entwined in many transactions of financial businesses. David Bradford addresses these issues in his chapter in this volume.

Although these problems with a VAT are difficult, there are also three decades of experience in other countries, particularly in Europe, on which to draw. In fact, of all the major industrialized countries, the United States is the only one that does not use a VAT. All European countries that use a VAT have retained sizable personal income taxes, however.

The European experience indicates that a VAT could raise enough revenue to replace the U.S. income taxes. The standard rate, applied to most goods and services, is 20 percent or more in several European

38. Cnossen (1994).

countries, and the revenue generated approaches the 10.4 percent of gross domestic product generated by the U.S. federal income taxes. VAT revenue as a percentage of GDP for seven countries is as follows: Denmark, 9.7; Finland, 9.3; Austria, 8.7; Norway, 8.7; France, 8.4; United Kingdom, 6.2; and Germany, 5.9.

The fact that VATs have been around a while, at levels comparable to what the U.S. would need to replace the income tax, brings both good and bad news. The good news is that the United States would not be stepping into unknown territory, as would be the case with a retail sales tax, flat tax, or personal consumption tax. The bad news is that other countries' experience is not encouraging about the possibility of actually realizing the simplification potential of a VAT. Few European countries levy a broad-base, uniform-rate VAT that promises maximum simplification. Instead the European VATs feature multiple rates that require difficult distinctions, invite abuse, and demand close monitoring.

In some cases, it appears that European countries' VATs are no simpler than their income taxes, although quantitative evidence is scarce. The ratio of collection cost to revenue raised was only slightly lower in Britain for the VAT than for the personal income tax—4.9 percent for the personal income tax (1.5 percent for administration, 3.4 percent for taxpayer costs), and 4.7 percent for the VAT (1.0 percent administration, 3.7 percent for taxpayer costs).[39] In Sweden the VAT is *more* expensive to operate than the income tax, costing 3.1 percent of revenue, compared with 2.7 percent for the income tax. This finding led its author to remark that "the VAT is evidently not the simple tax it has been marketed as."[40] Undoubtedly, in these two cases the failure of the VAT to achieve a collection cost advantage reflects both that actual VATs are more expensive than ideal VATs, and that European income taxes are apparently less costly to collect than the U.S. income tax.

Nor do enforcement problems disappear under the credit-invoice method of administering the VAT, despite its self-enforcement feature. Estimates of evasion range from 2 percent to 4 percent in the United Kingdom to 40 percent in Italy.[41] A VAT requires an enforcement system to monitor unregistered business, detect exaggerated refund claims, and

---

39. The corporation income tax was the lowest of the three at 2.7 percent of revenue (0.5 percent administration and 2.2 percent compliance). See Godwin (1995).

40. Malmer (1995, p. 258). The income tax cost was 1.0 percent for administrative cost, 1.7 percent for taxpayer cost. For the VAT it was 0.6 percent for administrative cost, 2.5 percent for taxpayer cost.

41. See Tait (1988, p. 304).

minimize unrecorded cash purchases, underreported sales, and false export claims.

The VAT holds the potential for major simplification compared with the current U.S. income tax. But the failure of European VATs to realize this potential suggests one should not compare the messy real world income tax with an ideal VAT that, at least so far, exists only in the imagination. More practically, European experience warns that if the United States adopts a VAT, it would be well advised to keep it simple and uniform.

The Flat Tax

Whatever its problems, the VAT achieves one fundamental simplification—no individual tax filing is required. In contrast, the flat tax does require returns by individuals who earn more than the filing thresholds. For this reason, it is bound to be more costly to operate than a VAT. Compared with the current income tax, though, its vastly simplified postcard personal tax return is perhaps its greatest attraction.

To estimate collection costs of a flat tax, one can estimate the additional cost of the flat tax relative to the VAT or the savings relative to the existing system. European-style VATs, with multiple rates and the complexity that engenders, appear to cost between 3 and 5 percent of revenue. The Congressional Budget Office estimates that a VAT with a single rate would cost about the same share of revenue as the European taxes if it raised $150 billion, but a substantially lower percentage of revenue at higher tax rates.

What does this imply about the flat tax? The business tax under the flat tax would be collected as a subtraction, rather than a credit-invoice, VAT, except that compensation to labor is deductible.[42] Both deviations from the European-style VAT will increase the collection cost ratio for the flat tax. The deductibility of payments to labor drastically reduces the business tax base, but does not reduce the collection cost at all and may increase it. Second, using the subtraction method sacrifices the nat-

---

42. Strictly speaking, the business part of the flat tax cannot use an invoice-credit system because a firm's deductions are not limited to sales from other businesses (labor costs are also deductible). Some of the purported self-enforcement advantages of the invoice-credit VAT could be maintained if invoices are required in order to claim deductions for nonlabor inputs; a similar system could, of course, be used under an income tax, as well.

ural enforcement advantages of the credit-invoice method. Furthermore, it makes exempting small businesses much more costly in terms of forgone revenue and the probable cutoff for exemption much lower. In fact, neither the Hall-Rabushka flat tax nor the Armey-Shelby plan mentions a small business exemption. Without it, the cost savings of ignoring the hardest-to-tax sector vanish.

For all these reasons it is impossible to confidently forecast the collection cost of the business part of the flat tax on the basis of observable systems, because none exists. Such vexing issues of business taxation as the distinction between an asset used for business and one used for consumption do not go away under a flat tax and may even be exacerbated by it.[43] Potential transition rules create additional uncertainty. From a political perspective, it is difficult to see how a flat tax could be passed if it simply extinguished the trillions of dollars of undepreciated basis in existing assets and debt.[44]

Compared with the current personal tax system, the flat tax indisputably represents radical simplification. The postcard tax return fairly conveys the simplification gains for many taxpayers from having to report only wages, salaries, and pension disbursements.[45] However, for the nearly 50 million taxpayers who now file a Form 1040EZ or 1040A, the simplification is not substantial.

What about the one number? I have placed the compliance cost of the individual income tax at $50 billion. I estimate that about one-third of that amount, $17 billion, is attributable to business operations of individuals. I have placed the compliance costs of incorporated businesses and the entity-level costs of partnerships at an additional $20 billion. If the flat tax cuts business compliance costs by one-third (from about $37 billion to $25 billion) and personal compliance costs by 70 percent (from about $33 billion to $10 billion), we are left with a flat tax for which the total compliance cost—$35 billion—is about half that of the current system. This estimate ignores any ugly transition rules.

43. Feld (1995).

44. See chapter 11 in this volume by Ronald A. Pearlman for an examination of transition issues.

45. The postcard-size business return of the flat tax does not fairly convey the complexity of a business return. The postcard is only the last stage of a process that, depending on the scale of the business, can still have a large information-gathering and record-keeping burden.

The Personal Consumption Tax

Under a personal consumption tax, consumption is income minus net saving. In theory, all income is included in the individual tax base—wages and salaries, interest receipts, dividends, and capital gains. What differentiates a personal consumption tax from an income tax is that the former allows an unlimited deduction for net saving, a kind of unlimited and unrestricted individual retirement account (IRA) that allows deduction of net additions to savings accounts, investments in stocks, bonds, mutual funds, life insurance, and other assets. As is true for IRAs, withdrawals from the accounts would be taxable at the appropriate marginal rate.

Unlike the other kinds of consumption tax discussed so far, the personal consumption tax would complicate tax matters for many individuals. It is true that some of the difficult compromises made by the current income tax—such as including capital gains in taxable income only upon realization—are handled easily by a personal consumption tax; for example, if accrued capital gains are left unrealized, they are both income and saving, so they have no tax consequences. However, the tax affairs of the average taxpayer, for whom the conceptual measurement difficulties of capital income are now of little concern, would be complicated by the addition to the tax base of borrowing and savings account withdrawals. If a consumed income tax handles borrowing uniformly, even credit card interest would have to be reported.

For families with little capital income, calculating taxable income can be simplified to the extent that assets are kept within the IRA-type accounts. However, some features of the new requirement of keeping track of net saving will be complex, and aspects of personal financial affairs that currently have no tax implications would have them under a personal consumption tax. Although a personal consumption tax is akin to having an unlimited, unrestricted IRA, IRA participation is voluntary. Keeping such records is significantly more difficult than reporting limited deposits to an IRA account and only reporting withdrawals during retirement.

A personal consumption tax raises a whole host of new enforcement issues and can generate complex avoidance schemes. Taxpayers would have an incentive to report all new saving and to conceal withdrawals or borrowing. The Treasury Department's 1984 study of this issue concluded that compliance with a personal consumption tax would require "a more extensive system of information reporting and monitoring than does an income tax," including "a comprehensive inventory of all existing wealth upon enactment of the tax, registration of private borrowing, and a far-reaching system of exchange controls to facilitate policing of foreign transactions."[46] Martin Ginsburg recently scrutinized the USA tax and found numerous ways that high-income taxpayers could manipulate net saving to avoid taxes. Bizarre situations could result in which "municipal bonds pay interest in even years only, executive compensation and the yield on at least one class of each corporation's stock is paid only in odd years, and the rich with borrowed money buy raw land or works of art they admire but may not keep forever."[47] Some of the problems arise from the particular transition rules, deductions, and compromises of the USA tax, but others are generic to any personal consumption tax. In its favor, a personal consumption tax eliminates the need for a complex business tax. It can stand alone or be accompanied by a VAT, the simplification advantages of which have already been discussed.

I place the personal consumption tax in the same category as the retail sales tax. Evidence on the cost of collection is beside the point. I believe that it is unenforceable at the standard of equity and the lack of intrusiveness that most American taxpayers would expect. If and when a workable version appears, a second look will be worthwhile.[48]

Income Tax Reform

In one sense, it is easier to estimate the collection cost implications of income tax reform than of replacements to the income tax, because one can proceed incrementally. In another sense, though, it is more difficult, because the number of possible variations on income tax reform is infinite, each with its own degree of simplification. Some income tax reforms add complexity, whatever their other merits. Examples include compre-

46. U.S. Treasury Department (1984, vol. 1, p. 585).

47. Ginsburg (1995, p. 21). Clifton Fleming Jr. (1995) concluded that the USA tax would be simpler than the current system but nevertheless "significantly intricate."

48. British economist Nicholas Kaldor, one of the strongest proponents of the personal consumption tax, thought it too complicated to be the backbone of a tax system. "Any attempt to replace [the income tax with a personal expenditure tax] suddenly by an untried system, whatever its potential merits, would be just as idealistic and unpractical as a sudden decision by the Railway Executive to abandon all steam locomotives in favor of a gas turbine which existed in the blue-print stage. In the case of the expenditure tax one can be fairly confident that because of its administrative complexities it would never be a suitable tax for [all] taxpayers. The most that can be hoped for therefore is to introduce a spendings tax that can be operated side by side with the income tax." Kaldor (1955, p. 224).

hensive inflation indexing for capital income, taxation of fringe benefits, and some forms of integration of the corporate and individual tax systems. Moreover, the collection cost implications of each tax reform depend on other reforms. By taking maximal advantage of withholding at source, a set of reforms to the income tax—including a single rate, a broad tax base, and integration—could achieve much of the collection cost savings possible under the flat tax.[49] However, such an income tax differs fundamentally from the existing system and is not currently a live policy option.

Rather than further explore the maximal simplification potential of an income tax, I will instead examine a streamlined alternative income tax of the type that may eventually be offered as a policy alternative to the radical plans based on consumption discussed earlier. It is not yet embodied in draft legislation, though its individual side bears some resemblance to the "10 percent tax" sketched out by Representative Richard A. Gephardt in July 1995.

This tax would establish a single rate for most, but not all, individual taxpayers and institute a return-free system for many individuals. It would eliminate all current itemized deductions except for mortgage interest, end the child care and elderly credit, restrict business deductions for fringe benefits, eliminate the exemption for state and local bond interest, and end all special savings incentives programs such as IRAs and Keogh plans. On the business side, it would eliminate the alternative minimum tax, simplify the taxation of foreign source income, and establish a dividend credit at the basic rate of individual tax.

The added revenue from base broadening would be used to pay for a reduced basic tax rate of 10 percent, which would apply to 75 percent of taxpayers. A second rate of 25 percent would apply to income above a certain level. The simplification of the base would allow the establishment of a return-free system, along the lines of the current British income tax, under which the combination of withholding by employers and interest payers and the dividend credit frees most basic-rate taxpayers of the need to file tax returns. Individuals with business income would still have to file returns.

Such a system would provide what I call "populist simplification"—a majority of taxpayers would be freed of the hassle of filing and preparing

---

49. Slemrod (1995).

tax returns.[50] Those with relatively complicated returns would continue to file, but the fraction who itemize would be cut substantially.

Only a few attempts have been made to go beyond back-of-the-envelope reasoning to measure the savings of such an incremental income tax reform. I have performed an econometric analysis of the data from Slemrod and Sorum; simulations based on the econometric results indicate that eliminating itemized deductions would reduce the use of professional assistance by slightly more than 10 percent and reduce expenditures on professional assistance by as much as one-third.[51] The estimated savings in compliance cost depended sensitively on the estimation procedure and ranged from negligible to 20 percent. Mark Pitt and I found that some taxpayers who would save money by itemizing do not bother to do so, presumably because of the cost of keeping track and documenting the deductible activities.[52] From this behavior we estimated that the private cost of itemizing in 1982 was $1.4 billion and the social cost was about $2 billion. These studies suggest that an income tax reform like the one I have outlined, which includes scaling back but not eliminating itemization, would reduce the compliance cost of the individual income tax by no more than 5 percent. However, neither study examines the cost saving of moving to a return-free system. Because the taxpayers with the simplest returns would be the ones affected by the return-free system, I believe an upper bound on this saving—net of the cost to employers and other institutions of implementing it—is an additional 10 percent of the compliance cost of the current individual income tax system.

With regard to business taxation, Blumenthal and I found that the alternative minimum tax (AMT) might add as much as 18 percent to the compliance cost for large corporations.[53] However, since the AMT is an issue mostly for the largest companies, the savings for the business sector as a whole must be much smaller. Blumenthal and I estimated that dealing with foreign-source income accounts for 40 percent of the total compliance cost of large multinational corporations.[54] As with the AMT, though, this is an issue predominantly for larger companies, and vaguely

---

50. A separate administrative system for remitting earned income credits might have to be established.

51. See Slemrod (1989); Slemrod and Sorum (1984). Part of the effect occurs because, in Slemrod (1989), ending itemization increased the price of professional assistance for those taxpayers who no longer itemize. The analysis uncovered no significant effect on compliance costs of moving to a single-rate system.

52. Pitt and Slemrod (1989).

53. Slemrod and Blumenthal (1996).

54. Blumenthal and Slemrod (1995).

specified simplifications of the tax treatment of foreign-source income cannot be counted on to save much. A reasonable estimate of the potential cost saving of this plan for business is 5 percent.

This set of income tax reforms does not seem to promise a large percentage saving in the resource cost of taxation, although the potential saving amounts to several billion dollars.[55] It does promise significant "populist" simplification.

Another, not mutually exclusive, strategy is to establish institutional checks on the growth of tax complexity in order to halt the apparently inexorable recent rise in compliance costs. In the past decade several countries have instituted a formal mechanism for introducing compliance costs into tax policymaking. Since 1985 the United Kingdom has required its officials to produce compliance cost assessments for all regulations affecting business, including tax regulations. Since 1985 Holland has required qualitative rather than quantitative compliance cost assessments for changes in tax legislation. The New Zealand government instituted in 1994 a similar proposal, and the Australian government announced in August 1994 its intention to attach tax impact statements addressing the compliance cost issues to all future tax legislation.

The United States has no such procedures, although for the past several years it has published estimated average times of completion of the major tax forms. The Internal Revenue Service has committed itself in its business master plan to reducing the time burden of paperwork from tax compliance by 7 percent and the expense by 3 percent by fiscal year 2001.

Conclusion

There are substantially less complex, and therefore less costly, ways to raise $730 billion than the current U.S. tax system. Whether one of these alternatives should be adopted depends on what the extra complexity is now buying. Some complexity buys the capacity to fine-tune tax liability—to "personalize" it—according to family characteristics. This capacity would certainly be lost under business tax–based tax systems

---

55. A 15 percent reduction in the compliance cost of the individual income tax, plus a 5 percent reduction for business, produces a cost saving of $8.5 billion out of a total compliance cost of $70 billion.

such as the VAT. Under either the flat tax or a clean-base income tax, much or all of this personalization would be eliminated, but the presence of individual returns means that it could easily be reintroduced if people wanted it. Some complexity—for example, that stemming from the alternative minimum tax—buys only perceived fairness. And some complexity buys nothing; misguided attempts to "encourage" particular activities often both distort the economy and cause complexity.

Some of the cost of the current tax system stems from the inherent structural difficulties of any comprehensive income tax system. Although the U.S. tax system compromises the principles of income taxation in many ways, difficult issues of capital income measurement remain—concerning capital gains, integration, and inflation—that a consumption-based tax completely avoids.

All the consumption tax systems exempt the ordinary return to capital, thus sidestepping these mismeasurement problems and the transactional complexity that inevitably arises when different ways of earning capital income are not taxed uniformly. The simplicity gain of consumption-based taxes, though, depends on the method of implementation.

The overriding question is whether replacing the income base with a consumption base is either necessary or sufficient for significant tax simplification. On both counts I think the answer is no. European experience with the VAT has shown that a consumption tax is not sufficient for simplification: real-life VATs are as costly to operate as a real-life income tax. The United States may pledge to "do it right," but tax system designs always look a lot simpler than actual tax legislation, especially when taxes are levied at high rates and equitably enforced. There are arguments on both sides about whether a flat tax would inherently be more susceptible to complexity than a VAT. Unfortunately, and perhaps tellingly, there is no historical experience with the flat tax that would inform this question.

Whether adopting a consumption base is necessary for substantial simplification is a much more difficult question. Depending on what is meant by "substantial," a consumption base is not necessary for substantial simplification because a clean-base, return-free income tax system with a single rate covering most of the taxpaying population achieves a lot. However, the transactional complexities that arise from the taxation of capital income would remain. A clean VAT or flat tax could provide major simplification. But a close look at the differences between the current system and these alternatives reveals that one important element of radical tax simplification is no secret at all.[56] Rather it has been the mantra for decades of many income tax reformers: to repeal the many implicit subsidies for programs that could never survive on their own, that try to fine-tune tax liability, or that serve as sops to politically powerful groups.

The corporate alternative minimum tax illustrates this potential. Big businesses cites this provision as the leading cause of unnecessary tax complexity.[57] It has nothing to do with any principle of income taxation and everything to do with an expedient, but exceedingly complex, way to avoid the politically embarrassing spectacle of large corporations that report ample profits to their shareholders but owe no tax. The same perceptual problem could certainly plague the business part of a flat tax or value-added tax, and there is no guarantee that an alternative minimum tax would not eventually emerge in these settings to spare tax legislators embarrassment.

The real secret to simplification under either a VAT or the flat tax is the potent combination of taxing all factor payments—except labor income, under the flat tax—at the business level with a flat rate. This structure allows most or all of the complicated issues of factor income measurement to be handled at the most efficient point—the business. Taxing capital income, as is required under an income tax, certainly adds complexity, but when handled entirely at the business level it is not an overwhelming problem.[58]

The flat rate is a key component of the simplicity of these plans, because it allows the business tax to be a final tax, rather than a withholding tax that must be fine-tuned at the personal level. Moreover, under a single-rate system, transactions between individuals or between government and individuals that do not generate income do not have tax consequences, which would not be true in a graduated-rate system.

Simplification should be one criterion on which tax system are judged, but it should not be the only one. There are important trade-offs between simplicity and fairness.[59]

56. Slemrod (1995).
57. Slemrod and Blumenthal (1996).
58. For an opposing view, see Bradford (1986).
59. As Musgrave (1994) has argued, if progressivity and personalization of the tax burden are abandoned as policy goals, the simplicity advantages of an impersonal business-level consumption tax like the VAT become compelling.

Appendix: The ADL Methodology for Measuring the Income Tax Compliance Cost of Business

In its report to the IRS, Arthur D. Little (ADL) presents two tables summarizing the average annual time spent by businesses on tax matters, broken down by their principal tax form (Form 1120, 1120S, or 1065), and by whether or not the business used a paid preparer (which accounts for 85 percent of firms). The key results from these tables are reported in table 10A-1.

Based on material presented in the appendixes to the final report, the total 1983 population for each type of return is listed in the fourth row of table 10A-1. Applying the average hours to the population figures yields an estimated aggregate of 546.7 million hours. Yet the final aggregate estimate of hours for 1983, calculated from the model created by Arthur D. Little, is 2,748 million hours, *five* times higher; this is the number on which the official paperwork burden estimates are based.

How is one to explain the discrepancy between the final burden estimate and the much lower estimate obtained by multiplying their own published averages by the total population size? No explanation is offered in the final report, nor is the discrepancy mentioned.

One thing is clear: the ADL methodology does *not* simply blow up the average figures by the population to obtain the aggregate. In part because one of their objectives was to produce a procedure that could automatically generate estimates of burden in the future as the tax law changed, they developed a model from which the burden could be built up form by form (over 200 forms in 1983) to produce the total burden. However, they did not have, nor could they reasonably obtain, survey estimates of burden form by form, as they asked in the survey only for estimates of six components of burden—record keeping, getting advice, obtaining materials, finding and working with a preparer, preparing the return, and

Table 10A-1. *Average Time Spent on Various Activities, by Type of Return and Preparer Status, 1983 Estimates*[a]

Type of preparer	Form 1120	Form 1120S	Form 1065
Paid preparer (hours)	138.82	125.78	86.83
Self-prepared (hours)	132.86	98.60	44.39
Weighted average (hours)	137.93	121.70	80.47
1983 population	2,422,705	646,794	1,663,237
Total estimated hours (millions)	334.2	78.7	133.8

Source: Arthur D. Little (1988, tables VIII-10, VIII-11).
a. Weighted data, although the results from the unweighted data are very close to the numbers reported here.

sending the return. ADL says that "it was not reasonable to expect businesses to be able to determine or estimate how much time they spent on each form. . . . Therefore, businesses reported burden by activity for the business' entire tax return."[60] These responses are the basis of the averages reported in table 10A-1.

In order to provide the IRS with a model that would allow them to easily estimate how the burden changed from year to year as the tax system changed, ADL devised several models of how these six components of the burden depended on readily observable variables. Although they investigated many variables and estimating equations, in the end they settled on highly simplified versions, in which each component of time is presumed to depend linearly (with no intercept term) on at most two of the following three observable tax form variables: F05, the number of line items on the form and in any worksheet; F21, the number of references in the form instructions to the Internal Revenue Code and Regulations, and F41, the number of "attachments" requested that are IRS forms. As an example, the predicting equation for the time spent on record keeping for any business using a paid preparer is simply 0.260 times F05. In 1983 the basic 1120 corporate income tax form had, by ADL's estimate, 294 line items, so that their estimate of burden *for any and every business* using a paid preparer is 76.44 hours (0.260 × 294). These equations were based on (apparently unweighted) OLS regressions in which the dependent variable was time per form and the independent variable(s) were line items, references, and attachments per form.

The ADL report refers to those models as "simplified" models (as opposed to "research" models), whose objective is to identify "practical, easy-to-use burden models that the IRS could employ to make burden estimates by activity and tax form."[61] But these simplified models are transparently implausible. Among other obvious problems, they presume that the record-keeping time it takes to prepare a given form depends only on the number of line items in that form, and is therefore exactly the same for General Motors as it is for Ma and Pa Groceries, Inc. Putting aside obvious specification flaws, one would expect that the predictive model should generate aggregate estimates that are consistent with the survey results. Instead, the model's predictions are a factor of five higher, with no explanation given for the discrepancy.[62]

60. Arthur D. Little (1988, p. VIII-11 to VIII-12).
61. Arthur D. Little (1988, p. VIII-11).
62. A small part of the discrepancy may be explained by the fact that the 2,748 million

Comment by Jane G. Gravelle

Joel Slemrod's chapter first presents measures of compliance costs, including a discussion of their limitations and various problems with estimates that have been made. His estimate of $75 billion seems to be as reasonable as one is likely to derive from the data, but that figure should be taken with a grain of salt given the weakness of survey data and the difficulty in identifying marginal costs. I suspect that people exaggerate the time they spend and also assign to tax compliance costs recordkeeping expenditures that are needed for business or financial planning in any case. I have no hard evidence of that suspicion, other than doubting that it takes an hour or more to copy and mail a simple tax return, as reported in the IRS paperwork statistics.

I also think it is helpful to understand more about the distribution of costs. For example, less than 16 percent of individuals report business or farm income, less than 9 percent rental income, and less than 5 percent partnership or Subchapter S income. Less than 30 percent itemize deductions, and more than 45 percent use one of the short forms. One of the most challenging issues—and one that illustrates the trade-off between simplicity and other objectives of the tax system—is the EITC, which appeared on 13 percent of returns in 1993 and is sure to rise. Almost certainly there are alternative ways of providing work subsidies (for example, payroll tax relief) that would not involve a computation by the individual of an EITC but would also not be as finely tuned to family circumstances.

---

hours includes the compliance cost for information reporting (Form 1099) and the forms for employee income and social security tax withholding. Whether tables VIII-10 and VIII-11 include such costs is not clear, although it arguably excludes them because the questionnaire asks how much time was spent on these forms separately and after the question about time spent overall on federal income tax forms. If this time was not considered by respondents in their answers to the first question on overall time spent, the 546.7 million hours is an underestimate of the true total time. According to the (flawed) ADL model, the information report and withholding forms accounted for 22.5 percent of the time spent on all the other forms; applying this percentage to the 546.7 million number inflates it to 669.9 million hours. If the respondents' answers to the first question about time included information reports and withholding forms, then the 546.7 million figure need not be so inflated. Finally, the 2,748 million hours' figure calculated by ADL inappropriately includes time spent on forms dealing with excise taxes, nonprofit organizations, estates, and trusts. According to ADL, this time accounts for 200.4 million of the 2,748 million hours. For pointing out these issues to me, I am grateful to Edith Brashares of the Office of Tax Analysis, U.S. Department of the Treasury.

Indeed, that is the major issue that I would like to raise: how to incorporate these compliance costs in the policymaking calculus, especially as we consider different elements of tax reform.

Simplification is only one of the objectives of tax reform along with efficiency and equity. It would be helpful to place the discussion more firmly within the framework of this trade-off. What types of changes have potentially important efficiency and equity considerations but are minor in their implications for compliance costs? What types of changes have significant trade-offs of all types?

Five major tax reform proposals are under consideration: retail sales tax; value-added tax, generally using the subtraction method; the Hall-Rabushka flat tax, the Nunn-Domenici USA tax, and a broader income tax base. I will not elaborate on Slemrod's discussion of the retail sales tax or the Nunn-Domenici USA tax. His suggestion that the former may be very difficult to implement in practice, and the latter would probably add considerably to complexity are reasonable characterizations of the feasibility of adopting these proposals.

Rather I turn my attention to perhaps the most popular major proposal at the moment, the flat tax. Subsumed in this tax revision proposal is a fundamental tax reform such as the Gephardt proposal; and, only one step away is a subtraction-method VAT. Indeed, the flat tax could be characterized as a subtraction-method VAT with a wage credit, accomplished by moving the locus of taxation of the wage piece of value added to the wage earner.

To explore its link to the income tax, however, consider the flat tax as composed of the following tax revisions, which begin with incremental reforms and then move on to more basic changes:

1. A general base broadening that eliminates itemized deductions, existing credits such as the EITC, the child credit, and other minor credits. Some fringe benefits would be taxed, notably health insurance, by disallowing deductions by the firm, along with repeal of the AMT. (One could nevertheless retain the EITC or perhaps shift the credit to the payroll tax or to the direct welfare system.)

2. An imposition of a single-level tax of capital income that shifts the locus of the tax to businesses. This move combines a corporate integration scheme with a shift in the taxation of earnings on debt-financed capital to the business. It leaves the individual worker or retiree with a tax only on wages and pensions unless that individual is self-employed.

3. Adoption of a territorial basis for capital income, eliminating foreign tax credits.

4. Adoption of a single flat rate, with an exemption for individuals.

5. A shift of the tax base from income to consumption by allowing expensing of all costs, including capital goods acquisitions and inventories.

At this point, only one more step would turn this system into a subtraction-method VAT: moving the locus of wage taxation to the firm and eliminating the exemption.

Now consider the simplicity issue and how it looms relative to the other issues of efficiency and equity.

Before turning to the flat tax itself, consider briefly the choice between VAT and flat. By moving to a VAT, one would be eliminating the need for the vast bulk of taxpayers to file a return, and the increase in complexity in the business return would be minor. However, the return to be filed by workers in the flat tax is extremely simple, with the most complex issue the determination of a dependent. A return-free tax system would seem to be quite feasible. Slemrod's back-of-the-envelope calculations suggest a savings of perhaps $10 billion or so from a VAT versus a flat.

In choosing a VAT over a flat tax, I suspect an overriding issue is whether to provide relief for lower-income individuals through exemptions and standard deductions—an issue largely of equity. Indeed, the flat tax is a clever way of providing some relief for lower-income people under a VAT. There would also be much greater pressure for a price accommodation with a VAT; in fact, the need for a large and disruptive price change may rule out a VAT as a substitute for the current income tax.

Now let us turn to elements of the flat tax. In the last step, the shift from an income tax base to a consumption tax base, compliance issues are probably very unimportant relative to other issues. If one works back from Slemrod's numbers, they seem to suggest that the flat tax as a whole might cut business costs by about $10 billion; hence these changes might be worth even less in compliance since one could, for example, eliminate the AMT or at least some foreign tax complications without resort to a consumption tax. In addition, most businesses keep depreciation and inventories and use accrual accounting for reporting to stockholders, sharing with partners, providing balance sheets data for purposes of loans, and presumably for measuring their own profitability for business planning purposes. Expensing will still require a different set of books, and for most firms, no great gain in simplicity appears. Small firms, by the way, can expense small equipment purchases and use cash accounting, although they must keep inventories.

Contrast the dramatic importance of the potential efficiency and equity concerns. Shifting to a consumption tax base radically alters the tax burden across generations by imposing a lump sum tax on old capital and presumably on old people. In part because of this lump-sum tax and in part because of the elimination of tax on new capital investment (which also equalizes the tax on different types of capital) there are potential gains in efficiency and consequences for growth.

This lump-sum tax on old capital, which has yet to be clearly recognized in the political arena, will be played out in many ways. The most obvious is demonstrated by the current attention in the debate to accumulated depreciation deductions on old capital, which will be lost. So too will the cost of existing inventory. With the flat tax, it will likely show up, for most people, in a decline in the value of the stock market. The burden of this tax will fall wholly on equity, since the flat tax imposes taxes only on physical assets and not financial ones. It is clear from conversations that concern about transition is mounting, suggesting that not everyone is wholly comfortable with this distributional shift. And if the result is to include complex transition results, the tax law for businesses could be made more complicated for many years.

I conclude that we should probably not let compliance costs weigh very heavily in choosing between a consumption and an income tax.

I think a similar conclusion is in order about the flat-tax rate. Actually calculating the tax is not complicated by a progressive rate structure since one only looks up one number in the tax table. Moreover, about 75 percent of taxpayers now have a flat rate with an exemption, and 96 percent face only two rates plus an exemption. At least one compliance cost of different rates is the tendency (assuming business incomes are assigned the top rates) for incomes to be characterized as wages at least to the point to being able to use the exemptions and lower rates. This problem already exists in the flat tax because of the large exemptions, however, and it seems a relatively minor affair. Self-employment income could just be added to the individual's tax schedule; it is hardly favored since all self-employment income is subject to payroll taxes. Even adding one rate greatly increases the flexibility of the system in obtaining a desired degree of progressivity, though with some efficiency cost.

Step 3 is a minor point in the tax system in general but an important point in some quarters, particularly for large U.S. firms. Although residence-based taxation is likely to be more efficient, I am not certain that a territorial method will simplify the system, because there will be even more pressure placed on transfer pricing rules. That is an issue that, I suspect, could benefit from some more exploration. It might be better to impose the tax more broadly by requiring constructive realization of the incomes of all foreign subsidiaries, which, combined with a per country foreign tax credit, would make tax havens far less attractive.

Steps 1 and 2 seem to me to be the places where the most gains in efficiency are likely to occur as they greatly reduce the complexity faced by individuals in reporting their incomes or in making economic decisions. If only these steps were undertaken, the nation would have a vastly simplified progressive income tax, which, if multiple rates were allowed, could produce any desired distributional pattern. This simplified tax is by the way quite different from the Gephardt proposal, which, although containing many base-broadening proposals, maintains the familiar structure of a separate corporate and individual income tax.

Item 2 is similar to the CBIT proposal studied by the Treasury Department under the Bush administration. One could make a somewhat less dramatic reform that would still be more efficient (although it would be more costly) than the current law by retaining the deductibility of interest for firms and the taxability by individuals. In that case, we would have a simplified form of integration by eliminating taxes on dividends and capital gains.

This is a simpler income tax system that undertakes a subset of the flat-tax revisions—if the flat tax were considered feasible, this set of changes should also be feasible since it involves a much less radical departure from the current tax system. If the goal is simplifying the tax structure and reducing compliance costs, this set of reforms seems to be the one to focus on. Most of the changes in this simplified tax also operate to increase economic efficiency, and while there would be a significant redistribution of the tax burden, such problems might be dealt with by some grandfathering rules. One of the most troublesome issues, of course, is the EITC, which plays an important role in the overall distributional policy. It is not easy to fix.

The remaining changes that move us from a simplified income tax to the flat tax should be judged almost entirely on their equity and efficiency implications.

References

Allers, Maarten. 1995. "Tax Compliance Costs in the Netherlands." In *Tax Compliance Costs: Measurement and Policy*, edited by Cedric Sandford, 73–95. Bath, U.K.: Fiscal Publications.

Arthur D. Little. 1988. *Development of Methodology for Estimating the Taxpayer Paperwork Burden*. Final Report to the Department of the Treasury, Internal Revenue Service (June).

Blumenthal, Marsha, and Joel B. Slemrod. 1992. "The Compliance Cost of the U.S. Individual Income Tax System: A Second Look after Tax Reform." *National Tax Journal* 45 (June): 185–202.

———. 1995. "The Compliance Cost of Taxing Foreign-Source Income: Its Magnitude, Determinants, and Policy Implications." *International Tax and Public Finance* 2 (May): 37–53.

Bradford, David. 1986. *Untangling the Income Tax*. Harvard University Press.

Cnossen, Sijbren. 1994. "Administrative and Complicance Costs of the VAT: A Review of the Evidence," reproduced at 94 *Tax Notes Today* 121–35, an online service of Tax Analysts, available on LEXIS.

Due, John F., and John L. Mikesell. 1994. *Sales Taxation: State and Local Structure and Administration*, 2d ed. Washington: Urban Institute Press.

Feld, Alan L. 1995. "Living with the Flat Tax." *National Tax Journal* 48 (December): 603–17.

Fleming, J. Clifton, Jr. 1995. "Scoping Out the Uncertain Simplification (Complication?) Effects of VATs, BATs and Consumed Income Taxes." *Florida Tax Review* 2(7): 390–443.

Ginsburg, Martin D. 1995. "Life under a Personal Consumption Tax: Some Thoughts on Working, Saving, and Consuming in Nunn-Domenici's Tax World." *National Tax Journal* 48 (December): 585–602.

Godwin, Michael. 1995. "The Compliance Costs of the United Kingdom Tax System." In *Tax Compliance Costs: Measurement and Policy*, edited by Cedric Sandford, 73–100. Bath, U.K.: Fiscal Publications.

Hall, Arthur. 1995. "Compliance Costs of Alternative Tax Systems." Testimony to the House Ways and Means Committee, June 6.

Iocozzia, James T., and Garrick R. Shear. 1989. "Trends in Taxpayer Paperwork Burden." In *1989 Update: Trend Analyses and Related Statistics*. Washington: U.S. Internal Revenue Service.

Kaldor, Nicholas. 1955. *An Expenditure Tax*. London: George Allen & Unwin, Ltd.

Malmer, Håkan. 1995. "The Swedish Tax Reform in 1990-1 and Tax Compliance Costs in Sweden." In *Tax Compliance Costs: Measurement and Policy*, edited by Cedric Sandford, 226–62. Bath, U.K.: Fiscal Publications.

Musgrave, Richard. 1994. "Progressive Taxation, Equity, and Tax Design." In *Tax Progressivity and Income Inequality*, edited by Joel Slemrod, 341–56. Cambridge University Press.

Payne, James L. 1993. *Costly Returns: The Burdens of the U.S. Tax System*. San Francisco: ICS Press.

Pitt, Mark, M., and Joel Slemrod. 1989. "The Compliance Cost of Itemizing Deductions: Evidence from Individual Tax Returns." *American Economic Review* 79 (December): 1224–32.

Sandford, Cedric T. 1995. *Tax Compliance Costs: Measurement and Policy*. Bath, U.K.: Fiscal Publications.

Slemrod, Joel. 1984. "Optimal Tax Simplification: Toward a Framework for Analysis." *1983 Proceedings of the Seventy-Sixth Annual Conference on Taxation Held under the Auspices of National Tax Association—Tax Institute of America*, 158–67. Columbus: National Tax Association—Tax Institute of America.

———. 1989. "The Return to Tax Simplification: An Econometric Analysis." *Public Finance Quarterly* 17 (January): 3–27.

———. 1995. "What Makes Some Consumption Taxes So Simple, and Others So Complicated?" Paper prepared for Conference on Fundamental Tax Reform, Center for Economic Policy Research at Stanford University, December 1.

Slemrod, Joel, and Marsha Blumenthal. 1996. "The Income Tax Compliance Cost of Big Business." *Public Finance Quarterly* (forthcoming).

Slemrod, Joel, and Nikki Sorum. 1984. "The Compliance Cost of the U.S. Individual Income Tax System." *National Tax Journal* 37 (December): 461–74.

Smith, Peter. 1991. "Lessons from the British Poll Tax Disaster." *National Tax Journal* 44 (December, pt. 2): 421–36.

Tait, Alan. A. 1988. *Value-Added Tax: International Practice and Problems*. Washington: International Monetary Fund.

Tanzi, Vito. 1995. *Taxation in an Integrating World*. Brookings.

U.S. Congressional Budget Office. 1992. *Effects of Adopting a Value-Added Tax*. (February).

U.S. General Accounting Office. 1993. *Value-Added Tax: Administrative Costs Vary with Complexity and Number of Businesses*.

U.S. Treasury Department. 1984. *Report to the President: Tax Reform for Fairness, Simplicity, and Economic Growth*. Vol. 1: *Overview*.

Vaillancourt, Francois. 1989. *The Administrative and Compliance Costs of the Personal Income Tax System and Payroll Tax System in Canada, 1986*. Toronto: Canadian Tax Foundation.

Yitzhaki, Shlomo. 1974. "A Note on 'Income Tax Evasion: A Theoretical Analysis.' " *Journal of Public Economics* 3 (May): 201–02.

CHAPTER 11

Transition Issues in Moving to a Consumption Tax: A Tax Lawyer's Perspective

Ronald A. Pearlman

A person who paid income taxes all his working life, and who retires [becoming a consumer] just as a consumption tax is introduced, isn't going to get the joke. Kenneth J. Kies[1]

Exempting the earnings on new saving is one thing, but exempting the earnings on all existing capital is quite another. Ernest S. Christian[2]

Some problems are so complex that you have to be highly intelligent and well informed just to be undecided about them. Peter's Almanac[3]

A government which robs Peter to pay Paul can always depend on the support of Paul. George Bernard Shaw[4]

SUPPOSE that Congress considers replacing the current individual and corporate income taxes with a low-rate, broad-based consumption tax. Suppose further that the proposed legislation would deprive individuals and businesses of the right to offset preenactment tax basis in business

In addition to the very helpful comments of the conference participants, I have benefited from discussions of transition issues among the members of the Tax Systems Task Force of the American Bar Association Section of Taxation, and especially from the comments of Michael Graetz; from work with Hap Shashy in identifying transition issues for the Task Force; and from discussions with Tom Barthold, John Buckley, Ed Cohen, Cliff Fleming, Don Fullerton, Dan Halperin, and Tom Terry; and my colleague, Brian Lebowitz. I also was fortunate to receive very able research assistance from Jennifer Averbuch during her tenure as a summer associate at Covington and Burling.

1. Kies, chief of staff, Joint Committee on Taxation, quoted in Lee A. Sheppard, "Consumption Tax Debunking at Tax Foundation Conference," *Tax Notes*, vol. 69, November 27, 1995, p. 1072.

2. Ernest S. Christian, "Good Intentions Do Not a Tax System Make," *Tax Notes*, vol. 69, November 20, 1995, p. 1044.

3. Peter (1982).

4. Shaw (1944, p. 256).

and investment assets against future gains realized on the disposition of these assets, and that borrowers, including homeowners, would no longer be entitled to deduct interest expense on their preenactment mortgages. In addition, suppose that members of Congress and the president find these effects unacceptable and modify the proposed legislation to include transition relief for tax basis, inventory costs, interest expense, and other financial situations affected by transition. Finally, suppose that a tax rate of 25 to 30 percent on a comprehensive consumption-tax base is necessary to maintain revenue.

Would such a plan be attractive to the American public and to policymakers?

This chapter examines issues that arise from the hypothetical replacement of the present U.S. tax system with a consumption-based tax such as the one proposed by Representative Dick Armey and Senators Richard C. Shelby and Larry E. Craig or by Senators Sam Nunn, Pete V. Domenici, and J. Robert Kerrey.[5] I use *flat tax* to refer to the Armey-Shelby-Craig bill and *USA tax* (unlimited savings allowance) to refer to the Nunn-Domenici-Kerrey proposal.

This chapter establishes a framework for thinking about transition and applies it to selected issues raised by the transition from an income tax to the flat tax or the USA tax. It then explains why transition is an important subject in the debate over tax reform and why the breadth and magnitude of the proposed changes ensure that transition issues will be at the center of the debate. The chapter discusses what I think is the proper scope of relief from the effects of transition and presents arguments for and against the use of "reliance"—taxpayers' claims that they undertook financial commitments in response to an incentive in current law—to justify relief. It enumerates factors relevant in evaluating the appropriateness of transition relief. The chapter then explores selected transition issues raised by the flat tax and USA tax, primarily the so-called tax on existing capital (frequently referred to as *old capital*), the related business depreciation issue, and the treatment of postenactment interest expense. I conclude that any enactable legislation must provide transition relief with respect to these items, and I assess the importance of the issues and possible transition options.[6] My analysis and conclu-

---

5. H.R. 2060 and S. 1050, 104 Cong., 1 sess. (1995); and S. 722, 104 Cong. 1 sess. (1995).

6. I have relied on Bradford (1995); Feldstein (1976); Graetz (1977, 1979, 1985); Levmore (1993); Sarkar and Zodrow (1993); U.S. Department of the Treasury (1977, chap. 6); and Louis Kaplow, "Recovery of Pre-Enactment Basis under a Consumption Tax: The USA Tax System," *Tax Notes*, vol. 68, August 28, 1995, pp. 1109–18.

sions are not those of an academic but rather of a practicing tax lawyer who has tried to assist clients in anticipating, analyzing, and adapting to changes in the tax law, and of an occasional government participant in the legislative process to alter tax laws.

The Importance of Transition

Transition issues nearly always loom large in the tax legislative process because changes in tax law directly affect individual and business tax liabilities and indirectly affect other individuals or sectors of the economy by changing the values of assets. Of course, some asset values may rise.[7] But not surprisingly, legislators focus on projected losses.[8]

Transition in the Current Consumption-Tax Debate

Transition is frequently neglected at the beginning of the tax legislative process. When a proposal is first offered, attention focuses on its broad impact. For example, when President Reagan transmitted his 1985 tax reform proposals to Congress, he acknowledged the inadequacy of the transition provisions but deferred to "the prerogative of the congressional tax-writing committees to design appropriate transition rules."[9] However, as it did in 1985, public attention soon turns to transition. People begin evaluating proposals in light of their particular circumstances. Indeed, frequently the attention is refocused entirely to the design of politically acceptable transition relief, depriving substantive changes of adequate analysis.

Although transition generally becomes the focus late in the legislative process, it has received attention early in the current tax reform debate and is likely to continue to do so. First, some taxpayers and policymakers believe that the lack of adequate transition relief in some recent tax legislation adversely affected the economy. Some observers, for example,

---

7. For example, in a shift from the current income tax to a low-rate consumption tax, receipts from preenactment private sector qualified pension and profit-sharing plans may be taxed under the new consumption tax at a lower rate than they would have been under the old income tax. See Institute for Fiscal Studies (1978, p. 190).

8. For a discussion of the short-lived "windfall recapture tax" proposal included as part of President Reagan's 1985 tax reform recommendations, see Zodrow (1988, p. 387).

9. *President's Tax Proposals to the Congress for Fairness, Growth, and Simplicity* (1985, p. 435); and see Roth (1996).

criticized the application of the passive loss rules of the Tax Reform Act of 1986 to pre-1986 investments and, because of expected reductions in the value and therefore the prices of certain residential and commercial real estate, predicted adverse effects on the financial condition of the real estate industry and on banks and thrifts.[10] And in 1993 those who sought repeal of the luxury tax on boats attributed job losses and financial troubles in the U.S. recreational boat manufacturing industry to enactment of the excise tax on higher-cost boats.[11] Whether or not these reactions are justified, many people believe the lack of adequate transition provisions caused adverse effects. As a result policymakers are likely to be particularly sensitive to future transition issues.

A second reason for the early emphasis on transition is that the flat tax and the USA tax call for changes to the U.S. tax system that would significantly affect the economy. These changes would be much more far reaching than President Reagan's 1985 tax reform proposals or even the predecessor recommendations of the Treasury Department known as Treasury I.[12] Because neither the United States nor any other industrialized country has experienced such a radical change in its tax system, the uncertainty is understandably great.

The development of transition rules during the legislative process might be characterized as the ultimate in representative government. It is constituent oriented, generally functions behind closed doors, and too often neglects broad principles of tax policy or the complexity and administrability of the transition relief. Consequently, the resulting legislative product may intensify public distrust of the process and disdain for the tax system. The adverse publicity directed to the hundreds of transition rules included in the Tax Reform Act of 1986 serves as an appropriate illustration.[13]

10. *Tax Reform Act of 1986*, 100 Stat. 2085, sec. 501. This provision took effect January 1, 1987, with a phased-in disallowance of passive losses of 35 percent in 1987, 60 percent in 1988, and 90 percent in 1990. John M. Berry and Albert B. Crenshaw, "Real Estate Faces Shake-Up: Senate Panel's Tax Bill," *Washington Post*, May 8, 1986, p. E1; Laurie P. Cohen, "Commercial Real Estate Market Is Hurt by Uncertainty over Tax Overhaul Bill," *Wall Street Journal*, July 10, 1986, p. 8; and Tom Furlong, "The Final Tax Bill—Property Real Estate Industry Finds Changes Devastating," *Los Angeles Times*, August 20, 1986, p. A16.

11. *Omnibus Budget Reconciliation Act of 1990*, 104 Stat. 1388, sec. 11221. See National Marine Manufacturers Association (1993, p. 1753). Several of the previously enacted luxury excise taxes, including the one on boats, were repealed in the *Revenue Reconciliation Act of 1993*, 107 Stat. 312, secs. 13161–62.

12. U.S. Department of the Treasury (1984).

13. See Donald L. Barlett and James B. Steele, "The Tax-Break Sweepstakes: Who

Criticism of how transition relief has been considered in past debates on tax legislation will no doubt affect future consideration of transition issues, but demands for relief will doubtlessly be a crucial part of any tax reform debate. Thus it is important to anticipate the transition issues and probable legislative responses should Congress mark up the flat tax or the USA tax. Confronting transition issues early will force policymakers and their advisors to concentrate on the economic, revenue, and design implications of transition relief.

The Scope of Transition Relief

Transition encompasses a broad spectrum of issues. I adopt a restricted sense of transition so that I can focus on several of the major ones. Tax policy addresses the effects of a change in the law on behavior adopted under previous law and behavior that is unrelated to the law previously in force. After a change to a consumption-based system, for example, repeal of the exclusion of state and local bond interest will change the behavior of the holders of existing securities, and the repeal of the home mortgage interest deduction will affect the behavior of existing mortgagees. For behavior unrelated to the law previously in force, the repeal of bond interest exclusion will affect the ability of state and local governments to raise funds in the capital markets and the repeal of the home mortgage interest deduction may turn away prospective home buyers.

Of course, preenactment and postenactment taxpayer effects are related. If repeal of the home mortgage interest deduction causes house prices to fall, both current owners and future home buyers will be affected. However, transition relief may not be as appropriate for taxpayers who buy houses after the new law takes effect as it is for taxpayers who bought houses before. I shall focus on transition issues resulting from effects of tax changes on prechange taxpayers.[14]

When Is Transition Relief for Prechange Taxpayers Appropriate?

With the exception of instances in which tax rates have increased, Congress has been very willing to provide transition relief when tax

---

Wins Round 2?" *Philadelphia Inquirer*, September 25, 1988, p. A1; and Barlett and Steele, "A Historic Hotel and Its Quest for a Tax Cut," *Philadelphia Inquirer*, September 26, 1988, p. A10.

14. See Feldstein (1976) for a theoretical statement in support of delayed effective dates.

provisions that favored taxpayers are narrowed or repealed.[15] Because tax liability equals the tax rate times the tax base, changes in tax rates affect liability as directly as does the repeal or modification of a deduction, credit, or exclusion. Although Congress seldom gives transition relief for rate increases, it does so often for changes to the tax base.

Two reasons explain these divergent responses. First, rate increases generally affect all taxable assets similarly. Because the relative value of a particular asset should not decrease, a particular taxpayer or taxpayer group should not suffer a disproportionate loss of wealth.[16] Accordingly, transition relief should be unnecessary.[17] But the repeal or modification of targeted tax incentives affects taxpayers and classes of assets differently and may result in disproportionate losses that justify transition relief.

The second reason for the historical difference between the treatment of the effects of changes in rate and base relates to perceptions of fairness or equity. Tax rates are not generally viewed as a tool for affecting taxpayer behavior except in the most general macroeconomic sense. But members of Congress typically believe transition relief is appropriate when people and businesses act because of their reliance on a targeted incentive in current law: these taxpayers should be protected from a subsequent change in the law. Thus "reliance" is central to any analysis of transition relief.

THE RELIANCE CLAIM. A claim for transition relief based on reliance rests on the premise that it is unfair to change a tax rule after a taxpayer acted because of that rule. The claim is strongest when a targeted tax incentive, enacted to induce specific behavior, is narrowed or repealed. In such cases taxpayers can often document that they relied on the tax incentive and that it induced their behavior.

15. Recent examples include the lengthening of the depreciable lives of real property by the *Deficit Reduction Act of 1984*, 98 Stat. 494, sec. 111, generally effective for property placed in service after March 15, 1984, and by the *Tax Reform Act of 1986*, sec. 201(a), generally effective for property placed in service after December 31, 1986. Legislative changes that reduce liabilities are more likely to be retroactive. Examples include the deductibility of bus operating authorities, effective for taxable years ending after November 18, 1982; rules relating to losses and certain kinds of interest income of insolvent financial institutions, effective for taxable years beginning after December 31, 1982; and the mortgage interest deduction of ministers and military personnel, effective for taxable years beginning before 1986, provided the statute of limitations on refund claims had not expired. *Tax Reform Act of 1986*, paras. 144, 243, 905.

16. See the section "Preexisting Commitments" later in this chapter.

17. See U.S. Department of the Treasury (1977, pp. 183–85).

For example, the low-income housing credit (section 42 of the Internal Revenue Code of 1986), which provides a tax credit for ten years following the construction of a qualifying project, was enacted to stimulate development of marginal housing projects. Many such projects were completed solely because the credit was enacted.[18] If Congress were to propose repeal of the credit, taxpayers who developed housing projects because of it within the preceding ten years could be expected to seek transition relief. In contrast, it would be quite difficult for owners of low-income housing projects to demonstrate that they had relied on a particular general tax rate. Such an argument would be more credible if they had enjoyed a preferred rate on a narrow category of investments.

In short, claims for transition relief based on reliance are generally stronger for narrowly targeted tax provisions and weaker for broad provisions. Members of Congress perceive a difference between the effect of a change in the base and a change in rates and, indeed, a change in rates is likely to produce broader effects than a change in a narrowly targeted provision. In addition, Congress has changed rates relatively frequently and seldom accorded relief. For these reasons, a reliance claim based on rates is hard to sustain.

Michael Graetz and others have challenged the appropriateness of transition relief based on fairness or reliance arguments, even in the case of narrowly targeted tax provisions.[19] Graetz points out that the fairness argument tends to focus on people who are nominally affected by a proposed change in the law. He suggests that if fairness is the standard, all who might have altered their behavior because of a particular pre-change tax rule should be protected.[20] He correctly characterizes the process of making transition rules. Generally, transition relief is accorded taxpayers whose tax liabilities are directly affected by a proposed change in the law. If the secondary effects are considered at all, they arise in connection with the overall merits of the proposed change rather than

18. See U.S. Congress, Joint Committee on Taxation (1987, pp. 152–53), which explains the reasoning behind enactment of the low-income housing credit.

19. Graetz (1977, p. 47; 1985, p. 1820); and Levmore (1993, p. 265). Graetz does not argue against the provision of transition relief, although he does think grandfathered relief should be avoided. Rather, he maintains that the appropriateness of relief should be based on an evaluation of changes in wealth and, specifically, the magnitude of taxpayers' economic gains and losses, without regard to reliance (1985, pp. 1823–26). In contrast, the Treasury Department argues that "transition rules need to be designed to minimize unfair losses, or undeserved windfalls, to individuals whose investment decisions were influenced by the provisions of the existing code." U.S. Department of the Treasury (1977, p. 181).

20. Graetz (1977, p. 77).

with how the change, if enacted, should be made effective. Graetz also denies that tax laws providing subsidies or other economic benefits should be construed as contractual obligations.[21]

I offer a different view. Tax incentives indeed do not necessarily have the legal force and effect of a formal contract.[22] But I believe that the legislature is obliged to honor its word whenever it is reasonable to infer such a contract.[23]

One need not endorse use of the tax code to provide economic incentives to conclude that those who reacted to tax incentives as the Congress intended should be entitled to know that the rules will not be changed midstream.[24] This reliance right exists not merely because transition relief has been given in the past, but because such relief is an appropriate obligation by a party to a contract.[25] If at a law's enactment Congress wants to signal that a tax provision is temporary and thereby forestall reliance, it can adopt a statutory sunset provision or explicitly caution against reliance in the legislative history.

21. Graetz (1985, p. 1824).

22. Possible legal claims to the contrary apparently are being considered in connection with certain thrift bailout transactions that were "marketed" by the Federal Savings and Loan Insurance Corporation (FSLIC) and the Federal Deposit Insurance Corporation (FDIC) in the late 1980s, in part on the basis that purchasers were entitled to certain tax benefits under the law then in effect. The *Revenue Reconciliation Act of 1993*, 107 Stat. 312, sec. 13224, changed certain of the rules governing the taxation of FSLIC assistance payments to distressed institutions and applied the changes (in future tax years) to transactions consummated before the legislation. For an example of a pending claim alleging that the FDIC breached its contract obligation to the purchaser of failed thrifts by supporting passage of the 1993 legislation, see *First Texas Bank* v. *FDIC*, U.S. District Court for the Northern District of Texas, Dallas Division, Civil Action No. 395-CV2584-H, filed October 31, 1995 (allegation no. 31, p. 12). See also *United States* v. *Winstar Corp.* (July 1, 1996), in which the Supreme Court upheld the lower court's determination that the government breached contracts with several acquirers of failed thrifts as a result of limits imposed by Congress in the *Financial Institutions Reform, Recovery, and Enforcement Act of 1989*, 103 Stat. 183 (on the inclusion of "supervisory goodwill" in regulatory capital).

23. For a recent articulation of this view, see Logue (1996, p. 1129).

24. Economists might argue instead that the market is the best place to deal with the financial risks of change. Political scientists might array themselves against transition relief based on reliance because a requirement that taxpayers who relied on current law must be protected from changes in the law would limit the ability of the government to alter policy.

25. If taxpayers are unsure that the promise of a tax benefit will be honored, they will discount its value and thereby undermine its effectiveness. See Feldstein (1976, p. 93), Fischer (1980, pp. 93–105), and Logue (1996, pp. 1138 ff). Reference to the existence of a contract is not intended to mean that transition relief is appropriate only when a formal contract exists between the parties. The enactment of a targeted tax incentive may create an implicit contract between the government and taxpayers that imposes obligations on the government if it chooses to change the terms.

Any test based on the concept of reliance will necessarily be subjective, and the extent of reliance in specific cases admittedly will be a matter of judgment. Nevertheless, as a matter of policy, not politics, it is appropriate to consider that an implicit contract exists between a taxpayer and the government when the taxpayer undertakes tax-induced behavior. This "deemed" contract is an initial element in the construction of a design for transition relief.

Transition relief may be appropriate if taxpayers can establish that they responded to a targeted tax provision before learning that the law was about to change. However, they may be expected to assert that they relied on the law as it was, even when substantial nontax factors prompted their behavior. Therefore, a careful evaluation of the reliance claim is necessary. This evaluation should seek to determine the extent to which the taxpayers' actions hinged on the tax provision; if it did, any financial damage resulting from the proposed law change should be ameliorated. In general, the correlation between the specificity of the tax provision and the extent of reliance will be strong.[26]

Transition relief is often focused on transactions that were the subject of a legally enforceable express contract or other binding commitment to undertake certain actions. For example, the repeal in 1995 of Section 1071 of the Internal Revenue Code of 1986, relating to the tax treatment of certain FCC-certified sales of minority-owned broadcast properties, did not apply to sales or exchanges that were the subject of binding written contracts entered into before January 17, 1995, provided that applications for the necessary FCC certificates also had been requested by that date.[27] In such cases taxpayers are likely to maintain that they are entitled to transition relief because they made commitments based on current tax law. Because contracts prevent them from altering their behavior after the law changes, these claims, which are based on reliance, evoke sympathy. Such a binding contract is relevant evidence in evaluating the merits of the reliance claim, but is not sufficient to justify transition relief. A contract that calls for multiyear actions by the taxpayer reinforces the claim and justifies particularly generous transition relief. In cases in which the commitment is undertaken without regard to the prechange tax rules, a binding contract does not strengthen the reliance claim.

---

26. A more extensive set of factors that are relevant in testing the validity of a reliance claim may be found in Goode (1987, pp. 159–62).

27. Self-Employed Health Insurance Act, H.R. 831, P.L. 104-7, sec. 2(d) (2) (1995).

If repeal of a targeted incentive raises the appeal of transition relief but an increase in tax rates generally does not, two questions remain: should transition relief ever be denied after the repeal of a targeted incentive or granted in the case of a rate increase, and what is the appropriate policy for changes in provisions that fall between these extremes?

If reliance were sufficient to justify transition relief, such relief would be appropriate in the case of every repeal or narrowing of a targeted tax incentive. In fact, no relief may be justified if other policy changes offset the effect on a taxpayer's financial condition of a change in a specific tax provision.

Assume, for example, that targeted tax legislation repeals the home mortgage interest deduction. Affected taxpayers could be expected to assert, probably on the basis of reliance, that repeal is unfair as applied to preenactment indebtedness. Now assume that in addition to repealing the home mortgage interest deduction, Congress also reduces tax rates enough to offset most homeowners' after-tax cash shortfall from the loss of future interest deductions. Further assume that the rate reductions cause increases in the demand for owner-occupied housing and house prices increase. Under these circumstances, homeowners may have lost little or nothing and transition relief may be inappropriate, even considering a taxpayer's reliance on the deduction.

Reliance is the beginning, not the end, of the analysis in evaluating the appropriateness of transition relief. One should look beyond the narrow effect of a change in a specific tax law to the overall effect of the proposed legislation on the taxpayer's wealth.

ANALYSIS OF RELEVANT WEALTH CHANGES. A wealth change represents the effect on capitalized value resulting from a change in the tax law.[28] A first-order effect is the impact of the change, if any, on the actual tax liability of an individual or business. However, a change in the value of a particular type of asset—a residence or a tax-exempt bond, for example—must also be considered. Analysis of wealth change should also include changes in interest rates, overall prices, investment, employment, and wages.[29]

---

28. References in the remaining discussion to wealth change or wealth effect are intended to encompass the impact of a change in tax law on the financial condition of an individual or group of individuals, including taxpayers directly affected by the change and others who are only indirectly affected. See Atkinson and Stiglitz (1980, pp. 27–28, 65–68).

29. U.S. Congress, Joint Committee on Taxation (1995b, pp. 85–87).

Tax policymakers are used to hearing about potential negative wealth effects. It is less common to see positive wealth effects considered in the legislative process. But relief is not justified if losses a taxpayer may suffer from one element of complex legislation are offset by gains from others. Transition relief is also questionable when it confers windfall gains. The possible increase in the value of state and local tax-exempt bonds that may be grandfathered in connection with the repeal of the interest exclusion is one example.[30] The benefit to the holders of capital assets with unrealized appreciation that was not subject to tax before conversion to a flat tax or other new proposal that does not tax capital gains is another.

A SECOND LOOK AT RATE CHANGES: WEALTH EFFECTS. Businesses and investors expect tax rates to change. They factor such expectations along with other market uncertainties into their economic decisionmaking. As a result, taxpayers generally expect no transition relief when rates increase and do not quarrel about the *prospective* effect of a rate change on an earlier economic decision.

Nevertheless, transition relief may sometimes be appropriate when rates increase. Once again, wealth effects are relevant in evaluating whether a rate increase may have so adversely affected taxpayers in general that relief—a phase-in, for example—is advisable.

EVERYTHING ELSE. Identifying clear cases of reliance—those stemming from provisions enacted to stimulate narrowly defined taxpayer behavior—is rarely easy. Occasionally a taxpayer group will suffer obvious losses that merit relief, even in the absence of reliance. Examples include the unlikely proposals to reduce the dollar amount of the personal exemption or standard deduction or the possible reduction in the earned income tax credit. The not-so-clear cases are more difficult. However, merely because it is difficult to identify specific instances in which transition relief is appropriate does not mean that there is no intellectual foundation for relief. Transition issues should not be viewed as essentially political, with the primary motive being how to defuse opposition to a proposed legislative change most effectively. Serious policymakers, intent on moderating the unanticipated negative and positive effects of a tax law change—the windfall losses and the windfall gains—should ignore assertions that transition relief is mere politics. They should seek accu-

30. Graetz (1977, pp. 61–63).

rately and reliably to identify appropriate adjustments for transition effects.

An Approach to Transition Relief

There are many potential legislative responses to claims for transition relief, ranging from no response to full grandfather relief that exempts affected taxpayers from the new law.[31] Relief may take such intermediate forms as a delayed effective date or the gradual phase-in of a new provision or phase-out of an old one.[32] And, it is possible to provide monetary payments or other direct financial support outside the tax system.

In selecting a form of relief, policymakers should try to minimize undesirable wealth effects and incentive problems (that is, taxpayer reactions to special features of a change before it is enacted) and make relief as simple and administrable as possible.[33] Relevant considerations include: does a valid reliance claim exist?[34] If such a claim is established, are any losses from one element of the tax bill offset by gains from other provisions? If there is a potential reliance claim, are negative wealth effects of a proposed change large enough to justify relief? How much revenue would the proposed relief cost? What will be the distributional effects of the proposed relief? Will it be possible to design and implement a workable transition rule without unduly complicating the law? The final issues concern timing. If through advance notice of a change in the law or a deferred effective date, taxpayers can act to mitigate their economic losses before the law changes, the case for transition relief is weakened.[35] Such considerations also bear on whether the appropriate effective date of a change in the law should be the date a member of

31. Grandfather transition is discussed in U.S. Department of the Treasury (1977, pp. 189, 200–01) and Graetz (1977, p. 60 ff).

32. Phased-in transition and delayed effective dates are discussed in Graetz (1979, p. 1650; and 1977, p. 63, n. 53); and in U.S. Department of the Treasury (1977, p. 191).

33. U.S. Department of the Treasury (1977, p. 188).

34. *Blueprints for Tax Reform* categorizes transition issues in terms of their carryover and price effects; U.S. Department of the Treasury (1977, pp. 181–85). Neither category directly incorporates taxpayer reliance, the most important influence on legislative transition relief, although *Blueprints* does consider equity issues in discussing the carryover and price effects. Because of the significance that I place on reliance and because I agree with Graetz that carryover and price effects generally are similar in effect (Graetz, 1979, p. 1650), I do not follow the *Blueprints* format.

35. U.S. Department of the Treasury (1977, p. 183). The potential incentive for acting before the effective date through a sale of an asset, for example, might result in a change in asset value.

Congress introduces a bill or the president announces a legislative recommendation or at some later date, such as the date that one of the tax-writing committees includes a provision in its bill?[36] The expectations of an individual or business will vary depending on the status of proposed legislation at the time a financial commitment is made and on the private sector's judgment regarding the time it will take for the tax change, if enacted, to be capitalized into the value of the relevant investment. Congress's willingness to provide transition relief will be influenced by the relationship between the time a taxpayer acted and the status of the proposed legislation at the time of the action.

Specific Transition Issues

The Armey-Shelby flat tax contains no provisions for transition. Robert Hall and Alvin Rabushka appear to dismiss transition provisions as an unfortunate intrusion of the political process into the design of an otherwise "good, practical tax system."[37] Presumably, the principal congressional sponsors of the flat tax were mindful of the very significant potential effects on the economy of such a dramatic change in the tax system.[38] Because I believe that effective transition relief is both an important part of the design of good tax legislation and good politics, I am puzzled about why transition is not addressed in the bill that was introduced. Perhaps the consideration of relief is omitted because it necessitates higher tax rates during the transition than are needed without it, and the sponsors wanted to be able to publicize a low tax rate and to present the big picture unencumbered by issues of transition.

In contrast to the flat tax, the USA tax deals specifically, although in my opinion unsatisfactorily, with transition, especially the issue of what

36. See Pearlman (1994, pp. 5–8) for a discussion of the "shifting" effect of a proposed change in the tax law from nominally prospective to nominally retroactive as it moves through the legislative process.

37. However, they do suggest transition relief for the unrecovered basis of depreciable property by means of a continuation of the present-law system of depreciation for pre-enactment assets. In addition, in informal remarks during the Brookings conference, Professor Hall indicated that he was troubled with the taxation of the service value of housing and suggested preserving the deduction for state and local property taxes as a way to reduce the impact of the proposed law change. Hall and Rabushka (1995b, p. 78).

38. See the statement by Doug Koopman, a member of Armey's staff, in Peter Passell, "Spending It; For Business, the Stakes Are High," *New York Times*, September 3, 1995, sec. 3, p. 7.

constitutes the preenactment tax basis. However, because it does not deal with other issues (the taxability of interest on preenactment debt, for example), the proposal only scratches the surface.

The following section is not a comprehensive review of the many potential transition issues raised by the flat tax and the USA tax. Instead, it has three purposes: to identify the most important transition issues, to consider them in light of the preceding analysis, and to speculate on how they might be dealt with during the legislative process.

Transition Wealth Tax

The most frequently discussed transition issue relating to a shift from an income tax to a consumption-based tax is the so-called one-time tax on existing capital.[39] Consider, for example, a recently retired person who has paid tax on earnings during years of active employment and has saved part of those earnings to acquire investment assets. The retiree has tax basis in the assets that would offset all or much of any proceeds should the assets be sold. To the extent the proceeds represent the recovery of basis, under the present income tax they could be consumed or reinvested as the owner chooses without further tax. However, under a consumed-income tax, flat tax, or value-added tax the gross sales proceeds that are used for consumption—and, under the USA tax, the net dissaving—would be subject to tax.

INAPPROPRIATENESS OF DOUBLE TAX ARGUMENT. Some analysts hold that the retiree would be subject to double taxation or a double tax.[40] In testimony before the House Ways and Means Committee Leslie Samuels, the former assistant secretary of the Treasury for tax policy, stated the problem more accurately than have those who characterize it as one of double taxation: "The most significant issue . . . is deciding how to treat

39. See U.S. Congress, Joint Committee on Taxation (1995b, pp. 84–85); Bradford (1995, p. 20); and Sarkar and Zodrow (1993, p. 359).
40. Louis Kaplow, "Recovery of Pre-Enactment Basis under a Consumption Tax: The USA Tax System," vol. 68, Tax Notes, August 28, 1995, pp. 1114, asserts that "any plausible norm consistently applied to the pre- and post-enactment periods would not favor the double-taxation of pre-enactment savings." Bradford (1995, p. 16) refers to tax basis as an accumulation of tax-prepaid claims on future consumption, a characterization that implies a double tax. See Ernest S. Christian and George J. Schutzer, "USA Tax System: Description and Explanation of the Unlimited Savings Allowance Income Tax System," Tax Notes, vol. 66, March 10, 1995, special supplement, p. 1565, which refers to the transition issue as a second taxation.

the postchange return to wealth that was accumulated out of after-tax income under the income tax."[41] A consumption tax may tax consumption out of preenactment wealth that had already been subject to the income tax when it was earned. Thus wealth may be subject to two taxes. But *double taxation* is a term of art intended to identify the multiple taxation of certain *behavior* or *economic activity*. Here, no economic activity is being taxed twice. An income tax, which seeks to tax the income-earning activity, differs fundamentally from a consumption-based tax, which seeks to tax the act of consumption.[42]

The label of double tax implies the necessity of a remedy without first examining whether application of the consumption tax without transition relief is inappropriate and without regard to the consequences of providing relief. Policymakers may ultimately conclude that subjecting a taxpayer to both the old income tax and the new consumption tax is unfair, but this conclusion is not the same as stating that a taxpayer's assets are double taxed.

EXPECTED REACTION. It is not surprising that so-called old capital receives so much attention. There is a lot of it—as much as $10 trillion—and it is owned disproportionately by the elderly.[43] Accordingly, some form of relief may be both appropriate and politically necessary. Tran-

---

41. Samuels (1995, p. 33).

42. Applying a similar argument in analyzing a retroactivity issue, Michael J. McIntyre, "Transition Rules: Learning to Live with Tax Reform," *Tax Notes*, vol. 4, August 30, 1976, p. 10, has stated, "No one seems to argue, for example, that a new sales tax (or an increase in the rate of an old one) is retroactive when it applies to purchases made from income already earned."

43. Eric Toder, deputy assistant secretary in Tax Analysis, Department of the Treasury, testified (1995, p. 17) that total U.S. household wealth is about $23 trillion and the adjusted basis is $10 trillion. See also Samuels (1995, p. 34). Some estimates are lower. Rudolph Penner, one of the consultants on the design of the USA tax, has stated (1994, pp. 25–26) that old wealth may not be such a great problem because savings rates are so low that few taxpayers have accumulated assets on which they previously have paid tax, particularly if housing and pension funds, which are deductible under current law, are disregarded. Notwithstanding Penner's observation, the Treasury's numbers will be very visible in the political debate. On the ownership of wealth, see chapter 3 by Eric M. Engen and William G. Gale in this volume and Fullerton (1985, pp. 5–10). Graetz (1977, p. 51, n. 16) commented that the impact of the shift to a consumption tax is the same on everyone with equal wealth and the same propensity to consume. Therefore, we should be concerned if the impact on a retiree is greater than on a younger person because of the inability of the retiree to work harder to compensate for the tax increase. According to the Joint Committee on Taxation, "The one-time tax on wealth introduced by the consumption tax may fall heavily on the elderly, who in the aggregate hold a large share of existing assets." U.S. Congress (1995b, p. 88).

sition relief for existing capital will likely be very attractive among legislators because the issue can be presented as one of "lost basis." Imagine the reaction of a member of Congress upon learning that a consumed income tax will fall on the full value of consumption financed by the sale of an asset without any offset for the asset's adjusted tax basis. (In fact, the USA tax does provide some transition relief for preenactment basis.) The reaction may well be different if the consumption tax is a retail sales tax that does not require a calculation of gain on the sale or disposition of a capital asset.

Because the decision on whether and how to tax existing capital is so important and affects so many people, it will receive a great deal of attention should Congress seriously consider a consumption-based tax. It is important, therefore, to consider whether and when transition relief is necessary.

Some economists argue that cold-turkey transition to a consumption tax is important precisely to take advantage of the lump-sum tax on existing capital, which does not distort economic behavior and holds down rates necessary to sustain revenue.[44] Despite this argument for efficiency, transition relief may still be necessary. Because I believe the tax law should not be changed without anticipating and, in appropriate circumstances, compensating groups of taxpayers or sectors of the economy for serious economic losses, transition relief that avoids inequities may be justified even if it reduces efficiency gains. However, so many variables must be considered in evaluating claims for transition relief that it is difficult to determine with confidence whether relief is appropriate and, if so, for whom and to what extent.

RELEVANT CONSIDERATIONS. The first consideration for the validity of transition relief is the extent of taxpayer reliance. Taxpayers will maintain that when they saved from after-tax income, they assumed they had satisfied their tax liabilities and that, except to the extent of appreciation after the passage of a new law, they are entitled to rely on a long tradition of no double tax. But this assertion is not a valid reliance claim. People will seek wealth regardless of the rules for taxing capital gains.

44. The corollary is that if the owners of old capital are accorded transition relief, the savings and other positive economic gains will be reduced. See chapter 2 by Alan J. Auerbach in this volume; see Engen and Gale in this volume. It may be wrong to assume that a tax on existing capital will cause no distortions. If taxpayers anticipate such a one-time tax, they will try to avoid it, and these actions would impose an efficiency loss.

To assert that the Internal Revenue Code includes a basis offset for capital assets to induce specific taxpayer behavior stretches the concept of a contract. I would, therefore, reject reliance as a justification for transition relief for existing capital. At the same time, arguments involving reliance, fairness, and equity will creep into the existing capital debate, and the political response to such claims may well be different.

The second consideration concerns the impact of tax reform on wealth. Ideally, an analysis of relative and overall wealth changes should facilitate decisions on when transition relief for existing capital is appropriate. Rather than analyzing the impact of a proposed change asset-by-asset or investment-by-investment, it may be possible, by focusing on a taxpayer's (or class of taxpayers') overall economic gains and losses as a result of the change in law, to identify factors favoring and opposing relief and thereby enable a more precise identification of which taxpayers deserve relief.

Certain provisions of the income tax may ameliorate effects of the tax on existing capital. For example, the deferral of tax on capital gains, the preferential rate on capital gains, and the consumption-tax treatment of private retirement plans may moderate or eliminate decreases in the after-tax cost of certain assets. If so, the burden on existing capital under the income tax would be less than is commonly perceived.[45] Moreover, many retirees will not liquidate their preenactment investment assets but will continue to hold them and earn interest and dividends. These returns, most of which are taxable under the income tax, would be completely free of current tax under the USA tax to the extent they are reinvested.[46] For high-bracket taxpayers, even taxable net dissaving would be subject to a significantly lower tax rate under the proposed legislation than it is under the present income tax.[47]

45. William G. Gale has suggested that the burden on old capital is somewhat ameliorated because the elderly, who would bear a relatively large portion of any tax on accumulated assets, receive large net benefits from medicare and, to some extent, social security; see "Building a Better Tax System: Can a Consumption Tax Deliver the Goods?" *Tax Notes*, vol. 69, November 6, 1995, pp. 781–86. Of course, "the elderly" is not a homogeneous class. The tax on old capital will burden the wealthy elderly. Most social security and medicare benefits accrue to people with modest assets and income. To treat the elderly as an undifferentiated class is misleading.

46. S. 722, sec. 50ff. (Unlimited Savings Allowance).

47. Hall and Rabushka (1995b, p. 41) describe tax reform as a tremendous boon to the economic elite. Moreover, they point out that if the consumption being financed by the sale of investment assets is the college education of a child of an individual still in the work

Macroeconomic effects will also influence changes in taxpayers' wealth. The effects of transition depend on changes in price levels and on the composition of taxpayers' investment portfolios.[48]

There are two significant problems with analyses of changes in wealth. First, they tend to address changes affecting broad segments of the population. Accordingly, they do not account for the many differences in circumstances and financial positions among individuals. For example, analysts agree that an implicit tax on existing capital will affect elderly retirees most harshly at a time when they are net dissavers.[49] Some retirees are dissavers, but many are not. Second, the reliability of analyses of the effects of a total replacement of the present U.S. tax system with an alternative system, a change with which we have no experience, is questionable.[50] It is very important, therefore, that analyses of changes in the financial condition of taxpayers be appropriately careful and that policymakers understand their limitations. For anyone to predict changes in individuals' wealth resulting from a massive change in the tax law without substantially qualifying the prediction would be irresponsible.

A one-time wealth tax would probably raise enough revenue to finance the adoption of a relatively low tax rate.[51] Conversely, if the Treasury Department's estimates are accurate, a transition rule that preserved some or all preenactment tax basis would significantly decrease revenues. Large swings in revenue might not cause legislators to reject claims for transition relief for existing capital, but they almost certainly would influence the design and the extent of any such relief.

A one-time tax on existing capital could permit a broad reduction in the rate structure of the new tax system and might be very progressive.[52] However, if transition relief were to be provided to existing capital, the resulting tax system would be equivalent to a wage tax.[53]

---

force, the returns on expenditures for higher education—that is, the increased earnings of the child—will also benefit from the lower rate.

48. Bradford (1995, pp. 24, 28–30).

49. See, for example, U.S. Congress, Joint Committee on Taxation (1995b, p. 88).

50. For example, Bradford (1995, p. 27) focuses on asset price effects. He states that they constitute an important component of the transition analysis. Not surprisingly, they are hard to predict.

51. Bradford (1995, p. 37).

52. Gale, "Building a Better Tax System," p. 785. See Levmore (1993, p. 307) for a general discussion of the feasibility of a broad retroactive tax in such circumstances.

53. It is worth noting that a "wage tax" analysis assumes that the discount rate used in determining the present value of expensing equals the assumed future rate of return (a normal or routine return). To the extent the return to new capital exceeds the assumed rate of return (in other words, an extraordinary return), characterization of the tax as a wage

Transition relief will inevitably complicate the law, even if only temporarily. Elaborate relief, such as a depreciation system with multiple-class recovery periods designed to provide deferred cost recovery, would add a great deal of complexity.[54] Complexity should not be considered merely a short-term postenactment difficulty. Preenactment assets will continue to exist for many years and will delay the move to a simplified tax system. Because the simplicity of consumption-based taxes is a major source of their appeal, transition deserves a close look. Otherwise, members of Congress and taxpayers affected by transition rules may be in for a big surprise.

Effective dates in a new law are important in evaluating how taxpayers will respond and thus the need for and design of transition relief. At the point that a wealth tax is understood and seriously anticipated, people may be expected to react, for example, by increasing consumption.[55] Other responses may be more devious. If taxpayers knew that the USA tax would take effect a year hence, they would be well advised to withdraw assets from bank accounts and liquidate other assets that have little or no accrued gain and redeposit or reinvest the proceeds following enactment.[56]

LIKELY LEGISLATIVE RESPONSE. Officials have recently displayed a healthy appreciation of these matters. Former Assistant Treasury Secretary Leslie Samuels has stated that the treatment of existing capital is the most significant issue in converting from an income tax to a consumption tax and has indicated the possible need to provide transition relief.[57] Kenneth J. Kies, chief of staff of the Joint Committee on Taxation, observed, "You really have to think about whether you're going to create significant generational inequities for people who have lived their entire lives under an income tax based system by putting them all on a consumption based system right before retirement."[58] In contrast, Ernest Christian, a designer of the USA tax, expressed the view that "exempting the earnings on new saving is one thing, but exempting the earnings on

---

tax is an overstatement. To the extent these analyses are correct, the effect of the transition relief can be expected to be regressive. Samuels (1995, p. 25); Bradford (1995, pp. 10–13); Grubert and Newlon (1995, p. 4). But also see Graetz (1979, p. 1655) and chapter 9 by Don Fullerton and Diane Lim Rogers in this volume.

54. Graetz (1979, p. 1655).
55. Bradford (1995, p. 37).
56. Gale, "Building a Better Tax System," p. 785.
57. Samuels (1995, pp. 25, 33).
58. Bureau of National Affairs (1995, p. G-5).

all existing capital is quite another."[59] This stance may be strategically appropriate from one of the principal architects of the USA tax, but it is neither wise policy nor sound politics. Indeed, the crafters of the USA tax seem to have acknowledged this by including some transition relief for preenactment basis as part of their individual-level tax.

It is difficult to believe that members of Congress would agree on some theoretical ground to expunge preenactment basis in assets. Therefore, although it is interesting to consider a cold turkey transition, such a development will be impossible. Thus, attention should turn to alternative relief measures and their costs.

FORMS OF TRANSITION RELIEF. Relief from a transition tax on wealth could take any one of many forms.[60] It could be asset specific, by means of an immediate deduction for preenactment basis or a system of depreciation or amortization. It could be taxpayer specific, compensating particularly affected taxpayers by providing them with some form of consumption-tax exemption or direct payments, possibly through the social security system.[61] And, at least theoretically, the new system could be phased in and run along with the present system for awhile.

The USA tax provides individuals with transition relief for preenactment basis.[62] Taxpayers with no more than $50,000 in basis in "qualified savings assets" would be entitled to an elective "transition-basis deduction" that could be amortized over three years.[63] Taxpayers who do not elect the transition-basis deduction or who own more than $50,000 in qualified savings assets may not amortize their basis but may reduce otherwise "taxable withdrawals" of previously saved income by preenactment basis.[64] Under this rule, basis would reduce tax liability only in a year in which a taxpayer is a net dissaver. If taxpayers were to sell investment assets and reinvest the sales proceeds in a year in which they

---

59. Christian, "Good Intentions," p. 1044.

60. Aaron and Galper (1986, pp. 99–101); Bradford (1995, p. 33); Graetz (1979, p. 1658); Christian and Schutzer, "Unlimited Savings Allowance (USA) Tax System," pp. 1566–68; and Kaplow, "Recovery of Pre-Enactment Basis under a Consumption Tax," p. 1110).

61. Henry J. Aaron and Harvey Galper, "Reforming the Federal Tax System," *Tax Notes*, vol. 24, 1984, pp. 285, 293; and Kotlikoff (1995, pp. 110–54).

62. As I later describe more fully, relief also is provided as part of the business-level tax.

63. S. 722, sec. 12. See also Christian and Schutzer, "Unlimited Savings Allowance (USA) Tax System," p. 1515.

64. S. 722, secs. 1(c), 1(e), and 54.

consume current earnings (wages, for example), taxable income in that year would not be reduced by preenactment basis.

To provide net consumers (net dissavers) more favorable transition relief than net savers is a curious policy result that invites planning designed to accelerate the use of otherwise deferred basis.[65] For example, by planning net dissaving and net saving in alternate years, a taxpayer might be able to ensure the relatively current use of transition basis even though total consumption over the period would be the same as if the saving and consumption occurred equally in each year.[66] This would be a wonderful world for creative tax lawyers. For this reason, I would be surprised if the USA tax transition mechanism survived the legislative process in its proposed form.

To this point, I have referred only to the USA tax because of the relevance of tax basis in the calculation of gain on saving assets. The basis issue does not arise for the flat tax at the individual level because gain on the sale or disposition of investment assets is not a component of individual taxable income.[67] But it does arise at the business level, a subject I address later. This difference is politically significant. Those who support transition relief for existing capital will find it much easier to focus policymakers on the proposed elimination of tax basis at the individual level than to explain and quantify the issue of existing capital at the business level under the flat tax.

My final comment on the wealth tax is a prediction. Enacting any form of consumption tax that includes gain on the sale or disposition of a capital asset without providing some form of transition relief for the preenactment basis of investment assets will be impossible. Although existing capital would be subject to a one-time tax under a retail sales tax, tax basis would be irrelevant and transition relief would therefore be much less certain. A deferred basis-recovery system would be costly, resulting in increased tax rates, and would be complex.

---

65. For discussions of the USA unlimited savings account, including operation of the transition rule, see Kaplow (1986), Ginsburg (1995, pp. 585, 596–97), and Alvin C. Warren, "The Proposal for an 'Unlimited Savings Allowance,'" *Tax Notes*, vol. 68, August 28, 1995, pp. 1103–08.

66. See Kaplow, "Recovery of Pre-Enactment Basis," p. 1111, n. 5.

67. H.R. 2060, sec. 1(b).

Preenactment Basis: Depreciation and Inventory

By far the most significant transition issue for business taxes under both the flat tax and the USA tax concerns preenactment basis. The flat tax provides no transition relief for preenactment basis or inventory. Robert Hall and Alvin Rabushka justify this position not on tax policy grounds, but rather as the way to facilitate the transition from a complicated and costly income tax system to a simple, efficient tax.[68] The USA tax, however, does include some transition relief.

THE "PROBLEM." Consider what could happen under both the flat tax and the USA tax.[69] A retail store has a $10,000 preenactment inventory that is sold immediately after the new law passes. The sales proceeds are includable in income.[70] Without transition provisions, no deduction for the preenactment inventory cost will be allowed. A one-time tax on existing capital will result.[71]

A similar situation arises with respect to the undepreciated value of equipment and structures used up in production or sales. Without transition relief the difference between the nominal taxation of the return on an old asset and the return on an asset acquired following enactment of the new law is stark. A business that owns assets acquired before the new law takes effect will have no opportunity to recover the undepreciated basis remaining on the effective date of the new law. Businesses that purchase assets following enactment will receive an immediate deduction for their capital investments. Two theories, if valid, might support a conclusion that no transition relief is appropriate.[72] First, a general value-added tax may lead to increased prices. If it does, the burden of any additional tax attributable to the disappearance of preenactment basis in business assets will be borne by consumers, not the owners of the business. Neither businesses nor their owners deserve any transition relief. Second, if one accepts the contention that expensing under a VAT permits the purchaser of inputs that are to be used in a trade or business to recoup the value-added tax embedded in the price of the purchased

---

68. Hall and Rabushka (1995b, p. 46).

69. S. 722, secs. 204(a)(1) and 205; and H.R. 2060, sec. 102(a) (proposed sec. 11(d)(1)(A) and (2)).

70. S. 722, sec. 203(A); and H.R. 2060, sec. 102 (proposed sec. 11(c)(1) and (2)).

71. See Bradford (1995, p. 20).

72. I particularly appreciate John Buckley's patience in guiding me through this analysis.

inputs, no transition relief is deserved because the price of preenactment assets did not include an embedded VAT. Recovery of preenactment basis is unnecessary to place old and new assets on the same footing.

Although these theories may be valid, they also are vulnerable. Not all analysts agree with the premise of the first argument that the incidence of a VAT is on the consumer. The staff of the Joint Committee on Taxation, for example, suggested that whether a consumption tax causes price increases or wage or profit decreases depends on monetary policy and cannot be predicted on the basis of economic theory.[73] Even those who accept the argument that consumers bear a value-added tax through increased prices should acknowledge that neither the flat tax nor the business component of the USA tax is exactly comparable.[74]

The second argument, which I find particularly interesting, assumes that expensing is a necessary component of a subtraction-method VAT solely to enable the business to recover the VAT embedded in the price of inputs. However, it also is frequently pointed out that a principal feature of all consumption taxes, including value-added taxes, is that the routine return on capital is exempt from tax. The ability to fully deduct the cost of inputs, including capital costs, in the year of acquisition under a subtraction-method VAT provides the business taxpayer with the desired capital income exemption. Viewed from the standpoint of the taxation of a future stream of income, it would appear that even though preenactment assets did not bear a value-added tax, owners of these assets will be treated less favorably than owners of postenactment assets if they are not entitled to offset the preenactment cost in calculating postenactment tax liability.

Because a business may expense the cost of postenactment inputs under a subtraction-method VAT, owners of preenactment assets are not likely to concede that the burden of the business-level tax necessarily falls solely on consumers and not on the owners of capital.[75] Nor are advocates of transition relief likely to agree that a present-value income exemption accorded the owner of newly acquired capital is fully offset because preenactment assets did not bear a VAT at the time of acquisition.

73. U.S. Congress, Joint Committee on Taxation (1993, pp. 48–54).

74. Jane G. Gravelle, "The Flat Tax and Other Proposals: Who Will Bear the Tax Burden?" *Tax Notes*, vol. 69, December 18, 1995, pp. 1517–27.

75. Indeed, if price levels increase, owners of capital in the form of fixed-income securities may be expected to suffer a windfall loss caused by the overall price increases.

MAGNITUDE. The amount of existing basis that may be the subject of business-level transition relief is very large. The Treasury Department estimates the existence of $3 trillion of undepreciated-cost basis.[76] For taxable year 1992, depreciation and amortization deductions for all corporations with net income totaled slightly over $287 billion.[77] At the current 35 percent corporation income tax rate, the tax effect of a single year's deduction would equal the total 1992 corporation income tax receipts (after credits), and this calculation does not take the basis of inventory into account. Even at the 19 percent rate proposed for the flat tax, the annual revenue cost of allowing continued depreciation deductions at the 1992 level would exceed $54 billion.

If tax receipts under any new law must equal those of present law, transition relief for the preenactment basis of business assets will have a significant influence on the new law's tax rates. Analysts have suggested that the flat tax rate would have to be increased 1 to 4 percentage points (to 23 percent) to maintain revenue neutrality.[78] One report alleges that transition relief contained in the USA tax accounts for as much as one-quarter of the tax rate necessary to maintain revenue.[79] Therefore the need for and design of transition relief for preenactment business assets significantly affects the rates of a proposed tax plan.

PROGNOSIS. I do not think it is particularly difficult to predict the likely congressional reaction to the existing basis problem. A *Fortune* article stated, "Were Washington to disallow deductions [for preenactment basis], every CEO-laden corporate jet in America would commence strafing Capitol Hill."[80] We should expect near unanimity that it will be necessary to provide some form of transition relief. First, businesses will

---

76. Louis Lyons, "The Populism of Tax Reform Is Leaving Business Behind," *Tax Notes*, vol. 70, March 11, 1996, pp. 1436, 1437.

77. Internal Revenue Service (1995, p. 65).

78. Hall and Rabushka (1995a, pp. 19–20) refer to 1992 personal and corporate depreciation deductions totaling $597 billion, with a revenue cost of $209 billion at an assumed 34 percent rate and $108 billion at an assumed 19 percent rate. They suggest that the 20.1 percent rate could be reduced after five years. I suspect that the calculation of the 20.1 percent rate did not include the revenue cost of allowing recovery of preenactment inventory costs. The 4 percentage point estimate comes from Brinner, Lasky, and Wyss (1995, p. 12).

79. Lee A. Sheppard, "Consumption Tax Debunking at Tax Foundation Center," *Tax Notes*, vol. 69, November 27, 1995, p. 1072.

80. Richman (1995, pp. 36, 44).

be able to point to the loss of tax basis.[81] Second, questions relating to tax incidence assumptions will not be satisfactorily resolved. Third, the disparity between the nominal taxation of income from pre- and post-enactment assets will likely be considered unacceptable. Although action of some kind is likely, there is no comparable historical precedent.[82] General assertions regarding the desirability of transition relief are easy, but revenue constraints will narrow transition relief options.

VALUE AS THE MEASURING ROD. The accepted view appears to be that a taxpayer is not entitled to transition relief for the value of an asset already deducted under the income tax. Indeed, Shounak Sarkar and George Zodrow maintain that if these assets were all given immediate consumption-tax treatment—through a deduction for existing basis, for example—some taxpayers would receive windfall gains because not all assets are subject to comprehensive income taxation under current law.[83]

This position is questionable. Even if the basis of a preenactment asset has been fully recovered under the income tax, such recovery may not be economically equivalent to a deduction for the cost of the asset under the new consumption tax. To the extent it is not, the return on the asset under a newly effective consumption tax would be subject to future tax, whereas the present-value routine return on a postenactment asset will not be subject to tax. Of course, if an asset that is fully depreciated under current law is still producing income, perhaps previous depreciation allowances have been too generous. But although this might be characterized as a defect under present law, it has little to do with the prospective taxation of income from these assets following a change in the law.

Consideration of this issue requires isolation of two transition effects: the effect of the old law on the value of preexisting assets and the effect of the new on the asset's value. Dealing only with unrecovered preenact-

---

81. Toder (1995, p. 2014) stated, "Denying deductions for pre-enactment basis means that income from these assets would be overtaxed. The windfall loss will place them at a competitive disadvantage." Christian and Schutzer (1995, p. 1534) wrote that businesses must be permitted to retain and recover the preenactment basis. Peter Passell reports that Doug Koopman, a member of Congressman Armey's staff stated that "we still have to work this out." See "Spending It," p. 7. Hall and Rabushka (1995a, b) acknowledge the problem of lost deductions under the flat tax.

82. The shift to a greatly accelerated depreciation system by the Economic Recovery Tax Act of 1981 was not accompanied by any relief for pre-ERTA assets, even though their owners suffered a windfall loss. (Of course, these owners did not lose basis, as would be the case under the flat tax as proposed.) Thus a more thorough examination of historical precedents would be worthwhile.

83. Sarkar and Zodrow (1993, p. 369).

ment cost is not a complete answer to transition issues that concern existing capital.[84]

VALUE VERSUS BASIS. A direct comparison of two assets with the same purchase price, one acquired immediately before enactment and one immediately after, reveals the size of the transition problem. If the tax treatment of these assets differs and one seeks the same treatment of the preenactment asset and the postenactment asset, the transition rule should permit purchasers of preenactment assets to expense their cost just as they could do with the cost of the postenactment asset. If this analysis is correct, transition relief should focus on the fair market value of the preenactment asset when the new law is passed, not on the historic tax basis of the asset, which may exceed or be less than date-of-enactment value.

TRANSITION LIMITED TO RECOVERY OF PREENACTMENT BASIS. If transition relief were limited to unrecovered basis, the new law would allow an immediate postenactment deduction for the undepreciated cost of old assets or for their value at the date of enactment.[85] Deferred deductions under a depreciation or amortization system would moderate but not eliminate the disparity in the taxation of the return on old and new assets.[86] Payment of interest on the unrecovered basis would eliminate the disparity on a present-value basis, but would not correct the disparity in cash flow.

Ernest Christian and George Schutzer conclude that if preenactment basis were immediately expensed, the USA business tax would raise no revenue in that year.[87] They realistically label the "immediate postenactment deduction" option as unacceptable on revenue grounds. Allowing a deduction at sale equal to the present value of the basis in the year of enactment is the economic equivalent of an immediate deduction, but it would reduce government revenue less in the short run.[88] If the asset were sold immediately after enactment, the taxpayer would receive a full basis

---

84. Bradford (1986, p. 320) suggests the possibility of an initial wealth loss for the preenactment asset, but it is not clear if he means to limit his statement to old assets with remaining, undepreciated basis.

85. Bradford (1995, p. 33); Graetz (1979, p. 1655).

86. Bradford (1995, p. 35). The statement assumes that the deferred deduction is not accompanied by an interest payment or other payment to compensate for the deferral.

87. Christian and Schutzer, "Unlimited Savings Allowance (USA) Tax System," p. 1534.

88. Aaron and Galper (1986, p. 100).

deduction. If the asset were sold in the future, the date-of-enactment basis would be indexed.

This method of responding to the revenue implications of an immediate postenactment deduction has some attractions, but it would probably be regarded as unacceptable. First, the cash-flow benefits to the government are mirrored by the cash-flow disadvantages to affected taxpayers, particularly those with long-lived assets, some of which will remain in use indefinitely.[89] Second, it would place considerable pressure on businesses to sell their old assets immediately. If they did so, the revenue advantage would be lost. If they did not, their inaction likely would be attributable to the enactment of objectionable antichurning rules. It also is likely that indexing would be criticized as being arbitrary, inherently inaccurate, and complex.

It is much more likely that some form of postenactment depreciation system would be adopted. Inevitably, any approach will make the new law more complex for a long time, probably more than the five years suggested by Robert Hall and Alvin Rabushka.[90] During this period, business taxpayers would be required to maintain separate records and methods of accounting for pre- and postenactment assets.

Designing a new depreciation system will be constrained only by imagination and revenue. The easiest approach might be to permit recovery of the cost of old assets under the preenactment income tax rules. Hall and Rabushka suggest this approach and propose to offset the revenue loss by limiting the taxpayer's postenactment expensing deductions, for example, to 50 percent.[91]

The USA tax proposes a "transition basis deduction."[92] A preenactment asset would be assigned to a new depreciable class, based on whether the asset was depreciable or amortizable under the income tax and, if so, the remaining recovery period as of the date of enactment. If the asset were depreciable and had a remaining recovery period of less than fifteen years, the unrecovered cost would be amortizable over ten years. If the remaining recovery period were fifteen years or more, the amortizable period would be thirty years. If the asset were nondeprecia-

---

89. I recognize that economists generally disregard analyses based on cash flow, but cash is a finite asset in every business. Unlike a computer model, the real world requires that taxpayers come up with the cash necessary to satisfy a tax liability, either by borrowing or diverting funds intended for some other purpose.

90. Hall and Rabushka (1995a, p. 20).

91. Hall and Rabushka (1995b, p. 46).

92. S. 722, secs. 290 et seq.

ble, the amortizable period would be forty years. Unrecovered inventory costs would be amortizable over three years.

Recognition in the USA tax of the importance of transition is very much preferable to the head-in-the-sand approach of the introduced version of the flat tax. The transition basis deduction is a constructive option if transition is to be accomplished by means of a depreciation system. However, the approach of the USA tax itself is arbitrary and would create disparities among preenactment assets. Why, for example, should inventory cost be recoverable over three years rather than one or two? Why should an asset with a remaining recovery period of fifteen years and one with a remaining recovery period of two years be placed on the same fifteen-year schedule for recovery of remaining basis?

Any system of deferred cost recovery will be imperfect and complex. Imperfections result from the inability to reconcile present-value cost and cash flow and from the disparities that will arise because of different depreciable lives or recovery periods.[93] The USA tax illustrates the arbitrariness of any transition relief and portends deep disagreements within the business community.

Changes in corporate and individual behavior will be inevitable, no matter what transition rules are adopted. If no immediate postenactment deduction is provided, for example, and if the proposed transition cost recovery system backloads relief, such as in the proposal by Henry Aaron and Harvey Galper described earlier, businesses may be expected to defer preenactment investment in new assets and will be encouraged to churn existing assets following enactment.[94]

Interest on Preenactment Indebtedness

Consistent with traditional consumption-tax theory, neither the USA tax nor the flat tax would permit the postenactment deductibility of interest. Both reflect a cold-turkey transition to the new law, with no relief for interest expense on preenactment debt.

BUSINESS INTEREST. Whether as a theoretical matter transition relief is needed will depend on the postenactment macroeconomic responses to

93. Bradford (1995, p. 35) points out that owners of short-lived assets are more fully protected than owners of those with longer lives.
94. Bradford (1995, p. 37); Auerbach and Kotlikoff (1987, p. 83). Kaplow (1995, p. 1112) argues that allowing basis recovery only when old assets are sold would encourage a postenactment one-time sale of all assets. Also see U.S. Department of the Treasury (1977, p. 188).

the legislation, in particular changes in price levels.[95] There is precedent for less than full relief.[96] Nonetheless, it is improbable that either tax proposal could be enacted without permitting some, possibly even generous, postenactment deductibility for interest expense on preexisting debt.[97]

Providing relief for interest payments might seem relatively easy and inexpensive. In fact, in discussing a transition option for home mortgage interest, Hall and Rabushka state, "If all deductions are completely matched with taxation on the other side, then a transition provision to protect existing interest deductions would have no effect on revenue."[98] In the real world, however, this conclusion is inaccurate. Interest income and expense will not be completely matched, even in the case of home mortgage interest.

The staff of the Joint Committee on Taxation determined that as of 1987 approximately 38 percent of the $1.2 trillion of corporate bonds was held by foreigners, private pension plans, and state and local government retirement funds.[99] (The data exclude trade debt, mortgages, and bank debt.) Unless Congress is prepared to tax these currently exempt holders, transition treatment cannot be symmetrical. And if Congress subjects interest income on existing debt to continued taxation, this debt likely will migrate to tax-exempt holders, thereby increasing the percentage of existing debt they own.

The lack of symmetry means that if transition relief is accorded existing debt, the government will sustain large revenue losses.[100] To the extent that preenactment lenders are allowed the benefit of the new law's exclusion from the tax on interest income, they will enjoy a windfall.[101]

---

95. Bradford (1995, p. 32).

96. A five-year phase-out of the deduction for personal interest was provided in sec. 511 of the Tax Reform Act of 1986. See Internal Revenue Code, secs. 163(h)(5) and (d)(6)(B).

97. Indeed, Bradford (1995, pp. 35–36) suggests that the commitment to pay fixed interest on preexisting debt would seem to be a particularly prominent candidate for special transition treatment. See also Grubert and Newlon (1995 p. 7) for a projection of an increase in the tax burden of debt-financed businesses.

98. Hall and Rabushka (1995b, p. 79). They also suggest a transition scheme designed to prompt the renegotiation of preenactment debt.

99. U.S. Congress, Joint Committee on Taxation (1989, table 1E).

100. IRS Statistics of Income for 1992 indicate that corporations with net income claimed interest expense deductions of approximately $114 billion on indebtedness with a term of one year or more. At a tax rate of 35 percent, the tax effect of these deductions represents approximately 40 percent of total 1992 corporate tax receipts.

101. U.S. Congress, Joint Committee on Taxation (1995a, p. 35). In addition to the

HOME MORTGAGE INTEREST. The USA tax preserves part of the home mortgage interest deduction. Interest on home equity loans would cease to be deductible.[102] Accordingly, the extent of transition relief for these items will be an issue. The flat tax repeals the home mortgage deduction and provides no relief.

Mortgagees may be expected to resist repeal of their future interest deductions. As Dennis Capozza, Richard Green, and Patric Hendershott point out in chapter 5 in this volume, elimination of the mortgage interest deduction, combined with repeal of the property tax deduction, will lower housing prices, although the duration and extent of the effect are subject to debate.[103] Second, loss of the deduction will affect the cash flow of millions of taxpayers. Nearly 27 million individual returns claimed $196.9 billion in mortgage interest deductions in 1992.[104] The Congressional Budget Office estimated that elimination of the mortgage interest deduction in the context of the current income tax would have raised the taxes of 28 million homeowners in 1996 by an average of $2,100.[105]

The home mortgage interest deduction has powerful, well-organized advocates in and out of Congress. I recall that within twenty-four hours after President Reagan appeared before a homebuilders group in 1984 on a campaign trip through the Southwest, he removed from future consideration any proposal to curb the home mortgage interest deduction.

The proposed elimination of the deduction for home mortgage interest will be one of the most hotly contested issues in the upcoming tax reform

---

direct effect of interest transition, there likely will be other transition anomalies resulting from the absence of an explicit deduction for preenactment debt. Warren, "Proposal for an 'Unlimited Saving Allowance,'" pp. 1107–08).

102. Section 163(h)(3)(A)(ii); and Christian and Schutzer (1995, p. 1523).

103. Grubert and Newlon (1995, p. 26) assume a shift of capital from housing but do not quantify it. Hall (1995b, pp. 223–38) projects a small, brief negative impact on housing prices and both a short- and long-run impact on land prices. Brinner, Lasky, and Wyss (1995) estimate that under a flat tax, the aggregate value of houses would decrease 15 percent (based on the capitalized value of the lost mortgage interest and state and local property tax deductions) and housing starts would drop 22.3 percent in the first year but would again begin to increase in 2000. For responses and critiques, see Schaefer (1995); and Bruce R. Bartlett, "Will the Flat Tax KO Housing?" *Wall Street Journal*, August 2, 1995, p. A10.

104. Internal Revenue Service (1995b, p. 75).

105. U.S. Congressional Budget Office (1995, p. 343). Although it is not clear from the text, this estimate likely was made by the staff of the Joint Committee on Taxation. The DRI/McGraw-Hill study projects that if 90 percent of home mortgage interest remained deductible, the 1996 tax rate under the flat tax would have to be 2 percentage points higher to retain revenue neutrality. See Brinner, Lasky, and Wyss (1995, p. 12).

debate. In the extremely unlikely event that the deduction is repealed, threats of a great many defaults (perhaps as many as 600,000 foreclosures a year and heavy losses for at least five years) will fuel the demand for such relief.[106] Relief will be based on claims of reliance and will likely involve grandfathering existing debt.

Other Transition Issues

A large number of other provisions of fundamental tax reform would trigger calls for transition relief.

STATE AND LOCAL BOND INTEREST EXCLUSION. The USA tax would continue to exclude interest on qualifying state and local bonds.[107] Coupled with a savings deduction on the purchase of these bonds, this provision is intended to maintain the preference of the present law.[108] The flat tax, however, would repeal the present exclusion. Is providing transition relief to existing bondholders under the flat tax necessary and appropriate?

The staff of the Joint Committee on Taxation speculates that taxpayers who purchased tax-exempt state and local bonds before enactment of a consumption-based tax would find the value of the bonds "sharply reduced" if the interest from them suddenly became subject to tax.[109] And another observer has stated, "State and local officials are an important and potentially powerful interest group whose concerns must be considered as tax reform unfolds."[110] If this view is widely held, transition relief will be provided.[111]

106. Bureau of National Affairs (1996, p. G-1).

107. S. 722, secs. 4(a)(4) and 91. Interest income otherwise is taxable under the USA tax individual tax. S. 722, secs. (3(a)(3)(A) and (4). But see Warren, "Proposal for an 'Unlimited Savings Allowance,'" p. 1107, example B, for the suggestion that because of the way the unlimited savings allowance operates, under certain circumstances tax-exempt income will nevertheless effectively be subject to tax.

108. Christian and Schutzer, "Unlimited Savings Allowance (USA) Tax System," p. 1564.

109. U.S. Congress, Joint Committee on Taxation (1995a, p. 27). See also Samuels (1995, p. 24), who commented that "existing holders of long-term municipal bonds would suffer a capital loss."

110. Friedlander (1995, p. 4).

111. State and local governments might benefit from the ability to advantageously redeem preenactment obligations that have decreased in value because they lacked transition relief. Nevertheless, I would expect that in addition to caring about prospective policy, these governments also will stand with their existing investors.

The form of relief will be very important, because the attempt to prevent windfall losses would create windfall gains. For example, if all currently exempt bonds are grandfathered, their value will increase as they mature and the supply dwindles.[112] Of course, a simple grandfathering would not be sufficient if all postenactment interest is excluded from income.[113]

ALIMONY AGREEMENTS. The allowance of an alimony deduction is merely one example of dozens of potential reliance-based transition issues. Under current law the person who pays alimony receives a deduction, and the recipient must include it as income.[114] The USA tax preserves the current system.[115] The flat tax provides no deduction for the payer and does not tax the recipient.

Myriad divorce and separation agreements have been negotiated in specific reliance on present law. The flat tax would impose a windfall loss on payers and provide recipients with a windfall gain. This is a classic invitation for reliance-based claims for transition relief.[116] Although payers may also benefit from any rate reduction, transition relief, probably grandfathered, will be necessary, complemented by the inclusion of the deducted amount in income of the recipient, as under present law.

RETIREMENT ASSETS. The postenactment tax treatment of current pension plan assets is yet another prominent matter of contention. Because these assets have received consumption-tax treatment under current law, tax reform proposals have treated them more favorably than pre-enactment after-tax savings. Accordingly, it has been suggested that pension benefits should reduce transition relief otherwise made available to owners of existing capital.[117]

---

112. U.S. Department of the Treasury (1977, p. 190).
113. See Graetz (1979, p. 1652).
114. Internal Revenue Code, secs. 71 and 215.
115. S. 722, sec. 5.
116. The reason for the reliance, however, is somewhat different in the case of the alimony deduction in the sense that it is a zero-sum game from the government's perspective. If rate differentials are ignored, any payments that are deducted by the payer are includable in income by the recipient. Thus, a payer who objects to the loss of a deduction will do so not because of a tax benefit enacted to induce certain behavior in exchange for a reduction in tax revenues, but because the Internal Revenue Code has adopted a taxing scheme for alimony payments that is intended to provide the kind of certainty on which parties may rely in reaching private agreements.
117. Institute for Fiscal Studies (1978, p. 190).

SOCIAL SECURITY BENEFITS. Under the flat tax, social security benefits would be nontaxable and, symmetrically, contributions would be non-deductible. Under current law, employee payroll taxes are not deductible, payroll taxes of the self-employed are partially deductible, and employers' payroll taxes paid on behalf of their employees are fully deductible. Part of social security benefits are included in personal income subject to tax. Perhaps the benefits should remain at least partly subject to tax following a change in the law, although the transition period would be long.

CAPITAL GAINS. Under the flat tax, capital gains, whenever accrued, would not be taxed when recognized. To put unrealized capital gains on a par with previously taxed capital, the unrealized gains should probably be taxed as of the date of enactment of the new law.[118] But no legislative effort to do so is likely to succeed.

PREENACTMENT TAX ATTRIBUTES. Net operating losses, foreign tax credits, alternative minimum tax credits, and suspended passive-activity loss credits are important tax assets. For publicly held businesses the financial accounting effects of eliminating certain of these tax assets could make these transition issues as important as any.[119] For example, under the flat tax, corporations with net operating losses would not be entitled to use them in computing postenactment taxable income. Because a net operating loss constitutes a prepaid tax asset for purposes of financial accounting, it is reflected in corporate net worth. Loss of preenactment net operating losses would reduce corporate assets and net worth. The same would be true of unused alternative minimum tax and foreign tax credits.[120]

The elimination of accumulated deferred tax liabilities in one year would offset corporate profits in that year.[121] Of course, a reduction in the corporate tax rate would have an offsetting positive effect on financial statements as deferred tax reserves were restored to income. The effect

118. U.S. Department of the Treasury (1977, p. 206). See also Zodrow (1987, p. 130) and U.S. Congress, Joint Committee on Taxation (1995a, p. 90).

119. Sullivan (1995, p. 207ff). See also Hal Gann and Roy Strowd, "Deferred Tax Accounting for Tax Reform Proposals," *Tax Notes*, vol. 68, July 3, 1995, pp. 111–16.

120. Under the flat tax the foreign tax credit is repealed, which is consistent with the adoption of a territorial system, and no provision for unused foreign tax credits is provided. Expiration of these credit carryovers could be expected to strongly affect the balance sheets of U.S.-based multinational corporations.

121. Sullivan (1995, p. 211).

of the loss of tax credits on cash flow and reported accounting profits would probably make some form of transition relief necessary. The revenue effect and the form of relief will be important considerations.

Conclusion

In a recent comment on the likely transition effects of a move to a consumption-based tax system, Representative Bill Archer, chair of the House Ways and Means Committee, was reported to have said that "three top economists" had told him that implementation of a consumption tax—presumably as a replacement for the present income tax—could be accomplished "in one fell swoop . . . without any major economic dislocation."[122] If the report is accurate and if such advice was given, it is unfortunate and irresponsible.

The staff of the Joint Committee on Taxation has expressed the view that "if a comprehensive tax reform proposal were enacted and made effective overnight, taxpayers would experience pronounced swings in after-tax income, wealth, and cash flow."[123] Senator Sam Nunn, a sponsor of the USA tax, recently stated, "Proposals for fundamental tax reform that do not address transition are not simple—they are simplistic because they are not complete. They have avoided the hard questions and the hard work which are essential for meaningful tax reform."[124] My experience at the Treasury Department with the Tax Reform Act of 1986 convinces me that we cannot begin to imagine the extent to which transition issues will arise in connection with any legislative consideration of any fundamental reform of the tax system, whether an income-based or consumption-based proposal. I am equally convinced that if any of these proposals proceeds to the legislative drafting stage, those charged with considering transition will have to do so without the benefit of much data or empirically supported analysis.

Some might try to derail current tax reform efforts by demonstrating that transition effects will be so large and efforts to craft acceptable transition rules so difficult that adopting a replacement system of taxation should be abandoned. Just as analysts should not trivialize potential transition effects, a serious discussion of transition issues should not have

---

122. Herzfeld (1996, p. G-3).
123. U.S. Congress, Joint Committee on Taxation (1995a, p. 27).
124. *Congressional Record*, daily ed., April 15, 1996, S2372.

as its purpose the destruction of what otherwise might be considered desirable tax reform. Rather, deliberations regarding changes in tax law will best be served by a careful analysis of inevitable transition effects.

Comment by Robert Hall

It is an encouraging sign that the issues surrounding the transition to a consumption tax have gained the attention of a leading practitioner of tax law. My own work, especially my joint book with Alvin Rabushka, gives only a sketchy treatment of the transition.[125] If consumption taxation is becoming more than a theoretical ideal, we must consider the transition issues seriously.

As Ronald A. Pearlman makes clear, the central issue of the transition to a consumption tax is the potential second taxation of wealth accumulated from after-tax income during an earlier income-tax regime. To the tax practitioner, this is the issue of lost basis. Taxpayers can lose basis in many circumstances, depending on the design of the consumption tax. For example, under an income tax, a taxpayer who recently purchased stock out of after-tax income (that is, not within a tax-sheltered vehicle such as a 401k) can sell the stock and consume the proceeds without incurring further tax. Under an individual cash-flow consumption tax, the sale would be taxable. Without a special transition provision to exempt assets acquired earlier under an income tax, a consumption tax will impose a second round of taxation on those assets.

The fundamental sources of lost basis are capital goods and claims on foreigners. The big numbers come from the undepreciated part of plant and equipment and from inventories (current tax law gives a deduction for cost of goods sold at the time they are sold). Housing may be another large issue, but not for consumption-tax designs, such as the flat tax, where the tax on housing is prepaid.

A consumption tax is a tax on noncapital income (mostly wages) plus a one-time capital levy. The central issue in the transition is the size of the capital levy. If the transition plan grants an immediate deduction equal to the book value of plant, equipment, and inventories (the most generous reasonable provision), the consumption tax will be close to a pure tax on noncapital income. The capital levy would apply only to the difference between the book and market values of the capital goods. An

125. Hall and Rabushka (1995b).

intermediate approach would be to give an immediate deduction equal to the present value of the deductions that would have been available under the income tax. More aggressive capital levies could be achieved by giving taxpayers smaller deductions.

Pearlman approaches the resolution of the question of the magnitude of the capital levy from a legal perspective primarily, though he also discusses the principles that economists have applied. One legal framework is the law of contracts.[126] If we view the provisions of the existing income tax as a contract, then the removal of deductions is a breach of the contract. Efficient breaches will occur if the breacher—the government—is required to compensate the counterparty—the taxpayer—for the value lost as a result of the breach. This standard legal principle would support the intermediate transition provision of a deduction equal to the present value of the lost future stream of deductions.

Pearlman also discusses the law of promises. The basic legal principle is that a promise becomes binding when the beneficiary relies on it. Hence Pearlman suggests that one criterion for determining if a taxpayer needs to be compensated for a lost deduction is whether the taxpayer relied on the existence of the deduction in making an earlier decision. It seems reasonable to infer reliance on the government's promise of subsequent deductions when firms invest in plant, equipment, and inventories. So the reliance principle would seem to call for transition measures that give firms something to replace lost depreciation and cost-of-goods-sold deductions.

The economic analysis of this issue has two contradictory elements—few economists have a balanced view of the two. The first is that a capital levy that takes taxpayers by complete surprise is an ideal neutral tax. It has no distortionary effects and permits a lower consumption tax rate. Because consumption taxes distort the choice between market and non-market activities, the deadweight burden of the tax system is reduced by imposing a one-time capital levy at the time of tax reform.

The second element starts from the observation that expectations of future capital levies have large deadweight burdens. Investment suffers a disincentive if business suspects that there will be a capital levy in the future. To induce efficient investment, government needs to commit itself credibly not to impose capital levies in the future.[127]

126. See Polinsky (1989).
127. See Fischer (1980).

How can government impose a one-time levy today without creating expectation of future levies? The levy today is the most efficient way to raise revenue, and the levy in the future is the least efficient. This is the central issue in Pearlman's chapter.

Private parties commit themselves through contracts, enforced by a powerful third party, the government. If taxes were a matter of contract between one private party and another, the transition issues would be clear. Cancellation of basis in capital would be a breach, resolved as I discussed earlier, with a cash payment to compensate the loser. The benefit of a strict contractual view of the relation between citizens and government is that contracts block on-the-spot opportunism, for example, exploiting the neutrality of an unexpected capital levy. Thus a long tradition in monetary economics suggests that the citizens should write a contract with the monetary authority to prevent the use of unexpected monetary expansion, which is a temptation because it may have benefits similar to those of an unexpected capital levy.

Pearlman notes that the question of the enforcement of government policies as if they were contracts has been considered by a number of courts recently (see note 22). The creation of government in the first place through contracts that are mutually advantageous is a libertarian dream because it forbids purely redistributional interventions. In a society organized on that view of government, a tax reform that denied previously promised deductions would be unthinkable. The switch to a purely contractual approach to government in the United States today would be less attractive, however, because it would require buying out interest groups that have been the beneficiaries of earlier programs that redistributed in their favor. The contractual approach to reforming agriculture policy, for example, would require an enormous lump sum, raised by distortionary taxes, to buy the nation out from expensive promises that are currently in place.

What transition issues must be considered with respect to the Hall-Rabushka flat tax? First, the flat tax does not raise any issue of stealing basis from taxpayers in the single largest component of national wealth, namely, owner-occupied housing. Proceeds from the sale of a house are not included in taxable cash flows in the proposal. Instead, the tax on the service flow of housing is imposed at the time the house is built, by including the creation of new houses in the business tax and not permitting a deduction for the purchase of a house. There is no retroactive tax on existing houses, so the transition effectively preserves basis by removing the tax. In fact, it goes beyond preserving basis because it eliminates the possibility that taxpayers face today of paying capital gains taxes on the appreciated portion of their house values.[128]

The central transition issue is just as Pearlman identifies: the potential loss of basis in plant, equipment, and inventories. Our basic plan, with a 19 percent tax rate and an exemption level of around $26,000 for a family of four, is revenue-neutral on the assumption that there is no hangover of depreciation and cost-of-goods deductions from the earlier income tax. We do give some illustrations of the tax rate that would be needed to finance that hangover if it were allowed.

The translation of the fundamental issue of lost basis in plant, equipment, and inventories into gains and losses for individuals involves many complexities. I can only sketch some of them here.[129] First, some consumption taxes—the VAT or national sales tax—would raise the price level discontinuously. Thus, upon transition to these taxes, debt holders absorb losses in proportion to the tax rate. The flat tax, however, does not raise the price level, so debt holders do not lose. In all consumption taxes, equity holders suffer the loss of basis. With the flat tax, the effect is magnified for leveraged corporations, because they do not enjoy any diminished real value of their debt.

Second, much wealth in the United States is held in zero-basis form in retirement accounts. Pearlman presumes that there is no special transition issue for this form of wealth. It would be taxed in the same way under income and consumption taxes. Under the transition to Hall-Rabushka, debt held in tax-deferred form enjoys a windfall. Because the price level does not rise, there is no diminution in value at the time of reform. But the taxpayer avoids the tax burden upon liquidation.

Finally, I concur with Pearlman's concern about announcement effects. Under a transition to a consumption tax of any type, between announcement and execution, there is an incentive to accumulate consumption goods and decumulate investment goods. Although the fundamental incentive is the same for all types of consumption taxes, the way the signal reaches decisionmakers is different. For VATs or sales taxes, hoarding of consumption goods would be the natural response to anticipated price increases. For the flat tax, avoidance of investment

---

128. Pearlman's note 37 mentions my remark that housing might be overtaxed after replacement of the existing federal tax system with the flat tax. This is not a transition issue, but a question of harmonizing existing heavy state and local taxation with a federal system extended to include the service value of housing.

129. See Hall (1995).

would be the natural response to the anticipated price decline for capital goods.

In general, in the search for guidance in designing a workable and fair transition, Pearlman has done an admirable job of discussing both the underlying central issue of lost basis and the legal considerations surrounding that issue. By contrast, many public finance economists simply presume that maximum exploitation of the one-time neutral capital levy is the right way to proceed. Though the flat tax looks less attractive once it is combined with a reasonable transition plan, I concede that the factors considered by Pearlman mandate a serious consideration of the transition.

References

Aaron, Henry J., and Harvey Galper. 1985. *Assessing Tax Reform*. Brookings.

Atkinson, Anthony B., and Joseph E. Stiglitz. 1980. *Lectures on Public Economics*. McGraw-Hill.

Auerbach, Alan J., and Laurence J. Kotlikoff. 1987. *Dynamic Fiscal Policy*. Cambridge University Press.

Bradford, David F. 1995. "Consumption Taxes: Some Fundamental Transition Issues." Working Paper 5290. Cambridge, Mass.: National Bureau of Economic Research (October).

———. 1986. *Untangling the Income Tax*. Harvard University Press.

Brinner, Roger E., Mark Lasky, and David Wyss. 1995. "Residential Real Estate Impacts of Flat Tax Legislation." Lexington, Mass.: DRI/McGraw-Hill (May).

Bureau of National Affairs. 1995. "Tax Reform Plans Raise Transition Issues: Possibility of Taxing Pensions, Benefits." *Daily Tax Report*, July 19, p. G-5.

———. 1996. "Loss of Mortgage Interest Break Would 'Flatten' Housing Market, Realtors Say." *Daily Tax Report*, January 23, p. G-1.

Feldstein, Martin. 1976. "On the Theory of Tax Reform." *Journal of Public Economics* 6 (July–August): 77–104.

Fischer, Stanley. 1980. "Dynamic Inconsistency, Cooperation and the Benevolent Dissembling Government." *Journal of Economic Dynamics and Control* 2 (February): 93–107.

Friedlander, George D. 1995. *Municipal Bonds and Tax Reform: Should Investors Be Concerned?* New York: Smith Barney (May).

Fullerton, Don. 1985. "The Consumption Tax versus the Income Tax." In *Real Tax Reform: Replacing the Income Tax*, edited by John H. Makin, 5–13. Washington: American Enterprise Institute.

Ginsburg, Martin D. 1995. "Life under a Personal Consumption Tax: Some Thoughts on Working, Saving, and Consuming in Nunn-Domenici's Tax World." *National Tax Journal* 48 (December 1995): 585–602.

Goode, Richard. 1987. "Disappointed Expectations and Tax Reform." *National Tax Journal* 40 (June): 159–69.

Graetz, Michael J. 1977. "Legal Transitions: The Case of Retroactivity in Income Tax Revision." *University of Pennsylvania Law Review* 126: 47–87.

———. 1979. "Implementing a Progressive Consumption Tax." *Harvard Law Review* 92 (June): 1575–1661.

———. 1985. "Retroactivity Revisited." *Harvard Law Review* 98 (June): 1820–41.

Grubert, Harry, and T. Scott Newlon. 1995. *The International Implications of Consumption Tax Proposals.* U.S. Treasury Department (September).

Hall, Robert E. 1995. "The Effects of Tax Reform on Prices and Asset Values." Paper prepared for "Tax Policy and the Economy," a conference sponsored by the National Bureau of Economic Research, Washington, November 7, 1995, reproduced at 95 *Tax Notes Today* 223–38, an online service of Tax Analysts, available on LEXIS.

Hall, Robert E., and Alvin Rabushka. 1995a. "The Flat Tax: A Simple Progressive Consumption Tax." Paper prepared for "Frontiers of Tax Reform," a conference sponsored by the Hoover Institution, Washington, May 11.

———. 1995b. *The Flat Tax.* 2d ed. Stanford, Calif.: Hoover Institution Press.

Herzfeld, John. 1996. "House Republicans Will Look For Way to Revive Tax 'Extenders,' Archer Says." *Daily Tax Report*, April 23, p. G-3. Bureau of National Affairs.

Institute for Fiscal Studies. 1978. *The Structure and Reform of Direct Taxation.* London: George Allen & Unwin.

Kaplow, Louis. 1986. "An Economic Analysis of Legal Transitions." *Harvard Law Review* 99 (January): 509–617.

Kotlikoff, Laurence J. 1995. "The Economic Argument for Consumption Taxation." Testimony before the House Ways and Means Committee, June 6, 1995, reproduced at 95 *Tax Notes Today* 110–54, an online service of Tax Analysts, available on LEXIS.

Levmore, Saul. 1993. "The Case for Retroactive Taxation." *Journal of Legal Studies* 22 (June): 265–307.

Lodin, Sven-Olov. 1978. *Progressive Expenditure Tax—An Alternative? A Report of the 1972 Government Commission on Taxation.* Stockholm: LiberFörlag.

Logue, Kyle D. 1996. "Tax Transitions, Opportunistic Retroactivity, and the Benefits of Government Precommitment." *Michigan Law Review* 94 (March): 1129–96.

National Marine Manufacturers Association. 1993. *Statement Regarding the Repeal of the 10% Federal Excise Tax on the Price of Boats Costing More Than*

$100,000. Committee Print. House Ways and Means Committee. Government Printing Office (March–April).

Pearlman, Ronald A. 1994. Testimony in Hearings before the Subcommittee on the Constitution of the Senate Judiciary Committee. August 4. 103 Cong. 2 sess.

Penner, Rudolph G. 1994. *Reducing the Tax Burden on Saving*. Washington: Investment Company Institute.

Peter, Laurence J. 1982. *Peter's Almanac*. William Morrow and Co.

Polinsky, A. Mitchell. 1989. *An Introduction to Law and Economics*. Little, Brown.

President's Tax Proposals to the Congress for Fairness, Growth, and Simplicity. 1985. Government Printing Office (May).

Richman, Louis S. 1995. "The Flat Tax; It's Hot, It's Now, It Could Change the Way You Live." *Fortune*, vol. 131 (June 12): 36–46.

Roth, William V., Jr. 1996. Senate Committee on Finance, press release 104–175 (March 29).

Samuels, Leslie B. 1995. Testimony in Hearings before the House Committee on Ways and Means. June 7. 104 Cong. 1 sess. U.S. Treasury Department.

Sarkar, Shounak, and George R. Zodrow. 1993. "Transitional Issues in Moving to a Direct Consumption Tax." *National Tax Journal* 46 (September): 359–76.

Schaefer, Rebecca S. 1995. "Ganging Up Again At 'Gucci Gulch': A Look at the DRI Flat Tax Study." Washington: Citizens for a Sound Economy (August 15).

Shaw, George Bernard. 1944. *Everybody's Political What's What?* Dodd, Mead, and Company.

Sullivan, Martin A. 1995. *Flat Taxes and Consumption Taxes: A Guide to the Debate*. Washington: American Institute of Certified Public Accountants (December).

Toder, Eric. 1995. Testimony before the Senate Budget Committee. February 22. 104 Cong. 1 sess. U.S. Treasury Department.

U.S. Congressional Budget Office. 1995. *Reducing the Deficit: Spending and Revenue Options*.

U.S. Congress, Joint Committee on Taxation. 1987. *General Explanation of the Tax Reform Act of 1986*. Government Printing Office.

———. 1989. *Federal Income Tax Aspects of Corporate Financial Structures*, JCS 1-89. Government Printing Office.

———. 1993. *Methodology and Issues in Measuring Changes in the Distribution of Tax Burdens*. JCS 7-93. Government Printing Office.

———. 1995a. *Discussion of Issues Relating to "Flat" Tax Rate Proposals*, JCS 7-95. Government Printing Office.

———. 1995b. *Description and Analysis of Proposals to Replace the Federal Income Tax*. JCS-18-95. Government Printing Office.

U.S. Department of the Treasury. 1977. *Blueprints for Basic Tax Reform.*

———. 1984. *Tax Reform for Fairness, Simplicity, and Economic Growth: The Treasury Department Report to the President* (November).

U.S. Internal Revenue Service. 1995a. *Statistics of Income 1992 Corporation Income Tax Returns.*

———. 1995b. *Statistics of Income 1992 Individual Income Tax Returns.*

Zodrow, George R. 1987. "Alternative Approaches to Progressive Expenditure Taxation." Reprint 87-3. Rice University, Institute for Policy Analysis.

———. 1988. "The Windfall Recapture Tax: Issues of Theory and Design." *Public Finance Quarterly* 16 (October): 387–424.

PART FIVE

Finance and International Effects

CHAPTER 12

Treatment of Financial Services under Income and Consumption Taxes

David F. Bradford

WhHY ARE financial institutions singled out for special attention in discussions of "fundamental" tax reform? Why not farms? Pharmaceutical manufacturers? State and local governments? Multinational companies? The economic activities of each of these would be profoundly affected by fundamental tax reform. Yet they do not receive special attention. The reason, I believe, is that three of the reforms now widely discussed include a business tax much like a value-added tax. Experts on the value-added tax have long recognized that it is difficult to apply to financial institutions the same tax system applicable to most other companies.

Four plans for restructuring the U.S. tax system have been the focus of discussion: institution of a federal retail sales tax, a value-added tax, a "flat" tax, and the USA (unlimited savings allowance) tax. Representative Bill Archer (Republican of Texas), chairman of the House Committee on Ways and Means, and Senator Richard Lugar (Republican of Indiana) are supporters of a sales tax, although no legislative proposal has yet been introduced. There have been a number of value-added tax proposals, including a highly detailed plan introduced by Representative Samuel Gibbons of Florida, ranking Democrat on the Committee on Ways and Means.[1] Representative Richard Armey (Republican of Texas), is a particularly well-known advocate of a flat tax; others have advanced similar proposals. All are modeled on the flat tax developed by Robert

I thank Richard Goode, Louis Kaplow, Jerome Kurtz, Paul McDaniel, Nils Matson, Peter Merrill, and conference participants. I also thank the John M. Olin Foundation and Princeton University's Woodrow Wilson School for financial support of research on transition and implementation issues. None of these individuals or organizations are responsible for the conclusions I express.
    1. See Gibbons (1993, 1996).

Hall and Alvin Rabushka. Senators Pete Domenici (Republican of New Mexico) and Sam Nunn (Democrat of Georgia) developed and introduced the USA tax in April 1995.[2]

At the heart of all four plans is a tax paid by businesses.[3] A retail sales tax requires businesses to pay tax equal to a percentage of the value of their sales to nonbusiness customers.[4] In the other three plans the business tax is a variant of a consumption-type value-added tax implemented by the subtraction method.[5]

Two features of a value-added tax are responsible for the problem in taxing financial services. First, financial transactions, such as the payment or receipt of interest or dividends or the sale or purchase of securities, are not counted in determining a business's value-added tax liability. Second, although a value-added tax is levied on all business sales, not just sales to nonbusiness customers, in one way or another a business customer gets a rebate of tax paid by its suppliers. Sales from one business to another generate no net revenue to the government because the tax paid by the seller just equals the reduction in tax for the business buyer. Final consumers get no such tax reduction. The net effect, therefore, is an indirect tax on individuals collected from businesses. This indirect measurement fails for some financial services.

The Problem

It is a matter of conventional wisdom that financial services create headaches for consumption-type taxes, which many people equate with value-

2. For useful discussions of current proposals see U.S. Congress, Joint Committee on Taxation (1995) and Arthur Andersen (1995). A detailed description of the USA tax, prepared by Alliance USA (1995), was published as a special supplement, Ernest S. Christian and George J. Schutzer, "USA Tax System: Description and Explanation of the Unlimited Savings Allowance Income Tax System," in *Tax Notes*, vol. 66, March 10, 1995. The actual legislative proposal was reproduced as a special supplement by the Bureau of National Affairs, April 26, 1995.

3. People, not impersonal entities, ultimately bear taxes. *Paid* is thus not the same as *borne*. As the example of the payroll tax paid by businesses illustrates, having companies pay taxes is simply a way to implement collection. It does not in itself determine the ultimate burden of a tax.

4. Rules on which sales count as retail sales vary greatly in actual versions of this tax.

5. *Subtraction method* means that tax is based on total sales and purchases, less total purchases from other businesses, rather than being built up from taxes on each transaction separately. Most of the world's value-added taxes are based on the invoice-and-credit method, under which tax is levied on each sale and a credit is given for documented taxes paid on purchases.

added taxes. It is less widely recognized that the difficulties are not confined to consumption taxes. Hall and Rabushka assert that "banks, insurance companies, and other businesses that bundle services with financial products present a challenge to any tax system."[6] I shall develop this point at some length later. But first, I should state my thesis: it is the visibility of the problem under value-added taxes (whether or not they are consumption taxes, as economists understand this term) that accounts for the attention paid to it. The economically equivalent difficulty shows up in any tax system, but it generally lacks political prominence.

The problem is created by the fact that banks, insurance companies, and other financial institutions receive at least some of their income from the difference between the rate of interest they earn on loans and the rate they pay to depositors and other providers of their funds. But financial transactions are normally not included in the base for determining a company's value-added tax. Value-added tax is not charged on interest received, nor is there any credit or deduction for interest paid. If a financial institution earned all its profits from the spread on financial transactions and had any deductible or creditable expenses, the business would be in a perennial *negative* tax position. If the tax were "refundable," even a profitable financial institution might forever qualify for a net refund. And if a company had enough ordinary sales to pay some tax or were consolidated with a company that had a positive tax liability, it would be obvious that financial institutions were paying less tax than apparently similar nonfinancial enterprises.

It may not be immediately obvious that the problem has nothing *inherently* to do with consumption rather than income as the basis for taxation. Consumption taxes differ from income taxes in the treatment of investment. Investment outlays such as the purchase of equipment or accumulation of inventory are deducted immediately under consumption taxes. Under an income tax they are deducted as income is earned. Current proposals are consumption taxes because investment expenditures are written off at once rather than depreciated over time.

Value-added taxes would become income taxes rather than consumption taxes if the costs of investment were deducted as investments depreciate instead of expensed. From this perspective, one can see that a financial institution can run a perennial loss for tax purposes as readily under an income-type value-added tax as under a consumption-type. The

---

6. Hall and Rabushka (1995, p. 73). For an excellent overview of the problems of taxing financial institutions, see Neubig (1984).

method of collecting the tax at the business level is what causes the problem. The problem exists under other approaches, but it is invisible and so of less political concern.

Solutions

Most countries that have a value-added tax exempt financial services.[7] Under an exemption, a financial institution's value added from financial services provided to customers is untaxed, but the institution is also denied any credit for taxes paid on purchased goods and services it uses in producing those financial services. For sales to households, as opposed to sales to businesses, exemption results in a somewhat lower tax than would be due if the financial services were treated like other sales. But because no credit is provided for taxes paid on inputs, all that is left out is the value added by the financial organization. Exemption in an invoice-and-credit value-added tax comes close to taxing financial services "correctly." The more the costs of the services derive from inputs purchased by the financial business from other companies (and the less from, for example, the financial company's own employees), the closer the approximation.

Exemption is no simple cure, however. For one thing, if financial services provided to households are undertaxed, financial services to other businesses are overtaxed because the businesses receive no credit for inputs used to produce the services. Furthermore, exemption requires distinctions among types of purchases and sales. The result is complexity and the unwanted incentives typical of line-drawing in a tax system. Merrill and Adrion observe that "the VAT rules applicable to financial services are among the most complex in the entire VAT system."[8]

Countries exempt financial services in invoice-and-credit value-added taxes to approximate the tax rate applied to other goods and services. But even if the result is close to "right," many countries impose separate

7. Tait (1988) covers the VAT thoroughly; Tait (1991) gives more compact treatment. See Messere (1993, chap. 13) for a history of value-added taxes as well as a description of the principal alternative systems. Good discussions of the invoice-and-credit method used in most countries to implement a value-added tax can be found, for example, in Aaron (1981), and Cnossen, Galper, and McLure (1993). For details of the treatment of financial services see Chant (1989), Henderson (1988), Hoffman (1988), and Peter R. Merrill and Harold Adrion, "Treatment of Financial Services under Consumption-Based Tax Systems," *Tax Notes*, vol. 68, September 18, 1995, pp. 1496–1500.

8. Merrill and Adrion, "Treatment of Financial Services," p. 1497.

taxes on financial products to offset the value-added tax exemption. Merrill and Adrion suggest that the combination probably taxes financial services more heavily than other goods and services.[9] The imposition of extra taxes to offset a tax advantage that may not really exist illustrates the political importance of appearances.

The Proposals' Approaches

U.S. retail sales taxes typically exclude financial services, whether the customer pays for them explicitly or accepts reduced interest. Even if explicit charges for financial services were subject to retail sales tax, a functionally similar charge imposed by paying below-market interest rates might attract little attention, because it would not put the financial company in a negative tax position. The value-added tax elements of the other three plans do, however, create this possibility, and they do incorporate special rules for financial institutions and services or both.

The USA tax is much the most explicit in this respect, as well as in others. For most businesses, the tax base would consist of the difference between sales and purchases from other businesses, with no account taken of financial flows. Banks and bank customers, insurance companies and their products, and investment conduits, such as mutual funds and real estate investment trusts, would all have special rules that resemble a conventional income calculation.[10]

Congressman Gibbons's value-added tax proposal is not specific on the details but asserts that procedures would be developed to tax financial services. It appears the intent is to use methods like those proposed in the USA tax.[11]

The flat tax would also provide special rules for banks and insurance companies. Banks would have to report the price of the services they provide to depositors, measured as "the difference between the market interest rate and the lower rate that the bank pays on accounts that have bundled services."[12] Similarly, the service element in mortgage interest charges, in the form of higher interest charged than the market interest

---

9. Merrill and Adrion, "Treatment of Financial Services," p. 1497. Emphasizing the great difference between the usual base of a tax on financial services and the theoretically correct value-added tax base, Weichenrieder (1994) reaches the same conclusion for the case of insurance in Germany.

10. Alliance USA (1995, pp. 201–43).

11. See Gibbons (1993, 1996).

12. Hall and Rabushka (1995, p. 74).

rate, would be added to the tax base of the bank. An analogous procedure is envisioned for insurance companies.

Taxation of Financial Institutions under Existing Law

The simplified examples of the tax treatment of various financial transactions presented below do not describe how financial institutions are now taxed. These details would be important in thinking through the consequences of major changes in the tax law for existing financial businesses. To compute corporation income tax liability, life insurance companies, for example, have to determine the policyholders' share of tax-exempt interest; and mutual insurance companies are subject to provisions designed to place them in a particular relationship to stockholder-owned companies.[13]

In spite of such complexities, however, two basic tax regimes apply to financial institutions. Some institutions such as mutual funds are treated as pass-through entities. Provided various requirements concerning distributions are satisfied, income from the business's portfolio is allocated to shareholders and taxed to them. Because income is net of administrative and management costs, services provided by such companies are excluded from the income tax base. The other regime, applicable to banks and insurance companies, applies the same income-measurement rules as the ones nonfinancial businesses face. The main difference, important primarily for insurance companies, is that they may set up deductible reserves for future losses (payouts on the policies for insurance companies, bad debts for banks). That is, they can deduct currently the value of expected future losses. Such a deduction results in the conceptually correct measure of the change in net worth of the business, but ordinary companies may not take such deductions. In this respect banks and insurance companies enjoy a tax advantage relative to ordinary companies.

Finally, life insurance offers individual policyholders a well-known tax advantage. The liability for death benefits or for future annuity that insurance companies may deduct corresponds to accruing income of the policyholder. The failure to impose income tax on policyholders for this "inside build-up" reduced federal revenues by an estimated $10 billion for fiscal 1995.[14]

---

13. For a compact discussion, see *U.S. Master Tax Guide, 1991* (1991, pp. 506–18).
14. *Budget of the United States Government, Fiscal Year 1997: Analytical Perspectives*, pp. 61–90.

This chapter recapitulates the challenge posed by the taxation of financial services and examines options for confronting it. A principal theme is that in most instances in which financial services might go untaxed under the reform plans (absent special, and complicating, rules), they are also free of tax under the current income tax. The locus of the nontaxation is shifted, however, from the individual to the business, and the problem thereby becomes more obvious. A second theme is that relatively simple techniques of cash-flow accounting would tax financial services consistently with other goods and services in consumption tax systems. Nevertheless, cash-flow accounting approaches have not yet proven attractive to policymakers in value-added tax countries, in part because cash-flow approaches raise transition issues that would need to be addressed in the design of tax rules.

The Canonical Case: Demand Deposits

Demand deposits illustrate the problem of taxing financial services.[15] Typically, banks pay little or no interest on demand deposit balances, but they provide checking services "free." More accurately, the depositor pays for the checking services by accepting a lower rate of interest than could be earned from other equally risky and liquid assets. For example, suppose the going interest rate is 10 percent, and the bank pays 4 percent on demand deposits, provided the depositor maintains an average monthly balance of at least $1,000. A carefully calculating depositor will keep, let us say, an average balance of $1,500, so the bank pays $60 a year in interest. In the meantime the funds are invested at 10 percent, yielding $150. The $90 difference covers the bank's noninterest costs; any net surplus accrues as profit. I shall assume that the $90 exactly covers the bank's costs, so that there is no profit and that the costs consist entirely of payments to companies that provide computer services.[16]

The Income Tax Problem

The income tax problem is that the depositor is not taxed on the service yield from the funds on deposit. If the bank paid the full 10

15. Hoffman, Poddar, and Whalley (1987) provide a useful discussion of the treatment of banks under a value-added tax.

16. As noted in the introduction, the problem vanishes to the extent that the bank's costs take the form of employee expenses, because these costs are not deducted from a value-added tax base.

Table 12-1. *Treatment of a Demand Deposit under the Income Tax*

Item	Value
Information	
Account average balance	$1,500
Cost of service	90
Service charge	0
Interest paid on account	60
Bank's taxes	
Interest received	150
Interest paid on deposit	(60)
Cost of providing service	(90)
Taxable income	0
Summing up	
Interest bank received	150
Tax bank pays	0
Interest paid on deposit	(60)
Costs	(90)
Net	0
Value of service in forgone after-tax interest in 30 percent bracket	$63

percent interest rate and charged for the services, the depositor would have an additional $90 in taxable income and have to pay an explicit charge of $90 for checking. A depositor in a hypothetical 30 percent tax bracket would owe $27 in tax. Table 12-1 summarizes the situation.

Under the familiar Schanz-Haig-Simons standard, income for tax purposes is the sum of the taxpayer's consumption and increase in wealth during the period. If one examines the typical depositor's accounts, to say that leaving out the financial services paid for by forgone interest is to say one is omitting some consumption. In effect, under existing rules the depositor obtains a deduction for the cost of the checking acount, which would (or might) be regarded as a personal expenditure and therefore not eligible for deduction in normal income tax usage. The effect is to subsidize checking account services at the depositor's marginal tax rate—a zero-bracket taxpayer gets no subsidy.

If checking account services are properly deductible, there is no economically interesting problem. Implicit interest that takes the form of services is not taxed, but neither would explicit interest payments associated with offsetting deductible charges. Since a large proportion of demand deposits, and of financial services in general, is for business customers, the income measurement difficulty is of less quantitative significance than might be thought. For the individual customers for whom a deduction would not be allowed, the problem is measured by their marginal tax rates and stock of deposits.

Exclusion of consumption of financial services is a problem for two reasons. First, the subsidy of demand-deposit services causes inefficiently large use of these services relative to other consumption goods and services. And the failure to tax income that takes the form of financial services necessitates higher tax rates to raise a given amount of revenue, thereby increasing the efficiency cost of the tax system.

Second, mismeasuring income from financial services raises the usual vertical and horizontal equity issues. The effect of mismeasurement on the average progressivity of the tax system could be corrected by lowering individual tax rates a little. The result would be no change in overall progressivity, but a redistribution from demand-deposit lovers to demand-deposit avoiders. If there is close correlation between income and tastes for demand deposits, the change in the distribution would be small. In that case the only issue would be the size of any efficiency gain from confronting individual taxpayer depositors with the true marginal cost of the services they consume.[17]

One may get a very rough idea of the efficiency stake from the figures compiled by the Commerce Department on "imputed interest" received by persons from banks, credit agencies, investment companies, life insurance carriers, and private noninsured pension plans. The estimate for 1993 of $350 billion includes $204 billion from life insurance and pension funds and $146 billion identified as "services furnished without payment" from the other financial intermediaries. The $204 billion presumably consists predominantly of the accrual of inside build-up and only secondarily of financial services. That would leave about $200 billion of the Commerce Department's 1993 estimate that might measure the phenomenon discussed in this chapter. Some, perhaps significant, part of this total may well be overstatement of nondeductible interest paid by households—mortgage interest of nonitemizers or interest on credit card

---

17. An adequate analysis of the efficiency consequences of various rules would take us into the realm of the second best. The usual presumption is that there would be an efficiency gain when the price to the depositor is brought closer to marginal cost. Theoretically, however, the subsidy to demand deposits could be offsetting some other incentive effects of the tax system; so removing the subsidy could reduce efficiency. These observations ignore general equilibrium effects of changed tax treatment on the prices of financial services (and other prices, for that matter). If demand-deposit services are provided at constant returns to scale and do not depend on highly specialized inputs, these further effects would be small. Any reduction in the equilibrium levels of demand-deposit services would be accompanied by redeployment of resources to other uses with similar value. Presumably, however, the short-run impact would be hard on demand-deposit providers, who might be expected to oppose higher taxes on financial services.

debt, for example (see the discussion of mortgage interest later). If, however, all of it is now excluded from the individual base and ought to be included, adding it to the individual income tax base and taxing it at an average marginal rate of 20 percent would add more than 6 percent to aggregate federal personal and corporate taxes of $661 billion. The $200 billion may also be compared with aggregate personal consumption in 1993 of $4,454 billion, so it would amount to more than 4 percent of consumption.[18] The figure seems implausibly large as a measure of excluded income in the form of financial services.

IS A FIX NEEDED? The significance of such income mismeasurement depends on the extent of differences in the use of demand deposits among taxpayers within income classes and on the extent of overconsumption of demand-deposit services (the elasticity of demand for demand deposits).[19] If members of each income class make similar use of demand deposits, the issue is wholly one of efficiency rather than equity as these terms are generally understood. In turn, efficiency needs to be assessed in relation to the difficulty of correcting the income measurement.

Before turning to possible fixes, one should consider whether demand-deposit services should be taxed. Are the services consumption? This question is not simply a technical one to which there is a correct technical answer.[20] It is instead a normative question about who should bear the tax burdens. Suppose banks are required to pay market interest on demand deposits and to charge fees that cover their costs. Should a person who has $90 of demand deposit fees bear the same tax burden as someone who has no demand deposit fees but instead $90 extra of other goods and services? The answer might be no if fees are regarded as a cost of earning a living. This answer may seem fanciful in the case of demand deposits, but not for itemized deductions for the cost of advice on how to manage a stock portfolio.[21] The use of demand deposits may increase

18. Imputed interest received by persons is taken from the *Survey of Current Business* (July 1994), table 8.17. Personal consumption for 1993 is taken from the *Economic Report of the President, February 1996*, table B-1; personal and corporate taxes are from table B-80.
19. For present purposes I can neglect the question that I have often stressed elsewhere of how one ought to classify people by ability to pay. See, for example, Bradford (1986).
20. Bradford (1986).
21. The Tax Reform Act of 1986 limited such miscellaneous deductions to the excess of a certain fraction of income (in addition to the usual restrictions on itemized deductions). The motivation was not principled income measurement but revenue and simplification.

income net of fees by economizing on other more costly methods of settling payments.[22]

ALTERNATIVE FIXES: IMPUTING INCOME. Methods of imputing in-kind financial services to the income tax base fall into two classes: depositor-side corrections and institution-side corrections. Within the latter, corrections may be institution specific—for example, applied to companies identified as banks—or transaction specific—for example, applied to demand-deposit services, by whomever provided.

Income mismeasurement occurs at the depositor level. If depositors face different tax rates, as they do under the current individual income tax, a precise correction would need to be made at the depositor level. Depositor income is understated by the explicit fee the bank would charge as an alternative to providing a lower financial return. To correct the error in income measurement, this forgone payoff to the depositor would be imputed as income subject to tax.

The problem is that this fee is not observed. Rather, it is inferred from the difference between the actual financial payoff to the depositor and the payoff if no banking services were involved. The benchmark payoff is presumably that of an asset as safe and liquid as a demand deposit but without its convenient services. Hall and Rabushka suggest the required amount is easily measured as the difference between the interest paid on the demand deposit and the Treasury bill rate.[23] This simple standard might work for demand deposits, whose security and liquidity are easy to observe. How this "interest imputation" approach would work in more complex cases is less clear.

---

22. One alternative to demand deposits—cash—raises the same issue of untaxed consumption services. If there is no way to reach this consumption, exempting the same consumption in the form of demand-deposit services may raise efficiency issues. See note 19. The attempt to put quantitative flesh on this argument would perhaps strain the analytical substance of the Schanz-Haig-Simons concept, which is not grounded in the welfare economics that economists usually deploy. (Does it matter, for example, whether time saved by using demand deposits instead of cash is devoted to extra paid work or to leisure?) The comparison to the expenses of managing a portfolio simply underscores that the "correct" treatment of demand-deposit fees is not clear-cut. Building on a model advanced by Foley (1970), Chia and Whalley (1989) (described also in Whalley, n.d.) argue that exempting financial services from tax may serve efficiency. See also the development of the Chia and Whalley analysis by Davies (1991). Grubert and Mackie (1996) have recently developed a similar argument.

23. Hall and Rabushka (1995).

Since income is imputed to the depositor, there would be no need to distinguish business from nonbusiness customers. A business customer would deduct the imputed service fee, just offsetting the imputed income.

Rules for taxing financial services often single out particular types of financial institutions as opposed to particular types of transactions. But business-level adjustments could be based on the nature of the transaction, whether carried out by a bank or by some other enterprise. Income would be imputed to the business instead of to the customer who actually enjoys it. This approach resembles the proposal to tax fringe benefits by denying a deduction to businesses that offer them. The transaction is taxed at the bank's marginal tax rate. If the bank's marginal tax rate approximates the highest depositor rate, this correction would overtax service income of all taxpayers in lower brackets. A distribution- and revenue-neutral correction requires reduced marginal tax rates on individuals at all levels. The choice between banking and other services would be unchanged for high-bracket depositors, but low-bracket depositors would have an incentive to substitute away from banking services.

One problem is that the institution-side correction is wrong for business depositors. An additional correction would be necessary for business customers. Business deposits could be identified and excluded from the adjustment, although mismeasurement would persist if businesses differ in their marginal tax rates. The administrative complications are obvious.

Imputing income to the institutions based on demand-deposit balances is a transaction-specific correction, triggered whenever the tax authorities observe the bundling of demand-deposit services with a financial return. The relevant rule could be stated in functional terms so that the same correction applies for a nonbank institution that provides a similar service. (A depositor-level correction would be necessarily specific to each transaction.)

Banks could be subjected to tax rules different from those applied to other businesses. The USA tax takes this approach. Current income tax law also applies special rules to particular classes of institutions, in part to permit deductions that are not allowed to ordinary businesses to handle future contingencies.

The Consumption Tax Problem: VAT Systems

Under the consumption tax, more than under the income tax, a variety of rules can achieve economically equivalent results. Furthermore, the rules may be mixed and matched if reasonable care is taken.[24] I focus on two main approaches to consumption taxation. Business-level taxes include the value-added tax and retail sales tax, the Hall-Rabushka flat tax, and the business tax component of the USA tax. The other approach is an individual tax on all cash inflow less cash outflow for the acquisition of assets—that is, saving. The individual tax component of the USA tax is in this category.[25]

The value-added tax base consists of a business's receipts from sales of goods and services less the purchases of goods and services from other businesses—a tax on real transactions. Such financial transactions as borrowing and lending, issue and repurchase of stock, and payments and receipts of dividends do not enter the tax base. What, exactly, is a real transaction? When tax liability turns on a distinction, that distinction will come under pressure. Consider an automobile dealer who sells a luxury car for only $5,000 but requires installment payments calculated at a very high rate of interest. The sale of the real product, the car, is bundled with a financial transaction, the installment loan. If the financial transaction is untaxed, the business can avoid tax by arranging for buyers to pay for purchases largely through untaxed interest on the installment loan.

One way to protect against tax avoidance using such bundled transactions would be to require separation of real and financial transactions, perhaps by mandating that the automobile seller and the lender be separately owned businesses. This requirement would go some way to ensuring the arm's-length quality of the financial transaction. Or tax law might require that the buyer always have the option to buy the car for cash for the price quoted in the installment contract.

Still easier would be to require that a bundled transaction be accounted for on a bundled, cash-flow basis. The seller of the car would treat as taxable income all cash paid by the buyer, whether characterized as principal or interest. This rule would not require adopting cash-flow accounting in any other respect. It would render the seller indifferent among payment schedules with the same discounted value and eliminate incentives to inflate the interest rate.

24. There is a voluminous literature on the various forms of consumption and income taxes. The magisterial Meade Committee report (Institute for Fiscal Studies, 1978) is particularly important. See also Bradford (1986, 1987, 1996) and Bradford and the U.S. Treasury (1984).

25. Another example is the cash-flow tax proposal described in Bradford and the U.S. Treasury (1984).

Table 12-2. *Treatment of a Demand Deposit under a Subtraction-Type Consumption Tax*

Item	Value
Information	
Account average balance	$1,500
Cost of service	90
Service charge	0
Interest paid on account	87
Bank's taxes	
Sales	0
Purchases (cost of services)	90
Net tax base	−90
Rebate of tax (assuming 30 percent tax rate)	27
Summing up	
Interest bank receives	150
Tax rebate to bank	27
Interest paid on deposit	−87
Costs	−90
Net	0
Value of service to client (forgone interest of $150 less interest of $87 received on the deposit)	$63

THE DEMAND DEPOSIT UNDER THE VAT. "Real" bank financial services, such as checking accounts and safe deposit boxes, are bundled with the financial return, the payment of interest. Table 12-2 shows the break-even situation corresponding to the income tax example. The bank has no identified real sales, but does have real expenses of $90.

Under the VAT the extra $1,500 in demand deposits gives rise to a $90 loss. If the tax is refundable or the bank owes enough tax on other transactions, its taxes are reduced by its marginal tax rate times this loss. If the tax rate is 30 percent, the saving is $27. The break-even interest payable on the demand deposit is increased, relative to the income tax case, by the tax saving: $87 instead of $60. Because the individual does not pay tax (or deduct expenses), the depositor nets $87 plus demand deposit services by forgoing interest, which I assume to be 10 percent, on $1,500. The implied value of services to the depositor is the difference between 10 percent of $1,500 and $87, or $63.

This example illustrates several points. Value-added tax accounting excludes the financial-service value of the demand deposit, which is implicit in the reduced rate of return paid to the depositor. For a taxpayer with the same marginal tax rate as the bank, the outcome is the *same* under uncorrected value-added tax and income tax regimes.

The effect of the tax rule on the cost of financial services to the depositor is independent of the depositor's marginal tax rate. That means, for example, that a shift from an uncorrected income tax regime to an uncorrected value-added tax regime would in this respect benefit low-bracket taxpayers. The implicit subsidy received by low-bracket depositors is lower under the income tax. A zero-rate depositor obtains no subsidy. Under the value-added tax, the implicit subsidy is the same for all and is at the value-added tax rate. The key point here is that the undertaxation of financial services is more or less the same in both direct income taxes and consumption taxes implemented at the company level. The principal difference is visibility. The undertaxation of financial services under the consumption tax shows up as negative taxable income. Because business depositors would be allowed to deduct any service fees that were assessed, the problem has to do only with services provided to households.

TRANSACTION-SPECIFIC CORRECTIONS UNDER THE VAT. If a VAT has a uniform tax rate, correcting the tax base to include the value of financial services is easier than it is in a graduated tax regime. If labor earnings, as in the flat tax, are the measure of ability to pay, it is not necessary to allocate services to particular depositors. The transaction-specific, institution-side corrections described in connection with the income tax could be extended to the value-added tax.

For example, the bank could be obliged to report as taxable sales some interest rate times deposits. Any payment made to depositors (whether labeled interest or toasters) would be taken as a deduction and treated as a rebate on sales. Alternatively, the estimated cost of providing deposit services could be imputed as sales by the bank (with payments to depositors netted). As with the income tax, these imputations would produce the wrong result for business depositors. Either the imputation would be omitted for them, or the imputed amounts would be reported to business depositors to be taken as deductions against their sales.

It is instructive to consider how the various methods for dealing with the automobile installment sale situation could be adapted to the treatment of demand deposits.[26] The simplest approach, as in the case of the

26. An obligatory separation of the real and financial transactions might be effected by setting up a collateral account at a separate financial institution to secure the interests of the bank providing demand-deposit services. Checks written by the depositor would be

Table 12-3. *Cash-Flow Treatment of a Demand Deposit*

Item	Value
Information	
Account average balance	$1,500
Up-front tax on deposit	450
Yield on remainder at 10 percent	105
Cost of service	90
Service charge	0
Premium paid on account	60
Bank's taxes	
Sales	−60
Less purchases (cost of services)	90
Net tax base	−150
Tax rebate to bank	45
Summing up	
Interest bank receives	150
Tax rebate to bank	45
Expenses	−90
Premium on account	−60
Net	0
Value of service to client (forgone interest of $150 less premium of $60 on the deposit)	90

car dealer, would be to require cash-flow accounting. The bank would treat all incoming cash as taxable sales and all outgoing cash as purchases. The depositor would be treated symmetrically. A business would take a deduction for all deposits and include all withdrawals.

I did not mention cash-flow accounting as a possible method for correcting the income tax base, although by adding imputed interest to balances it might be feasible. It is, however, a natural approach in a consumption-tax world. The transaction-specific approach would be identified with any bundled transaction involving a financial product and financial service, not with institutions. Any business providing a bundled service could be obliged to use cash-flow reporting.

Table 12-3 illustrates the cash-flow approach. The bank's tax rate is assumed to be 30 percent. Accordingly, it owes $450 in tax on the original deposit of $1,500. As before, the depositor receives $60 in in-

---

made good by transfers from the independently maintained collateral account. (This would correspond to obliging the car purchaser to obtain an installment loan from an institution with no interest in the sale of the car.) It is harder to come up with an analogue to obliging the car dealer to stand ready to sell for cash at the quoted price that is the nominal amount of the installment loan.

terest, relabeled a premium payment. This premium, along with the costs of servicing the account, is deductible. The result is a current year's loss of $150 (larger than in the conventional case), which qualifies for $45 in tax rebate at the bank's 30 percent marginal rate. The key to that result is that, although it is carrying a liability of $1,500 in demand deposits, the bank is able to earn interest on only the net $1,050 left after the deposit tax. The break-even requirement that interest earned less net taxes equals premiums paid to depositors plus the costs of serving the account results in a net payoff to depositors of the excess of interest over costs. As a consequence, the depositor pays the full cost of serving the account in the form of forgone interest, net of any premium earned on the account.

CASH-FLOW TREATMENT: PERCEPTION, CASH-FLOW, AND TIMING PROBLEMS. The cash-flow method precisely measures income but raises perception problems. In the example the current loss to the bank is even greater than it is with no adjustment. Could policymakers grasp the effect of the front-loaded tax paid at the time a deposit liability is created?

The initial tax payment is a hidden asset that purchases future tax deductions. In the example the deduction for liquidating the deposit currently would be $450. The bank loses the income—$45 at an assumed interest rate of 10 percent—on this asset, which accrues to the government, exactly offsetting the rebate claimed by the bank, which is breaking even.

One objection to this approach is the requirement for a large tax payment by the bank when an account is created, coupled with a large deduction from the base of a business depositor. The effect is reversed when the deposit is drawn down. Apart from start-up situations, balances would typically be sufficiently stable to moderate this problem. Alternatively both sides of the tax transactions could be treated as compulsory loans to and borrowing from the government. The bank would not actually pay tax on net deposits. Instead, it would obtain a balance of tax due on the tax authorities' books, on which it would pay nondeductible interest annually.

I have not mentioned a necessary condition for the efficacy of the cash-flow method: the same rate must apply to deposits and withdrawals. If rates change, powerful incentives arise to manipulate balances. An anticipated rate hike would boost the value of future tax deductions from reductions in balances. The same incentive effects of anticipated changes in tax rates apply more broadly to investment decisions in a value-added tax.[27]

To avoid the incentive effect of an anticipated change in rates, an account built up of inflows when the tax rate is 25 percent would have to be segregated from accounts built up when the rate is 30 percent. This solution brings problems of its own—the difficulty of policing the segregation of different vintages. It is not clear whether this problem is solvable.

Morley English and Satya Poddar describe an analogous method for dealing with time-varying tax rates.[28] A tax calculation account (TCA) would be established to serve as a clearing device to which taxes due on cash inflows are credited and taxes refundable on cash outflows would be debited. The taxpayer would be charged interest on a positive balance and receive interest on a negative balance. (To assist with the perception problem, these payments might be called taxes.) Otherwise no taxes would be paid except for periodic settling up. They deal with tax rate changes by adjusting balances in the TCA. If rates change, balances would be adjusted so that the bank's position on reaching a zero deposit balance would be unchanged. In the example given in table 12-3, the bank starts with a balance of $450 after receiving the demand deposit. If the tax rate is cut to 20 percent, the balance would be multiplied by 0.20/0.30, so that upon liquidation of the deposit, the bank would owe no tax. The effect is to neutralize the incentives (and redistributions) that would otherwise be set up by anticipated changes in tax rates.

INSTITUTION-SPECIFIC CORRECTIONS. Countries using credit-and-invoice value-added taxes have generally chosen a transaction-specific, institution-side correction. Designated financial services are *exempted* from the value-added tax, while the credit otherwise available for value-added tax paid on purchased inputs is denied. Value-added tax is paid on the inputs to financial services that are purchased from other businesses, but not on the labor and perhaps profits of the financial institution. This approach has a number of more or less serious drawbacks, particularly in its failure to distinguish between business and nonbusiness clients. Since it is virtually impossible to identify financial services rendered *within* a business (to itself), this role creates an incentive to shift such activities away from specialized financial institutions.

27. Bradford (1996).
28. English and Poddar (1995). For a discussion of the problem in its general form, see Boadway and Bruce (1984).

The Consumption Tax Problem: Individual Cash-Flow Taxes

Individual-level cash-flow taxes raise other problems of measuring financial services. Individuals would pay tax on all cash receipts and deduct saving.[29] Capital purchases are immediately expensed. Financial assets would be treated in a way analogous to today's individual retirement account. Flows into so-called qualified accounts are deductible; flows from the account to the taxpayer are included in taxable income. This framework indirectly measures consumption. Any cash that comes in that is not saved must be consumed.

In some cases the exact opposite treatment of saving and its future payoff may be desirable. Financial assets acquired outside of qualified accounts are ignored for tax purposes. No deduction is allowed, and no inclusion of any return flow in future taxable income is required. Called the prepayment approach, this method produces the equivalent result.

Qualified Account Treatment of Demand Deposits

At the individual level the prepayment method is likely to be applied to demand deposits. An effective tax would be imposed on financial services paid for in the form of reduced interest received by the depositor.[30]

Cash-flow accounting for a demand deposit, which implements a tax on services when it is applied to the bank, gives the opposite result when it is applied to individuals. Consider a depositor who is allowed a deduction for a deposit. Subsequent withdrawals are included in the depositor's tax base. The withdrawals are, however, net of the bank's implicit charges that are netted from the interest that would otherwise be credited. Consequently, the return to the depositor consists of a financial component that is included in the depositor's tax base and a service component that is not, just as in the present income tax. The depositor-side corrections discussed in connection with the income tax can counter the same problem in an individual cash-flow tax. The tax prepayment treatment of demand deposits deals with the problem more simply, however. Since the return is not taxed, the depositor will view financial and service returns as equally valuable.

---

29. The approach described here is that proposed for the cash-flow tax in Bradford and the U.S. Treasury (1984).
30. Bradford and the U.S. Treasury (1984).

Other Financial Services

Problems with respect to other financial services tend to crop up in both individual and business taxes, but in different places.

Mortgage Loans

The value of financial services associated with a mortgage loan can easily be missed under a value-added tax. Mortgage loans provide an opportunity to charge for financial services in the guise of interest. Hall and Rabushka note that there is about a 3 percentage point spread between the "pure" interest rate and the lending rate for bank loans.[31] This differential seems rather high for bookkeeping and similar services and may incorporate default risk. If it is possible to identify the value of the financial service, and if one decides to tax it, the alternatives are clear-cut.

CURRENT LAW. In deducting interest, an itemizer deducts any embedded financial service charges. So the consumption element is excluded from the tax base. For nonitemizers, implicit charges for financial services remain in the tax base and are taxed like other consumption.

SUBTRACTION VAT. If the bank treats mortgage payments as purely financial, they are not included in the bank's tax base. The nonfinancial costs of providing those services, however, are deductible. The analogy with the demand deposit is clear.

Without a correction, VAT rules would extend the exclusion from itemizers to all taxpayers. Although the result would have the appearance of a tax break for wealthy banks, under competitive conditions, relative to the preexisting income tax, the benefit would flow mostly to lower-income individuals and tax-exempt borrowers. Consequently, any correction (such as imputing a service charge) would work to the disadvantage of lower-income individuals and tax-exempt borrowers.

Once again the problem is confined to transactions between business lenders and nonbusiness borrowers. Interbusiness transactions are self-correcting. Transactions purely among households do not register in the tax base.

---

31. Hall and Rabushka (1995, p. 75).

The various options for dealing with demand deposits can be adapted to mortgage and other loans. One difficulty that does not apply to demand deposits concerns measurement of outstanding liability, because the contractual amounts may differ from market values. The cash-flow method could be applied and would include financial services in the tax base. The bank would deduct the amount loaned and take into income all repayments, which would have to cover service as well as financial costs. Note that it is not necessary to contemplate special rules for selected institutions. The rules could be based on economic function (bundling of a loan and financial services) and apply to all institutions.

INDIVIDUAL CASH-FLOW TAXES. If individuals borrow on a qualified basis, the bank could set up a line of credit run through a qualified account with interest charged to the debit balance. To use the line of credit, the borrower withdraws from the qualified account. As with all other withdrawals, the amount is included in the borrower's income. Repayments, whether called principal or interest, take the form of deposits to the qualified account and are deductible. It should be apparent that the qualified account approach would permit taxpayers to deduct the value of financial services associated with a loan.

Under the prepayment approach, neither the loan proceeds nor repayments have any tax consequence. So the prepayment approach includes financial services in the taxpayer's base.

Obliging taxpayers to adopt the prepayment approach to demand deposits has few drawbacks. In the case of mortgage borrowing there are policy reasons for allowing flexibility. With progressive rates, a large withdrawal from a qualified account to buy a house might drive the taxpayer into a higher bracket. Allowing borrowing on a tax-prepayment basis would eliminate this problem. Consequently, if it were deemed worthwhile to seek equivalence in the treatment of financial services under the two approaches, one of the other methods for imputing the value of services would have to be deployed.

Property-Casualty Insurance

A property-casualty insurance contract can be thought of as consisting of two elements: a wager with the insurance company and a loan to the insurance company. The wager aspect is evident in what are called short-tailed policies, in which any payoff occurs within a year or two. A long-tailed policy adds the element of time. It involves a loan of the policy premium by the policyholder to the insurance company. The company pays the loan back as compensation for the insured-against events and, perhaps, in the form of premium rebates. The risk part is the same as for a short-tailed policy. The loan part is best understood by abstracting from risk.

CURRENT LAW. The taxation of a property-casualty policy, other than for business purposes, is somewhat peculiar. Casualty losses that exceed fairly high limits are generally deductible under the individual income tax. Loss payments that exceed the insured loss are included in income. Since the policyholder cannot deduct policy premiums, but loses the deduction for loss to the extent of the insurance payoff, there is an implicit tax on the insurance policy.

The tax treatment of the insurance policy ignores nondeductible loss. The policyholder pays the premium, net of any payback, on an after-tax basis. For a short-tailed policy, the service fee embedded in the premium is thereby included in taxable consumption.

On long-tailed policies companies may provide a financial return net of service costs. The tax rules that treat premiums received by insurance companies as gross income and allow deduction of expenses, loss payments, and the increase in the discounted value of expected future payouts (reserves) mean that the implicit yield on policy premiums will be the before-tax interest rate.[32] The result is a small tax advantage, depending on the marginal rate of the policyholder. If the premium is regarded as a pure loan to the company, the payback will be net of service costs. So it is like the demand deposit. The fact that such long-tailed policies as malpractice insurance are primarily issued to business clients presumably means the tax-free service value in property-casualty policies is of no importance as a matter of policy. Any benefit to one side of the transaction is offset by the disadvantage to the other.

SUBTRACTION VAT. Under a VAT the problems for property-casualty insurance are the same as for bank loans.[33] If the insurance premium and

---

32. For a discussion of the connection between the taxation of property-casualty insurance companies and competitive premiums, see Bradford and Logue (1995). See also Main (1983).

33. Barham, Poddar, and Whalley (1987) and Thomas S. Neubig and Harold L. Adrion, "Value-Added Taxes and Other Consumption Taxes: Issues for Insurance Companies," *Tax Notes*, vol. 61, November 22, 1993, pp. 1001–11, provide useful discussions of insurance in the context of value-added taxation.

the payoffs on the policy are regarded as financial, the company will have expenses but no income. A VAT does not tax household interest receipts. So the long-tailed lines lose their interest-tax advantage, especially for high-bracket taxpayers. For low-bracket policyholders and on all short-tailed policies, the exclusion of service value would rise. Cash-flow treatment of the premium and payoffs by the company would correct the income measure. Since insurance companies currently treat premiums as gross income and deduct loss payments, this practice would depart less from current practice than would the same treatment of bank deposits. The main change would be eliminating the reserve deduction. It should be possible to implement such treatment on a transaction-specific rather than company-specific basis.

INDIVIDUAL CASH-FLOW TAXES. Qualified account treatment of property-casualty insurance results in the exclusion of the insurance company's services from the policyholder tax base. A simple corrective would be to apply prepayment rules, with no deduction of premium and no inclusion of proceeds. (This would be independent of the treatment of casualty losses.)

LIFE INSURANCE. Life insurance raises essentially the same issues, with the same implications, as property-casualty insurance.[34] In contrast with a property-casualty policy, where the insured-against event has a monetary value, there are no natural limits on the amount of life insurance. This feature heightens the tax advantage of long-tailed insurance that results from the failure to include accruing value in policyholder income. So long-tailed life insurance is extensively held by individuals.

CURRENT LAW. A term life insurance policy has no effect on income tax for the policyholder. Premiums are not deductible. Proceeds paid at death are not taxed to either the decedent or the beneficiary. Since the payoff is net of the insurance company's costs, the costs must be reflected in the price to the policyholder. In other words, for a term policy the financial service is taxed.

A long-term policy that accumulates cash value has an additional benefit for the policyholder—the accruing value of the policy, the "inside

---

34. The tax treatment of both property-casualty and life insurance companies was substantially overhauled in 1984. For a discussion of some of the anomalies in pre-1984 tax rules for life insurance, see Aaron (1983).

build-up," is not taxed. The payoff at death is free of tax and the payoff by redemption (or annuity) enjoys deferral of tax. In either case the service charge comes out of the payback to the policyholder and is not subject to policyholder-level tax. Just like the bank account, the long-tailed life policy provides a setting for service value to go untaxed.

VAT AND INDIVIDUAL CASH-FLOW TAXES. Under the VAT an insurance policy would be treated as a financial transaction. There would be costs of servicing policies but neither receipts nor deductions associated with the premiums and loss payments. Like the bank, the break-even insurance company will appear to be running losses. Insurance with cash-value buildup will be relatively less attractive than it now is because all interest, not just the implicit interest in a life insurance policy, will be free of tax. For low-bracket taxpayers and all term insurance, the net effect is to increase the extent of service value excluded from the tax base. Cash-flow treatment of the premium and payoffs by the company would correct the income measure. Although these transactions would typically (perhaps only) be entered into by identifiable insurance companies, the tax treatment could be specified functionally on a transaction-specific rather than company-specific basis. For the individual cash-flow tax, the story is the same as for the property-casualty insurance company.

Conclusion

There are broadly similar tax problems under the existing income tax system and potential alternative, consumption-type tax systems for all services that may be charged for through implicit reductions in interest paid to lenders or interest charged to borrowers. The problems show up at different places—at the company level rather than at the individual client level. Where the client is a business and tax rates are the same, the problem typically nets out between the two sides of the transactions. In many respects, producing consistent tax consequences of financial contracts and instruments is easier under consumption-type than income-type taxes.

Problems relate to services rendered to households. Where these problems seem to require solutions—even where similar problems go unaddressed in the income tax—cash-flow approaches promise relatively simple solutions.

Comment by John B. Shoven

This chapter is about an important topic, but not one of the most important topics regarding taxation. My list of the "top five" problems concerning taxation and tax reform (not necessarily in order) would include the following:

—Our inability to value leisure and nonmarket activity (for example, we fail to distinguish between two different families each of whom has $50,000 of income; one achieves that income with three jobs and the other does the same with one job;

—The nontaxation of the imputed return to owner-occupied housing;

—The double taxation of corporate equity income through the corporation income tax;

—The trade-off between equity and efficiency, particularly determining the optimal progressivity of marginal tax rates; and

—The choice of tax base between consumption and income.

The taxation of financial services is of second-tier importance relative to these matters, but nonetheless financial services account for 8 percent of GDP, and their appropriate taxation is definitely worth considering.

David Bradford's chapter makes several useful points about the taxation of financial services with either an income tax or a consumption tax. The primary message of the chapter is that an income tax has at least as much difficulty in taxing financial services as does a particular type of consumption tax, the value-added tax. Bradford goes through the case of demand deposits in complete detail. Depositors receive both explicit cash interest and implicit interest in the form of in-kind services such as check clearing services and free safe deposit boxes. The income tax applies only to the explicit interest income and therefore effectively subsidizes the in-kind services at the depositor's marginal income tax rate. This subsidy is not unlike the tax treatment of fringe benefits from employment or other nontaxed perks available with some employment situations. Bradford goes over the alternative income tax corrections for this situation (and draws attention to the fact that there is no problem with the income tax treatment for business depositors). The only total correction in an income tax economy involves imputing income to the recipients of the financial services. He also shows that a value-added tax would fail to tax the services associated with demand deposits. The tax shortage in this case takes place at the level of the financial institution (the bank or the savings and loan), but if these institutions face competition, the net result for depositors is exactly the same as with an equal-rate income tax. In both cases, unless corrections are made, financial services are underpriced relative to other forms of consumption, potentially leading to inefficiencies and inequities between large users of demand deposits and small users. Bradford argues that the example of the demand deposit generalizes to most of the other cases of taxing financial services. In general the problems come about from the bundling of taxable transactions and untaxed services.

Bradford asserts that the consumption tax corrections would be simpler than the corrections with the income tax. To be honest, I am not convinced. One of the mechanisms that he suggests is the imposition of a cash-flow tax on financial service transactions. There are several problems with such cash-flow taxation. First, their appearance can be quite different from their actual economic incidence, and this can make them less politically viable. The corporate taxation of mutual life insurance companies can be viewed as equivalent to that of the stock mutuals with this kind of cash-flow logic, the so-called prepayment analysis. Nonetheless, an extra tax was imposed on the mutuals (section 809) in order to level the playing field. Second, it is not simple to change the tax rates with cash-flow taxation and maintain the desirable neutrality properties. Bradford argues that transactions of different vintages and tax rate regimes can be kept separate, and this move would permit flexibility in setting tax rates. Although I cannot prove it, my guess is that establishing and policing such vintage accounts would prove complicated.

I am convinced by David Bradford's main point—namely, that taxing financial services is at least as difficult with an income tax as with a consumption tax. Therefore there is no reason to use financial services taxation as a reason not to consider adopting a national consumption tax. However, I am unconvinced that taxing financial services appropriately is simple or easy in either tax regime. We have not made the corrections called for in an income tax environment, presumably because they are in fact difficult to implement. For example, we do not impute income to users of demand-deposit accounts, just as we do not impute income to owner-occupants. I also have my doubts that the corrections necessary to appropriately tax financial services in a consumption tax environment would indeed be made. The choice between a consumption tax and an income tax should probably be made with other considerations in mind, particularly those regarding equity considerations and those evaluating the impact of the tax system on labor and capital markets. The taxation of financial services is an important detail, but a detail nonetheless.

References

Aaron, Henry J., ed. 1981. *The Value-Added Tax: Lessons from Europe.* Brookings.

———. 1983. *The Peculiar Problem of Taxing Life Insurance Companies: A Staff Paper.* Brookings.

Alliance USA. 1995. "The USA Tax System." Washington.

Arthur Andersen. 1995. "Tax Reform 1995: Looking at Two Options." Office of Federal Tax Services (May).

Barham, Vicky, S. N. Poddar, and John Whalley. 1987. "The Tax Treatment of Insurance under a Consumption Type, Destination Basis VAT." *National Tax Journal* 40 (June): 171–82.

Boadway, Robin, and Neil Bruce. 1984. "A General Proposition on the Design of a Neutral Business Tax." *Journal of Public Economics* 24 (July): 231–39.

Bradford, David F. 1986. *Untangling the Income Tax.* Harvard University Press.

———. "On the Incidence of Consumption Taxes." 1987. In *The Consumption Tax: A Better Alternative*, edited by Charles E. Walker and Mark A. Bloomfield, 243–61. Ballinger. (Revised version published as "What Are Consumption Taxes and Who Bears Them?" *Tax Notes*, vol. 39, April 18, 1988, pp. 383–91.)

———, ed. 1995. *Distributional Analysis of Tax Policy.* Washington: AEI Press.

———. 1996. "Consumption Taxes: Some Fundamental Transition Issues." In *Frontiers of Tax Reform*, edited by Michael J. Boskin, 123–50. Stanford, Calif.: Hoover Institution Press.

Bradford, David F., and Kyle D. Logue. 1995. "The Effects of Tax Law Changes on Prices in the Property-Casualty Insurance Industry." Princeton University.

Bradford, David F., and the U.S. Treasury Tax Policy Staff. 1984. *Blueprints for Basic Tax Reform*, 2d ed. Arlington, Va.: Tax Analysts (original edition published as a U.S. Treasury study, 1977).

Chant, John F. 1989. "Financial Institutions and Tax Reform." In *The Economic Impacts of Tax Reform*, edited by Jack Mintz and John Whalley, 223–54. Toronto: Canadian Tax Foundation.

Cnossen, Sijbren, Harvey Galper, and Charles E. McLure Jr. 1993. *The Value Added Tax: Coming to America?* Washington: Tax Analysts.

Chia, Ngee Choon, and John Whalley. 1989. "Should Banks Be Taxed?" University of Western Ontario.

Davies, James B. 1991. "The Treatment of Financial and Non-Financial Intermediation under a Value-Added Tax." University of Western Ontario.

English, Morley D., and Satya Poddar. 1995. "Taxation of Financial Services under a VAT: Applying the Cash-Flow Approach."

Foley, Duncan K. 1970. "Economic Equilibrium with Costly Marketing," *Journal of Economic Theory* 2 (September): 276–91.

Gibbons, Sam M. 1993. "A Proposal for a New Revenue System for the United States Incorporating a Value-Added Tax." Paper prepared for the Ways and Means Committee Annual Issues Seminar, March 12–14.

——. 1996. "The Value-Added Tax: A Revenue System for America's Future." Washington.

Grubert, Harry, and James Mackie. 1996. "An Unnecessary Complication: Must Financial Services Be Taxed under a Consumption Tax?" Office of Tax Analysis, U.S. Treasury Department.

Hall, Robert E., and Alvin Rabushka. 1995. The Flat Tax, 2d ed. Stanford, Calif.: Hoover Institution Press.

Henderson, Yolanda K. 1988. "Financial Intermediaries under Value-Added Taxation," New England Economic Review (July–August): 37–50.

Hoffman, Lorey Arthur. 1988. "The Application of a Value-Added Tax to Financial Services." Canadian Tax Journal/Revue Fiscale Canadienne 36 (September–October): 1204–24.

Hoffman, Lorey Arthur, S. N. Poddar, and John Whalley. 1987. "Taxation of Banking Services under a Consumption-Type, Destination Basis VAT." National Tax Journal 40 (December): 547–54.

Institute for Fiscal Studies. 1978. The Structure and Reform of Direct Taxation: Report of a Committee Chaired by Professor J. E. Meade. London: George Allen & Unwin.

Main, Brian G. M. 1983. "Corporate Insurance Purchases and Taxes." Journal of Risk and Insurance 50 (June): 197–223.

Messere, Kenneth C. 1993. Tax Policy in OECD Countries: Choices and Conflicts. Amsterdam: IBFD Publications BV.

Neubig, Thomas S. 1984. "The Taxation of Financial Institutions after Deregulation." National Tax Journal 37 (September): 351–59.

Tait, Alan A. 1988. Value-Added Tax: International Practice and Problems. Washington: International Monetary Fund.

——, ed. 1991. "Value-Added Tax: Administrative and Policy Issues." Occasional Paper 88. Washington: International Monetary Fund.

U.S. Congress, Joint Committee on Taxation. 1995. Discussion of Issues Relating to "Flat" Tax Rate Proposals. JCS-7-95. Government Printing Office.

U.S. Master Tax Guide. 1991. Chicago: Commerce Clearing House.

Weichenrieder, Alfons J. 1994. "Mehrwertsteuer, Versicherungssteuer und Risikoallokation [VAT, Insurance Tax, and Risk Allocation]." University of Munich.

Whalley, John. n.d. "Taxation and the Service Sector." Canadian Tax Paper 93. In Taxation to 2000 and Beyond, edited by Richard M. Bird and Jack M. Mintz, 269–97. Toronto: Canadian Tax Foundation.

CHAPTER 13

Fundamental Tax Reform in an International Setting

James R. Hines Jr.

FUNDAMENTAL REFORMS of the U.S. tax system are typically conceived in closed-economy settings and with domestic goals in mind. Some domestic goals become more costly to achieve, and others less so, as economies are exposed to the rest of the world. The openness of the American economy in the 1990s suggests that tax reforms are likely to succeed only if they are tailored to the international situation of the U.S. economy.

This chapter contrasts the international features of tax reform proposals with current U.S. law. It also analyzes the effect of domestic reforms on macroeconomic variables including interest rates, exchange rates, and the current account; indicates how tax reforms will affect behavior of multinational corporations, in particular transfer pricing, financial flows, technology transfer, and foreign direct investment; explains the effects of tax reforms on the international activities of individuals, including their willingness to work or invest abroad; and shows the effect of grafting onto existing tax reform plans an alternative treatment of foreign source income—border cash-flow taxation.

Support for consumption taxation in the United States is motivated in part by the potential of such taxes to simplify compliance and enforcement by avoiding complications associated with measuring capital income. Consumption taxes are also thought to encourage saving and investing by removing differences between before-tax and after-tax returns to savers. At the same time, the reforms are controversial, in part because they would change the distribution of tax burdens.

International considerations motivate fundamental tax reform proposals much less than do domestic considerations although many people hope to use tax reform to enhance the worldwide competitiveness of

American businesses. The proposition that consumption-oriented tax reforms would boost the competitiveness of U.S. companies is complex, quite apart from the usual difficulty in defining "competitiveness." Proposed tax reforms would do many things that are likely to influence the competitiveness (somehow defined) of American companies. Only a very small part of the overall effect stems from the border price adjustments contained in some of the plans. Instead, tax reforms influence competitiveness by changing after-tax capital costs at home and abroad, by removing various taxes and subsidies embodied in current law, and by giving businesses and individuals incentives to change financial practices. The net effect of fundamental tax reforms on the international position of the U.S. economy is very difficult to predict, since it is the product of many forces that are currently only partially understood.

One conclusion that emerges is that simple partial-equilibrium reasoning about either the domestic or the international effects of fundamental tax reforms in open economies may be misleading. While it does not follow that the effects of fundamental tax reforms are completely unpredictable, minor differences in the behavior of international markets can have major implications for the effects of proposed tax reforms.

Current Tax Rules and Alternatives

I examine four proposed alternatives to the current tax system: the national retail sales tax (as proposed by Senator Richard Lugar, Republican from Indiana), the flat tax (as proposed by Representative Richard Armey, Republican from Texas, and Senator Richard Shelby, Republican from Alabama), the value-added tax (as proposed by Representative Sam Gibbons, Democrat from Florida), and the USA (unlimited savings allowance) tax (as proposed by Senators Sam Nunn, Democrat from Georgia, and Pete Domenici, Republican from New Mexico). Any of the four proposals would, if adopted, fundamentally change the U.S. tax system, principally by reducing taxes on capital income.

The Current U.S. Tax System

The federal income tax in the United States currently taxes income on a residence basis.[1] Corporations and individuals resident in the United

1. Parts of the following description of U.S. tax law are excerpted from Hines and Hubbard (1995).

States owe taxes to the U.S. government on all of their worldwide income. To avoid double taxation, U.S. law permits U.S. multinational businesses to claim tax credits for income taxes (and related taxes) paid to foreign governments.[2] The U.S. corporation income tax rate is currently 35 percent. Under the foreign tax credit system, a U.S. corporation that earns $100 in a foreign country that has a 15 percent tax rate pays a tax of $15 to the foreign government and $20 to the U.S. government, since its U.S. corporate tax liability of $35 (35 percent of $100) is reduced to $20 by the foreign tax credit of $15.

DEFERRAL OF U.S. TAXATION. Unrepatriated profits earned by foreign subsidiaries of U.S. companies are temporarily excluded from the rule that businesses must pay tax to the U.S. government on their worldwide incomes. The deferral lasts until those profits are paid as dividends to the U.S. parent.[3] This deferral is available only on the active business profits of American-owned, separately incorporated subsidiaries in foreign countries. The profits of unincorporated foreign businesses, such as those of U.S.-owned branch banks in other countries, are taxed immediately by the United States.

To illustrate deferral, consider a U.S.-owned subsidiary that earns $500 in a foreign country that has a 10 percent tax rate. This subsidiary pays taxes of $50 to the foreign country (10 percent of $500) and might remit $100 in dividends to its U.S. parent, using the remaining $350 ($500 minus $50 of taxes minus $100 of dividends) to reinvest in its own, foreign, operations. The U.S. parent must then pay U.S. taxes on the $100 of dividends it receives (and is eligible to claim a foreign tax credit for the foreign income taxes its subsidiary paid on the $100).[4] But

2. The U.S. government is not alone in taxing the worldwide income of its resident companies while permitting companies to claim foreign tax credits. Other countries with such systems include Greece, Italy, Japan, Norway, and the United Kingdom. Under U.S. law, U.S. businesses may claim tax credits for taxes paid abroad by foreign affiliates of which they own at least 10 percent. Only those taxes that qualify as income taxes are creditable.

3. Deferral of home-country taxation of the unrepatriated profits of foreign subsidiaries is a common feature of systems that tax foreign incomes. Other countries that permit this kind of deferral include Canada, Denmark, France, Germany, Japan, Norway, Pakistan, and the United Kingdom.

4. If the parent company does not have excess foreign tax credits (on which more shortly), it is eligible to claim a foreign tax credit of $11.11, representing the product of foreign taxes paid by its subsidiary and the subsidiary's ratio of dividends to after-tax profits [$50 × ($100/$450) = $11.11]. The foreign tax credit is added to dividends received in calculating taxable foreign-source income.

the U.S. company owes no U.S. taxes on the $350 that the subsidiary earns abroad and does not remit. If the subsidiary later paid a dividend of $350, the parent would then owe U.S. tax, less foreign tax credits, on that amount.

U.S. tax law contains provisions designed to prevent American businesses from delaying the repatriation of lightly taxed foreign earnings. These tax provisions apply to foreign corporations that are at least 50 percent–owned by U.S. businesses holding stakes of at least 10 percent each. Certain income of controlled foreign corporations is "deemed distributed," and therefore immediately taxable by the United States, even if not repatriated as dividend payments. This Subpart F income consists of income from passive investments, such as interest and dividends received from investments in securities; foreign base company income that arises from using a foreign affiliate as a conduit for certain types of international transactions; income that is invested in U.S. property; money used offshore to insure risks in the United States; and money used to pay bribes to foreign government officials. American businesses with foreign subsidiaries that earn profits through most types of active business operations and that subsequently reinvest those profits in active lines of business are not subject to the Subpart F rules; they may therefore defer U.S. tax liability on their foreign profits indefinitely.

EXCESS FOREIGN TAX CREDITS. The U.S. government permits U.S. businesses to claim foreign tax credits, doing so with the understanding that this policy reduces U.S. revenue. The foreign tax credit is intended to reduce international double taxation, which could deter most international business if nothing were done about it. But U.S. policy is crafted to prevent U.S. businesses from using foreign tax credits to reduce taxes on profits earned *within* the United States. The foreign tax credit cannot exceed the tax that would have been due if the income had been earned in the United States. For example, with a U.S. tax rate of 35 percent, a U.S. corporation with $200 of foreign income faces a foreign tax credit limit of $70 (35 percent of $200). If foreign income tax is no more than $70, the corporation can claim foreign tax credits for all of its foreign taxes paid. If, however, the business pays more than $70 in foreign taxes, it could claim no more than $70 of foreign tax credits.

Businesses with foreign tax payments above the foreign tax credit limit have excess foreign tax credits. Under some circumstances, companies can use excess foreign tax credits in one year to reduce their taxes for other years. They may apply excess foreign tax credits against their U.S.

tax obligations for up to the two previous or five succeeding years.[5] U.S. law requires businesses to use all of their worldwide foreign income to calculate the foreign tax credit limit. They have excess foreign tax credits if the sum of their worldwide foreign income tax payments exceeds this limit. This procedure is known as worldwide averaging.[6]

WITHHOLDING TAXES ON INTEREST, ROYALTIES, AND DIVIDENDS. Governments commonly impose withholding taxes on cross-border flows such as interest payments, royalties, and dividend remittances. These taxes are formally the obligations of the recipients, but those who make the cross-border payments of interest, royalties, or dividends actually pay them.[7] The United States permits U.S. taxpayers to claim foreign tax credits for withholding taxes imposed by foreign governments on cross-border flows. The United States imposes 30 percent withholding taxes on interest (other than portfolio interest, which is untaxed), royalties, and dividends, but is very willing to reduce withholding through bilateral tax treaties. Other countries have similar withholding tax systems and exhibit similar eagerness to conclude bilateral agreements, which is why the United States currently has more than forty income tax treaty partners. The terms of U.S. income tax treaties vary, but they often reduce U.S. interest and royalty withholding tax rates to zero and dividend withholding tax rates to 5 percent.[8]

Payers may usually deduct, and recipients must usually include, interest and royalty payments in calculating taxable incomes. For example, a royalty payment from a foreign subsidiary to its U.S. parent reduces the subsidiary's taxable income in the foreign country and increases the tax-

---

5. Foreign tax credits are not adjusted for inflation, so taxpayers generally find them to be most valuable if claimed as soon as possible. Barring unusual circumstances, companies apply their foreign tax credits against future years only when they are not able to apply them against either of the previous two years. The most common reason why companies cannot apply excess foreign tax credits against either of the previous two years is that they have unused excess foreign credits in *those* years.

6. Not all countries that grant foreign tax credits use worldwide averaging. For example, while Japan uses worldwide averaging, the United Kingdom instead requires its companies to calculate foreign tax credits on an activity-by-activity basis. The United States used to impose separate foreign tax credit limits for each country to which a taxpayer had paid taxes. Worldwide averaging dates from the mid-1970s.

7. This design permits recipients to claim foreign tax credits while affording governments sufficient leverage over the withholding agents located in their countries to ensure that the taxes are actually paid.

8. Hines and Willard (1992) report that the average dividend withholding tax rate in U.S. tax treaties is 10.7 percent.

able income of the U.S. parent. Interest payments affect taxable incomes similarly. Royalties and interest received from foreign payers are considered to have foreign source, so U.S. taxpayers can apply any excess foreign tax credits against the associated U.S. tax liabilities. Since royalties and interest reallocate taxable incomes among jurisdictions with possibly very different tax rates, multinational companies frequently have incentives to pay excessive royalties or interest from affiliates in high-tax locations to affiliates in low-tax locations. Governments are aware of this incentive and require that royalties correspond to market values of patents, trademarks, or other intangible assets for which royalties are paid. Similarly, intracompany interest payments must be based on market interest rates.

INCOME DETERMINATION. Tax authorities prescribe regulations that determine the location of income earned by multinational corporations. Businesses with operations in many locations have incentives to relocate profits from high-tax to low-tax jurisdictions. They can do so if companies in low-tax jurisdictions pay low prices for intracompany purchases and receive high prices for intracompany sales on transactions with subsidiaries, parents, or parallel entities in high-tax jurisdictions. Most countries, including the United States and other OECD members, require that transfer prices equal the prices that would have been paid in transactions between unrelated parties. On many occasions, however, such prices are unavailable. Government regulations then provide alternative methods of determining transfer prices, but enforcement can be difficult.

A second income determination issue concerns the allocation of expense deductions among operations located in different jurisdictions. Certain expenses, such as those for interest and research and development (R&D), may enhance profitability in jurisdictions outside of those in which affiliates incur the expenses. Under U.S. law, multinational companies may deduct only a portion of their U.S. interest and R&D expenses against U.S. taxable incomes, allocating (for U.S. tax purposes) the remainder against their foreign incomes. If companies have deficit foreign tax credits, this allocation reduces their U.S. tax liabilities on foreign income by the same amount that it increases their U.S. tax liabilities on domestic income and consequently has no effect on total U.S. tax liabilities. If companies have excess foreign tax credits, however, this expense allocation increases U.S. liabilities on domestic income without any offsetting reduction in U.S. tax liabilities on foreign income (which are zero because of excess foreign tax credits). Hence, companies with excess foreign tax credits face higher costs of domestic borrowing and R&D than do companies with deficit foreign tax credits.

IMPORTS AND EXPORTS. U.S. tax law treats imports as deductible expenses and exports as taxable income. In addition, American exporters may use one of two methods that reduce U.S. taxation of export income. They may treat up to half of export profits as having foreign source. If the exporter has excess foreign tax credits, this option effectively exempts that portion of profits from U.S. tax. Or they may export goods through foreign sales corporation subsidiaries, which may indefinitely defer U.S. tax on part of export profits.

INDIVIDUALS. Under current law, American individuals, like businesses, are taxed on all of their worldwide income and may claim foreign tax credits for income taxes paid to foreign governments. Alternatively, Americans working and living abroad may exclude from their taxable U.S. incomes up to $70,000 a year of foreign-source earnings.[9]

Alternatives

The flat-tax plan advocated by Representative Armey and Senator Shelby (and embraced by many others)[10] would scrap the current federal income tax, replacing it with a modified value-added tax (VAT) on businesses and an individual tax at the same rate on wage income. Under the Armey-Shelby tax, businesses deduct wages as well as the cost of inputs—including investment—purchased from other businesses. Interest of nonfinancial businesses is neither reportable nor deductible. The flat tax is territorial in the sense that it applies only to income earned in the United States. Foreign-source income of U.S. taxpayers would be exempt from U.S. taxation, but value added (net of wages) by foreign-owned businesses operating in the United States would be taxed. The Armey-Shelby tax treats imports and exports in the same way that they are currently treated: export receipts are included as part of taxable income, and import expenses are deducted from taxable income.

---

9. The $70,000 exclusion is subject to various requirements, and taxpayers facing very high costs of foreign housing can deduct excess housing costs from their foreign-source incomes before excluding $70,000 for U.S. tax purposes. See Redmiles (1994) for a description of current U.S. law.

10. Hall and Rabushka (1995), who are the original architects of the plan, describe and analyze the principal version of the flat tax currently under consideration.

The value-added tax embraced by Representative Sam Gibbons is a flat-rate tax on business value added. It differs from the Armey-Shelby plan in that businesses do not deduct wages in calculating their taxable incomes, and individuals do not pay the tax at all. In contrast to the Armey-Shelby plan, the Gibbons VAT would rebate taxes on export sales and impose tax on imports. Foreign-source income of U.S. businesses and individuals is exempt from taxation under Representative Gibbons's plan; in this respect the Gibbons VAT resembles European VATs.

The USA tax includes a business VAT and a progressive personal tax. As in the Armey-Shelby tax, companies would deduct input costs (including capital purchases); nonfinancial businesses would exclude interest receipts, but could not deduct interest payments. The USA tax retains the deductibility of mortgage interest in its individual tax component. Like the Gibbons VAT, the USA tax is border adjustable. Value added abroad by foreign subsidiaries of U.S. companies is also exempt from U.S. taxation under the USA plan. The plan does, however, require individuals to pay U.S. tax on foreign-source income (net of foreign tax credits for income taxes paid to foreign governments).

The sales-tax plan proposed by Senator Lugar envisions replacing federal income taxes (other than the social security payroll taxes) with a national sales tax. This sales tax would be applied on sales to domestic consumers, not to businesses. The system is territorial only in the sense that sales to foreigners are not taxed. The base of the Lugar tax is domestic consumption, whether financed by income earned in the United States or income earned abroad.

The Armey-Shelby flat tax, Gibbons VAT, and Lugar sales tax plans are silent on their intentions for the 30 percent U.S. withholding taxes, but it appears that they would unilaterally eliminate them.[11] In contrast, the Nunn-Domenici USA tax would maintain these taxes. The withholding tax changes introduced by the Armey-Shelby, Gibbons, and Lugar tax plans are of course not quite as dramatic as would be the elimination of withholding taxes under the current U.S. tax system, since the plans do not permit businesses to deduct interest payments, and the Armey-Shelby flat tax and the Gibbons VAT do not permit deductions for royalties paid to foreigners. The Nunn-Domenici USA tax also removes the deductibility of interest and royalties paid to foreigners, but at an 11 percent business tax rate, this change is less consequential than it would be with the current U.S. tax rate of 35 percent.

---

11. Grubert and Newlon (1995) make this observation.

Differing Philosophies

The current U.S. income tax takes as its tax base the incomes of American residents. To be sure, the current system offers numerous credits and exclusions for the foreign-source incomes of American companies and individuals, but it does so as concessions to source taxation by other governments and out of concern over double taxation. The guiding principle, however, is a desire to tax the *worldwide* incomes of Americans. The tax bases in the Armey-Shelby and Gibbons proposals are income— other than capital income—*earned* in the United States. The tax base in the Lugar proposal is *individual consumption* in the United States, which is almost the same as consumption by individual Americans. The tax base in the Nunn-Domenici proposal is individual consumption of Americans along with business cash flow from U.S. activities. Table 13-1 summarizes the major differences among the international features of the plans.

These tax base differences are responsible for differing treatments of foreign transactions and for differing degrees to which international transactions affect tax revenue. There are numerous areas of overlap; for example, the taxation of consumption in the United States indirectly taxes some of the foreign-source incomes of Americans. Income taxation is typically thought to entail more enforcement difficulties than does consumption taxation, since income often is harder for authorities to observe than is consumption. In addition, taxpayers may have far greater abilities to reallocate income in response to tax rate differences than they do to reallocate consumption. Below I examine these differences in specific situations.

Impact on Macroeconomic Activity

A shift to consumption taxation may affect interest rates and the current account. It will also influence foreign direct investment, an activity that is almost exclusively undertaken by multinational corporations.

INTEREST RATES. Much of the attraction of consumption-oriented tax reforms stems from the removal of any differences between the before-tax and the after-tax returns to saving. By removing these differences, these reforms are likely to stimulate domestic saving.[12] Some analysts argue that increased U.S. savings will cause U.S. interest rates to fall,

---

12. Hall (1996).

Table 13-1. *Alternative U.S. Tax Treatments of International Transactions*[a]

		Tax regime			
Type of transaction	Current system	Armey-Shelby flat tax	Gibbons VAT	Nunn-Domenici USA tax	Lugar sales tax
Individuals					
Foreign investment income	Taxed (FTC)	Untaxed	Untaxed	Untaxed	Untaxed
Foreign labor income consumed abroad	Taxed (FTC & excl.)	Taxed	Untaxed	Taxed (FTC)	Untaxed
Foreign labor income consumed in the U.S.	Taxed (FTC)	Taxed	Taxed	Taxed (FTC)	Taxed
Domestic labor income consumed abroad	Taxed	Taxed	Untaxed	Taxed	Untaxed
Corporations					
Foreign-source dividends, interest, and royalties	Taxed (FTC)	Untaxed	Untaxed	Untaxed	Untaxed
Export receipts	Taxed (partially)	Taxed	Untaxed	Untaxed	Untaxed
Import expenses	Deductible	Deductible	Nondeductible	Nondeductible	Nondeductible

a. The table describes the treatment of income sources under current U.S. tax law and four proposed alternatives. The qualifier (FTC) indicates that foreign tax credits can be used to offset some or all of associated U.S. tax obligations; the qualifier (FTC & excl.) indicates that taxpayers can exclude a certain portion of foreign income from U.S. taxation or apply foreign tax credits against associated U.S. tax obligations; and the qualifier (partially) indicates that only a part of receipts need be included in taxable income.

thereby stimulating business investment and partially compensating homeowners for the removal of tax deductibility of mortgage interest.[13] Robert E. Hall and Alvin Rabushka estimate that domestic real interest rates would fall by approximately one-fifth if the United States were to adopt the Armey-Shelby plan.[14]

Others note that consumption-oriented tax reforms simultaneously raise after-tax returns to both saving and investing, thereby boosting the demand for capital as well as its supply, making their effects on interest rates indeterminate.[15] Empirical studies usually find the demand for capital to be more interest rate–sensitive than is the supply of capital. Martin Feldstein argues that the effect of tax reform on capital demand is stronger than its effect on saving, particularly in the short run.[16] He calculates that domestic real interest rates would nearly double in the very short run and remain higher than pre-reform interest rates over longer horizons.

In an open-economy setting, major tax reforms may affect pre-tax interest rates little or not at all, even if they change domestic saving and investment by large amounts. The reason is that the domestic market for capital may represent only a small part of the world market that determines world interest rates and what businesses and individuals can borrow or save abroad. Fundamental tax reforms in the United States do not directly influence demand for capital deployed in foreign countries, nor do they affect foreign supply of capital, since foreigners are not currently (and would not be in any of the reform scenarios) taxed by the United States on portfolio interest received from U.S. sources.

Of course, international variations in interest rates reflect differences in underlying inflation rates and other considerations. From the standpoint of lenders, what matters are risk-adjusted nominal interest rates corrected for anticipated exchange-rate appreciation or depreciation.[17] If

13. See, for example, Hall (1995, 1996), Hall and Rabushka (1995), and Eric Toder, "Comments on Proposals for Fundamental Tax Reform," *Tax Notes*, vol. 66, March 27, 1995, pp. 2003–15.

14. Hall and Rabushka (1995).

15. Bradford (1996) and Grubert and Newlon (1995).

16. Feldstein (1995).

17. This condition holds only if the tax treatment of foreign-source capital income is unaffected by its decomposition into interest and foreign exchange gains and losses. The tax systems of some countries (including the United States) distinguish these two sources of return, thereby creating incentives for investors that differ based on expected exchange rate movements. See Levi (1977), Hartman (1979), Wahl (1989). Consequently, uncovered interest parity only approximates the equilibrium condition for lenders from some countries.

risk-free interest rates in a country exceed those available elsewhere, and if the country's currency is not expected to depreciate relative to others, then the country will quite naturally attract capital in search of high returns. The inflow of capital ultimately depresses local interest rates (or creates a situation in which the local currency is expected to depreciate), thereby equalizing expected returns in different locations.

ONE QUALIFICATION. The inability of domestic policies to affect interest rates that are determined on world markets is subject to an important qualification. This conclusion follows from two closely related conditions. The first is covered interest parity, in which differences between spot and futures prices of foreign exchange perfectly offset interest rate differences. The second is uncovered interest parity, in which interest rate differences equal anticipated changes in relative exchange rates. Covered interest parity is an arbitrage relationship, in the sense that adept investors could earn risk-free profits should it fail to hold. By contrast, uncovered interest parity is not an arbitrage relationship, and therefore its absence generally cannot be exploited by investors without exposure to associated exchange-rate risk.

Quantitative studies of foreign-exchange markets generally confirm the existence of covered interest parity,[18] but they present a decidedly mixed picture of uncovered interest parity. Standard tests of market equilibrium find that large deviations from uncovered interest parity can occur and are correlated with observable variables, making them predictable to rational investors.[19] Many analysts have tried to explain deviations from uncovered interest parity with risk aversion or expectational errors on the part of investors.[20] These efforts suggest that the evidence might be consistent with equal risk-adjusted expected real interest rates across countries, but only if unlikely circumstances (such as enormous risk aversion in foreign exchange markets) prevail. The more likely interpretation is that interest rates are not perfectly equalized across countries.

If true, this result implies that investors could improve their returns by reallocating some of their capital among countries. Their failure to do

18. Frankel (1991) notes that observed deviations from covered-interest parity typically occur in countries with capital controls.

19. Examples include Bilson (1981), Fama (1984), Campbell and Clarida (1987), Giovannini and Jorion (1987), and Cumby (1988).

20. An alternative possibility is that the statistical tests were flawed, possibly because of "peso problems." See, for example, Dominguez (1986), Engel (1984, 1992), Frankel (1986), Froot and Frankel (1989), Kaminsky (1993), and Lewis (1989).

so is puzzling and may be related to an aversion to owning foreign assets. Kenneth R. French and James M. Poterba document a very strong investor preference for domestic securities.[21] They attribute this preference to subjective and quite possibly irrational beliefs that foreign investments are riskier than domestic investments. Martin Feldstein and Charles Horioka found that national saving and investment are highly correlated, from which they inferred that capital is somewhat immobile internationally.[22] Subsequent studies report similar correlations of saving and investment rates but offer the alternative interpretation that correlated omitted variables of one kind or another, rather than capital immobility, could account for this pattern.[23]

Consequently, the evidence on capital mobility is at least consistent with the possibility that risk-adjusted national real interest rates could deviate from world real interest rates without stimulating fully offsetting capital movements. This conclusion does not, however, mean that sizable differences are *likely* to persist over significant periods of time. Central banks may adjust national monetary policies in response to international interest rate differentials if they seek to prevent excessive capital movements. Consequently, a tax reform that changes net domestic capital demand (at given interest rates) may not lead to sizable interest rate changes if monetary policies adjust to forestall international capital movements.

A SECOND QUALIFICATION. Even if international interest rates are equal, the U.S. economy may be so large that U.S. tax policy can influence U.S. interest rates through its effect on world interest rates. In 1992 the United States produced 25.4 percent of world output and accounted for 16.8 percent of world saving and 18.2 percent of the world investment.[24] Whether these shares are large enough for U.S. policies to affect world interest rates is a difficult question. But they suggest that the much larger world capital market is likely to absorb most of the effect on interest rates of changes in the United States.

---

21. French and Poterba (1991).
22. Feldstein and Horioka (1980).
23. These studies are surveyed by Frankel (1991).
24. The 1992 figures for GDP, saving, and investment are reported in World Bank (1994). These statistics suffer from many limitations, not the least of which is the difficulty of translating separate national accounts into common currencies; nevertheless, these numbers offer useful indicators of orders of magnitude.

Exchange Rates and the Current Account

The ability of U.S. exporters to compete in world markets is understandably important to U.S. policymakers, and fundamental tax reforms are often evaluated on the basis of their effect on U.S. export performance. Tax reforms would probably influence the volume and composition of American exports, though the sources of this influence may be subtler than at first appears.

BORDER ADJUSTMENTS. The reform proposals differ markedly in their treatment of imports and exports. The Gibbons, Nunn-Domenici, and Lugar plans all exclude export sales by American businesses from taxable income and directly or indirectly tax import purchases as consumption in the United States. The exclusion of export sales and the inclusion of imports are known as "border adjustments." The Armey-Shelby plan is similar to the current U.S. tax system in that profits from export sales are taxable, while business purchases of imports are deductible.

There is no theoretical reason to expect border adjustments to influence trade patterns because the exchange rate can move to perfectly offset the effect of border adjustments.[25] Consider, for example, the consequences of somehow removing border adjustments from the Nunn-Domenici plan so that export sales were included in taxable income (and therefore subject to an 11 percent tax), while businesses were permitted to deduct expenditures on imports. A simultaneous 11 percent depreciation of the dollar would perfectly offset the removal of U.S. border adjustments, since an 11 percent weaker dollar makes it possible for foreigners to purchase U.S. exports at prices that include the 11 percent tax now imposed on exports but at no greater cost as measured in their own currencies. U.S. exporters will receive unchanged after-tax returns if their export prices (measured in dollars) rise by 11 percent when border adjustability is removed; and importers, too, are unaffected if import prices (measured in dollars) rise by 11 percent due to a currency depreciation at the same time that imports become deductible against a tax rate of 11 percent. If markets are in equilibrium before the removal of border adjustments, they can be expected to remain in equilibrium by a simultaneous fall in the value of the dollar.[26] Consequently, differences

25. Grossman (1980), Dixit (1985), and Feldstein and Krugman (1990) elaborate this well-known feature of border adjustment.

26. This line of reasoning ignores any effects on trade of changes in asset portfolios caused by exchange rate changes.

in the treatment of exports and imports in different tax reform plans should not influence U.S. export performance.

A COMPLICATION. While this reasoning is sound, it presumes that exchange rates are determined by purchasing power parity (PPP), a theory that is not consistent with all of the available evidence. PPP implies that exchange rates move to equate the prices of goods in different markets; if PPP does not hold, then buyers of internationally traded goods can reduce their costs by reconfiguring their purchases. Since normal market pressures gradually erode such price disparities, PPP should hold over the long run, and possibly at every point in time. In fact, PPP seems to hold over very long time horizons, but an average of four years is required for market prices to converge halfway to PPP once significant deviations appear.[27]

It is difficult to draw strong lessons from this evidence for the effect of tax changes, since little is known about why exchange rates deviate from PPP. The fact that PPP does not always hold does not necessarily mean that removing U.S. taxes on export revenues will stimulate exports. It is *conceivable*, for example, that PPP does not hold because exchange rates overreact to tax changes. In that case the exclusion of export income from the tax base could make U.S. exports less competitive in world markets. It is perhaps more likely that tax changes that affect domestic price levels do not generate immediate offsetting exchange-rate movements. For example, the introduction of a Gibbons-style VAT, which taxes imports and exempts exports, may require U.S. dollar appreciation to maintain trade balance. As a short-run matter, exchange rates may not offset tax changes entirely, but the evidence also suggests that they are likely to do so over a period of several years.

While the border adjustments may not affect international trade over the long run, other tax changes are likely to do so. Fundamental reforms remove current U.S. tax subsidies for exports through the foreign-sourcing rules and foreign sales corporations and could change U.S. factor endowments by encouraging capital accumulation in the United States. Theory predicts that countries will export commodities that use intensively the factors in which they are relatively well endowed. An increased U.S. capital-labor ratio should encourage U.S. exports of capital-intensive goods and U.S. imports of labor-intensive goods. This

27. See, for example, Abuaf and Jorion (1990), Johnson (1990), Frankel (1991), Wei and Parsley (1995), and Froot, Kim, and Rogoff (1995).

theory has difficulty explaining many observed trade patterns,[28] but it may indicate the likely effect of the proposed tax changes. The Armey-Shelby and Gibbons plans would also remove the advantaged tax treatment of owner-occupied housing. Owners for whom housing suddenly becomes more expensive may be inclined to change their investment and consumption patterns. While even the direction of the resulting effect on net exports is difficult to predict, it could be quite important.

International trade theory suggests that tax reforms influence long-run trade patterns by changing domestic factor supplies and commodity demands, not through border adjustments. The same theory also requires that countries not run long-run current account surpluses or deficits, since doing so implies that some debts would remain unpaid over long time horizons. The theory, therefore, rules out any effect of tax policies—or any other policies—on net exports over the long run, since trade must be balanced. The issue of competitiveness, if viewed as one of maintaining net export surpluses, is then strictly a short-run consideration—and a questionable one at that, since trade surpluses must, in time, be replaced by trade deficits. If competitiveness is instead interpreted as a profitability condition, then fundamental tax reforms should be evaluated according to their impact on the activities and returns of businesses and individuals.

Impact on Multinational Corporations

Tax policies influence most activities of multinational corporations. Empirical studies indicate that U.S. businesses own more capital in low-tax countries and less capital in high-tax countries than they would in the absence of tax differences and that they structure their finances to reduce tax obligations.[29] In addition, specific U.S. tax provisions, such as the export tax subsidies and the tax penalties for foreign bribery and foreign boycott participation, also influence the behavior of U.S. companies.[30]

The responsiveness of multinational businesses to tax incentives suggests that fundamental tax reforms might significantly change how businesses operate in the United States and U.S. companies do business

28. See Leamer and Levinsohn (1995) for a recent survey of empirical tests of theories of international trade that focus on factor endowments.

29. Hines (1996) surveys this literature.

30. See Kemsley (1995), Hines (1995b), and Redmiles (1992).

around the world.[31] Tax changes influence several closely related practices of multinational companies.

Effect on Financial Activities of Multinational Companies

The financial practices of multinational companies reflect many objectives, including a desire to avoid taxes. Fundamental tax reform would affect the profitability of different financial policies, therefore influencing which ones businesses adopt. The choice of transfer pricing strategy is among the most important. Transfer prices are the prices used in transactions among entities—a parent and its foreign subsidiaries, for example—located in different countries but within the same controlled group. Government regulations limit company discretion on transfer pricing but are notoriously difficult to interpret and enforce. As a result, businesses retain some latitude to set prices to reduce their own tax liabilities.

By taxing only domestic consumption, the retail sales tax would greatly encourage multinational companies to set transfer prices in order to shift profits to the United States, where they would be untaxed, instead of to foreign countries that retain taxes on profits. The incentives created by the Armey-Shelby flat tax, the Gibbons VAT, and the Nunn-Domenici USA tax plans are similar, though smaller, because businesses would pay U.S. taxes, although at rates much below the current 35 percent corporate profits tax. If foreign governments keep their current tax systems, then the U.S. business tax rate—whichever plan is adopted—would be much lower than rates in other countries where most foreign operations of U.S. businesses are located.[32] The same incentives would apply to foreign-chartered businesses operating in the United States.

At the same time, the Armey-Shelby, Gibbons, and Nunn-Domenici plans terminate the foreign tax credit. This change would encourage U.S. companies to shift foreign source profits to foreign tax haven countries

31. Some argue that the actions of certain multinational companies are motivated as much by nationalism as by desires to maximize after-tax profits and that nationalism is responsible for their willingness to pay significant taxes to home-country governments in order to avoid smaller tax obligations to host-country governments. There is no systematic evidence of this type of behavior in practice.

32. Hines and Rice (1994) calculate a 31 percent unweighted mean foreign tax rate paid by U.S. multinationals in 78 countries 1982. In deriving this figure Hines and Rice oversample tax havens, so a weighted mean tax rate would be considerably higher.

as well as to the United States. Under current law, the foreign tax credit desensitizes U.S. taxpayers to foreign liabilities, because those taxpayers know that U.S. credits will be available when the income is repatriated. Repeal of the foreign tax credit, with this offset no longer available, would increase the attractiveness of tax havens. Given the small share of U.S. business activities located in tax havens, however, the net effect of fundamental reform is likely to be one of shifting profits from foreign countries into the United States.

The current practices of U.S. and foreign businesses indicate the rough magnitude of likely reactions to fundamental U.S. tax reform. Royalty payments by foreign subsidiaries to their U.S. parent companies are quite sensitive to withholding tax rates on royalties.[33] Profitability of foreign subsidiaries of U.S. parents varies negatively with local tax rates after controlling for various inputs and local conditions.[34] Only half of the reported low profitability of foreign-owned companies in the United States can be explained by observable inputs, suggesting that the other half could represent aggressive transfer pricing by businesses eager to avoid U.S. tax liabilities.[35] U.S. parents with foreign subsidiaries in tax havens have unusually low U.S. tax liabilities.[36] The reduction in the U.S. corporation income tax rate in 1986 was associated with a sharp rise in reported returns on equity in the United States among companies with foreign operations.[37]

The quantitative evidence suggests that multinational businesses are capable of reducing taxable incomes in high-tax locations and raising them in low-tax locations. This evidence by no means implies violation of transfer pricing laws, though of course it does not rule out that possibility. It means that current laws allow some shifting of taxable profits. Indeed, it is noteworthy that companies do not reduce tax liabilities in high-tax locations more than they do. Even the highest estimated responsiveness of reported profits to tax rates indicates that multinational companies have only limited capacity to relocate their profits. Eric M. Rice and I report that the elasticity of pre-tax profits with respect to tax rates is well below unity when evaluated at the mean.[38]

33. Kopits (1976), Hines (1995a), and Grubert (1995).
34. Grubert and Mutti (1991) and Hines and Rice (1994).
35. Grubert, Goodspeed, and Swenson (1993).
36. Harris and others (1993).
37. Klassen, Lang, and Wolfson (1993). Hines (1996) offers a critical survey of the quantitative transfer pricing literature.
38. Hines and Rice (1994).

Transfer pricing practices reflect the historical behavior of businesses, itself a function of government enforcement efforts. If the United States were to adopt the Lugar sales tax, then transfer pricing would become irrelevant from a U.S. tax standpoint, and the U.S. government would certainly devote far fewer (if any) resources to enforcing international transfer pricing rules. Consequently, the responsibility for defending their tax bases would fall entirely on foreign governments, which may or may not be well positioned to evaluate transfer pricing issues involving U.S. affiliates. Furthermore, intergovernmental consultations that are often helpful in resolving transfer pricing disputes would become less interesting to the United States. As a result, companies would probably have greater abilities to select transfer prices that reduce their worldwide tax burdens. The same considerations would apply, though to a lesser degree, if the United States adopted any reform that significantly reduced U.S. business tax rates.

One type of transfer pricing change is not likely to enhance U.S. revenues—the treatment of interest income under the Armey-Shelby flat tax. U.S. exporters would have incentives to relabel taxable export receipts as untaxed interest receipts if possible, since doing so would reduce U.S. tax liabilities. There is an open question of whether the relatively low rate under the Armey-Shelby plan creates an incentive worth risking enforcement penalties in order to undertake such a relabeling, particularly since existing transfer pricing regulations can probably be used to prevent pure tax avoidance through this channel.

Transfer pricing would still be important even if fundamental tax reform effectively eliminated U.S. taxation of new investment income. Transfer pricing remains important to U.S. tax collections to the extent that business income remains taxable, as under the Armey-Shelby flat tax or the USA tax. In addition, the ability to avoid tax by adjusting transfer prices affects the desirability of locating business operations in various jurisdictions. In becoming a low-tax country with weak transfer price enforcement, the United States also becomes more attractive to investors as long as other countries do not do the same.

Tax reform will also influence other financial aspects of the operations of multinational businesses. The treatment of corporate debt finance would change dramatically with fundamental tax reform and with it the treatment of the financing of foreign affiliates with debt.[39] Since interest

39. This issue is examined in Hines (1994), Grubert (1995), Altshuler and Mintz (1995), and Froot and Hines (1995).

receipts would not be taxable in the United States, while interest payments would remain deductible abroad, U.S. companies would have incentives, to the extent permitted by thin capitalization rules, to replace equity with debt finance of their foreign affiliates. Foreign companies operating in the United States would generally be loath to finance their U.S. affiliates with debt, since the favorable U.S. tax rate would reward locating as much taxable income as possible in the United States.

By removing U.S. taxation of foreign-source income, fundamental tax reforms would eliminate the incentives U.S. multinationals currently have to defer repatriation of their foreign profits and remit dividends from abroad on a selective and generally inefficient basis.[40] In addition, fundamental reform would make the United States a very attractive country for the corporate residence of multinational companies. There is evidence of some mobility on the part of multinational companies seeking to avoid home-country taxation of their foreign earnings.[41] Fundamental tax reform would position the United States to attract such companies.

Effect on Direct Investment

Fundamental tax reform would change after-tax returns to many activities in ways that directly or indirectly influence levels of U.S. direct investment abroad and foreign direct investment in the United States. The exemption of foreign-source income from U.S. tax would encourage U.S. companies to invest abroad, but the simultaneous removal of U.S. capital taxation would make the United States a more attractive location for capital, perhaps thereby reducing foreign investment by American businesses. The net effect of the legislation therefore turns on the extent to which domestic and foreign investment may substitute for or complement each other.

High tax rates appear to discourage investment by multinational companies.[42] While the many empirical studies use different data and meth-

40. For evidence of the impact of taxation on dividend payments by the foreign subsidiaries of U.S. multinationals to their parent companies, see Hines and Hubbard (1990), Altshuler and Newlon (1993), and Altshuler, Newlon, and Randolph (1995). The evidence suggests that tax incentives are largely responsible for the very skewed pattern of dividend payments in practice; Hines and Hubbard report that 84 percent of the foreign subsidiaries of U.S. multinationals paid zero dividends to their American parents in 1984.

41. See, for example, Hines (1991) and Collins and Shackelford (1995).

42. See Boskin and Gale (1987); Young (1988); Slemrod (1990); and Hines (forthcoming) for evidence of strong tax effects on foreign direct investment in the United States. Studies of U.S. direct investment abroad include Boskin and Gale (1987); Grubert and Mutti (1991); Harris (1993); and Hines and Rice (1994).

ods, they suggest that the elasticity of foreign direct investment with respect to after-tax returns is about one.[43] On net, eliminating the capital income tax is likely to make the United States a more attractive place for investment by both domestic and foreign companies. Initially, capital inflows are likely to cause the U.S. dollar to appreciate, reducing the volume of U.S. exports and increasing imports. In time the U.S. dollar will appreciate to support the repatriation of profits to foreign investors in the United States.

Investors from foreign tax credit countries now can claim foreign tax credits for their U.S. tax obligations. Whether U.S. taxes would continue to be creditable after fundamental tax reform is debatable, since credits are typically granted only for income taxes, and the United States would no longer impose an income tax. Businesses are exempt from retail sales tax, so there is nothing to credit. The flat tax, VAT, and USA taxes are somewhat more complex cases, and controversy persists over their potential creditability.[44]

Even if the new taxes could not be credited, fundamental reform would nevertheless enhance the attractiveness of the United States as an investment location for foreign investors. Creditability would be a minor issue for two reasons. Expensing of investment so greatly reduces business tax obligations that little U.S. tax would remain to credit, and this remainder represents taxes on investment returns in excess of the normal rate of return. The second is that less than half of foreign direct investment in the United States comes from countries that grant foreign tax credits. Of the countries listed in table 13-2, only three—Italy, Japan, and the United Kingdom—use foreign tax credit systems. These three countries account for less than 40 percent of foreign-owned property, plant, and equipment in the United States in 1992 and also less than 40 percent of U.S. employment by foreign-owned companies.

Effects on Other Activities

Fundamental tax reform is likely also to influence the location of R&D, the extent to which companies choose to transfer technologies abroad, and the degree to which they export from the United States instead of producing goods abroad for sale in foreign markets. As a

43. Hines (1996) critically reviews the evidence on foreign direct investment.
44. Avi-Yonah (1995) and McIntyre (1996) argue that they would not be creditable. McLure and Zodrow (1996) and Grubert and Newlon (1995) believe that they would be.

Table 13-2. *Foreign Activity in the United States, by Country of Ultimate Beneficial Owner, 1992*

| Country | Property, plant, and equipment | | Employment | |
	1992 $ (billions)	Percent of foreign total	Thousands	Percent of foreign total
Australia	$19.1	2.94	137.8	2.99
Belgium	12.6	1.94	99.6	2.16
Canada	96.6	14.85	587.9	12.75
France	44.7	6.87	358.7	7.78
Germany	55.4	8.52	519.5	11.27
Italy	5.9	0.91	42.3	0.92
Japan	133.5	20.53	728.2	15.79
Kuwait	8.8	1.53	9.6	0.21
Netherlands	61.2	9.41	306.1	6.64
Saudi Arabia	6.8	1.05	10.2	0.22
Sweden	12.6	1.94	157.0	3.40
Switzerland	25.7	3.95	295.1	6.40
United Kingdom	114.0	17.53	961.4	20.85
Venezuela	5.1	0.78	15.8	0.34
Total other foreign	150.9	23.20	382.2	8.29

Source: United States Department of Commerce, Bureau of Economic Analysis (1994). The first column reports gross book values of foreign-controlled property, plant, and equipment (PPE) as of year-end 1992; the third column reports U.S. employment of foreign-controlled affiliates in the United States. Dollar amounts are billions of dollars; employment figures are thousands of full-time employees. The table entries include all countries with $5 billion or more of PPE at year-end 1992.

general rule, the ability to avoid all U.S. tax on foreign operations, along with the ability to claim a tax deduction for 100 percent of R&D expenses incurred in the United States, would enhance the attractiveness of the United States as a location in which to perform R&D, particularly if multinational companies can use technologies developed in the United States to enhance the profitability of affiliates in low-tax foreign countries or if royalties received from abroad are not included in U.S. taxable income. The removal of the special tax treatment of export income would discourage U.S. exports, but this change, along with others, must be evaluated in the context of the much more dramatic change introduced by removing the tax on capital income in the United States.

Cross-Border Activities of Individuals

Fundamental tax reform would change the incentives for individuals to work and consume abroad. For high-income Americans who live in low-tax foreign countries, or for any Americans with opportunities to work there temporarily, current U.S. law imposes tax burdens not incurred by local workers. Furthermore, U.S. taxation of foreign-source capital income gives Americans incentives to invest in securities paying the highest pre-tax rates of return because foreign withholding taxes are creditable against U.S. tax liabilities. Such taxes do not affect the total tax liabilities of individual recipients of foreign-source capital income, but they do reduce U.S. tax collections.

All of the consumption-oriented tax reforms would significantly change the incentives of individuals. By taxing only domestic consumption, the sales tax, the Armey-Shelby flat tax, and the Gibbons VAT encourage individuals to select foreign employment based on after-foreign-tax compensation (as well as lifestyle considerations); their treatment of foreign labor income is similar to what current U.S. law would be if it asserted territorial, rather than worldwide, jurisdiction.

The USA tax retains U.S. taxation of foreign-source income while providing foreign tax credits in a manner similar to that of the current U.S. tax system. But the USA tax changes the U.S. personal income tax base and personal income tax rates. It is likely, therefore, to affect the foreign tax credit status of individuals with foreign-earned income. In particular, if foreign tax credits are calculated in a manner akin to current procedure, many people will find themselves with excess foreign tax credits. This result is particularly likely for high-income savers, whose taxable incomes shrink under the Nunn-Domenici plan; and Americans living abroad tend (at least currently) to be well compensated.[45] Consequently, the USA tax is likely to eliminate U.S. tax on foreign earnings of some individuals, while for others the removal of the $70,000 exclusion would create new U.S. tax liabilities on their foreign-source incomes. The net *aggregate* effect of the Nunn-Domenici plan on U.S. taxation of foreign-source labor income is unclear.

Removing U.S. taxation of capital income will raise the after-tax returns Americans receive from investing both in the United States and abroad. Now individuals pay the same tax on investment income wherever it is earned, as long as the foreign tax credit offsets foreign liabilities. Under a consumption tax, no U.S. tax on capital income would be imposed. But the repeal of the foreign tax credit would mean that U.S.

---

45. Data reported in Redmiles (1994) indicate that filers of Form 2555—Americans who live and work abroad—had average foreign incomes of $73,000 in 1991.

net effect would be to encourage U.S. taxpayers to shift investments home from abroad.

A different logic applies to the allocation of labor supply by Americans. While the United States currently taxes little of the foreign-source labor earnings of Americans,[46] tax on labor income consumed abroad would be removed under the fundamental reforms. Furthermore, the introduction of a consumption tax would create a new disincentive to consume in the United States. For this reason, tax reform might increase the attractiveness of foreign employment relative to domestic employment. How much this incentive influences employment and labor hours depends, of course, on the responsiveness of labor supply to differences in after-tax compensation. Male labor supply is generally thought to be unresponsive to compensation differences (with female labor supply somewhat more so), but very little is known about the elasticity of international employment substitution.

Whatever the tax incentives created by fundamental reforms, the apparent reluctance of Americans to work abroad (or at least to report doing so)[47] suggests that the effects would be small. It is conceivable, but hardly likely,[48] that fundamental tax reforms could so stimulate capital accumulation in the United States that the productivity of U.S. workers would rise enough to offset or reverse the effect of the tax change on after-tax wages. Furthermore, any effects from capital deepening are likely to appear slowly.

Consumption-oriented tax alternatives such as the sales tax and the VAT can encourage taxpayers who earn income in one country to consume it in other countries that have lower tax rates. Americans could avoid a sales tax or a VAT by consuming outside the United States. In contrast, the USA tax falls on worldwide consumption, and the personal component of the Armey-Shelby flat tax falls on earnings, rather than on consumption. While the sales tax and the VAT encourage people to consume in low-tax countries, doing so on a large scale would be costly.

46. Redmiles (1994) reports that Americans living and working abroad had total foreign-source salaries and wages of $16.0 billion in 1991. After excluding $9.7 billion from U.S. taxable income, and applying $0.8 billion of foreign tax credits, their aggregate U.S. tax liability on this income was $0.9 billion.

47. The $16.0 billion of foreign-source wage and salary income of Americans living abroad in 1991 reported by Redmiles (1994) contrasts with $2.7 trillion of total 1991 wage and salary incomes of Americans reported by Gross (1993).

48. See chapter 2 by Alan J. Auerbach and chapter 3 by Eric M. Engen and William G. Gale in this volume.

Americans spent $43.6 billion while traveling abroad in 1994, while foreigners traveling in the United States spent $60.4 billion.[49] The introduction of a national sales tax in the United States might encourage a reversal of these numbers, but even such a change would not have large effects on the U.S. economy.

Transition

International assets are affected by the transition, but their small relative size makes transition issues somewhat less important than they are for domestic assets. To the extent that a transition from income- to consumption-oriented taxation affects returns to domestic investments, there will naturally be some spillover into foreign investment activity.

One major transition issue concerns unused depreciation allowances and whether reforms such as the Armey-Shelby flat tax would be designed to compensate existing companies for depreciation allowances that would otherwise be lost. Foreign owners of U.S. assets would bear a nontrivial fraction of the transition incidence of plans that fail to compensate existing owners for depreciation allowances never claimed; whether or not this fact enhances the desirability of transition relief depends on complex considerations. Foreign owners of U.S. capital would experience similar capital losses in a transition to a Gibbons-style VAT, but the border adjustments could cause some increase in the value of the U.S. dollar and ameliorate transition losses.

Another international redistribution created by the transition is the loss of deferred U.S. tax liability on the unrepatriated foreign profits of American businesses. The aggregate stock of this future liability was about $29 billion in 1986.[50] The very rapid subsequent growth of the foreign earnings of U.S. corporations implies that, in spite of the reduction of the U.S. corporate tax rate from 46 percent to 35 percent, this unpaid tax liability is surely much higher now. Reform plans (such as the Armey-Shelby flat tax) that exempt from U.S. taxation the foreign incomes of American businesses would provide windfalls to existing owners of foreign subsidiaries.

49. See Mann and Barges (1995).
50. Hines (1991).

Policy Formation and Coordination

Fundamental U.S. tax reforms that influence the attractiveness of the United States as a location for multinational businesses to earn their profits may also encourage other governments to reconsider their own tax systems. Very little is known about how they would respond. Germany remains a high-tax country surrounded by low-tax competitors in an open European market. But countries can retaliate if they think U.S. tax policies will cause multinational companies to shift operations abroad or use various devices to shift tax base abroad.

Forecasting the reactions of other governments is hard because so many economic and political considerations influence tax policy formation. Many countries reduced tax rates and broadened bases in the mid-1980s at about the same time the United States enacted the Tax Reform Act of 1986. But it is not necessarily correct to infer that competitive pressures from the United States were responsible for these reforms. The U.S. tax reform in part reflected an international consensus on appropriate principles of tax reform, and U.S. actions underscored to international observers their potential value.

One of the interesting international questions raised by fundamental tax reform is its effect on the U.S. tax treaty network. Reuven S. Avi-Yonah's prediction that other countries would respond to U.S. tax reform by abrogating their treaty agreements with the United States is unlikely on three grounds.[51] Treaty-provided withholding tax reductions generally benefit countries that reduce rates and would be even more beneficial if the United States abolished its foreign tax credit. In addition, it is probably a mistake to view tax treaty negotiations in isolation from other diplomatic connections between countries. Finally, the nondiscrimination provisions of tax treaties might be of great value to foreign investors after fundamental tax reform, thereby making foreign governments reluctant to forgo treaty opportunities with the United States.[52]

Border Cash-Flow Taxation

Current tax reform proposals, other than Representative Gephardt's modified income tax, exempt foreign-source income from direct U.S.

51. Avi-Yonah (1995).
52. Grubert and Newlon (1995).

taxation. This feature creates some knotty enforcement issues because exemption of foreign-source income gives some businesses incentives to recharacterize cross-border payments to avoid taxes.

Border cash-flow (BCF) tax treatment of border transactions could be incorporated within some of the plans to address these issues. The idea underlying BCF is to treat any cash flow across the border as a taxable event, with resources flowing out of the United States constituting deductions and resources flowing into the United States constituting income. Under BCF, as under the current U.S. tax system, export receipts are taxable and import expenses are deductible. Border cash-flow taxation treats capital transactions the same way it treats exports and imports of inventory property. Hence, capital funds invested abroad in equity or debt are deductible against current income. Any receipts from abroad—dividends, interest, royalties, or loan repayments—are taxable. The simplest version of BCF applies to transactions between U.S. companies and their wholly owned foreign subsidiaries; more complex rules would be necessary for less than wholly owned subsidiaries.

BCF taxation breaks with a tradition, exemplified by the foreign tax credit, under which U.S. tax policy aimed to encourage U.S. taxpayers to invest in projects with the highest before-tax yield, wherever the investment might be located in the world. The foreign tax credit thereby encourages behavior that is consistent with maximizing world welfare. Under BCF, U.S. taxpayers would, in effect, receive a deduction for foreign taxes rather than a credit. For this reason, U.S. taxpayers would choose among investments based on a comparison of after-foreign-tax returns of foreign investments with before-tax returns of U.S.-based investments. BCF taxation encourages behavior that is consistent with maximizing U.S. economic welfare.

Taxable income under BCF taxation is the net flow of funds into the United States, regardless of form. Under BCF taxation, a U.S. company would owe the same tax inside the United States whether it earns $200 abroad, repatriating $50, or earns $50 in the United States and $150 abroad, repatriating none. Such a system greatly simplifies U.S. tax enforcement. It also sharply reduces incentives of American multinationals to shift profits to offshore tax havens. Such companies would have to pay tax if they repatriated overseas profits to the United States. But if funds were later required overseas, the transfer would be deductible. Accordingly, there would be no reason to delay repatriating the funds, which would avoid even the low capital income taxes levied in tax havens. Because BCF taxation provides only a deduction, not a credit, for foreign capital income taxes, it would encourage U.S. multinationals to use transfer pricing to report profits in the United States rather than abroad. The same would be true of foreign multinationals that anticipate making net investments in the United States.

It is instructive to contrast the BCF system to the exemption of foreign income provided under the USA tax. By allowing a deduction for funds invested abroad, the BCF system effectively imposes U.S. taxes on above-normal returns earned abroad by U.S. companies, where *above-normal returns* is understood to represent returns net of foreign tax. This tax system can be thought of as treating excess foreign returns as though they had U.S. origin and were therefore taxable by the United States. The BCF system is, in this sense, quite consistent with the philosophy of the Armey-Shelby flat tax, though it is much easier to implement together with the border adjustments in the Gibbons VAT and Nunn-Domenici USA taxes.

It is possible to introduce the BCF system without fundamental reform of the U.S. tax system, though BCF fits most neatly within the reform frameworks because of their effective removal of the taxation of capital income. Of course, the introduction of a BCF system together with a domestic income tax requires extensive accompanying regulation to prevent U.S. companies and individuals from parking funds abroad in passive investments routed through tax havens that could accumulate indefinitely without U.S. income taxation. Some expansions of the current Subpart F and PFIC (Passive Foreign Investment Company) rules would be necessary—in particular treating passive investment principal and not simply its return—as deemed distributed to U.S. investors. Even with such regulation, U.S. companies would in many cases have increased tax incentives to invest abroad rather than at home, since foreign investments become effectively expensed for U.S. tax purposes.

The net effect on U.S. tax revenue of BCF taxation combined with income taxes is ambiguous, since any substitution of foreign for domestic investment reduces U.S. tax collections, while the transfer pricing incentives and improved (from the U.S. standpoint) allocation of U.S. direct investment resources enhance U.S. tax collections.

Conclusion

International considerations increasingly influence economic policies. Fundamental consumption-oriented tax reforms are usually defended on the basis of their domestic consequences, but it is clear that they could have very important international consequences as well. In the absence of stronger evidence, it is, however, difficult to predict exactly what direction these consequences will take. At the same time, international market conditions significantly influence the degree to which fundamental reforms will reach the domestic objectives they are designed to achieve.

One of the dangers of embarking on wholesale policy reform in an open economy is that unforeseen international complications may undermine otherwise desirable results. The observed responsiveness of foreign direct investment, international trade, corporate financing, and many other activities suggests that minor missteps may have major consequences for governments concerned about their economies and their tax bases. In particular, there is little basis for the proposition that fundamental tax reform will greatly enhance the international competitiveness of an economy. Judgments on the desirability of fundamental reforms should rest on the incentives they introduce and the incentives they replace. In an open economy, international markets generate certain incentives that may not be affected by national tax reforms in even the largest countries.

Choosing a tax base is not simply a matter of selecting the most effective means of raising revenue. Taxes imposed on different bases can have very different distributional consequences, thereby greatly influencing their desirability. The U.S. political system over the past century exhibits a strong preference for taxing on the basis of income (including capital income), which may reflect the distribution of income in the United States or simply lack of imagination in designing tax reforms. In evaluating the consequences of sweeping reform, it is appropriate to consider its effect on all of the economy—including its international component—as well as on all of the affected individuals.

Comment by J. Gregory Ballentine

I suspect that specialists in international taxation and international economics are somewhat chagrined by the continued great need for a chapter such as the one by James R. Hines in this volume. For what Hines does so very well is to remind us gently that the U.S. financial capital market is linked to worldwide markets; exchange rates are adjustable and those adjustments can largely offset the effects of border tax adjustments; and economically relevant concepts of "international competitiveness" bear little relationship to the size or sign of the trade balance.

Even if his chapter were limited to these and similar points, Hines's contribution would be very valuable. He also makes many other important points, however. I discuss one of those points here, the impact of fundamental reform on transfer pricing and then turn to an issue not addressed by Hines.

To understand the impact of fundamental tax reform on the return to transfer price manipulation, one needs to ignore the mechanics of setting transfer prices and focus on the effect. That is, to determine if transfer pricing manipulation could be a tax administration problem in the presence of any particular type of fundamental tax reform, ask whether a multinational firm can make a tax gain by simply declaring a million dollars more or less of taxable income in a foreign jurisdiction with a corresponding change in U.S. taxable income.[53]

It is crucial that this question be set in the context of an assumption that there be no change in the actual business activities of the firm in either jurisdiction. The extent that substantial business activities will relocate to a low tax rate jurisdiction consequent upon fundamental tax reform is a matter of the responsiveness of investment to tax incentives, not transfer pricing. Transfer pricing controversies focus on whether shifts of income have occurred that are inconsistent with the shift in actual business activity.[54] To focus clearly on whether there can be gains to transfer pricing manipulation, rather than effects on investment incentives, it is necessary to frame the question as stated above—is there a benefit to a shift of one million dollars of income into or out of the United States with no change in business activity?

53. The fact that a firm may have a potential tax gain from shifting income does not imply that income has been shifted. Nor does the absence of a tax benefit for a firm imply that the tax authorities will not adjust that firm's transfer prices. Indeed, there are numerous cases in which the IRS has alleged that income has been shifted from the United States to a higher tax-rate jurisdiction. Transfer price disputes generally revolve around whether the income reported in different jurisdictions is consistent with the business activities, risks, investments, and other conditions in those jurisdictions. This is a difficult issue and as long as a government can gain revenue by proposing an adjustment to transfer prices, disputes over transfer prices will remain. In this discussion I am focusing on the incentives of firms to shift income through transfer pricing policies. In my experience, the problem of tax authorities' trying to shift income through transfer price adjustments is more severe.

54. Transfer price disputes are so difficult to resolve because, in the disequilibrium world of an individual business entity, there can be large differences in the arm's-length income associated with given investments and activities.

The answer to this question depends on the disparity, if any, in the statutory tax rates applied to business receipts in the two jurisdictions. It does not depend directly on the effective tax rate on new investment in either jurisdiction. There can still be a sizable advantage to shifting income out of the United States under a regime that has a zero effective tax rate on new investment if that zero rate is achieved by expensing rather than exemption. There is a clear tax benefit to expensing an investment at one tax rate and paying tax on the income at a lower rate.[55]

This point is not an academic quibble. In the past, many of the most contentious tax disputes have revolved around investments that bore a zero (or lower) effective tax rate in the United States. That is, they involved controversy over the location of income from investments in research and development (R&D) done in the United States. Recently, the Internal Revenue Service has expressed concern that U.S. subsidiaries of foreign companies have taken deductions under the U.S. tax system for advertising expenditures incurred to promote sales in the United States, the income from which has been improperly shifted to the parent company, which is subject to tax rules of the home country. Since both R&D and advertising expenditures are expensed, both of these types of disputes deal with zero taxed investments.

It might seem, therefore, that if the United States is to achieve a zero tax rate on new investment, it should do so through an exemption system, thereby virtually eliminating the interest of shifting U.S. income abroad through transfer price manipulation. Indeed, Hines suggests this when he concludes that "transfer pricing remains important to U.S. tax collections to the extent that business income remains taxable."

I think that is wrong. It is true that if some business income taxation remains, there can be an effect on U.S. tax collections from transfer price changes. The effect on tax collection is not the relevant factor to gauge the economic importance of transfer pricing issues, however.[56] The main

55. In principle, I suppose that transfer price type manipulations could provide a tax gain if statutory tax rates are the same, but deductibility rules differ. That is, one could shift an expense to a jurisdiction that allowed immediate deduction from one that delayed the deduction. In general, however, differences in the timing of deductions relate to depreciation of physical assets, and it is difficult to shift depreciation deductions without changing the geographic location of the assets themselves.

56. I believe this conclusion of Hines's is one of the very few, if not the only one, in the entire conference in which the level of tax collections, as opposed to the structure of the tax system, had any consequence. As mentioned at the end of my comment, I think a more general focus on the possible impact of tax reform on tax collections is called for.

economic effect of tax-based transfer pricing planning and disputes is a deadweight loss of resources.[57] The resources devoted to such planning and disputes generally will rise with an increase in the geographic disparity of statutory rates on business receipts. (This follows simply because the gain from shifting income rises as statutory rate differentials increase.) Thus, if the United States exempts business income from taxation, the worldwide deadweight loss from transfer pricing disputes, possibly including that borne directly by U.S. multinational firms, will rise.[58]

Hines gives another reason for the importance of transfer pricing under fundamental tax reform, which is that the United States will become more attractive to investors. As indicated by the way I phrased the question of the significance of transfer pricing—what is the effect of a shift in income with no shift in business activities—I also disagree with Hines on this conclusion. If the United States becomes more attractive to investors because of fundamental tax reform, that is a matter of the effect of tax incentives on the geographical location of investment, not transfer pricing. The very nature of a transfer pricing dispute is whether there has been a shift in income that is not consistent with a shift in business investment.

In the context of the relocation of investment, Hines concludes that fundamental tax reform may cause R&D activities to shift from other locations to the United States. This is because of "the ability to avoid all U.S. tax on foreign operations, along with the ability to claim a tax deduction for 100 percent of R&D expenses incurred in the United States." Although this may be what is implied by some of the proposals today, I think it is very unlikely that any final reform would allow this to happen. There is a very strong tradition in the United States, and in other jurisdictions, I believe, against allowing full deductions for all R&D, with no taxation of the income from the international use of the resulting technology. (Notice that the effective tax rate from such treatment is $-t/(1-t)$, where t is the statutory rate.)

If fundamental tax reform still matches expenditures and income from international use of R&D, then deductions not matched with expenditures would only occur to the extent that non-arm's-length transfer prices

57. Clearly, this conclusion does not apply to setting transfer prices to provide the appropriate internal management incentives.

58. I do not mean to imply that this loss is large relative to any gains that might otherwise occur from fundamental tax reform. I have not attempted to measure the deadweight loss from transfer pricing disputes. I have observed, however, that a dispute over transfer pricing is often the most costly and prolonged dispute in a multinational firm's tax audit.

are used. Of course that can occur under the current system. Indeed, as mentioned above, the possibility that such a mismatch has occurred has been a major factor in transfer pricing disputes. Under fundamental tax reform, however, with lower statutory rates in the United States, the gains from non-arm's-length pricing of the benefits of international use of U.S. R&D are lower. Thus, if matching of expenditures and income is required, the only incentive to locate R&D in the United States would arise from non-arm's-length pricing, and that incentive would be lower than under the current system.

As I mentioned at the outset, much of Hines's chapter is a valuable reminder of the importance of the international economy to the effects of U.S. tax changes. That is valuable not because other participants at the conference believed that the impact of taking into account the international economy is trivial. It is just that difficult problems such as the impact of fundamental tax reform have to be addressed in pieces, and not every analysis in this volume will take into account all aspects of the problem. The piecemeal approach is not a deficiency, indeed it is an advantage, as long as all of the major pieces are addressed by someone.

In my view, Hines and others have left out an important piece, however. They followed a time-honored tradition in public finance of examining the structure of the tax system as if that structure could be changed in radical ways with no impact on the level of taxation. Thus, the possibility that fundamental tax reform could only be politically feasible if it resulted in a tax reduction is ignored. This seems to me especially problematic when some of the reforms would remove the veil of business taxes and shift all taxation to a form perceived by voters to fall on individuals.

I recognize the danger in having high-quality, objective economic analyses, such as the ones in this volume, veer off into political speculation. Nonetheless, it seems to me that an examination of the effects of fundamental tax reforms on capital accumulation, national saving, international capital flows, and trade flows that ignores the possible effects of increases in the federal budget deficit has left out an important piece of the problem. Perhaps at least part of a future analysis should, as Hines's analysis reminds us of the role of the international economy, remind us of the role and consequence of the possible interaction between the level of taxation and changes in the structure of taxation.

References

Abuaf, Niso, and Philippe Jorion. 1990. "Purchasing Power Parity in the Long Run." *Journal of Finance* 45 (March): 157–74.

Altshuler, Rosanne, and Jack M. Mintz. 1995. "U.S. Interest-Allocation Rules: Effects and Policy." *International Tax and Public Finance* 2 (May): 7–35.

Altshuler, Rosanne, and T. Scott Newlon. 1993. "The Effects of U.S. Tax Policy on the Income Repatriation Patterns of U.S. Multinational Corporations." In *Studies in International Taxation*, edited by Alberto Giovannini, R. Glenn Hubbard, and Joel Slemrod, 77–115. University of Chicago Press.

Altshuler, Rosanne, T. Scott Newlon, and William C. Randolph. 1995. "Do Repatriation Taxes Matter? Evidence from the Tax Returns of U.S. Multinationals." In *The Effects of Taxation on Multinational Corporations*, edited by Martin Feldstein, James R. Hines Jr., and R. Glenn Hubbard, 253–76. University of Chicago Press.

Avi-Yonah, Reuven S. 1995. "The International Implications of Tax Reform in the United States." *Tax Notes International*, November 27, 1447–60.

Bilson, John F. O. 1981. "The 'Speculative Efficiency' Hypothesis." *Journal of Business* 54 (July): 435–51.

Boskin, Michael J., and William G. Gale. 1987. "New Results on the Effects of Tax Policy on the International Location of Investment." In *The Effects of Taxation on Capital Accumulation*, edited by Martin Feldstein, 201–22. University of Chicago Press.

Bradford, David F. 1996. "Consumption Taxes: Some Fundamental Transition Issues." In *Frontiers of Tax Reform*, edited by Michael J. Boskin, 123–50. Hoover Institution Press.

Campbell, John Y., and Richard H. Clarida. 1987. "The Term Structure of Euromarket Interest Rates: An Empirical Investigation." *Journal of Monetary Economics* 19 (January): 25–44.

Collins, Julie H., and Douglas A. Shackelford. 1995. "Corporate Domicile and Average Effective Tax Rates: The Cases of Canada, Japan, the United Kingdom, and the United States." *International Tax and Public Finance* 2 (May): 55–83.

Cumby, Robert E., 1988, "Is It Risk? Explaining Deviations from Uncovered Interest Parity." *Journal of Monetary Economics* 22 (September): 279–99.

Dixit, Avinash K. 1985. "Tax Policy in Open Economies," in Alan J. Auerbach and Martin Feldstein, eds. *Handbook of Public Economics*, vol. 1, 313–74. Amsterdam: North-Holland.

Dominguez, Kathryn M. 1986. "Are Foreign Exchange Forecasts Rational? New Evidence from Survey Data." *Economics Letters* 21: 277–81.

Engel, Charles M. 1984. "Testing for the Absence of Expected Real Profits from Forward Market Speculation." *Journal of International Economics* 17 (November): 299–308.

Engel, Charles M. 1992. "On the Foreign Exchange Risk Premium in a General Equilibrium Model." *Journal of International Economics* 32 (May): 305–19.

Fama, Eugene F. 1984. "Forward and Spot Exchange Rates." *Journal of Monetary Economics* 14 (November): 319–38.

Feldstein, Martin. 1995. "The Effect of a Consumption Tax on the Rate of Interest." Working Paper 5397. National Bureau of Economic Research (December). Cambridge, Mass.

Feldstein, Martin, and Charles Horioka. 1980. "Domestic Saving and International Capital Flows." *Economic Journal* 90 (June): 314–29.

Feldstein, Martin, and Paul Krugman. 1990. "International Trade Effects of Value-Added Taxation." In *Taxation in the Global Economy*, edited by Assaf Razin and Joel Slemrod, 263–82. University of Chicago Press.

Frankel, Jeffrey A. 1986. "The Implications of Mean-Variance Optimization for Four Questions in International Macroeconomics." *Journal of International Money and Finance* (supplement) 5 (March): S53–S75.

———. 1991. "Quantifying International Capital Mobility in the 1980s." In *National Saving and Economic Performance*, edited by B. Douglas Bernheim and John B. Shoven. University of Chicago Press.

French, Kenneth R., and James M. Poterba. 1991. "Investor Diversification and International Equity Markets." *American Economic Review* 81 (May): 222–26.

Froot, Kenneth A. and Jeffrey A. Frankel, 1989. "Forward Discount Bias: Is It an Exchange Risk Premium?" *Quarterly Journal of Economics* 104 (February): 139–61.

Froot, Kenneth A., and James R. Hines Jr. 1995. "Interest Allocation Rules, Financing Patterns, and the Operations of U.S. Multinationals." In *The Effects of Taxation on Multinational Corporations*, edited by Martin Feldstein, James R. Hines Jr., and R. Glenn Hubbard, 277–312. University of Chicago Press.

Froot, Kenneth A., Michael Kim, and Kenneth Rogoff. 1995. "The Law of One Price over 700 Years." Working Paper 5132. Cambridge, Mass.: National Bureau of Economic Research (May).

Giovannini, Alberto, and Philippe Jorion. 1987. "Interest Rates and Risk Premia in the Stock Market and in the Foreign Exchange Market." *Journal of International Money and Finance* 6 (March): 107–23.

Gross, Edward B. Jr. 1993. "Individual Income Tax Returns, Preliminary Data, 1991." *Statistics of Income Bulletin* 12 (Spring): 6–22.

Grossman, Gene M. 1980. "Border Tax Adjustments: Do They Distort Trade?" *Journal of International Economics* 10 (February): 117–28.

Grubert, Harry. 1995. "Royalties, Dividends, and R&D." In *Proceedings of the Eighty-Seventh Annual Conference on Taxation*. Columbus, Ohio: National Tax Association.

Grubert, Harry, Timothy Goodspeed, and Deborah Swenson. 1993. "Explaining the Low Taxable Income of Foreign-Controlled Companies in the United States." In *Studies in International Taxation*, edited by Alberto Giovannini, R. Glenn Hubbard, and Joel Slemrod, 237–75. University of Chicago Press.

Grubert, Harry, and John Mutti. 1991. "Taxes, Tariffs and Transfer Pricing in Multinational Corporate Decision Making." *Review of Economics and Statistics* 73 (May): 285–93.

Grubert, Harry, and T. Scott Newlon. 1995. "The International Implications of Consumption Tax Proposals." *National Tax Journal* 48 (December): 619–47.

Hall, Robert E. 1995. "The International Consequences of the Leading Consumption Tax Proposals." Stanford University (November).

Hall, Robert E. 1996. "The Effects of Tax Reform on Prices and Asset Values." In *Tax Policy and the Economy*, edited by James M. Poterba, vol. 10, 71–88. MIT Press.

Hall, Robert E., and Alvin Rabushka. 1995. *The Flat Tax*. 2d. ed. Hoover Institution Press.

Harris, David G. 1993. "The Impact of U.S. Tax Law Revision on Multinational Corporations' Capital Location and Income-Shifting Decisions." *Journal of Accounting Research* Supplement 31: 111–40.

Harris, David, and others. 1993. "Income Shifting in U.S. Multinational Corporations." In *Studies in International Taxation*, edited by Alberto Giovannini, R. Glenn Hubbard, and Joel Slemrod, 277–307. University of Chicago Press.

Hartman, David G. 1979. "Foreign Investment and Finance with Risk." *Quarterly Journal of Economics* 93 (May): 213–32.

Hines, James R. Jr. 1991. "The Flight Paths of Migratory Corporations." *Journal of Accounting, Auditing, and Finance* 6 (Fall): 447–79.

———. 1994. "Credit and Deferral as International Investment Incentives." *Journal of Public Economics* 55 (October): 323–47.

———. 1995a. "Taxes, Technology Transfer, and the R&D Activities of Multinational Firms." In *The Effects of Taxation on Multinational Corporations*, edited by Martin Feldstein, James R. Hines Jr., and R. Glenn Hubbard, 225–52. University of Chicago Press.

———. 1995b. "Forbidden Payment: Foreign Bribery and American Business after 1977." Working Paper 5266. Cambridge, Mass.: National Bureau of Economic Research (September).

———. 1996. "Tax Policy and the Activities of Multinational Corporations." Working Paper 5589. Cambridge, Mass.: National Bureau of Economic Research (May).

———. Forthcoming. "Altered States: Taxes and the Location of Foreign Direct Investment in America." *American Economic Review*.

Hines, James R. Jr., and R. Glenn Hubbard. 1990. "Coming Home to America: Dividend Repatriations by U.S. Multinationals." In *Taxation in the Global Econ-*

omy, edited by Assaf Razin and Joel Slemrod, 161–200. University of Chicago Press.

———. 1995. "Appendix." In *Taxing Multinational Corporations*, edited by Martin Feldstein, James R. Hines Jr., and R. Glenn Hubbard. University of Chicago Press.

Hines, James R. Jr., and Eric M. Rice. 1994. "Fiscal Paradise: Foreign Tax Havens and American Business." *Quarterly Journal of Economics* 109 (February): 149–82.

Hines, James R. Jr., and Kristen L. Willard. 1992. "Trick or Treaty? Bargains and Surprises in International Tax Agreements." Working Paper. Harvard University.

Johnson, David R. 1990. "Co-Integration, Error Correction, and Purchasing Power Parity between Canada and the United States." *Canadian Journal of Economics* 23 (November): 839–55.

Kaminsky, Graciela. 1993. "Is There a Peso Problem? Evidence from the Dollar/Pound Exchange Rate, 1976–1987." *American Economic Review* 83 (June): 450–72.

Kemsley, Dean. 1995. "The Effect of Taxes on the Choice between Exports and Foreign Production." Working Paper. Columbia University.

Klassen, Kenneth, Mark Lang, and Mark Wolfson. 1993. "Geographic Income Shifting by Multinational Corporations in Response to Tax Rate Changes." *Journal of Accounting Research* (Supplement) 31: 141–73.

Kopits, George F. 1976. "Intra-Firm Royalties Crossing Frontiers and Transfer-Pricing Behavior." *Economic Journal* 86 (December): 791–805.

Leamer, Edward E., and James Levinsohn. 1995. "International Trade Theory: The Evidence." In *Handbook of International Economics*, vol. 3, edited by Gene M. Grossman and Kenneth Rogoff. Amsterdam: North-Holland.

Levi, Maurice D. 1977. "Taxation and 'Abnormal' International Capital Flows." *Journal of Political Economy* 85 (June): 635–46.

Lewis, Karen K. 1989. "Changing Beliefs and Systematic Rational Forecast Errors with Evidence from Foreign Exchange." *American Economic Review* 79 (September): 621–36.

Mann, Michael A., and Sylvia E. Barges. 1995. "U.S. International Sales and Purchases of Private Services." *Survey of Current Business* 75 (September): 68–105.

McIntyre, Michael J. 1996. "International Aspects of Kemp Commission Report." *Tax Notes International*. (February 5) 12 (6): 417–20.

McLure, Charles E. Jr., and George R. Zodrow. 1996. "The Economic Case for Foreign Tax Credits for Cash Flow Taxes." Stanford University.

Redmiles, Lissa. 1992. "International Boycott Participation, 1990." *Statistics of Income Bulletin* 12 (Fall): 88–89.

———. 1994. "Individual Foreign-Earned Income and Foreign Tax Credit, 1991." *Statistics of Income Bulletin* 14 (Fall): 113–22.

Slemrod, Joel. 1990. "Tax Effects on Foreign Direct Investment in the United States: Evidence from a Cross-Country Comparison." In *Taxation in the Global Economy*, edited by Assaf Razin and Joel Slemrod, 79–122. University of Chicago Press.

United States Department of Commerce, Bureau of Economic Analysis. 1994. *Foreign Direct Investment in the United States: 1992 Benchmark Survey, Preliminary Results.*

Wahl, Jenny Bourne. 1989. "Tax Treatment of Foreign Exchange Gains and Losses and the Tax Reform Act of 1986." *National Tax Journal* 42 (March): 59–68.

Wei, Shang-Jin, and David C. Parsley. 1995. "Purchasing Power *Dis*-Parity during the Floating Rate Period." Working Paper. Harvard University.

World Bank. 1994. *World Tables 1994.* Johns Hopkins University Press.

Young, Kan H. 1988. "The Effects of Taxes and Rates of Return on Foreign Direct Investment in the United States." *National Tax Journal* 41 (March): 109–21.

Contributors

With their affiliation at the time of the conference

HENRY J. AARON
Brookings Institution

ALAN J. AUERBACH
University of California, Berkeley

J. GREGORY BALLENTINE
KPMG Peat Marwick

B. DOUGLAS BERNHEIM
Stanford University

DAVID F. BRADFORD
Princeton University

DENNIS R. CAPOZZA
University of Michigan

CHARLES T. CLOTFELTER
Duke University

DAVID CUTLER
*Harvard University and National
   Bureau of Economic Research*

ERIC M. ENGEN
Federal Reserve Board

DON FULLERTON
University of Texas

WILLIAM G. GALE
Brookings Institution

JANE G. GRAVELLE
Congressional Research Service

RICHARD K. GREEN
University of Wisconsin

JONATHAN GRUBER
*Massachusetts Institute of
   Technology and National
   Bureau of Economic Research*

ROBERT HALL
Hoover Institution

PATRIC H. HENDERSHOTT
Ohio State University

JAMES R. HINES JR.
*Harvard University and National
Bureau of Economic Research*

DOUGLAS HOLTZ-EAKIN
Syracuse University

SCOTT HOUSER
University of Wisconsin

HILARY WILLIAMSON
HOYNES
*University of California, Berkeley,
and National Bureau of
Economic Research*

R. GLENN HUBBARD
Columbia University

LAURENCE J. KOTLIKOFF
Boston University

BRUCE K. MACLAURY
Brookings Institution

RONALD A. PEARLMAN
Covington and Burling

JAMES POTERBA
*Massachusetts Institute of
Technology and National
Bureau of Economic Research*

DIANE LIM ROGERS
Congressional Budget Office

RICHARD L. SCHMALBECK
Duke University

JOHN KARL SCHOLZ
University of Wisconsin

LOUISE SHEINER
Council of Economic Advisers

JOHN B. SHOVEN
Stanford University

JOEL SLEMROD
University of Michigan

ROBERT K. TRIEST
Federal Reserve Bank

Participants

With their affiliation at the time of the conference

BERNARD AIDINOFF
Sullivan and Cromwell

WILLIAM ANDREWS
Harvard University Law School

MICHAEL H. ARMACOST
Brookings Institution

MICHAEL BOSKIN
Stanford University

DANIEL FEENBERG
National Bureau of Economic Research

HARVEY GALPER
KPMG Peat Marwick

MARTIN D. GINSBURG
Georgetown Law Center

ROGER GORDON
University of Michigan

DANIEL HALPERIN
Georgetown Law Center

KENNETH KIES
Joint Committee on Taxation

ALICIA MUNNELL
Council of Economic Advisers

RUDY PENNER
KPMG Peat Marwick

LESLIE SAMUELS
U.S. Treasury Department

EUGENE STEUERLE
The Urban Institute

EMIL SUNLEY
International Monetary Fund

ERIC TODER
U.S. Treasury Department

ALVIN WARREN
Harvard University Law School

GEORGE ZODROW
Rice University

Index

Aaron, Henry J., 420
Abraham, Jesse M., 191, 195
Accountants: demand for, 269, 363, 379
Adjusted gross income (AGI), 285, 285n
Adjustment costs: of investing, 303; of tax reform, 61–64
ADL. *See* Arthur D. Little
Adrion, Harold, 440, 441
AFDC. *See* Aid to families with dependent children
A. Foster Higgins, 127
Age groups: differential consumption tax rates, 116–17; distribution of value-added taxes, 260; effects of mortgage interest deduction elimination, 174, 201; impact of consumption tax, 322; impact of flat tax, 63, 294, 297, 388; impact of tax reform, 64–65, 84, 90, 333, 338, 350; saving motivations, 92–94; saving rates, 59, 84, 90, 90n; transition issues, 59, 407–08, 409n; welfare gains with tax reform, 331–35, 337. *See also* Retirees
Aid to families with dependent children (AFDC), 252, 272–73
Alimony: tax treatment, 424, 424n
Alternative minimum tax (AMT), 39–40, 382; compliance costs, 379–80; repeal of, 386
AMT. *See* Alternative minimum tax
Archer, Bill, 426, 437

Armey, Dick. *See* Armey-Shelby flat tax
Armey-Shelby flat tax, 44–45; base, 473; with charitable deduction, 292; charitable deduction eliminated, 223, 230; estate and gift taxes eliminated, 223, 230–31; exempt organizations, 226; foreign tax credit eliminated, 481–82; impact on Americans working abroad, 487; impact on asset values, 60, 63; impact on efficiency, 61; impact on health insurance, 136–38, 139, 141, 152, 153; impact on housing prices, 194–95; impact on interest rates, 475; impact on medicaid spending, 144; impact on output, 59, 63, 66; impact on saving rate, 59; impact on state taxes, 137n; impact on transfer prices, 481, 483; impact on wages, 152; on interest income, 483; lack of transition relief, 405; with mortgage interest deduction, 181, 200, 292; mortgage interest deduction eliminated, 173–74, 178–79, 188, 422; progressivity, 61; rates, 24–25, 46, 288, 293–94; transition relief, 55, 59, 61, 63, 181, 489; treatment of exports and imports, 478, 483; withholding taxes eliminated, 472; zero-bracket amounts, 72. *See also* Flat tax

507